THE JOSSEY-BASS
READER ON CONTEMPORARY ISSUES IN ADULT EDUCATION

THE JOSSEY-BASS
READER ON CONTEMPORARY ISSUES IN ADULT EDUCATION

Sharan B. Merriam, André P. Grace

JOSSEY-BASS
A Wiley Imprint
www.josseybass.com

Published by Jossey-Bass
A Wiley Imprint
989 Market Street, San Francisco, CA 94103-1741—www.josseybass.com

Jossey-Bass books and products are available through most bookstores. To contact Jossey-Bass directly call our Customer Care Department within the U.S. at 800-956-7739, outside the U.S. at 317-572-3986, or fax 317-572-4002.

Jossey-Bass also publishes its books in a variety of electronic formats. Some content that appears in print may not be available in electronic books.

Library of Congress Cataloging-in-Publication Data

The Jossey-Bass reader on contemporary issues in adult education / [edited by] Sharan B. Merriam, André P. Grace.—1st ed.
       p. cm.
    Includes bibliographical references and index.
  ISBN 978-0-470-87356-4 (pbk.)
  1. Adult education—United States. I. Merriam, Sharan B. II. Grace, André P., 1954– III. Jossey-Bass Inc.
  LC5251.J775 2011
  374′.973—dc22

2010051344

FIRST EDITION

PB Printing 10 9 8 7 6 5 4 3 2

The Jossey-Bass
Higher and Adult Education Series

Contents

PART FOUR
THE CHANGING LANDSCAPE OF ADULT LEARNING

Sources

Chapter 1

From Lindeman, E. C. (1961/1926). *The Meaning of Adult Education*. Montreal: Harvest House. pp. 3–9. Reprinted by permission of Sage Publications.

Chapter 2

From Locke, A. L. (1933). *The American Negro*. American Library Association. Used with permission from the American Library Association.

Chapter 3

Excerpted from Freire, P. (1970). *Pedagogy of the Oppressed*. New York: Seabury. © 1970, 2000. Reprinted with permission of the publisher, the Continuum International Publishing Group.

Chapter 4

Grace, A. P. (1999). Building a knowledge base in U.S. academic adult education (1945–1970). *Studies in the Education of Adults, 31*(2), 220–236. Used by permission of the NIACE.

Chapter 5

Glowacki-Dudka, M., & Helvie-Mason, L. B. (2004). Adult education at the margins: A literature review. In M. Wise & M. Glowacki-Dudka (Eds.), *Embracing and enhancing the margins of adult education* (pp. 7–16). New Directions for Adult and Continuing Education, No. 104. San Francisco: Jossey-Bass.

Chapter 6

Johnson-Bailey, J. (2006). African Americans in adult education: The Harlem Renaissance revisited. *Adult Education Quarterly, 56*(2), 102–118. Copyright © 2006 American Association for Adult and Continuing Education. Reprinted by permission of Sage Publications.

Chapter 7

Gordon, W., & Sork, T. J. (2001). Ethical issues and codes of ethics: Views of adult education practitioners in Canada and the United States. *Adult Education Quarterly, 51*(3), 202–218. Copyright © 2001 American Association for Adult and Continuing Education. Reprinted by permission of Sage Publications.

Chapter 8

Jarvis, P. (2008). Rediscovering adult education in a world of lifelong learning. *International Journal of Critical Pedagogy, 1*(1). Used by permission.

Chapter 9

Griffin, C. (2006). Research and policy in lifelong learning. *International Journal of Lifelong Education, 25*(6), 561–574. Reprinted by permission of the publisher (Taylor & Francis Ltd., http://www.informaworld.com).

Chapter 10

Walters, S. Social movements, class, and adult education. In T. Nesbit (Ed.), *Class concerns: Adult education and social class.* New Directions for Adult and Continuing Education, No. 106. San Francisco: Jossey-Bass.

Chapter 11

Choules, K. (2007). Social change education: Context matters. *Adult Education Quarterly, 57*(2), 159–176. Copyright © 2007 American Association for Adult and Continuing Education. Reprinted by permission of Sage Publications.

Chapter 12

Fiallos, C. A. (2006). Adult education and the empowerment of the individual in a global society. In S. B. Merriam, B. C. Courtenay, & R. M. Cervero (Eds.), *Global issues and adult education: Perspectives from Latin America, Southern Africa, and the United States* (pp. 15–29). San Francisco: Jossey-Bass.

Chapter 13

Gouthro, P. A. (2007). Active and inclusive citizenship for women: Democratic considerations for fostering lifelong education. *International Journal of Lifelong Education, 26*(2), 143–154, reprinted by permission of the publisher (Taylor & Francis Ltd., http://www.informaworld.com).

Chapter 14

Nesbit, T. (2005). Social class and adult education. In T. Nesbit (Ed.), *Class concerns: Adult education and social class* (pp. 5–14). New Directions for Adult and Continuing Education, No. 106. San Francisco: Jossey-Bass.

Chapter 15

van der Veen, R., & Preece, J. (2005). Poverty reduction and adult education: Beyond basic education. *International Journal of Lifelong Education, 24*(5), 381–391. Reprinted by permission of the publisher (Taylor & Francis Ltd., http://www.informaworld.com).

Chapter 16

Daley, B. J. (2006). Aligning health promotion and adult education for healthier communities. In S. B. Merriam, B. C. Courtenay, & R. M. Cervero (Eds.), *Global issues and adult education: Perspectives from Latin America, Southern Africa, and the United States* (pp. 231–242). San Francisco: Jossey-Bass.

Chapter 17

Bierema, L. L. (2009). Critiquing HRD's dominant masculine rationality and evaluating its impact. *Human Resource Development Review, 8*(1), 68–96. Copyright © 2009 Sage Publications. Reprinted by permission of Sage Publications.

Chapter 18

Owenby, P. H. (2002). Organizational learning communities and the dark side of the learning organization. In D. S. Stein & S. Imel (Eds.), *Adult learning in community* (pp. 51–60). New Directions for Adult and Continuing Education, No. 95. San Francisco: Jossey-Bass.

Chapter 19

Excerpted from Cervero, R. M., & Wilson, A. L. (2006). *Working the planning table: Negotiating democratically for adult, continuing, and workplace education* (pp. 80–102). San Francisco: Jossey-Bass.

Chapter 20

Newman, M. (1994). *Defining the enemy*. Sidney: Stewart Victor. Republished online 2007 at www.michaelnewman.info, Chapter 28, Reflection Disempowered. Used by permission of the author.

Lyrics for "Silver Dagger" copyright Chandon Music, used by permission.

Excerpt from *Death and the Maiden* by Ariel Dorfman used by permission of Nick Hern Books, www.nickhernbooks.co.uk

Lyrics for "Joe Hill," music by Earl Robinson, words by Alfred Hayes, copyright © 1938 (renewed) by Music Sales (ASCAP) and MCA Music Publishing for the United States. International copyright secured. All rights secured. Used by permission. Words and music by Earl Robinson and Alfred Hayes, Copyright © 1938, 1942 Universal Music Corp. Copyright renewed and assigned to Universal Music Corp. and Music Sales Corporation. All rights reserved. Used by permission. Reprinted by permission of Hal Leonard Corporation.

Chapter 21

Cranton, P. (2006). A theory in progress. In *Understanding and promoting transformative learning: A guide for educators of adults* (pp. 39–56). San Francisco: Jossey-Bass, 2006.

Chapter 22

Niewolny, K. L., & Wilson, A. L. (2009). "Social learning" for/in adult education? A discursive review of what it means for learning to be "social." In R. L. Lawrence

(Ed.), *Proceedings of the 50th Annual Adult Education Research Conference*. Chicago: National-Louis University. Used by permission of the authors.

Chapter 23
Dirkx, J. M. (2008). The meaning and role of emotions in adult learning. In J. Dirkx (Ed.), *Adult learning and the emotional self* (pp. 7–18). New Directions for Adult and Continuing Education, No. 120. San Francisco: Jossey-Bass.

Chapter 24
Guy, T. C. (2006). Adult education and the mass media in the age of globalization. In S. B. Merriam, B. C. Courtenay, & R. M. Cervero (Eds.), *Global issues and adult education: Perspectives from Latin America, Southern Africa, and the United States* (pp. 64–77). San Francisco: Jossey-Bass.

Chapter 25
Merriam, S. B., & Kim, Y. S. (2008). Non-western perspectives on learning and knowing. In S. B. Merriam (Ed.), *Third update on adult learning theory* (pp. 71–81). New Directions for Adult and Continuing Education, No. 119. San Francisco: Jossey-Bass.

Chapter 26
Chapman, V. (2005). Attending to the theoretical landscape in adult education. *Adult Education Quarterly, 55*(4), 308–312. Copyright © 2005 American Association for Adult and Continuing Education. Reprinted by permission of Sage Publications.

Chapter 27
Sandlin, J. A. (2007). Popular culture, cultural resistance, and anticonsumption activism: An exploration of culture jamming as critical adult education. In E. J. Tisdell & P. M. Thompson (Eds.), *Popular culture and entertainment media in adult education* (pp. 73–82). New Directions for Adult and Continuing Education, No. 115. San Francisco: Jossey-Bass.

Chapter 28
Kilgore, D. (2004). Toward a postmodern pedagogy. In R. St. Clair & J. Sandlin (Eds.), *Promoting critical practice in adult education* (pp. 45–53). New Directions for Adult and Continuing Education, 102. San Francisco: Jossey-Bass.

Chapter 29

Hill, R. J. (2004). Activism as practice: Some queer considerations. In R. St. Clair & J. Sandlin (Eds.), *Promoting critical practice in adult education* (pp. 85–94). New Directions for Adult and Continuing Education, No. 102. San Francisco: Jossey-Bass.

Chapter 30

Grace, A. P., & Wells, K. (2007). Using Freirean pedagogy of just ire to inform critical social learning in arts-informed community education for sexual minorities. *Adult Education Quarterly, 57*(2), 95–114. Copyright © 2007 American Association for Adult and Continuing Education. Reprinted by permission of Sage Publications.

Preface

There's something of a contradiction when speaking of the field of adult education. On the one hand, adult education programs are everywhere—in the workplace, hospitals, libraries, communities, colleges and universities, and online. On the other hand, adult education as a professional field of practice is nearly invisible, with many educators of adults unaware that they are part of a larger enterprise. This paradox also encompasses adult learners themselves. While the most recent U.S. survey revealed that 44% of adults participated part-time in formal adult education activities and 70% were learning informally (NCES, 2007), most adults don't consider themselves learners unless they are "taking a class."

These contradictions are not surprising given that the field of adult education has never been easily captured within one definition, one history, or even one theory. Whether we are talking about diverse adult populations, practices, philosophical perspectives, program planning models, or theories about how adults learn, there has always been a colorful collage of various and sometimes competing components comprising adult education as a field of practice. Professional adult educators do believe, however, that there is some common ground that links us together as a field. Learning, for example, is something human beings do throughout their lives; it is indeed lifelong and lifewide. Further, adult education can be a positive force in our lives and can contribute to individual betterment and a more just and equitable society for all.

As with professionals in other fields of practice, adult educators learn to become educators through experience and study. For example, a nursing supervisor in a hospital might be asked to develop a program to train others in the use of new medication; a community resident might organize other residents to help educate the community about safety concerns; an experienced worker might be tapped for some on-the-job mentoring of a new employee; or a carpenter might teach a woodworking class at the local community school. These are all examples of adult education in practice in real-life situations.

While many do learn to be adult educators through experience, others combine experience with formal study, sometimes on their own, but more likely as students in master's and doctoral programs. It is in these programs that learners are systematically exposed to the literature in the field. And as with the field itself, there is a wide diversity of resources with which to study the field. There are numerous research and practice-oriented journals; magazines and newsletters; online resources; a *Handbook of Adult and Continuing Education* that is published every ten years; a monograph series titled *New Directions for Adult and Continuing Education*; and dozens of textbooks on various aspects of the field including program planning, adult learning, theory building, philosophy, and history. There is, however, no single volume that functions as a reader on contemporary issues and trends in this very dynamic field of practice.

The Jossey-Bass Reader on Contemporary Issues in Adult Education is designed to be both a stand-alone reader for those self-directed adult educators who want to sample some of the thinking about adult education, and a reader that surveys an array of historical and contemporary issues important to study and critique in undergraduate or graduate courses in adult education. *The Jossey-Bass Reader* is particularly appropriate for introductory, overview, or social context courses in graduate programs of adult education. Such introductory courses not only provide the base for other courses in the curriculum, but they also typically explore issues and trends in the field.

OVERVIEW OF THE CONTENTS

Two selection processes took place to develop *The Jossey-Bass Reader on Contemporary Issues in Adult Education*. First, a panel of North American adult educators was invited to brainstorm a list of current issues and trends in the field. These lists varied from four and five broad issues to more than twenty more specific possibilities. A close study of these lists revealed five themes in common, and these structure the book. The next step was to decide on selections for each theme.

The two editors independently suggested possibilities for each theme; these lists were combined, and both editors read all the nominated pieces. Finally, the editors decided on selections to be included; this list had to be further adjusted to stay within space allocations. There are a total of 30 selections distributed across five topics, each topic with between five and seven selections.

Part One, "Defining a Field of Practice: The Foundations of Adult Education," contains selections related to social justice, ethics, and the historical evolution of the field. Three pieces are by historical "giants" in the field— Eduard C. Lindeman, Alain Locke, and Paulo Freire. Four pieces by contemporary scholars reflect upon the marginal place of the field in universities and society, African American adult education during the Harlem Renaissance, the evolution of the knowledge base, and ethics in the field.

Part Two is titled "Positioning Adult Education in a Global Context." While globalization, or the movement of goods, services, people, and ideas across national boundaries, is not new, the speed with which this movement is occurring is unprecedented. Part Two contains readings that consider the position of adult education in today's world from various perspectives including lifelong learning, policy, women's roles, social movements, and individual empowerment.

Part Three, "Adult Education's Constituencies and Program Areas: Competing Interests?", presents a sampling of the diversity of constituencies and program areas. As there were dozens of possibilities for this section, we tried to select pieces that went beyond description; rather, the selections we chose are thought-provoking, raising questions about an area of practice that we might not have considered before. There are readings on social class and adult education, poverty and its link to adult basic education, the need to bring health promotion and health education together, a feminist critique of human resource development, the "dark side" of the learning organization, and finally, program planning considered from the perspective of negotiating power and interests.

Part Four, "The Changing Landscape of Adult Learning," addresses the heart of all adult education practice. Adult learning is the key to understanding how areas as diverse as adult literacy programs, continuing professional education, workplace learning, and a nature hike in a national park could all come under the umbrella of adult education. As with other parts in this reader, our selections are intended to offer a sample of ways to look at and think about adult learning. There are readings on the changing meaning of reflection, transformative learning, and social learning. The final three selections consider the role of emotions in learning, how mass media is a global system of informal adult learning, and what non-Western perspectives have to tell us about learning and knowing.

Part Five is a selection of readings that we've aptly titled "New Discourses Shaping Contemporary Adult Education." Adult education has always been a dynamic and changing field of study and practice, one informed by various disciplines and philosophical schools of thought. In Part Five we offer a sampling of new thinking about our field. The first piece sets the stage by considering the role of theory in adult education. The other four selections explore anticonsumption activism, what it means to engage in a postmodern pedagogy, queer pedagogy, and critical social learning.

Finally, in our prefaces to each of the five parts, we introduce each of the selections in more detail so that readers will have an idea of what to expect as they engage in the readings. At the end of each preface, we have included several reflection and discussion questions to further engage readers in issues germane to adult education today.

ACKNOWLEDGMENTS

This reader is the brainchild of David Brightman, our editor at Jossey-Bass, who had a vision of what this book might be. David and editorial coordinator Aneesa Davenport have been enormously supportive in helping us bring this book to fruition. We thank you for your assistance throughout the project. We also want to thank the panel of North American adult educators who helped us brainstorm themes and issues—Ralph Brockett, Tal Guy, Cathy Hansman, and Vanessa Sheared. Finally, we are indebted to our colleagues in adult education from across the globe who authored the selections we chose for this reader. Without your work, this book would not exist, nor would our field be such an exciting and dynamic place to be!

Sharan B. Merriam
André P. Grace
January, 2011

REFERENCE

National Center for Education Statistics (NCES) (2007). Adult education participation in 2004-2005. Retrieved August 2010, from http://nces.ed.gov/pubs2006/adulted/

The Editors

Sharan B. Merriam is professor emeritus of adult education and qualitative research at the University of Georgia in Athens, Georgia, U.S. Merriam's research and writing activities have focused on adult and lifelong learning and qualitative research methods. For five years she was coeditor of *Adult Education Quarterly*, the major research and theory journal in adult education. She has published 26 books and over 100 journal articles and book chapters. She is a four-time winner of the prestigious Cyril O. Houle World Award for Literature in Adult Education for books published in 1982, 1997, 1999, and 2007. Her most recent books are *Learning in Adulthood* (2007), *Non-Western Perspectives on Learning and Knowing* (2007), and *Qualitative Research: A Guide to Design and Implementation* (2009). In 1998 she was a Fulbright scholar to Malaysia, and in 2006 she was a distinguished visiting scholar at Soongsil University in South Korea. From 2009 to 2010 she was a senior research fellow at the Institute for Social Sciences, University Putra Malaysia.

André P. Grace is a professor in educational policy studies and director of the Institute for Sexual Minority Studies and Services in the Faculty of Education, University of Alberta, Edmonton, Canada. He is a past president of the Canadian Association for the Study of Adult Education, and he is also a past chair of the Steering Committee for the Adult Education Research Conference in the U.S. His work in educational policy studies primarily focuses on comparative studies of policies, pedagogies, and practices shaping lifelong learning as critical action, especially in the contexts of Organization for Economic Cooperation and

Development (OECD) countries. Within this research he includes a major focus on sexual minorities and their issues and concerns regarding social inclusion, cohesion, and justice in education and culture. He and Tonette S. Rocco, coeditors of the Jossey-Bass book *Challenging the Professionalization of Adult Education: John Ohliger and Contradictions in Modern Practice,* won the 2009 Phillip E. Frandson Award for Literature in the Field of Continuing Higher Education from the University Continuing Education Association in the U.S. At the 2010 Standing Conference on University Teaching and Research in the Education of Adults, University of Warwick, UK, he won the Ian Martin Award for Social Justice for his paper entitled *Space Matters: Lifelong Learning, Sexual Minorities, and Realities of Adult Education as Social Education.*

About the Contributors

Laura L. Bierema is professor of adult education and human resource and organizational development at the University of Georgia, Athens.

Ronald M. Cervero is professor in the Department of Lifelong Education, Administration, and Policy, associate dean for Outreach and Engagement in the College of Education, and codirector of the Institute for Evidence-Based Health Professions Education at the University of Georgia, Athens.

Valerie-Lee Chapman was assistant professor in the Department of Adult and Community College Education at North Carolina State University.

Kathryn Choules is social justice consultant for the Edmund Rice Institute for Social Justice in Fremantle, Australia.

Patricia Cranton is visiting professor of adult education at Penn State University at Harrisburg and adjunct professor at Teachers College, Columbia University.

Barbara J. Daley is professor and department chair of the Department of Administrative Leadership at the University of Wisconsin-Milwaukee.

John M. Dirkx is professor of higher, adult, and lifelong education at Michigan State University and editor of the *Journal of Transformative Education*.

Cecilia Amaluisa Fiallos is a specialist in adult education and former National Director of Lifelong Popular Education at the Ministry of Education, Ecuador.

Paulo Freire was a Brazilian educator and influential theorist of critical pedagogy.

Michelle Glowacki-Dudka is assistant professor of adult, higher, and community education at Ball State University in Muncie, Indiana.

Wanda Gordon is former program head of health sciences at University of the Fraser Valley, Chilliwack, British Columbia.

Patricia A. Gouthro is a professor at Mount Saint Vincent University in Halifax, Nova Scotia.

Colin Griffin is Honorary Visiting Senior Fellow in the Department of Politics at the University of Surrey, where he previously worked in the School of Educational Studies.

Talmadge C. Guy is associate professor in the Department of Lifelong Education, Administration, and Policy at the University of Georgia, Athens.

Lora B. Helvie-Mason is assistant professor of communication studies at Southern University at New Orleans.

Robert J. Hill is associate professor of adult education at the University of Georgia, Athens.

Peter Jarvis is professor of continuing education at the University of Surrey.

Juanita Johnson-Bailey is professor of adult education and women's studies at the University of Georgia, Athens.

Deborah Kilgore is a research scientist in the Center for Engineering Learning and Teaching at the University of Washington.

Young Sek Kim is a lecturer at Dong-Eui University, Busan, South Korea.

Eduard C. Lindeman was an American educator, serving nearly all his years as a professor at the New York School of Social Work, later part of Columbia University.

Alain Locke was an American writer, philosopher, educator, patron of the arts, and the chair of the department of philosophy at Howard University in Washington, D.C., for most of his career.

Kim L. Niewolny is assistant professor of adult and community education in the College of Agriculture and Life Sciences at Virginia Polytechnic Institute and State University.

Michael Newman is an educator, author, and consultant in the field of adult education.

Tom Nesbit is associate dean of continuing education at Simon Fraser University, Vancouver, British Columbia.

Phillip H. Owenby is an educator and consultant in Knoxville, Tennessee.

Julia Preece is professor of adult and continuing education and honorary senior research fellow at the University of Glasgow.

Jennifer A. Sandlin is associate professor in the School of Social Transformation at Arizona State University, Tempe.

Thomas J. Sork is a professor of adult education and associate dean of External Programs and Learning Technologies in the Faculty of Education at the University of British Columbia.

Ruud van der Veen is adjunct professor of adult learning and leadership at Teachers College, Columbia University.

Shirley Walters is professor of adult and continuing education and director of the Division for Lifelong Learning at the University of Western Cape, South Africa.

Kristopher Wells is a researcher at the Institute for Sexual Minority Studies and Services, University of Alberta.

Arthur L. Wilson is professor of adult education and chair of the Department of Education at Cornell University, Ithaca, New York.

PART ONE

DEFINING A FIELD OF PRACTICE: THE FOUNDATIONS OF ADULT EDUCATION

Giroux (1996) asserts, "History is not an artifact" (p. 51). From this perspective, the history of adult education is alive, bringing issues of who is represented and who works for change to bear on theorizing, research, and practice. In our field of study and practice, a turn to history enables us to explore people, politics, and ideas that have defined modern practice. It becomes a way to reflect on what has been perceived as a divide exacerbating fragmentation of our field. On one side is adult education's tradition as social education in the spirit of initiatives like the Highlander Folk School and the Antigonish Movement. These social-learning endeavors variously focused on education for citizenship, community building, recovering from economic and other hardships, and fighting oppression in the name of social justice. On the other side is the field's pragmatic tendency to respond to outside pressures to become more instrumental and vocational in nature. However, we view engaging field history as more than investigating this divide: It provides us opportunities to explore the degree to which adult education can be spacious and filled with possibility as we set goals to meet the instrumental, social, and cultural needs of learners. As well, a turn to history also enables us to think about what adult education might look like in the future:

> At issue here is a vision of the future in which history is not accepted simply as a set of prescriptions unproblematically inherited from the past. History can be named and remade by those who refuse to stand by passively in the face of human suffering and oppression. (Giroux & McLaren, 1988, p. 176)

This vision, aimed at extending human possibilities, situates foundational studies as dynamic, open, unsettled, subject to revision, and worth struggling over.

Such a view of history is reflected in the selections in this section that includes pieces from the original writings of three field icons: Eduard Lindeman, Alain Locke, and Paulo Freire. In Chapter 1, Lindeman, framing education as life, positions the field as a potentially liberating space for adult learners as he engages what adult education means. He provocatively suggests that adult education begins where vocational education ends. His work will appeal to reflective practitioners concerned with holistic forms of learning and education that address current economic, social, and cultural turmoil. Throughout his influential book *The Meaning of Adult Education,* Lindeman (1926/1961) cast true adult education as social education that helps learners thrive as citizens living in community with others. From this perspective, Chapter 1 considers motivations, concepts, and methods that shape the learning process as it focuses on situations that require learners to draw on their experiences as they participate in problem solving.

In Chapter 2, Locke, a social and cultural educator who became the first Black president of the American Association for Adult Education from 1945 to 1946 (Stubblefield & Keane, 1994), contests the historical notion of the Black American as a "problem" and speaks to the transformation of modern Blacks in early 20th century U.S. culture through migration augmenting urbanization and the intensification of race consciousness and solidarity. Locke's work will speak to readers interested in the social history of recovery of Black morale through political participation aimed at attaining civil rights. Importantly for those interested in revising the place of Black citizens in U.S. social history, his work explores the emergence of the Black American amid deterrents to this recovery including racial tensions, injustices, and the rapid spread of policies of segregation.

In another classical contribution to our field of study, Freire in Chapter 3 presents his "banking" concept of education as a springboard to think about the roles and interactions of educators and learners in adult education, where the key goal of social education is justice for all that starts from building critical consciousness of worldly realities and systems. Freire's anti-oppression work has been a major influence on critical pedagogy and critical adult education in North America. What reflective practitioners can gain from this piece is a set of themes to guide the development of a democratic social practice of adult education. These themes include education as the practice of freedom, education as transformation through praxis, and education as a proactive space for problem solving. These themes are central to Freire's goal for adult education: to help educators and learners build partnerships through critically reflective dialogue and action to create a better world.

In Chapter 4, Grace explores the emergence of U.S. academic adult education during the quarter century following World War II when knowledge production was deeply influenced by an array of economic and cultural transitions. This article is informative to those exploring how adult education has to readjust to cope with the fallout from the ongoing economic crisis that hit with full force in the fall of 2008. While the present is different, the article and the current crisis both raise the same basic question for adult educators: What knowledge has most worth? Grace considers how adult educators answered this question pragmatically after World War II so they might increase the presence and value of adult education in mainstream education and culture. This article, exploring such constructs as liberal adult education, provides food for thought for those concerned with the decline of social education and its emphases on democracy, freedom, and social justice in a more instrumentalized lifelong learning world.

In a social historical analysis in Chapter 5, Glowacki-Dudka and Helvie-Mason locate adult education at the margins of the university and society. Their work speaks to readers concerned with assaults on academic adult education. Glowacki-Dudka and Helvie-Mason reflect on purposes and goals of adult education tied to the dichotomy of adult education as social education and as a professionalized practice. For readers concerned that adult education is a weather vane responding to social, cultural, and economic change forces, their analysis leads to a hopeful conclusion: While adult education is a marginalized enterprise, it can be energized by the field's natural tendencies toward collectivity, flexibility, and diversity.

Johnson-Bailey's Chapter 6 parallels themes in Locke's analysis. She explores the steady and committed participation of African Americans in adult education, surveying available research on the sociopolitical and cultural aspects of this educational movement. In particular, she focuses on African-American involvement in the Harlem Renaissance (1920–1945). Themes emerging from her study include education for assimilation (linked to addressing the Black "problem"); education for cultural survival (associated with Black efforts to build self-esteem and cultural importance in the context of nation); and education for resistance (focused on minority rights and addressing injustices). For educators and learners who may think adult education is neutral, Johnson-Bailey's article challenges them to interrogate the field's political nature and the ways that modern practice has been exclusionary.

Any reflection on the foundations of adult education ought to include a focus on ethical issues and practices. In Chapter 7, Gordon and Sork consider arguments for and against the development of codes of ethics across professional practices. They compare views of Canadian and U.S. adult educational practitioners regarding the scope and functions of codes of ethics. They survey practitioner encounters with ethical issues and dilemmas, listing frequently cited issues like confidentiality and learner-adult educator relationships. Gordon and Sork's research will have import for reflective practitioners grappling with codes of ethics, attitudes toward them, and their implications for the field of study and practice.

As the selections in this section demonstrate, traditional adult education has been marked by a commitment to education for social purposes. The social history of the field reminds us of a long-standing critical concern with issues of democracy, freedom, social justice, and ethics. Sometimes these issues have been sidelined in instrumental moves to professionalize modern practice. We hope that readers consider the selections in this section to be an appetizer for further engagement with the foundations of adult education.

▨ FOR REFLECTION AND DISCUSSION

1. Inspired by the theme *living and learning for a viable future: the power of adult learning,* the UNESCO-sponsored Sixth International Conference on Adult Education (CONFINTEA VI) was held in Bélem do Pará, Brazil, December 1–4, 2009. CONFINTEA VI noted that a significant portion of adult learning and education is deeply rooted in everyday life, local contexts, and grassroots initiatives focused on addressing social, cultural, and environmental challenges

(UIL, 2010). Provide some examples of such contemporary adult education from your own knowledge and experience. How does adult education today compare to ways it was constructed in the historical articles in this section?

2. While CONFINTEA VI positioned *diversity* as a necessity in adult learning and education, does it exacerbate field fragmentation? Are there ways to value diversity and still describe the field as strong, coherent, and organized?

3. How might we address the long-standing divide positioning adult education for social and cultural purposes against adult education as a professionalized practice tied to economic interests? Do social and economic interests have to be in opposition?

4. How might learning from the history of education for Black adults in the United States inform and revitalize more dynamic and inclusive contemporary forms of adult education focused on social justice?

5. How important is it for the field of adult education to have a code of ethics? With the enormous diversity of programs and constituencies that exist, is it even possible or realistic to have a code of ethics?

REFERENCES

Giroux, H. A. (1996). Is there a place for cultural studies in colleges of education? In H. A. Giroux, C. Lankshear, P. McLaren, & M. Peters (Eds.), *Counternarratives: Cultural studies and critical pedagogies in postmodern spaces* (pp. 41–58). New York: Routledge.

Giroux, H. A., & McLaren, P. (1988). Teacher education and the politics of democratic reform. In H. A. Giroux (Ed.), *Teachers as intellectuals: Toward a critical pedagogy of learning* (pp. 158–176). New York: Bergin & Garvey.

Lindeman, E. C. (1926/1961). *The meaning of adult education*. Montreal: Harvest House.

Stubblefield, H. W., & Keane, P. (1994). *Adult education in the American experience*. San Francisco: Jossey-Bass.

UNESCO Institute for Lifelong Learning (UIL). (2010). *CONFINTEA VI – Sixth international conference on adult education: Final report*. Hamburg, Germany: Author.

CHAPTER 1

For Those Who Need to Be Learners

Eduard C. Lindeman

"We need, then, to reintegrate, to synthesize, to bind up together the different forces and influences in our national life. We need a greater courage: seriousness, a greater courage in self-knowledge, a greater unity, and changes in the machinery of our education which leave our religious and political life in their existing incoherence, or even add to it, will not serve our purpose."
—A. E. ZLMMERN

"The principle we wish to establish is that the important thing in this connection is an increased demand on the part of all kinds of people for educational facilities, which may roughly be termed non-vocational, since they are concerned really with restoring balance to a man who has, of necessity, developed to a great extent one or other of his characteristics for the purposes of his livelihood or for the satisfaction of his reasonable desires."
—ALBERT MANSBRIDGE

Education conceived as preparation for life locks the learning process within a vicious circle. Youth educated in terms of adult ideas and taught to think of learning as a process which ends when real life begins will make no better use of intelligence than the elders who prescribe the system. Brief and rebellious moments occur when youth sees this fallacy clearly, but alas, the pressure of adult civilization is too great; in the end young people fit into the pattern, succumb to the tradition of their elders—indeed, become elderly-minded before their time. Education within the vicious circle becomes not a joyous enterprise but rather something to be endured because it leads to a satisfying end. But there can be no genuine joy in the end if means are irritating, painful. Generally therefore those who have "completed" a standardized regimen of education promptly turn their faces in the opposite direction. Humor, but more of pathos lurks in the caricature of the college graduate standing in cap and gown, diploma in hand shouting: "Educated, b'gosh!" Henceforth, while devoting himself to life he will think of education as a necessary annoyance for succeeding youths. For him, this life for which he has suffered the affliction of learning will come to be a series of dull, uninteresting, degrading capitulations to the stereotyped pattern of his "set." Within a single decade he will be out of touch with the world of intelligence, or what is worse, he will still be using the intellectual coins of his college days; he will find difficulty in reading serious books; he will have become inured to the jargon of his particular profession and will affect derision for all "highbrows"; he will, in short, have become a typical adult who holds the bag of education—the game of learning having long since slipped by him.

Obviously, extension of the quantity of educational facilities cannot break the circle. Once the belief was current that if only education were free to all, intelligence would become the proper tool for managing the affairs of the world. We have gone even further and have made certain levels of education compulsory. But the result has been disappointing; we have succeeded merely in formalizing, mechanizing, educational processes. The spirit and meaning of education cannot be enhanced by addition, by the easy method of giving the same dose to more individuals. If learning is to be revivified, quickened so as to become once more an adventure, we shall have need of new concepts, new motives, new methods; we shall need to experiment with the qualitative aspects of education.

A fresh hope is astir. From many quarters comes the call to a new kind of education with its initial assumption affirming that *education is life*—not a mere preparation for an unknown kind of future living. Consequently all static concepts of education which relegate the learning process to the period of youth are abandoned. The whole of life is learning, therefore education can have no endings. This new venture is called *adult education*—not because it is confined to adults but because adulthood, maturity, defines its limits. The concept is inclusive. The fact that manual workers of Great Britain and farmers of Denmark have conducted the initial experiments which now inspire us does not imply that adult education is designed solely for these classes. No one, probably, needs adult education so much as the college graduate for it is he who makes the most doubtful assumptions concerning the function of learning.

Secondly, education conceived as a process coterminous with life revolves about *non-vocational* ideals. In this world of specialists everyone will of necessity learn to do his work, and if education of any variety can assist in this and in the further end of helping the worker to see the meaning of his labor, it will be education of high order. But adult education more accurately defined begins where vocational education leaves off. Its purpose is to put meaning into the whole of life. Workers, those who perform essential services, will naturally discover more values in continuing education than will those for whom all knowledge is merely decorative or conversational. The possibilities of enriching the activities of labor itself grow less for all workers who manipulate automatic machines. If the good life, the life interfused with meaning and with joy, is to come to these, opportunities for expressing more of the total personality than is called forth by machines will be needed. Their lives will be quickened into creative activities in proportion as they learn to make fruitful use of leisure.

Thirdly, the approach to adult education will be via the route of *situations,* not subjects. Our academic system has grown in reverse order: subjects and teachers constitute the starting-point; students are secondary. In conventional education the student is required to adjust himself to an established curriculum; in adult education the curriculum is built around the student's needs and interests. Every adult person finds himself in specific situations with respect to his work, his recreation, his family-life, his community-life, et cetera—situations which call for adjustments. Adult education begins at this point. Subject-matter is brought into the situation, is put to work, when needed. Texts and teachers play a new and secondary role in this type of education; they must give way to the primary importance of the learner. (Indeed, as we shall see later, the teacher of adults becomes also a learner.) The situation-approach to education means that the learning process is at the outset given a setting of reality. Intelligence performs its function in relation to actualities, not abstractions.

In the fourth place, the resource of highest value in adult education is the *learner's experience.* If education is life, then life is also education. Too much of learning consists of vicarious substitution of someone else's experience and knowledge. Psychology is teaching us, however, that we learn what we do, and that therefore all genuine education will keep doing and thinking together. Life becomes rational, meaningful, as we learn to be intelligent about the things we do and the things that happen to us. If we lived sensibly, we should all discover that the attractions of experience increase as we grow older. Correspondingly, we should find cumulative joys in searching out the reasonable meaning of the events in which we play parts. In teaching children it may be necessary to anticipate objective experience by uses of imagination but adult experience is already there waiting to be appropriated. Experience is the adult learner's living textbook.

Authoritative teaching, examinations which preclude original thinking, rigid pedagogical formula—all of these have no place in adult education. "Friends educating each other," says Yeaxlee, and perhaps Walt Whitman saw accurately with his fervent democratic vision what the new educational experiment implied when he wrote: "Learn from the simple—teach the wise." Small groups of aspiring adults who desire to keep their minds fresh and vigorous; who begin to learn by confronting pertinent situations; who dig down into the reservoirs of their experience before resorting to texts and secondary facts; who are led in the discussion by teachers who are also searchers after wisdom and not oracles: this constitutes the setting for adult education, the modern quest for life's meaning.

But where does one search for life's meaning? If adult education is not to fall into the pitfalls which have vulgarized public education, caution must be exercised in striving for answers to this query. For example, once the assumption is made that human nature is uniform, common and static—that all human beings will find meaning in identical goals, ends or aims—the standardizing process begins: teachers are trained according to orthodox and regulated methods; they teach prescribed subjects to large classes of children who must all pass the same examination; in short, if we accept the standard of uniformity, it follows that we expect, e.g., mathematics, to mean as much to one student as to another. Teaching methods which proceed from this assumption must necessarily become autocratic; if we assume that all values and meanings apply equally to all persons, we may then justify ourselves in using a forcing-method of teaching. On the other hand, if we take for granted that human nature is varied, changing and fluid, we will know that life's meanings are conditioned by the individual. We will then entertain a new respect for personality.

Since the individual personality is not before us we are driven to generalization. In what areas do most people appear to find life's meaning? We have only one pragmatic guide: meaning must reside in the things for which people strive, the goals which they set for themselves, their wants, needs, desires and wishes. Even here our criterion is applicable only to those whose lives are already dedicated to aspirations and ambitions which belong to the higher levels of human achievement. The adult able to break the habits of slovenly mentality and willing to devote himself seriously to study when study no longer holds forth the lure of pecuniary gain is, one must admit, a personality in whom many negative aims and desires have already been eliminated. Under examination, and viewed from the standpoint of adult education, such personalities seem to want among other things, intelligence, power, self-expression, freedom, creativity, appreciation, enjoyment, fellowship. Or, stated in terms of the Greek ideal, they are searchers after the good life. They want to count for something; they want their experiences to be vivid and meaningful; they want their talents to be utilized; they want to know beauty and joy; and they want all of these realizations of their total personalities to be shared in communities of fellowship. Briefly they want to improve themselves; this is their realistic and primary aim. But they want also to change the social order so that vital personalities will be creating a new environment in which their aspirations may be properly expressed.

CHAPTER 2

The Negro in America

Alain Locke

INTRODUCTION

One-tenth of the population of "these United States" is black, brown or yellow, of Negro descent and remotely of African derivation, and, according to the relative rates of population growth, this racial ratio promises to remain nearly constant indefinitely. To visualize this ratio, it has been aptly suggested that we think of the Negro as "America's tenth man." But the Negro's true significance only becomes evident when to this numerical importance we add that which he has always had as a national issue and which he still has as a present-day minority problem. As the "bone of contention" in the slavery controversy, the "ward of democracy" throughout the Reconstruction, and the "problem" of interracial adjustment in the contemporary social order, the Negro has been by some irony of fate throughout American history the human crux of our practical problems of political and social democracy.

The importance of being a problem, however, is a handicapping, not a stimulating, importance, and the black minority would gladly be relieved of it. Yet not until social justice and consistent democracy are worked out in America will the Negro as America's most chronic social problem cease to have an unnatural and disproportionate prominence. This summary and outline reading course are designed to help the reader interested in the problem of the Negro minority achieve historical perspective, social insight and progressive understanding with respect to it, and, equally important, to lead him to some acquaintance with the human elements and achievements of the people behind the problem.

If ever the story of the American Negro can be divorced from the controversial plane of the race problem—and some day it will—the story will then be told and appreciated as one of the impressive epics of human history. For, in the final analysis, it is a great folk-epic. In order that the reader may have panoramic perspective, let us review the main stages of this racial epic in its tragic, but momentous and inspiring three-hundred-year course through the decades of American history. We review it not solely to gratify historical curiosity or to evoke sentimental interest, but because the one safe intellectual approach to a social problem is through a sound historical perspective. Since this, too, is a most effective cure for prejudice and social misunderstanding, the wide-scale cultivation of such an approach seems obviously one of the outstanding practical hopes of the Negro and one of the great progressive needs of democracy.

To comprehend the Negro in America one must trace his path for seven or eight human generations through a long inferno of slavery and a yet unfinished social purgatory of testing struggle and development. The black man's Odyssey began with the terrific toll of a wholesale transplanting from Africa, rapidly succeeded by burdensome, yet transforming, tasks. The Negro endured titanic toil, the complete transformation of his ways of life, and the stress of an unplanned, begrudged, but quite redeeming, assimilation of the white man's civilization and religion. Patience, adaptability, loyalty and smiling humility gave him the subtle victory of survival against great odds; and the first act of slavery climaxed with the welding of patriarchal ties between master and slave.

But the tragic second act was already pushing the first off the historical scene. Slavery deepens and spreads; the black victim must descend to its abysses in the Lower South, nurturing almost hopelessly, but for religion, the underground hope of freedom. And then, as the vexing question of human property begins to divide the political and legal councils of the nation, the fugitive slave sets fire to the tinder of abolitionism and moral reaction, and suddenly out of the first great crisis comes the Civil War and slave emancipation.

But after the first blind leap of the black masses into the hopeful chaos and opportunities of freedom, Negro life was destined to drag through the Reconstruction and its heavy series of ordeals. First there was the difficult lesson of self-maintenance, clumsily but ploddingly learned; then the still heavier task of education, feverishly and unevenly achieved; then confusion and setback, patiently endured, under the storm of Reconstruction reaction and mob violence; then a slow, dogged retreat from serfdom and partial defeat on the tenant farms to the labor marts of the towns and cities; more patient endurance of the loss of the newly won franchise and the civil rights of full citizenship; and eventually a new mass concentration and survival in the city's black ghettos, under steady odds of economic discrimination and segregation.

Finally, with another war, another crisis and its new opportunities came. This time it was the surge forward into the World War's rapid expansion of life and labor, and a consequent enlargement of life, economic and cultural, in the new centers. But the anticipated rewards of the Negro's patriotic response to the idealism of the "War to Save Democracy" were not measurably realized and, spurred by the bitter disillusionments of post-war indifference, there came that desperate intensification of the Negro's race consciousness and attempt at the recovery of group morale through a racialist program of self-help and self-determination which has been the outstanding development in Negro life during this generation. With this phase came the beginnings of independent economic enterprise, a growing disposition for political action and the recovery of civil rights and political participation; and finally on the horizon a mounting wave of new social and economic realism. It is with this new temper and attitude that the Negro confronts the present crisis, with its crossroads dilemma of either slow progress by patient advance and interracial cooperation or of problematic but tempting quick progress through joining issues with the forces of radical proletarian reform. This is the point at which we contemporary spectators stand, survey and wonder. Certainly the past of the Negro in America has been an epical adventure, pursued against great odds and opposition, but favored, almost providentially at critical times, by saving alliances with the forces of moral and social liberalism, all combining to achieve a gradually ascending scale of achievement and progress.

On the other side, the story is equally dramatic if read in forward-looking perspective. It is the long Odyssey of the white mind, wandering through the mazes of self-made dilemmas, in search of a way out into the consistent practice of democracy.

Out of the Civil War, inevitable consequence of the deepening hold of slavery, emancipation came as a strategic blow at the seceded South; half a national economy had to be overturned and the freed Negro masses became the helpless, burdensome wards of the Federal government. Meshed in with the aftermath of war and slavery came then a conflicting flow and ebb of forces, now favorable, now unfavorable, to the interests of the Negro.

In 1895, however, a leader in black reconstruction caught the approval of the South and the favor of Northern captains of industry by an appeal for advancing the South through improving the industrial and economic condition of the Negro. There followed a great revival of philanthropic interest and aid in the education of the Negro; but along with it a very prevalent and possibly dangerous acceptance of Booker Washington's strategic compromise of bi-racialism: "In all things vital and economic, we can be one as the hand, while in things social we can be separate as the fingers." There followed a decade and more of common, constructive, enthusiastic effort to truss up the sagging economy of the rural Southern Negro, but the odds of a bad system of land tenant farming, an unscientific type of agriculture, continued exploitation and the inroads of the growing industrialization of the South all combined to cause a steady trek of the Negro population from the land toward the cities. This caused or coincided with another reaction of Southern opinion and a flare of race riots and increased racial tension, bridged only at a desperate moment in 1919 by the adoption of the new machinery of local interracial commissions to allay popular antagonism and bring the better elements of both races together in common counsel and constructive community effort.

To this movement we owe the emergence of the new liberal South. But the large-scale migration of Negroes from the South to Northern centers shortly afterward led to increased friction in these communities, and merely shifted the areas and issues of racial tension. In fact, a problem conventionally regarded as sectional suddenly and unmistakably became national, and a new phase of the race problem began. We still confront a seriously divided white mind, no longer split sectionally, but divided now into nation-wide liberal and reactionary camps. A liberal element in the South, small but influential, has recanted the traditional antagonisms and code of the old régime, and in liberal circles, North and South, an enlightened minority is showing an increased willingness to welcome Negro advance, to join cooperatively with Negro leadership in programs of racial and community improvement, and to extend recognition and reciprocity to the advance-guard elements of Negro life. Over against this, however, is a white mass mind still reactionary and strongly racial; this time largely over labor rivalry and for economic reasons. In fact, segregation policies and labor discrimination have now become the crucial practical issues in the contemporary racial situation. And although this reactionary body of opinion is not as militant as the older traditional opposition, its wide distribution, North and South, is a threatening aspect in the present and near future.

These are but highlights in the history of the shifting attitudes of the white majority mind, as it has grappled and fumbled, relaxed and grown tense again, in reaction to the steadily changing situations of the steadily advancing black minority.

Students of the question are generally agreed that the effect of the Negro's presence in this country has been about as marked as the admittedly great and transforming influence of America upon the Negro. There is this double strand running through the whole scheme of the American race problem, and the student should bear constantly in mind the parallelism by which every white move has its black counterpart, every black stitch, its white counter-stitch. Whenever we think of the situation as a minority problem, we must instantly think of it also in its other aspect as a majority problem. This is factual warrant for preferring to regard the dilemmas and difficulties of this minority-majority interaction as the American race problem rather than as the "Negro problem." In every historical crisis its consequences have turned out to be just as national as they have been racial; and it should be obvious that from no one side of the equation alone can its progressive solution be carried forward.

THE PRESENT-DAY PROBLEM (CIRCA 1933)

The transformation of the Negro during the last two decades is founded on two motives, one physical, the other, spiritual. Migration has been the physical mainspring of the change, and a new spirit of race consciousness and solidarity has been the regenerating spiritual force. Out of the combination has come both a "New Negro," and a new frontage of the Negro on American life.

All through his history since emancipation, the Negro has been responding to unfavorable conditions by migration, but this last series of mass movements has been upon an unprecedented scale. It had begun before the outbreak of the World War, but was heavily increased by the demands of industry during the war for the replacement of the European immigrant labor supply. This has been estimated as a movement northward of over a million and a half of the Negro population. But to this must be added that phase of the Negro migration which is not inter-sectional between North and South, but from the rural to the urban centers within comparatively short range. Two results are outstanding, the rapid urbanization of the Negro, a serious shift in the areas feeling the stresses of race contacts and their difficulties, a decided extension of new phases of the race situation to cities of the North and Mid-West, and a closer alignment of the race issue with the problems of labor competition and economic adjustment.

It has already been pointed out that a decided increase in race tension and a rapid spread of policies of segregation have accompanied this mass movement. But the movement has had its positive gains; large masses of the Negro population have been subjected to the galvanizing shocks of change and have thus been stimulated to rapid progress. Because of the new concentrations in city areas, there has been a marked heightening of the sense of group solidarity and common interests. This will prove to be the most potential and powerful factor in the whole situation, if ever the exigencies of Negro life should demand large-scale mass action. And if the present heavy social and economic pressure on the Negro should increase or even be maintained, such demands will undoubtedly arise. There have also been great drawbacks in this urban movement, chiefly the unfavorable conditions in the almost ghetto-like city centers where so many of the migrant masses have been forced to congregate, and the precarious marginal position of the Negro on the fringe of the labor market, faced at present, as he is, by comparative indifference or hostility from the ranks of organized white labor.

Though fraught with danger, this is an entirely new alignment, likely within half a generation to change the whole basic aspect of the race question. There is a school of younger Negro thought which, viewing the increasing emphasis of the situation upon the economic condition of the Negro masses, regards the race question as likely to resolve itself into the issues of the economic class struggle and proletarian radicalism. There is a main obstacle, however, for the present, in the conservative temper of social thinking now prevalent among Negroes, although in very recent years there are increasing signs of a slow drift toward the spirit and doctrines of social radicalism. Certainly the only likely factors in a possible shift of any large section of the Negro masses in the direction of radical social action would be those of extreme pressure from intolerable mass conditions in the city areas or desperate reaction in the face of continued exclusion from the ranks and opportunities of progressive and organized white labor.

A feature of great importance, however, is the swing of the race situation in the South toward this same condition of increasing economic discrimination and labor antagonism. This is a direct result of the recent industrialization of the South and the simultaneous shift of the Negro population to city and town centers. At first the northward migration of the Negro had a favorable influence on the Southern situation. There was a greater appreciation of the Negro as an economic asset and as a potential labor supply. Considerable improvement followed in the policy of Southern communities, resulting in the improvement of school and civic facilities for Negroes in the South. But in spite of heavy increases in state expenditure for public school facilities for Negroes in the South, still more equitable division of the public school funds is obviously necessary, since with all this rapid improvement only 69 per cent of the Negro children of school age are enrolled and the general per capita expenditure averages for the whole South only one-third of the average expenditure for white children, with of course many communities falling considerably below this general average.

When all favorable progress has been taken into account, therefore, there is still much injustice to be remedied: the persistence of lynching and mob-terrorism, the increasing tension and competition of white and Negro unskilled and semi-skilled labor, the crowding of the Negro out of the higher ranks of labor, some of which he occupied earlier in the century, the continuation of the traditional policies of segregation in public, civic and educational activities, the inequitable distribution of the Negro share in public tax funds for schools and civic improvements, and continued lack of respect for the advancing class of Negroes, except from the few enlightened liberal elements in the Southern communities.

Summarizing the whole situation, we may see that although the Negro has made amazingly rapid gains in the last few years, the race situation in both the North and the South is intensified, indeed partly because of these gains. For mass opinion among whites still interprets this rapid advance as social and economic encroachment, and seldom looks at it in its deeper constructive aspect of common advance and the lifting of the level of civilization. So, unless liberal white opinion in both sections, in cooperation with intelligent Negro leadership, can rapidly widen opportunities and lessen artificial handicaps, the mass momentum of Negro advance must produce serious race conflict. Short of the bitter extremities of ruthless economic conflict or resolution of the mass feud between black and white through the discovery of common proletarian interests, there lies one intermediate way of realistic hope, since, after all, America has kept herself an institutional democracy in spite of her treatment of the Negro. The Negro, though still heavily disfranchised, is potentially a citizen with the corrective power of the ballot. Two things encourage this hope: the revival of the Negro's interest in reclaiming the ballot along with political independence in its use, and the fact that by his recent migrations to border states, he has acquired unexpectedly considerable re-enfranchisement and latent political power. This, intelligently used, might remove enough of the restrictions to his progress to forestall serious race conflict, and might lead to the steady progressive adjustment so desirable and so desired by all but the extreme social reactionaries and the extreme social radicals.

The Negro's Americanism

A solution of the race problem within the institutional framework and the traditional ideals of American democracy would be most congenial and welcome to the Negro, for on the whole his Americanism is unquestioned and unquestioning. Both by temperament and group policy, the Negro has been conformist throughout his history in this country. His values, his ideals, his objectives, have been peculiarly and unreservedly American. Racialism has rarely, if ever, been a direct mood for the Negro, but only an enforced counter-attitude in the face of proscription and discrimination. And, even then, this racialism has never set up separate or different values or loyalties, but has only been a practical social device to secure on a separate basis and by another route the common values and ends which prejudice more directly denied or curtailed. Except for superficial physical dissimilarities, by and large, the Negro would be indistinguishably American, and it is unlikely that a foreign observer would believe himself in the presence of a different race. What overtones of emotional difference there are, in fair comparison with the mass similarities, would seem negligible, making the prevalent social sense of difference all the more contrary to reason and ironical. On historical, psychological and cultural grounds, the Negro minority is entitled to the fullest share in American civilization, and has less real impediments and separatist tendencies than any other of the many component minority elements in America.

CHAPTER 3

Pedagogy of the Oppressed

Chapter 2

Paulo Freire

A careful analysis of the teacher-student relationship at any level, inside or outside the school, reveals its fundamentally *narrative* character. This relationship involves a narrating Subject (the teacher) and patient listening objects (the students). The contents, whether values or empirical dimensions of reality, tend in the process of being narrated to become lifeless and petrified. Education is suffering from narration sickness.

The teacher talks about reality as if it were motionless, static, compartmentalized, and predictable. Or else he expounds on a topic completely alien to the existential experience of the students. His task is to "fill" the students with the contents of his narration—contents which are detached from reality, disconnected from the totality that engendered them and could give them significance. Words are emptied of their concreteness and become a hollow, alienated, and alienating verbosity.

The outstanding characteristic of this narrative education, then, is the sonority of words, not their transforming power. "Four times four is sixteen; the capital of Pará is Belém." The student records, memorizes, and repeats these phrases without perceiving what four times four really means, or realizing the true significance of "capital" in the affirmation "the capital of Pará is Belém," that is, what Belém means for Pará and what Pará means for Brazil.

Narration (with the teacher as narrator) leads the students to memorize mechanically the narrated account. Worse yet, it turns them into "containers," into "receptacles" to be "filled" by the teachers. The more completely she fills the receptacles, the better a teacher she is. The more meekly the receptacles permit themselves to be filled, the better students they are.

Education thus becomes an act of depositing, in which the students are the depositories and the teacher is the depositor. Instead of communicating, the teacher issues communiqués and makes deposits which the students patiently receive, memorize, and repeat. This is the "banking" concept of education, in which the scope of action allowed to the students extends only as far as receiving, filing, and storing the deposits. They do, it is true, have the opportunity to become collectors or cataloguers of the things they store. But in the last analysis, it is the people themselves who are filed away through the lack of creativity, transformation, and knowledge in this (at best) misguided system. For apart from inquiry, apart from the praxis, individuals cannot be truly human. Knowledge emerges only through invention and re-invention, through the restless, impatient continuing, hopeful inquiry human beings pursue in the world, with the world, and with each other.

In the banking concept of education, knowledge is a gift bestowed by those who consider themselves knowledgeable upon those whom they consider to know nothing. Projecting an absolute ignorance onto others, a characteristic of the ideology of oppression, negates education and knowledge as processes of inquiry. The teacher presents himself to his students as their necessary opposite; by considering their ignorance absolute, he justifies his own existence. The students, alienated like the slave in the Hegelian dialectic, accept their ignorance as justifying the teacher's existence—but unlike the slave, they never discover that they educate the teacher.

The *raison d'être* of libertarian education, on the other hand, lies in its drive towards reconciliation. Education must begin with the solution of the teacher-student contradiction, by reconciling the poles of the contradiction so that both are simultaneously teachers *and* students.

This solution is not (nor can it be) found in the banking concept. On the contrary, banking education maintains and even stimulates the contradiction through the following attitudes and practices, which mirror oppressive society as a whole:

a. the teacher teaches and the students are taught;
b. the teacher knows everything and the students know nothing;
c. the teacher thinks and the students are thought about;
d. the teacher talks and the students listen—meekly;

e.   the teacher disciplines and the students are disciplined;

f.   the teacher chooses and enforces his choice, and the students comply;

g.   the teacher acts and the students have the illusion of acting through the action of the teacher;

h.   the teacher chooses the program content, and the students (who were not consulted) adapt to it;

i.   the teacher confuses the authority of knowledge with his or her own professional authority, which she and he sets in opposition to the freedom of the students;

j.   the teacher is the Subject of the learning process, while the pupils are mere objects.

It is not surprising that the banking concept of education regards men as adaptable, manageable beings. The more students work at storing the deposits entrusted to them, the less they develop the critical consciousness which would result from their intervention in the world as transformers of that world. The more completely they accept the passive role imposed on them, the more they tend simply to adapt to the world as it is and to the fragmented view of reality deposited in them.

The capability of banking education to minimize or annul the student's creative power and to stimulate their credulity serves the interests of the oppressors, who care neither to have the world revealed nor to see it transformed. The oppressors use their "humanitarianism" to preserve a profitable situation. Thus they react almost instinctively against any experiment in education which stimulates the critical faculties and is not content with a partial view of reality but always seeks out the ties which link one point to another and one problem to another.

Indeed, the interests of the oppressors lie in "changing the consciousness of the oppressed, not the situation which oppresses them," (de Beauvoir, 1963, p. 34) for the more the oppressed can be led to adapt to that situation, the more easily they can be dominated. To achieve this the oppressors use the banking concept of education in conjunction with a paternalistic social action apparatus, within which the oppressed receive the euphemistic title of "welfare recipients." They are treated as individual cases, as marginal persons who deviate from the general configuration of a "good, organized and just" society. The oppressed are regarded as the pathology of the healthy society which must therefore adjust these "incompetent and lazy" folk to its own patterns by changing their mentality.

These marginals need to be "integrated," "incorporated" into the healthy society that they have "forsaken."

The truth is, however, that the oppressed are not "marginals," are not living "outside" society. They have always been "inside" the structure which made them "beings for others." The solution is not to "integrate" them into the structure of oppression, but to transform that structure so that they can become "beings for themselves." Such transformation, of course, would undermine the oppressors' purposes; hence their utilization of the banking concept of education to avoid the threat of student *conscientização*.

The banking approach to adult education, for example, will never propose to students that they critically consider reality. It will deal instead with such vital questions as whether Roger gave green grass to the goat, and insist upon the importance of learning that, on the contrary, Roger gave green grass to the rabbit. The "humanism" of the banking approach masks the effort to turn women and men into automatons—the very negation of their ontological vocation to be more fully human.

Those who use the banking approach, knowingly or unknowingly (for there are innumerable well-intentioned bank-clerk teachers who do not realize that they are serving only to dehumanize), fail to perceive that the deposits themselves contain contradictions about reality. But sooner or later, these contradictions may lead formerly passive students to turn against their domestication and the attempt to domesticate reality. They may discover through existential experience that their present way of life is irreconcilable with their vocation to become fully human. They may perceive through their relations with reality that reality is really a *process,* undergoing constant transformation. If men and women are searchers and their ontological vocation is humanization, sooner or later they may perceive the contradiction in which banking education seeks to maintain them, and then engage themselves in the struggle for their liberation.

But the humanist revolutionary educator cannot wait for this possibility to materialize. From the outset, her efforts must coincide with those of the students to engage in critical thinking and the quest for mutual humanization. His efforts must be imbued with a profound trust in people and their creative power. To achieve this, they must be partners of the students in their relations with them.

The banking concept does not admit to such partnership—and necessarily so. To resolve the teacher-student contradiction, to exchange the role of depositor, prescriber, domesticator, for the role of student among students would be to undermine the power of oppression and serve the cause of liberation.

Implicit in the banking concept is the assumption of a dichotomy between human beings and the world: a person is merely *in* the world, not *with* the world or with others; the individual is spectator, not re-creator. In this view, the person is not a conscious being (*corpo consciente*); he or she is rather the possessor of a consciousness: an empty "mind" passively open to the reception of deposits of reality from the world outside. For example, my desk, my books, my coffee cup, all the objects before me—as bits of the world which surround me—would be "inside" me, exactly as I am inside my study right now. This view makes no distinction between being accessible to consciousness and entering consciousness. The distinction, however, is essential: the objects which surround me are simply accessible to my consciousness, not located within it. I am aware of them, but they are not inside me.

It follows logically from the banking notion of consciousness that the educator's role is to regulate the way the world "enters into" the students. The teacher's task is to organize a process which already occurs spontaneously, to "fill" the students by making deposits of information which he or she considers to constitute true knowledge.[1] And since people "receive" the world as passive entities, education should make them more passive still, and adapt them to the world. The educated individual is the adapted person, because she or he is better "fit" for the world. Translated into practice, this concept is well suited for the purposes of the oppressors, whose tranquility rests on how well people fit the world the oppressors have created and how little they question it.

The more completely the majority adapt to the purposes which the dominant majority prescribe for them (thereby depriving them of the right to their own purposes), the more easily the minority can continue to prescribe. The theory and practice of banking education serve this end quite efficiently. Verbalistic lessons, reading requirements,[2] the methods for evaluating "knowledge," the distance between the teacher and the taught, the criteria for promotion: everything in this ready-to-wear approach serves to obviate thinking.

The bank-clerk educator does not realize that there is no true security in his hypertrophied role, that one must seek to live *with* others in solidarity. One cannot impose oneself, nor even merely co-exist with one's students. Solidarity requires true communication, and the concept by which such an educator is guided fears and proscribes communication.

Yet only through communication can human life hold meaning. The teacher's thinking is authenticated only by the authenticity of the students' thinking. The teacher cannot think for her students, nor can she impose her thought on them.

Authentic thinking, thinking that is concerned about *reality,* does not take place in ivory tower isolation, but only in communication. If it is true that thought has meaning only when generated by action upon the world, the subordination of students to teachers becomes impossible.

Because banking education begins with a false understanding of men and women as objects, it cannot promote the development of what Fromm calls "biophily," but instead produces its opposite: "necrophily."

> While life is characterized by growth in a structured functional manner, the necrophilous person loves all that does not grow, all that is mechanical. The necrophilous person is driven by the desire to transform the organic into the inorganic, to approach life mechanically, as if all living persons were things.... Memory, rather than experience; having, rather than being, is what counts. The necrophilous person can relate to an object—a flower or a person—only if he possesses it; hence a threat to his possession is a threat to himself, if he loses possession he loses contact with the world.... He loves control, and in the act of controlling he kills life. (Fromm, 1966, p. 41)

Oppression—overwhelming control—is necrophilic; it is nourished by love of death, not life. The banking concept of education, which serves the interests of oppression, is also necrophilic. Based on a mechanistic, static, naturalistic, spatialized view of consciousness, it transforms students into receiving objects. It attempts to control thinking and action, leads women and men to adjust to the world, and inhibits their creative power.

When their efforts to act responsibly are frustrated, when they find themselves unable to use their faculties, people suffer. "This suffering due to impotence is rooted in the very fact that the human has been disturbed" (Fromm, 1966, p. 31). But the inability to act which causes people's anguish also causes them to reject their impotence, by attempting

> ....to restore [their] capacity to act. But can [they], and how? One way is to submit to and identify with a person or group having power. By this symbolic participation in another person's life, (men have] the illusion of acting, when in reality [they] only submit to and become a part of those who act. (Fromm, 1966, p. 31)

Populist manifestations perhaps best exemplify this type of behavior by the oppressed, who, by identifying with charismatic leaders, come to feel that they themselves are active and effective. The rebellion they express as they emerge in the historical process is motivated by that desire to act effectively. The dominant elites consider the remedy to be more domination and repression, carried out in the name of freedom, order, and social peace (that is, the peace of the elites). Thus they can condemn—logically, from their point of view—"the violence of a strike by workers and [can] call upon the state in the same breath to use violence in putting down the strike" (Niebuhr, 1960, p. 130).

Education as the exercise of domination stimulates the credulity of students, with the ideological intent (often not perceived by educators) of indoctrinating them to adapt to the world of oppression. This accusation is not made in the naïve hope that the dominant elites will thereby simply abandon the practice. Its objective is to call the attention of true humanists to the fact that they cannot use banking educational methods in the pursuit of liberation, for they would only negate that very pursuit. Nor may a revolutionary society inherit these methods from an oppressor society. The revolutionary society which practices banking education is either misguided or mistrusting of people. In either event, it is threatened by the specter of reaction.

Unfortunately, those who espouse the cause of liberation are themselves surrounded and influenced by the climate which generates the banking concept, and often do not perceive its true significance or its dehumanizing power. Paradoxically, then, they utilize this same instrument of alienation in what they consider an effort to liberate. Indeed, some "revolutionaries" brand as "innocents," "dreamers," or even "reactionaries" those who would challenge this educational practice. But one does not liberate people by alienating them. Authentic liberation—the process of humanization—is not another deposit to be made in men. Liberation is a praxis: the action and reflection of men and women upon their world in order to transform it. Those truly committed to the cause of liberation can accept neither the mechanistic concept of consciousness as an empty vessel to be filled, nor the use of banking methods of domination (propaganda, slogans—deposits) in the name of liberation.

Those truly committed to liberation must reject the banking concept in its entirety, adopting instead a concept of women and men as conscious beings, and consciousness as consciousness intent upon the world. They must abandon the educational goal of deposit-making and replace it with the posing of the problems of human beings in their relations with the world. "Problem-posing" education, responding to the essence of consciousness—*intentionality*—rejects communiqués and embodies communication. It epitomizes the special characteristic of consciousness: being *conscious of,* not only as intent on objects but as turned in upon itself in a Jasperian "split"—consciousness as consciousness of consciousness.

Liberating education consists in acts of cognition, not transferals of information. It is a learning situation in which the cognizable object (far from being the end of the cognitive act) intermediates the cognitive actors—teacher on the one hand and students on the other. Accordingly, the practice of problem-posing education entails at the outset that the teacher-student contradiction to be resolved. Dialogical relations—indispensable to the capacity of cognitive actors to cooperate in perceiving the same cognizable object—are otherwise impossible.

Indeed problem-posing education, which breaks with the vertical characteristic of banking education, can fulfill its function of freedom only if it can overcome the above contradiction. Through dialogue, the teacher-of-the-students and the students-of-the-teacher cease to exist and a new term emerges: teacher-student with students-teachers. The teacher is no longer merely the-one-who-teaches, but one who is himself taught in dialogue with the students, who in turn while being taught also teach. They become jointly responsible for a process in which all grow. In this process, arguments based on "authority" are no longer valid; in order to function authority must be *on the side of* freedom, not *against* it. Here, no one teaches another, nor is anyone self-taught. People teach each other, mediated by the world, by the cognizable objects which in banking education are "owned" by the teacher.

The banking concept (with its tendency to dichotomize everything) distinguishes two stages in the action of the educator. During the first he cognizes a cognizable object while he prepares his lessons in his study or his laboratory; during the second, he expounds to his students about that object. The students are not called upon to know, but to memorize the contents narrated by the teacher. Nor do the students practice any act of cognition, since the object towards which that act should be directed is the property of the teacher rather than a medium evoking the critical reflection of both teacher and students. Hence in the name of the "preservation of and knowledge" we have a system which achieves neither true knowledge nor true culture.

The problem-posing method does not dichotomize the activity of teacher-student: she is not "cognitive" at one point and "narrative" at another. She is always "cognitive," whether preparing a project or engaging in dialogue with the students. He does not regard objects as his private property, but as the object of reflection by himself and his students. In this way, the problem-posing educator constantly re-forms his reflections in the reflection of the students. The students—no longer docile listeners—are now critical co-investigators in dialogue with the teacher. The teacher presents the material to the students for their consideration, and re-considers her earlier considerations as the students express their own. The role of the problem-posing educator is to create, together with the students, the conditions under which knowledge at the level of the *doxa* is superseded by true knowledge at the level of the *logos*.

Whereas banking education anesthetizes and inhibits creative power, problem-posing education involves a constant unveiling of reality. The former attempts to maintain the *submersion* of consciousness; the latter strives for the *emergence* of consciousness and *critical intervention* in reality.

Students, as they are increasingly posed with problems relating to themselves in the world and with the world, will feel increasingly challenged and obliged to respond to that challenge. Because they apprehend the challenge as interrelated to other problems within a total context not as a theoretical question, the resulting comprehension tends to be increasingly critical and thus constantly less alienated. Their response to the challenge evokes new challenges, followed by new understandings; and gradually the students come to regard themselves as committed.

Education as the practice of freedom—as opposed to education as the practice of domination—denies that man is abstract, isolated, independent, and unattached to the world; it also denies that the world exists as a reality apart from people. Authentic reflection considers neither abstract man nor the world without people, but people in their relations with the world. In these relations consciousness and world are simultaneous: consciousness neither precedes the world nor follows it.

> La conscience et le monde sont dormés dun même coup: extérieur par essence à la conscience, le monde est, par essence relatif à elle. (Sartre, 1947, p. 32)

In one of our culture circles in Chile, the group was discussing (based on a codification[3]) the anthropological concept of culture. In the midst of the discussion, a peasant who by banking standards was completely ignorant said: "Now I see that without man there is no world." When the educator responded: "Let's say, for the sake of argument, that all the men on earth were to die, but that the earth remained, together with trees, birds, animals, rivers, seas, the stars... wouldn't all this be a world?" "Oh no," the peasant replied. "There would be no one to say: 'This is a world.'"

The peasant wished to express the idea that there would be lacking the consciousness of the world which necessarily implies the world of consciousness. *I* cannot exist without a *not-I*. In turn, the *not-I* depends on that existence.

The world which brings consciousness into existence becomes the world of that consciousness. Hence, the previously cited affirmation of Sartre: *"La conscience et le monde sont dormés d'un même coup."*

As women and men, simultaneously reflecting on themselves and on the world, increase the scope of their perception, they begin to direct their observations towards previously inconspicuous phenomena:

> In perception properly so-called, as an explicit awareness [*Gewahren*], I am turned towards the object, to the paper, for instance. I apprehend it as being this here and now. The apprehension is a singling out, every object having a background in experience. Around and about the paper lie books, pencils, inkwell and so forth, and these in a certain sense are also "perceived," perceptually there, in the "field of intuition"; but whilst I was turned towards the paper there was no turning in their direction, nor any apprehending of them, not even in a secondary sense. They appeared and yet were not singled out, were posited on their own account. Every perception of a thing has such a zone of background intuitions or background awareness, if "intuiting" already includes the state of being turned towards, and this also is a "conscious experience", or more briefly a "consciousness of" all indeed that in point of fact lies in the co-perceived objective background. (Husserl, 1969, pp. 105–106)

That which had existed objectively but had not been perceived in its deeper implications (if indeed it was perceived at all) begins to "stand out," assuming the character of a problem and therefore of challenge. Thus, men and women begin to single out elements from their "background awareness" and to reflect upon them. These elements are now objects of their consideration, and, as such, objects of their action and cognition.

In problem-posing education, people develop their power to perceive critically *the way they exist* in the world *with which* and *in which* they find themselves; they come to see the world not as a static reality, but as a reality in process, in transformation. Although the dialectical relations of women and men with the world exist independently of how these relations are perceived (or whether or not they are perceived at all), it is also true that the form of action they adopt is to a large extent a function of how they perceive themselves in the world. Hence, the teacher-student and the students-teachers reflect simultaneously on themselves and the world without dichotomizing this reflection from action, and thus establish an authentic form of thought and action.

Once again, the two educational concepts and practices under analysis come into conflict. Banking education (for obvious reasons) attempts, by mythicizing reality, to conceal certain facts which explain the way human beings exist in the world; problem-posing education sets itself the task of demythologizing. Banking education resists dialogue; problem-posing education regards dialogue as indispensable to the act of cognition which unveils reality. Banking education treats students as objects of assistance; problem-posing education makes them critical thinkers. Banking education inhibits creativity and domesticates (although it cannot completely destroy) the *intentionality* of consciousness by isolating consciousness from the world, thereby denying people their ontological and historical vocation of becoming more fully human. Problem-posing education bases itself on creativity and stimulates true reflection and action upon reality, thereby responding to the vocation of persons as beings only when engaged in inquiry and creative transformation. In sum: banking theory and practice, as immobilizing and fixating forces, fail to acknowledge men and women as historical beings; problem-posing theory and practice take the people's historicity as their starting point.

Problem-posing education affirms men and women as beings the process of *becoming*—as unfinished, uncompleted beings in and with a likewise unfinished reality. Indeed, in contrast to other animals who are unfinished, but not historical, people know themselves to be unfinished; they are aware of their incompletion. In this incompletion and this awareness lie the very roots of education as an human manifestation. The unfinished character of human beings and the transformational character of reality necessitate that education be an ongoing activity.

Education is thus constantly remade in the praxis. In order to *be,* it must *become.* Its "duration" (in the Bergsonian meaning of the word) is found in the interplay of the opposites *permanence* and *change.* The banking method emphasizes permanence and becomes reactionary; problem-posing education—which accepts neither a "well-behaved" present nor a predetermined future—roots itself in the dynamic present and becomes revolutionary.

Problem-posing education is revolutionary futurity. Hence it is prophetic (and as such, hopeful). Hence, it corresponds to the historical nature of humankind. Hence, it affirms women and men as beings who transcend themselves, who move forward and look ahead, for whom immobility represents a fatal threat, for whom looking at the past must only be a means of understanding more clearly what and who they are so that they can more wisely build the future. Hence, it identifies with the movement which engages people as beings aware of their incompletion—an historical movement which has its point of departure, its Subjects and its objective.

The point of departure of the movement lies in the people themselves. But since people do not exist apart from the world, apart from reality, the movement must begin with the human-world relationship. Accordingly, the point of departure must always be with men and women in the "here and now," which constitutes the situation within which they are submerged, from which they emerge, and in which they intervene. Only by starting from this situation—which determines their perception of it—can they begin to move. To do this authentically they must perceive their state not as fated and unalterable, but merely as limiting—and therefore challenging.

Whereas the banking method directly or indirectly reinforces men's fatalistic perception of their situation, the problem-posing method presents this very situation to them as a problem. As the situation becomes the object of their cognition, the naïve or magical perception which produced their fatalism gives way to perception which is able to perceive itself even as it perceives reality, and can thus be critically objective about that reality.

A deepened consciousness of their situation leads people to apprehend that situation as a historical reality susceptible of transformation. Resignation gives way to the drive for transformation and inquiry, over which men feel themselves to be in control. If people, as historical beings necessarily engaged with other people in a movement of inquiry, did not control that movement, it would be (and is) a violation of their humanity. Any situation in which some individuals prevent others from engaging in the process of inquiry is one of violence. The means used are not important; to alienate human beings from their own decision-making is to change them into objects.

This movement of inquiry must be directed towards humanization—the people's historical vocation. The pursuit of full humanity, however, cannot be carried out in isolation or individualism, but only in fellowship and solidarity; therefore it cannot unfold in the antagonistic relations between oppressors and oppressed. No one can be authentically human while he prevents others from being so. Attempting *to be more* human, individualistically, leads to *having more,* egotistically: a form of dehumanization. Not that it is not fundamental *to have* in order *to be* human. Precisely because it *is* necessary, some men's *having* must not be allowed to constitute an obstacle to others' *having,* must not consolidate the power of the former to crush the latter.

Problem-posing education, as a humanist and liberating praxis, posits as fundamental that the people subjected to domination must fight for their emancipation. To that end, it enables teachers and students to become Subjects of the educational process by overcoming authoritarianism and an alienating intellectualism; it also enables people to overcome their false perception of reality. The world—no longer something to be described with deceptive words—becomes the object of that transforming action by men and women which results in their humanization.

Problem-posing education does not and cannot serve the interests of the oppressor. No oppressive order could permit the oppressed to begin to question: Why? While only a revolutionary society can carry out this education in systematic terms, the revolutionary leaders need not take full power before they can employ the method. In the revolutionary process, the leaders cannot utilize the banking method as an interim measure, justified on grounds of expediency, with intention of *later* behaving in a genuinely revolutionary fashion. They must be revolutionary—that is to say, dialogical—from the outset.

NOTES

1. This concept corresponds to what Sartre calls the "digestive" or "nutritive" concept of education, in which knowledge is "fed" by the teacher to the students to "fill them out." See Jean-Paul Sartre, "Une idée fundamentale de la phénomenologie de Husserl: L'intentionalité," *Situations I* (Paris, 1947).
2. For example, some professors specify in their reading lists that a book should be read from pages 10 to 15—and do this to "help" their students!
3. Codification
    a. Simple:
        visual channel: pictorial, graphic
        tactile channel
        auditive channel
    b. Compound: simultaneity of channels

REFERENCES

de Beauvoir, S. *La Pensée de Droite, Aujord'hui* (Paris); *El Pensamiento Politico de la Derecha* (Buenos Aires, 1963), p. 34.

Fromm, E. *The Heart of Man.* (New York, 1966).

Husserl, E. *Ideas-General Introduction to Pure Phenomenology.* (London, 1969.

Niebuhr, R. *Moral Man and Immoral Society.* (New York, 1960).

Sartre, J-P. "Une Idée Fundamentale de la Phénoménologie de Husserl: L'intentionalité," *Situations I* (Paris, 1947).

CHAPTER 4

Building a Knowledge Base in U.S. Academic Adult Education (1945–1970)

André P. Grace

INTRODUCTION

The construction, exchange, and distribution of knowledge in U.S. academic adult education (1945–70) is at the heart of the matter when it comes to understanding the social and cultural formation of the U.S. field during this period. These turbulent years fit neatly into what Jameson (1991: xx) calls "the brief 'American century' (1945–73)." This he describes as a time of fast changes in which technology transformed capitalism, and economic and cultural development raced along courses that were neither separate from nor in synch with one another. Jameson warrants that the basic technology necessary to support the new and radically different system, which he calls late capitalism, existed by 1945. He discusses the emergence of this system in terms of the economic and cultural preconditions necessary to produce such phenomenal change. First, he asserts that the economic precondition for the new system, which became a global economic system, was established in the U.S.A in the 1950s. During these years a seemingly boundless consumerism and vast creativity resulting in new products and technologies began to blur distinctions between the cultural and the economic. Second, he contends that the cultural precondition for the new system, providing an absolute break with the past and resulting in the transformation of the lifeworld, was more properly fulfilled in the 1960s. The vast social and

33

psychological transformations during this decade indicated wide-ranging change, which was reinforced by a generational rupture that indelibly marked this time. Jameson claims that the short-lived American century collapsed in 1973 when the economic and the cultural crystallized in the wake of a series of crises to reveal a new and different system, which was already functioning in a permanent and all-pervasive way. These crises, including the world oil crisis and the end of the international gold standard, revealed a U.S. economy vulnerable to the whims of the global economy it had helped to create.

The years 1945 to 1970 also fit neatly into the third period of Cotton's (1968) field periodisation model delineating the era of the modern practice of adult education. The first period of his model (1919–29) begins with the 1919 Report released by the Adult Education Committee of the British Ministry of Reconstruction after World War I. This seminal report is taken to signal the beginning of organised modern practice globally. The first period ends with the stock market crash of 1929, while the second period (1930–46) covers the years of the Great Depression and World War II. The third period is dated from 1947, the year the Truman Commission on Higher Education issued the report *Higher Education for American Democracy* (Grattan, 1959). For the purposes of this work, it is modified to cover field emergence to 1970, the year when the design and content of a new U.S. handbook of adult education signaled that the techno-scientisation and professionalisation of adult education—at least in its U.S. academic form—were complete (Wilson, 1995). The third period proved a time of escalating field expansion, predicted by Locke in the foreword to the 1948 U.S. handbook of adult education where he claimed that "the corporate age of adult education confronts us" (Knowles and DuBois, 1970: xxi). This expansion was made possible by government, business, and industry. They poured resources into adult education, which they saw as an educational vehicle to help meet the demands of a knowledge and service economy emerging in the face of techno-scientific change.

During the years 1945 to 1970, knowledge production became a primary focus in adult education's quest for space (a recognised and useful presence) and place (a respected and valued position) in the new economic system developing in the emerging post-industrial society. Skill was the bedrock of status in this society in which theoretical (read techo-scientific) knowledge had prime value as the chosen cultural currency in the evolving military-industrial complex (Bell, 1967; Thompson and Randall, 1994). In this paper, I investigate field knowledge production in the light of competing cultures of adult learning vying for recognition and value at a time when on the one hand, knowledge seemed to be fleeting, momentary and fragmented and on the other, a culturally productive force with power to control. I begin by analysing the constitution of the field's productive knowledge base, which focused on method and process in an effort to provide order to a transient and unstable construction. Next I explore the evolution of U.S. adult education's knowledge base in relation to a post-war knowledge explosion that equated knowledge with productivity in a way that raised serious questions debating which knowledge was of most worth. I reflect critically on the cultural politics of field knowledge production, which equated building a techno-scientific knowledge base with building collateral to leverage dominant cultural space and place. Then I examine the location of liberal education as well as the location of history and philosophy as foundational knowledges in the emerging culture of techno-scientific learning. I follow this analysis with an assessment of the status of U.S. adult educational research (1945–70) in relation to the professionally installed need for a productive knowledge base and the larger cultural need for a more encompassing research project. I conclude with a postscript suggesting the cultural space and place of U.S. academic adult education in 1970.

KNOWLEDGE PRODUCTION AS CULTURAL PRODUCTION: THE CONSTITUTION OF A PRODUCTIVE KNOWLEDGE BASE IN U.S. ACADEMIC ADULT EDUCATION (1945–70)

A knowledge explosion rocked U.S. society after World War II and spurred on the growth and development of post-industrial society (Bell, 1967). This set the stage for the evolution of an increasingly systematised modern practice of adult education. As a more instrumentalised practice emerged, dual foci on method and the process of learning how to learn became signifiers of order and control. However, content had become unglued in this practice as productive knowledge became a transitory construction associated with education for now and learning for the moment. In this unstable learning culture, citizen learners were unsteadied by the fleeting nature of what they could know. Intimating that process had indeed seized the day, Seay (1958: 24) argued, "The startling realization that much content of today is outmoded for tomorrow is taking the 'punch' out of the current argument for a return in … education to content emphasis." Adding to the crisis of content was the fact that the expansion of the knowledge base was accompanied simultaneously by its erosion, as obsolete knowledge was discarded. White (1970: 125) alluded to the transient nature of this knowledge production:

> It may be there are eternal and unchanging truths to be learned by adults. Or it may be that knowledge is so chimerical that nothing is learned forever for certain. Or it may be that Thoreau had the matter well in hand when he remarked that he stood precisely where the two eternities met—the eternity of the past and the eternity of the future. His stance at any moment was an absolute truth, but as he bit into the eternity of the future it changed. So did the eternity of the past as days and experiences were added to it.

As the notion that nothing was learned forever for certain took hold, post-industrial days in adult education became days of process when knowing "how to" seemed to be the only way out, the only way to experience some degree of control. Blakely and Lappin (1969: 19) located productive knowledge in this how-to learning world:

> In our society the relationship between knowledge and action is altering, with consequent changes in the nature of both. Knowledge is becoming organized around application. Action is coming to be guided by knowledge—knowledge purposively and systematically taught and learned.

With this emphasis on systematic application, the emphasis on method in a culture of learning driven by productive knowledge seemed but a logical corollary. However, a focus on method resulted in an adult-education curriculum that was "need-meeting but not goal-fulfilling" (Jensen et al., 1964: vii). In other words, this focus located citizen learners as consumers whose instrumental rather than expansive human potential had to be developed. It advanced a cultural politics of learning that failed to situate skills training within the "big picture" of learner needs and desires. This politics venerated the "Isation Syndrome"—techno-scientisation, professionalisation, institutionalisation, and individualisation—and it supported systematisation as a necessary and valuable dynamic in the burgeoning knowledge economy. It worked to keep the dominant culture-power nexus intact. Thus it opposed a more comprehensive cultural politics supporting an emancipatory educational project that would integrate needs for instrumental learning with needs for social and cultural learning. Adult education required such a broader project if it was to shape the adult learner as an agent who could engage both productive knowledge and productive action in a change culture of crisis and challenge.

However, the need to develop a broader project that would take place in the intersection of instrumental, social, and cultural education was overshadowed by the desire to secure a more valuable space and place in the emerging change culture. Indeed, a growing cohort of academic adult educators intensified efforts to systematise modern practice (Verner, 1961, 1964a, b). They were intent on producing knowledge with mainstream cultural worth. They were willing to turn to the social sciences to write analytical and interpretive accounts of adult education and to promote an empirical approach to problem-solving (Verner, 1960). However, this move to establish adult education as an ordered and orderly enterprise was not a new venture. The tendency to systematise adult education in the era of U.S. modern practice can be traced back at least to professionalisation moves in the middle and late 1930s (Cotton, 1968).

After World War II, academic adult educators proceeded with new vigour in their efforts to professionalise modern practice and institutionalise a techno-scientific knowledge base. It was an attempt to achieve greater space and place for a field that had traditionally been marginalised not only by the larger U.S. culture and society but also by the discipline of education itself (Jensen et al., 1964).

However, another cohort of academic adult educators, whose position is represented, for example, by the work of Bergevin (1967), approached the turn to a more systematic modern practice more judiciously. Remembering the field's historical role as social education, they remained sentinels on guard against the erosion of the social in U.S. adult education. While they realised that modern practice could not ignore instrumental education, they knew that social and cultural forms of adult education were needed also to enhance life, learning and work possibilities for ordinary citizen learners. As a consequence, two relatively divergent camps of U.S. academic adult educators can be identified in the post-war period. The predominant group, intent on systematising the field through professionalisation and techno-scientisation, focused on creating a culture of adult learning derived from an emphasis on knowledge as a productive cultural force. In this mainstream learning paradigm, the citizen learner was treated as a consumer of techno-scientific knowledge, which can be construed as a commodity serving the interests of capitalist democracy. The other group, intent on remembering the social purpose of adult education, critically questioned this emerging culture of learning. They focused on reinvigorating a traditional culture of adult learning historically constructed within an emphasis on productive action in the social and cultural realms. In this learning paradigm the citizen learner was cast as a change agent who worked in community with the citizen educator to improve life, learning and work possibilities through frontline social action and cultural work. Serving the interests of ordinary citizens and their communities was the primary concern.

The focus on productive knowledge, with its concomitant focus on process and method, raised a key question in U.S. academic adult education—was knowledge an end or the means to an end? Despite the sorry status of the field's own knowledge, debate around this question proceeded vigorously. Udvari (1972: 235–6) suggests, "the body of knowledge surrounding adult education between 1928 and 1960 is small and unimpressive when contrasted with [public education] ... Grossly lacking ... [are] philosophy, theory, and goals for adult education." He supported this assertion by turning to Liveright's often repeated list of "four problems which characterize adult education in the United States: (1) lack of sound philosophy; (2) irrelevance of content or subject matter; (3) under-utilization of resources; and (4) absence of a sound and accessible theory base." In the 1960 U.S. handbook of adult education, Verner (1960: 162) addressed other problems when he assessed the status of the field knowledge base:

> Like the field itself, the literature about adult education ranges widely over a vast array of topics in a highly disorganized manner ... Very little of this material can be classified as great or even highly significant to the field, but all of it has been timely.

He concluded that the general literature defied orderly classification. Moreover, it was repetitive and defensive in its attempt to justify adult education. He noted that the bulk of material in libraries was not catalogued under adult education or some recognisable heading. He also remarked that the readership for adult education literature (when it was read at all) was generally limited to adult educators themselves.

Despite these various problems existing in a field seeking to increase the cultural currency of its knowledge base, Verner (1960) remained hopeful. He suggested, "Perhaps the constructive use of the literature of adult education will increase as the field itself becomes unified and acquires a sense of common identity through which the dispersed parts gain a perception of their relationship to the whole" (p. 164). Linking systematisation to building a productive knowledge base, he predicted that an observable increase in the rate of production of adult education materials, coupled with more frequent use of the literature by professional adult educators, would result in improvements in library practices. To expand readership, Verner wanted academic adult educators to move in a new, more productive direction that would increase the cultural utility of adult education. He challenged those who produced field literature to stop preaching the lifelong learning sermon to the converted and to move away from the "impressionistic propaganda" (p. 166) dominating the literature. He asked them to focus instead on building a consistent and systematic knowledge base so they would know more about "the basic elements of their craft" (p. 166).

This set quite a task for adult education, which was still a fledgling enterprise with a knowledge base in genesis. Indeed, the knowledge base could still be depicted as scattered and diffuse at the end of the 1960s (Axford, 1969). Nevertheless, nearly 50 years into modern practice, there was evidence of a developing and expanding knowledge base in the U.S. field. The Library of Continuing Education at Syracuse University provided an example, albeit an isolated one, of the kind of data-retrieval system needed to support theory building and practice in adult education (Axford, 1969). There was also a growing volume of literature addressing "the shadowy zones between adult educational practice and such other fields of inquiry or application as anthropology, economics, history, philosophy, social work, librarianship, social psychology, sociology, human development, and physiology" (Houle, 1972: 238). This turn to other disciplines and sources of knowledge to build a field knowledge base was important. It indicated that "the content of adult education has neither horizontal nor vertical limits—that is instances of adult education can be found that touch every body of knowledge known to man [*sic*]" (Schroeder, 1970: 34).

KNOWLEDGE IS POWER TO CONTROL POWER: LOCATING KNOWLEDGE AS A PRODUCTIVE FORCE IN POST-INDUSTRIAL SOCIETY

A knowledge base is a power tool built in the intersection of culture, ideology, politics and history. Understood this way, the construction, exchange and distribution of knowledge is dynamic and evolving, affected by producer disposition, contexts and relations of power as well as by the cultural currency given to the production. Friedenberg (1983) argues that the answer to the question "which knowledge is most worthwhile?" is inherently shaped by culture; therefore, it is concomitantly caught up in ideology and cultural practices. He believes that any attempt to answer this difficult question must begin with a careful explication of the ideological implications of knowledge production. Tierney (1992) asserts that knowledge is a political construction, tentative in nature, which is shaped by individual beliefs and values as well as by the social and historical contexts. Thus characterised, knowledge production is seen as provisional, discursive and located in particular ways. This suggests that the construction, exchange and distribution of knowledge need to be interrogated and problematised to reveal the nature and limits of knowledge production as a cultural production. Since, in turn, this production shapes educational forms and functions, the analysis must be extended so that education is open to challenge and rethinking as a cultural formation (Usher and Edwards, 1994). This intimates that, in adult education as a field of study and practice, questions must be raised continuously concerning what academic adult educators believe and value as they produce knowledge and shape educational practices.

This focus on method in U.S. academic adult education was part of the drive to build a productive knowledge base and shape a techno-scientific practice for post-industrial times. It was caught up in a field politics more concerned with expanding system capacity than with enhancing learner capacity. When this politics took up questions of "what for?" and "for whom?," it usually did so in dominant cultural terms. It tended to forget the larger social and cultural needs of ordinary citizen learners in the rush to concentrate on their instrumental learning needs. From this perspective, it can be argued that academic adult educators supported a public pedagogy for mainstream practice that can be aptly referred to as a pedagogy of submission. Within this pedagogy, productive knowledge supplanted productive action (read social activism and cultural work) as the means to solve life, learning and work problems. This knowledge bound the citizen learner in ways that shaped the culture of techno-scientific learning as a culture to concentrate and control power. In this culture the adult learner as consumer displaced the adult learner as agent.

In their analysis of institutional arrangements and organisational patterns in adult education, Blakely and Lappin (1969) maintained that knowledge was power to control power. This notion of a knowledge-power nexus only reiterated what Lindeman (1926/1961: 25) had argued much earlier: "The assimilation of knowledge ... is synonymous with power." In this light, the attempt to build a productive knowledge base in order to align neatly with the values of post-industrial society can be understood as recognition of the inextricable linkage between knowledge and power in post-war U.S. academic adult education. This recognition helps to explain turns to professionalisation and techno-scientisation since, as Lindeman also argues, "the urge to power ... [is] a many-faceted motivation for ... behavior." In addition, it helps to explain adult education's tendency toward systematisation in the post-war period. During this time government, universities and other institutions claimed various pieces of the adult educational enterprise in their quest to solve problems in the interest of maintaining the status quo. As these institutions invested in adult education, the mainstream field seemed ready to submit to building a productive knowledge base that would enhance its dominant cultural space and place. Academic adult educators appeared willing to appropriate and assimilate techno-scientific knowledge to ensconce academic adult education as a valued field of study and to elevate the larger enterprise to the status of a broadly appealing and valuable cultural formation. The politics of submission appeared to be a way forward in a post-industrial culture where productive knowledge had become the prime currency in the emerging knowledge economy. This knowledge had given rise to a noetic society where the fundamental problem was sharing knowledge, which concomitantly meant sharing power (Blakely, 1970). For the cohort of academic adult educators working to systematise modern practice, the development of a techno-scientific educational project was a way to have space and place in this sharing. However, for the cohort more concerned with productive action as a way out for citizen learners, the assimilation of techno-scientific knowledge appeared at odds with the production of other useful knowledge that remembered a field history as social education for ordinary citizen learners.

Which knowledge was of most worth in U.S. academic adult education (1945–70) seemed to depend on whether one desired the field's historical cultural place as social education or a post-industrial cultural place focused on contributing to the growing knowledge economy. Yet any attempt to place academic adult educators neatly into opposing camps in this period is difficult for at least two reasons. First, even Bergevin (1967) as a leader among those favouring productive action, saw some advantage in turning to psychology as a culturally valued techno-scientific discourse in order to help build a productive knowledge base to inform adult education. However, he was explicit in warning adult educators about the dangers of a psychologistic turn, which, he suggested, raised issues around the control of the learning environment and learner freedom. Indeed, he cautioned the field to be aware of its potential capacity to "manipulate other people to . . . [its] advantage by using some of the very psychological insights that might be used to release [them]" (Bergevin, 1967: 163). Second, it is apparent that certain prominent U.S. academic adult educators defied location in a particular camp by working to find common ground in the intersection of historical field values and the emerging cultural values in this period. For example, London (1964) built a bridge of sorts between academic adult educators with divergent views when he contextualised the psychological within the social and the cultural in his work. His turn to social psychology helped to constitute field knowledge of social change, its sources, and its enabling and inhibiting factors. Through his work he pressed field players to think about the social (structural and organisational patterns) and cultural (behavioural patterns) contexts shaping institutional behaviour and affecting participation in adult education.

THE SPACE AND PLACE OF LIBERAL ADULT EDUCATION AND THE HISTORICAL AND PHILOSOPHICAL FOUNDATIONS OF ADULT EDUCATION IN THE CULTURE OF PRODUCTIVE KNOWLEDGE

The Location of the Liberal Tradition in University Adult Education (1945–70)

In their account of the liberal tradition in university adult education, Taylor et al. (1985) state two general purposes of liberal adult education: (a) to promote intellectual growth and development; and (b) to carry out education for citizenship. They also list key characteristics. First, liberal adult education is focused on the progress of the individual who uses different perspectives to analyse social and personal location as a first step in building new knowledges and understandings. Second, it situates education as a dialogic and dialectical encounter in which individuals learn to engage in critical analysis as a way to question ideas, assertions, explanations and interpretations to continue this knowledge-building process. Third, it emphasizes an educational praxis where the educative process benefits from a mutual engagement with the lived (experience) and learned (expertise) knowledges of both educator and learner. Fourth, it locates the classroom as a participatory democratic site where learners work with the educator to make decisions about content, process, priorities and time allocations as the course proceeds.

How did liberal adult education fare in the new cultural and economic milieu emerging after World War II? While university adult education was grounded in the liberal tradition in the U.S.A and England, Taylor et al. argue that its post-war forms were shaped predominantly to meet perceived economic needs defined by government, industry and the professions. This threatened the space and place of liberal adult education, which, historically, had occupied a non-utilitarian realm. The danger was perhaps greater for English liberal adult education since it used a more delimited definition of liberal education that excluded the utilitarian as it implies the vocational or technical. Though both English and U.S. liberal adult education have shared the purposes and characteristics outlined above, the liberal tradition has functioned quite differently in both countries. This is because England has not veered from its historically delimited definition of liberal adult education while the U.S.A has expanded its definition to include utilitarian functions in keeping with its devotion to the idea of service. Lowe (1970) credits the 1919 Report with sustaining the cultural value that England gave to its circumscribed kind of liberal education. Nearly 50 years after the release of the report he maintained that England remained "virtually alone among nations" (p. 23), defining adult education as "*non-vocational* [his italics] education voluntarily undertaken by people over eighteen" (p. 23), even though a good deal of technical and vocational education existed in the country.

While English liberal adult education may have been in a more precarious position in the face of post-war cultural and economic transformations, Fieldhouse (1985) affirms that it remained a small but requisite part of education for social and cultural change. It enjoyed this location until the early 1970s. Taylor et al. contend that English liberal adult education had extensive value because it encompassed individual and social education as well as education for citizenship. It retained a broad understanding of education for citizenship aligned with different educational purposes along an individualist/collectivist continuum. On the one hand, it focused on liberal individualism, educating citizens to make informed personal choices as participants in democratic processes. On the other hand, it also focused on collective social change, educating groups, especially working-class students, to be intellectually and politically prepared to participate fully in democratic society.

In contrast to the English liberal tradition, Taylor et al. suggest that U.S. liberal adult education was strongly utilitarian, pragmatically placing the education of professionals above the education of workers in the interests of serving government, industry, and the professions. They argue that this location of liberal adult education aligned with the assumption that U.S. liberalism adhered to the dominant discourse of democracy promoting the U.S. system of government and its establishment values. In keeping with this assumption, they suggest that, with the exception of the 1960s, government service was considered consistent with achieving social purpose goals in U.S. society. "Perhaps nothing so fully captures the difference between the U.S.A and England than the idea of service as the American interpretation of social purpose" (Taylor et al, 1985: 26). From this perspective, U.S. liberal adult education was cast as an instrument of social reform as government dictated and supported it. Thus, when it took on education for citizenship, it engaged in Americanization, valuing service to government, the economy, and techno-science. Such service was considered to guarantee individual advancement in a supposedly class-free U.S. society.

Culturally Refitting Liberal Education for Space and Place in Postindustrial Adult Education

In a report focusing on the emergence of liberal, non-vocational adult education in the era of U.S. modern practice, Brunner et al. (1959) remarked that the evolution of U.S. adult education encompassed predominantly liberal forms of adult education, with some attention given to vocational education. However, the historical emphasis on liberal education had declined and, by the 1950s, it was vocational education that was prominent in the field. Liberal education, without apparent utility in the mainstream techno-scientific learning world, had to struggle for space and place in this culture. Learner needs, traditionally asserted in terms of a broader emancipatory liberal project, were now stated in terms decidedly synchronised to a post-industrial adult learning culture wanting room in the emerging military-industrial complex. Taylor et al. (1985: 170) frame the descent of liberalism and its emancipatory project in the face of academic adult education's turn to techno-scientism:

> The key to democracy becomes conformity and unity, not freedom; equality becomes advancement of those able to benefit from contact with the elite; service is to vested interests, not to the cries for change; and excellence means the survival of academe—control through the scientific, rational method as the only legitimate form of knowledge—not the capacity for critical reflection or social transformation.

Podeschi (1994) suggests that this erosion continued in U.S. adult education in the 1960s as turns to professionalisation and techno-scientisation became even more pronounced. He adds that this erosion was intensified by federal involvement in education and by a new progressivism emphasising individual freedom. A de-emphasis on values and interdisciplinary foundational knowledge, both foci of liberal education, accompanied this erosion. Thus the struggle of history and philosophy for a recognised and valued presence in adult education can be understood as a consequence of the declining cultural currency of liberal education in post-industrial society. Adult education's growth and development were marred in this period because the enterprise failed to turn adequately to historical and philosophical foundations that would guide the clarification of the field's form and function (Welton, 1991).

The Fugitive Space and Place of Historical Knowledge in the Culture of Productive Knowledge

In a discussion of the historical construction of knowledge in U.S. adult education, Jensen (1964) related that a base had been built using two primary sources. First, the field had constructed principles or generalisations informed by experience with problems in everyday practice. Second, the field had borrowed and reformulated knowledge drawn from other disciplines to answer similar questions of concern in adult educational practice. A concern with productive knowledge and its application, as well as a generally pragmatic approach to practice, ensured that the field's knowledge base would continue to be built using knowledge from the first source. Such leanings also ensured a turn to disciplines like psychology, which were viewed as sources of useful knowledge. However, the effect on knowledge drawn from foundation disciplines like history and philosophy was a declining emphasis on building a knowledge base from the second source. History and philosophy inhabited the realm of non-practical (and thus apparently non-productive) knowledge. They were devalued currency when it came to deciding what knowledge had cultural worth.

With respect to history, there is evidence from a number of sources to support this contention. The minor presence or noticeable absence of history in adult educational discourse is mentioned frequently in period literature. For example, Verner (1960) related that literature on the history of the field was fragmentary and generally limited to local histories of institutions and particular geographical areas. "Far too many of these historical studies have been issued in pamphlet form, with the result that they quickly become fugitive and all but lost to the field" (p. 167). Similarly, Whipple (1964) concluded that adult educators, for the most part, had not seen the usefulness of history to the development of the field. He argued that history was important to reveal the complexity of adult education, to help build its knowledge base, and to assist adult educators to execute responsibly their functions in the present. Despite these worthwhile uses of historical knowledge, he noted the absence of history in supposedly inclusive works such as Brunner et al.'s (1959) *Overview of Adult Education Research*. This absence provided an example of a field thinking only in "present" terms and turning (when it turned at all) to disciplines other than history to answer its questions. Whipple's reflection generally speaks to the fugitive space and place that history has occupied in adult education as a field of study and practice. In a conspectus of post-World War II modern practice, Rockhill (1976) recounts that histories of adult education have been few and far between in knowledge production. She captures part of its problem when she describes the history of adult education as "a history that had to wait" (p. 199) because it is secondary to the formal schooling of children in the scheme of education. She captures another part when she notes (p. 197) the difficult task of the adult education historian writing a history of a field with unfixed borders:

> We know little about how adult education functions as a reality in the lives of people ... Adult education is not synonymous with an institution or set of institutions, nor is it coterminous with a level or fourth tier of learning. Thus, its conceptualization and history are necessarily complex and difficult to integrate.

A Good Thing—The Space and Place of Philosophical Knowledge in the Culture of Productive Knowledge

If philosophy appeared sidelined to a lesser extent than history in post-industrial adult education, it was because a vocal contingent of academic adult educators worked hard to profile it as rudimentary to the formulation of the field's "big picture." For example, Axford (1969: 96) declared that philosophy was essential "to develop a clear image of adult education ... It is the responsibility of the educator of adults to philosophize." White (1970: 121) concluded that adult education should have an affinity for philosophy because both fields of study wanted the same things: "Philosophy is concerned with such basic problems as freedom and social justice, equal opportunity—in civil rights and power—and the participation of citizens in great decisions. So is adult education."

Despite these declarations of the value of philosophy, there still remained a clear need for increased philosophical inquiry and debates as adult educators came to terms with the question "What is adult education?" Powell (1960: 41) contended that the lack of debate, not the fact of debate, around philosophies of adult education should be a matter of key concern:

> The truth is that people in this field of endeavor have done much more educating than philosophizing about it. This is probably as it should be in a growing enterprise, and it is certainly characteristic of the American way of getting things done.

This explanation notwithstanding, Powell felt strongly that adult educators needed to philosophise in order to advance the field. For him, the process of "continuous philosophizing" (p. 42) was more important than the determination of any particular philosophy of adult education. He concluded that "there is only one basic philosophy about adult education: that it is a good thing, and more of it would be better" (p. 43).

Powell (1956: 231) saw a commonality of concerns beyond the polarity permeating field philosophical discourse. He maintained:

> All expressions of the "philosophy of adult education" come to focus on three key concepts: the Individual [his emphasis], who is the subject of concern and the agent of growth; the Community, which is the focal environment of his [sic] efforts; and the Democratic Process, which is the guarantor of his freedom and of his value as a man [*sic*].

However, Powell's attempt to converge philosophies of adult education around this focus belied the fact that these concepts were differently understood and valued in the field. The philosophy of adult education was contested terrain. Adult educators provided a spectrum of competing purposes for a field still in genesis. The range covered the gamut from individual security and self-actualisation to community development and social emancipation. Apps (1973) tried to weaken the opposition between individual and social purposes, claiming it was a false binary. He drew on Freire who suggested that individual growth and development occurred within a larger process of transforming society. Individual freedom was a subset of social responsibility. Bergevin (1967) agreed, promoting self-actualisation of the individual within the context of becoming a responsible and responsive citizen. "Each of us has an important part to play in the social drama ... We can't very well learn our part in isolation. It is learned in relationship with others" (p. 34). Bergevin (1967: 30) believed adult education should help the individual "grow and develop as a contributing member of the social order that will in turn present him [sic] with continuing opportunities to fulfill his particular purpose in life." He provided (pp. 30–31) five major goals of adult education intersecting individual and social concerns:

> (a) To help the learner achieve a degree of happiness and meaning in life; (b) To help the learner understand himself [sic], his talents and limitations, and his relationships with other persons; (c) To help adults recognize and understand the need for life-long learning; (d) To provide conditions and opportunities to help the adult advance in the maturation process spiritually, culturally, physically, politically, and vocationally; (e) To provide, where needed, education for survival, in literacy, vocational skills, and health measures.

He knew these goals were difficult to achieve in a society that gave only "a perfunctory nod to adult education" (p. 36). He warned against a cultural politics of learning where "someone will always come to the fore ... to take from us the burden of thinking and responsibility, only to replace it with one of submission" (p. 36). He wanted adults to see the complexity of problems and to be cautious of adult education that presented "one side, the 'right' side" (p. 37). Bergevin warned that this expert kind of adult education made adults complacent and ready to accept fast and neat answers to difficult problems. It amounted to a pedagogy of submission that disabled the adult learner as agent.

The debates around the philosophy of adult education revealed the lack of unity around field purposes. However, as Axford (1969) stated, not every adult educator worried about disunity of purpose. Some saw the lack of cohesiveness as an advantage and a reflection of the pluralism characterising 1960s' society. For them, adult education's diverse "programs represent[ed] ... [the field's] objectified philosophy" (p. 96). To keep a multi-purpose field strong, they wanted to develop and nurture philosophy in general because any programme would only be as good as the philosophy guiding its design. Yet, despite this desire and a prevalent discourse valuing philosophical inquiry, a sad state of affairs remained as the 1970s began: "75 per cent of all adult learning in the United States proceed[ed] along its old familiar lines ... without much concern or knowledge about the newer outreach of either philosophy or practice" (Knowles and Klevins, 1972: 13).

Diffusion of Responsibility, Diffusion of Effort: U.S. Adult Educational Research as a Source of Productive Knowledge

As post-industrial society emerged, U.S. academic adult educators were challenged continuously to emphasise theory building and research in their work to build a knowledge base with cultural worth (Kreitlow, 1970). This emphasis is clear in the 1960 U.S. handbook of adult education. Pointing to the value of formal knowledge, Verner (1960) noted a rapid growth in research literature and declared its potential for helping the field advance. In fact, the 1960 handbook reified the scientific as the body and soul of systematic adult educational theory, research, and practice (Wilson, 1995). It enforced the notion that professional adult educators engaged the methods of science to problem-solve in practice, moving adult education from its traditional location as a field of practice closer to its desired location as a field of study (Wilson, 1995).

In their overview of adult-education research, published the year before the handbook, Brunner et al (1959) described the burgeoning research output as chaotic. Brunner and his associates related that adult educators focused on method when they engaged in research. This seemed a natural focus for an emerging field of systematic study. They also noted that a significant amount of available research had typically been carried out by social scientists bringing theories and methodologies from other disciplines to bear on adult education. Kreitlow (1960) reiterated this point, reporting that a bulk of the enterprise's understanding came from outside but related studies in sociology and psychology. A decade later he repeated: "As a field of professional study, adult education borrows and reformulates knowledge from other disciplines" (Kreitlow, 1970: 145). This intimated that academic adult educators themselves had not yet assumed a role as primary producers in research knowledge production in their own field. Brunner et al (1959) listed a number of factors to explain this situation. First, there was the pressure of large and growing enrollments after World War II, and the concomitant tendency for adult educators to focus on practice rather than research in the face of this pressure. Second, there was the newness of adult education as a profession. Academic adult education in particular had yet to produce the contingent of graduates needed to expand the research knowledge base. However, graduate students in adult education tended to be older and established in careers. If these students focused on research at all, they wanted it to be applicable to their own work situations. Third, there was the profusion of agencies involved in adult education with the enterprise generally having only marginal status in them. Moreover, while these agencies generally took up a wide range of subject matter, many of them conducted no research or peripheral research to meet administrative or service ends. Brunner's group (1959: 4) concluded:

> There is a great diffusion of responsibility, for adult education has never developed, and probably in our type of culture never can develop, a single institutional pattern comparable to the pre-adult, university, or cooperative extension pattern of education. There is, therefore, a diffusion of professional effort.

Fourth, there was a lack of financial support for adult education research, with available funding generally going to operations rather than research. Fifth, research focus was on descriptive studies and narrative accounts with limited applicability. Brunner et al (1959: 6) reported a lack of empirical research and "an exceedingly liberal definition of what constitutes research." Yet they also upheld the merits of descriptive research: "Description is the first step in the development of research in any discipline. It lays the foundation for later effective and definitive research by suggesting hypotheses and lines of inquiry" (p. 6). Kreitlow (1960: 112) concurred:

The last two decades of adult education research might be identified as "the age of description." One should not be too pessimistic about what the age of description has done for the future outlook in adult education research. It has provided an important basis for further study.

Brunner et al. also identified key areas for future research to vitalise a more encompassing culture of adult learning. They highlighted the need to study how adults learn and the necessity to connect this research to a revision of adult-education methods. They argued for research projects into learner motivation, interests and participation as well as the requirement for longitudinal studies that investigated group changes over time. Kreitlow (1960) also emphasised the need for longitudinal studies in the field. In line with the move to formalise modern practice, he called for more empirical research in order to build a sound knowledge base. Like Brunner and his associates, he was concerned with the development of a body of systematic research into adult education methods. He called on adult educators to conduct more research into the teaching of adults. In the 1960 handbook, Kreitlow suggested six areas for future adult education research which were clearly designed to entrench adult education as a separate field of study with its own distinctive learning culture:

- the needs and desires of individuals and groups in the community;
- adult education agency purposes and planning in relation to community goal setting;
- the resources of adult education and the community and their interconnectedness;
- agency operations in terms of administrative structural set up and community coordination, instructional development, and the nature of the community;
- methods of teaching adults and instructor characteristics; and
- the objectives and outcomes of adult education.

In his presentation of ideas to enhance adult education's learning culture, Axford (1969) provided perspectives in line with Kreitlow's vision of a future field of study. He wanted professional adult educators to be well trained in research methodology and to use an interdisciplinary approach, which drew on social science research. Adult educators needed to access research findings in various disciplines in order to build a field-nourishing theory and practice. Axford (1969: 211) was particularly concerned about the enterprise's weak theoretical foundation: "There ... appears a lack of structure and theory which would be the basis for new research and for integrating the research done to date." A growing body of research would provide insights into adult learning. It would aid understanding of adult education as it teased out how the field functions within social, political, and economic contexts. This research would highlight the mutuality of theory and practice. It would nurture a field of cultural politics accentuating the interdependency of researchers and practitioners in the process of making sense of a very complex and diverse enterprise. It would recognise that the enterprise was attached to institutions and therefore caught up in the dynamics of institutional growth, adaptation and decay.

However, there were barriers to meeting this responsibility and enabling the knowledge production, exchange and distribution process. First, cooperation and dialogue did not sufficiently mark the relationship between researchers and practitioners. Udvari (1972: 237) described this failure to communicate and its consequences:

> Perhaps the most obvious problem in adult education today is the wide gulf in the dialogue process ... between the researcher and the practitioner. One reason for the gulf is that ... [practitioners] are too busy meeting practical programmatic require-ments. Their knowledge and theories are generally intuitive. They create innovations by acting on hunches whose validity is untested. Consequently, innovations in adult education take many years to be identified by theorists, tested by researchers, and disseminated as valid theory, methods, and techniques among practitioners.

Second, the university had a poor track record in supporting adult education as a field of study inextricably linked to a wider field of practice. Kreitlow (1970) argued that the university had presented a barrier to the advancement of adult educational research in the 1950s and 1960s. Indeed, adult education was in the precarious position of becoming part of an institution that did not wholeheartedly support it. Traditional forms of support were still needed to ensure survival in academe. Kreitlow (1970: 144) put it bluntly:

> It should be clearly stated that the increase in graduate study and the advance in research were not accomplished solely by a response on the part of the universities to the social climate. Leadership from the great foundations (Ford, Kellogg, Carnegie) and the federal government was essential. The universities were concerned, but there is little evidence to show they would have made the major advances without the federal government and the foundations teasing them along.

Arguing that research efforts needed to focus more broadly on the roles and purposes of adult education, he listed "three major and interrelated categories of application" to be investigated: "They are 1) the adult as an individual and a learner; 2) the adult's response to socio-cultural phenomena; [and,] 3) the adult education enterprise" (ibid: 142). He contended that knowledge in these three areas should form a core knowledge base for those entering the profession. To do this work properly, he declared that basic philosophical questions needed to be addressed and the notion of community needed to be emphasised. However, the 1970 handbook generally cloned concerns important in the 1960 handbook. It emphasised the reporting of systematic research as its key function and it continued to see techno-scientisation as the road to the professionalisation of the field. Wilson (1995) relates that the emphasis on research reflected the continuing need for increased, higher quality research efforts. It also indicated the need for a more encompassing field-research project attentive to the spectrum of prevailing instrumental, social and cultural concerns. As the 1960s drew to a close, adult education's state of affairs was reflected by these unsatisfied needs.

POSTSCRIPT: WHAT KNOWLEDGE IS OF MOST VALUE?

Post-industrial academic adult education's drive to build a productive knowledge base can be understood as an attempt to gain cultural place by reshaping its role and purpose within a culture of techno-scientific learning. While U.S. academic adult education certainly made progress in building a knowledge base (1945–70), it had been selective in determining which knowledge was of most value. Thus it still had much work to do. As the 1970 U.S. handbook of adult education indicates, the extent of common knowledge in adult education, and the degree to which it was possible to have a common knowledge base, were still much-debated topics. In part, this is understandable because efforts to build such a base had only begun in earnest in the 1920s. From 1945 to 1970 these efforts were complicated by the field's struggle for cultural space and place in a rapidly changing socio-political and economic milieu where a post-industrial knowledge economy was reconfiguring culture. Indeed, it would be fair to say that, in 1970, U.S. academic adult education was still learning to crawl.

REFERENCES

Apps, J. W. (1973). *Toward a Working Philosophy of Adult Education*, Syracuse, NY: Syracuse Publications in Continuing Education.

Axford, R. W. (1969). *Adult Education: The Open Door*, Scranton, PA: International Textbook Company.

Bell, D. (1967). "The post-industrial society: a speculative view," in E. Hutchings and E. Hutchings (eds.), *Scientific Progress and Human Values*, New York: American Elsevier Publishing Company.

Bergevin, P. (1967). *A Philosophy for Adult Education*, New York: The Seabury Press.

Blakely, R. J. (1970). "New needs, new contents, new forms," in W.L. Ziegler (ed.), *Essays on the Future of Continuing Education Worldwide*, Syracuse, NY: Syracuse University Publications in Continuing Education.

Blakely, R. J. and Lappin, I. M. (1969). *Knowledge is Power to Control Power: Institutional Arrangements and Organizational Patterns for Continuing Education*, Syracuse, NY: Syracuse University Publications in Continuing Education.

Brunner, E. de S., Wilder, D. S., Kirchner, C. and Newberry, Jr J. S. (1959). *An Overview of Adult Education Research*, Chicago: Adult Education Association of the U.S.A.

Cotton, W. E. (1968). *On Behalf of Adult Education: A Historical Examination of the Supporting Literature*, Boston: Center for the Study of Liberal Education for Adults.

Fieldhouse, R. T. (1985). *Adult Education and the Cold War: Liberal Values Under Siege 1946–51*, Leeds, UK: University of Leeds.

Friedenberg, E. Z. (1983). "Education," *American Quarterly*, *35*, (1 and 2), 205–16.

Grattan, C. H. (1959). *American Ideas about Adult Education 1710–1951*, New York: Bureau of Publications, Teachers College, Columbia University.

Houle, C. O. (1972). *The Design of Education*, San Francisco: Jossey-Bass.

Jameson, F. (1991). *Postmodernism, or, the Cultural Logic of Late Capitalism*, Durham, NC: Duke University Press.

Jensen, G. (1964). "How adult education borrows and reformulates knowledge from other disciplines," in G. Jensen, A. A. Liveright and W. Hallenbeck (eds.), *Adult Education: Outlines of an Emerging Field of Study*, Washington, DC: Adult Education Association of the U.S.A.

Jensen, G., Liveright, A. A. and Hallenbeck, W. (1964). "Adult education," in G. Jensen, A. A. Liveright and W. Hallenbeck (eds.), *Adult Education: Outlines of an Emerging Field of Study*, Washington, DC: Adult Education Association of the U.S.A.

Knowles, M. S. and DuBois, E. E. (1970). "Prologue: the handbooks in perspective," in R. M. Smith, G. F. Aker and J. R. Kidd (eds.), *Handbook of Adult Education*, New York: Macmillan.

Knowles, M. and Klevins, C. (1972). "Resume of adult education," in C. Klevins (ed.), *Materials and Methods in Adult Education*, New York: Klevens Publications Inc.

Kreitlow, B. W. (1960). "Research in adult education," in M. S. Knowles (ed.), *Handbook of Adult Education in the United States*, Washington, DC: Adult Education Association of the U.S.A.

Kreitlow, B. W. (1970). "Research and theory," in R. M. Smith, G. F. Aker and J. R. Kidd (eds.), *Handbook of Adult Education*, New York: Macmillan.

Lindeman, E. C. (1926/1961). *The Meaning of Adult Education*, Montreal: Harvest House.

London, J. (1964). "The relevance of the study of sociology to adult education practice," in G. Jensen, A. A. Liveright and W. Hallenbeck (eds.), *Adult Education: Outlines of an Emerging Field of Study*, Washington, DC: Adult Education Association of the U.S.A.

Lowe, J. (1970). *Adult Education in England and Wales*, London: Michael Joseph.

Podeschi, R. (1994). "The rise and fall of liberal adult education: CSLEA at mid-century," Proceedings of the 35th Annual Adult Education Research Conference, The University of Tennessee, Knoxville, TN, pp 300–05.

Powell, J. W. (1956). *Learning Comes of Age*, New York: Association Press.

Powell, J. W. (1960). "Philosophies of adult education," in M. S. Knowles (ed.), *Handbook of Adult Education in the United States*, Washington, DC: Adult Education Association of the U.S.A.

Rockhill, K. (1976). "The past as prologue: toward an expanded view of adult education," *Adult Education*, *26*, 4, 196–207.

Seay, M. F. (1958). "Centers for continuing education," in H. C. Hunsaker and R. Pierce (eds.), *Creating a Climate for Adult Learning*, Purdue University: The Division of Adult Education.

Schroeder, W. L. (1970). "Adult education defined and described," in R. M. Smith, G. F. Aker. and J. R. Kidd (eds.), *Handbook of Adult Education*, New York: Macmillan.

Taylor, R., Rockhill, K. and Fieldhouse, R. (1985). *University Adult Education in England and the U.S.A*, London: Croom Helm.

Thompson, J. H. and Randall, S. J. (1994). *Canada and the United States: Ambivalent Allies*, Montreal and Kingston, ON: McGill-Queens University Press.

Tierney, W. G. (1992). *Official Encouragement, Institutional Discouragement: Minorities in Academe–The Native American Experience*, Norwood, NJ: Ablex Publishing Company.

Udvari, S. S. (1972). "Applied research innovations and ideas," in C. Klevins (ed.), *Materials and Methods in Adult Education*, New York: Klevens Publications Inc.

Usher, R. and Edwards, R. (1994). *Postmodernism and Education*, New York: Routledge.

Verner, C. (1960). "The literature of adult education," in M. S. Knowles (ed.), *Handbook of Adult Education in the United States*, Washington, DC: Adult Education Association of the U.S.A.

Verner, C. (1961). "Basic concepts and limitations," in J. R. Kidd (ed.), (1963) *Learning and Society*, Toronto: Canadian Association for Adult Education.

Verner, C. (1964a). "Definition of terms," in G. Jensen, A. A. Liveright and W. Hallenbeck (eds.), *Adult Education: Outlines of an Emerging Field of Study*, Washington, DC: Adult Education Association of the U.S.A.

Verner, C. (1964b). *Adult education*, New York: The Center for Applied Research in Education.

Welton, M. (1991). "What's new in the history of adult education," *HSE/RHE*, *3*, 2, 285–97.

Whipple, J. B. (1964). "The uses of history for adult education," in G. Jensen, A. A. Liveright and W. Hallenbeck (eds.), *Adult Education: Outlines of an Emerging Field of Study*, Washington, DC: Adult Education Association of the U.S.A.

White, T. J. (1970). "Philosophical considerations," in R. M. Smith, G. F. Aker and J. R. Kidd (eds.), *Handbook of Adult Education*, New York: Macmillan.

Wilson, A. L. (1995). "The common concern: controlling the professionalization of adult education," in S. B. Merriam (ed.), *Selected Writings on Philosophy and Adult Education* (2nd edn), Malabar, FL: Krieger.

CHAPTER 5

Adult Education at the Margins

A Literature Review

Michelle Glowacki-Dudka and Lora B. Helvie-Mason

A dult education as a field has a complex history, with roots in social movements and concurrent pressures to formalize the process of vocational education. This chapter situates adult education at the margins within academic disciplines and as an educational vocation. We draw on literature from within adult education, as well as reflecting on the broader social context.

HISTORICAL UNDERPINNINGS

A recognized literary foundation for the field of adult education in the United States is Lindeman's work *The Meaning of Adult Education,* first published in 1926. Lindeman defines adult education as the place "where vocational education leaves off. Its purpose is to put meaning into the whole of life" (1926, p. 5). He explains that adult education "will be via the route of situations, not subjects," that the "resource of highest value in adult education is the learner's experience," and that "authoritative teaching, examinations which preclude original thinking, rigid pedagogical formulae—all have no place in adult education" (p. 6). Adult education is "friends educating each other." With these guiding assumptions, the field of adult education shook off traditional methods of teaching and learning and assumed a position at the margins from the beginning.

These ideas, emerging from pressures on teachers to support vocational education and to carry the work of the university into the workplace, took shape in formal courses of study beginning in 1918 with adult education methodologies taught at Columbia University. In 1930 Columbia established the first department of adult education, and since that time adult education has grown as a field of study (Milton, Watkins, Studdard, and Burch, 2003). In the year 2000, departments of adult, continuing, and community education existed in seventy-four institutions in the United States, with thirty-eight doctoral programs and seventy-two master's degrees offered (*Peterson's,* 2000). Yet with tightening budgets and shifting priorities, the number of institutions offering adult education degrees has decreased by 29 percent between 1992 and 2002 (Milton, Watkins, Studdard, and Burch, 2003).

The field of adult education consists of three tiers of leadership (Houle, 1956). At the top of the pyramid sit the adult education professionals who work in academia or other settings; they are primarily concerned with the field itself. The next tier includes professionals whose duties include adult education (for example, nurse educators, librarians, museum directors, and workplace coordinators). The largest group of adult educators is made up of the lay educators (practitioners) who serve adults directly and may not even recognize that a specific discipline of adult education exists (Imel, Brockett, and James, 2000). This group includes community workers, training staffs, union activists, and so on (Houle, 1956).

Recognizing the field's leadership dynamics, Houle (1956) suggested that academic programs should prepare the field professionals (those who will be professors) to work with the second and third levels of educators as a central responsibility. Thus, the debate around professionalization of the field began.

In 1962 Knowles noted that as adult education becomes increasingly recognized as a discrete activity, adult educators in each segment of the field look to other adult educators as allies in a national struggle for recognition, power, and financial support. He explained that "the marginality of the adult educational role in most institutional settings induces an era to seek mutual support, status, and problem-solving help across institutional lines" (p. 265). Yet as adult educators work across these institutional boundaries and welcome multiple disciplines, philosophies, and methods into the field, they can become confused about the balance between their roles as educators and as representatives of their disciplines. Because adult education casts a wide net, professionals and practitioners must balance philosophical agendas, social pressures, and competing educational goals.

Historically, adult education trends reflect changes in society, from the social action movements of the 1920s to federally sponsored programs in the 1930s, from the GI bill in the 1940s to the civil rights movement in the 1960s. The term *lifelong learning* emerged in the 1960s with intentions to integrate adult education into wider public policy (Stubblefield and Keane, 1989). Since then government and business have used the concept of lifelong learning to signify constant retraining for vocational changes, rather than the original intent to value voluntary learning across the lifespan (Collins, 1991).

PURPOSES OF ADULT EDUCATION

Adult education mirrors and at times facilitates change in society, as Beder (1989, p. 37) explained with the "basic purposes of Adult Education":

1. To facilitate change in a dynamic society
2. To support and maintain a good social order
3. To promote productivity
4. To enhance personal growth

Although these purposes are at times contradictory, they accurately reflect the roles that adult education takes on in the United States. The location and context of adult learning may assign each of these goals to mainstream or marginal positions. For example, adult education programs in the workplace will mainstream the goals of productivity and support of the social order but may marginalize goals for personal growth and social change. A political action committee may mainstream the social change agenda while setting the others at the margins. A religious institution or health club may make personal growth the focus and marginalize productivity.

Currently the adult education field within academia focuses on issues related to continuing education, community education, adult basic education (English as a second language and literacy), lifelong learning, human resource development and training, as well as critical education issues related to identity politics (race, class, gender, and so on). The field of adult education also includes methods of social research (qualitative and quantitative), educational leadership, and uses of educational technology to support teaching and learning, among others (Knox, 1993; Merriam and Cunningham, 1989; Hayes and Wilson, 2000).

ADULT EDUCATION AT THE MARGINS

"One must recognize that adult education programs are often marginalized within the academic institutions and often within the very colleges and departments in which they exist" (Imel, Brockett, and James, 2000, p. 634). At recent meetings of their professional groups, the American Association for Adult and Continuing Education, the Commission of Professors of Adult Education, and the Adult Education Research Conference have considered as a leading topic the theme of how to integrate adult education within colleges of education and at the same time keep its own identity. Milton, Watkins, Studdard, and Burch (2003) suggest that program integration (which they define as "the integration of adult education into the main focus of education," p. 37), responsiveness to change, and internal leadership are key factors in the strength and wellness of adult education programs. Although "deans don't support what they don't understand," these scholars write (p. 38), it is up to the adult education faculty members to educate their colleagues and administration in higher education to demonstrate and articulate the value of adult education.

The perception of marginal status stems from the lack of specific credentials for entrance to the field and from the ambiguous definition of adult education. Although scholars often repeat the arguments for and against certification in adult education (James, 1992; White, 1992; Boshier, 1988; Galbraith and Gilley, 1985), Boshier (1988, p. 69) strongly suggests that although "profound dangers [are] associated with training people along 'specific and rigid' lines," adult educators need training in program planning and teaching adults. These two topics are often at the core of graduate studies in adult education along with historical, philosophical, and sociological foundations and an overview of educational research (Knowles, 1988; Commission of Professors, 1988). Other issues of race, gender, and class certainly fit into the adult education curriculum. Therefore, the question of what the credentials in adult education are can be partially answered by looking at the graduate degrees available.

ADULT EDUCATION AS A PROFESSION

The debate over whether adult education should be professionalized continues today with leaders in the field still disagreeing. Some argue that professionalism contributes to improved practice; others see professionalism "narrowing the parameters as to who can practice and what defines 'good practice'" (Merriam and

Brockett, 1997, p. 220). Collins (1992, pp. 41–42) invites us to "place emancipatory interests above the technical rationality" and "to counter this apolitical profession-alizing tendency" by "incorporating a questioning of all authoritative, professional assumptions into our pedagogy."

Although adult education is an academic discipline and professional field, the adult education faculty follows certain standards and attempts to fit into the status quo in order to hold status within the university and with other professions. Now in 2004 adult education has become a legitimate field of study with many graduate programs, thousands of graduates, and hundreds of books and articles being pub-lished each year for both academicians and practitioners (Griffith, 1992). Although it remains a stepchild to more dominant, better-funded programs such as K–12 education, educational administration, and human resources, it is a recognized field (Sticht, 2001). In the 1980s the concept of lifelong learning helped to push adult education into the limelight, and other disciplines took it up to forward their own agendas (for example, workforce development, just-in-time education). The term was written into grants in order to sell adult education as a product; thus, "lifelong learning as a guiding principle became a debased currency" (Collins, 1991, p. 7). As other disciplines adopted this idea, adult education returned to its position at the margins.

Some would argue that adult education is now established and is no longer a marginal field of practice (Ilsley, 1992). Yet this chapter argues that adult education will never be mainstreamed, that we should embrace its position at the margins and use that position for social change. We agree with Sheared and Sissel (2001, p. 330) that "rather than spending time debating whether adult education is a legitimate discipline, we perhaps ought to revel in the fact that it is marginal; and more importantly, an alternative explanation for its marginalization in relation to the merging of these two words—*adult and education*—ought to be explored."

ADULT EDUCATION AS SOCIAL ACTION

Many authors (Collins, 1991; Ilsley, 1992; Cunningham, 1992) are concerned that adult education focuses too heavily on the individual's learning and should push for social justice and equality. Ilsley (1992, p. 33) writes:

> Adult education has tremendous drive, but no direction.... We do not have to be guided by the status quo.... Today social change commands attention.... It is to

our advantage that adult education is a constantly moving, tension-filled and fluctuating field of practice, for this dynamism and flexibility enable us to discuss and respond to a myriad of social problems. But as long as we employ a content-centered approach to teaching adults, as if facts are neutral and values lie beyond our domain, the prominence of the values of the dominant culture is inevitable and implicit agreement with the vision of the status quo is maintained.

From its position at the margins, adult education has a great opportunity to work for change, both as an insider within organizations and as an outsider looking into issues with a critical and reflective eye (Hayes and Wilson, 2000). Much of the social research in adult education lately uses this position to speak about uses of power and politics as well as to add marginalized voices to the dialogue of education (Cervero and Wilson, 1994; Cervero, Wilson, and associates, 2001; Sheared and Sissel, 2001). "Every adult educator is a social activist regardless of his or her particular vision of society" (Cervero, Wilson, and associates, 2001, p. 13).

Most adult education happens beyond the view of traditional educational activities. Therefore, the forces at work to marginalize the field reflect forces in society. Apple (2001, p. ix) states that "our social system is crisscrossed by axes of class, gender, race, age, nationality, region, politics, religion, and other dynamics of power," creating a "complex nexus of power relations." Adult education sits in this mix as an ever present entity negotiating adult learning, but it seldom appears in the limelight.

MULTIPLE GOALS FOR ADULT EDUCATION

Determining the numbers of adult educators is difficult, yet in his work "Future Directions for Adult and Continuing Education: A New Plateau," Knox (2004) found fifty "separate and robust national associations of people who work in the field" and that support "lifelong learning as central throughout society." He seeks to collaborate with these practitioners of adult education in other disciplines "to provide leadership in our provider agencies and in the field."

These practitioner areas embrace multiple perspectives and philosophies. Although it is difficult to identify a concrete and single direction, the diversity of populations served through collaborative relationships strengthen adult education research and practice. At times adult educators see commonalities across disciplines that others choose not to see. For example, leaders in human resource development choose to see their field as parallel to adult education, although adult education and human resource development leaders often use the same skill sets with differing guiding philosophies (Kuchinke, 1999). Cervero (1992, p. 48) reminds us "to recognize that different (and to some extent competing) purposes, knowledge and ideologies underlie the work of adult education"; however, "we must not trivialize the knowledge and practice of those who work outside the mainstream."

Each year business and industry, federal and state governments, and nonprofit and community groups spend billions of dollars on educating adults (U.S. Department of Education, 2001). Although each activity serves distinct audiences and purposes, all these programs share core adult education components.

Early on, Knowles (1962) recognized that adult educators needed to be connected to each other and other organizations. He described forces promoting coordination such as "overlapping markets of adult education services" and "the marginality of adult education in most institutional settings"; and he wrote that, "advances in knowledge and method occurring in one element of the field have implications for other elements" (p. 265). Yet Knowles was aware of the pressures on adult educators not to coordinate too much, such as "the lack of agreement on ultimate goals for adult education"; limits to "personal resources"; "differences in vocabularies, theoretical and philosophical positions, and differences in methodological approaches that interfere with communication"; and difficulty in "construct[ing] a coordinative organizational structure where the component parts of the field feel represented" (p. 266).

Even as the Future Directions project (Knox, 2004) seeks to link professional organizations, the field of adult education is becoming more divergent. Graduate programs often incorporate this diversity by collaborating with other departments to offer interdisciplinary degrees. One could take courses in departments such as human geography, philosophy, educational leadership, statistics, management, gerontology, sociology, curriculum and instruction, nursing, and women's studies. Heaney (2000, p. 561) explains that "individual practitioners do not define the field of adult education, nor do the experts. A definition of the field of practice is the social product of many individuals who negotiate the value and meaning of what they come to see as serving a common purpose over time."

As adult educators come to claim the position at the margins as their own, they will be in a better position to negotiate their work's values and meaning. Only by embracing the position at the margins can we shift the boundaries to value and include everyone's contribution: "We must go beyond the 'academy walls' in order to hear the voices of the other and make space for those in the margins, as well as in the center. It is this shifting of margins and centers that will allow for and create a new reality built on a foundation of inclusion of the multiple and varied realities of us all" (Sheared and Sissel, 2001, p. 330).

◾ EMBRACING THE MARGINS

How can adult education take advantage of and embrace its position at the margins? Adult education's position at the margins does not have to be detrimental. At times "marginality may render decision-making susceptible to external influences" (Clark, 1968, p. 149), yet working with stakeholders beyond its own control can be beneficial. Cervero and Wilson (1994, p. 4) understand that "adult educators are not free agents.... Rather their planning is always conducted within a complex set of personal, organizational, and social relationships of power among people who may have similar, different, or conflicting sets of interest."

The nature of lifelong learning, and of adult education itself, defines it as a collective activity, not a singular reality. Although adult educators may wish to create their own independent field of study, a number of groups share the underlying theories, methods, and philosophies for adult teaching and learning.

Adult educators revel in flexibility that allows them to adapt teaching and learning applications to the situation. However, Brockett (1989, p. 117) identified the primary challenge of adult education as "balancing unification and specialization," because without an awareness of the need for unification, adult education will "inevitably continue to suffer from fragmentation and lack of professional identity."

With diverse ideas and ideals, we develop allies but may struggle for a common direction. This also makes the voice of adult educators politically unheard by being so drowned out by multiple interests (Griffith, 1992).

Jarvis (1992), on the other hand, wishes to expand the scope of leadership in the field. "By having more leaders who are conversant with these debates, we can help make our field more mainstream. If leaders are drawn from the wider field, they would bring different perspectives and understandings that can only enrich our field" (p. 57).

Although marginality may be a "prime source of insecurity" (Clark, 1968, p. 149), it is also a position in which collaboration across groups is essential to promoting growth. Only by recognizing the power at the margins will adult educators be able to shift the debate and change the view from the center.

REFERENCES

Apple, M. "Foreword." In R. M. Cervero and A. L. Wilson (eds.), *Power in Practice: Adult Education and the Struggle for Knowledge and Power in Society.* San Francisco: Jossey-Bass, 2001.

Beder, H. "Purposes and Philosophies of Adult Education." In S. Merriam and P. Cunningham (eds.), *Handbook of Adult and Continuing Education.* San Francisco: Jossey-Bass, 1989.

Boshier, R. "A Conceptual Framework for Analyzing the Training of Trainers and Adult Educators." Reprinted in S. Brookfield (ed.), *Training Educators of Adults: The Theory and Practice of Graduate Adult Education.* Routledge: New York, 1988.

Brockett, R. G. "Professional Association for Adult and Continuing Education." In S. Merriam and P. Cunningham (eds.), *Handbook of Adult and Continuing Education.* San Francisco: Jossey-Bass, 1989.

Cervero, R. M. "Adult and Continuing Education Should Strive for Professionalization." In R. G. Brockett and M. W. Galbraith (eds.), *Confronting Controversies in Challenging Times: A Call for Action.* New Directions for Adult and Continuing Education, no. 54. San Francisco: Jossey-Bass, 1992.

Cervero, R. M., and Wilson, A. L. *Planning Responsibly for Adult Education: A Guide to Negotiating Power and Interests.* San Francisco: Jossey-Bass, 1994.

Cervero, R. M., Wilson, A. L., and associates. *Power in Practice: Adult Education and the Struggle for Knowledge and Power in Society.* San Francisco: Jossey-Bass, 2001.

Clark, B. *Adult Education in Transition: A Study of Institutional Insecurity.* Berkeley: University of California Press, 1968.

Collins, M. *Adult Education as Vocation: A Critical Role for the Adult Educator.* New York: Routledge, 1991.

Collins, M. "Adult and Continuing Education Should Resist Further Professionalization." In R. G. Brockett and M. W. Galbraith (eds.), *Confronting Controversies in Challenging Times: A Call for Action.* New Directions for Adult and Continuing Education, no. 54. San Francisco: Jossey-Bass, 1992.

Commission of Professors of Adult Education. "Standards for Graduate Programmes in Adult Education." Reprinted in S. Brookfield (ed.), *Training Educators of Adults: The Theory and Practice of Graduate Adult Education.* Routledge: New York, 1988.

Cunningham, P. "Adult and Continuing Education Does Not Need a Code of Ethics." In R. G. Brockett and M. W. Galbraith (eds.), *Confronting Controversies in Challenging Times: A Call for Action.* New Directions for Adult and Continuing Education, no.54. San Francisco: Jossey-Bass, 1992.

Galbraith, M. W., and Gilley, J. W. "An Examination of Professional Certification." *Lifelong Learning,* 1985, *9*(2), 12–15.

Griffith, W. S. "Has Adult and Continuing Education Fulfilled Its Early Promise?" In B.A. Quigley (ed.), *Fulfilling the Promise of Adult and Continuing Education.* New Directions for Continuing Education, no. 44. San Francisco: Jossey-Bass, 1992.

Hayes, E., and Wilson, A. (eds.). *Handbook of Adult and Continuing Education*. San Francisco: Jossey-Bass, 2000.

Heaney, T. W. "Adult Education and Society." In E. Hayes and A. Wilson (eds.), *Handbook of Adult and Continuing Education*. San Francisco: Jossey-Bass, 2000.

Houle, C. "The Development of Leadership." Chap. 4 in *Liberal Adult Education*. White Plains, N.Y.: Fund for Adult Education, 1956.

Ilsley, P. "The Undeniable Link: Adult and Continuing Education and Social Change." In R. G. Brockett and M. W. Galbraith (eds.), *Confronting Controversies in Challenging Times: A Call for Action*. New Directions for Adult and Continuing Education, no. 54. San Francisco: Jossey-Bass, 1992.

Imel, S., Brockett, R. G., and James, W. B. "Defining the Profession: A Critical Appraisal." In E. Hayes and A. Wilson (eds.), *Handbook of Adult and Continuing Education*. San Francisco: Jossey-Bass, 2000.

James, W. B. "Professional Certification Is Not Needed in Adult and Continuing Education." In R. G. Brockett and M. W. Galbraith (eds.), *Confronting Controversies in Challenging Times: A Call for Action*. New Directions for Adult and Continuing Education, no. 54. San Francisco: Jossey-Bass, 1992.

Jarvis, P. "Leaders of Adult and Continuing Education Should Come from Outside the Field." In R. G. Brockett and M. W. Galbraith (eds.), *Confronting Controversies in Challenging Times: A Call for Action*. New Directions for Adult and Continuing Education, no. 54. San Francisco: Jossey-Bass, 1992.

Knowles, M. S. *The Adult Education Movement in the United States*. Austin, Tex.: Holt, Rinehart and Winston, 1962.

Knowles, M. S. "A General Theory of the Doctorate in Education." Reprinted in S. Brookfield (ed.), *Training Educators of Adults: The Theory and Practice of Graduate Adult Education*. Routledge: New York, 1988.

Knox, A. B. *Strengthening Adult and Continuing Education: A Global Perspective on Synergistic Leadership*. San Francisco: Jossey-Bass, 1993.

Knox, A. B. "Future Directions for Adult and Continuing Education." AAACE-sponsored Web page. [http://www.aaace.org/futures/] (accessed Oct. 1, 2004).

Kuchinke, K. P. "Adult Development Towards What End? A Philosophical Analysis of the Concept as Reflected in the Research, Theory, and Practice of Human Resource Development." *Adult Education Quarterly*, 1999, *49*(4), 148–162.

Lindeman, E. *The Meaning of Adult Education*. Montreal, Quebec: Harvest House, 1926.

Merriam, S., and Cunningham, P. (eds.). *Handbook of Adult and Continuing Education*. San Francisco: Jossey-Bass, 1989.

Merriam, S. B., and Brockett, R. G. *The Profession and Practice of Adult Education: An Introduction*. San Francisco: Jossey-Bass, 1997.

Milton, J., Watkins, K. E., Studdard, S. S., and Burch, M. "The Ever Widening Gyre: Factors Affecting Change in Adult Education Graduate Programs in the United States." *Adult Education Quarterly*, 2003, *54*(1), 23–41.

Peterson's Graduate and Professional Programs: An Overview 2000. Lawrenceville, N.J.: Peterson's, 2000.

Sheared, V., and Sissel, P. A. (eds.). *Making Space: Merging Theory and Practice in Adult Education.* New York: Bergin & Garvey, 2001.

Sticht, T. G. "The Power of Adult Education: Moving the Adult Education and Literacy System of the United States from Margins to Mainstream of Education." Summary paper, California, January 2001. (ED 457410). [Available at http://www.nald.ca/fulltext/sticht/power/cover.htm.]

Stubblefield, H., and Keane, P. "The History of Adult and Continuing Education." In S. Merriam and P. Cunningham (eds.), *Handbook of Adult and Continuing Education.* San Francisco: Jossey-Bass, 1989.

U.S. Department of Education, National Center for Education Statistics. Chap. 4 in *Digest of Education Statistics:* "Table 369. U.S. Department of Education Appropriations for Major Programs, by State or Other Area: Fiscal Year 2001." [http://nces.ed.gov/programs/digest/d02/tables/dt369.asp] (accessed Oct. 5, 2004).

White, B. "Professional Certification Is a Needed Option for Adult and Continuing Education." In R. G. Brockett and M. W. Galbraith (eds.), *Confronting Controversies in Challenging Times: A Call for Action.* New Directions for Adult and Continuing Education, no. 54. San Francisco: Jossey-Bass, 1992.

CHAPTER 6

African Americans in Adult Education

The Harlem Renaissance Revisited

Juanita Johnson-Bailey

The involvement of African Americans in the annals of adult education in the United States has been one of consistency and commitment. Yet, it has also been a presence that has remained largely unknown to many adult educators, practitioners, and students. The educational history of African Americans in the United States has been primarily one of exclusion. For approximately 300 years (1619 to 1868), during which the critical masses of African Americans were enslaved, it was illegal or unacceptable to educate people of African ancestry in most of the states in the Union. After the War Between the States, the federal government made a meager effort to educate the newly freed Black populace, which included many adults, through the Bureau of Refugees, Freedmen, and Abandoned Lands (Freedmen's Bureau). This effort, Reconstruction, occurred from 1864 to 1876 and quickly disintegrated as the mood of the country changed and sympathy for the former slaves dissipated (DuBois, 1903/1953; Woodson, 1915).

Although the efforts of the Freedmen's Bureau and groups such as the American Missionary Association and the Quakers were significant post-Reconstruction adult education efforts, the phase of the post-post-Reconstruction remains one of the most vital and important times in the adult education movement of African Americans (Denton, 1993; DuBois, 1903/1953; Franklin, 1963). This era, 1920 through 1945, represents a quarter of a century when African Americans made meaningful strides in self-education and self-governance. The period of freedom prior to the 1920s was spent laboring toward economic survival and political autonomy. Researchers recognize the second decade of the 1900s as an important one for Blacks (Colin, 1989; Peterson, 1996; Sitkoff, 1978). During this period, institutions and groups such as the Universal Negro Improvement Association, Tuskegee University (through the summer institutes), sororities (Alpha Kappa Alpha and Delta Sigma Theta), fraternities (Omega Psi Phi and Alpha Phi Alpha), and the National Colored Women's Clubs were introducing programs to educate adults of African ancestry. Yet, little research has been done on this specific time period in adult education.

This study has significance given the limited research done on the topic. To date, three major texts are currently in print and available for use in adult education programs throughout the United States on African American adult education. *Freedom Road: Adult Education of African Americans* (Peterson, 1996) is an edited work containing six chapters that outline the lives and adult education endeavors of six prominent African Americans. The first publication by Neufeldt and McGee (1990), *Education of the African American Adult: An Historical Overview*, is also an edited book, consisting of three sections exploring Black adult education from the 1700s through 1980. The book includes 13 chapters that give a sketched overview of specific adult education programs. *Education of the Black Adult in the United States: An Annotated Bibliography* (McGee & Neufeldt, 1985) contains 367 citations and a one-paragraph synopsis of each article and book cited. Although the McGee and Neufeldt text of annotated citations includes extensive listings, these entries are of limited value because the authors have set such broad parameters as to render many of the citations useless according to adult education as identified in the adult education handbooks. Adding to this small body of accessible literature on the history of the African American adult education movement are three unpublished dissertations on three prominent adult educators: Marcus Garvey (Colin, 1989), Nannie Helen Burroughs (Easter, 1992), and Alain Locke (Guy, 1993). These three texts and three dissertations comprise a sizeable bulk of the book-length contributions on African American adult education in the United States (Johnson-Bailey, 2001). In addition, there are approximately 100 journal articles that examine this subject.

The unknown and essentially unrecorded efforts of this populace are a meaningful part of the American adult education history. Furthermore, the stories of struggle and self-governance inherent in the efforts of a group of learners and educators who developed and administered programs in an unaccepting environment speaks to the fundamental beliefs and democratic ideals of the contemporary adult education movement (Cunningham, 1996; Freire, 2000). Inclusion of more history from this group adds to the dimension of the exciting portrait of adult education by broadening the dialogue to include issues of power and access.

CONCEPTUAL FRAMEWORK AND METHOD

The purpose of this study was to examine, describe, and analyze one quarter of a century (1920 to 1945) of African American adult education programs. It is believed that this research broadens the existing literature on African Americans in adult education by examining primary sources in an effort to produce a comprehensive listing and description of adult education programs and writings that resulted from these educational efforts. This study endeavored to describe the programs by including mission statements, objectives, and activities, also focusing on the sociocultural factors.

This study's conceptual framework is based on Black feminist thought (Collins, 1989), especially the critical race components encompassed in the theory (Bell, 1992; hooks, 1989). The resulting frame influenced the research in that Black feminist thought's focus on power and positionality led to the development of research questions that asked (a) whose interests were being served in the programs, (b) how sponsorship affected program development, and (c) how the societal context played into the educational leadership, program development, and missions. Directly connected to accepting the diffusive nature of power as central to Black feminism, the theoretical frame affected data analysis and data collection. This perspective necessitated that the racial and gendered context of the time inform the analysis and be juxtaposed against a contemporary critique of the data that centered on issues of gender, race, and class.

Data were collected in two ways. First, I used program areas as ways to delineate or categorize the data. Emphasis was placed on primary sources from African Americans, and when pamphlets or conference materials were used, every effort was made to determine the race of the program directors or instructors. Only pamphlets or programs that were generated by African Americans were used. This was ascertained by triangulating with photos or through separate archival searches. Second, I used chronological and thematic methods as a way of bringing order to the archival materials.

Data Collection for the Archival Searches

The sites for archival data collection were the following institutions: the New York Public Library's Schomburg Center for Research in Black Culture, the Moorland-Spingarn Archives at Howard University, and the Hollis Burke Frissell Library at Tuskegee University in Tuskegee, Alabama. These locations were the main sites because an examination of the *National Union Catalog of Manuscript Collections* suggested these sites as the most appropriate and abundant for information pertaining to the educational history of African Americans.

Data Analysis

Data analysis was inductive and involved sifting through large amounts of data in an effort to categorize the data by identifying common topics. After identifying the applicable holdings through the *National Union Catalog of Manuscript Collections* and from the audit trails of historical studies on African Americans, I consulted the archivist at each of the selected libraries and reviewed the abstracts of each of the collections that covered the 25-year period under review. The data were originally cataloged chronologically and by archival site. This data management technique proved inadequate and counterproductive for analysis because it prohibited the emergence of themes. Only when the data were grouped by preliminary and loosely defined categories did cohesive themes become apparent. All data that involved the teaching and learning of adults were tagged for copying and then organized thematically.

FINDINGS

Three major themes emerged from this archival search. The most readily observable and robust theme was *education for assimilation*. The second most frequently occurring theme was *education for cultural survival*, and the third theme, which was infrequent, was *education for resistance*.

In the collected data (which exceeded 3,000 pages), the themes of cultural assimilation and resistance were immediately recognized, especially given the direct political messages contained in the records. Many of the holdings openly debated the need for the Blacks of the period to assimilate, be hardworking, and of service to the White population as a means of survival. The theme education for assimilation uses the term *assimilation* according to its sociological definition as defined by Banks (1997) and refers to an ethnic or racial group's efforts to relinquish its characteristics in favor of the characteristics and norm of the dominant group. The idea of America as a melting pot where all new immigrant groups are encouraged to conform to an ideal that resembles a British expatriate citizen has been popular in American culture since the early 1800s and was first expressed as a formal concept in *The Melting Pot*, a 1908 play by Zangwill. In this study, the concept of education for assimilation refers to the efforts of African Americans to use education as a means of reshaping their group out of a culture that celebrated communal knowledge and consensus and into Anglo-Protestant cultural norms that honor individualism and competition (Guy, 1999).

The second theme, education for cultural survival, is akin to the ideals posited by Booker T. Washington and his Tuskegee Institute (Denton, 1993). Primarily, the education would also be aimed at providing steady and essential employment. Consequently, its goal would be to provide an economic base that would uplift the race from poverty into a working class and a possible segregated middle-class status. The group would survive as a cultural entity while maintaining a deeply rooted folk culture. Physical and spiritual survivals are also included under this theme.

The third and final theme, education for resistance, is closely associated with education for cultural survival but differs in that it recognizes the value of the culture and gives credit to the contributions of African Americans as a viable and respectable group. Several means of resistance are evident in the data: Avoid assimilation, safeguard physical harm to the group and to the individual, and work toward equity on the political and social levels. This theme is recurrent in the data and journal articles studied, and it is seen as the precursor to what became the modern civil rights movement.

Education for Assimilation

The most constant of the themes to emerge from the data, education for assimilation, is self-explanatory and easily understood as a first line of defense to America's new citizens: We must be like the previous immigrant groups, we must fit in, and we must not be the White man's burden. Finding their way to better social skills and better job skills through education was thought of as the trustworthiest way to make it in this land of opportunity. Programs and curricula of the time included offerings on social etiquette, proper speech for formal and informal occasions, hygiene, homemaking, budgeting, and literacy.

It was a widely held belief that the Negro was a burden to the American White populace. In 1924, the Commission on Interracial Co-Operation, which included such African American leaders as Robert Moton, president of Tuskegee Institute from 1915 through 1935, issued a report stating that "The relations of Whites and Negroes in the United States is our most grave and perplexing domestic problem." It further expressed the belief that the answer to the problem lay in the hands of the "Negro":

> Solutions . . . are being brought about—as alone they could be brought about by a transformation in the point of view of the local white community towards the local colored community. But in each case this change has been based on a transformation in the colored community itself which warranted it. (Locke, n.d.)

The dilemma of the African American was a national issue addressed by President Calvin Coolidge in a 1924 correspondence (personal letter). Coolidge's idea that the solution to the Negro problem lay in the Hampton-Tuskegee concept is again set forth in a Hampton-Tuskegee promotional brochure, *Except They Be Sent*: "to build up, by teaching Negroes to work better, live better and think better, that fundamental self-respect and character alone can win for any race the true and lasting respect of others" (Locke, 1924). Implicit in the communication from Coolidge is the acceptance of the idea that the Negro is at fault and that the race of Blacks are deficient and require instruction.

Although Coolidge's letter was a private correspondence, feelings about the inadequacy of the new Black citizens and their responsibility for their status were openly expressed in print. Meritocracy was held out as the American ideal, and it was stated repeatedly that if the Blacks did not succeed it was because they did not wish to succeed. A Young Men's Christian Association (YMCA) training pamphlet gave directions to Blacks on how to succeed and implicitly chided them as lazy:

> Clear eyes indicate an alert, trained mind; a sound forceful body; clean thoughts and living—character. These coupled with steady, cheerful, persistent effort in his chosen work bring success to *any* man regardless of race or color.

> The "color discrimination" excuse for not achieving is outworn. Those who—forgetting color—catch the vision of accomplishment, dream of achievements—and press forward confidently, quietly, steadily, rarely fail to make their mark. DON'T PITY YOURSELF because you are colored. LET THE "Y" SHOW YOU HOW TO TURN EVERY HANDICAP INTO AN ASSET. (Moorland, n.d.-a)

It is interesting that within the body of this 1927 YMCA brochure the circumstance of being a Negro is referred to twice as a handicap to be overcome. The YMCA, a national organization with a somewhat standardized curriculum, was a major sponsor of adult education programs for African Americans. The YMCA often had Black and White branches that even when housed in the same building were segregated along racial lines. (It was noted in data analysis that from the 1930s forward, the YMCA and government-sponsored programs began to include an element of racial pride in the accomplishments of African Americans.) One of its more aggressive programs relied heavily on volunteers to give back to their own communities. Through a 1930s program called "The Three R League," volunteer literacy instructors were asked to make the following pledge: "I promise to teach one or more illiterates a year the rudiments of Reading, Writing and Arithmetic as part of a Five Year Program of the Three R League of the Young Men's Christian Associations" (Moorland, n.d.-c).

Another prominent push to educate the African American adult was headed by the Institute on Adult Education of Negroes. It was sponsored by the U.S. Office of Education with the cooperation of the American Association for Adult Education and the National Conference on Adult Education and the Negro, with the financial assistance of the Carnegie Corporation of New York. This initiative occurred in reaction to the 1940 census that revealed that 3 million Negroes, one quarter of the Negro population, were functionally illiterate. A study based on the census report set forth how functional illiteracy affected the Negro race: "(1) limited and warped personality development; (2) high morbidity and death rates; (3) occupational inefficiency and limitations; (4) ineffective citizenship; (5) unwholesome and disorganized home and family life; and (6) general social and economic maladjustments" (Caliver, 1946, p. 1).

A search of YMCA brochures revealed that many of the teachers and administrators of the YMCA programs were in fact African Americans. Another surprising revelation found in the data was that many prominent Black educators shared similar opinions on the condition of African Americans. Ambrose Caliver, an African American and the head of the Project for the Special Education of Negroes, which was funded by the Carnegie Corporation in cooperation with the U.S. Office of Education, was considered an education specialist in matters related to the higher education of African Americans. He was vocal in placing partial liability on Blacks for their current impoverished circumstances. Caliver believed, as did Washington and Carver and other leading African American educators, that their people should pull themselves up by their bootstraps. Caliver (n.d.) believed that Blacks had been severely corrupted by their experiences in slavery:

> The attitude of Negroes toward work has been greatly colored by his experiences during slavery. Forced to act as a beast of burden and to toil ceaselessly from dawn to dusk at hard physical labor, he has attached an opprobrium to all manual work, even after the conditions producing this "complex" have ceased to exist.

Across many national programs, such as the YMCA, church programs, and government programs (e.g., the Works Progress Administration [WPA]), it was professed that any education for the Blacks should include certain principles in order to counteract this programmed laziness. These beliefs are again reflected in a 1932 document from Miner Teachers College that stated that some of the most important points to be remembered when dealing with Black students was a need to use "rigid discipline" and to attempt to instill in them a sense of responsibility for the "reputation of the race" (Caliver, 1932).

It was also well accepted that this education needed to center on several areas. Routinely, these foci included any combination of the following areas: home life, vocations, citizenship, leisure, health, and ethics and morals. However, what is particularly interesting is that evidence exists that the "man on the street," the everyday African American, believed herself or himself to be in need of re-education in order that they progress. The *Annual Report of the Director 1938–1939 of the American Association for Adult Education* reasoned that the sales of their booklets in the Black community were so successful because Blacks believed and readily accepted the messages of group responsibility and improvement contained in the booklets.

Education for Cultural Survival

The theme *education for cultural survival* is defined by its historical context. By 1920, African Americans were only 55 years away from enslavement and thought of themselves as a contained cultural group that needed to establish a united effort to prosper in a country that granted them full citizenship after a 300-year wait. Amid an environment of the Black press, thriving periodical publications, an organized club movement, and church denominations (The Colored Methodist Episcopal Church, African Methodist Episcopal Church, and the Baptist Church), a powerful and sustained discourse thrived about the status of the Negro. It was noted in one periodical series produced by the National Council of the YMCA called *The*

Ninth Man that 1 in every 10 American males was a Black man. Although the authorship of pamphlets such as *The Ninth Man* cannot be identified, analysis of the data revealed that African Americans were represented among the segregated programs, teachers, and leadership. This fact, along with the stated beliefs of African American leaders such as Moton, Caliver, Washington, and Carver, can lead one to believe the ideas expressed in *The Ninth Man* were a common part of the African American rhetoric: that Blacks were an important and indispensable part of American society, and their survival and that of America were inextricably bound. The popular pamphlet series addressed the issue thus:

> One out of every nine men in the United States is a colored man. With his destiny the fate of others is intertwined. All nine rise or fall together. What manner of person is this ninth man? He came to this country with the early settlers, and to his labor may be credited an important share in its development and growth. He has served his country with ungrudging loyalty at every call to arms. As a citizen, he has made distinguished progress under severe and acknowledged handicaps. Only 62 years removed from slavery, he has reduced his illiteracy to 22.9% and his mortality from 24.2% in 1910 to 19.4% in 1920. His group has produced more than one composer whose works, judged solely on their merit, have won international recognition; a singer of international fame; a distinguished biologist; a novelist of great power; a scientific agriculturist whose original discoveries have attracted nation-wide attention; a leading American critic and anthologist; and one of the world's greatest industrial educators. (Moorland, n.d.-b)

The idea of the contributions of Blacks was also taken up in other venues. In 1937, a WPA adult education program examined "The Role of the Negro in Shaping America" and how "The Negro Saved the Union."

In addition, survival was conceptualized in terms of economic, spiritual, and physical survival. Economic survival is most often discussed and focused on in the educational programs of this period 1920 to 1945. Overall, the masses of freed people were economically disadvantaged when compared to other segments of society (Franklin, 1963). A great deal of energy was consumed attempting to find employment that paid a living wage. Putting one's nose to the grindstone had certainly been trumpeted as the way that other immigrant groups had progressed. Usually, economic survival was tied to physical survival. However, there was another dimension to physical survival. During this tumultuous time in the United States, the Ku Klux Klan and the Regulators were patrolling many states in an effort to keep African Americans "in their place." Infamous for their night rides, cross and property burnings, and mob justice, such groups posed a physical threat to Blacks. Entire families, including, men, women, and children, were driven out and lynched for alleged offenses: being impudent, appearing lascivious, or encroaching on territory or rights belonging to White citizens (Sitkoff, 1978).

The third type of survival, spiritual survival, is referred to often in the literature regarding this time period, but it was meagerly supported in this archival data. Christianity as the dominant religion of the slave masters became the religion of the former slaves. Routinely, Black ministers addressed the congregation about remaining "righteous" in the face of inhumane conditions and treatment. In songs and in literature of the time, depictions of the falsely accused and long-suffering Black are typical: "Nobody knows the trouble I've seen. Nobody knows but Jesus." Black denominations, in particular, were at the forefront of organized educational activities for their adult congregants.

Another aspect of education for cultural survival dealt with feeling a sense of pride in the accomplishments of the racial group and in its cultural norms, folkways, and mores. A concerted effort by Black anthropologists began in the early 1900s to preserve the narratives, poems, songs, and artifacts of African Americans. The Associates in Negro Folk Education illustrate a prime example. In 1934, they prepared a project for the preparation of materials on Negro history, life, and culture for the use of adult education groups for submission to the American Association for Adult Education. The endeavor was undertaken at the suggestion of Alain Locke, a prominent adult educator and Howard University professor who would later become the first African American president of the American Association for Adult Education. Locke's survey report on the world of the Harlem and Atlanta projects in Negro adult education was influential in the creatively artistic heyday of the Harlem Renaissance. He set forth several goals, including,

a. To publish 9 or 10 syllabi outline or study booklets as authorized by the grant.
b. To influence a constructive program and policy with respect to the extension of adult education work and opportunities among Negroes and to stimulate the study of Negro life and culture by adult education groups in general (Images and Recorded Sound, n.d.).

His general conclusions were summative in nature and directly spoke to a readiness in the African American community to embrace and honor the culture formed in this adopted land.

Locke, the consummate adult educator, set forth strategies and curricula recommendations. Foremost among his suggestions was the need to develop special materials on popular subjects that were of special interest to adult Blacks. In response to his advice, the Washington, D.C.–based Associates in Negro Folk Education organized an independent project "for the use of adult education groups on Negro life, history, and culture." Sponsored by a $5,250 grant from the Carnegie Corporation through the American Association of Adult Education (AAAE), the famous *Bronze Booklets* included the following: "Negro Art: Past and Present"; "Experiments in Negro Adult Education"; "The Negro in American Fiction"; "Negro Drama and Poetry"; and "An Outline of Negro History and Achievement." (See Peterson, 1996, for a more thorough discussion of the *Bronze Booklets*.)

Other aspects of education for cultural survival as they pertain to physical and spiritual survival were harder to identify and support with data because they were represented more on the community level than on the national level. For example, the antilynching campaigns discussing the political context of mob violence, which worked on the local levels to effect change through local law enforcement officials in conjunction with the White women's and Black women's club organizations, are documented primarily in city newspapers and through local church and civic organizations. The educational programs that addressed spiritual growth included a combination of Bible study and literacy classes and are referenced in the literature and archival data as being abundant in occurrence among Black churches, but few existing church programs were found in the archives examined.

Education for Resistance

It is important to note that resistance in the context of this study occurred in 1920 to 1945 and does not resemble the resistance of racial groups of the 21st century. Resistance as found and used in the African American educational programs analyzed can best be viewed as preparatory steps that were necessary to today's concept of judicious defiance. This concept is easily evidenced in a 1940 press release from Howard University, in which Professor Rayford W. Logan outlined the needs of minority groups at the third annual Conference on Adult Education and the Negro. He declared,

> The problems of no one minority race will be settled permanently until the problem of all of them are solved. The first need of minorities in this crisis . . . is to determine as accurately as possible how much they must surrender temporarily in order to pre-serve the balance and prepare for future gains. . . . A Third need is the realization by all minorities that no one of them can obtain permanent security so long as any

other minority is held down. Indeed I am not sure which is the greater tragedy, the opposition of minorities by majorities or the oppression of one minority by another. (McClarrin, 1940)

Considering the words of Logan in the historical context of the time, it is evident that his speech is a theoretical call to arms that lays out a plan for peaceful struggle against an unjust system. Words such as these more commonly occur in the data from collegiate and community leaders near the later part of the time period studied. This reinforces them as definite precedents to the stirring civil rights speeches that would move a nation to end legally sanctioned Jim Crow.

Another famous Black contemporary of Logan's and a proponent of subtle resistance was Rufus Ballard Atwood, the president of Kentucky State Industrial College for Colored Persons. He placed great emphasis on the need to formally educate adult African Americans beyond the basics of reading and writing for survival. Although he often presented his ideas ensconced in the rhetoric of assimilation and cultural survival, his crucial message was that striving for the intellectual higher ground would set the race on a path toward equality. He stated the following in his speech, "Public Sentiment Toward the Education of Negroes":

> It is clear at first sight that the attitudes toward the education of Negroes are not generally favorable. There is, of course, variation from state to state and often from district to district with these units, still the laws, policies and expression of public servants, together with the voice of the press indicate attitudes usually hostile or generally indifferent. As for the attitudes of the public press, efforts should be directed through the owners, editors, influential citizens, and readers of these periodicals...but until Negroes do exert themselves through the ballot and the other techniques of political and economic activity, the strongest pressure which may be brought against hostile or indifferent attitudes is a plea. And too well do we know that begging for consideration has proved one of the most ineffective levers toward the placing of education of Negroes in its proper place. (Atwood, n.d.)

Atwood is clearly presenting a rationale for working toward desegregation by building a power base, but he makes this proposal in an indirect manner. Implicit in this plan is political autonomy and self-governance. Ultimately, the African Americans of the day would benefit from economic, educational, and social benefits. Even though Atwood does not directly imply that integration is his goal, it is evident that the changes for which he is calling will revolutionize America and set the African American on a new role to economic and social equality.

An example of the marginalization of resistance as a somewhat unpopular perspective for African American adult educators of the Harlem Renaissance era is seen in the fact that the *Bronze Booklets* were carefully scrutinized for political perspective prior to publication. According to Peterson's (1996) seminal work, *Freedom Road: Adult Education of African Americans*, the publishing body for the *Bronze Booklets*, the AAAE, refused to print manuscripts by DuBois and Bunche because they represented their respective pan-Africanist and Marxist perspectives in their booklets.

▓ DISCUSSION

Adult education during the Harlem Renaissance was a vigorous enterprise when compared to today's scattered efforts (see Johnson-Bailey, 2001, for an in-depth discussion of African American adult education in the second half of the 20th century). Overall, the legally sanctioned segregation of the 1920s and the desperate circumstances of African American people were responsible for fostering a receptive and growing environment for adult education within the African American communities.

The three themes of education for assimilation, education for cultural survival, and education for resistance were evident throughout the searches of archival data from the Schomburg, the Moorland-Spingarn, and the Hollis Burke Frissell sites. The themes seem endemic of African American existence during the period of 1920 to 1945 and invariably appear in contemporary educational literature on African Americans in adult education (Guy, 1999; Peterson, 1996). Johnson-Bailey and Cervero (2000), in their survey of the field's handbooks, present the color-blind, multicultural, and social justice perspectives as themes that have been evident relative to African Americans in adult education throughout the handbooks' existence, 1934 to 2000. These perspectives are compatible with assimilation, cultural survival, and resistance, respectively.

Implicitly embedded in the first theme of cultural assimilation is the requirement that Blacks relinquish any markers of their former culture that do not serve their new citizenship, a dressed-up version of their old slave status. According to education for assimilation, African Americans are to be trained for menial and laborious work. Furthermore, their education is to be confined to basic literacy, elementary mechanical skills, and the rudimentary elements of service work. Programs such as the YMCA's directly chastised Negroes to be "alert," work hard, and rise above the "handicap" of their race. Cultural assimilationists told White

America and African Americans that the unfortunate plight of the Black race, lower-class economic status, low educational attainment, high illiteracy rates, and high morbidity were the result of laziness and poor choices. In one sense, the former slaves and their descendants were being told that their 300-year unfortunate enslavement and its resulting consequences no longer mattered. Therefore, if Blacks were not currently succeeding, they were to blame. No responsibility was placed on the advantaged White citizenry that had enslaved Blacks or benefited from their enslavement.

The assimilationists were embracing a position that still exists in contemporary American society. As Lipsitz (1998) writes of modern-day race relations,

> Because American society has not acknowledged the ways in which we have created a possessive investment in whiteness, the disadvantages of racial minorities may seem unrelated to the advantages given to whites. Minority disadvantages are said to stem from innate deficiencies, rather than from systematic disenfranchisement and discrimination. (p. 24)

The concept of assimilation remains connected to education, as noted by Apple (2002) when he contends that the hegemonic intent of modern-day education is to reproduce the status quo so that the disenfranchised are always relegated to subservient positions. Woodson (1933/1990), who was writing shortly after the Harlem Renaissance, succinctly explains the importance of disempowering and keeping the undereducated in their place:

> If you can control a man's thinking you do not have to worry about his action. When you determine what a man shall think you do not have to concern yourself about what he will do. If you make a man feel that he is inferior, you do not have to compel him to accept an inferior status, for he will seek it himself. If you make a man think that he is justly an outcast, you do not have to order him to the back door. He will go without being told; and if there is not a back door, his very nature will demand one. (p. 84)

Freire (2000) explains that the oppressor must keep the masses demoralized in order to subjugate them. Essential to this suppression is the myth of meritocracy that promotes the idea that if the masses are not succeeding, then the fault must lie with their deficiencies and their dissimilarities to the oppressor. Therefore, education for assimilation is invested in continuing the old routine under the guise of a new system and new unlimited opportunities for those willing to rise above their circumstances and work to reach the carrot that is always beyond their reach.

Education for cultural survival, the second theme, embodies the knowledge that African Americans of the Harlem Renaissance were a distinct cultural group that had unique mores and folkways. The proponents of this perspective celebrated the literature, music, food, art, and existence of African American people as a triumph.

African American scholars of the day who were advocates of education for cultural survival, such as Alain Locke, Arturo Schomburg, Nannie Burroughs, Ira Reid, and Sterling Brown, all believed that it was essential to preserve the culture. The protection of the culture included teaching it to those who were not acquainted with its scope and recording it for future generations. The data were filled with examples of education for cultural survival that focused on keeping the essence of the culture alive. The Negro Folk Education Project, the Negro As Artist, and the *Bronze Booklets* are prominent examples of education for cultural survival. Others who worked toward the survival of the cultural group placed their emphasis on economic and physical survival of the individual and the group. These adult education leaders included Booker T. Washington and George Washington Carver.

In locating cultural survival in a modern context, the educational efforts of the civil rights era, such as SNCC's (Student Non-Violent Coordinating Committee) and the Black Panthers' educational programs, and present-day efforts such as Marva Collins's all-Black Westside Preparatory School come to mind. The founders of these programs created curricula that celebrated African American culture, and they posited that it is imperative to wrap empowering education in a multicultural curriculum. Prominent African American adult educators (Colin & Guy, 1998; Peterson, 1996; Sheared, 1994) continue this tradition by stressing the importance of including the contributions and traditions of African Americans in the core curriculum of adult education.

The third and final theme, education for resistance, was the most easily identifiable and the most infrequent in occurrence throughout the data. It has appeal because of its applicability to the modern context of the African American. And it has additional allure given the bravery that it took in the setting of the early 1900s to speak these words:

> The silently growing assumption of this age is that the probation of races is past, and that the backward races of to-day are of proven inefficiency and not worth having. Such an assumption is the arrogance of peoples irreverent toward Time and ignorant of the deeds of man.... Two thousand years ago such dogmatism, would have readily welcomed, would have scouted the idea of blond races ever leading civilization.

So woefully unorganized is sociological knowledge that the meaning of progress, the meaning of "swift" and "slow" in human doing, the limits of human perfectibility, are veiled, unanswered sphinxes on the shores of science.... Your country? How came it yours? Before the Pilgrims landed we were here. Here we have brought our three gifts and mingled them with yours: a gift of story and song—soft, stirring melody in an ill-harmonized and unmelodious land; the gift of sweat and brawn to beat back the wilderness, conquer the soil, and lay the foundations of this vast economic empire two hundred years earlier than your weak hands could have done it; the third, a gift of the Spirit. Around us the history of the land has centered for thrice a hundred years; out of the nation's heart we have called all that was best to throttle and subdue all that was worst; fire and blood, prayer and sacrifice, have billowed over this people and they have found peace only in the altars of the God of Right. (DuBois, 1903/1953, p. 189)

Advocates of education for resistance appealed and in some instances demanded an equitable education that would provide access and opportunity of training to African Americans. It was then expected that education would eventually lead to their full participation as persons of equal ability and background and would therefore result in the overthrow of segregation. Programs that centered on resistance were more commonly sponsored on the local level and according to the data studied were always self-sponsored by African Americans for African Americans. Typical programs that used education for resistance as their basis were citizenship programs that encouraged the new Black citizens to vote and run for public office and programs that promoted higher education and scholarly training over vocational training.

Education for resistance is akin to the social justice perspective that represents a growing presence in the field of adult education. Central to the social justice assembly is a growing body of adult educators speaking from feminist (Flannery, 1994; Johnson-Bailey, 2003; Tisdell, 1995) and poststructuralist perspectives (Baptiste, 2000; Grace, 2001). These scholars are conscious resisters to the majority Eurocentric perspective, which focuses on the experiences of middle-class, White America. These scholars represent the views from the margins. In addition, Brookfield (2003), a seminal theorist in adult education, reminds us of the importance of acknowledging the influence and importance of works by such Black theorists as Outlaw (1983) and DuBois (1903/1953) to the philosophical tradition of emancipatory education.

This study enhances the literature on historic African American adult educators that was begun by researchers like Colin, Guy, and Peterson by adding the names of prominent activist educators, Moton, Atwood, and Caliver. Exploration of the lives of such leaders and the programs of the time stand poised, ready to be mined for data that could significantly contribute to our knowledge base on African Americans' place in the field.

This study also provides historical evidence for understanding the contemporary status and duplicity of the debates on the place and importance of multicultural and social justice education to the field. Unfortunately, this illuminates the position that we are where we were more than 50 years ago—still discussing the chasm created by racial divides. This position is made clear by a survey of the field's eight handbooks of adult and continuing education that extricates adult education's unchanging perspective (Johnson-Bailey & Cervero, 2000). As adult educators, we are persistent in acknowledging our roots of education for social change. Yet, programs such as Highlander are part of our history rather than part of our present. Cunningham (1996) calls on the field to make good on our professed beliefs by reviving our transformational legacy.

To work toward change, it seems essential to be informed as to how past events play a part in present circumstances. It is believed that the death knell to a vigorous adult education program among African Americans was sounded by integration (Colin, 1989; Guy, 1999; Neufeldt & McGee, 1990). Laws passed in the 1950s and 1960s provided a deceptive environment of equal access and opportunity by appearing to assure African Americans equity in employment, education, and housing, seemingly making adult education for African Americans a less urgent issue. In addition, integration destroyed a vital component of the African American community—a visible leadership and role-model structure that trained future community members and provided culture-specific understandings and solutions. Without this base, which was abandoned for the greener pastures of White communities with improved facilities, full coffers, and extensive opportunities, the identity held by Blacks that they were a distinct and interdependent community eroded.

The catalogued data from this study could provide, along with other previously mentioned resources, an audit trail for examining the political context of African American participation and African American contributions to adult education. Furthermore, based on the data in this study, it is apparent that the adult educators in the union-organizing and civil rights movements as well as social justice proponents and feminist scholars are but part of a long-established tradition that includes the African American adult educators of the Harlem Renaissance as one set of unacknowledged foreparents.

REFERENCES

Apple, M. W. (2002). *Official knowledge: Democratic education in a conservative age.* New York: Routledge.

Atwood, R. B. (n.d.). *Public sentiment toward the education of Negroes* (John W. Davis Papers, Box 168-4, Folder 10). Howard University, Moorland-Spingarn Research Center, Manuscript Division, Washington, DC.

Banks, J. (1997). *Teaching strategies for ethnic studies.* Boston: Allyn & Bacon.

Baptiste, I. (2000). Beyond reason and personal integrity: Toward a pedagogy of coercive restraint. *Canadian Journal for the Study of Adult Education, 14,* 27–50.

Bell, D. (1992). *Faces at the bottom of the well.* New York: Basic Books.

Brookfield, S. D. (2003). Racializing the discourse of adult education. *Harvard Educational Review, 73*(5), 497–523.

Caliver, A. (n.d.). *Article III of the fundamentals in the education of Negroes: An interpretation of the objectives adopted by the National Conference on Fundamental Problems in the Education of Negroes* (A. Caliver Papers, Box 171-29, Folder 24). Howard University, Moorland-Spingarn Research Center, Manuscript Division, Washington, DC.

Caliver, A. (1932). *Miner Teacher's College: Outline of a vocational education, a brief survey course, second semester, topic VIII* (A. Caliver Papers, Box 171-37, Folder 9). Howard University, Moorland-Spingarn Research Center, Manuscript Division, Washington, DC.

Caliver, A. (1946). *Institute on Adult Education of Negroes, Hampton Institute* (A. Caliver Papers, Box 171-47, Folder 25). Howard University, Moorland-Spingarn Research Center, Manuscript Division, Washington, DC.

Colin, S.A.J., III. (1989). *Voices from beyond the veil: Marcus Garvey, the Universal Negro Improvement Association, and the education of African Ameripean adults.* Unpublished doctoral dissertation, Northern Illinois University, DeKalb.

Colin, S.A.J., III, & Guy, T. C. (1998). An Africentric interpretive model of curriculum orientations for course development in graduate programs in adult education. *PAACE Journal of Lifelong Learning, 7,* 43–55.

Collins, P. H. (1989). The social construction of Black feminist thought. *Signs, 14*(4), 745–773.

Cunningham, P. M. (1996). Race, gender, class, and the practice of adult education in the United States. In P. Wangoola & F. Youngman (Eds.), *Towards a transformative political economy of adult education: Theoretical and practical challenges* (pp. 139–159). DeKalb, IL: Leps Press.

Denton, V. L. (1993). *Booker T. Washington and the adult education movement.* Gainesville, FL: University Press.

DuBois, W.E.B. (1903/1953). *The souls of Black folk.* Greenwich, CT: Fawcett.

Easter, O. V. (1992). *Nannie Helen Burroughs and her contributions to the adult education of African-American women.* Unpublished doctoral dissertation, Northern Illinois University, DeKalb.

Flannery, D. (1994). Changing dominant understandings of adults as learners. In E. Hayes & S.A.J. Colin, III (Eds.), *Confronting racism and sexism* (pp. 17–26). New Directions for Adult and Continuing Education, No. 61. San Francisco: Jossey-Bass.

Franklin, J. H. (1963). *From slavery to freedom: A history of American Negroes.* New York: Knopf.

Freire, P. (2000). *Pedagogy of the oppressed* (new rev. 30th-anniversary ed.). New York: Continuum.

Grace, A. P. (2001). Using queer cultural studies to transgress adult educational space. In V. Sheared & P. A. Sissel (Eds.), *Making space: Merging theory and practice in adult education* (pp. 257–270). Westport, CT: Bergin & Garvey.

Guy, T. C. (1993). *Prophecy from the periphery: Alain Locke's philosophy of cultural pluralism and adult education.* Unpublished doctoral dissertation, Northern Illinois University, DeKalb.

Guy, T. C. (1999). Adult education and democratic values: Alain Locke on the nature and purpose of adult education for African Americans in America. In L. Harris (Ed.), *The critical pragmatism of Alain Locke: A reader on value, theory, aesthetics, community, culture, race, and education* (pp. 219–234). Lanham, MD: Rowman & Littlefield.

hooks, b. (1989). *Talking back: Thinking feminist, thinking Black.* Boston: South End Press.

Images and Recorded Sound. (n.d.). *Survey report on the world of the Harlem and Atlanta Projects in Negro adult education.* New York Public Library, Schomburg Center for Research in Black Culture, NY.

Johnson-Bailey, J. (2001). The road less walked: A retrospective of race and ethnicity in adult education. *International Journal of Lifelong Education, 20*(1–2), 89–99.

Johnson-Bailey, J. (2003). Everyday perspectives on feminism: African-American women speak out. *Race, Gender & Class, 10*(3), 82–99.

Johnson-Bailey, J., & Cervero, R. M. (2000). The invisible politics of race in adult education. In A. L. Wilson & E. R. Hayes (Eds.), *Handbook of adult and continuing education* (pp. 147–160). San Francisco: Jossey-Bass.

Lipsitz, G. (1998). *The possessive investment in Whiteness: How White people profit from identity politics.* Philadelphia: Temple University Press.

Locke, A. (n.d.). *Progress in race relations: A survey of the work of the Commission on Interracial Co-Operation for the year 1923–1924* (A. Locke Papers, Box 164-176, Folder 29). Howard University, Moorland-Spingarn Research Center, Manuscript Division, Washington, DC.

Locke, A. (1924). *Except they be sent* (A. Locke Papers, Box 164-176, Folder 18). Howard University, Moorland-Spingarn Research Center, Manuscript Division, Washington, DC.

McClarrin, O. (1940). *Howard University professor outlines the needs of minority groups at the Third Annual Conference on Adult Education.* Washington, DC: Howard University, Secretary's Office, Press Service.

McGee, L., & Neufeldt, H. (Eds.). (1985). *Education of the Black adult in the United States: An annotated bibliography.* Westport, CT: Greenwood.

Moorland, J. E. (n.d.-a). *Clear eyes achieve success* (J. E. Moorland Papers, Box 126-42). Howard University, Moorland-Spingarn Research Center, Manuscript Division, Washington, DC.

Moorland, J. E. (n.d.-b). *The ninth man* (J. E. Moorland Papers, Box 126-42). Howard University, Moorland-Spingarn Research Center, Manuscript Division, Washington, DC.

Moorland, J. E. (n.d.-c). *The three R league* (J. E. Moorland Papers, Box 126-42). Howard University, Moorland-Spingarn Research Center, Manuscript Division, Washington, DC.

Neufeldt, H. G., & McGee, L. (Eds.). (1990). *Education of the African American adult: An historical overview*. New York: Greenwood.

Outlaw, L. T., Jr. (1983). Race and class in the theory and practice of emancipatory social transformation. In L. Harris (Ed.), *Philosophy born of struggle: Anthology of Afro-American philosophy from 1917* (pp. 117–129). Dubuque, IA: Kendall/Hunt.

Peterson, E. A. (Ed.). (1996). *Freedom road: Adult education of African Americans*. Malabar, FL: Krieger.

Sheared, V. (1994). Giving voice: An inclusive model of instruction: A womanist perspective. In E. Hayes & S.A.J. Colin, III (Eds.), *Confronting racism and sexism* (pp. 27–38). San Francisco: Jossey-Bass.

Sitkoff, H. (1978). *A new deal for Blacks— The emergence of civil rights as a national issue: The Depression decade*. New York: Oxford University Press.

Tisdell, E. J. (1995). *Creating inclusive adult learning environments: Insights from multicultural education and feminist pedagogy* (Information series No. 361). Columbus, OH: ERIC Clearinghouse on Adult, Career, and Vocational Education. (ERIC Document Reproduction Service No. ED 384 827)

Woodson, C. G. (1915). *The education of the Negro prior to 1861*. New York: The Knickerbocker Press.

Woodson, C. G. (1933/1990). *The mis-education of the Negro*. Trenton, NJ: Africa World Press.

CHAPTER 7

Ethical Issues and Codes of Ethics

Views of Adult Education Practitioners in Canada and the United States

Wanda Gordon and Thomas J. Sork

In recent years, the ethics of practice has been a popular discussion topic in many professional fields, including adult education. Dozens of articles and chapters have been written during the past 20 years on the ethics of practice in adult education, including debates about the desirability and feasibility of developing codes of ethics. Among those who have argued for the development of codes of ethics are Boulmetis and Russo (1991), Griffith (1991), Connelly and Light (1991), Siegel (2000), and Sork and Welock (1992). Arguments supporting the development of ethics codes have focused on the need to protect the public from harm inflicted by unscrupulous or incompetent practitioners, the value of developing a common moral framework to guide practice, the expectation of self-regulation in maturing fields of social practice (one aspect of which is having and enforcing a code of ethics), and the commitment to ethically responsible practice that adopting a code represents.

There have also been strong arguments against developing codes of ethics, including those presented by Carlson (1988), Collins (1991), and Cunningham (1992). These arguments have included the decontextualized nature of codes and their consequent irrelevance to many problems of practice, the privileging of elites who usually hold positions of power that enable them to develop and enforce codes, and the impossibility of developing a meaningful code that is broadly acceptable, relevant, and enforceable given the diversity of the field. The debates on codes of ethics have largely been between academics. While these debates have continued, several practitioner groups in the United States have developed codes of ethics or guidelines for developing codes of ethics, including the Pennsylvania Association for Adult Continuing Education (n.d.), the Coalition of Adult Education Organizations (1993), theLearning Resources Network (1994), Michigan Adult and Community Educators (Mallet, 1994), the Association for Continuing Higher Education (Lawler, 2000a), and the Academy of Human Resource Development (1999). Although not presented as a code of ethics, Wood (1996) proposed nine ethical responsibilities that adult educators have to society, learners, organizations, and the profession. Most recently, Siegel (2000) proposed a universal code of ethics for adult educators consisting of 10 principles derived from other published work. The existence of these efforts to codify ethical principles and the reasons they were developed are strong indirect indicators that practitioners are encountering troubling ethical issues in practice and are seeking help in how to address them.

The purpose of this study was to identify the ethical issues experienced by adult education practitioners in British Columbia (BC) and their views about the need for a code of ethics for the field of adult education. The study was an approximate replication of a research project reported by McDonald and Wood (1993) that surveyed a variety of adult education practitioner groups in Indiana. We believed that it was important to do this study for several reasons. BC represents a different cultural context for the practice of adult education, and therefore, we wondered if the ethical issues faced by practitioners here would differ from those faced by practitioners doing similar work in Indiana. We also wondered if opinions about the role and desirability of a code of ethics would be similar because, as far as we know, no codes of ethics have been developed by adult education groups in Canada, and two of the strong critics of codes of ethics (Carlson, 1988; Collins, 1991) are based in Canada. There are also precedents for surveying practitioners about ethical issues to better understand the issues they most often encounter (Barber, 1990) and as a preliminary stage leading to the development of a code of ethics (Lawler, 2000a). In addition, knowing what ethical issues, concerns, and dilemmas practitioners experience provides the basis for planning professional development activities.

LITERATURE REVIEW

Discussion of the ethics of practice is a relatively recent phenomenon in adult education. Most of the literature that explicitly addresses the ethics of practice was published in the past 20 years. A good portion of this literature has focused on ethical issues that are likely to be encountered in specific areas of practice, such as program planning (Brockett & Hiemstra, 1998; Cervero & Wilson, 1994; Singarella & Sork, 1983; Sork, 1988), teaching (Caffarella, 1988; Lenz, 1982; Merriam & Caffarella, 1999; Pratt, 1998), administration (Pearson & Kennedy, 1985; Price, 1997; Sisco, 1988), marketing (Burns & Roche, 1988; Martel & Colley, 1986), counseling and advising (Day, 1988), evaluation (Brookfield, 1988), using mediated forms of instruction (Holt, 1996, 1998; Reed & Sork, 1990), and continuing professional education (Lawler, 2000b). Other literature has addressed ethics more broadly, including a recent book by Jarvis (1997) in which he made a strong argument for the universal "good" of respecting persons as an overriding moral principle that should guide all educational practice.

Empirical studies of the ethics of practice have been rare. In early studies, Clement, Pinto, and Walker (1978) and Maidment and Losito (1980) reported on surveys of training and development professionals and the kinds and frequencies of ethical issues they encountered in practice. Knudson (1979) surveyed professors of adult education in the United States and Canada regarding unethical situations with the goal of gaining insight into potential future directions for the development of ethical guidelines. Barber (1990) reported on a survey conducted to identify the perceived importance of ethical issues and how frequently these issues were experienced by extension professionals. More recently, Lawler (1996) surveyed members of the Association for Continuing Higher Education seeking member consensus about ethical dilemmas and principles to be used in addressing these dilemmas. The results of this survey were used to construct a code that was approved by the association in 1997 (Lawler, 2000a). In 1993, the results of a survey of adult education practitioners in Indiana were published by McDonald and Wood. This survey was designed to determine the extent to which practitioners confronted ethical issues in their practice, the kinds of issues confronted, and their views toward codes of ethics as tools to help them address ethical issues. Rather than summarize their findings here, we instead compare the Indiana findings with those of our study in BC.

RESEARCH DESIGN

As in McDonald and Wood's (1993) original study, we used survey methodology to determine the views of adult education practitioners about the types and natures of ethical issues, concerns, and dilemmas they experienced and about the need for a code of ethics. The BC study surveyed practitioners from four organizations that were roughly equivalent to the groups surveyed in Indiana: adult basic education instructors and administrators listed with Literacy BC, members of the British Columbia Association of Continuing Education Administrators, BC members of the American Society for Training and Development, and BC members of the National Society for Performance and Instruction. In the Indiana study, the sample was drawn from adult basic education instructors listed with Indiana's Department of Education, members of four Indiana chapters of the American Society for Training and Development, and members of the Indiana Council of Continuing Education. Because the membership (population) of the four BC adult education organizations was considerably smaller than the population from which the Indiana sample was drawn, all members of the British Columbian organizations were included in the survey. Of the 460 potential respondents identified, 122 were continuing education administrators, 158 were adult basic educators, and 180 were training and development practitioners. In contrast, McDonald and Wood (1993) used a stratified random sampling technique to obtain 454 potential respondents. Of this total, 248 adult basic educators and 177 trainers were included in the sample. All 29 members of the Indiana Council for Continuing Education were included in the sample due to the small number of potential respondents.

The survey questionnaire used in the BC study was adapted with permission from the original questionnaire developed by McDonald (1991). Adaptations were made to McDonald's questionnaire because of the limitations of the original survey and the need to modify language reflecting the Canadian context. Both the original and adapted questionnaires were divided into three major sections: demographics, experiences and perceptions regarding codes of ethics, and personal encounters with ethical issues and dilemmas. In the BC survey, closed-ended questions regarding demographic characteristics included primary role in current position, age, sex, education, and years worked in the field. Section Two contained seven closed-ended questions including yes/no, Likert-type, and multiple-choice items. One of these questions was "Should there be a code of ethics for the field of adult education?" All respondents were asked to explain their answers to this question. These explanations were then analyzed and clustered into common themes. In the final section of the questionnaire, respondents were asked to share examples of ethical issues, concerns, or dilemmas from their practice settings. The nature of these examples raised questions about what is the proper, right, fair, or responsible thing to do within the context of decisions or actions that affect other people. The questionnaire concluded with an opportunity for respondents to add any "additional comments" regarding ethics and codes of ethics in adult education.

The questionnaire used in the original Indiana study was pretested for face validity and field tested with a convenience sample of adult educators from the sample frame. It was also subjected to expert critique for content validity. Because the questionnaire used in the BC study had been modified from the original tool, field testing with a convenience sample of 12 adult educators was also employed, resulting in minor wording and format changes.

In early November 1995, 460 questionnaires were mailed to potential respondents in BC. A follow-up of nonrespondents was completed with a second mailing at the end of November. As a result of the initial and follow-up mailings, 261 usable surveys were received (an overall response rate of 60% after correcting for nondeliverable surveys). By comparison, the Indiana study was based on 249 usable surveys (a 56% response rate).

Table 7.1 summarizes the proportion of respondents who were members of each type of organization included in the two samples. The relative proportions of respondents from the three types of organizations were more evenly distributed in the BC sample than in the Indiana sample. Continuing education administration was better represented among respondents to the BC survey than to the Indiana survey.

As in the Indiana study, three statistical tools were used to analyze and interpret the data. These were descriptive statistics, chi-square tests of significance, and one-way analysis of variance tests. Responses to open-ended questions were categorized and frequency counts made for each category. Although clustering narrative data is subject to errors of categorization, we are confident that such errors were minimal due to the clarity and uncomplicated character of the responses. Further detail about both the study's methodology and results can be found in Gordon (1997).

Table 7.1. Respondents by Organizational Membership

	BC Survey		Indiana Survey	
Type of Organization	n	%	n	%
Adult basic education/literacy	97	37.2	113	45.4
Continuing education administration	71	27.2	23	9.2
Training and development	93	35.6	113	45.4
Totals	261	100.0	249	100.0

Note: BC = British Columbia.

▓ RESULTS

Responses to key survey questions and comparable data from the Indiana study are presented to reflect the similarities and differences in study results.

Demographics

In the BC study, 58% of respondents were female and 42% were male. In the Indiana study, 59% were female and 41% were male. In BC, the largest number of respondents (44%) reported that their primary roles were manager or administrator, whereas in Indiana, the largest number (43%) reported that their primary roles were instructor or trainer. In BC, the largest number of respondents (39%) held bachelor's degrees, whereas in Indiana, the largest number (45%) held master's degrees. In both studies, the largest percentage of respondents (52% in BC and 37% in Indiana) indicated that they had worked in the field of adult education for more than 10 years. In BC, the largest percentage of respondents (51%) were between the ages of 40 and 49. Age was not included as a variable in the Indiana study.

Practitioner Views About Codes of Ethics

Should there be a code of ethics? The major research question asked in both the BC and Indiana studies focused on adult education practitioners' views about the need for a code of ethics for the field of adult education. Fifty-two percent of the individuals surveyed in the Indiana study answered "yes" to the question, "Do you believe there should be a code of ethics for you as an adult educator?" In the BC study, 73% of respondents answered "yes" to a similar question: "Do you believe there should be a code of ethics for the field of adult education?" Table 7.2

Table 7.2. Beliefs About the Need for a Code of Ethics for the Field of Adult Education

Belief About the Need for a Code of Ethics	BC Survey		Indiana Survey	
	n	%	n	%
Yes	190	72.8	130	52.2
No	18	6.9	37	14.9
Not sure	53	20.3	70	28.1
Missing cases	0	0	12	4.8
Totals	261	100.0	249	100.0

Note: BC = British Columbia.

presents a comparison of study results. Although the wording of the BC study question was somewhat broader than the Indiana study question, the magnitude of the "yes" responses was surprising. Respondents were asked to briefly explain their "yes," "no," and "not sure" responses. The explanations provided were similar in both the BC and Indiana studies.

In the BC study, the most common theme supporting the need for a code of ethics was that a code should act as a guideline or reference point for acceptable behavior and ethical decision making. The following comments extracted from the survey reflect this general theme:

- I think it is important for any profession to have a code of ethics which states the principles and values to guide practitioners. A code sets boundaries for acceptable ethical and professional behavior.
- Public declarations such as a code of ethics provide an important frame of reference for our behavior and can be used as a basis for decision making by both teachers and administrators.
- A set of guidelines is definitely needed in this field to assist practitioners in making decisions about what is right or wrong.

The second most frequently occurring theme noted by respondents to the BC survey was that the primary focus of any code of ethics for the field of adult education should be the learners or clients. This theme is illustrated by these comments:

- A code of ethics should assure that each student is treated equally and fairly.
- I believe we owe the learners a standard of conduct that allows them to learn in an atmosphere of honesty and integrity.
- A code of ethics should be essential for all fields of work when dealing with people's lives is involved.

Other frequently cited reasons for supporting a code of ethics included the following: A code helps to deter unethical behavior, a code enhances the credibility of the profession, and a code increases professionalism and accountability.

The two primary reasons respondents gave for believing that there should not be a code were that the existence of a code does not ensure ethical practice and that the diversity of the field of adult education precludes applicability to all settings. Two examples of comments from respondents who believed there should not be a code are as follows:

- I believe people who enter this field generally have a high degree of internalized moral values, so they don't need a code. For those who don't have values, no code will assure ethical professional practice.
- The field of adult education is huge and varied. I doubt any general code of ethics could be devised that would apply to such diversity.

Reasons respondents gave for feeling unsure about the need for a code included concerns about content, construction, and enforcement and issues related to the diversity of the adult education field. The following examples reflect these themes:

- The specific content of a code would determine a more specific answer. If a code protects the student/learner, I would say yes. If the code only protects the interests of the adult educator, I would give a definite no. Protection of an inept educator at the expense of student/learners absolutely angers me.
- I would like to see the content. It may or may not be useful depending on the wording, intended uses, enforcement policy, etc.

Functions of a code of ethics. Practitioners' beliefs about the functions of a code of ethics obtained through an eight-item Likert-type scale provided similar results in both the BC and Indiana studies. The majority of respondents in both studies either agreed or strongly agreed with the following statements:

- "A code of ethics instructs the practitioner about what is good practice."
- "A code of ethics gives the profession integrity or credibility."
- "A code of ethics contributes to the identification of the occupation as a profession."
- "A code of ethics for adult education is as important as a code of ethics for practitioners in law, medicine, and other professions."
- "A code of ethics influences people to restrain themselves from engaging in unethical practices."

There was no clear majority agreement in either study (50% in BC and 48% in Indiana) with the statement, "A code of ethics ensures clients that professional services are rendered with high standards." More than two thirds (69%) of the respondents in Indiana and more than three fourths (83%) in BC were either undecided about or disagreed with a statement regarding codes of ethics deterring government regulation of the profession. Fifty-eight percent of respondents in Indiana and 68% in BC either disagreed or strongly disagreed with the statement, "A code places power in the hands of an elite group of professionals who control the majority of practitioners."

ANOVA, employed to examine the relationship between how respondents felt about the function of codes of ethics and whether they believed there should be a code of ethics for the field of adult education, produced similar results in both BC and Indiana. Respondents who agreed or strongly agreed with statements about the functions of codes of ethics were more likely to respond "yes" to the need for a code of ethics than those who were undecided about or disagreed with the statements ($p \leq .05$).

Currently Operating Under a Code

Additional questions in the survey measured practitioners' knowledge of existing codes and whether they were currently operating under codes. In both studies, less than 50% of respondents knew of the existence of a code of ethics to guide their practice in adult education. In the BC study, 40% answered "yes" to this question, whereas 27% in the Indiana study answered "yes." Fifty percent of the BC sample and 34% of the Indiana sample indicated that they were presently operating under some code of ethics.

Issues a Code Should Address

Those respondents who answered "yes" or "not sure" to the question of whether a code of ethics was needed for the field of adult education were asked to respond to the question, "What issues should a code address?" It is noteworthy that in both studies, learner-focused issues were cited most frequently. Client confidentiality and treatment of the learner were the two most frequently identified areas of concern that both BC and Indiana respondents believed should be included in a code. In both studies, the greatest number of ethical issues, concerns, or dilemmas encountered by practitioners had to do with confidentiality, so it was not surprising that they believed that a code should address this issue. Interestingly, the least frequently mentioned issues in both studies were determining program fees, misuse of funds, copyright infringement, and professional development. These issues typically have fewer direct consequences for learners, whereas those more frequently mentioned have more direct and potentially more serious consequences for learners.

Creation, Regulation, and Enforcement of a Code

Further noteworthy findings include the responses to questions about the creation, regulation, and enforcement of a code of ethics. In both studies, the professional association was the most frequently indicated organization that the practitioners believed should create and disseminate a code of ethics. In response to the question, "Should a code of ethics for adult education practitioners have a regulating function?" it was not clear to adult educators whether a code of ethics should have this function. Of the 242 respondents in BC answering this question, 39% responded "yes" whereas 37% responded "not sure." Of the 199 respondents in Indiana answering this question, 36% responded "yes" whereas 43% responded "not sure." Of those respondents who believed that a code of ethics should have a regulating function, differences were evident in study responses to the follow-up question of who should have primary responsibility for code enforcement. In the BC study, the professional association was the most frequently cited organization, whereas in the Indiana study, the employing organization was most frequently identified.

When demographic variables were cross-tabulated with respondent beliefs about the need for a code of ethics, and the chi-square test was applied, the only variable that indicated a significant difference in the Indiana study was respondent education ($p = .045$). Individuals without bachelor's degrees were more likely to respond positively to the need for a code of ethics. The only demographic variable that indicated a significant difference in the BC study was the respondents' primary roles in their current positions ($p = .026$). Teachers and trainers were more likely to respond positively to the need for a code of ethics. Managers and administrators were more likely to be unsure of the need for a code.

When the chi-square tests were applied to respondents' knowledge of the existence of a code, whether they were currently operating under codes, and how they answered the question on their beliefs about the need for a code of ethics, both the BC and Indiana studies produced similar results. Those respondents who knew of the existence of a code of ethics to guide their professional practice were more likely to believe that there should be a code of ethics (BC results: $p = .000$; Indiana results: $p = .004$). Similarly, those respondents who were presently operating under codes believed that there should be a code of ethics for the field of adult education (BC results: $p = .006$; Indiana results: $p = .000$).

When the chi-square tests were applied to citing issues that a code should address and practitioner group affiliation, both studies indicated similarities and differences. In both studies, adult basic educators (ABEs) believed more than the other practitioner groups that treatment of the learner and the needs of the learner should be addressed. In both studies, training and development (T&D) practitioners believed that copyright infringement should be addressed. In the BC study, T&D practitioners believed more than the other practitioner groups that the issue of credentials should be addressed. In the Indiana study, T&D practitioners believed more than the other groups that honesty in advertising and conflicts of interest should be addressed. Table 7.3 provides a summary comparison of significant values for issues that a code of ethics should address by practitioner group affiliation.

In response to the questions about the creation, regulation, and enforcement of a code of ethics, differences were evident in the study results. However, although differences in selected results were noted, the ABE group was consistently responsible for the statistically significant differences in both studies. In the Indiana study, when the chi-square tests were applied to responses about who should create and disseminate a code by group affiliation, the ABE group believed that a code should be developed by the employing organization more than the other two groups ($p = .014$). In the BC study, a statistically significant difference was found between responses of ABEs and the other two groups on the regulating function of a code of ethics. ABEs felt more positively about the regulating function than the other two practitioner groups ($p = .025$). In the Indiana study, a statistically significant difference was found between responses of ABEs and the other two groups on who

Table 7.3. Summary of Significant Values: Issues a Code Should Address by Practitioner Group

Issue (practitioner group)	Significant (p) Values	
	BC Survey	Indiana Survey
Needs of learner (ABE)	.037	.002
Treatment of learner (ABE)	.006	.025
Copyright infringement (T&D)	.000	.000
Credentials (T&D)	.048	*ns*
Honesty in advertising (T&D)	*ns*	.011
Conflicts of interests (T&D)	*ns*	.001

Note: BC = British Columbia, ABE = adult basic educator, T&D = training and development.

should be responsible for code enforcement. ABEs believed more strongly than the other groups that the employing organization should be responsible for code enforcement ($p = .003$). No significant differences were noted in the BC study.

Personal Encounters with Ethical Issues and Dilemmas

In BC, 55% of respondents cited examples of situations that created ethical issues, concerns, or dilemmas for them (a somewhat broader question than that used in the Indiana study). In Indiana, 30% of respondents cited examples of situations that created ethical dilemmas in their practice. Of the 143 respondents in the BC study, 13 provided more than one example. Ten of these respondents provided two examples and 3 respondents provided three examples each. The organizing scheme used by McDonald (1991) in the original study was applied to the data. As content areas emerged from the analysis, it was clear that the original 10 domains used in the Indiana study generally fit the data. Additional categories were established through content analysis to reflect differences in the types of data obtained. The number of responses to this question allowed the creation of enough categories that grouped analytically similar examples without masking differences by using too large or gross ones. Thirteen domains resulted from the categorization of examples provided by BC respondents. The three additional categories that were not evident in the original Indiana study were credential issues, learner–adult educator relationship issues, and intraorganizational issues. Table 7.4 presents the frequencies of ethical issues by practitioner group.

The most frequently cited issue across all three groups of practitioners was confidentiality, with the majority of dilemmas arising from issues around the provision of student information to "others" (family members, funding agencies, other students or teachers). T&D practitioners focused particularly on the issue of creating a "safe place" during training and experienced dilemmas when, for example, "the adult learner's manager or supervisor wants to know details re: the learner's comments, participation etc. during a training program." Confidentiality was also the most frequently cited ethical dilemma in the Indiana study.

The second most frequently cited ethical issue involved learner–adult educator relationships. This domain focused on examples where respondents experienced, were aware of, or had witnessed student complaints about faculty, power imbalances, role conflicts, and socially intimate instructor-student relationships. Both continuing educators and ABEs expressed specific concerns about socially intimate student-teacher relationships centering on such questions as "how friendly should teachers behave with students," "to date or not to date," "how much extracurricular

Table 7.4. Major Domains of Ethical Issues, Concerns, and Dilemmas

Issue	Practitioner Groups			
	Continuing Education	Training and Development	Adult Basic Education	Total
Confidentiality	11	13	20	44
Learner–adult educator relationship	6	0	15	21
Finance	6	5	5	16
Professionalism and competence	2	4	8	14
Conflicts of interest	7	6	1	14
Evaluating student performance	3	3	4	10
Ownership of instructional materials	1	7	1	9
Intraorganizational concerns	3	1	5	9
Credentials	2	3	2	7
Unsound training design	2	3	0	5
Employment practices	1	1	2	4

socialization is acceptable," and finally, the dilemma of being aware of student-teacher sexual relationships.

Financial issues were the next most frequently cited category and included examples involving program fees, allocation of resources, and billing clients. For continuing educators and ABEs, prioritizing programs in "budget cutting" exercises was a particular concern.

Professionalism and competence issues and conflicts of interest were the fourth and fifth most frequently cited categories. ABEs were particularly concerned about instructor competence. One respondent asked, "How do you deal with someone who is not committed to doing a good job?" Issues of professional integrity concerned T&D practitioners. One consultant noted that during an organizational review, "the underlying intent was that I would recommend firing an individual." Across all three groups, conflicts of interest most often involved individuals with training or consulting businesses generating second incomes. One respondent noted, "Colleges have to compete with their own faculty who are moonlighting as consultants and trainers." Also included in this domain were examples of "perks" for business or services provided.

Evaluating student performance was the next most frequently cited ethical issue. Examples in this domain focused primarily on dilemmas associated with equitable standards, "bending rules," or waiving academic requirements.

The seventh most frequently cited category was ownership of instructional materials. This was clearly of greatest concern to T&D practitioners. One respondent noted that "a major issue for educators at all levels is copyright infringement. Because as educators we believe in the free and open dissemination of information, we tend to justify unauthorized use of copyrighted materials!"

Intraorganizational issues were the next most frequently cited category, primarily concerning those practitioners employed in public institutions. Within this domain, compromising personal codes of ethics due to administrative decisions and whether to "report or not report a colleague" provided ethical dilemmas for respondents.

Credentialing issues were related primarily to teachers misrepresenting their qualifications or being awarded contracts based on reasons other than their credentials, and unsound training design issues were related primarily to the appropriateness of training. One continuing educator wrote, "I have declined to deliver training that did not clearly benefit the recipient or is clearly not the solution to a problem."

The next category providing ethical issues for practitioners was employment practices. This domain focused on questionable hiring practices (personal favoritism) and concerns about layoff procedures. One practitioner experienced the dilemma of "being asked by one's institution to engage in budget planning which inevitably limited the job security and opportunities of colleagues."

Enrollment and attendance issues were of concern to four practitioners. Two continuing educators wrote of their dilemmas in advising students regarding "enrolling in courses to boost lagging enrollment or boost budget numbers."

Additional Comments Regarding Ethics and Codes of Ethics

As in the Indiana study, respondents to the BC study were given the opportunity to add further comments about ethics or codes of ethics in adult education. Thirty-eight individuals in the BC survey and 41 in the Indiana survey chose to add their comments. Common themes evident in the BC study included the protection and needs of the learner, recognition of the diversity of the field and the associated challenges of a common code, and concerns about code enforcement. A continuing education administrator made the following comment: "A code of ethics has value as a set of guiding principles, however, I am concerned that enforcement by a professional body will lead to unnecessary bureaucracy and limitations on credentialing." Across all three groups of practitioners, support for a code of ethics was also a common theme.

◾ DISCUSSION

The results of the BC study clearly confirm positive practitioner attitudes toward codes of ethics and support the findings reported in the Indiana study. Although this is not surprising because the respondents in both studies were from roughly equivalent practitioner groups, the magnitude of the BC response was surprising. Certainly, in the time since the original Indiana study, the visibility of ethics and ethical issues has increased in society generally. As Leskinen (1993) noted, "Hardly a day goes by without news about unethical behaviour by our elected officials, our fellow educators, business leaders, and ordinary citizens" (p. 6). This increased general awareness may stimulate adult educators to reflect on the issues and dilemmas that confront them in their everyday practice. Within this context of practice, the potential benefits of codes of ethics may be reinforced. The strength of the BC response may also be the result of greater experience with codes of ethics. Whereas 34% of the Indiana respondents indicated that they operated under codes of ethics, 50% of the BC respondents indicated this status.

Although there is a high degree of practitioner support for codes of ethics, the respondents in both studies were not clear whether a code of ethics should have a regulating function. This is not surprising, because code enforcement has been a consistent issue in other professions. The many procedural issues that code enforcement raises (who should regulate, what practitioner actions are considered unethical, what disciplinary measures or sanctions would be developed) may affect responses to the enforcement issue. Perhaps the notion of regulation or enforcement is a premature component in the process of code development. As Connelly and Light (1991) argued, "the development of enforcement procedures is a later stage in the process of building a code of ethics" (p. 239).

In both the BC and Indiana studies, examples of situations that created ethical issues or dilemmas for the respondents clearly demonstrate the existence of complex, profound, and varied problems facing practitioners. As noted previously, more than half of the respondents in the BC study cited ethical situations from practice, and although the response rate was surprising given the open-ended question format, it was the description of the examples that was more surprising. The length and detail of the responses clearly conveyed the often difficult decisions that confront adult educators in diverse practice settings. The willingness of practitioners to share their experiences with ethical issues highlights the need for continuing dialogue within the field about the ethics of practice.

To those who are critics of the professionalization of the field, this study might represent little more than confirmation that practitioners, especially those who belong to professional organizations such as those whose members were surveyed, support the development of a code because it represents the values of the dominant and elite group to which they belong. A code freezes in time what the dominant group considers "responsible practice," thus reinforcing and reproducing the status quo. It is troubling to note that some of the codes of ethics that have been produced for adult education contain clauses that call for "following existing rules, policies, and laws." These clauses would effectively render unethical the work of social activists such as Paulo Freire and Miles Horton, who deliberately broke rules, policies, and laws that were unjust and oppressive. So, there is reason to be cautious about developing any code of ethics that prevents work that challenges unjust, oppressive structures. It is also the case that codes of ethics developed in Eurocentric cultures privilege a Western, liberal political philosophy. This marginalizes those from non-Western cultures and those with more radical philosophies and may result in adult education becoming a less inclusive field.

Although we recognize that these are real concerns, we cannot use them as excuses to avoid dealing with the ethics of practice. The important thing is that we are aware of the problems associated with professionalization and avoid the pitfalls that thoughtful critics have identified.

Implications

The findings of this study have a number of implications for the field of adult education. To those who may wish to continue the debate about whether or not there should be codes of ethics for adult educators, the BC study conveys a strong message from the perspective of practitioners. If practitioners' views are seen as important and valuable, then serious consideration should be given to continuing dialogue about the process of developing codes of ethics. Clearly, the ethical issues cited by the study respondents attest to the need for addressing ethical problems and the potential role of codes of ethics to guide professional practice. Professional associations and organizations related to adult education may wish to consider providing opportunities for their members to discuss and debate issues of code development. Additionally, through this process, support for practitioners in dealing with ethical issues and dilemmas could be a positive outcome. As McDonald and Wood (1993) asked, "Where are practitioners to find support and insight for recognizing and addressing such dilemmas . . . if not with the professional leadership . . . then with whom?" (p. 256).

To those who teach in adult education graduate programs, these findings suggest that explicit discussion of ethical issues and some experience with ethical problem solving might be useful additions to the curriculum. Ethical issues will not disappear. Whether graduates are employed as teachers, administrators, or program planners, their practice will involve dealing with ethical issues and dilemmas. If those engaged in the preparation of adult educators are not addressing the ethical dimensions of practice, they are not being responsive to the needs for assistance expressed by practitioners in both BC and Indiana.

Although the findings of the BC study strongly confirm positive practitioner attitudes about the need for a code of ethics for the field of adult education, further research should be done to confirm these findings. Conducting similar studies with other groups of adult educators may be valuable in gaining different perspectives on the issues addressed in the BC and Indiana surveys. Research into exploring workable regulatory mechanisms could provide clearer direction on the issue of code enforcement. Qualitative research studies that explore the lived experiences of practitioners may provide new insights into the ethical dimensions of practice and are suggested to further extend the findings of this study.

If there are still serious questions about the desirability or feasibility of developing codes of ethics for adult education, it would seem prudent to craft some alternative response to the pleas for help reflected in both the BC and Indiana studies. Adult educators have a proud tradition of responding to the educational needs of adult learners, but it seems that there is a strongly felt but unmet need among practitioners for knowledge and skills related to professional ethics. If there is no systematic response to this need, serious questions can be raised about adult educators' collective commitment to ethically responsible practice.

REFERENCES

Academy of Human Resource Development. (1999, May). *Standards on ethics and integrity*. Baton Rouge, LA: Author.

Barber, S. L. (1990). Ethical issues and perceptions of importance and frequency by adult educators in the cooperative extension system. *Dissertation Abstracts International, 50*(11), 34–45 A.

Boulmetis, J., & Russo, F. X. (1991). A question of ethics. *Community Education Journal, 18*(2), 15–18.

Brockett, R. G., & Hiemstra, R. (1998). Philosophical and ethical considerations. In P. S. Cookson (Ed.), *Program planning for the training and education of adults: North American perspectives* (pp. 115–133). Malabar, FL: Krieger.

Brookfield, S. (1988). Ethical dilemmas in evaluating adult education programs. In R. G. Brockett (Ed.), *Ethical issues in adult education* (pp. 88–102). New York: Teachers College Press.

Burns, J. H., & Roche, G. A. (1988). Marketing for adult educators: Some ethical questions. In R. G. Brockett (Ed.), *Ethical issues in adult education* (pp. 51–63). New York: Teachers College Press.

Caffarella, R. S. (1988). Ethical dilemmas in the teaching of adults. In R. G. Brockett (Ed.), *Ethical issues in adult education* (pp. 103–117). New York: Teachers College Press.

Carlson, R. A. (1988). A code of ethics for adult educators? In R. G. Brockett (Ed.), *Ethical issues in adult education* (pp. 162–177). New York: Teachers College Press.

Cervero, R. M., & Wilson, A. L. (1994). *Planning responsibly for adult education: A guide to negotiating power and interests*. San Francisco: Jossey-Bass.

Clement, R. W., Pinto, P. R., & Walker, J. W. (1978). Unethical and improper behavior by training and development professionals. *Training and Development Journal, 32*(12), 10–12.

Coalition of Adult Education Organizations. (1993). *Guidelines for developing a code of ethics for adult educators*. Manhattan, KS: Author.

Collins, M. (1991). *Adult education as vocation: A critical role for the adult educator*. New York: Routledge.

Connelly, R. J., & Light, K. M. (1991). An interdisciplinary code of ethics for adult education. *Adult Education Quarterly, 41*, 233–240.

Cunningham, P. M. (1992). Adult and continuing education does not need a code of ethics. *New Directions for Adult and Continuing Education, 54*, 107–113.

Day, M. J. (1988). Educational advising and brokering: The ethics of choice. In R. G. Brockett (Ed.), *Ethical issues in adult education* (pp. 118–132). New York: Teachers College Press.

Gordon, W. M. (1997). *Ethical issues and codes of ethics: Views of adult education practitioners in British Columbia*. Unpublished master's thesis, University of British Columbia, Vancouver, Canada.

Griffith, W. S. (1991). Do adult educators need a code of ethics? *Adult Learning, 2*(8), 1, 4.

Holt, M. E. (1996). Adult educators in cyberspace: Ethical considerations. *Adult Learning, 8*(2), 15–16, 25.

Holt, M. E. (1998). Ethical considerations in Internet-based adult education. In B. Cahoon (Ed.), *Adult learning and the Internet* (New directions for adult and continuing education, no. 78, pp. 63–69). San Francisco: Jossey-Bass.

Jarvis, P. (1997). *Ethics and education for adults in a late modern society*. Leicester, UK: National Institute for Adult and Continuing Education.

Knudson, R. S. (1979). *A philosophical analysis of* The Flies *with ethical implications for adult education*. Unpublished doctoral dissertation, University of Wisconsin–Madison.

Lawler, P. A. (1996). Developing a code of ethics: A case study approach. *Journal of Continuing Higher Education, 44*(3), 2–14.

Lawler, P. A. (2000a). The ACHE code of ethics: Its role for the profession. *Journal of Continuing Higher Education, 48*(3), 31–34.

Lawler, P. A. (2000b). Ethical issues in continuing professional education. In V. Mott & B. Daley (Eds.), *Charting a course for continuing professional education* (New directions for adult and continuing education, no. 86, pp. 63–70). San Francisco: Jossey-Bass.

Learning Resources Network. (1994). *Learning Resources Network code of ethics.* Manhattan, KS: Author.

Lenz, E. (1982). *The art of teaching adults.* New York: Holt, Rinehart & Winston.

Leskinen, H. (1993). Ethical dilemmas. *Adult Learning, 5*(2), 6.

Maidment, R., & Losito, W. F. (1980). *Ethics and professional trainers.* Madison, WI: American Society for Training and Development. (ERIC Document Reproduction Service No. ED 186 980)

Mallet, R. H. (1994). Quality means being ethical. *Adult Learning, 5*(6), 13–14.

Martel, L. D., & Colley, R. M. (1986). Ethical issues in marketing and continuing education. *New Directions for Continuing Education, 31,* 91–101.

McDonald, K. S. (1991). *A study of the attitudes of adult education practitioners about codes of ethics.* Unpublished doctoral dissertation, Ball State University, Muncie, Indiana.

McDonald, K. S., & Wood, G. S. (1993). Surveying adult education practitioners about ethical issues. *Adult Education Quarterly, 43,* 243–257.

Merriam, S. B., & Caffarella, R. S. (1999). *Learning in adulthood: A comprehensive guide* (2nd ed.). San Francisco: Jossey-Bass.

Pearson, G. A., & Kennedy, M. S. (1985). Business ethics: Implications for providers and faculty of continuing education. *Journal of Continuing Education in Nursing, 16*(1), 4–6.

Pennsylvania Association for Adult Continuing Education. (n.d.). *Statement of ethics.* Harrisburg: Author.

Pratt, D. D. (1998). Ethical reasoning in teaching adults. In M. W. Galbraith (Ed.), *Adult learning methods: A guide for effective instruction* (2nd ed., pp. 113–125). Malabar, FL: Krieger.

Price, D. W. (1997). Ethical dilemmas in administrative practice. *Adult Learning, 9*(1), 15–17.

Reed, D., & Sork, T. J. (1990). Ethical considerations in distance education. *The American Journal of Distance Education, 4*(2), 30–43.

Siegel, I. H. (2000). Toward developing a universal code of ethics for adult educators. *PAACE Journal of Lifelong Learning, 9,* 39–64.

Singarella, T. A., & Sork, T. J. (1983). Questions of value and conduct: Ethical issues for adult education. *Adult Education Quarterly, 33*(4), 244–251.

Sisco, B. R. (1988). Dilemmas in continuing education administration. In R. G. Brockett (Ed.), *Ethical issues in adult education* (pp. 64–87). New York: Teachers College Press.

Sork, T. J. (1988). Ethical issues in program planning. In R. G. Brockett (Ed.), *Ethical issues in adult education* (pp. 34–50). New York: Teachers College Press.

Sork, T. J., & Welock, B. A. (1992). Adult and continuing education needs a code of ethics. *New Directions for Adult and Continuing Education, 54,* 115–122.

Wood, G. S., Jr. (1996). A code of ethics for all adult educators? *Adult Learning, 8*(2), 13–14.

PART TWO

POSITIONING ADULT EDUCATION IN A GLOBAL CONTEXT

The inaugural *Global Report on Adult Learning and Education* (GRALE) was released in 2009. Based on input including national reports from 154 UNESCO member states, the report surveys the purposes, trends, challenges, and benefits of adult education as it advocates for encompassing and inclusive adult learning (UIL, 2009a). Unfortunately, as the report emphasizes, adult learning and education still lack adequate investment and significant recognition across most nations. There is low and inequitable participation due to socioeconomic, demographic (notably gender and age), and geographical factors. To overcome these barriers, GRALE calls for an emphasis on adult learning and education to meet the diverse needs of an array of learners in terms of basic education (mainly adult literacy programs that currently constitute the dominant form of education for adults globally), life-skills education, vocational and job-related education, the socialization and political participation of people, continuing professional development, and knowledge production. As the report focuses on issues of provision, participation, and quality in adult learning and education, it positions adult learning and education within a lifelong learning framework that accentuates building human capacity to assist mediation of the instrumental, social, and cultural domains shaping life and work. Specifically, GRALE (2009) locates adult learning and education at the core of "a necessary paradigm shift towards lifelong learning for all as a coherent and meaningful framework for education and training provision and practice" (UIL, 2009b, p. 14).

This trend to nest adult learning and education in a lifelong learning framework has been evident since the 1990s. However, as several authors in this part suggest, the trend is more indicative of the desire of policymakers to promote a new instrumentality and vocationalism aimed at advancing economic interests. It does not indicate altruism that seeks to lift the prominence of adult learning and education in culture and society. Indeed, policymakers often see adult learning and education as remedial or catch-up education as they extol the virtues of higher education and schooling for children and youth. They emphasize education that advances the knowledge and global economies that have emerged in recent decades under neoliberalism—an ideology and longtime global policy emphasizing knowledge production, worker performance, privatization, and economic output. Within neoliberal economies, knowledge is reduced to information, thus making it variously transferrable, replaceable, and disposable. In this milieu, the space and place of adult education appears even more tenuous. The articles in this section of the book variously speak to these issues and the problems created for adult learning and education. In sum, the authors call for a return to traditional forms of adult learning and education that emphasize social education for diverse learners. They also highlight the tension between social education and the more professionalized and instrumentalized adult learning and education associated with advancing the global economy.

Speaking to this tension in Chapter 8, Jarvis, locating us in an Age of Learning, speaks to differences in the concepts of lifelong learning and adult education in times when lifelong learning appears to subsume all kinds of learning. He argues that lifelong learning is emerging uncritically in a neoliberal world marked by globalization and a totalistic advanced capitalism, both shaped by rapid changes in information technology. In sum, these transitions have cultural and ethical consequences, leaving Jarvis to call for a return to traditional adult education and the perspectives it can provide in preparing adults to be responsive and responsible in everyday life.

In Chapter 9, Griffin shifts our thinking to the realm of policy, accusing adult and lifelong educators of having little effect on educational policymaking internationally. Like Jarvis, he bemoans the move away from adult education's historical emphasis on advocacy to a focus on implementing lifelong learning in more instrumental terms. During this move, Griffin contends that notions of *policy* and *research* have been reconceptualized while policymaking as a process has become increasingly problematic. He suggests that the root of this problem is the tendency of policymakers to embrace lifelong learning itself as policy, which leads to its implementation in forms that many lifelong educators do not support. He uses The Learning Society program in Britain as a case study to demonstrate the impact that the neoliberalization of lifelong learning has had on policy and research.

In Chapter 10, Walters takes us back to a focus on more traditional adult education in her article providing a historical analysis of social movements and class and their effects on organizational and educational practices in South Africa. Situating social movements as opportune voluntary associations that respond to particular forces affecting civil society, she considers what it means to participate and learn in social movements in order to get ready for change or resist it. Of interest to reflective practitioners exploring the value of informal adult learning, she concludes that social movements are privileged spaces where knowledge can be produced and exchanged.

In Chapter 11, Choules complements Walters's perspectives and analyzes the impact of context on social change education that addresses injustices. Importantly, she considers how much contemporary social change education derives from Freirean pedagogy or popular education, as it is called in Latin America. After discussing what constitutes popular education as a participatory, radically democratic, and liberatory pedagogy, Choules provides readers with key insights regarding how the application of Friere's foundational work in different social, cultural, economic, and political contexts is problematic, perhaps most especially in the West where the tendency has been to conceal oppression. She also provides readers with knowledge of what constitutes popular education instruction as she considers the meaning of *concientization* (critical consciousness), the position of the educator, the role of student experience, the role of dialogue and democratic processes, and the acknowledgment of political objectives. Here she speaks in practical terms to ways of dealing with difficulties that arise when applying aspects of popular education in a Western context.

From an Ecuadorian perspective, in Chapter 12 Fiallos discusses the impact of neoliberal globalization, relating how the global economy has impoverished her country through translocation—the extraction and transfer of national wealth—and left a culture of harm in its wake. Linking these conditions to deterrents to prosperity and security in everyday living, she challenges adult education to have an important primary goal: to engage in education for citizenship focused on relearning critical consciousness so citizens are aware of their rights and responsibilities in local and global contexts. With the intention of making the lived realities of people better, Fiallos offers a thought-provoking view on development as freedom. This view places value on the revitalization of public responsibility as it focuses on the achievement of results including the elimination of poverty, the advancement of civil and cultural rights, and the improvement of the health of citizens. She ends the chapter with a challenge to adult educators to engage in a more ethical practice by taking responsibility to inform learners about the realities of neoliberal globalization. Here the pedagogical task would be to have learners think critically about individual, institutional, and societal responsibilities to make a better world.

In another selection remembering the social purpose tradition in adult education, Gouthro in Chapter 13 focuses specifically on the challenges of creating deliberative democratic learning spaces for women across differences in order to accent critical dialogue and advance active and inclusive citizenship. She provides readers concerned with the parameters and dynamics of education for women with a reflective analysis of structural inequalities that negatively impact women's access to and participation in lifelong learning. Here she also considers impediments for women imposed by a narrow neoliberal definition of lifelong learning that focuses on advancing local and global economies. Of importance to inclusive adult educators, Gouthro speaks to our need to develop a more intricate understanding of gender as a concept before we discuss possibilities for lifelong learning that promote the involvement of women as citizens in education and society. Drawing on her own research in Canada, Gouthro provides adult educators with suggestions for democratizing pedagogical practices and informing more inclusive lifelong-learning policymaking that focuses on the redistribution of resources and the recognition of women.

Through these selections focused on challenges and possibilities for adult learning and education, we hope that readers will reflect on the many contexts and complexities shaping a global learning culture where adult learning and education still fight for space and place. We also hope that readers valuing our field of study and practice will consider how adult learning and education might face the challenge of clarifying our purposes and fortifying our presence at a time when the field requires renewal of its direction amid the educational new wave of interest in lifelong learning.

FOR REFLECTION AND DISCUSSION

1. Do adult learning and education have to be territorial and segregationist in order to survive? Can adult learning and education be reinvented as a core element of lifelong (from cradle to grave) and lifewide (for living and working) learning that has as much currency as higher education or schooling for children and youth?

2. In a world where credentialism, accreditation, and performance outcomes drive much of adult learning and education, how might we develop forms of education emphasizing democracy, freedom, and justice that will be valued in 21st century adult education?

3. How might we address the issue of low and inequitable participation as a perennial feature of adult learning and education?

4. How should adult learning and education tackle contemporary challenges interfering with the right of women to literacy and further learning in order to address issues of their participation, equity, empowerment, and citizenship globally?

5. To what degree should the state be politically committed to and responsible for funding adult learning and education? Why? To what degree should individuals and corporations be responsible? Why?

REFERENCES

UNESCO Institute for Lifelong Learning (UIL). (2009a). *Global report on adult learning and education: Executive summary*. Hamburg, Germany: Author.

UNESCO Institute for Lifelong Learning (UIL). (2009b). *Global report on adult learning and education*. Hamburg, Germany: Author.

CHAPTER 8

Rediscovering Adult Education in a World of Lifelong Learning

Peter Jarvis

I consider it a great honour to have been asked to contribute to this remembrance of Pato—a great friend to many people and an especial member of the Centre for Social and Educational Research (CREA). I was unsure, however, about what I should write. I wondered whether I should read more of his writing and try to comment on what he had said, but I felt this inappropriate since he had already written it, and so I decided to look at the present situation in adult education and seek to understand why adult educators like Pato and other members of CREA are important in today's world. Sadly, in losing Pato we have lost an outstanding adult educator. I was also influenced by a comment that Marta once made to me about how Pato had hated the type of repressive regime of Franco from which Spain had emerged, but I do not think that we have actually emerged from totalism and even from some forms of repression.

We live in an "Age of Learning" (Jarvis, 2001)—lifelong learning. In many ways lifelong learning was the ideal of many adult educators of previous generations (Hutchins, 1968; Husen, 1972) and it is still the ideal for others (Longworth, 1996)—but the questions must be asked at this time in history: have the ideals of those early adult educators been fulfilled, and is what we now have in lifelong learning the fulfillment of those aspirations? In this brief paper I want to argue that despite an apparent synthesis between the two concepts of lifelong learning and adult education, there are also important differences that must now be recognised,

113

and these have become more apparent and more important because of the way that society is changing. I want to suggest that the advanced capitalist world is becoming more totalistic than ever before and that this form of totalism is being supported uncritically by lifelong learning despite some of its more questionable practices and procedures, and so we need to rediscover traditional adult education in order to provide a more critical perspective. The paper has three brief parts: the first examines the globalised capitalist society, the second looks very briefly at the idea of totalism, and finally the place of lifelong learning and adult education is examined.

PART I: GLOBAL CAPITALISM

Many theories of globalisation exist; Sklair (1991, pp. 27–36), for instance, classified these into five:

- imperialist and neo-imperialist;
- modernization and neo-evolutionalist;
- neo-Marxist (including dependency theories);
- world system (and the new international division of labour theory);
- modes of production theory.

All of them throw some light on globalisation, but none explain it fully and only by combining and modifying them can globalisation in contemporary society be explained. Starting with the neo-Marxist, the economic institution no longer alone constitutes the substructure of society, but there is still a substructure and it now includes technology, especially information technology, which has enabled the re-alignment of space and time. Indeed, when this combined with rapid transport systems, the world changed into a global village—a process of standardization (Beck, 1992) or McDonaldization (Ritzer, 1993). But this enabled the imperialist approach to have even more validity in the past decade since the U.S.A. has exerted itself as the single global imperial power (Americanisation) and became part of the substructure (see Jarvis, 2007 for a fuller discussion of this point).

Consequently, the concept of globalisation might best be understood as a socioeconomic and political phenomenon that has profound cultural and ethical implications. From an over-simplistic perspective, globalisation can be understood by thinking of the *world* as having a substructure and a superstructure, whereas the simple Marxist model of society was one in which each *society* had its own substructure and a superstructure. For Marx, the substructure was the economic institution and the superstructure everything else in social and cultural life—including the state, culture, and so on. Those who owned the capital, and therefore the means of production, could exercise power throughout the whole of their society. But over the years the significance of ownership declined as more mechanisms to control un-owned capital emerged. Now those who control the substructure exercise tremendous power throughout the globe, resulting in the centralisation of power and Westernisation (Americanisation) of the world. Supported by the political and military might of America, tremendous advances in information technology dominate the facilitation of these global processes. Consequently these globalising forces exercise standardising pressures on all societies. Once the power of the state looks diminished, as it has almost everywhere except the U.S.A., it is hardly surprising that the state must respond to the demands of the substructure, especially those of the large transnational companies whose economies are greater than those of many countries in the world. At least two things result from this: there is a standardising effect on the world and people begin to lose respect for its politicians, as the European Commission (EC, 2001) recognised. The politicians now talk of power sharing, but few people who have power are prepared to share it unless they are forced to do so, and many of those who actually have it care little for what others claim in public! If this process affects states and cultures, then it becomes self-evident that it also affects the educational process.

The power of the substructural forces has become even more concentrated and politicians seem unable to control their activities, as Korten (1995) argues when he suggests that corporations will rule the world (see also Monbiot, 2000). This power is to be seen in almost every walk of life—advertising on TV, sponsoring cultural events, pressurised sales, conformity to the consumer culture—as Bauman (1999, p. 156) suggests:

> Once the state recognizes the priority and superiority of the laws of the market over the laws of the *polis,* the citizen is transmuted into the consumer, and a "consumer demands more and more protection while accepting less and less the need to participate" in the running of the state. (*italics* in original)

The exertion of similar forces on each people and society is beyond doubt despite their different histories, cultures, languages, and so on, but these forces do not exist unopposed since different cultural groups seek to retain their own ways of life. In addition, some states and national governments still seek to oppose or modify the forces of globalisation. This gives rise to both convergence and difference.

The control of the substructure advertising and the control—overt and covert—exercised by employers over employees reinforce the process, and the influence it has on the educational system all point in the direction of Western society becoming totalistic. But it is Western society. For capitalism to be successful it needs to be lean and this demands an unemployed potential labour force in each country, even more so in the global society. There are the poor even in the rich countries and even more poor in the poor countries of the world—it is an unequal place, a place where the poor have no power and depend upon the moral responsibility of the wealthy.

PART II: TOWARDS A TOTALISTIC SOCIETY

At least three approaches to totalism can be detected in the literature. Arendt (1976, p. ix) talks of totalitarianism as "the only form of government with which coexistence is not possible"; in her studies of Soviet Communism and German Nazism, she is careful in her use of the term and she is well aware that in both of these societies the regime was never monolithic (p. xiv) and that there was a dual authority of the party and the state (p. 93). The absolute authority in both cases lay with the leader and neither party nor state disputed with that authority. What is significant here is the separation of party and state—that totalitarianism is not monolithic.

In a similar tone, Lifton's (1961) focus is on ideological totalism in communist China; he (pp. 477–497) examines eight criteria by which any environment can be judged as to the level of its brainwashing: milieu control, mystical manipulation, the demand for purity, the cult of confession, the "sacred" science, loading the language, doctrine over person, and the dispensing of existence. In a sense, some of these reflect the research that he carried out on people brainwashed in communist China, but we can also see that in contemporary Western global capitalism there is milieu control, the play on desire and the need to fulfil it, the sacred science of rationality and the scientific, the use of language to carry the values of capitalism, the idea that maximising the profit of the system is more important than the person and some people (the poor and those who live in countries that are of little or no use to global capitalism, except as a potential reserve army of labour) are non-persons, dispensable and forgettable—perhaps!

In contrast, Levinas (1961, p. 38) recognises that when the stranger becomes a face, there is the beginning of ethics and he sees that totality is problematic in the relationship between the same and the Other. For him, society is necessary and in some ways it is important that everybody is part of the totality, but he (1961, p. 61) goes on to say that "the knowing subject is not part of the whole" because it is the individual who is morally responsible for the other—although no individual should expect reciprocity in the matter of moral responsibility. The totalisers seek always to place individuals into wholes (systems—if you like) and so that individual responsibility for the other is lost—to reach for infinity is to transcend the totality in relationship with the other—in a relationship of concern for the other. While we can agree that the whole is more than the sum of its parts (totality) in some ways, we can also say that the parts are more than the totality in other ways because each individual is a morally responsible agent for the other. What we find, however, in the literature of the learning society (Lave and Wenger, 1991; Ranson, 1994: Longworth, 1996; Wenger, 1998), and much of the current management literature (Senge, 1990) is an emphasis on systems rather than individual responsibility. We need to rediscover the latter—a not very visible value in the language of lifelong learning.

PART III: LIFELONG LEARNING AND ADULT EDUCATION

Since the 1990s, the term "adult education" has seemed to disappear and lifelong learning assumed prominence. Lifelong learning emphasises that we are able to learn throughout the whole of our lifespans and that we need to keep on learning in order to keep abreast with the developments in contemporary society. In the first instance, the "discovery" that we learn throughout our lives is to be applauded and with it the new emphasis on providing opportunities for adults to learn. However, much of what they learn—either through television and other forms of advertising—focuses upon the need for individuals to be consumers. Indeed, capitalism cannot survive unless it continues to create consumers, at whatever cost to the consumers, and sell its products and generate profit and capital. In addition, most of the emphasis on lifelong learning is on vocational learning—learn in order to get a job, learn in order to be a member of the corporation (the whole), learn in order to keep abreast with the latest developments so that individuals can play their part in the production process. Capitalism needs workers and consumers who can accept in an unquestioning manner its ideology and so it colonized the education and learning processes—both institutional and non-institutional. Naturally, in an industrial world, it is necessary to learn in order to function as a member of society but it has become morally reprehensible ever to speak out against the whole, even though the culture of the totality is imposed on the whole by those who have the power to do so. In this sense, we are all members of the totality and are all part of its totalising influence—sociologists have long recognised that we are both socialised and over-socialised (Wrong, 1963) into society. In this one sense, lifelong learning is in all of its manifestations a totalising force and an agent of totalisation but a very necessary one in today's society—but not the only one!

Adult education is something else! Adult education is about treating individuals as adults and educating them so that they may mature and develop as responsible persons playing their full part in the world. It is about being prepared in adult life to act in the cause of right because we are free individuals (Freire, 1972), even to be prepared to learn to resist (Newman, 2006) the powers that be. Adult education is about responsibility for the other without seeking to exercise power over the other. It emphasises the individual within the totality and what Levinas sees as the possibility to transcend the totality. Indeed, Peperzak (1993, p. 36) nicely sums up Levinas' position by suggesting that he saw God "as 'he' who left a trace in *an*archical responsibility" in individuals. Critical adult education looks at the totality from the viewpoint of individuality and the potentiality of infinity.

CONCLUSIONS

Contemporary global capitalism is a totalising force creating totalities, and its power co-exists with that of the politicians. Indeed, it supersedes it. Such an approach to society demands the types of lifelong learning that we have and this approach to learning is both necessary and can be very beneficial at times. But the global capitalist world has not created a utopia—we have the third world and the third world in the first world. While we may need capitalism as an efficient production and distribution process, we also need individuals who are morally responsible. We need lifelong learning in order to produce an efficient system that can be of service to the whole world, but we also need to rediscover adult education which can help us realise our individual freedom and exercise our own moral responsibility to the other in an imperfect world.

It is this approach to the education of adults that I believe was embodied by Pato and which is to be found in the work of many critical adult educators—it is also, I think, a reflection of the philosophy of CREA.

REFERENCES

Arendt, H. (1976). *Totalitarianism*. San Diego: Harvest Book, Harcourt (Part 3 *The Origins of Totalitarianism*).

Bauman, Z. (1999). *In Search of Politics*. Cambridge: Polity.

Beck, U. (1992). *Risk Society*. London: Sage.

European Commission. (2001). *European Governance: a white paper*. Brussels: COM(2001) 428 final.

Freire, P. (1972). *Cultural Action for Freedom*. Harmondsworth: Penguin.

Husen, T. (1974). *The Learning Society*. London: Methuen.

Hutchins, R. (1968). *The Learning Society*. Harmondsworth: Penguin.

Jarvis, P. (ed.). (2001). *The Age of Learning*. London: Kogan Page.

Jarvis, P. (2007). *Globalisation, Lifelong Learning and the Learning Society: sociological perspectives*. London: Routledge

Korten, D. C. (1995). *When Corporations Rule the World*. London: Earthscan.

Lave J., and Wenger, E. (1991). *Situated Learning*. Cambridge: Cambridge University Press.

Levinas, E. (1991[1969]). *Totality and Infinity*. AH Dordrecht: Kluwer.

Lifton, R. Jay. (1961). *Thought Reform and the Psychology of Totalism*. Harmondsworth: Penguin.

Longworth, N. (1999). *Making Lifelong Learning Work: learning cities for a learning century*. London: Kogan Page.

Monbiot, G. (2000). *The Captive State*. London: MacMillan.

Newman, M. (2006). *Teaching Defiance*. San Francisco: Jossey Bass.

Peperzak, A. (1993). *To the Other: An Introduction to the Philosophy of Emmanuel Levinas*. West Lafayette: Purdue University Press.

Ranson, S. (1994). *Towards the Learning Society*. London: Cassell.

Ritzer, G. (1993). *The McDonaldization of Society*. Thousand Oaks: Pine Forge.

Senge, P. (1990). *The Fifth Discipline*. New York: Doubleday.

Sklair, L. (1991). *Sociology of the Global System*. Hemel Hempstead: Harvester Wheat-sheaf.

Wenge, R. E. (1998). *Communities of Practice*. Cambridge: Cambridge University Press.

Wrong, D. (1963). The Over-Socialized Conception of Man in Modern Sociology in *American Sociological Review*, vol. 26, pp. 183–193.

CHAPTER 9

Research and Policy in Lifelong Learning

Colin Griffin

INTRODUCTION

The failure of adult and lifelong educators to exercise much influence over national education policies has been a perennial concern of the *International Journal of Lifelong Education* almost from the beginning, and it is an issue that has been raised in editorial comment on many occasions. Adult educators have not been successful in defending liberal and humanistic adult education, and lifelong educators have witnessed the frequent assimilation of a holistic concept of lifelong learning into human resource development for employment in a competitive global economy.

This article is concerned with these apparent failures to influence policy, particularly in the context of the relation between research and policy. It is suggested that one way of addressing these issues is to consider lifelong educators and policy-makers as constituting distinct communities of practice or professional groups, or to identify them along a continuum of different roles and categories of intellectuals in society. The focus upon research evidence in relation to policy is, of course, much narrower than the total possibilities and forms that influences upon policy may take. Nevertheless, in so far as research evidence has traditionally represented a major element in policy formation, it is suggestive of much wider transformations in the meanings of both "policy" and "research" itself, which in turn may throw some light upon the central issue of failures in influence upon national policies for lifelong learning.

A recent edition of the Journal was, in fact, focused on policy studies in lifelong learning, on the grounds as the editors said, that "Lifelong educators need to be studying and publishing widely on policy so that they may be active in seeking to influence governmental policy" (Editorial, *IJLE* 2004: 515). The evidence from the national studies that follow, of South Africa, France, Singapore, Aotearoa New Zealand and Hong Kong, confirm that lifelong educators have had little influence on policy. The question posed by this article is whether influence is possible or, at least, where do its limits lie?

However, from a study of the articles in the Journal, some preliminary problems in the relation between the lifelong educators and the policy-makers become apparent. For example, with the exception of the study of Hong Kong, none of the articles in this policy-focused issue of the Journal pays much attention to the problematic policy process itself. While they contain much valuable description and analysis of policy documents, and much by way of policy implementation and especially evaluation, the actual processes in which failures of influence are manifested are not examined and the mechanics of failure not explored. As a result, we learn *that* but not *why* there has been a failure of influence on the part of lifelong educators.

Again, most of us have read academic reviews that conclude with the recommendation of the work to "policy-makers," and publishers in the field rarely exclude them from the list of groups who need to read the book in question. But who exactly *are* the "policy-makers"? In particular, can they be said to constitute a distinct community of practice or profession? Conflicts over the abstract meaning of "lifelong learning" in policy literature, which are often remarked on, simply reinforce the need to know who the "policy-makers" are. It would seem that from the point of view of adult and lifelong educators, policy-makers are always "other" than themselves, which in terms of the complexity of the policy process does not do justice to the role of those who implement policy in the actual formation of it. One of the aims of this article is to raise the issue of identity in the case of both researchers and policy-makers, and to look at these relations in the light of distinct categories of intellectuals in society or communities of practice or professions. This may throw some light on the failure of adult and lifelong educators to exercise the kinds of influence over policy that have been of concern for so many years. Conflicts of meaning attributed to "lifelong learning" may also be addressed in terms of their origins in the function of policy discourse itself, rather than in terms of philosophical abstraction.

Almost 20 years ago, Brendan Evans argued that the reasons why adult educators in Britain failed to have much impact on policy were clear. His argument was contexted in what he termed "radical" adult education, by which he meant adult education with some kind of social transformation element, rather than the kind of liberal adult education that addressed individual learning needs but reproduced existing relations of society: obviously, "radical" then stood for a wide range of possible ideological positions. In any case, even if "radical" only referred to a demand for substantially increased public funding, it was unlikely, in Evans' opinion, to have much influence on policy-makers. This was because, in countries such as Britain, the political system did not accommodate rapid social transformation: "The political system ensures that policy change is incremental, and that policies are determined by bureaucrats and officials who are more responsive to the interests of major economic groups in society than to educationalists" (Evans, 1987: 224). In other words, adult educators needed to be more realistic about the likely possibilities for change and, in fact, to rule out any realistic possibility of a policy for radical adult education.

However, this kind of analysis does not convey the situation in which adult and lifelong educators find themselves today. For one thing, Evans tended to think in terms of a "policy community" for adult education, which no longer exists in the same way. Also, the problem nowadays is precisely that national governments and international organisations actually *have* embraced lifelong learning *as* policy: they simply have not implemented it in forms that many lifelong educators themselves advocate. In this sense, lifelong learning remains too radical an idea in the face of the overriding economic imperatives of employment and global competition. The implication of which is that a more "incremental" approach is more likely to succeed, and no doubt this could be derived from the enormous range of policy documents for lifelong learning that have been produced in the last few years. At least, Evans' theory of incrementalism did attempt an answer to the question of *why* there may be a failure of influence.

In fact, the difference between *adopting* radical adult education policies and *implementing* lifelong learning further helps to refine the central issue of this article. Even in this postmodern age of de-differentiation, the distinction between adopting and implementing policy remains fundamental to our concept of "policy-making" and, of course, "policy-makers." From this it would seem that lifelong learning is not too radical to adopt as policy, but it is too radical to implement in practice. For example, in the case of European countries, the European Commission's own report *National Actions to Implement Lifelong Learning in Europe* (EC, 2001) makes clear that at the strategic level lifelong learning is being implemented in terms of basic education, human resource development and qualifications frameworks, as a master strategy for a competitive European workforce for the global economy.

The reasons why adult education has been superseded by lifelong learning are not in dispute, having to do with skills training for employment, global competition, neo-liberal politics and so on. But the fact that "policy-maker" is being used to include such diverse functions as policy adoption and implementation suggests that this is far too heterogeneous a group to identify for purposes of influence and advocacy. As in the case of "research," we are dealing with concepts in need of much greater clarity. In fact, "policy-makers" could reasonably include more or less anyone connected with policy, from Evans' politicians, administrators and bureaucrats down to heads of organisations and teachers in classrooms. The focus on policy *process* rather than product is crucial: a great deal of policy has unintended consequences—it is resisted, incorporated and subverted and, as we have seen in the case studies in this Journal, appropriated by national governments for their own purposes. Above all, people who "make" policy seldom have complete control over the final outcome.

So there are elements of Evans' analysis that remain valid. However, he did not pay the kind of attention to the role of research evidence in policy formation that nowadays we need for purposes of explanation. Since then, the background to the issue has changed: we need to consider public perceptions of research in relation to policy generally, together with changes in the significance and meaning of both "research" and "policy" during the years since radical adult education was the issue.

BACKGROUND

Like it or not, we live in an age of acute public scepticism with regard to the significance of research evidence in relation to public policy. Rightly or wrongly, research evidence is regarded as inconsistent, inconclusive, tentative, incomplete, or even as something appropriated by governments for political purposes and forming simply another "spin" on political agendas. This credibility gap takes many forms and contains instances from both natural and social scientific research. One of the most obvious is the failure of the "intelligence" that was "spun" to justify the invasion of Iraq. But there are many others, such as the health risks posed by smoking or mobile phones, criminal and immigration statistics, global warming, genetic engineering and so on. In all these cases, the appropriation of research evidence by governments, political parties or business and industry suggests that there is no longer a clear and unambiguous concept of either research processes or research evidence. Research itself, like lifelong learning, has been appropriated and, like knowledge, has been commodified.

In these circumstances, it is hardly surprising that the policy process is more complex and ambiguous now than when statistical data or empirical evidence were regarded as constituting matters of "fact" or statements of "truth." The "cultural" turn has meant that consultancy, lobbying, and in particular the manipulation of media and communications systems has overtaken appeals to evidence, truth or fact in the "making" of policy. It continues to be true, as Evans suggested, that educationalists would not be able to exercise the same degree of influence over policy as that of major economic groups. But to this analysis must be added other kinds of interests. In Britain, the government at election time has ignored the recommendations of the Tomlinson Report (DfES, 2004) for the abandonment of some narrowly academic awards in favour of a more equitable balance of academic and vocational qualifications. It may well be that this was because traditional (and parental) influence counts for more than an education profession which widely welcomed the Report. If so, then this is further evidence of the need to grasp the policy process and identify the policy-makers in order to better understand the process of influence itself.

However, we have to try to determine the degree to which reports, such as the Tomlinson Report, are actually based upon research evidence. It is not always clear that the kinds of evidence upon which policies may be formed can count as "research" at all: in other words, where does the concept of "research" begin and leave off? Many such reports are supported by research evidence, but the degree to which they are can vary very widely. So it is important to consider the ambiguity of the concept of research as well as its public appropriation and ultimate commodification. In postmodern conditions are we not all researchers and do we not all create knowledge? In the end, it is a matter of belief and credibility: what, for example, disposes us to believe or disbelieve research evidence from tobacco companies about the health risks of smoking or environmental groups about global warming? We are always, such being the nature of research as we understand it, able to claim that the sample was too small, or that in one way or another, the research was "flawed." At least, these are the customary ways in which to dismiss claims to factual evidence or the "truth" of the matter.

As with policy, we have to see research as both process and product. In this case, we can begin to identify the differences between research and policy communities. As far as researchers are concerned, research is the professional *process* by which they are identified as a community. As far as policy-makers are concerned, research is a *product* that may or may not be fit for policy purpose. This distinction, between research as process and product, suggests the contrast between the value rationality which underpins research itself, and the instrumental rationality according to which policy-makers act in regard to research findings.

It is therefore possible to make an initial distinction between researchers and policy-makers, reflecting the respective value and instrumental rationality of their practices. In this sense, but only perhaps in this sense, they display the characteristics of joint enterprise, mutuality and shared repertoire which constitute the basic features of all communities of practice (Lave and Wenger, 1991). However, it will be argued that there are reasons for thinking that researchers constitute a community of practice in other ways which policy-makers do not.

As far as social science is concerned, the identifying characteristic of the research community of practice is its value rationality with regard to methodology (the case of natural science is also increasingly seen as incorporating a dimension of ethical, or value rationality too). This is important for several reasons, not least because the concept of evidence-based practice has arrived in many professional contexts, among which is educational policy (Thomas and Pring, 2004). In the context of school education at least, policy research for practitioners is a well developed field (Ozga, 1999).

Apart from the trend towards the use of research or evidence-based practice in such cases as these, there has been for some years a trend towards much wider and inclusive concepts of research methodology, the value rationality of which, it is suggested, constitutes one of the identifying characteristics of researchers as a community of practice. The turn towards qualitative methods has led to extremely diverse conceptions of the nature of the research process and of meanings of "evidence" or "validity." Indeed, the traditional claims of neutrality or objectivity with regard to the research process have long been abandoned. This is true again, especially in the case of education (Griffiths, 1998, 2003). Research validity and evidence are constituted as much by narratives and fictions (Clough, 2002) or life histories (Goodson and Sikes, 2001) as what was traditionally regarded as "empirical" data.

If meaning-making and story-telling constitute valid research methods and bases for evidence-based practice, what are the implications of this for the instrumental rationality of the policy community? On the one hand there has been a commodification and bureaucratisation of research, but on the other a flowering of considerable methodological diversity which suggests that value rationality continues to characterise the research community of practice.

Changes in the meaning of "research" provide an example of what is meant by a community of practice, but it also suggests that this may have implications for communication with other such communities such as policy-makers. After all, research is something that is "done," whereas policy is something that is "made."

However, what is true of developments in the meaning of research is to some extent paralleled by changes in the meaning of "policy" and "policy-making" itself. The process of commodification and bureaucratisation of research can be put alongside changes in the way we conceptualise the policy process itself. By this is meant that the traditional formulations of the policy process, consisting of elements such as aims, objectives, formation, implementation, outcomes, evaluation and so on, have been superseded by more discursive or Foucauldian formulations (Ball, 1990). This generates a sceptical attitude towards the literal analysis of policy and takes policy texts as themselves constituting those relations of power which they purport to describe, a perspective which permits an analysis of "policy-making" in much more reflexive terms. It also has major implications for the concept of "policymakers," which thus becomes much more problematic. Unsurprisingly, the prolific policy texts of lifelong learning itself have been read as metaphor (Nicoll and Edwards, 2000) and as rhetoric (Edwards and Nicoll, 2001). But what is true for policy texts is true also of the research process itself. Just as knowledge and power are constructed through the discourses of policy, so research itself is a discursive practice whereby the researcher constructs and problematises reality in the form of "evidence" (MacLure, 2003). Nowhere is this more evident than in the case of research conducted within qualitative methodological perspectives with their particular spin on "truth." In a way, this article is concerned with trying to identify and bring into some kind of relation the discursive practices embedded in the texts of both researchers and policy-makers. Discursive practice is an approach conspicuously absent in the case of typical national studies of lifelong learning policy, such as were cited at the outset.

The policy process, understood in this way, *appears* more transparent than ever, by way of media exposure, consultation, opinion polling, democratisation and so on, but at the same time it continues to reproduce the existing relations of power and status in society. Thus, the kind of radical adult education with which Evans was concerned has itself been incorporated into policy: instead of the "working class community" of radical adult education we have equal opportunities, social inclusion and "opportunity for all." Simultaneously, traditional academic values and their distinction from vocational education are reasserted in the same policy process. According to this kind of analysis, research has to be contexted in the discourses of policy if it is to serve the instrumental rationality of policy-makers. And perhaps the journalistic term "spin" is little more than a popular take on policy discourse.

The background against which we need to context the relations between research and policy, and therefore between adult and lifelong educators and policy-makers, has changed greatly. During all the years when it was observed that educators exercised little influence over policy, these changes have completely altered the terms on which our understanding of the situation needs now to be based. If, as it is frequently asserted, lifelong educators should try to influence policy, then they need to do so on very different terms from those in which adult educators were failing to do so 20 years ago. Most significantly, we have seen that whereas radical adult educators were trying to influence policy in the direction of the adoption of radical policies, lifelong educators are trying to influence policy-makers to implement a policy they have already adopted in very public forms. Lifelong learning has not been rejected as being too "radical," but has been incorporated and appropriated by governments to serve purposes other than those which some educators think it should. To understand this, and act upon it, we need to rethink the significance of research and reconceptualise policy-making in the light of the kind of developments that have been outlined.

The background to any exploration of the relation between research and policy-making in lifelong learning therefore consists of a global crisis of confidence on the part of the public in the capacity of research evidence to constitute a necessary and sufficient direction for policy, together with changes in the meaning of both research evidence and policy-making themselves.

To return to the original question, which concerned the ways in which adult and lifelong educators might exercise some influence with policy-makers, it has been argued that the once clear distinction between research-evidenced advocacy and the attempt to influence on other terms no longer holds good. What counts as research evidence is now capable of taking a variety of forms, following upon the diversity of methodological values held by researchers and which constitutes the value rationality of researchers as a community of practice. Influence could take the form of appeals to social justice or political principle, or simply the self-defeating character of some kinds of bureaucratic surveillance, as much as to statistical or empirical evidence. However, instrumental rationality, which is what would constitute policy-makers as a community of practice, will determine the kind of influence that prevails in the end. In the case of commissioned research, upon which so much lifelong learning policy is evidenced, this could be construed as reflecting the instrumental rationality of the policy process rather than the value rationality of the researchers themselves. The concern of policy-makers is with research as product, whereas that of researchers is with research as process and practice. Policy-makers control or "spin" research as product. The concern of researchers as a community of practice is with control over the integrity of the process of research: researchers decide what is to count as "research," which has been described in terms of their value rationality. The degree of control maintained by researchers over what counts as "research" is one reason perhaps to think of researchers as constituting a profession rather than a mere community of practice. Policy-makers may be indifferent with regard to the actual process by which research evidence is assembled, which seems to have been the case with the invasion of Iraq.

So the meaning of "research" has changed to the extent that there is no longer an identifiable difference between research evidence-based advocacy and other possible forms of influence. It may also be the case that "policy-makers" is too vague a category for practical purposes of influencing them (especially without basic distinctions between those who decide or adopt policies and those concerned with implementing them). The question "who are the policy-makers?" has its equivalent in the question policy-makers might ask of research, namely, "what is it?"

To put the issue in its most extreme form, it might be suggested that educators do not know who the policy-makers are and policy-makers do not know what research is. Obviously, this is not literally true, but it does express a fundamental problem in trying to grasp the complexity of the relations between research, advocacy, influence, policy formation and implementation. In order to do this, however, it is necessary to look at the various ways in which adult and lifelong educators, researchers and policy-makers might be located in relation to one another: as professional communities of practice, or in other ways which might help to explain the function of research and influence in the policy process.

RESEARCHERS, EDUCATORS AND POLICY-MAKERS

From the outset, it has been suggested that "policy-makers" is too vague and heterogeneous a description of all the possible roles people play in relation to "policy." The particular example of the distinction between those who decide or adopt policies and those whose role is to implement them has been cited to argue that "policymaking" covers too wide a range of professional relations people have with the policy process to be useful to anyone trying to influence it. The complexity of the process means that many different roles are involved, from formulation to adoption to implementation and evaluation. And at each of these stages the process is characterised by ambiguity, resistance, incorporation and appropriation: all of these go into the "making" of policy. Obviously, the first condition of successful influence would be to identify the role where influence is relevant, or at least most likely to succeed. This was, in fact, Evans' prescription.

It does not seem useful therefore to think of policy-makers as themselves constituting a community of practice. Apart from a shared instrumental rationality with respect to the policy process, such a diverse collection of people are unlikely to have a sense of joint enterprise, mutuality or repertoire of resources. In fact, they are quite unlikely to fall into such a category: their orientation to the process is one of a means to the end of adoption, implementation, resistance, incorporation or whatever.

Probably, in any case, the concept of the community of practice is only useful in a context of adult learning: it has only limited sociological value as applied to professional communities as is the case here, since it conveys little sense of the relations of power, status and control over resources that professionalism invariably involves. The concept has more of a functionalist than an analytical potential.

Nevertheless, in the case of researchers or educators it may be that their identity does include a community of practice element. Educators share joint enterprise, mutuality and repertoire in learning, as do researchers in their commitment to and control over the concept of methodology. However, all of our groups have a common social identity as professionals and intellectuals in society, and it may be fruitful to explore their shared and diverse characteristics in these terms rather than as members of communities of practice. This may throw more light on the kinds of relationships that exist between them. There is no reason why such a framework of analysis should not be relevant in the all-too-vague category of social policy-makers.

About the time when Brendan Evans was constructing his political critique of radical adult education in relation to policy, the radical schooling movement was flourishing both in Britain and the U.S.A. In this tradition, Aronowitz and Giroux (1986) considered the role of the intellectual in a book that, although concerned with the debate about the public school system in America, was dedicated to Paulo Freire. Contained in their argument is an attempt to reformulate the role of teachers as public intellectuals in an analysis that may illuminate the roles of lifelong educators and researchers in relation to those of policy-makers. Thinking of these categories as constituting communities of practice or professional bodies does not, in itself, address issues of communication between them. But thinking about them as public intellectuals, and in particular as characterised by alternative professional rationalities, may take the analysis a little further.

In particular, Aronowitz and Giroux were concerned with the relationship between policy and the changing roles of educators, academics and researchers, which is the subject of this article:

> With the advent of the twentieth century, the administration and organization of public schools were increasingly brought under the influence of the instrumental ide-ologies of corporate business interests; moreover, the growing professionalization of academics and their respective disciplines resulted in a redefinition of the theoretical nature of the social sciences. Increasingly, university social scientists shifted from the terrain of social reform to the role of expert as policy advisor. Within this context, the relationship between knowledge and power took on a new dimension as the develop-ment of social science became closely linked to supporting the ideological and social practices of a business society. (Aronowitz and Giroux, 1986: 25)

They argue that this process of appropriating education to corporate or instrumental ideology has had the effect of imposing a kind of technical rationality upon the role of the teacher and the academic. This seems particularly important (and relevant to the purpose of this article) in the conception of the academic in the role either of social reformer or policy advisor: these are clearly seen as distinct by Aronowitz and Giroux. There is therefore a gap between this policy instrumentality and the critical pedagogy or reflective practice necessary for the performance of educational roles in a democratic society. As a result, they argue that it is necessary to reconceptualise the roles of teachers and academics as intellectuals along the lines initiated by Gramsci, whereby intellectuals are regarded as a social category rather than, for example, a social class. Aronowitz and Giroux develop his analysis of intellectuals in order to understand the general role of teachers in the reproduction and transformation of social practice. Adapting Gramsci's theory, they identify four categories of intellectuals in society and specifically in their roles with regard to education:

1. *Transformative intellectuals.* "Central to the category of transformative intellec-tuals is the task of making the pedagogical more political and the political

more pedagogical … Within this view of schooling, critical reflection and action become part of a fundamental social project to help students develop a deep and abiding faith in the struggle to overcome injustices and to change themselves."

2. *Critical intellectuals.* "Critical intellectuals are ideologically alternative to existing institutions and modes of thought, but they do not see themselves as connected either to a specific social formation or as performing a general social function that is expressively political in nature. Their protests constitute a critical function, which they see as part of their professional status or obligation as intellectuals."

3. *Accommodating intellectuals.* "Accommodating intellectuals generally stand firm within an ideological posture and set of material practices that support the dominant society and its ruling groups. Such intellectuals are generally not aware of this process in that they do not define themselves as self-conscious agents of the status quo … This category of intellectuals … define themselves in terms that suggest they are free-floating, removed from the vagaries of class conflicts and partisan politics."

4. *Hegemonic intellectuals.* "Hegemonic intellectuals do more than surrender to forms of academic and political incorporation, or hide behind spurious claims to objectivism; they self-consciously define themselves through the forms of moral and intellectual leadership they provide for dominant groups and classes. This stratum of intellectuals provides various factions of the dominant classes with a homogeneity and awareness of their economic, political, and ethical functions." (Aronowitz and Giroux, 1986: 36–39)

Although theoretically any individual could fit into any category, nevertheless membership of a community of practice or a profession would clearly limit the scope for action in any particular category.

So such a scheme is only suggestive. And yet it is possible to recognise ways in which adult and lifelong educators, together with researchers and policy-makers, might be located somewhere along the projected continuum of transforming and hegemonic intellectuals. Those influential gurus Freire and Habermas, for example, seem to be identifiable as respectively transformative and critical intellectuals.

In particular, Evans' radical adult educators, together with all of those inspired by Freire's liberation pedagogy, would seem to fulfill the conditions of transformative intellectuals in society. Academic researchers might traditionally fall into the category of critical intellectuals, although the wider scope of methodological perspectives makes this less apparent than it once was. Adult and lifelong educators, insofar as there is any agreement as to what lifelong education or learning is, can be more or less transformative or more or less hegemonic: certainly the literature permits us to identify concepts of lifelong education and learning across the whole continuum of intellectual categories. As for policy-makers, the "other" of the lifelong education literature, these as a group we can more confidently identify as hegemonic or at least accommodating intellectuals.

The whole point of the exercise is to help us explore possibilities for seeing these groups in relation to one another, reflecting their alternative rationalities or intellectual functions in society. Evans' theory ran to the effect that radical adult educators as transformative intellectuals would have little influence on policy-makers who constituted hegemonic intellectuals in an incremental policy process. In the current context of lifelong education, a more holistic, transformative or redistributive vision of what this might mean is likely to make little headway for the same reasons, even though as policy it might be universally adopted: policy-makers as accommodating intellectuals will of necessity distinguish between adopting and implementing lifelong learning as has happened in so many countries.

The position of policy in relation to research evidence can also be located in terms of alternative rationalities and intellectual categories. For example, commissioned research, upon which so much lifelong education policy is based, constitutes the accommodation or incorporation of the research process into the policy process itself. As Aronowitz and Giroux point out, the bureaucratisation of education and research has changed the academic function away from critical towards accommodating intellectual modes, a process which can be discerned in the fate of radical adult education (or even of adult education *per se*) since the time of Evans' critique. The fact that the meaning of "research," like that of "policy," is much more problematic, contested and ambiguous than it was has contributed to the process whereby policy-makers may incorporate it, appropriate it, or merely "spin" it for their own purposes.

Such speculations as these may help us to understand better why lifelong education and learning have been almost universally adopted as policy, while at the same time they have been almost universally subverted or accommodated to other policy aims and objectives, taking research along with them. We saw at the outset that this has happened in many countries, but the situation in the UK is particularly characteristic, having witnessed a classic evolution of adult education into lifelong learning policies according to an incremental and research-evidenced process.

CASE STUDY: THE LEARNING SOCIETY PROGRAMME IN BRITAIN

The advent of the New Labour government in Britain was supposed to herald a new era of "evidence-based policy and practice," and one consequence of this was a major policy-focused research project into lifelong learning and the learning society, which ended in the year 2000.

This provides a most relevant commentary on the analysis that this article has been concerned with, particularly in the form of the selection of research findings edited by Frank Coffield under the title *Speaking Truth to Power* (Coffield, 1999). The title of the book itself is significant, in the light of the argument that research produces evidence rather than abstract "truth," and also that policy-makers (whoever these are) are unlikely to be exercising "power." There is more of truth perhaps in the full title of the government's project, which was *The Learning Society: Knowledge and skills for employment*, since skills and employability have, as we saw, been the most widely implemented concept of lifelong learning in many societies around the world. The case of this project clearly demonstrates that researchers and policy-makers simply had different concepts of what the object of the exercise was, since there are so many meanings of the learning society and lifelong learning to choose from. Indeed, the final research findings from the project were published under the title *Differing Visions of a Learning Society* (Coffield, 2000).

The study also bears out the analysis of researchers and policy-makers as communities of practice reflecting alternative rationalities. The *Learning Society* research project was funded by government, and the researchers also had meetings with "policy-makers." This means that the research was sponsored by government and implicitly incorporated into its own policy projects. However, the outcome was precisely the opposite, since what the researchers turned up was a powerful critique of the government's own lifelong learning policies. In other words, the researchers retained control over the integrity of the research process itself and did not produce findings to serve the instrumental rationality of the policy-makers. The value rationality of researchers, as Coffield himself expressed it, means that they may well "stick unwelcome findings under the nose of government" (Coffield, 1999: 7). Optimistically perhaps, he hoped that such findings might contribute to more of a "learning society" mode of government itself.

Having said this, however, it is important to consider that all research projects are contexted in the political conditions prevailing at the time. With hindsight, it is easy to understand that the New Labour project, so eagerly embraced by centre-left and social democratic sympathisers (including academics), in fact contained little or no redistributive element. It was not necessary to do research to discover as much. As David Clark said: "[Brown's] strategy of delivering a 'maximalist equality of opportunity' through lifelong learning cannot succeed unless there is also concerted action to redress the cumulative, inter-generational inequalities of outcome that are the inevitable by product of an unfettered free-market economy" (Clark, 2003). Similarly, the fashionable concept of globalisation (and its spurious developments such as "glocalisation"), which formed the bedrock of lifelong learning policy discourse in the 1990s, is also now superseded in our understandings by the US global hegemony project, rather than as some more mutual economic, social or cultural process.

It has, of course, long been recognised that relations between communities of researchers, policy-makers and practitioners were problematic, and Coffield cites models of alternative visions of research functions in relation to policy, such as that of Bell and Raffe (1991). However, it is necessary to account for the changing context of research such as this, and especially to problematise both the identity of the "policy-makers," who seem most unlikely to constitute an identifiable community of practice, and also the policy process itself. Since New Labour, this identity and process have to be reformulated in terms of the functions of policy advisers and media specialists (colloquially called "spin-doctors"), and the research function needs relocating in quite different policy processes and contexts than was even recently the case.

Lifelong and adult educators, in failing to exercise much influence over policy, may take comfort from the fact that the application of research findings to educational policy has been very slight. As one of the most distinguished practitioners in the field, Maurice Kogan, put it:

> I have conducted research on policy-related issues for about 30 years now, yet in the watches of the night I find it difficult to say how far any of my work or that of my colleagues has contributed to policy. (Kogan, cited in Coffield, 1999: 11)

Kogan goes on to explore this issue, observing that governments have not displayed much willingness to be influenced by research findings, and even less to "apply" them in policy: "election legitimises the weakest and craziest of policy beliefs. They derive from value preferences that can, but need not be, affected by knowledge" (cited in Coffield, 1999: 11). In a rare reflection on the relation of research and policy in the real world, Kogan goes on to review the situation in education over the last few decades. Obviously, there have been instances where education policy has coincided with the state of knowledge or prevailing values, for example in the case of human capital theory and social mobility, where selection processes appeared to embody criteria of social justice. However, such policies were often quickly reversed in the wake of other states of knowledge that may or may not have reflected research findings. In other words, "there are severe epistemological and operational problems in connecting policy and research," and there is little possibility of a "linear" model of application of research findings to policy formation. Much more likely to work, Kogan argues, is the kind of knowledge generated in practice by practitioners, which is of a far more immediate and authentic nature than that produced by research.

What was happening at the time Kogan was presenting this analysis was that the policy process itself was beginning to change in a postmodern direction. The process was becoming much more one involving consultants, advisers and media "spin." Increasingly, certainly in education, it was taking the form of systems of surveillance and control, inspection and audit, which left little room for the direct application of research findings to policy-making. And, although in his own review Kogan does not mention it, the example of the *Learning Society* project demonstrated the fundamentally critical position that research findings might generate in relation to government policy, which was not a state of affairs likely to encourage future public funding.

Kogan's analysis is authoritative, and yet it still reflects the kind of "application" model of the research and policy relationship. More importantly, however, it also reflects a fairly unproblematic concept of the policy-making process and the identity of the "policy-makers" themselves. What it does strongly suggest is that the process of policy formation is much more likely to be susceptible to the influence of practitioner-generated knowledge and pressure, in the face of the shrinking scope for traditional research in postmodern policy conditions.

CONCLUSION

At least in relation to research findings, lifelong and adult educators find themselves in the same situation as other professional workers when it comes to influencing policy, and it seems unlikely that this situation will change. The analysis presented in this article suggests that there is less scope than there used to be for thinking of lifelong educators, researchers, practitioners or policy-makers as constituting some kind of identifiable professional community, or culture, or community of practice. Particularly in the case of policy-makers, this seems a wholly unexamined concept in any case. It seems more useful to look at their relations as expressing positions along a range of intellectual relations of society, with lifelong educators and practitioners often representing transformative positions (Evans' radical adult educators), researchers as critical intellectuals, and policy-makers as accommodating or hegemonic intellectuals.

In the exercise of influence, we need to consider that the meanings of both "research" and "policy" have changed, to the extent that the findings of research are much less distinguishable from other forms of influence on policy. This is partly because of changes in the research process itself, but also because of changes in the policy process to the extent that consultancy, advice and media presentation are much more significant now than the so-called "knowledge" or "evidence" upon which the process was supposed to be based.

Of course, there is still scope for adult and lifelong educators to influence policy, but it is not down this route. As Kogan observed, policy implementation, if not formation, can still be affected by the kinds of knowledge generated exclusively in professional practice: for example, in this case, the motivations of adult learners. Perhaps it is only *post-facto* influence, but it can make a difference as it did with the bureaucratic distinction of liberal learning and vocational skills, and the evident connections between learning and citizenship, social inclusion, personal development and so on.

Thus there is evidence of successful practitioner resistance to excessive surveillance and the kind of bureaucratic audit that defeats the purposes of policy and brings about unintended and unwelcome consequences. Perhaps this is a kind of counter-factual evidence from practice. This in Britain at least has been the case with police, nurses, social workers and teachers. Unfortunately, adult and lifelong educators do not have the critical mass or weight of such groups of workers as these, and are unlikely ever to be able to wield this degree of influence. But it is well to remember that resistance, appropriation and incorporation are all part of the policy process, and that in this sense we all "make policy."

REFERENCES

Aronowitz, S. and Giroux, H. A. (1986). *Education Under Siege: The conservative, liberal and radical debate over schooling.* (London: Routledge and Kegan Paul).

Ball, S. J. (1990). *Politics and Policy Making in Education: Explorations in policy sociology.* (London: Routledge).

Bell, C. and Raffe, D. (1991). Working together? Research, policy and practice. In G. Wolford (ed.), *Doing Educational Research* (London: Routledge).

Clark, D. (2003, November 8). *The Guardian*, p. 20.

Clough, P. (2002). *Narratives and Fictions in Educational Research.* (Maidenhead: Open University Press).

Coffield, F. (ed.). (1999). *Speaking Truth to Power: Research and policy on lifelong learning.* (Bristol: Policy Press).

Coffield, F. (ed.). (2000) *Differing Visions of a Learning Society: Research findings.* (Bristol: Policy Press).

Department for Education and Skills (DfES). (2004). *14–19 Curriculum and Qualifications Reform: Final report of the Working Group on 14–19 reform.* (The Tomlinson Report) (London: DfES Publications).

Editorial. (2004). *International Journal of Lifelong Education, 23*(6), 515–516.

Edwards, R. and Nicoll, K. (2001). Researching the rhetoric of lifelong learning. *Journal of Education Policy, 16*(2), 103–112.

European Commission, Cedefop, Eurydice [EC]. (2001). *National Actions to Implement Lifelong Learning in Europe.* (Brussels: Eurydice).

Evans, B. (1987). *Radical Adult Education: A political critique.* (London: Croom Helm).

Goodson, I. F. and Sikes, P. (2001). *Life History Research in Educational Settings: Learning from lives.* (Buckingham: Open University Press).

Griffiths, M. (1998). *Educational Research for Social Justice: Getting off the fence.* (Buckingham: Open University Press).

Griffiths, M. (2003). *Action for Social Justice in Education: Fairly different.* (Maidenhead: Open University Press).

Lave, J. and Wenger, E. (1991). *Situated Learning: Legitimate peripheral participation.* (Cambridge: Cambridge University Press).

MacLure, M. (2003) *Discourse in Educational and Social Research.* (Maidenhead: Open University Press).

Nicoll, K. and Edwards, R. (2000). Reading policy texts: Lifelong learning as metaphor. *International Journal of Lifelong Education, 19*(5), 459–469.

Ozga, J. (1999). *Policy Research in Educational Settings: Contested terrain.* (Buckingham: Open University Press).

Thomas, G. and Pring, R. (eds). (2004). *Evidence-Based Practice in Education.* (Maidenhead: Open University Press).

CHAPTER 10

Social Movements, Class, and Adult Education

Shirley Walters

ocial movements are movements of people in civil society who cohere around issues and identities that they themselves define as significant (Martin, 1999). The following quotation describes a group of poor women in South Africa, a group calling itself People's Dialogue, who are mobilizing around their need for houses. They are part of a social movement of women and men internationally who are collectively struggling for access to land and houses.

> Women are singing
> Ululating, dancing,
> Marching
> Carrying placards for their different housing associations,
> Wearing T shirts which read—
> People's Dialogue for Housing and Shelter
> We Want!
> Power! Money! Knowledge!
> The songs they sing tell of the hardships they endure in the shacks, the threat from fire, rain and the wind from eviction even under a new government.
>
> Now they have started to build houses by saving R2 [two South African rands (equivalent to 35 U.S. cents)] a day.
>
> These women are marching to the mass meeting in Hout Bay settlement, Imizamo Yethu. The atmosphere is electric, there is lots of energy, excitement and anxiety as

the different housing savings groups take the courage to say enough is enough, we are tired of this kind of life, and don't want to die in fires any longer and they say, "We work with all our hearts to do the good work and do not want to be pitied and we will rebuild our lives as we build our homes" (Ismail, 2003, p. 94).

The fact that the women from People's Dialogue are poor, they speak IsiXhosa, and they are women shapes very much what they do and how they do it. This chapter will examine how particularly notions of class affect the education in and the learning fostered by social movements. I will begin with a discussion of what social movements are and what adult education and learning means in relation to them. I will then focus in on South African social movements as a "mirror and lens" (Crowther, Martin, and Shaw, 1999, p. 2) in order to draw out key issues. In this era of globalization, South Africa is a microcosm of wider processes at work in other societies. It is a middle-income country that has recently emerged from a protracted liberation struggle; and its reentry into the global economy is heightening the tensions between economic development, equity, and redress. As such, South Africa is both a mirror reflecting these processes and a lens through which to examine them.

▪ WHAT ARE SOCIAL MOVEMENTS?

Social movements are voluntary associations of people and organizations within civil society that rise and fall in response to particular social, economic, ideological, and political changes and issues often driven by the state or the market. They are reactive and are sustained by their relationships to the particular issues or circumstances. A common feature of much social-movement activity is its oppositional or alternative nature. Social movements are the lightning rods of society. They can be either conservative reactionary forces or progressive. The focus in this chapter is on the latter.

Welton (quoted in Martin, 1999) identifies three general characteristics of social movements: they articulate a collective identity, which means that their members subscribe to a common cause that the movement expresses collectively; they exist in an antagonistic relation to an opposed group or interest; they have a normative orientation, which means that they embody a mobilizing ethic, moral code, or set of beliefs that reflect shared values and purposes.

Social movements have a long history around the world, for example, within anticolonial struggles, among peasants and workers, the urban poor, black people, and women. Oppressed and exploited people have fought back against their harsh material realities through collective organizing. Many social movements have historically organized around class-related issues. Eyerman and Jamison (1991, p. 62) say that social movements are "at once conditioned by the historical contexts in which they emerge, their particular time and place, and, in turn, affect that context through their cognitive and political praxis." To understand the workings of particular social movements, you therefore have to locate them quite particularly.

Melucci (quoted in Badat, 1999, p. 29) argues that we should see social movements as "action systems operating in a systemic field of possibilities and limits . . . . Social movements are action systems in that they have structures: the unity and continuity of action would not be possible without integration and interdependence of individuals and groups." In many instances a social movement comprises various smaller interdependent organizational structures, working toward a particular social goal. The social movement in turn may well form a coalition with other social movements, in order to create a united front to oppose an issue or promote an idea.

Through participation in social movements, people prepare for change or resistance to it by challenging or confirming the ways in which they think and feel and act politically. Their moral or counterhegemonic work may become the common sense of an era. As Martin (1999, p. 10) states, "in this sense social movements are intrinsically educative both for the participants and for the broader society."

SOCIAL-MOVEMENT LEARNING

Eyerman and Jamison (1991) have made a seminal contribution to understanding learning in social movements. They state (p. 14): "Social movements are not merely social dramas; they are the social action from where new knowledge including worldviews, ideologies, religions, and scientific theories originate." Because adult education is integral to social processes and therefore social movements, it is not surprising that it gains in prominence at heightened political or economic moments in response to actions within the state, civil society, or the private sector.

Social-movement learning includes both learning by people who participate in social movements and learning by people outside of social movements through the impact they make (Hall and Clover, 2005). Learning through a movement can occur informally through participation or through intentional educational interventions. The educational and organizational practices intertwine. The cultural, gender, class, and ethnic locations of the individuals or groups involved shape the educational and organizational practices, just as they are shaped by the particular historical conjuncture. Social movements are exceedingly rich learning environments. So in those movements organized around class-related issues such as working conditions, housing, health, and other social services, participants come to realize that collective action and solidarity, as captured in the workers' slogan "an injury to one is an injury to all," is the most effective approach to overcome social and economic hardships.

I turn now to explore what these ideas mean in a specific context through a description of social movements in South Africa, with a particular focus on the ways that social class shapes organizational and educational practices.

SOCIAL MOVEMENTS IN SOUTH AFRICA

Over the last hundred years in South Africa, civil society has responded to political, social, cultural, and economic hardships through mobilizing people across social class, ethnicity, gender, and geography into social movements. During the 1970s, 1980s, and early 1990s, the political social movements for democracy were particularly prominent. These movements adopted innovative organizational and educational processes to encourage women and men of all classes and racial categories to participate actively in the movement for change. In 1994 national liberation was achieved. More recently social movements have again formed in response to economic and social hardships in relation to land and privatization of basic services (like water), HIV/AIDS, and violence against women and children; some have strong links to international social movements. Each of the social movements has a different composition of membership depending on its social purposes. Some, for example, are rooted very particularly among the landless and the poor, others among middle-class, working-class, and poor women. The composition of movements shapes profoundly the organizational and educational activities within them. I will draw on a study (Walters, 1989) of self-education within the social movements in the 1980s, which shows this clearly.

The history of resistance in South Africa from the early twentieth century involves a complex interplay between national political organizations and social-movement struggles; Abrahams (1996) provides a succinct description of this. The social-movement struggles have had a significant effect on the development of strategic perspectives of political organizations. When the African National

Congress (ANC) was formed in 1912, it reflected an attempt to unite people, who until then had resisted colonialism in scattered and disparate ways, into a national political movement. The development of capitalism in South Africa in the latter half of the nineteenth century had destroyed the traditional precapitalist social formations of the indigenous people. The political, social, and economic institutions that emerged during those early years gave the South African social formation its peculiar racial capitalist character. The early national liberation movement, mainly made up of the ANC, whose leadership came almost entirely from the ranks for the emergent African middle class, had no mass membership and in many ways represented the social and political outlook of that social class. As Abrahams argues, this outlook sharply circumscribed the political strategies and tactics the ANC advocated and employed.

In mass protests women resisted an attempt to extend the notorious pass laws to them, forcing the state to drop the idea temporarily. (Pass laws prescribed who could enter, live, and work in certain areas. The common result was that black men and women had to carry a pass on them at all times or face punishment and imprisonment.) The conservative ANC leadership was forced to respond to social-movement struggles engineered and led by people in communities and in the mines. The Communist Party of South Africa, formed in 1921, provided a very important theoretical input that helped shape the early perspectives of the nascent liberation movement. One of the factors that made class alliances possible was a shared oppression that all black people in South Africa experienced.

In the early 1940s, numerous social movements of the poor emerged in response to people's worsening economic, social, and political positions. The enormously exploitative conditions that oiled the wheels of white capitalism meant that issues such as housing, cost of living, fuel, transport, and clothing all became highly contentious political issues for black people. Numerous grassroots social movements emerged in the urban slums, arising out of local frustrations at appalling conditions. Their emerging leadership was not of the same social class or outlook as that of the existing political organizations. However, they began processes that effectively pushed organizations like the ANC toward the left. Such social movements were defensive responses by the working class and poor to socioeconomic crises. They tended to have short life spans. The ANC began to provide the glue to bond them into a sustainable movement to end white minority rule, a movement that conformed to the three characteristics of social movements that Welton (quoted in Martin, 1999) identified: a collective identity of oppressed people, an antagonistic relationship with the white minority government, and a vision of a nonracial democratic state.

In this early period, the impact of poor and working-class people on the shape and form of the liberation movement was marked. They influenced what the movement took up and how. Evidence of this influence was visible in the 1950s when the ANC changed into a mass-based organization that adopted strikes, boycotts, mass protests, and general civil disobedience as its new weapons. Seeking the destruction of white minority rule necessitated creation of the broadest front of resistance because it affected people across class, social, and racial lines. It thus laid the basis for the potential unity of those social forces and classes. Among the white people were also those prepared to throw in their lot with the oppressed in pursuit of nonracial democracy.

The 1960s was a quiet period because the state had banned political organizations and jailed their leadership. The ANC set itself up in exile and established its military wing. The social movements of the 1970s and 1980s can be traced back to these earlier periods. As Melucci (quoted in Badat, 1999, p. 32) states, it is important to recognize the relationship between the visible and latent dimensions of collective action: during the latency phase, "the potential for resistance or opposition is sewn into the very fabric of daily life. It is located in the molecular experience of the individuals and groups who practice the alternative meanings of everyday life. Within this context, resistance is not expressed in collective forms of conflictual mobilizations. Specific circumstances are necessary for opposition and therefore of mobilizing and making visible this latent potential." Thus, phases of latency, far from being periods of inaction, are crucial to the formation and development of abilities and capacities for mobilization and struggle.

The formation of the United Democratic Front (UDF) in 1983 was a culminating point of the reemergence of popular struggles in the 1970s and responses to the state's restructuring. The UDF comprised thousands of sector organizations nationally. Two of the most significant social-movement formations within the UDF were the trade union movement and community-based residents' associations that formed around specific issues. The independent trade union movement was emphasizing the importance of worker democracy within the unions and the workplace as an essential part of the broader struggle for democracy; this movement did not join the UDF until later. Its participants saw community organizations as unaccountable and were at times critical of middle-class leadership.

Through the collective struggles with community organizations, the differences between the forms and functions of trade unions and other organizations came into focus. The unions initially argued against affiliation to the UDF because they saw the different class composition of the various affiliates as leading to different possibilities for organizational forms and strategies. There were ideological struggles in the unions themselves between those who emphasized organizing in the workplace and those who argued for closer worker-community solidarity. Harsh repression from the state forced closer work among and across organizations.

Besides differences across class and organizational forms, racial differences intersected with class. Within the apartheid hierarchy, the African townships were the most impoverished; and Webster (in Walters, 1989) found that the working class and the poor devised all sorts of strategies to cope with their poverty and oppression. Many people were engaged in informal sector activities such as brewing beer and hawking food, and they fleshed out their inadequate income through small self-help groups like burial societies and credit societies. They were defensive responses. Molefe (quoted in Walters, 1989, p. 120) found that it was more difficult in African areas to establish more structured community organizations: "We see less of a natural drift towards committees or formal styles of organizations." He comments on the lower levels of repression in the Indian and Coloured areas than in African areas. (The racial hierarchy privileged white, then Indian, then Coloured, then black Africans. This meant that residential areas reflected the degree of privilege and deprivation in that order.) Organizations were therefore less vulnerable. The level of repression also forced many Africans to believe that the only viable option was a military one. Thus, the repression aided recruitment for the liberation army rather than for small-scale relatively reformist community struggles. Molefe's third point was that the greater degree of material deprivation created organizational possibilities. There were limited resources for people to draw on. People who had overcome the struggle for survival had more time and inclination to engage in other struggles. These realities played out in the ways that organizations operated. For example, in African townships people were mobilized mainly through mass meetings; in Coloured areas there was more door-to-door organizing. The symbolic and cultural forms that organizations used also varied across ethnic groups. Singing, dancing, and ululating were integral to African-led organizations, as we see in the opening quotation.

Within organizations like the United Women's Organisation, an important affiliate of the UDF, the class and cultural alliances among women were significant. The organization was formed into branches based in geographical areas in Cape Town. Because of the ecology of the apartheid city, this meant that each of the branches adopted a distinctive profile in terms of racial, language, and class differences. The older African women and some Coloured women, who had status from their close involvement with the liberation movement, provided the political leadership. The white middle-class women played a support role, although each branch had the autonomy to shape its own activities. So the participants' biographies influence particular branches' activities. For example, one branch of mainly white women did a popular history project to highlight the devastating effects of the Group Areas Act, while an African branch organized a march to the local shop against hikes in bread prices. The white women, because of their privileged class positions, were able to provide transport and other organizational infrastructure to support organizing in the poor working-class areas.

Learning within the social movements was conscious. Most of the affiliated organizations promoted participatory democratic practices as a way of building members' capacities. Originating in the Black Consciousness Movement was the imperative for black people to gain confidence and capacity to lead. Within the nascent women's movement was the commitment to develop women, particularly black working-class women. In the trade unions was the need to build worker leadership. The emphasis was on collective leadership and learning by doing. However, as Walters (1989) describes in great detail, the participatory democratic practices were shaped by the origins and purposes of the organization, the members' biographies, and members' theoretical understandings of their actions. Those who were most closely allied to the movement in exile had stronger accountability to that; whereas others emphasized the importance of the collective inside the country, township, or organization. The tensions between accountability to the collective within one affiliate and to the broader movements, both inside the country and in exile, were palpable. These often had racial, class, and other historical dimensions.

The influence of ideologies and philosophies from international social movements on the ways of organizing was also apparent. The works of the Italian Marxist Gramsci and Brazilian Freire, among others, were widely read. The radical students, worker, women's, and black movements in North America and Europe were also influential, as were the anticolonial struggles in Africa.

The contemporary social movements in South Africa are influenced by the intense social mobilizing of the earlier years of struggle. There are both continuities and breaks with the past. As Ismail (2003, p. 100) describes the women of the South African Homeless People's Federation, "They sing various hymns, slogans, traditional songs, which they often combine with protest songs from the struggle days, and new protest songs from the Federation. They sing about the hardship of being in shacks that are prone to rain and evictions." What is new is that they have strong relationships internationally as they build "globalization from below" (Marshall, 1997, p. 57). They have, for example, special relations with the National

Slum Dwellers Federation in India, and their education has been enriched through exchange programs with them. The people's development strategies resonate with working-class and poor women's pedagogy in other parts of the world (Walters and Manicom, 1996; Foley, 1999). Although the hegemony of the neoliberal global economy ensures that the struggles continue for poor and working-class women and men in South Africa, they are reacting in new and creative ways.

IN CLOSING

Social movements are privileged locations for the creation of new knowledge. They are, as Eyerman and Jamison (1991, p. 10) have said, "epistemic communities." They stress the historical and social construction of ideas and the active role that social movements play in knowledge production. Cognitive praxis, they argue, "does not come ready-made to a social movement. It is precisely in the creation, articulation, formulation of new thoughts and ideas—new knowledge—that a social movement defines itself in society" (p. 10). Knowledge is produced through debates over meeting agendas, the planning of meetings, campaigns and demonstrations, and exchanges over strategies and tactics. It is also generated, as Badat (1999) argues, in interaction with old movements, old traditions, concepts, and values and in the recombination and reinterpretation of intellectual roles and practices. The South African social movements through action over many years generated the hope and possibility of a new democratic, nonracial, and nonsexist order.

As we have seen, the social movements were molded within the particular historical conjunctures. The alliances across class, ethnicity, gender, and race forged organizational and educational practices. The setting of the agenda of the movements over time was shaped very directly by the economic conditions of the poor. They challenged the middle-class leadership of the ANC in the 1930s and 1940s and influenced directly what the movements did and how they operated. In the 1970s and 1980s, the organized working class strongly influenced what and how movements organized, but other working-class and poor people organizing in their localities contested this. Contestations among working-class and middle-class leadership were also reality. Old and new cultural forms shaped the movements' symbolic and expressive moments.

It is not possible to isolate the influence of class alone on the pedagogy and politics of social movements because class is so intertwined with other social categories. However, the social locations of the members and their relative degrees of wealth or poverty will, of course, have profound effects on their consciousness, which will shape what issues they take up and in whose interests they mobilize. For example, in the environmental movements in various parts of the world, there is at times deep difference of opinion between communities of environmental activists, depending on their socioeconomic circumstances. Some indigenous communities struggling for survival have sometimes asked whether an endangered animal is more significant than their endangered community.

So for adult educators and activists, this discussion on class and social movements raises several key questions:

- How is the mode of organizing within social movements going to encourage or inhibit people of different economic and social backgrounds from participating?
- Who is giving leadership? What are their socioeconomic circumstances? And how will this shape what issues the movement takes up when and where?
- What is the different cultural, ethnic, gender, and class mix of the social movement? How can the movement give expression to the range of cultural practices among women and men in order to maximize their participation?
- What are the historical class-related traditions within particular social movements that participants can build on?
- How does my own social and economic class position influence my own practices as adult educator and activist?

REFERENCES

Abrahams, D. "South Africa: Social Movements, Coalitions, and the Struggle for Democracy." In Philippines-Canada Human Resource Development Program, *From Resistance to Transformation: Coalition Struggles in Canada, South Africa, the Philippines and Mexico.* Ontario: Philippines-Canada Human Resource Development Program, 1996.

Badat, S. *Black Student Politics, Higher Education and Apartheid: From SASO to SANSCO, 1968–1990.* Pretoria: HSRC, 1999.

Crowther, J., Martin, I., and Shaw, M. (eds.). *Popular Education and Social Movements in Scotland Today.* Leicester, England: National Institute of Adult Continuing Education, 1999.

Eyerman, R., and Jamison, A. *Social Movements: A Cognitive Approach.* Oxford: Polity Press, 1991.

Foley, G. *Learning in Social Action: A Contribution to Understanding Informal Education.* London: ZED Books, 1999.

Hall, B., and Clover, D. "Social Movement Learning." In L. English (ed.), *International Encyclopedia of Adult Education.* London: Palgrave Macmillan, 2005.

Ismail, S. "A Poor Woman's Pedagogy." *Womens Studies Quarterly*, 2003, *31*(3/4), 94–112.

Marshall, J. "Globalization from Below: Trade Union Connections." In S. Walters (ed.), *Globalization, Adult Education and Training: Impacts and Issues*. London: ZED Books, 1997.

Martin, I. "Introductory Essay: Popular Education and Social Movements in Scotland Today." In J. Crowther, I. Martin, and M. Shaw (eds.), *Popular Education and Social Movements in Scotland Today*. Leicester, England: National Institute of Adult Continuing Education, 1999.

Walters, S. *Education for Democratic Participation*. Bellville, South Africa: University of the Western Cape, 1989.

Walters, S., and Manicom, L. *Gender in Popular Education. Methods for Empowerment*. London: ZED Books, 1996.

CHAPTER 11

Social Change Education

Context Matters

Kathryn Choules

The thinking in this article crystallized as a result of attending the Third International Conference of the Popular Education Network, Braga, Portugal, in December 2004. At the conference, there were diverse presentations dealing with social change education. Most of the educational projects discussed were located in economically overdeveloped countries (First World) with a minority being located in economically underdeveloped countries (Third World). In relation to the educational projects located in the overdeveloped world, there were some projects that worked with sectors of the community that were significantly marginalized from the dominant culture. Others worked with mixed groups of students, including members of the dominant culture. Notwithstanding significant differences in context, all these projects were presented under the general descriptor of "popular education," motivating me to analyze the implications here.

Social change education, whether labeled popular education, critical pedagogy, or something else, generally uses an instructional methodology based on the foundational work of Paulo Freire (Campbell, 2001; Lather, 1998). Popular education is the name by which social change education is known in Latin America (Austin, 1999; Rogers, 2004). Critical pedagogy is the label under which much social change education locates itself in the West (Brookfield, 1995; Giroux, 2004; Lather, 1998; McLaren, 1989). Notwithstanding the differences between popular education and critical pedagogy discussed below, the common denominator is that the pedagogy is employed as a tool for engaging people to transform unjust social, economic, and political conditions.

149

Critical pedagogy arose in the Western academy. It has a well-developed social justice vision and sociological critique (in particular of capitalism and the ways that education systems perpetuate the inequalities that are present in society) but lacks a coherent body of work as to how it can be implemented in a concrete educational setting (Kincheloe, 1991). It is often criticized for its complexity and inaccessibility beyond the academy (Brookfield, 1995). Popular education, on the other hand, arose from the lived experience of working with groups denied access to resources and power. It has a stronger focus on its methodological aspects—on the "how to" or the instructional form that it takes. Critical pedagogy's greater focus on sociological critique rather than instructional practice has facilitated the adoption in the West of the instructional form developed by popular education in Latin America.

In a context different to that of Latin America, a wholesale adoption of popular education's instructional approach can cause significant problems for social change education in the West. By context, I take a broad interpretation that includes the socioeconomic, cultural, and political situation of the country, the country's position relative to the rest of the world, the particular location of the educational initiative, the (lack of) institutional support for the educational initiative, and the positioning of the facilitator and students in terms of factors such as race, class, wealth, gender, sexuality, language, education levels, and (dis)ability. This interest in the issue of context is the result of my engagement with social change education, both in practice and with the literature. Having spent 3 years working in popular education in Guatemala (with marginalized communities as well as with teachers and students in the formal education system), I then returned to Australia. There, I struggled to apply Freirean principles in a variety of contexts. These contexts included working with school groups on global development, with trainee prison officers on the nature and purpose of prisons, with people with disabilities on disability rights, with Australian residents on asylum-seeker issues, and with social change activists on global issues. This article seeks to explore the main issues that have arisen in my practice when working in a Western context.

The need to modify popular education (or Freirean pedagogy) has been raised by other social change educators working in economically overdeveloped countries such as the United States (Evans, Evans, & Kennedy, 1987). Various writers in the critical pedagogy tradition have critiqued the unthinking application of popular education's instructional practices when working in the context of Western formal education (Cale & Huber, 2001; George, 2001; Lewis, 1990; Luke, 1992). Nonetheless, it continues as Western educators, such as myself, (re)discover

Freire, not always aware of Freire's (1985) own warning against transplanting his pedagogy.

The way that social change pedagogy is experienced, understood, and responded to differs significantly depending on the positioning of the students. A significant issue is whether the social change vision of the pedagogy furthers the interests of the students or challenges their status, power, and wealth. In crude terms, when working with oppressed, excluded, or marginalized groups, the social change vision is more likely to be shared by students and the facilitator because its realization is seen to benefit the students. When working with the dominant social group, or those who benefit from existing inequitable systems, the social change vision may well not be shared. Realization of the vision may well threaten students' status, power, and wealth. I found that this occurred when working with mainstream Australians on an educational program that challenged the oppressive dominant discourse on asylum seekers. There was a significant group that resisted any suggestion that Australian society benefited from the presence of a diversity of cultural groups. They felt that their privileged position as part of the dominant cultural group (White Anglo-Australians) was threatened by the changes to society brought about by multiculturalism and even more so by the arrival of unauthorized asylum seekers. A compassionate response to asylum seekers was in conflict with their need to feel in control.

In noting the importance of the students' and facilitator's positioning, it is vital to recognize that due to each person's complex intersubjectivity, individuals have multiple positionings. At times a person may be part of a marginalized group and on other occasions within the dominant group. As Patti Lather and Elizabeth Ellsworth (1996) say,

> identity categories are positioned as multiple, fluid and often contradictory, both internally and externally. Sometimes we are these women, for example, but sometimes it is race or sexual orientation or class location that carries the most weight in a situation. (p. 70)

As such, it is an oversimplification to describe students as *either* part of the dominant cultural group *or* part of excluded or marginalized groups. At times, however, I do this in order to facilitate the focus on context. Whether the students are excluded from the dominant social group or firmly within it, the challenge for social change education is to respond to these different contexts and speak to all students in order to engage them to seek a more just world.

This article briefly describes popular education as developed in Latin America and then turns West to look at the issues that face the implementation of social change pedagogy there. It then hones in on five instructional techniques of popular education and looks at how they need to be adapted when working with students from the dominant social group. Most of us who are educators in the West often find ourselves working with students from the dominant social group. Thus, I hope that this discussion contributes to any educational effort that seeks to invite students to a new awareness of domination, wherever it shows itself.

POPULAR EDUCATION—ORIGINS AND CHARACTERISTICS

To understand some of the dangers that can arise from a wholesale adoption of popular education's methodology in different contexts, this article first looks at what constitutes popular education. The Popular Education Network, a network of mostly university-based educators, describes popular education as being

rooted in the real interests and struggles of ordinary people;

overtly political and critical of the status quo; and

committed to progressive social and political change in the interests of a fairer and more egalitarian society. (Popular Education Network, n.d., Plans and Purposes section)

The network states that popular education has the following characteristics:

Its curriculum comes out of the concrete experience and material interests of social movements and communities of resistance and struggle.

Its pedagogy is collective and democratic, focused primarily on group rather than individual learning and development.

It attempts to forge a direct link between education and social change. (Popular Education Network, n.d., Plans and Purposes section)

Although it is not explicit, these definitions *assume* that popular education will be conducted with the "popular sectors." Examples of popular education carried out in the West within this definition include educational projects with public housing residents on tenancy issues and programs with nonunionized casual labor on the importance of a collective response to industrial issues. In one collaborative project of this nature, we worked with the disability sector and sought to make explicit the links that exist between localized discrimination against people with disabilities and broader global and economic injustice. Such efforts seek a collective response to injustice experienced by the groups with whom the educational work is undertaken.

The link with the popular sectors is generally made very clear in Latin American literature on popular education. Freire (1997) called his form of pedagogy, among other things, *educación cultural popular*. The pedagogy explicitly refers to the role of the popular sectors, as can be seen from the various quotes of current Latin American popular educators collected by Robert Austin (1999):

> Popular education in the Latin American context can be understood as an educative practice located within a wider process that intends that the popular sectors constitute themselves as organized and conscious political subjects (García-Huidobro, 1983:2) . . . . In this sense, it is a Gramscian construction (Gramsci, 1992: 82–89) . . . . Two of the most eloquent voices of popular education's agenda (Rodríguez and Vío, 1990:9) describe it thus:

> The interaction between education and democracy constitutes a permanent challenge which refers as much to the order of values, attitudes and characteristic knowledges of the educational process as to the importance which the distinct formal and non-formal proposals of education have in the development of civic existence.

> CEAAL's [El Consejo de Educación de Adultos de América Latina—Latin American Advisory Body on Adult Education] current president defines popular education (Nuñez, 1992:55) as

> a process of education and training carried out politically from a class perspective that forms part of or is articulated with action organized by the people, by the masses, in order to achieve the objective of constructing a new society in accord with their interests . . . [It] is a continuous and systematic process implying moments of reflection on and study of the group and organization . . . . It is theory emerging from practice, not theory about practice. (pp. 43–44)

The main form of oppression that popular education has historically sought to combat is economic oppression. After all, the oppression resulting from extreme inequality of access to resources in Latin America is an overwhelming phenomenon. The political, economic, and social exclusion resulting from poverty affects the majority of the population. A second issue that has been addressed by much popular education in Latin America is the construction of active peace and democratic societies after decades of civil wars and dictatorships. The strengthening of civil society and increased political participation are key objectives in this work. This was a key feature of the popular education projects I participated in, in Guatemala in the late 1990s. We worked with students, parish groups, and teachers on ways to promote active peace and engage civil society in the dissemination of the peace accords (negotiated after 36 years of civil war).

There are two well-developed, interrelated aspects of Latin American popular education: first, its neo-Marxist economic analysis of oppression, and second, the instructional aspects of implementing popular education in practice. It is impossible to describe definitively any theoretical movement, as there is always evolution as well as diverging opinions within its loose boundaries. However, some key understandings on which popular education in Latin America is based include that human beings are meant to be free, work collectively, and seek justice; that human beings have agency and are capable of transforming the world; that power and its oppressive use are located with the ruling class; and that oppression is perpetuated by economic and cultural structures and the ideologies supporting them. Through unmasking hegemonic forces and understanding the reality behind ideology, popular education works toward the transformation of society by the people (the masses). Related more to the *practice* of this pedagogy, the starting point of the educative process is the valuable knowledge and experience of oppressed peoples. The practice of education must be participative, radically democratic, and reject all forms of authoritarianism. There must be coherence between political objectives and practice. In popular education, the educator disappears as the source of authority and a horizontal relationship is established in which students and teacher educate each other. The educator works to achieve critical awareness followed by transformative action, through loving dialogue and problem posing. A critical, ongoing praxis of reflection and transformative action is a central practice of popular education (Freire, 1987, 1998; Johnston, 2005).

The objective of popular education is the transformation of oppressive systems and the liberation of those oppressed. In social change education in the West, this objective is often implicit rather than explicit. One of the reasons for this is that social change education is often practiced with those who are not in need of liberation in the traditional sense, as they are part of the dominant group who benefit from unjust socioeconomic relations.

■ MOVING WEST—A DIFFERENT CONTEXT

Unlike Latin America, countries in the economically overdeveloped West generally have a reasonable social security system. Where there is adequate social security, no one has to live in abject poverty. In addition, political freedoms are better respected, and the countries are characterized by relatively stable representative democracies. The oppression, marginalization, and exclusion that occur within these countries are less acute and apply to a smaller percentage of the population than in Latin America (Smith, 1994). The worst off in these societies are significantly better off (in a material sense) than the majority in the underdeveloped world (O'Sullivan, 1999). A broadly defined, materially comfortable middle class consisting of the majority of the population makes up the largest social group. Oppression is largely invisible and unrecognizable to the majority of the population. The experience of the majority, however, is in contrast to the discrimination and marginalization faced by those who are not part of the dominant cultural group, such as indigenous people, refugees, nonnative English speakers, people with disabilities, and those who are not heterosexual. The invisibility of oppressive discourses has major consequences for social change education as it is commonplace to deny the existence of oppression in the West (Evans et al., 1987). The question for educators following the Latin American experience would be Where are the masses, the people with whom to work, and what needs to be transformed?

There are many examples of marginalized or excluded groups in economically overdeveloped countries. In Australia, for example, they include Aborigines, non-Whites, new immigrants, and Muslims. They are not, however, the popular sectors or the masses, comprising only a small percentage of the population. Working with these populations, although important, may have minimal impact on society as a whole. On the other hand, working for social change with the comfortable dominant group has the potential to engage more people, and people with greater resources. So why not work with those who are situated in the dominant culture? It is true that Freire (1987) believed that in order for members of the dominant class to participate in the struggle for justice they need to, in effect, commit class suicide and unite with the workers. However, such an absolutist and modernist view of freedom and liberation is not common in social change education now. Other popular educators in Latin America have seen that a more flexible approach is possible. Carlos Aldana Mendoza and Carlos Nuñez (2002) move from the specific instances of things that need to be transformed in Latin America, such as inadequate health services, housing, and roads, to a broader vision: "We transform society when we make it more just, more equal, more democratic, more educational, and healthier for all that live in it" (p. 11, translated from the original by the author).

A broad social change vision can be worked toward from a variety of starting points. Although popular educators usually work with the popular sectors, even in Latin America they have been working with other sectors of the community.

For Aldana Mendoza and Nuñez (2002), the crux of popular education is its orientation, purposes, and objectives:

> Whether we do popular education in the countryside, or in the city; whether we do it with school, college or university students or with peasants, workers, community leaders, illiterate people; with poor people or with people who are not poor, it will still be popular education *if its essence or orientation is social transformation.* (p. 20, translated from the original by the author)

Unfortunately, Aldana Mendoza and Nuñez did not describe the different ways to respond pedagogically when working in the various contexts they mention. In the next section, I discuss the different issues that may arise when working with different student groups and contexts.

POPULAR EDUCATION APPLIED TO A WESTERN CONTEXT

To illustrate some of the problems that occur with a wholesale application of popular education techniques to contexts different from those in which it originated, I now turn to look at some specific instructional aspects of popular education. I will explore how they fare when applied in a Western context where the students in the educational process belong to the dominant social group rather than being "more or less, a homogenous group of oppressed people" as anticipated by popular education (Cale & Huber, 2001, ¶1). Possible ways of addressing the difficulties that can arise are also examined. The instructional aspects that I will examine here are

the practice of ideology critique and concientization,

the educator's authority and positioning,

the role of student experience,

the role of dialogue and democratic processes, and

the acknowledgement of political objectives.

Practice of Ideology Critique and Concientization

The popular education process of *concientization*—which incorporates an analysis and critique of a particular social, economic, and historical situation, the raising of awareness, and is followed by transformative action—is an embodied application of critical theory's process of ideology critique (Allman, 1988). Conscientization and ideology critique seek "to penetrate the givens of everyday reality to reveal the inequities and oppression that lurk beneath" (Brookfield, 2000, p. 38). As Stephen Brookfield (2000) describes it, through this process

> People learn to recognize how uncritically accepted and unjust dominant ideologies are embedded in everyday situations and practices . . . [and] come to an awareness of how capitalism shapes social relations and imposes—often without our knowledge—belief systems and assumptions (that is, ideologies) that justify and maintain economic and political inequity . . . . An important element in this tradition is the thought of Antonio Gramsci (1978) whose concept of hegemony explains the way in which people are convinced to embrace dominant ideologies as always being in their own interests. (p. 36)

Ideology critique is an important analytical tool for social change education. Applied in countries with extremes in wealth and poverty, ideology critique's economic analysis of capitalism makes good sense to the people oppressed by that economic system—it "feels" right. Where the country has a widely available social security system, low levels of unemployment, and a reasonable basic wage, capitalism's inequities are less easily understood, both from an emotional and an intellectual perspective. Freire noted this, stating, "Because it is so difficult to work with the non-poor in this kind of experience, I prefer to work with the people of the *favelas* and the slums. They have much more knowledge for understanding all this" (interview contained in Evans et al., 1987, p. 222). The rational process of ideology critique will rarely have the same positive *affective* component for a person from the dominant group. Ideology critique must be accompanied by other ways of knowing and learning, particularly when working with members from the dominant cultural group.

To connect affectively with those who do well out of oppressive relations, reproductive values of connection, relationship, and caring need to be emphasized, perhaps more so than the rational (reasoned logic) process embodied in ideology critique (Shapiro, 2000). Rather than utilizing reasoned logic, Annette Baier's "progress of sentiments," as championed by Richard Rorty (1998, p. 181), may be how the dominant group can be engaged in social change processes. Even though "it is revolting to think that our only hope for a decent society consists in softening the self-satisfied hearts of a leisure class," Rorty (1998) says that the moral progress of the past two centuries is not a

> deepening understanding of the nature of rationality or of morality, but rather . . . one in which there occurred an astonishingly rapid progress of sentiments, in which it

has become much easier for us to be moved to action by sad and sentimental stories. (p. 185)

Ideology critique can be applied to expose the belief systems and assumptions that support forms of social exclusion as well as economic exclusion. Racism, sexism, ableism, and other bases on which certain groups are marginalized can also be subject to the process of ideology critique. Even though ideology critique is a useful tool for understanding how injustice is perpetrated and maintained within a society, it has the disadvantage of focusing on processes of oppression and the position of the marginalized. This may not be so helpful when dealing with groups that include members of the dominant group, comfortable with the existing status quo. To engage students who see injustice as being nothing to do with them, an analysis of privilege may prove a useful addition to ideology critique. In discussing the relationship between oppression and White privilege, Barbara Applebaum (2003) says,

> Resistance and lack of understanding work hand-in-hand to maintain the invisibility that is the sine qua non of white privilege. Dominant affiliated group members will not be able to appreciate how the marginalized are discriminated against nor will they be able to acknowledge their complicity in sustaining such systems, I submit, without an understanding of how privilege and oppression are systemically interrelated and mutually reinforcing. (p. 8)

As Applebaum highlights, the same structures that result in oppression also maintain privilege. Whether based on economic, racial, gender, or other differences, the privileges of a dominant group can usefully be analyzed in this way. A useful equivalent of *conocimiento de la realidad* ("understanding reality" practiced in Latin America) is to work to expose privilege with those who have it and gain awareness of what is happening behind the hegemonic façade. The need to include an analysis of privilege was highlighted in training I undertook of volunteers who wished to work with refugees. I was surprised to discover within the volunteers, whom I would otherwise expect to have a high awareness of the various forms of racism, a denial of institutional or systemic racism and a denial of how racism privileges the dominant White culture. Exercises that highlighted how racial privilege operated had some success there. For social change to occur, an analysis of privilege, as with ideology critique, is just the starting point. It needs to be followed by action to transform the unjust situation.

Educator's Authority and Positioning

The traditional relationship between educator and student is radically transformed in Freirean pedagogy. Some educators, looking for ways to create democratic learning processes, have used phrases such as the "withering away" of the teacher (Shor, 1987, p. 94). This comes in large part from Freire's (1987) horizontal relationship of teacher–student that he explains as follows:

> The teacher-of-the-students and the students-of-the-teacher cease to exist and a new term emerges: teacher-student with students-teachers. The teacher is no longer merely the-one-who-teaches, but one who is himself taught in dialogue with the students, who in turn while being taught also teach. In this process, arguments based on "authority" are no longer valid. (p. 67)

This relationship between educator and student assumes that the educator and students are in a similar position vis-à-vis oppressive power relations; that both educator and students are from the popular sectors and working for the same goals (or that the educator has committed class suicide in solidarity). Where there is a common purpose, there is a much-reduced need for the educator to rely on any form of institutional authority. This reduces the tension that arises in trying to achieve a democratic and collective process through the employment of authority. A high degree of democratic decision making about the educational content and a significant degree of student control are possible where this shared positioning exists. Such a situation facilitates the pedagogical goals and permits the educator to have a lower profile. Even in those situations, however, Freire, in conversation with Ira Shor (Shor & Freire, 1987), recognized that there was "a permanent tension in the relation between authority and liberty" and that the educator needed "responsibility, directiveness, determination, discipline, objectives" (p. 16). Where there is no common purpose between educator and students, the issue of how the educator exercises her or his institutional authority becomes even more significant. If students are located within the dominant group, there arises potential conflict between pursuing particular social change objectives and the popular education aim of democratic processes and horizontal relations between educators and students.

There are significant risks that an educator runs in seeking to have fully democratic processes where the participants come from a range of positions. With the presence of students from the dominant social group, a failure by the educator to exercise authority can allow exclusionary processes to exist and the dominant discourse to assert itself. As Brookfield (1995) notes,

> Students told me that my unwillingness to intervene too directly in class discussions for fear of overemphasizing the power of my own voice was actually allowing for the perpetuation of differences of class, race, and gender that existed outside the classroom. (p. xi)

Feminists have been at the forefront of reclaiming the importance of asserting institutional authority when the alternative is to allow oppressive patriarchal relations to be perpetuated (Weiler, 1994). Their situation shares much common ground with that of social change educators working with the dominant social group. Magda Lewis (1990), in analyzing the role of the educator, has "no problem justifying the use of [her] institutional power to create the possibility for privilege to face itself...Using power to subjugate is quite different from using power to liberate" (p. 480). The exercise of authority for counterhegemonic purposes will be experienced differently arising from the relative positioning of students and educator. It is potentially less confronting for those comfortable in their privileged position to be challenged by someone who is necessarily challenging his or her own privileged position at the same time. Given the fears bound up with contemplating a loss of privilege, it is less threatening to undertake this in the shared space of cultural commonality. My experience working with dominant groups confirms that to have an educator from a marginalized group challenge structural inequalities allows the dominant group to dismiss the educator as biased and resentful, thus justifying nonengagement with the message. This is not to discount the powerful effect of the voices and presence of people from marginalized groups but rather to raise one potential problem that occurs. Minority educators are significant forces for change but have to cope with dominant ideological prejudice.

The benefits of having the educator share the same privileged positioning as the students was apparent in a program I ran for Australian residents that challenged the dominant discourse on asylum seekers. We were all in the same privileged position of being citizens of a safe, stable, and materially comfortable country. Sharing this privileged position, it was less threatening for the participants when I discussed the conflict I felt from being part of a society that sanctioned the violation of asylum seekers' human rights.

Role of Student Experience

The life experiences of students are the starting point in popular education. In Latin America, the dominant culture tries to render the experience and even existence of the workers and peasants invisible. Using their experiences and knowledge as an integral part of the educational process challenges the silencing of their stories. This validates the experiences and existence of those marginalized in society and becomes a counterhegemonic process, especially when accompanied with problem posing and dialogue designed to show the situation not as "fated and unalterable, but merely as limited" (Freire, 1987, p. 72). As Henry Giroux (1985) wrote,

> [Freire] argues that educators have to work with the experiences that students, adults, and other learners bring to schools and other educational sites. This means making these experiences in their public and private forms the object of debate and confirmation; it means legitimating such experiences in order to give those who live and move within them a sense of affirmation and to provide the conditions for students and others to display an active voice and presence. (pp. xxi–xxii)

The incorporation of student experience into the educational process is much more delicate when working with members of the dominant group. For example, most people have experienced instances of prejudice and discrimination, and it is not uncommon for members of the dominant group to feel fear in relation to certain marginalized groups. Instances of "reverse racism" are often heard in teaching Aboriginal studies in Australia where students may have been subject to abuse or witnessed violence against Whites by Aborigines. When such students assert experiences of individual discrimination against themselves, this can result in an individualized discourse around discrimination and a denial of structural oppression and discrimination. It also allows the dominant group to (mis)position itself as the victim in relation to a particular social justice issue. It is vital, whether working with the dominant group or popular sectors, that discussion of the experiences of the students be followed by a process of abstraction and theorizing. Brookfield (1995) comments on the importance of guided reflection on experience:

> Myles Horton lamented the fact that people misinterpreted his valuing of adults' experiences as implying that the educator's task was to dignify experience in a reverential, uncritical way. As he said to Paulo Freire, "Often when I say you start with people's experience, people get the point that you start and stop with that experience ... There's a time when people's experience runs out" (Horton and Freire, 1990, p. 128). When this happens, the role of the skillful educator is to be a critical animator who asks provocative questions, and who supplies alternative interpretations or new information, without breaking the connection to the experiences that are being analyzed. (pp. 223–224)

Related to the need to critically theorize from student experience are Carmen Luke's (1992) words of warning. This is in keeping with other feminist scholars who have moved away from feminism's initial uncritical embrace of the experience of women as being the site for liberation. This caution is particularly relevant when working with groups generally comfortable with the dominant discourse. As Luke explains,

> Privileging experience as foundational to knowledge, or as a transparent window to the "real," denies its situatedness in discourses that constitute subjectivities in the first place, and that enable articulation of experience from discursively constructed subject positions . . . [C]ritique and action, deployed at the classroom level without critique of the metanarratives that theoretically and practically sustain the structures and discourses of schooling in the liberal state, may miss the point altogether. (p. 36)

Where there is no commonality of experience highlighted in groups of mixed positioning, an emphasis on experience will bring out the differences, divisions, and conflict that exist in society. An educator working with groups where the students come from different positions of privilege and oppression must expect this. As Kathleen Weiler (1994) says, "It raises again the problems left unaddressed by Freirean pedagogy—the overlapping and multiple forms of oppression revealed in 'reading the world' of experience" (pp. 33–34). Furthermore, with different student positions, their experiences will serve to ground different types of analysis in a social change pedagogy. For those excluded from full participation in society, dialogue and problem-posing about their experiences needs to be part of an analysis of *oppression*. For those located within the dominant social group, problematizing their experiences can be used to theorize their *privilege*.

Role of Dialogue and Democratic Processes

Dialogue is the central learning process in popular education. It is a dialogue of equals, and through this social process, knowledge and learning are generated (Freire & Macedo, 1995). The more authoritarian the cultural and political context in which the educational process is located, the more radically democratic will be the experience of dialogical education. Dialogue puts into practice in the educational setting the political outcome sought: radical democracy. Through this practice, we can learn to participate democratically, something that can translate beyond the educational setting, for the purpose of transforming society (Aldana Mendoza & Nuñez, 2002).

Using democratic dialogue carries with it dangers that are heightened when working with students from the dominant group. Democratic dialogue has been critiqued on the basis that it "requires and assumes a classroom of students unified on the side of the subordinated against the subordinators, sharing and trusting in an 'us-ness' against 'them-ness'" (Ellsworth, 1989, p. 315). Gary Cale and Conni Huber (2001) go as far as saying, "to teach effectively for democratic social change a different set of practices may be required which violate cherished humanistic and liberal adult education practices" (para. 3). When at least some students come from the dominant group, a practice in which all voices are treated equally has every likelihood to result in Marcuse's repressive tolerance: "An all-embracing tolerance of diverse views always ends up legitimizing an unfair status quo" (as discussed by Brookfield, 2002, p. 274). The results of this are seen by social change educators working with the dominant group. As discussed by Cale & Huber (2001), "Once I allowed the 'common sense' of the dominant ideology to be voiced, nothing could disarm it…'Democratic' discussions generally offered opportunities for students to attack and silence oppositional thinkers, including myself" (Findings from Practice, Cale section, para. 20–21).

The practice of democracy through dialogue with members of the dominant group must be carried out carefully and in anticipation that the dominant discourse will be asserted strongly. As educators, we must prepare ourselves for this, practicing a lighthanded problematization of that dominant discourse in a way that does not shut off dialogue but highlights the hidden injustice. Facilitators can turn the dialogue back on themselves or ponder out loud what it means for those who are disadvantaged by the discourse and what they would do if they were in that situation. For example, during a workshop with mainstream Australians on asylum seekers, a participant suggested to me that Australia had ruined multiculturalism because although it was fine for the world to be multicultural, it was not good for a country. He stated that Asians should go back to their original place, Arabs to theirs, and Africans to theirs. I posed, with mock horror, "Oh no, what does that mean for me? Where do I go, a White Australian?" This depersonalized challenge to the racism behind the comment allowed the participant to remain engaged and continue with the process. The "ideologically skewed nature of particular contributions" needs to be deconstructed in a depersonalized way (Brookfield, 2002, p. 276). Given the myths and misinformation that support oppressive discourses, it is vital that when these are voiced, the educator has accurate information with which to respond, or to ask the students to investigate.

Dialogue, as with ideology critique, is understood by popular education to be a process based on reason. It assumes that the students have the characteristics of the idealized autonomous, rational Enlightenment man—something we know is not true of any person. The warnings from Ellsworth (cited in Briton, 1996) on this score are important to keep in mind:

> [We cannot] assume rationalized, individualized subjects capable of agreeing on universalizable "fundamental moral principles" and "quality of human life" that become self-evident when subjects cease to be self-interested and particularistic about group rights.... [S]ocial agents are not capable of being fully rational and disinterested; and they are subjects split between the conscious and unconscious and among multiple social positionings. (p. 97)

A distinct problem from that raised by Ellsworth is the greater likelihood that with a heterogeneous group, a dialogical process will allow for the reproduction of the oppressive *relations* that characterize society—sexism, racism, ageism, and others. Dialogue favors individuals who are confident, articulate, and educated. Those who dominate societal relations, such as men, Whites, and the wealthy, are able to dominate dialogue in an educational space. Alison Jones (1999) argues that dialogue in a mixed group can be a recolonizing process in which the only people who gain are those from the dominant group as they gain access to the experiences of others. She highlights the difficulties that such dialogue poses for the students from marginalized groups, supporting Freire's (1987, p. 76) view that dialogue cannot occur between those who want to name the world and those who do not want this naming.

An educator can help heterogeneous groups to become aware of the inequalities that can be produced through dialogue. While students are unlearning the patterns of dialogical domination and becoming committed to undoing undemocratic practices of communication, other practices can be considered. For example, small groups of a more homogeneous character may work together more democratically as issues of societal power and prejudice are minimized within that grouping (Ellsworth, 1989). Giving students "thinking time" before requiring a response may level the playing field somewhat for students who do not think so quickly on their feet (Brookfield, 1995). Adaptations of the jigsaw technique (Aronson & Gonzalez, 1988) in which the participation of each person is important in order for the group goal to be achieved may also be useful. This is not to discount democratic dialogue as an important educative process. Rather, it is to understand it as an important educative *goal* that must be deliberately worked toward given the patterns of domination that exist.

◼ ACKNOWLEDGMENT OF POLITICAL OBJECTIVES

In Latin American popular education, the social change objectives are generated by, or at least shared by, the popular sectors with whom the education occurs. Attainment of the political and educational objectives is in the interests of the students. This facilitates a relatively uncontested process moving from understanding the reality of the oppressive situation, critiquing the oppressive situation, and committing to transform the oppressive situation. Through the clear enunciation by the educator of the political goals, a strengthening of solidarity arises. It is a very different situation where the students are very comfortable and happy in their privileged position. They enter the educational process with very different political objectives and no shared ideology with the educator. In such a situation, if the educator were to make a clear declaration of her or his position and the political objectives sought, alienation and rejection could well be among the principal reactions from students.

Where the educator's political objectives are not shared by the students, issues arise that were largely irrelevant to Freire and those working with popular sectors. I explore here whether there is an ethical imperative that requires the educator to declare her or his position. In arguing for a declaration of political beliefs, Freire does not see the existence of political beliefs as operating against the freedom of his students. He says, "I have never had the need to hide or the fear of hiding my political beliefs. Making my beliefs bare does not constitute, in my view, a form of imposition" (Freire & Macedo, 1995, p. 387). This may not be how a student might experience such declaration. In the different context of working in Western universities, Ellsworth (1989) acknowledges that it is common practice to disguise the political objectives of social change education. In naming a new course for students committed to combating racism, Ellsworth stated,

> I wanted to avoid colluding with many academic writers in the widespread use of code words such as "critical," which hide the action political agendas I assume such writers share with me—namely antiracism, antisexism, anti-elitism, anti-heterosexism, anti-ableism, anticlassism, and anti-neoconservatism.... I wanted to be accountable for naming the political agenda behind this particular course's critical pedagogy. (pp. 300–301)

It is important to note that both Freire and Ellsworth (in the specific course she was discussing above) were working with students who shared their political commitment. This context is distinct from that of working with people happy with the status quo. Ian Baptiste (cited in Brookfield, 2002) is explicit in arguing that in the second situation there is no need for transparency. On the contrary, social change educators will need "to engage in some form of manipulation—some fencing, posturing, concealment, maneuvering, misinformation, and even all-out deception as the case demands" (Brookfield, 2002, p. 273). Similarly strategic are the words of Michael Apple (2002) when looking at how to engage in critical pedagogy and social action post September 11 (and the attacks on the World Trade Center in New York and on Washington). He states that it "required a very strategic sense of how to speak and act, both in my teaching and in my appearances on national media" (p. 1763). Clearly, any declaration of position needs to be carefully crafted so as not to alienate a significant proportion of the students.

My preference when working on social change education with mixed groups is to acknowledge the variety of ideological positions present, acknowledge that our distinct positions are the result of our identity and experiences, and acknowledge that an openness to being challenged is fundamental to all defensible positions. Although I have a particular political position, I do not expect everyone to share that position. My educational goals are that we become aware of the existence of the dominant discourse or hegemonic ideology, how it is constructed, and the impact that is has on different groups. Thus, it is important for all of us to own our personal political ideology.

CONCLUSION

A social change education process will be experienced and responded to differently by students depending on how they are positioned in relation to the dominant culture and its economic and cultural systems. The popular sectors, excluded and marginalized by the dominant culture, are the origin of popular education, and as a result its methodology contemplates that students are drawn from these sectors. Their life experiences are anticipated by the pedagogy. Popular education's instructional practices do not anticipate the life experiences of members from the dominant culture. However, when members of the dominant culture examine their own experience in a popular education or dialogical process, they can be invited and challenged by that process to see the inequities, injustices, and domination systems in their experience and to envision, as Freire (1987) puts it, "the creation of a world in which it will be easier to love" (p. 24).

Because of the significant differences when undertaking social change education in the West, the instructional practices of popular education need modification. It may be preferable to use the term "popular education" only in the more limited context of working with groups excluded from the dominant culture. This would have the effect of reminding us that the wholesale application of one form of pedagogy to a new and different context is problematic. A change in the context in which a pedagogical tradition is to be applied requires changes to the pedagogical practices.

REFERENCES

Aldana Mendoza, C., & Nuñez, C. (2002). *Educación popular y los formadores políticos* [Popular education and political facilitators]. Guatemala City, Guatemala: Instituto Centroamericano de Estudios Politicos.

Allman, P. (1988). Gramsci, Freire and Illich: Their contributions to education for socialism. In T. Lovett (Ed.), *Radical approaches to adult education: A reader* (pp. 85–113). London: Routledge.

Apple, M. (2002). Patriotism, pedagogy, and freedom: On the educational meanings of September 11th. *Teachers College Record, 104*(8), 1760–1772.

Applebaum, B. (2003). White privilege, complicity, and the social construction of race. *Educational Foundations, 17*(4), 5–20.

Aronson, E., & Gonzalez, A. (1988). Desegregation, jigsaw, and the Mexican American experience. In P. A. Katz & D. Taylor (Eds.), *Eliminating racism: Profiles in controversy* (pp. 301–314). New York: Plenum.

Austin, R. (1999). Popular history and popular education: El Consejo de Educación de Adultos de América Latina. *Latin American Perspectives, 26*(107), 39–68.

Briton, D. (1996). *The modern practice of adult education: A postmodern critique.* Albany: State University of New York Press.

Brookfield, S. D. (1995). *Becoming a critically reflective teacher* (1st ed.). San Francisco: Jossey-Bass.

Brookfield, S. D. (2000). The concept of critically reflective practice. In A. L. Wilson & E. R. Hayes (Eds.), *Handbook of adult and continuing education* (pp. 33–49). San Francisco: Jossey-Bass.

Brookfield, S. D. (2002). Reassessing subjectivity, criticality and inclusivity: Marcuse's challenge to adult education. *Adult Education Quarterly, 52*(4), 265–280.

Cale, G., & Huber, C. (2001, October). *Teaching the oppressor to be silent: Conflicts in the "democratic" classroom.* Paper presented at the Proceedings of the 21st Annual Alliance/ACE Conference, Austin, TX. Retrieved November 2, 2004, from http://www.ahea.org/conference/ proceedings/2001/proceedings01.pdf

Campbell, P. (2001). Introduction. In P. Campbell & B. Burnaby (Eds.), *Participatory practices in adult education* (pp. 1–12). Mahwah, NJ: Lawrence Erlbaum.

Ellsworth, E. (1989). Why doesn't this feel empowering? Working through the repressive myths of critical pedagogy. *Harvard Education Review, 59*(3), 297–324.

Evans, A. F., Evans, R. A., & Kennedy, W. B. (1987). *Pedagogies for the non-poor.* Maryknoll, NY: Orbis.

Freire, P. (1985). *The politics of education: Culture, power and liberation.* Westport, CT: Bergin & Garvey.

Freire, P. (1987). *Pedagogy of the oppressed* (M. B. Ramos, Trans.). New York: Continuum.

Freire, P. (1997). *La educación como práctica de la libertad* [Education as the practice of freedom] (45th ed.). Mexico DF: Siglo Veintiuno Editores.

Freire, P. (1998). *Pedagogy of freedom: Ethics, democracy, and civic courage* (P. Clarke, Trans.). Lanham, MD: Rowman & Littlefield.

Freire, P., & Macedo, D. P. (1995). A dialogue: Culture, language, and race. *Harvard Educational Review, 65*(3), 377–402.

George, A. (2001). Critical pedagogy: Dreaming of democracy. In G. Tate, A. Rupiper, & K. Schick (Eds.), *A guide to composition pedagogies* (pp. 92–112). New York: Oxford University Press.

Giroux, H. A. (1985). Introduction. In *The politics of education: Culture, power and liberation* (pp. xxi-xxii). Westport, CT: Bergin & Garvey.

Giroux, H. A. (2004). Critical pedagogy and the postmodern/modern divide: Towards a pedagogy of democratization. *Teacher Education Quarterly, 31*(1), 31–47.

Johnston, R. (2005). Popular education and the academy: The problems of praxis. In J. Crowther, V. Galloway, & I. Martin (Eds.), *Popular education: Engaging the academy—International perspectives* (pp. 63–76). Leicester, UK: National Institute of Adult Continuing Education.

Jones, A. (1999). The limits of cross-cultural dialogue: Pedagogy, desire and absolution in the classroom. *Educational Theory, 49*(3), 299–316.

Kincheloe, J. (1991). *Teachers as researchers: Qualitative inquiry as a path to empowerment.* New York: Falmer.

Lather, P. (1998). Critical pedagogy and its complicities: A praxis of stuck places. *Educational Theory, 48*(4), 487–497.

Lather, P., & Ellsworth, E. (1996). This issue: Situated pedagogies—Classroom practices in postmodern times. *Theory into Practice, 35*(2), 70–71.

Lewis, M. (1990). Interrupting patriarchy: Politics, resistance and transformation in the feminist classroom. *Harvard Education Review, 60*(4), 467–488.

Luke, C. (1992). Feminist politics in radical pedagogy. In C. Luke & J. Gore (Eds.), *Feminisms and critical pedagogy* (pp. 25–53). New York: Routledge.

McLaren, P. (1989). *Life in schools: An introduction to critical pedagogy in the foundations of education.* New York: Longman.

O'Sullivan, E. (1999). *Transformative learning: Educational vision for the 21st century*. London: Zed Press.

Popular Education Network. (n.d.). *Plans and purposes*. Retrieved September 21, 2005, from http://www.neskes.net/pen/plans.htm

Rogers, A. (2004). *Non-formal education: Flexible schooling or participatory education?* Hong Kong: The University of Hong Kong, Comparative Education Research Centre.

Rorty, R. (1998). Human rights, rationality, and sentimentality. In *Truth and progress: Philosophical papers* (Vol. 3, pp. 167–185). Cambridge, UK: Cambridge University Press.

Shapiro, S. (2000). Peace or hate? Education for a new millennium. *Tikkun, 15*(1), 59–61.

Shor, I. (1987). *Critical teaching and everyday life*. Chicago: University of Chicago Press.

Shor, I., & Freire, P. (1987). What is the "dialogical method" of teaching? *Journal of Education, 169*(3), 11–31.

Smith, M. K. (1994). *Local education: Community, conversation, praxis*. Bristol, PA: Open University Press.

Weiler, K. (1994). Freire and a feminist pedagogy of difference. In P. McLaren & C. Lankshear (Eds.), *Politics of liberation: Paths from Freire* (pp. 12–40). London: Routledge.

CHAPTER 12

Adult Education and the Empowerment of the Individual in a Global Society

Cecilia Amaluisa Fiallos

This is an important chapter because it is being read by intellectually cultivated human beings, sensitive and capable of promoting changes in a society of globalized economy and culture (Velasco, 2004). Lamentably, instead of thinking and acting constantly to achieve the integral welfare of all the human beings of the planet, many of these people are concentrating exclusively on how to increase the financial worth of multinational corporations and of the countries of the world having greater economic growth, and on how to satisfy the unlimited ambitions of powerful groups and individuals. This chapter is important also because it focuses reflection on a South American country, located on the Pacific coast, latitude $0°$ (equatorial line), very rich, ecologically diverse, multicultural and multiethnic, in whose territorial surface of 254,000 square kilometers live twelve million inhabitants. In counterpoint, this country, Ecuador, is one of the countries of the Third World with a high index of lack of basic necessities (65 percent), which affects the majority of the population (Banco Mundial, 2004). It is a country with a dollarized economy and an external debt of $17 billion, which extracts approximately 42 percent of the national budget for repayment (Acosta, 2002a, 2002b).

Countries such as Ecuador are subject to a global economy and culture that obliges translocation of economic wealth and focusing of thought and vision outside itself while trying to follow a path that is not its own nor truly the most expedient one. Translocation signifies extracting the wealth of a country and transferring it elsewhere, diminishing the resources of some and increasing the wealth of others. As a result of this pattern of movement of wealth, those who were poor become poorer, and those who were wealthy become even richer, generating a lifestyle of overabundance and extravagance for some and profound necessity for others. This style of wealth accumulation is based on an archetype of nonequivalent economy (Peters, 1999) that is not new in the history of humanity, producing inequality and lack of solidarity without resolving the great problems of the world. Far from promoting the development of humanity, this model devalues it by changing it into an insatiable machine of depredation and waste that leads to its own self-destruction (Dieterich, 1999). Logic and reason as well as humanist ethics indicate that it is not beneficial for the world that the currently wealthy and the impoverished countries continue widening this gap. Nor is it beneficial, for example, to continue exploiting natural resources, polluting the environment with enormous quantities of carbon dioxide (Tréllez, in press), producing and using great quantities of weapons (Palmitesta, 2001), and promoting harmful activities and policies on the part of governments and individuals.

It is illogical that, although we live in a society of knowledge, the level of critical conscience and human coherence decreases instead of developing positively. This is one of the challenges of adult education, because beyond the multiple and diverse learning that we can have or promote most important of all is to motivate learners and teachers to relearn a citizenship based on local and global rights and responsibilities, in search of common welfare for all the people who inhabit our planet, in terms of equality. This does not mean learning to be "charitable" toward those who are considered "poor," or to be intolerant toward those who are perceived as being "different," but rather learning to think and work as conscientious human beings, civilized, coherent, disconnected from evil greed—in synthesis, learning to be and to live as truly intelligent and superior beings.

CONCEPTUAL BASES THAT SUPPORT GLOBAL SOCIETY

Development and economic growth continue in this century to be the principal motive of conflict on our planet. Control of resources is the primordial factor that motivates hegemonic control of territories, of government and international institutions. The motive, as has already been stated, is not fulfillment of vital necessities of all humanity but rather accumulation of wealth. Natural resources and the goods and services created by human beings are finite. Nevertheless, the want suffered by millions around the world is not for lack of these resources but rather because these are unequally distributed (Dieterich, 1999).

Peters (1999) shares the conviction of other great scientists—from the early socialists to Marx and Chomsky—that a market economy inevitably is exploited by human beings, toward polarization of social wealth and estrangement of the subject. Aristotle characterizes this process as "crematistic," perversion of the economy, of a subsystem in service of society into machinery that yields a profit at the cost of the majority. In the opinion of various economic analysts, the twentieth century and the beginning of the twenty-first century are characterized by superabundance, opulence, the capacity for excessive consumption and at the same time the deepening impossibility of escaping from problems stemming from deprivation, poverty, and oppression (Sen, 2000). The globalized economy, far from producing global welfare, generates greater impoverishment, at least among peoples with economies based in primary production who open their doors to liberalization of markets without any type of protection (Muradian, 2004).

The focus on income-centered development, the growth of the gross national product, the increase of personal income, industrialization, technological advancements, and social modernization, in addition to departing conceptually from other important aspects of the cultural development of humanity, do not allow nations to concern themselves with good quality of life for their inhabitants (Streeten and others, Morris, and Sen, all as cited in Garcia de la Sienra, 1990). The word *globalization* designates a superior force that acts in numerous dimensions and overcomes the will of individual or collective participants, local as well as national. As Sztompza (cited in Machado, 2001) has indicated:

> The ancient societies were constituted by a complex mosaic of social units, that frequently lived in isolation and were extremely diversified. The principal form of domination was conquest by way of invasion, war, or treaties.... There were multiple political entities separated until the relatively recent form of domination, the nation-states.... There were independent economies, closed, self-ruled, and there were various indigenous cultures that conserved their unique identities, often mutually unintelligible and incommensurable.... The present society demonstrates a completely different picture. (pp. 111–112)

Neoliberal globalization reduces the capacity of governments to make decisions about their territories, resources, and policies. It questions any national governmental initiative that could be considered interference; it preaches fulfillment of an agenda of privatization and defends the redefining of governmental activities in economic and social terms to the minimum level (Kacowicz, as cited in Machado, 2001). In my understanding, globalization as an extremely powerful economic and political force inhibits and distorts the development of many individual and collective freedoms. The only possible freedom is that of the market and of all that favors it: science, technology, laws, and education. For example, advertising for the automobile market reflects the real need for transporting people from one place to another. But instead of exerting pressure so that mass transportation systems can be enlarged or improved, it influences preference for acquiring a personal automobile, with which consumption of energy resources and pollution grow uncontrollably. Another example is the great influence that large transnational companies exercise in extracting petroleum, with corresponding ecological and social consequences, and use of those resources from exportation of petroleum to acquire weapons or luxury goods, instead of investing in quality education and public health.

The free market society changes human values such as kindness, solidarity, and ethics into expressions that are emptied of real content and are accommodated to the interests of the users—as occurs when announcements with great pathos on television newscasts recount the number of deaths of soldiers from a particular country. This leaves the impression that the deaths of soldiers on the other side of the conflict do not matter because they are evil. Some attack; others only defend themselves, and the economic and political reasons that cause war and death remain hidden, for example. This also occurs in discourse about gender equality with its advertising and cultural counterpart of the free market society, so that instead of promoting equality of valuation, development, welfare, and respect for all women (as indicated by human, civil, economic, cultural, and gender rights), the discourse promotes images of machismo and exploitation of women. We should ask, then, What or who controls the education of citizens, both inside and outside of school?

Linked to this economic, social, and political topic is another issue around which debate actively continues. It relates to determining which general and superior necessities of a human being and application of mechanisms allow measurement of the fulfillment of those necessities. According to Peters, the economic focus of the market centers in strengthening the market. Profitability is not the true objective of an economy that is devoted to the art of acquisition (Erwerbskunst) and satisfaction of the general necessities of family and government. This was the original key concept of Aristotle, who considered that the true sense of the word economy (Oikonomie) lies in fulfillment of need, not any art of acquisition, which is not a natural part of economy but rather the crematist phenomenon of producing wealth. According to Peters (1999), Aristotle held that

> many people believe that acquisition and amassing wealth are synonyms, but they are not. For Aristotle, this amassing of wealth [crematistic] is the unnatural use of human abilities, a perversion of the economy. In contrast with "crematism," which is insatiable, the fulfillment of need has a natural limit. The economy according to Aristotle is not autonomous, that is, it does not have its own individual laws, but rather of the government. In this way, economy will always be a theory about government and human beings, for which the most important knowledge, superior to any other, is politics on which the economy depends, in the same way as war strategy or rhetoric. Aristotle did not dedicate any particular study to economy, since he considered it as a part of his books about ethics and politics. (pp. 25–26)

Within this focus, individuals and peoples have the liberty to act and choose the type of life they want to lead. The concept of development as wealth originated within the framework of the individualist and liberal philosophy of law and government, and it was widely accepted during the eighteenth century. The idea of wealth refers, in effect, to a potentially optimal situation that could be reached, or what might be considered a limit, if society were organized according to a "natural" individualistic order, such that nothing would hinder full access to available resources (Sunkel & Paz, 1970). In contrast, participation in the market establishes a quantitative scale that labels people and nations as rich or as poor. Those who sell more at a higher price, and those who buy more at a lower price, are definitely those who have greater opportunity to accumulate wealth. From there, control of markets and their expansion constitutes the cornerstone of focusing on income-centered development.

In this way, the struggle against poverty and international policies (and also governmental politics), instead of being concerned with fulfillment of the general and superior necessities of the inhabitants, focuses on creating strategies that build up and maintain an active market, especially a global market. The Indian economist Amartya Sen (2000), winner of the 1998 Nobel Prize in economics, suggests that human necessities are not only material or what he calls "general necessities" but also "superior necessities," in which are included cultivation of the intellect, spirit, kindness, and commitment to support the cultural development of humanity. These two kinds of necessity are at the foundation of his concept of development as freedom. Sen states that solving the problems originating in lack of fulfillment of these necessities, principally health and education, constitutes a fundamental part of exercising development. He also indicates that it is necessary to recognize the role that freedom of various types plays in opposing these evils (Sen, 2000). Without strong local and national markets, without producers who constantly extract great quantities of resources, and without compulsive buyers, the system is not sustainable.

In the same way, the concept of sustainability that supports conservation of natural resources to guarantee the survival of present and future generations (UICN/PNUMA/WWWF, 1991) also points to regeneration of natural ecosystems, especially in countries with primary economies and high biodiversity, because the extensive system of extraction is not sustainable. This was analyzed in the Brundtland Report, produced by the World Commission on Environment and Development of the United Nations in 1983, which pointed to the necessity of undertaking a vast restructuring of the world economy since it was indispensable to change the lifestyle of many nations and individuals, to adopt a concept of austerity that would consider the common future of humanity to be of greatest importance (Brundtland, 2004).

In 1983, under the auspices of the past secretary general of the United Nations, Pérez de Cuellar, the Norwegian Gro Harlem Brundtland organized and directed the report of the World Commission on Environment and Development, entitled Our Common Future, known also as the Brundtland Report, through which was established the concept of sustainable development, which since then has been incorporated into all political and economic programs. The activities of the Brundtland commission led to convocation of the Earth Summit held in Rio de Janeiro in 1992. In the article written by Brundtland (n.d.), "Those Who Pollute Should Pay," she writes, "We are members of the first generation that confronts the challenge of satisfying the necessities of an infinite number of future generations. For this, we should leave enough 'environmental space' to those who will come, and recognize that our planet has a limited capacity to absorb industrial by-products." In the same way, in the first session of the Earth Summit (Rio + 5) there was renewed call to "dismantle a world order based on the survival of the strongest" (Reuters, AFP, DPA, and PL, 2002).

From this point of view, current local and global societies focus attention and efforts on ensuring the sustainability of an economic model that is not sustainable, causes global damage, and augments world conditions unfavorable to life. In his book *Anatomy of Human Destructivity*, Erich Fromm (1976) differentiates societies that affirm life, aggressive societies that are not destructive, and destructive societies. In his books *The Fear of Freedom* (1980) and *To Have or to Be* (1978), he demonstrates how the advent of liberal society and the market economy produces great anxiety in human beings because they have lost some of the certainty provided by a community that is concerned for its members. Individualization and the daily struggle to gain access to goods and symbols of power and security push human beings to generate individual and collective strategies of self-defense, expressed as barriers to communication and annulment of the rights of others (Fromm, 1976, 1978, 1980).

Various types, levels, and dimensions of violence, repression, and suffering operate actively in the majority of cultures and peoples, provoking permanent anxiety and a desperate search for compensation in whose pursuit human destructiveness forms an almost natural part of life. Fromm profoundly analyzes the conditions that provoke humanity's defensive aggression and genuine destructivity, the base of which is found in unfulfillment of existential needs (Fromm, 1976, 1978).

This focus, in contrast to the viewpoint of the global market society, is gaining a following. Nevertheless, this is not a sufficient counterweight to the power of the large corporations and countries that advocate a life-style based on accumulation and that promote the model of globalization. In China, for example, economists debate the new content of development, not as "elimination and struggle but as a force capable of generating harmony among persons, between human beings and nature, among regions and among social levels" ("Economistas Chinos," 2004, p. 1). In Latin American countries, not only does social protest endorse an inclusive rather than exclusive and destructive economic scheme; there is also deepening debate about structural and democratic reorganization of the global society of the future. One of many examples of this is the reflective group called the New Historical Project (NPH), which published a series of articles in The End of Global Capitalism (Dieterich and others, 1999).

AN ALTERNATIVE FOCUS ON DEVELOPMENT AND GLOBALIZATION

Sen (2000) suggests that development can be thought of as a process of expansion of the real freedoms that individuals enjoy. The determining factors in this process are social and economic institutions (such as educational and medical services), as well as political and human rights (such as the freedom to participate in debates and elections). In this process, industrialization, technological progress, and social modernization are means and instruments. He points out that this concept of development focuses the attention of governments and individuals on the results of development rather than on aspects of the process. This focus on development demands elimination of the principal sources of deprivation of freedom, which are poverty and tyranny, scarcity of economic opportunities, systematic social deprivation, abandonment of public services, and intolerance or excessive intervention on the part of repressive governments (Sen, 2000). I add here that this focus contributes to the effort among individuals, institutions, and governments to recognize and eradicate the vices that contribute to greed and lack of solidarity.

Second, education and health; human, civil, economic, and cultural rights; reduction of poverty; and fomenting of democracy all form part of the global agendas subscribed to by governments, international organisms, and organizations of civil society. But it is in precisely these areas where there is the least amount included in national budgets, especially in countries with the least economic development. The external debt leaves only a small portion of the budget for education, health, and basic infrastructure in mostly rural areas. Categories such as defense and military equipment, current costs, and refinancing of payments of the external debt receive the most funding. It is well said that the countries indebting themselves commit this grave error through their lack of experience or knowledge. But what is inadmissible is that they do it with the technical assistance of multilateral organizations of credit and under the management of the International Monetary Fund. Joseph E. Stiglitz (2002), who was awarded the 2001 Nobel Prize in economics, tells how, on the first day he went to work as chief economist and vice president of the World Bank, he was impressed by the slogan at the entrance to the huge building: "Our dream is a world without poverty"(p. 7). In my opinion, this is a clear example of a phrase emptied of content that expresses a half-truth about reality. That is, the World Bank lends money to countries that later repay with enormous quantities of resources extracted from the national budget, as in the previously mentioned case of Ecuador (Stiglitz, 2002). In this sense, it is common for plans and programs of government to include the essential elements in Sen's concept of development as freedom (2000); nevertheless, the majority of these programs do not go beyond proposals containing half-truths, while the democratic system of representation and politics reacts to them weakly.

The concept of development as freedom suggests taking into account not only fundamental factors but others that permit long lives and living well, not just in economically less-developed countries but in all nations. In my judgment, this supposes vigilance for humane treatment, practice of respect among people, good neighborly relationships between peoples and nations, and promotion of conditions of security and diverse opportunities for what Krishnamurti (1984) called the "flowering" of the person. This expression is used by Krishnamurti to refer to the quality of education that schools should provide and the type of environment that should exist for students as well as teachers. In his "Letters to the Schools' he writes, "the schools do not only have to be excellent from the academic point of view, but rather much more than this; they have to be interested in the cultivation of the total human being." In the context of the book, it is suggested that all societies in all areas should contribute to this flowering (Krishnamurti, 1984, p. 8).

Those who are responsible for this flowering process are families—fathers and mothers, together or separately—who should fully occupy themselves with physical and affective care, the flowering of kindness, and a sense of equality and austerity in their children—small children, adolescents and youths, girls and boys. In the same way, communities, institutions of society, governments, business, churches, and politicians need to place their daily activity within this same focus. If they do not all collaborate in a conscious and sustained manner, who else can contribute to expanding fundamental and superior freedoms that all the individuals on our planet—women and men—require?

A third aspect of this concept is related to the role of what Sen (2000) calls the market mechanism, with which it is absurd to disagree in a generic sense. Nevertheless, it is indispensable to recognize that this relational mechanism of society is greater than merely economic. Sen says that the market is an exchange that includes words, goods, or gifts, but growing unemployment in economically developed societies and the persistent lack of this "freedom" in nonindustrialized countries, as well as labor conditions, constitute a way of impeding the participation of individuals in this market mechanism of interchange (Sen, 2000).

In nonindustrialized countries with small markets, the quantity of jobs and the quality of wages (or social retribution for productive labor, as in, for example, the case of unsubsidized rural producers) in no way favor fulfillment of the "conditions necessary to live for many years and to live well as long as one lives" (Sen, 2000, p. 25), as Sen advocates in the concept of development as freedom. This question has more profound consequences than the mere lack of goods and services. It affects self-concept and belief in one's own capabilities; it annuls productive and creative potential and internal motivation. It inhibits participation and the capacity to commit oneself to higher goals. It generates desperation and chronic boredom, and the noxious tendency toward aggression, violence, destruction, and self-destruction (Fromm, 1976).

Following Sen's thinking, insufficient economic freedom plays a part in lack of social and political liberty. Unfortunately, a disconnected way of responding to these diverse necessities impedes the concept of development as an integrated process of expansion of fundamental freedoms interrelated among themselves and in a global sense. This is probably the key point in the proposal of development as freedom, since

> it allows the simultaneous appreciation of the vital role that many and different institutions play in the process of development, among which are found the markets and the organizations related to them: governments and local authorities, political parties and other civic institutions, the educational systems and the opportunities for dialogue and public debate (including the role of the media) . . . it also allows us to recognize the role of social values and traditions that can influence the freedoms that individuals enjoy and who have reasons to value them. . . . These shared norms can influence some social issues such as gender equality, types of child care, family size, birth control, care of the environment and many institutions and results. . . . Current social values and customs also affect the presence or absence of corruption and the role that trust plays in economic, social, or political relationships. (Sen, 2000, pp. 25–26)

In summary, this concept of development as freedom offers elevated value to the capacity for reasoning and sensitivity in human beings, limiting economic compulsion and envy and in its place favoring environments, relationships, and institutions that empower the individual and a free and liberating global society.

Within this perspective, development as freedom supposes "the capacity to live for many years (without dying in the flower of life) and to live well as long as one lives (and not to live in misery and deprived of freedom), ideals that almost all of us would greatly value and fervently desire" (Sen, 2000, pp. 29–30).

Reasoning with good judgment, one concludes that development cannot conceive of economic growth as an end in itself; rather, development should be about improving the life we lead and the freedoms we enjoy. Of course, this supposes viewing the globality of nations and their inhabitants with a sense of equality, responsibility, and solidarity. It does not make sense, then, to develop some nations and individuals at the cost of impoverishing others, nor pursue the process of elimination and struggle, as Wi Jie of Qinghua University in China says: "What the new concept of development in China underlines, is that it should be readjusted, it should not lend attention to one aspect and overlook the rest. It should not emphasize one sector and neglect the others in the treatment of different industries, regions, and social levels. The content of development is not elimination but rather harmony. For example, regarding the phenomenon of high, medium, and low incomes that are presented now, what is proposed is not to eliminate high incomes but rather to augment low incomes and to encourage their increase" ("Economistas Chinos," 2004, p. 2).

In the same way, neither would it make sense for some more powerful nations or blocs of nations to pressure or direct the global economy toward satisfying the insatiable interests of accumulation of wealth. It falls to intellectually cultivated, sensitive, and honest human beings to see that each individual, local, national, or global decision contributes to the common good and in no way endangers anyone or offers privileges to the stronger as an intrinsic value of global human society.

ROLES AND RESPONSIBILITIES OF ADULT EDUCATION

The view of development as freedom that we have explained in these pages lends special attention to expansion of the capacity of individuals to live a life that gives them value and reasons to value themselves, and to be responsible people in and of themselves and toward all that surrounds them and depends on them (Sen, 2000). To reinforce this idea, let us take up the reflections proposed by Fromm (1976) about the great contribution of Sigmund Freud's psychoanalytical theory (as cited in Fromm, 1976) in discovering the forces at work in human character and their internal contradictions. Fromm wrote: "The discovery of the unconscious processes and of the dynamic concept of character was radical because it extended to the roots of human behavior; and that was unsettling because now no one could hide behind their good intentions; and it was dangerous, because if everyone knew everything when they could know themselves and others, society would be shaken to its very foundations" (p. 14).

For the purpose of our reflection, if education in general and that of adults in particular could reveal the underlying bases of the character of the global market society, certainly it would be possible to promote at least a more ethical rebuilding of the concepts that drive individuals, institutions, and society, in search of greater coherence. If growth in these capacities can depend on public means, they could be enlarged even more by broadening and deepening critical thought and the capacity of participation and conscious, responsible intervention of individuals, in order to influence individual decision making in private and collective concerns and their results, whether on a local or a global level.

The normal focus that adopts development as freedom considers that individual and fundamental freedoms are essential; the success of a society must be evaluated from this viewpoint, primarily in the function of the enjoyment of various freedoms on the part of all its members. Instead of fixing attention on variables such as utility or strategies for attaining freedom or real income, what is important is to evaluate the freedom that one has to do the things that we need to value, for two reasons: one, it is our right; and two, because it is important to increase the opportunities for individuals to obtain valuable results (Sen, 2000).

This reflection carries us toward evaluating opportunities for success and deprivations, understanding that development of individual initiative and social effectiveness forms an important part of the expansion of freedoms. If we see only success and failure in increasing or decreasing income, we do not consider the global focus of development as freedom, which, as has already been stated, is evaluated according to the efficiency of social return in global terms of equality and solidarity. The text of Amartya Sen that we are following does not explicitly include the terms "equality and solidarity"; nevertheless we interpret his vision to include these values.

Even when these expressions contain a level of generalization and focus on the globality of nations and human beings, great importance is given to the development of freedoms for each individual, with which it is not the real character of the individualistic and competitive society being reiterated but rather the development of individual freedom as a social obligation. This assumes development of the "agency" of the individual:

> An agent or the agency of the individual ... in a higher sense signifies that he or she acts and produces changes whose achievements can be judged in function of his or her own values and objectives, whether we evaluate them or not in the function of some external criteria ... which refers to the role of the agency of the individual as a member of the public and as a participant in economic, social, and political activities that extend from participation in the market to direct or indirect intervention in individual or joint activities in political and other types of terrain. [Sen, 2000, p. 35]

This proposal for development as freedom points to individual responsibility as a basis for the effective and efficient social responsibility of government. When this responsibility is transferred to the government, all of the individuals and groups easily tend to question it and blame it for all kinds of faults, thereby excusing the citizens from responsibility, who then become accomplices and deceivers by will or omission. In other words, and using expressions from the field of psychology (Fromm, 1978), it is essential to develop the responsibility of individuals so they can take charge of what corresponds directly to them and of what is in hand to contribute by way of their agency. The transformation of the world, beginning with the small space where we live, cannot be the responsibility of others, but rather of ourselves. To avoid this responsibility signifies becoming indolent, comfortable, passive, and incapable of developing as free agents. If we avoid the task of judging the state of things and what must be done to provide ourselves and others with the conditions to live long enough and well, we are creating the stage for human degradation.

The concept of development as freedom suggests that "as reflective creatures, we have the capacity to contemplate the life of others. Our sense of responsibility does not have reason to refer only to the afflictions that our own behavior can cause (although this can also be very important), but rather, in more general terms, toward the misery that we see around us and that is within our power to remedy" (Sen, 2000, pp. 338–339).

The feminist perspective has explored this concept in a profound way, in search of achieving equality of rights and opportunities between men and women, a condition that, applied to adult education, demands substantive trans- formation of social institutions and of cultural practices as well as a progressive process of empowering women (Deere & León, 2002) and of other forms of masculine empowerment, allowing both to reach a full freedom and the possibility of exercising a wide sense of responsibility in service of society (Sen, 2000).

Nothing of what has been said to here could become an agent without the fully conscious, direct, sustained intervention of educational services as well as the role of educator of society through institutions and daily life. Adult education in every part of the world, whether in countries with a high educational level or in countries with a high rate of illiteracy, needs to assume the role of agent, to obtain the satisfaction of general necessities as well as superior necessities, as explained by Sen. Global society is obligated to facilitate development, while understanding it as an expansion of the freedoms of the human being. Seen in this way, adult education in a globalized society could be sufficiently creative to contribute to the cultural development of humanity. The processes of adult education that do not focus on this political and ethical role of society can be effective transmitters of knowledge, though without consciousness that they are reaffirming the values supported by the current inequitable global society.

Recalling the teachings of the Brazilian educator Paulo Freire (1958), we agree that the basic content of adult education that we need to promote "constitutes the comprehension of the human condition and the possibilities of overcoming cultural limits, not only for a greater understanding, but also to intervene further and to generate new mental dispositions that will allow it to function more effectively in its historical and cultural context" (p. 25).

Many educators in Latin America suggest the necessity of building communities of learning in all areas of individual life, which includes all types of institution and social space (Torres, 2004).

In connecting the various emphases and currents of thought that coexist in formulating educational proposals for adults, we could say that the existing global society requires an educational intervention of enormous magnitude; this is not strictly linked to the development of basic skills or useful learning of any type or depth. It includes the educated and the learners, professionals and those with broad experience, those who are studious and those who had few opportunities to develop intellectually. It refers to a global educational necessity with an orientation of empowerment or expanding freedoms for all human beings. Global society presents incredible opportunities; nevertheless, they do not benefit all human beings, given the problems that we have analyzed.

No change in the focus of income-centered development will be possible, nor can the globalization of wealth become a global theme, if individuals and their communities do not empower its capacity as an agent. This is one of the most important challenges in adult education because beyond the multiple and diverse learning experiences we can have or promote, the most important of all is that of relearning citizenship on the basis of individual, local, and global rights and responsibilities, in pursuit of the common welfare in terms of equality. In this way, we will have the opportunity to provide ways in which adult education can help people and communities (including all of its members, institutions, businesses, and authorities) to achieve the goal of becoming responsible individuals.

REFERENCES

Acosta, A. La deuda externa, un problema político global (III): Algunas reflexiones para construir soluciones alternativas [The external debt, a global political problem (III): Some reflections in order to construct alternative solutions]. *Diálogos La Insignia*. [http://www.lainsignia.org/2002/septiembre/dial_006.htm]. 2002a.

Acosta, A. Deuda externa y migración: Una relación incestuosa (III) [External debt and migration: An incestuous relationship (III)]. *Diálogos La Insignia*. [http://www.lainsignia.org/2002/septiembre/dial_006.htm]. 2002b.

Banco Mundial. Evolución, naturaleza, y distribución de la pobreza en el Ecuador, 1990–2002 [Evolution, nature, and the distribution of poverty in Ecuador, 1990–2002]. [http://www.bancomundial.org.ec/downloads/folletodifusion.pdf]. 2004.

Brundtland, H. Our common future. In *World commission on environment and development: United Nations Brundtland Commission*. [http://www.rulers.org/indexb5.html]. 2004.

Brundtland, H. *Paga quien contamina* [Those who pollute should pay]. [http://www.eumed.net/cursecon/textos/ghg-paga_quien_contamina.htm]. n.d.

Deere, C. D., & León, M. (2002). *Género, propiedad y empoderamiento: Tierra, Estado y mercado en América Latina* [Gender, property and poverty: Earth, the State and the market in Latin America]. Mexico City, México: PUEG y FLACSO Sede Ecuador.

Dieterich, H. (1999). Teoría y praxis del Nuevo Proyecto Histórico [Theory and praxis of the New Historical Project]. In H. Dieterich & others (Eds.), *Fin del capitalismo global: El nuevo proyecto histórico* [The end of global capitalism: The new historical project]. Buenos Aires, Argentina: Editorial 21.

Dieterich, H., Dussel, E., Franco, R., Peters, A., Stamer, C., & Zemelman, H. (Eds.). (1999). *Fin del capitalismo global: El nuevo proyecto histórico* [The end of global capitalism: The new historical project]. Buenos Aires, Argentina: Editorial 21.

Economistas chinos: Nuevo año, nuevo concepto de desarrollo [Chinese economists: New year, new development concept]. *Diario del Pueblo*. [http://spanish.peopledaily.com.cn/spanish/200401/05/sp20040105_71405.html]. May 1, 2004.

Freire, P. A. (1958). *Educação de adultos e as populações marginais: Mocambos* [Education of adults and marginal populations: The Mocambos]. Recife, Brasil: Centro Paulo Freire: Estudos e Pesquisas.

Fromm, E. (1976). *Anatomía de la destructividad humana* [Anatomy of human destructiveness]. Mexico City, Mexico: Siglo XXI Editores.

Fromm, E. (1978). *Tener o ser* [To have or to be]. Mexico City, Mexico: Fondo de Cultura Económica.

Fromm, E. (1980). *El miedo a la libertad* [The fear of freedom]. Buenos Aires, Argentina: Paidos.

García de la Sienra, A. *El concepto de desarrollo* [The concept of development]. Hemeroteca Virtual ANUIES. [http://www.hemerodigital. unam.mx/ANUIES]. 1990.

Krishnamurti, J. (1984). *Cartas a las escuelas* [Letters to the schools]. London: Edhasa.

Machado, J. Concepto de globalización [The concept of globalization]. [http://www.forum-global.de/bm/articles/inv/concglob.htm]. 2001.

Muradian, R. (2004). Integración económica y medio ambiente en América Latina [Economical integration and environment in Latin America]. In F. Falconí, M. Hercowitz, & R. Muradian (eds.), *Globalización y desarrollo en América Latina*. Quito, Ecuador: FLACSO.

Palmitesta, R. La escena geopolítica: El creciente armamentismo y la globalización de la violencia" [The geopolitical scene: The increasing armament and global violence]. [http://colombia.analitica.com/internacionales/6259946.asp]. 2001.

Peters, A. (1999). El principio de la equivalencia como base de la economía global [The principle of equivalence as a bases of global economy]. In H. Dieterich & others (Eds.), *Fin del capitalismo global: El nuevo proyecto histórico* [The end of global capitalism: The new historical project]. Buenos Aires, Argentina: Editorial 21.

Reuters, AFP, DPA, and PL. Johannesburg: Nota de prensa de la Cumbre de la Tierra.'' [www.lajornada.org]. 2002.

Sen, A. (2000). *Desarrollo y libertad* [Development and liberty]. Barcelona, Spain: Editorial Planeta.

Stiglitz, J. E. (2002). *El malestar en globalización* [The bad of globalization]. Buenos Aires, Argentina: Editorial Taurus.

Sunkel, O., & Paz, P. (1970). *El subdesarrollo latinoamericano y la teoría del desarrollo* [The underdevelopment of Latin America and the theory of development]. Mexico City, Mexico: Editorial Siglo XXI Editores.

Torres, R. M. Conversatorio acerca de la creación de comunidades de aprendizaje [Dialogue about the creation of learning communities]. [http://espanol.groups.yahoo.com /group/debateducacion]. 2004.

Tréllez, E. (in press). *La ciudadanía ambiental global: Manual para docentes de educación básica de América Latina y el Caribe* [The global community of citizenship: A manual for basic education teachers of Latin America and the Caribbean]. Quito, Ecuador: PNUMA-UICN-SUR.

UICN/PNUMA/WWWF. (1991). *Cuidar la tierra: Estrategia para el futuro de la vida* [Caring for the earth: A strategy for the future of life]. Gland, Suiza: Union Mundial para la Naturaleza.

Velasco, F. J. (2004). Globalización, desarrollo sustentable y identidad cultural [Globalization, sustainable development, and cultural identity]. In F. Falconí, M. Hercowitz, & R. Muradian (Eds.), *Globalización y desarrollo en América Latina [Globalization and development in Latin America].* Quito, Ecuador: FLACSO.

CHAPTER 13

Active and Inclusive Citizenship for Women

Democratic Considerations for Fostering Lifelong Education

Patricia A. Gouthro

Recent discourses in lifelong learning (Elliott 2000, Welton 2001, Martin 2003) have focused on the importance of active and inclusive citizenship. This paper examines factors to create a more inclusive learning environment for women to engage as active citizens within both educational contexts and the broader society. (This paper uses a critical feminist theoretical approach to argue that systemic concerns around equity, social justice and access need to be taken up by educators, administrators and policy makers in order to address democratic considerations for fostering lifelong learning for women.) I begin by examining how the concept of deliberative democracy has been taken up in discourses in lifelong learning, drawing upon critical feminist theory to consider criticisms regarding how democratic approaches to lifelong learning have been undermined by the effects of globalized capitalism. Challenging the focus on lifelong learning and the marketplace (Gouthro 2002a), this paper explores three democratic considerations to foster lifelong learning for women: a) structural gendered inequalities that situate women at a disadvantage in accessing and participating fully in educational contexts, b) a narrow definition of lifelong learning that focuses on the marketplace which serves to exclude, overlook, and diminish women's learning potentiality and c) the need to consider gender as a complex variable within the broader discourse of education for inclusion. My paper is informed by a current SSHRC (Social Science and Humanities Research Council) funded research study that examines lifelong learning trajectories for women in Canada and a current CCL (Canadian Council on Learning) funded grant on women and active citizenship in Nova Scotia. I conclude with recommendations regarding pedagogical practices for democratic educators and suggestions to inform policy development in lifelong education.

DELIBERATIVE DEMOCRACY, ACTIVE CITIZENSHIP AND LIFELONG LEARNING

The importance of democracy is a consistent theme that emerges in discussions around adult education. Lifelong learning is linked with developing an active and engaged citizenship, through what many critical theorists (Welton 1998, Habermas 2001, Gutmann and Thompson 2004) term "deliberative democracy." The capacity to develop well reasoned arguments, to critically assess evidence and to participate in dialogue with other citizens are all fundamental prerequisites for an active and engaged citizenship. Habermas (2001: 278–279) clarifies how democratic will-formation informed by discourse theory derives its legitimacy from "on the one hand, the communicative presuppositions that allow the better arguments to come into play in various forms of deliberation and, on the other, procedures that secure fair bargaining conditions." Therefore, decision-making is a dialogical process, whereby all participants must be provided with opportunities to participate equitably, in order to make decisions in a reasoned manner. Gutmann and Thompson (2004: 3) state that "most fundamentally, deliberative democracy affirms the need to justify decisions made by citizens and their representatives." Welton (1998: 370) argues that the notion of "deliberative democracy" is consistent with "core values" in "socially responsible adult education," as "we have a commitment to the enlightened, relatively autonomous and reflective learner; that social learning processes are central to the formation of the active citizen; and that we have an obligation to foster discussion, debate and dialogue among citizens." However, as Fraser (1995) and other feminists (Landes 1995, Pitanguy 2002, Preece 2002) have pointed out, women have frequently been marginalized or excluded from public deliberation, thus diminishing their ability to participate fully as active citizens.

Lifelong education has often garnered support as a means of ensuring that citizens can participate actively in the broader society, by fostering literacy and employment skills, as well as the capacity of individuals to make more informed decisions around issues such as health care, parenting and governance. Stromquist (2006: 9) argues that literacy can be regarded as a political project to assist women to engage more actively as citizens. Attaining literacy skills places women in a better position to advocate for their rights regarding income and health care, while challenging the underlying gender ideologies that put women in a more vulnerable position in society, by addressing concerns such as sexual assault and domestic violence.

In the 1970s, the pivotal UNESCO report, *Learning to Be* (Faure et al. 1972) argued that opportunities for lifelong education should be considered a basic human right. Lifelong learning was perceived to have many ameliorative effects that could serve to improve the conditions of humans across the globe.

Over recent decades, however, broader democratic goals have gradually been eroded by the rising influence of the marketplace on educational discourses. Increasingly, the support that governments, universities and corporations lend to lifelong education ventures is based on the belief that citizens need to continually learn new skills and adapt to a rapidly evolving global marketplace (Edwards 1997, Methven and Hansen 1997). While broader notions of lifelong learning outside of the paid workplace may be acknowledged, the main focus, rationale and willingness to provide financial support for education is usually connected to a bottom-line mentality that focuses primarily on "learning for earning."

Within this context, education is no longer perceived to be primarily a responsibility of the government for all of its citizens. In examining UK policies, Ian Martin argues that (2003: 568) "essentially, as the state has sought to reduce its role in the provision of services, so it has encouraged citizens to become more self-sufficient (and self-interested) consumers or customers—as distinct from supposedly dependent welfare clients." When education is perceived as an individual responsibility, each person must situate him/herself in the most advantageous position within what Beck (1992) has named a "risk society." Under these conditions, predictably, marginalized groups are increasingly disenfranchised. A competitive and individualistic approach towards lifelong education minimizes the importance of social justice considerations when fostering educational opportunities further disadvantaging women and minority groups.

In their research on lifelong learning, Gorard et al. (1999) discuss how individuals must map their own learning trajectories throughout their lifetime. Preliminary research from my SSHRC study on women's lifelong learning trajectories in Canada reveals some of the factors that complicate "individual" learning pathways, indicating that the model of the autonomous learner is more a reflection of masculine than feminine experience. Women's life courses and decisions around education are intricately linked with gendered responsibilities as they respond to the needs of others—husband's careers, children's education and care for elderly parents.

Recent discussions on educational policy take up Giddens (1998) concept of the "Third Way." Perkins et al. (2004: 1) explain that the Third Way has been presented as an alternative "between neo-liberalism and the post-war welfare state." It is based on notions of human capital theory, with the assumption that there will be economic payoffs if a society broadens access and opportunities for lifelong learning. However, as some critics (Lister 2003: 433) point out, the focus of these policies, particularly with regards to providing additional support to children, emphasizes the value of "the future *worker*-citizen more than *democratic*-citizen who is the prime asset of the social investment state." While Lister (2003) believes that this is still an improvement on previous social policy in the UK as it provides additional resources that will benefit children, it is still problematic because the primary focus on learning is linked with the marketplace. While having an educated workforce is a good thing, as Perkins et al. (2004: 15) note,

> Valuing families, communities, cultural practices, the environment and those population groups ill-suited to the labour market calls for broader social policy goals and a recognition of other forms of contributions as well as the simple one of economic participation.

As the divide between the rich and the poor widens, and many citizens feel excluded from deliberations around democracy (Martin 2003), adult educators need to carefully assess what they mean when they take up notions of citizenship and learning. When we invest in lifelong education, what kind of learning is being fostered?

Using a critical feminist perspective, I argue there is a need for broader, democratic beliefs to inform educational practices and policies. Critical theorists in adult education have drawn upon the work of the German philosopher, Jürgen Habermas, to envision a communicative approach towards learning that supports democratic ideals. Michael Welton (2001: 32) argues that "the central question for civil societarian adult educators and citizens is simply this: who can place issues on the agenda and determine what direction the lines of communication take?" Are practices in policies in lifelong learning to be determined through the mechanistic, utilitarian directives of the marketplace, or can critical educators shape a broader, more holistic view of what should encompass a learning society?

Similarly, critical feminists such as Nancy Fraser raise important questions about justice and inclusion issues, paramount to democratic educational practices. Fraser (2003: 9) believes that concerns around redistribution (sharing resources) and recognition (politics of identity) are often pitted against one another in what she perceives to be "false antitheses," arguing that "justice today requires *both* redistribution and recognition." Both of these factors must be taken up by feminists (and supporters) to address democratic concerns and to provide more inclusive learning opportunities for women to engage as active citizens.

STRUCTURAL INEQUALITIES FOR WOMEN

There are still many structural inequalities that limit women's ability to participate fully in lifelong learning, supporting Fraser's argument that both "redistribution" and "recognition" are key factors to be negotiated for women to attain equitable participation in society. These inequities are rooted in patriarchal social structures and unfortunately seem to exist in virtually all societies, to a greater or lesser extent. Structural social inequalities include lesser access to citizenship rights, including financial and educational resources, as well as less support and fewer opportunities to attain positions of power and authority within government, industry, religious and educational institutions. In addition, women continue to carry disproportionately greater burdens of unpaid labour in all societies. Violence that targets women, ranging from sexual harassment to rape and murder, still casts a dark shadow of patriarchy over the lives of all women (and men who genuinely care about them).

Within the larger global context, there are still many women who are not allowed even basic citizenship rights. For instance, Mona Laczo (2003: 77) points out that in Nepal citizenship is passed down through blood relationships from fathers to their sons and daughters. At the age of sixteen, Nepalese can apply for a Certificate of Citizenship, but a women's application has to be supported by her father or husband, creating a situation of vulnerability and dependence for women. Laczo (2003: 77) also notes that "thousands of Nepalese women are denied rights of citizenship because they have been trafficked against their will, or they belong to ethnic minorities, or they are refugees." Refugees are stateless, and thus have no citizenship protection, while children of mixed marriages who do not have Nepalese fathers are not eligible for citizenship. Women survivors who have been trafficked are frequently ostracized by their families and communities, and put in the problematic position of having to go to the same male relatives who sold them for permission to attain citizenship! Without basic citizenship rights, many Nepalese women have limited access to employment, education and health care, and the prospects for their children's future are limited.

Women who live in developed countries and who have obtained full citizenship rights have many privileges in comparison to women in situations such as this, but they still face many structural social barriers that limit their ability to participate fully as active citizens. While women have made great progress in obtaining further education and working in the paid labour force, an emphasis on competition and individualism factors out structural inequalities that need to be addressed for more equitable and democratic learning opportunities.

As critical theorists (Welton 2001, Gouthro 2002a) have noted, discourses in lifelong learning are increasingly shaped by the language of the global marketplace, that denotes learners as clients and education as a commodity. Jackson (2003) argues that when the agenda for lifelong learning is shaped primarily by market forces, women are frequently disadvantaged. In listening to women's life histories in my SSHRC research, it is clear that women's commitments to other family members means that women will frequently either limit, delay or struggle under adverse circumstances to continue their education. Women generally have responsibilities and connections to the homeplace that lead them to have different lifelong learning trajectories than men. Women consistently maintain a disproportionate responsibility for caring labour, such as motherwork (Hart 1997). Selwyn and Gorard (2003: 176–177) point out that having children disadvantages women in the labour force and in their pursuit of educational goals far more than men, as can be seen in recent research on participation rates in adult education in the UK where "a male with a child is 1.6 times as likely to participate as a woman with a child." Crittenden (2001) and Budig and England (2001) note that the "costs" of raising children are primarily borne by women, resulting in lower incomes and less opportunity for advancement. Women are more vulnerable to the caprices of an unforgiving marketplace if they take time out for caring labour (which they are socially assigned), and in the case of divorce, their income is likely to drop substantially (while a man's is likely to increase significantly). The same inequalities that hamper workplace advancement impact detrimentally on educational opportunities for women.

Bird (1999) notes that lifelong education is often an important venue for the transition between unpaid and paid labour commitments, when women shift as employees back into the marketplace. Due to the devaluation of women's unpaid labour, and the competitive individualized context predominant in current educational discourses, there is often a remedial approach towards women "return-ers." Hayes and Smith (1994) found that women are often treated as though they are deficient in adult education contexts. It is difficult to change prevailing and ubiquitous assumptions about gender roles that over time have become ingrained into our social fabric. As I have noted in earlier research (Gouthro 2002b), challenging entrenched ideas of what constitutes a "committed" or "productive" learner in academe is problematic. These definitions are frequently linked with a marketplace orientation that is so pervasive and taken-for-granted, it is diffi-cult for people to envision alternative perspectives that would validate women's unpaid labour contributions. Similarly, Hart (1997) argues that educators need to develop recognition for learning in more holistic contexts that validates women's subsistence labour, such as *motherwork*.

BROADENING OUR UNDERSTANDING OF LIFELONG LEARNING

A broader emphasis on lifelong learning that occurs in a wide range of contexts may be beneficial for all learners, but it is particularly important for women. A critical feminist perspective points to the need to recognize learning that occurs in the realm of what Habermas (1987) has termed the *lifeworld*—the everyday world of taken-for-granted activities, where our connections to others and understanding of the world is first formed. While it is important not to idealize the lifeworld (since there are also gendered dimensions to the lifeworld realm), learning in the home-place (Gouthro 2005), in community and civil society organizations (Welton 2001) all serve important purposes in promoting active citizenship.

Critical educators such as Welton (2001) and Johnston (1999) have pointed out the need to consider lifelong learning as a means to advance civil society and citizenship. These are important realms for sustaining democracy. Welton (2001: 33) argues that "Habermas's recent reflections on civil society and the public sphere are richly suggestive for adult learning theorists and practising adult educators who are designing intervention strategies for a just and honest learning society." Concerns around challenging what Habermas would term "system imperatives" (forces of the marketplace) that are encroaching into the realm of the lifeworld (our everyday world of home, local community, and civil society) must be taken up by educators committed to democratic practices.

Rennie Johnston (1999) explains that there are four overlapping approaches towards education and citizenship that can be examined from the social purpose tradition in adult education. First, adult learning for *inclusive citizenship* addresses economic and social exclusion. Secondly, adult learning for *pluralistic citizenship* recognizes concerns of identity and difference. Thirdly, Johnston (1999: 184) states that there is adult learning for *reflexive citizenship* whereby "adult learners [can] engage more actively and critically with the idea of both citizen's rights and their responsibilities." Finally, there is adult learning for *active citizenship* that has the opportunity to bring together divergent groups of citizens to actively work together in groups towards initiating social change. Johnston (1999: 186) argues that "common to all these groups, is that they are involved in learning and in different ways they promote and develop their individual and collective voice." Our understanding of the purposes of lifelong learning shifts if we investigate learning that occurs in lifeworld realms—from the homeplace to civil society organizations.

At the same time, it is essential to explore how within these different categories of citizenship, gender shapes social expectations around participation. Preece (2002: 21) argues that the concepts of citizenship and governance are gendered, which

> means that the way men and women learn what is valued in terms of active citizenship and participation in decision making determines their identity as citizens, their perceived entitlements as members of a given society and their perceived role within society.

For instance, Fraser (1995) notes that citizenship for men has often been linked with military service, which is often perceived as a valuable contribution to the larger society. Yet as many feminists argue, one of the main roles for many women—that of being mother—also provides many benefits to the state and is essential for raising the next generation of citizens, but it is generally overlooked in discussions around citizenship. In my CCL grant, one of the challenges in deciding upon who to approach to be participants has been to consider what constitutes active citizenship for women, as the contributions that women make to society are often not as publicly visible as the work that men do.

The historical exclusion of women from full citizenship cannot simply be addressed by broadening the definition of citizen to include women as well as men. Stromquist (2006: 8) claims that

> feminist theories have demonstrated that not only is the state gendered (through the prevailing presence of men in multiple public institutions and the presence of male leaders), but that citizenship itself is also gendered.

One of the problems with understanding concerns around citizenship is the all too frequent public conflation of "citizen" with "taxpayer," which is particularly problematic for women outside of the paid labour force. Elliott (2000) points out the need to recognize gendered forms of discrimination that could serve to disadvantage women if the model for citizenship participation does not acknowledge inequities in circumstances. Elliot (2000: 15) argues that "entry into the public sphere alone does not ensure 'equality' for women." It is important to recognize the value of unpaid labour, as well as provide support for women to access paid labour.

Nancy Fraser (2003) notes the dual concerns that frequently create tensions in resolving issues of inequality. Demands for parity (everyone has the same rights, privileges and access to resources) are often countered against the uniqueness of identity (the special considerations that particular groups wish to have recognized). From a critical feminist perspective, we can see the need for women to have equal access to learning opportunities, but at the same time there needs to be recognition for differences in experience, i.e. the focus in many women's lives on caring labour. These concerns are not mutually exclusive. Both approaches towards equity have to be addressed in order to create democratic opportunities for full participation in lifelong learning.

IDENTITY AND DEMOCRATIC INCLUSION

To understand the concept of active citizenship, we need to not only assess how women participate as citizens, but also the ways in which concerns that impact primarily upon women have been systematically ignored or trivialized within discourses around citizenship.

The historical precedents of democracy are exclusionary, as women, the poor and minority groups were generally not allowed to participate in decision-making processes around governance. As Bertrand Russell (1996, c. 1946: 574) points out, Locke's [1690] "social contract" which discussed the concept of civil society as the

> rule of the majority, unless it is agreed that a greater number shall be required...sounds democratic, but it must be remembered that Locke assumes the exclusion of women and the poor from rights of citizenship.

Even fairly recent critical discourses around the topic of citizenship often overlook or marginalize women's contributions and experiences. Landes (1995) points out that Habermas's (1987) discussion of the bourgeois public sphere where citizens (primarily men) participate was set up to exclude many issues that were relegated to the private (women's) sector, as these were considered to be particularistic rather than universal concerns. As Stromquist (2006: 8) notes, "citizenship must consider not only public but private realms." Landes (1995: 97) argues that while Habermas acknowledged there were some problems with the bourgeois public sphere "attaining its stated goals of equality and equal participation," this was perceived to be "a limitation of actual existing society, not of the model of a universal public according to which pre-existing social inequalities are bracketed." Bringing a feminist perspective to critical theory challenges the assumption that the exclusion and/or marginalization of women as fully participating, active citizens is not just an oversight that needs to be addressed by widening the parameters of discussion, but rather it is an intrinsic component of a society that does not value women's contributions and concerns as much as it values men's contributions and concerns. In her feminist analysis of Habermas's (1987) work, Nancy Fraser (1995: 36) argues that citizenship "has an implicit subtext" as long as the concepts of "worker" and "childrearer" are perceived as fundamentally different and incompatible.

A democratic approach towards learning needs to take into account the unique differences and situations of all learners, recognizing women are often expected to fulfill different social obligations and responsibilities. Fostering policies in lifelong education that address these concerns is important to create inclusive learning contexts.

At the same time, gender is just one variable that needs to be addressed if we are to consider what inclusion means in all learning contexts, and to assess how privilege too frequently defines educational goals. Adult educators who are motivated to support democratic practices need to critically reflect upon the policies and pedagogical environments that they are involved with to consider how the particular needs and challenges of their learners are being addressed.

Women of colour, lesbians, poor women and other women in minority positions have multiple challenges in attaining equity and recognition. For example, in developing civil society, feminists have often had to struggle to have issues pertaining particularly to women included on the agenda for social change. In her examination of the development of civil society in Latin America's southern cone countries (Argentina, Chile and Uruguay), Jaqueline Pitenguy (2002: 807) points out that feminists "had to struggle simultaneously to re-establish democracy and to widen the democratic agenda beyond classical civil and political rights to include gender inequality as a central democratic theme." Similarly, Bannerji *et al.* (2001: 21) note that

> women in anti-colonial nationalist movements also occupied subject positions that were multiply determined by notions and practices of gender, class, racism, and ethnicization. As potential citizens of emerging nations, they possessed plausible claims to political, legal and social equality with men. As women in patriarchal and class-based societies, however, they were often legally defined as the property of husbands and fathers.

Minority women face multiple barriers that hinder full democratic participation, barriers that are often played out in more subtle ways in different learning contexts. Educators need to acknowledge and address these concerns if they are to create what bell hooks (2003) calls a "teaching community." hooks recognizes that educators can never promise a completely safe learning environment, but she argues that creating a space where people can genuinely participate, listen and learn from one another can provide a constructive place where important learning can occur.

IMPLICATIONS FOR POLICY, PEDAGOGY AND PRACTICE

Democracy can either be fostered or stifled in different educational contexts. Critical and feminist educators recognize the need to continually reflect upon their own teaching practices. Brookfield (1995: 25) states that "in our classrooms, students learn democratic or manipulative behaviour. They learn whether independence of thought is really valued or whether everything depends on pleasing the teacher." A democratic learning space is one that is characterized by open, dialogical relationships. Fraser (2003: 44) explains the complicated and intertwined demands of creating dialogical opportunities for learning:

> Fair democratic deliberation concerning the merits of recognition claims requires parity of participation for all actual and possible deliberators. That in turn requires just distribution and reciprocal recognition. This circularity . . . faithfully expresses the reflexive character of justice as understood from the democratic perspective.

To address concerns of both redistribution and recognition, educational policies, institutional structures, and underlying values that shape educational practices have to be carefully examined. For example, although women's participation in higher education has increased dramatically over the past few decades, women still only comprise a third of all doctoral students. They are less likely to be in higher ranking, tenured positions in universities (Stalker and Prentice 1998, Hannah 2002). Women are still more likely to be primary caregivers for children and other family members, which disadvantages them as they move up the increasingly competitive ranks in universities. Issues of redistribution need to be taken up to address this—such as the lesser financial support and time constraints that women experience because of domestic obligations. In addition, there are issues of recognition to consider. Women's lives do not mirror men's, and the differences in their experiences should be valued so that they are not perceived as being "deficient." There needs to be greater respect for the contributions that women make to society through unpaid labour, which is still devalued.

Some policies in higher education are beginning to address these concerns. For instance, SSHRC (Social Science and Humanities Research Council) scholarship applications allow applicants to explain extenuating circumstances if there has been a break in their career trajectory, such as taking time out for caregiving activities. In my current SSHRC research study, women point out changes in higher education that have made learning opportunities more accessible, such as having opportunities to take courses on-line. However, there is still a need for more comprehensive changes to be made to create more equitable opportunities for women. Many doctoral programs still require full-time residency for a period of a year or longer. There are few funding opportunities for women who opt to take their degree part-time. Childcare on campus is often set up for full-time care during the daytime, while many courses are offered in the evenings.

A critical feminist framework for understanding active citizenship and lifelong learning raises many questions about our taken for granted assumptions around fairness, equity and justice. It challenges educators to be critical of the overarching influence of the marketplace on educational endeavours, and to think about the gendered nature of all aspects of life.

For instance, when Perkins et al. (2004: 8) discuss the concept of the "Third Way," they explain that advocates of this approach state that there should be "no rights without responsibilities." From a critical feminist framework I have to ask, what does this mean? If there are to be no rights unless you fulfill your obligations and responsibilities, how are the unpaid labour contributions, done primarily by women, taken into account? As Hart (1997) notes in her research on poor black women in the U.S. inner city, the time and energy that these women spend on raising their children is not valued or considered as work. With regards to the notion of responsibility, it does not seem to suggest that everyone will be engaged in labour that is conducted in an ecologically and environmentally sustainable fashion. Nor does it imply that men should be equally responsible for caregiving activities by taking time from their paid work careers to be involved in raising children and caring for the sick, disabled or elderly members of our population. If the notion of responsibility is defined within a masculine, market-oriented framework, then women will increasingly be disenfranchised as citizens.

A critical feminist framework points out that in any critical analysis of citizenship or civil society movements, there has to be a recognition that power is mediated through our societies in complex and interlocking ways. Our understanding of how societies are structured and therefore, how they can be changed, is limited if we leave out considerations around gender (as well as race, ability, age and other social/structural factors).

By bringing a feminist lens to critical perspectives in lifelong education, we gain insights into the different values that motivate social action. For instance, in previous work (Gouthro 2000) I examine how women's participation in civil society movements often emerges from their caregiving roles i.e. mothers who take on multinational corporations because of their concerns that toxic waste dumped in their community is impacting detrimentally on their (and their family's) health. One of the reasons I was motivated to apply for my current CCL grant is that I believe it is important to celebrate the unique ways that women have contributed to the evolution of active citizenship. For instance, in Canada there is a group of older women activists named the "Raging Grannies." Roy (2004) details how this social movement emerged as an eclectic group of women who came together to challenge the government on allowing nuclear submarines to land within the port of Victoria (on the western coast of Canada). These women use humour and wit to critique what they perceive to be unjust government policies, and to advocate for social change. For example, Roy (2004: 11) cites one of their poems:

The bad old days

Refrain: We're the women who did the work, So men could get the credit.
We said "Leave it to us," And wished we'd never said it.
No, I don't mind staying late, I'll type another stencil
Can I bring you coffee now? Let me sharpen your pencil
I'm sorry the baby cried, I'm sorry that she wet you
I'm sorry she threw up on you, I'm sorry she upset you.
Politics was not for us, We left that to our spouses
But now we know a women's place, In Parliamentary Houses.
. . .

We're prepared to work, But we want more than credit
Equal pay for equal Work, We'll sing until we get it.

When taking a global perspective on active citizenship, a critical feminist perspective encourages educators to conceptualize citizenship in a broader and more inclusive way. For instance, the notion of global citizenship could push people to think beyond the narrow parameters of their own nation-state, to realize that issues such as environmental sustainability and just labour practices are the responsibility of all people. In principle, everyone, including displaced refugees, should be able to access basic citizenship rights—so how can this difficult mandate be carried out?

Deliberative democracy suggests that there is a need to work towards developing a more active and engaged citizenship. Through dialogue, raising awareness of social issues, and encouraging participation by citizens in informing the development of social policies and practices, learners can be motivated to work towards social change. As educators, we must reflect upon the challenges of creating the capacity for our learners to engage proactively as citizens, taking into account the power differentials that still impact on women with regards to how we take up notions of citizenship.

Ultimately, Nancy Fraser (1995: 46) questions:

> Should the roles of worker, childrearer, citizen and client be fully degendered? Can they be? Or do we, rather, require arrangements that permit women to be workers and citizens as *women*, just as men have always been workers and citizens as *men*?

There are still many concerns that need to be addressed to create equitable and inclusive opportunities for women to participate as active citizens and in lifelong learning contexts. The current trend to support an individualistic and market oriented approach towards learning needs to be challenged by critical and feminist educators in order to create more democratic opportunities for women to engage fully in a learning society.

REFERENCES

Bannerji, H., Mojab, S. and Whitehead, J. (2001). *Of Property and Propriety: The Role of Gender and Class in Imperialism and Nationalism.* (Toronto, ON: University of Toronto Press).

Bird, E. (1999). Lifelines and Life Lines: Retraining for Women Returning to Higher Level Occupations—Policy and Practice in the UK. *International Journal of Lifelong Education,* 18(2), 203–216.

Beck, U. (1992). *Risk Society: Towards a New Modernity*. (M. Ritter, Trans.) (London: Sage Publications).

Brookfield, S. (1995). *Becoming a Critically Reflective Teacher*. (San Francisco, CA: Jossey-Bass).

Budig, M. J. and England, P. (2001). The Wage Penalty for Motherhood. *American Sociological Review, 66*, 204–215.

Crittenden, A. (2001). *The Price of Motherhood: Why the Most Important Job in the World Is Still the Least Valued*. (New York: Henry Holt & Co.).

Edwards, R. (1997). *Changing Places? Flexibility, Lifelong Learning, and a Learning Society*. (London: Routledge).

Elliott, J. (2000). The Challenge of Lifelong Learning as a Means of Extending Citizenship for Women. *International Journal of Lifelong Education, 32*(1), 6–21.

Faure, E., Herrera, F., Kaddoura, A. R., Lopes, H., Petrovsky, A. V., Rahnma, M. and Ward, F. C. (1972). *Learning to Be: The World of Education Today and Tomorrow*. (France: UNESCO).

Fraser, N. (1995). What's Critical About Critical Theory? In J. Meehan (ed.), *Feminists Read Habermas: Gendering the Subject of Discourse*. (New York: Routledge), pp. 21–56.

Fraser, N. (2003). Social Justice in the Age of Identity Politics: Redistribution, Recognition, and Participation. In N. Fraser and A. Honneth (eds.), *Redistribution or Recognition? A Political-Philosophical Exchange*. (London: Verso), pp. 7–109.

Giddens, A. (1998). *The Third Way: The Renewal of Social Democracy*. (Cambridge: Polity Press).

Gorard, S., Reeves, G. and Fevre, R. (1999). Two Dimensions of Time: The Changing Social Context of Lifelong Learning. *Studies in the Education of Adults, 31*(1), 35–48.

Gouthro, P. A. (2000). Globalization, Civil Society, and the Homeplace. *Convergence, XXXIII*, 1–2, 57–77.

Gouthro, P. A. (2002a). Education for Sale: At What Cost? Lifelong Learning and the Marketplace. *International Journal of Lifelong Learning, 21*(4), 334–346.

Gouthro, P. A. (2002b). What Counts? Examining Academic Values and Women's Life Experiences From a Critical Feminist Perspective. *Canadian Journal for Studies in Adult Education, 16*(1), 1–19.

Gouthro, P. A. (2005). A Critical Feminist Analysis of the Homeplace as Learning Site: Expanding the Discourse of Lifelong Learning to Consider Adult Women Learners. *International Journal of Lifelong Education, 24*(1), 5–19.

Gutmann, A. and Thompson, D. (2004). *Why Deliberative Democracy?*. (Princeton, NJ: Princeton University Press).

Habermas, J. (1987). *The Theory of Communicative Action: Volume Two Lifeworld and System: A Critique of Functionalist Reason*. (T. Mccarthy, Trans.) (Boston, MA: Beacon Press).

Habermas, J. (2001). *Between Facts and Norms: Contributions to a Discourse Theory of Law and Democracy*. (W. REHG, Trans.) (Cambridge, MA: MIT Press).

Hannah, E. (2002). *Women in the Canadian Academic Tundra: Challenging the Chill.* (Montreal, QC: McGill-Queens University Press).

Hart, M. (1997). Life-Affirming Work, Raising Children, and Education. *Convergence, XXX*(2/3), 128–135.

Hayes, E. R. and Smith, L. (1994). Women in Adult Education: An Analysis of Perspectives in Major Journals. *Adult Education Quarterly,* 44(4), 201–221.

hooks, B. (2003). *Teaching Community: A Pedagogy of Hope.* (New York: Routledge).

Jackson, S. (2003). Lifelong Earning: Working-Class Women and Lifelong Learning. *Gender and Education,* 15(4), 365–377.

Johnston, R. (1999). Adult Learning for Citizenship: Towards a Reconstruction of the Social Purpose Tradition. *International Journal of Lifelong Education,* 18(3), 175–190.

Laczo, M. (2003) Deprived of an Individual Identity: Citizenship and Women in Nepal. *Gender and Development.* 11(3), 76–82.

Landes, J. B. (1995). The Public and the Private Sphere. In J. Meehan (ed.), *Feminists Read Habermas: Gendering the Subject of Discourse.* (New York: Routledge), pp. 91–116.

Lister, R. (2003). Investing in the Citizen-workers of the Future: Transformations in Citizenship and the State under New Labour. *Social Policy and Administration,* 37(5), 427–443.

Locke, J. (1690). *The Second Treatise of Civil Government.*

Martin, I. (2003). Adult Education, Lifelong Learning and Citizenship: Some Ifs and Buts. *International Journal of Lifelong Education.* 22(6), 566–579.

Methven, P.J.B. and Hansen, J. J. (1997). Half a Revolution: A Brief Survey of Lifelong Learning in New Zealand. In M. J. Hatton (ed.), *Lifelong Learning: Policies, Practices, and Programs.* (Toronto, ON: School of Media Studies), pp 2–17.

Perkins, D., Nelms, L. and Smyth, P. (2004). Beyond Neo-Liberalism: The Social Investment State? *Social Policy Working Paper No. 3.* Available online at: http://www.bsl.org.au /pdfs/beyong_neoliberalism_social_socialinvestment_state.pdf The Centre for Public Policy (accessed 20 January 2006).

Pitanguy, J. (2002). Bridging the Local and the Global: Feminism in Brazil and the International Human Rights Agenda. *Social Research,* 69(3), 805–820.

Preece, J. (2002). Feminist Perspectives on the Learning of Citizenship and Governance. *Compare,* 32(1), 21–33.

Roy, C. (2004). *The Raging Grannies: Wild Hat, Cheeky Songs, and Witty Actions for a Better World.* (Montreal, QC: Black Rose Books).

Russell, B. (1996, c. 1946). *History of Western Philosophy.* (London: Routledge).

Selwyn, N. and Gorard, S. (2003). Reality Bytes: Examining the Rhetoric of Widening Educational Participation via ICT. *British Journal of Educational Technology,* 34(2), 169–181.

Stalker, J. and Prentice, S. (1998). (eds.) *The Illusion of Inclusion: Women in Post-Secondary Education.* (Halifax, Nova Scotia: Fernwood).

Stromquist, N. P. (2006). Women's Right to Adult Education as a Means to Citizenship. *International Journal of Educational Development,* 26(2), 140–152.

Welton, M. (2001). Civil Society and the Public Sphere: Habermas's Recent Learning Theory. *Studies in the Education of Adults,* 33(1), 20–34.

Welton, M. R. (1998). Educating for a Deliberative Democracy. In S. M. Scott, B. Spencer and A. M. Thomas (eds.), *Learning for Life: Canadian Readings in Adult Education* (Toronto, ON: Thompson Educational), pp. 365–372.

ADULT EDUCATION'S CONSTITUENCIES AND PROGRAM AREAS: COMPETING INTERESTS?

I t is not our intention in this part of the book on constituencies and program areas to provide a comprehensive examination of the various program areas and practices that characterize the current field of adult education. There is much better coverage of program areas in the 2010 *Handbook of Adult and Continuing Education*. Rather, we offer a selection of readings that touch on a sample of constituencies, program areas, and issues. These readings are provocative and cause us to ponder some of the questions with regard to the *practice* of adult education, especially in times when many learners, particularly those on the margins, are questioning the meaning and value of education in their lives. To that end, the six selections in Part Three address two issues: social class and poverty; three program areas: human resource development, health education, and organizational learning communities; and practice in terms of Cervero and Wilson's well-known program planning model, which speaks to the complexity of dealing with a spectrum of learners and their needs.

In Chapter 14 on social class and adult education, Nesbit traces the development of the concept of *class* and how this concept has changed over the years. Class is very much tied to economics with Marx's famous two-class system of owners of the means of production (the bourgeoisie) and workers (the proletariat). Nowadays we talk about upper, middle, and lower class and perhaps an "underclass" of the most poor. While Americans pride themselves on not attending to class, most still claim to be "middle class." Nesbit links class to education and adult education, which he points out, is a middle-class endeavor. Not only do most programs reflect middle-class values and culture, upper- and middle-class adults are twice as likely to engage in learning activities than working-class adults.

Intersecting with economics and social class is poverty. In Chapter 15, van der Veen and Preece explore the linkages between poverty and adult education from a global perspective. Citing the United Nations' Millennium Development Goal of reducing by half the people living in extreme poverty by 2015, they point out that 70% of the poor are women and 75% of those with disabilities live in developing countries. As formal educational systems are hampered by state regulations, they recommend more informal and nonformal adult education in the areas of literacy and basic education, agricultural extension, vocational training, and community development training to deal with extreme poverty.

Of the program-specific readings in this part, Daley's Chapter 16 on health promotion is most clearly responsive to social and community needs. In fact she points out that according to UNESCO, health is a "social construct: it is created in the interaction between people and their environments in the process of everyday life." Daley first traces the different roots of health promotion (health education and public health) and adult education, then makes a case for aligning the two fields more closely for their mutual benefit. She then discusses three specific strategies—program planning, teaching and learning, and research—that can foster collaboration between the two fields to everyone's benefit.

A major area of practice for educators of adults is at the work setting. Human resource development (HRD) historically has three emphases—training of workers, career development, and organizational development. HRD has become so big that some consider it a separate field of its own; we include it here however, as HRD is first and foremost about adult learning that is embedded in work. In Chapter 17, Bierema critiques the practice of HRD from a feminist perspective. She critically assesses HRD's dominant masculine rationality and performative outlook that privileges management and that marginalizes women HRD practitioners and learners. Bierema concludes that HRD's "skewed focus toward masculine, managerial, and monetary interests results in abandonment of its humanitarian roots."

Learning communities and learning organizations are two other areas of practice for adult educators. Learning communities can be separate stand-alone geographic sites, professional development communities, and even a community within a formal class. Further, an entire organization can decide to become a learning organization. In Chapter 18, Owenby reviews different types of learning networks in organizations and then explores some of the issues of learning communities, what he calls "the dark side." These issues center on who has the power and whose interests are being served. He suggests engaging in critical reflection and action inquiry to deal with these "blind spots" in organizational learning communities.

Chapter 19 is from Cervero and Wilson's book *Working the Planning Table* (2006). Unlike other program planning models which tend to focus on the technical dimensions of assessing needs, developing a program, and evaluating it, their model situates the technical aspects in a social and political context. There are four key "dynamics" that play out in any program planning context: power relations, people's interests, ethical commitments, and negotiation, which is "the central practical action at the table." Their model has changed the way many practitioners approach planning.

In summary, the six selections in Part Three do more than describe some aspect of adult education practice. From the role of social class and poverty, to program areas of health education, HRD, learning communities, and the social and ethical nature of program planning, the selections raise important issues for reflective practitioners to consider. Collectively, the readings remind us of the complexity of adult education as a field of study and practice where competing constituencies, programs, and issues vie for attention and space.

▓ FOR REFLECTION AND DISCUSSION

1. Areas of practice engaged in by adult educators range from teaching people how to read to HRD in global corporations. What are the differences in these two areas of practice in terms of goals and objectives, learners and sociocultural contexts? What do they have in common, if anything?

2. Some adult educators are dismayed that the field of adult education lacks a distinctive identity that is easily communicable to people outside the field. Daley's chapter on health education and adult education is a good example of

this confusion. How can adult education be conceptualized to be recognizable as a distinctive field of practice?

3. Program planning is a core activity for adult educators in all aspects of the field. How does Cervero and Wilson's model account for the realities of program planning across all types of settings?

4. Consider your practice as an adult educator. How do some of the issues raised by the chapters in Part Three intersect with your practice?

CHAPTER 14

Social Class and Adult Education

Tom Nesbit

conomic, social, and cultural factors profoundly influence how we live and what we do. The societies we live in, the relationships we have and create with other people, the ways we accommodate or resist unfairness and oppression, and the ways we choose to think about these phenomena are both limited and enabled by our place in the economic structure of society. Whether we like it or not, at individual, community, and societal levels, everything we believe and everything we do is influenced by our place in an economic and social order. So education, like all other areas of social activity, operates within a set of social, cultural, and economic relations and is shaped by cultural and economic influences (Althusser, 1971; Gramsci, 1971).

Education also shapes how we experience social, cultural, and economic forces. It's through education that we first come to understand the structures of society and the ways that power relations permeate them. Educational systems are thus one of the most important vehicles for *hegemony,* the process by which a society inculcates and maintains dominant ideas by portraying them as natural and normal. Because of this, groups and individuals regularly use the systems, institutions, policies, approaches, and practices of education to perpetuate positions of privilege and power. Two ways to do this are to favor technical rather than emancipatory knowledge and skills (Habermas, 1972) and to socialize people into accepting particular economic systems and cultural traditions. In doing so, dominant groups reproduce existing patterns of social relations and reinforce unequal distribution of power and privilege. Ironically, the education system also legitimates its role in social reproduction by deflecting attention away from the process. However, education can also counter hegemony by helping people understand how they might resist and challenge social structures and by suggesting ways to do so.

These relations establish the environments in which adult educators work. As Habermas (1972) also indicated, adult education is a moral and political endeavor as much as it is a technical practice, and it is thus affected by its role in maintaining or challenging the social order. Do adult education policies and practices reproduce existing relations of dominance and oppression? Alternatively, do they contribute to social as well as personal change? Answering such questions involves exploring the extent to which adult educators acknowledge notions of class and the related demands of capitalist ideology.

Capitalism seems a far cry from the common situations and interactions of adult educators, yet capitalist ideas are so insidious and pervasive that they affect every aspect of our work. Capitalist societies commodify human activity by subjecting all aspects of peoples' lives and social relations to market requirements. These relations are then normalized and made to seem natural. In capitalist societies, our prestige and status is related to productive ability; society values us by how much we earn. Such basic aspects as where we live, how we earn a living, who our friends are, and what access we have to healthcare and education are all dependent on our ability to produce wealth and other resources. Of course, these attributes are not fixed permanently; because the distribution of resources is unequal, people strive to maintain or enhance their own share. Thus, people's struggle for access to and control of resources is dynamic. Capitalist societies are stratified into *classes,* hierarchies of power and privilege related to the ownership and control of various forms of capital. Capitalist systems of structured inequality continue because society portrays them as normal or inevitable: the system encourages its victims to blame themselves for their failure to be successful. In this way dominant groups are able to maintain the status quo and the hegemony of their own ideas without facing too strong a challenge from those less powerful.

So understanding the relationships between class and educational policies and practices is important to a full appreciation of adult education. In this introductory chapter, I outline these various relationships. I first distinguish some ideas about class and then explore how they inform educational practices in general. Next, in focusing specifically on discussions of class in adult education, I chart the ground for the remaining chapters to explore in greater detail.

▮ WHAT IS CLASS?

Although Aristotle identified the segmenting of society by economic, social, and cultural distinctions, the concept of class is fairly recent. Its present use dates from mid-eighteenth–century France. At that time the *Encylopédistes,* a group of intellectuals who sought to assemble all available knowledge, developed a systematic classification first of plants, animals, minerals, and natural phenomena and then of the social and economic positions of people in society (Seabrook, 2002).

The concept of class later gained wider currency with the industrial revolution and the changes it brought about. By the mid-nineteenth century, Marx was using class as the foundational concept for explaining social organization in terms of understanding the ownership, means, and control of work processes and material wealth (Marx and Engels, [1845] 1970). He claimed that societies consisted of two classes: the bourgeoisie (which owned and controlled the mills, mines, and factories) and the proletariat (workers with little more than their labor power to sell). The relationship between these two classes is essentially unequal, exploitative, and beneficial mainly to the bourgeoisie. Those who own capital reinvest their profits to earn even more; those who don't must sell their ability to work in order to survive. Wealth thus returns to the owners, and workers perpetuate their own dependence. That is, though the working class generates surplus wealth, it does not equally profit from it. Because the bourgeoisie own the means of production and distribution of resources, that class disproportionally appropriates and accumulates wealth.

As modes of production and types of work became more complex, many came to regard the division of society into two opposing classes as overly reductionist and outmoded. Industrial societies shifted from a principally manufacturing basis toward the inclusion of more service- and knowledge-based industries. Forms of work became more elaborate and thus confounded existing notions of class. Intermediate class positions developed, and European societies soon settled into the now more familiar structuring of three classes—upper, middle, and lower, though these are still largely related to occupation and income. Most recently the concept of a fourth class, an underclass, has arisen. This rather unfortunately named group consists of those whom society considers outside of or largely excluded from the established economic order, such as the certifiably insane, the long-term unemployed, drug addicts, recent immigrants, prisoners, and others with certain so-called pathological deficiencies who are significantly dependent upon state welfare (Morris, 1994).

Of course, the explanatory and analytic power of class as a concept relates more to the notion that society is still stratified in ways that link individuals and groups with the economic order of production than it does to the specific number of different classes, their definition, or even the people who form them. So whether there are two, three, four, or even more classes, every division of society by class continues to stigmatize the less well-off and to define them as responsible for their own demise. Class still exists. As in Marx's time, all social life continues to be marked by the struggles and conflicts over access to the generation and distribution of wealth and status.

Not everyone regards class in such materialistic terms. Weber ([1920] 1968), for instance, argued that class is better defined by also including notions of culture, values, politics, and lifestyle. People who fall within the same economic class may nevertheless occupy different social-class positions and have differing opportunities for acquiring work, earning income, developing skills, obtaining education, and owning property. For Weber one's class is based more on these life chances, cultural background, status, and life outside of work than on one's relationship to the ownership and control of the means of production. Rather than see society as a two-class system, Weber posited a system of social stratification of many different classes that sometimes overlap. Classes need not be formally organized along such rigid lines. In other words, people from similar backgrounds need not communicate directly with one another in order to maintain their lifestyle, status, and prestige. In essence, they can act in concert without organizing themselves to do so.

This less-deterministic approach is also visible in the work of Bourdieu, for whom a class is any grouping of individuals sharing similar conditions of existence and tendencies or dispositions (Bourdieu and Passeron, 1977). Equally important as one's location in an economic order is the possession of various forms of capital—economic, cultural, social, or symbolic—that can constellate differently in different societies. Bourdieu's concept of class thus takes into account other stratifying factors, such as gender, race, ethnicity, place of residence, and age. Finally, these class structures are not predetermined or imposed from without but more subtly reproduced. For example, people with like dispositions can discriminate (often unwittingly) against those who have different lifestyles and personal characteristics. Note that both Weber and Bourdieu allow more scope for human agency than did Marx but still regard external class structures as fundamental and quite constant. In other words, class relationships transcend the individuals who occupy the positions: people may move around or stay put, but society is still structured along class-based axes of inequality and exploitation.

These two broad views have shaped the development of the concept of class in European and North American countries. In Europe, throughout the social upheavals of industrialization, older ideas of rank continued to affect definitions of class. The so-called lower orders, the laboring classes, and the middling ranks of society (such as merchants or teachers) existed alongside the aristocracy and the gentry. However, as the stratification of industrial society became less rigid, these definitions settled into the more familiar classification of working, middle, and upper class. Most recently, scholars have recognized that this depiction treats class as essentially static. Although it underlines the fundamentally economic nature of class, such a definition ignores the dynamic and shifting nature of the relationships between those who possess wealth and power and those who do not. Class has now come to be regarded more as a relation that is constantly changing. As British historian Thompson (1968, pp. 9–10) puts it, "class is not a category ... but rather an historical relationship between one group of people and another.... It is defined by men *[sic]* as they live their own history."

North American countries—which, since colonization, have largely developed in response to European feudalism—see themselves as relatively free from such archaic categories as aristocracy and the lower orders. Especially in the United States, one commonly hears that class has ceased to exist or that everyone is middle class. For Zweig (2000, p. 4), class is one of the nation's best kept secrets; any serious discussion of it is "banished from polite company." Instead, the ethics of self-reliance and mobility and the ideologies of individualism, egalitarianism, and meritocratic achievement have been more powerful forces than class solidarity. Nowadays existential rather than social factors tend to influence who Americans think they are. For example, it is far more common for people to define themselves as black, gay, Jewish, Latino, lesbian, or mobility-challenged than to refer to themselves in terms of class.

One of the so-called successes of capitalist ideology has been to reinforce the notion that individual identity is unrelated to such supposedly hidden forces as class. Identity politics (commonly based on individualistic claims of importance) represent the success of this misconception. Identity and other subjective politics (usually less overtly opposed to capitalism) are also more readily comprehensible and therefore more appealing. So even though vast institutionalized social inequalities persist in the United States, the discussion of class remains relatively ignored. Scholars tend to discuss social stratification more in terms of identity, inequality, or status rather than of opposing social classes. Paul Fussell (1992, p. 18) describes class as the "dirty little secret" of the United States, for, when compared with such categories as race or gender, class appears invisible. Of course, it's precisely this invisibility that, when linked with its apparent naturalness, allows an unfair class system to reproduce itself continually. Ironically, even though people might not discuss class much, it still remains a subjectively relevant category in their minds. Studies repeatedly indicate that, when asked, people have little difficulty placing themselves into a class and identifying strongly with it (Beeghley, 2000).

Given these different perspectives and ambiguities about class, examining it can often be difficult. Wright (1979) identifies four major approaches to understanding class: a functional differentiation of positions within a society, groups unified by their common position in a hierarchy of power or authority, groups with different market capacities that result in different life chances, and a shared location in the social organization of production. However, whatever one's orientation, an attention to class and class analysis reveals several general principles. First, a class analysis focuses on materialist concepts regarding the production and reproduction of social life and the importance of human activity in shaping both material subsistence and consciousness. Second, a class analysis highlights the fundamental and dynamic relationships between economic and social structures; the ideologies that frame our world; and the ways we experience, understand, and shape the world. Third, a class analysis suggests that we cannot explain social phenomena by their surface manifestations nor by the ways that individuals experience them but as, instead, representations of external divisions of power. Fourth, a class analysis provides a basis for explaining why people organize themselves into collective forces to resist injustice and exploitation. Finally, for those with a commitment to social justice, a focus on class also raises several important questions: How do we negotiate or internalize dominant ideologies and relations of ruling? How might alternative ones develop? How can marginalized people, silenced by social, economic, and cultural relations of power, recover their voices and the right to be heard? Because we can address these questions educationally, I now turn to exploring the relationships between class and education.

CLASS AND EDUCATION

Education is meant to inculcate dominant values, not confront them. Because educational institutions are generally a middle-class domain, their policies and practices are weighted strongly in favor of middle-class values. So capitalist societies, in which class operates as the primary structuring of social inequality, usually ignore or bury class perspectives. As such, many adult educators are uncertain about how their work reflects underlying political structures, let alone economic systems. Observing the effects of power and privilege is far easier than determining their causes. Yet a number of studies explore how education reproduces existing patterns of power. Economists Bowles and Gintis (1976) demonstrated how educational systems are part of a system of broader capitalist class relations. Their correspondence theory explains how, in general, schools reproduce the social relations that capitalist production requires. As Bowles and Gintis describe, capital requires two things: workers of specific types and relative social stability and ideological acceptance of class relations. The capitalist class thus has a broadly shared set of interests pertaining to educational systems and the capacity to promote such interests.

Some find the correspondence theory too mechanistic or reductive; it allows little agency for those involved. One less-deterministic approach came from Bourdieu (Bourdieu and Passeron, 1977) who suggested that education serves the interests of the privileged by structuring learners' access to and uses of various forms of social and cultural capital. Others have introduced notions of struggle and resistance into this process. Most notably, Willis (1977) showed how several working-class teenage lads consciously resisted and rebelled against school and classroom authority. Tellingly, however, this resistance worked better within school than outside it: when the lads left school, they remained unable to find anything but unskilled and unstimulating jobs. The work of McLaren (1995) and Apple (1996) also shows how individuals can resist and contest social and cultural oppression in educational settings. They document the complex relationships between cultural reproduction and economic reproduction and explore how class interrelates with the dynamics of race and gender in education.

All these studies indicate the essential role of education in promoting and maintaining the social relations required for capitalist production. Further, they suggest that we can fully understand education only as part of a broader capitalist class system. Although we now recognize that the relationships between educational practices and political structures are much more complex than correspondence theory suggests, adult educators who work in such areas as Adult Basic Education, literacy, vocational education, and the pernicious welfare-to-work programs will recognize how often their work, the policies about it, and the textbooks and curricula they use are still much more closely tied to employers' needs than to their adult or working-class students' interests (D'Amico, 2004; Kincheloe, 1999; Livingstone, 1999; Rose, 1989).

▪ FOCUSING ON ADULT EDUCATION

Adult education is not divorced from these trends. Together with K–12 and higher education counterparts, it is now firmly established as central to the smooth functioning of economic systems and societies. As such concepts as lifelong learning and the knowledge society gain prominence, education and training become key vehicles for preparing people to be adaptable to economic changes in society. Even though the aim of adult education is generally to ameliorate the social disadvantages that class and background produce, nowadays adult education often serves to exacerbate those disadvantages.

Despite this, scholars have left social class and its effects relatively underexplored, especially in North American adult education. For example, although ideas of class clearly inform several of the contributions to the two most recent editions of the *Handbook of Adult and Continuing Education* (Merriam and Cunningham, 1989; Wilson and Hayes, 2001), overall, the handbooks treat the topic only tangentially. Further, when we compare studies of class with the related analytic vectors of gender and race, we see that scholars do not explore class so rigorously. Recent ERIC searches combining the descriptors *adult education* with *gender, race,* and *social class* produce totals of 531, 322, and 85 hits, respectively. Assuming that the number of ERIC references roughly correlates with researchers' interests, why do researchers acknowledge class so significantly less than its counterparts? Why is class so underrepresented in social and educational theory? Why is it ignored as the elephant in the room (hooks, 2000)?

Of course, some adult educators have addressed issues of class more overtly. Most of the North American studies contained in the ERIC database focus on the consequences or experiences of class and explore such issues as the participation, access, and attainment of different groups. In documenting how social class affects participation in adult education programs, those studies consistently underscore how far social class remains a key determinant of adult participation in organized learning. To give just one recent example, Sargent and Aldridge (2002) indicate that upper- or middle-class adults are twice as likely to engage in some sort of learning activity than are those from the working class.

However, although they detail that class is a major factor affecting adult education participation, most studies in the ERIC database do not really explore how class works. From a conceptual perspective, they add little to London's classic study (London, Wenkert, and Hagstrom, 1963, p. 3), which explored the important contribution that adult education makes to larger society, specifically for those deemed "less educated and less skilled." London and his colleagues found a strong connection between social class and people's abilities to prosper in a rapidly changing world. Class not only affected participation in adult education activities but also was closely related to such other facets of social life as jobs, vocations, and leisure pursuits. Anticipating the subsequent debates about lifelong learning, London's report called for adult education and training to "become a continuing part of everyone's life" (p. 148), providing "both education for work and education for leisure" (p. 153).

This concentration on the results rather than the causes of class is perhaps understandable. Individuals tend to internalize the conflicts within hierarchical systems, especially those individuals without much power. Also, people usually closely experience class at the same time as other, more recognizable forms of oppression. These factors, when combined with the scarcity of class scrutiny, ensure that people do not always have readily available concepts to identify—let alone analyze—the class aspects of their experiences. So scholars continue to overlook class in the theoretical lexicon.

Thankfully, some adult educators have taken up the challenge of making class more explicit. In recent years North American scholars Collins (1998), Livingstone (1999), Sawchuk (2003), Schied (1993), and Welton (1995) have each provided sophisticated and complex analyses of class by examining the dynamic relationships between it and the associated practices, policies, and discourses of adult education. Elaborate explorations of class and adult education are more prevalent abroad. In addition to the authors of the following chapters, Allman (2001), Freire (1985), Stromquist (1997), Thompson (2000), Westwood and Thomas (1991), and Youngman (2000) all provide rich empirical and theoretical studies that tie adult education practices to class and the increasingly globalized nature of capitalism. Discussions of adult education and social class are also available outside of the traditional adult education literature; the concluding chapter of this sourcebook suggests some further examples and provides a more extensive reading list. Finally, because the authors of subsequent chapters come from different geographic areas and foci of interest, their reference lists also contribute to a comprehensive resource for further study.

▨ SUMMARY

Although social class is rarely evident in adult education discourse, no one should doubt its existence. All adults know that life chances and social opportunities differ greatly. Some are born into illiterate families; others into households fit around shift work, seasonal employment, or poverty. Others are raised with enough money, mobility, and access to feel encouraged and engaged. Economic sufficiency deeply affects all manner of human experience. And access to education remains the best hope for most adult learners, regardless of class, to secure economic stability and become more fully engaged citizens—a concern that lies at the heart of most adult education policies and practices. Because of this and specifically because of the general lack of awareness of class issues, adult educators should strive to find ways to discuss it. Regardless of individual political orientation, all adult educators need to find ways to link individual experiences with their social causes. Such persistent examination can help develop what some have called a sociological imagination—the ability to see the connection between the immediate, individual experience and societal, complex structures (Mills, 1967). In capitalist societies this means understanding the power and reach of social class. Though we commonly hear that class has largely disappeared, continuing to accentuate it helps us resist and challenge what Allman (2001, p. 209) has called the postmodern condition: "skepticism, uncertainty, fragmentation, nihilism, and incoherence." It can also provide an antidote to the social amnesia, self-absorption, and apolitical theorizing that pervades much of current adult education discourse.

REFERENCES

Allman, P. *Critical Education Against Global Capitalism. Karl Marx and Revolutionary Critical Education.* New York: Bergin & Garvey, 2001.

Althusser, L. "Ideology and Ideological State Apparatuses." In B. Brewster (ed.), *Lenin and Philosophy.* London: New Left Books, 1971.

Apple, M. W. *Cultural Politics and Education.* New York: Teachers College Press, 1996.

Beeghley, E. L. *The Structure of Social Stratification in the United States.* Needham Heights, Mass.: Allyn & Bacon, 2000.

Bourdieu, P., and Passeron, J. C. *Reproduction in Education, Society, and Culture.* Thousand Oaks, Calif.: Sage, 1977.

Bowles, S., and Gintis, H. *Schooling in Capitalist America.* New York: Basic Books, 1976.

Collins, M. *Critical Crosscurrents in Education.* Malabar, Fla.: Krieger, 1998.

D'Amico, D. "Race, Class, Gender, and Sexual Orientation in Adult Literacy: Power, Pedagogy, and Programs." In J. Comings, B. Garner, and C. Smith (eds.), *Review of Adult Learning and Literacy*, vol. 4: *Connecting Research, Policy, and Practice.* Hillsdale, N.J.: Erlbaum, 2004.

Freire, P. *The Politics of Education: Culture, Power, and Education.* New York: Bergin & Garvey, 1985.

Fussell, P. *Class: A Guide Through the American Status System*. New York: Touchstone, 1992.

Gramsci, A. *Selections from the Prison Notebooks*. (Q. Hoare and G. N. Smith, trans. and ed.) New York: International, 1971.

Habermas, J. *Knowledge and Human Interests*. Portsmouth, N.H.: Heinemann, 1972.

hooks, b. *Where We Stand: Class Matters*. New York: Routledge, 2000.

Kincheloe, J. L. *How Do We Tell the Workers? The Socioeconomic Foundations of Work and Vocational Education*. Boulder, Colo.: Westview Press, 1999.

Livingstone, D. W. *The Education-Jobs Gap*. Boulder, Colo.: Westview Press, 1999.

London, J., Wenkert, R., and Hagstrom, W. O. *Adult Education and Social Class*. Berkeley: University of California, Berkeley Survey Research Center, 1963.

Marx, K., and Engels, F. *The German Ideology*. (C. J. Arthur, trans. and ed.) London: Lawrence and Wishart, 1970. (Originally published 1845.)

McLaren, P. L. *Critical Pedagogy and Predatory Culture*. New York: Routledge, 1995.

Merriam, S. B., and Cunningham, P. M. (eds.). *Handbook of Adult and Continuing Education*. San Francisco: Jossey-Bass, 1989.

Mills, C. W. *The Sociological Imagination*. New York: Oxford University Press, 1967.

Morris, L. *Dangerous Classes: The Underclass and Social Citizenship*. London: Routledge, 1994.

Rose, M. *Lives on the Boundary: The Struggles and Achievements of America's Underprepared*. New York: Free Press, 1989.

Sargent, N., and Aldridge, F. *Adult Learning and Social Division*. Leicester, England: National Institute of Adult Continuing Education, 2002.

Sawchuk, P. H. *Adult Learning and Technology in Working-Class Life*. New York: Cambridge University Press, 2003.

Schied, F. M. *Learning in Social Context*. DeKalb, Ill.: LEPS Press, 1993.

Seabrook, J. *The No-Nonsense Guide to Class, Caste and Hierarchies*. Oxford: New Internationalist Publications, 2002.

Stromquist, N. P. *Literacy for Citizenship*. Albany, N.Y.: SUNY Press, 1997.

Thompson, E. P. *The Making of the English Working Class*. Oxford: Oxford University Press, 1968.

Thompson, J. *Women, Class and Education*. New York: Routledge, 2000.

Weber, M. *Economy and Society: An Outline of Interpretive Sociology*. (G. Roth and C. Wittich, eds.; E. Fischoff, trans.) New York: Bedminster Press, 1968. (Originally published 1920.)

Welton, M. R. *In Defense of the Lifeworld: Critical Perspectives on Adult Learning*. Albany, N.Y.: SUNY Press, 1995.

Westwood, S., and Thomas, J. E. (eds.) *Radical Agendas? The Politics of Adult Education*. London: National Institute of Adult Continuing Education, 1991.

Willis, P. *Learning to Labour: How Working-Class Kids Get Working-Class Jobs*. Farnborough, England: Saxon House, 1977.

Wilson, A. L., and Hayes, E. R. (eds.). *Handbook of Adult and Continuing Education* (New Edition). San Francisco: Jossey-Bass, 2001.

Wright, E. O. *Class Structure and Income Determination*. San Diego, Calif.: Academic Press, 1979.

Youngman, F. *The Political Economy of Adult Education*. London: Zed Books, 2000.

Zweig, M. *The Working-Class Majority*. Ithaca: Cornell University Press, 2000.

CHAPTER 15

Poverty Reduction and Adult Education

Beyond Basic Education

Ruud van der Veen and Julia Preece

While global wealth has increased during previous decades, poverty persists. One of the Millennium Development Goals declared by the United Nations in 2000 was to reduce by half the population of people living in extreme poverty, by 2015. In order to focus donor support, all low-income countries are now required to submit Poverty Reduction Strategy Papers (PRSPs). Adult education has not featured significantly in these papers, and not all national governments implement the recommended 6% of education budgets for adult education.

The trend in adult education policies (where they exist at all) has been to focus on literacy or basic education. Research has shown, however, that basic literacy skills are not in themselves sufficient to make a significant impact on poverty reduction, though they do help (Raditloaneng 2004). Adult education is potentially much more than literacy or basic education. Successful adult education includes also agricultural extension, vocational education, community development and training for active citizenship. Moreover, our central argument will be that developing countries not only need a more extended system for adult education, but also a more flexible and more targeted system than the rather traditional practices of most developing countries.

Within the constraints of a short article we can only touch on each form of adult education briefly. Moreover, the literature of adult education practices to alleviate poverty is mainly a description of cases of best practice. These cases demonstrate some important strengths and weaknesses of the current adult education practice to reduce poverty but much more solid research is needed.

Before we can develop this main argument further, we have to focus for a moment on the notions of poverty, poverty reduction, learning and adult education.

POVERTY REDUCTION

Poverty

The most common method to measure poverty is to define a poverty line, based on either statistical or policy standards, and then to calculate the percentage of a population that has an income below that line. For instance, the World Bank counts the number of people with an income less than $1 a day. The most recent figures (Worldbank Development Indicators 2004) show that between 1981 and 2001, poverty declined from 40% of the population in developing countries to 21%. This is due mainly to the economic growth in eastern Asia (mainly China) and southern Asia (mainly India). But in, for instance, sub-Saharan Africa and some countries in eastern Europe, poverty has increased.

Also rather common are deprivation index approaches, where poverty is not defined in terms of income alone, but also by dimensions like health, employment, housing conditions and human capital. Kaul and Tomaselli-Mochovits (1999) provide such indices for health, nutrition and food supply, and education.

Thirdly, poverty has non-material dimensions, such as discrimination, exploitation, fear, lack of power and shame. Such dimensions are best described in ethnographic research. An outstanding example is the three part series Voices of the Poor, coordinated by Narayan (2002) and based on participatory and qualitative research methods (small group discussions, in-depth interviews, etc.) in 60 countries.

Poverty Reduction

In as far as developing countries focus on education as a poverty reduction strategy, the bulk of their initiatives focus on basic education, including literacy programmes for adults (see section on basic education below). Nevertheless, the main focus of this article is on forms of adult education beyond literacy programmes that can contribute to poverty reduction.

The field of adult education is at the same time a political movement for social justice and a profession. As a political movement, it is divided by different ideologies. Instead of taking a stance for one of these ideologies, we try to cover the whole spectrum by sub-dividing the quest for poverty reduction in three broad strategies:

- The first strategy focuses on the role of the market and how expanding markets can reduce poverty by creating employment, often labelled as neo-liberal strategy (Rodrik 1999). Within such a strategy, two sub-strategies for adult education come to the fore. On the one hand, agricultural extension and, on the other hand, mainly in urban regions, systems for vocational education and training (see section on vocational education below).
- The second strategy focuses on the role of the civil society, NGOs and particularly the local community in creating social capital through self-organization and mutual help. Recently many have started to refer to this strategy as a social capital strategy (Saegert and Thomson 2001; Grootaert and van Bastelaer 2002) (see section on community development below).
- The third strategy for poverty reduction, often labelled as political-economical strategy, focuses on the role of the state in creating and distributing wealth (Fine 2001; Wilenski 2002) (see section on governance below).

Learning and Adult Education

The concept of learning related to poverty reduction strategies refers in the first place to the learning of social systems, such as learning corporate organizations, learning local communities and learning government agencies. Inherently this means that much of the learning we discuss here is informal learning. Coombs and Ahmed (1974: 8) define such informal learning as:

> The life-long process by which every person acquires and accumulates knowledge, skills, attitudes and insights from daily experience and exposure to the environment—at home, at work, at play; from the example and attitudes of family and friends; from travel, reading newspapers and books; or by listening to the radio or viewing films or television.

Adult education covers only part of that much broader informal learning. Learning, as the intended outcome of education, has been defined by Illeris (2002: 13–21) as all processes that lead to relatively lasting changes of capacity, whether it be of a motor, cognitive, emotional, motivational, attitudinal or social character. The heart of the matter is the question of effectiveness of each form of adult education. Under which conditions and to what extent is informal and/or formal education indeed effective? A complicating difficulty is how to measure effectiveness in the context of poverty reduction strategies. This difficulty is closely linked to the problems around defining and measuring poverty itself, as described above. Should effectiveness be measured only in terms of an increasing income after education or do we include other indicators that refer for instance to better health, employment, housing conditions, human and social capital? For the time being, if any research has been done, there is hardly any quantitative research that measures effectiveness; research so far consists of qualitative case studies. To prove that adult education can be effective in poverty reduction much more research is urgently needed.

Basic Education

In 1990 UNESCO started the Education for All programme to promote literacy. *Education for All: Is the World on Track?* (UNESCO 2002: 60–67) reports the following data:

> Past decades saw steady growth of the literate share of the adult world population from roughly 70% in 1980, 75% in 1990 to 80% in 2000. But a closer look tells us that there is slightly slackening pace, so acceleration is needed … In absolute numbers, the gains appear even more modest. In 1980 the world numbered approximately 870 million illiterates. This number grew to 880 million in 1990, as the reduction of illiteracy did not keep pace with population growth. Around 2000 it was down to roughly 860 million…. In 2000, close to two-thirds of all illiterates were female, and the gap is closing exasperatingly slowly…. Sub-Saharan Africa, the Arab states and North Africa, and South and West Asia have come a long way, starting from an adult literacy rate of 40% in 1980…Adult literacy rates in these regions now hardly reach 60%.

Beyond Reading and Writing

Both primary education for children and basic education for adults are potentially more than just learning to read and write. Firstly, there is a tendency to define literacy as functional literacy. Programmes for functional literacy integrate reading and writing skills with other life skills. For instance, the evaluation of the functional adult literacy programme in Uganda includes questions with respect to politics, health, local organizations and so on (Okech et al. 1999: 118–138). Functional literacy is at its best a broad preparation for the modernization tendencies in developing countries.

Secondly, beneath the manifest training of skills there is a latent learning of modernist attitudes. Traditionally, primary education taught children attitudes of obedience and diligence. In modern primary education and even more in basic education for adults there is a shift to facilitation of learning critical communication. A typical example is the literacy method of Paolo Freire. The principles of Freire have influenced many other modern methods for adult basic education. A typical example is the "Reflect" method, developed by ACTIONAID, which combines the principles of Freire with methods of community self-survey as developed in agricultural extension.

Thirdly, adult basic education includes more and more post-literacy courses. A typical example of post-literacy methods is initial and non-formal vocational training. Raditloaneng (2004) mentions in her research in Botswana for instance courses in bee keeping, screen printing and sewing, vegetable gardening, basketry and pottery.

Non-formal Education

Adult education theory makes a distinction between formal and non-formal education. Formal education has to comply with state regulations as a condition for financing and/or certification. Non-formal education is flexible; it adapts its content and methods to the wants of its stakeholders (initiators, teachers, participants). Very often, although not necessarily so, non-formal education is relatively short, for instance courses that last a couple of days or that consist of one session a week during a limited term. In the case of non-formal literacy and post-literacy courses this is a serious disadvantage. Moser (1996: 140), in an Ecuador case study, concludes:

> Despite [an] apparent proliferation of training courses, community members identified a number of problems. Among courses identified as useful, such as the electricity and literacy courses, people complained that the short duration (usually only 3 months) was not sufficient to gain real proficiency.

> Courses run specifically for women, such as dressmaking and crafts, were identified as inappropriate since they rarely resulted in the generation of income.

This does not mean that we plead for a formal "school" system for adult basic education. On the contrary, we support flexible, often non-formal systems of adult education with a high level of self-organization by participants. But that is something different from a cheap inefficient buy-off of legitimate learning needs of participants.

Vocational Education

Traditional Versus Flexible Practices

In urban areas in particular, there is a need for vocational education beyond basic education, both technical education (for instance electronics, metal work) and commercial education (for instance bookkeeping and secretarial work). Unfortunately the existing systems are rather inflexible. For instance, Nwagwu (2004) describes how such a traditional system in Nigeria consists of five different types of vocational schools and colleges and that it takes years to earn a degree. Because of this long duration, these schools are expensive and the state cannot afford to pay specialized staff and up-to-date equipment. Moreover, these schools often train more people for particular vocations than are asked for in the market. In Nigeria this often means that even after having earned a degree, people have to start from scratch in the labour market. Efforts to build a trained working class can also become futile in countries with decreasing incomes. For instance, Owusu (2001) described that in Ghana, even many salaried workers now earn an income below the level that is needed for subsistence, creating a class of working poor.

Gill, Fluitman and Dar argue that instead more flexible practices of Vocational Education and Training (VET) should be developed. These practices are both effective by targeting on those who will most benefit from them and by partnering with private suppliers. In more detail:

- Regardless of the mechanisms through which VET is supplied (public or private, subsidized or unsubsidized private), it is critical that these programs target groups that will most benefit from them.... In most cases VET programs are more expensive than alternatives, such as general education and job search assistance.
- Preoccupied with providing or financing VET, many governments have neglected their roles as providers of information about the availability and effectiveness of vocational programs.
- The experience of our sample countries indicates that when VET policies are designed to encourage rather than to replace the private sector (either private training providers, NGOs, or public-private partnerships) a vigorous private supply response can be forthcoming.... Experience also shows that for shorter courses that led trainees directly to jobs, clear and balanced legislation seems to be even more important than government subsidies.
- Political will, not institutional capacity, is the main obstacle to comprehensive reform of VET systems. (Gill, Fluitman and Dar 2000: 33–35)

Agricultural Extension

About two-thirds of the 1.1 billion people living on less than $1 a day are in rural areas (Worldbank Development Indicators 2004). Environmental degradation continues to deepen poverty and, over time, poor people can become trapped in a downward spiral. Lack of access to resources such as technologies, roads and social services (e.g. health) are exacerbated by market distortions that reduce profits (IFAD 2002). Agricultural extension services to alleviate poverty of farmers could be a solution, but as Narayan reports in her worldwide study *Voices of the Poor* (2000: 49–50):

> Few villages mention agricultural extension services as institutions of local importance. Where they exist, these services are often viewed as unresponsive. Residents in some communes of Ha Tinh Province in Vietnam complain that extension services have to be paid in advance rather than on credit and that the new seeds and pesticides being promoted do not perform as well as traditional crops and husbandry. All the same, they would value better guidance on pest control and training on new agricultural techniques. In Nchimishi, Zambia people say the local extension officer sells very expensive but ineffective drugs to fight tick-borne diseases in their cattle, but "the cattle continues to die."

But as Narayan adds, although people do not value external services much they value their own local organizations. Parthasarathy and Chopde (2000) describe an example of how a rural community in India capitalized on an experimental introduction of a new strain of pigeon pea seeds into the cropping system to make it more sustainable. In the absence of state support for the innovation, local farmers used kinship, community and other informal networks to produce and distribute the seeds. A pigeon pea cultivar had been introduced by a seed corporation to counteract local disease and create resistance to wilt. The cultivar could be utilized without additional technology such as irrigation systems and could be planted at the same time as traditional crops are planted. The company failed to release the seed commercially after trials, but local farmers shared it with friends. After finding success they passed on the news to others, undertaking production and distribution through kin and community networks, resulting in widespread adoption over time. The seed helped to stem production loss, increased yields and improved profits.

ICT

Only recently have some started to argue that lack of access to information and communications technologies (ICT) is an element of poverty. But, as Adeya (2003: 7–9) states, advocates of ICT must first understand the existing information systems of the poor, "how they interact with more formal information and the best way to strengthen them before intervening with new information sources." In Africa, for example, rural communication is largely oral so modern communication channels should take this into consideration. The most frequently quoted example of successful adaptation of technology is the Grameen Bank in Bangladesh. This is now a village-based microfinance organization. Cell phones are rented to villagers who become sellers and buyers of services (Adeya 2003: 19). Cecchini and Shah (2002) cite further examples. In Latin America, Africa and India, even illiterate adults have learned to use icon-based web services. In India there now exists an information-based health-care delivery that empowers health-care workers to provide timely care and information using an icon-based navigation system to cater for the literacy levels of workers.

Community Development

Beyond Communitarianism

In recent years development policy makers have begun to recognize that poverty reduction requires more than economic growth and more than economic skills development (Mitlin 2000; ARTC 2003). The World Bank is also now a proponent of strengthening social capital. Social capital represents the assets that are gained through social networks (Coleman 1994; Putnam 2000). Unfortunately there is a tendency to narrow this renewed interest in the local community towards an ideology of communitarianism, which focuses exclusively on the immediate village or neighbourhood, school and family. Moreover, Cleaver (2002: 4) provides evidence that a narrow interpretation of the concept of social capital also reproduces structural inequalities. She says that social isolation, difficulties in accessing help from relatives, insufficient labour and ineffective coping strategies, influenced by disproportionate burden of disease amongst the poor, often disable people from either building or accessing their social capital. Mayer and Rankin (2002) say that the World Bank, in practice, is only interested in social capital as a resource for financial discipline and peer pressure. So in problem neighbourhoods the function of civil society is simply to mobilize them for entrepreneurship activity, rather than conscientize them. But social capital is nevertheless a potential resource for bridging boundaries between state and civil society, between the middle classes and the poor.

Non-governmental Organisations (NGOs)

NGOs in particular became a popular resource in the 1980s and 1990s as a route to poverty alleviation. NGOs are legally formed autonomous organizations that possess non-profit status and whose primary motivation is to improve the well-being of the people. NGOs view development in terms of a participatory process of capacity building and empowerment of communities to improve their socio-economic well-being (SADC 2002). Nevertheless, Porter (2003: 134) states that a common problem in NGOs is that local understandings about poverty are often overridden by programmes of partnership that erode local confidence in home-grown ideas. NGOs are often forced to satisfy donor demands first, and many NGO programmes work with the relatively better-off. NGOs may also impose their own agendas on the self-help organizations they work with.

In spite of these caveats there are many instances where marginalized social groups and communities have demonstrated success in improving their capability, psychological and material circumstances. For instance, in urban regions, few have access in times of trouble to the social networks of trust and reciprocal relationships that are prevalent in rural communities. Therefore urban agriculture is important to women of low-income households beyond monetary gain. Slater (2001: 647–648) describes an initiative that demonstrates that food gardening can be a refuge also from the emotional and psychological strains of violence and a resource for creating social networks and community development, and raising consciousness.

Some 600 million urban dwellers in the South are living in inadequate housing, with inadequate basic services. Low-income residents are rarely consulted about city improvement plans but NGOs can provide integrated learning programmes that work with communities to collectively reduce water and electricity costs. Mitlin (2000) describes how NGOs assisted squatters to obtain land legally by learning how to negotiate with state or land owners and acquire loan programmes to obtain capital and improve their homes. Similarly with health services, Brehony (2000) describes how an NGO that decided to set up a community-based health-care project used *munnomu kabi* (friend in need) groups already in villages. The natural village organizational structure was used as a starting point to train people to look after the sick at home, using munnomu kabi as a building block for the project.

Target Groups

There are some groups that require specific, targeted support because of their marginality, extreme experiences or minority status, even amongst the poor. Women, even though they represent 50% of the population, still constitute 70% of the world's poorest. Women often suffer, not just from lack of income, but also from lack of access to services and opportunities for human development, lack of voice in political life and decision making, social subordination and exclusion (DFID 2000a). Research has shown the benefits to women's social and economic development if they participate in educational programmes (ADB 2003; USAID 2003). In spite of this evidence, gender was not found to be a cross-cutting issue in any of Millennium Development Goal reports in an analysis of 13 countries. Only five made specific reference to gender inequality as a source of poverty (UNDP 2003).

An even more marginalized face of poverty can be seen amongst people with disabilities. Three out of four people with disabilities live in a developing country and may account for one in five of the world's poorest (DFID 2000b: 2). Only 2% of people with disabilities have access to rehabilitation and appropriate basic services. Disability is both a cause and consequence of poverty. It increases isolation and economic strain since both education and employment are harder to access.

The most frequently cited success stories on this basis have been in India. The Young India Project in Andhra Pradesh (YIP) is an NGO. It has facilitated the formation of self-help groups who can support each other and campaign for their rights. It has also helped people with disabilities to access bank loans and education (DFID 2000b; Seeley 2001). Action on Disability and Development India (ADD-India) is another NGO that works in rural South India and supports savings, credit and income generation for people with disabilities. Its adult education role has been largely informal, through awareness campaigns, employing people with disabilities as consultants and advisors in policy design and implementation for development initiatives (Seeley 2001).

Governance and Active Citizenship

Protagonists of the political-economical strategy advocate a "structural" solution of poverty by creating a welfare state that guarantees the social rights of citizens (Marshall 1992). Nevertheless, socialist experiments, also in underdeveloped countries, demonstrated that this can easily lead to an ineffective bureaucracy that hinders overall economic growth. To overcome this dilemma it is necessary to build states that on the one hand develop a strong social planning but on the other hand are built on the control and participation of citizens. As adult educators, we shall focus below on the second requirement—the participation of citizens in social planning. Below we will briefly discuss four strategies to increase the influence of the poor in social planning.

Democracy

Firstly, in many countries there is an urgent need for a strategy to support truly representative democracy. The United Nations Development Program (UNDP 2002: 15) concludes that progress has been made. Since 1980, 81 countries have taken significant steps toward democracy and 140 of the 200 countries in the world now hold multiparty elections, more than at any time in history. Nevertheless there are in fact only 82, with 57% of the world's people, that are fully democratic.

Civil Society

Secondly, we agree with Wilensky (2002) that strong welfare states are also characterized by strong civil organizations on the national level, which collaborate and negotiate with governments for higher income, better education and social provisions crucial for the poor. Civil organizations include both special interest organizations in the economical domain, like the trade unions, and social-cultural organizations engaged in education and social work, such as the churches. Unfortunately, networks of such civil organizations on the national level are under-developed in many poor countries. For instance, 51 countries have not ratified the International Labour Organization's Convention on Freedom of Association, and 39 have not ratified its Convention on Collective Bargaining (UNDP 2002: 15). As far as adult education is involved in building a civil society, it is often limited to NGOs working on the local level (see section on community development).

Participation

Thirdly, effective social planning is participatory. Not only the failure of the socialist countries but also the crisis in the Western welfare state has demonstrated that national planning has a tendency to become static and therefore ineffective. Mannheim (1940: 369–381) defended 'planning for freedom', in which the goals and broad strategies for planning are set on the national level, but everyday planning is delegated to lower levels of the government. But decentralization is not enough. In fact, local authorities in many developing countries are typically autocratic and inefficient (Narayana et al. 2000 vol. 2: 209–211). For instance, in 1995 Bolivia introduced its Participación Popular policy to counterbalance this tendency to autocratic governance. Although the policy has been successful in delegating responsibilities, such a huge societal learning process of course also causes all sorts of problems in its early years (von Gleich 2000: 126–127).

State Efficiency

Last but not least, there is the huge problem of inefficient state agencies. The Voices of the Poor research project documents the fundamental problems (Narayan et al. 2002 vol. 1: 82–110). Barriers in access to government services include bureaucratic hurdles, incomprehensible rules and regulations, difficulties in accessing necessary information, humiliation of the poor by officials and widespread corruption. For example, India has one of the world's largest programmes of basic services and public assistance for the poor, lower castes and tribal groups; nevertheless it often fails to implement these rights in practice. Adult education should support, and is potentially very effective, by improving the public information.

CONCLUSION

Here we summarize our results in the form of hypotheses to be tested in future research and practice.

With respect to adult education in the economic domain, evidence from the case studies leads to the hypothesis that a more extended and more targeted system for basic education, agricultural extension and vocational training is urgently needed to help people to generate income. In particular, targeting to the real needs of the poor in a collaborative process between all stakeholders, employers, small business and employees is required.

With respect to adult education in the community, evidence from the case studies leads to the hypothesis that the development of social capital can indeed contribute to poverty reduction, both in terms of income and developing trust and reciprocity. But again it is important to target the adult education contribution precisely to the groups most in need, such as women and disabled groups.

With respect to adult education in the political domain, evidence from the case studies leads to the hypothesis that the current dominance of autocratic institutions is highly ineffective. There is an urgent need to develop governance processes, which constitute planning as a learning process involving all stakeholders actively, including organizations acting on behalf of the poor. The contribution of adult education to this much needed transformation of the state includes: (1) better information about the rights of the poor; (2) training of communication skills of the less educated; and (3) raising awareness that participation matters.

REFERENCES

ADB. (2003). *Gender and Development: Gender and development issues in the Asian and Pacific region.* http://www.adb.org

Adeya, C. N. (2003). *ICTs and Poverty: A literature review.* http://network.irdc.ca

Appeal Resource and Training Consortium. (ARTC). (2003). *Income Generating Programmes for Poverty Alleviation Through Non Formal Education: Summary of research studies on innovative approaches to income generating programmes for poverty alleviation.* (Bangkok: UNESCO).

Brehony, E. (2000) Whose practice counts? Experiences in using indigenous health practices from Ethiopia and Uganda. *Development in Practice*, 10(5), 650–662.

Cecchini, S. and Shah, T. (2002). *Information and Communications Technology as a Tool for Empowerment. World Bank Empowerment Source Book: Tools and practices 1.* Available online at: htttp://www.worldbank.org/poverty/empowerment/toolsprac/tool01.pdf

Cleaver, F. (2002). The inequality of social capital: Agency, association and the reproduction of chronic poverty. Paper presented at the Manchester University Conference, Staying Poor: Chronic Poverty and Development Policy, April.

Coleman, J. S. (1994). *Foundations of Social Theory.* (Boston: Harvard University Press).

Coombs, P. and Ahmed, M. (1974). *Attacking Rural Poverty: How nonformal education can help.* (Baltimore: Johns Hopkins University Press).

Department for International Development (DFID). (2000a). *Poverty Elimination and the Empowerment of Women.* (London: DFID).

Department for International Development (DFID). (2000b). *Disability, Poverty and Development.* (London: DFID).

Fine, B. (2001). *Social Capital versus Social Theory, Political Economy and Social Science at the Turn of the Millennium.* (London: Routledge).

Gill, I. S., Fluitman, F. and Dar, A. (eds.). (2000). *Vocational Education and Training Reform, Matching Skills to Markets and Budgets.* (New York: Oxford University Press).

Grootaert, C. and van Bastelaer, T. (eds.). (2002). *The Role of Social Capital in Development: An empirical assessment.* (New York: Cambridge University Press).

Illeris, K. (2002). *The Three Dimensions of Learning: Contemporary learning theory in the tension filed between the cognitive, the emotional and the social.* (Leicester: NIACE).

International Fund For Agricultural Development (IFAD). (2002). *IFAD and NGOS: Dynamic partnerships to fight rural poverty.* (Rome: IFAD).

Kaul, C. and Tomaselli-Mochovits, V. (1999). *Statistical Handbook on Poverty in the Developing World.* (Phoenix: Oryx Press).

Mannheim, K. (1940). *Man and Society: In an age of reconstruction.* (London: Routledge).

Marshall, T. H. (1992). *Citizenship and Social Class.* (London: Pluto Press).

Mayer, M. and Rankin, K. N. (2002). Social capital and (community) development: a north/south perspective. *Antipode*, 34(4), 804–808.

Mitlin, D. (2000). Addressing urban poverty: increasing incomes, reducing costs and securing representation. *Development in Practice*, 10(2), 204–216.

Moser, C. (1996) Urban poverty: how do households adjust? In *Ecuador Poverty Report* (Washington, DC: The World Bank), pp. 111–140.

Narayan, D. and Petesch, P. (eds.). (2002). *Voices of the Poor. Vol. 3. From many lands.* (New York: Oxford University Press).

Narayan, D. and Walton, M. (eds.). (2002). *Voices of the Poor. Vol. 1. Can anyone hear us?* (New York: Oxford University Press).

Narayan, D., Walton, M. and Chambers, R. (eds.). (2002). *Voices of the Poor. Vol. 2. Crying out for change.* (New York: Oxford University Press).

Nwagwu, J. U. (2004). Alleviating poverty through vocational education: The Nigerian experience. Paper presented at the Adult Education and Poverty Reduction Conference, Gabarone.

Okech, A., Carr-Hill, R. A., Katahoire, A. R., Kakooza, T. and Ndidde, A. N. (1999). *Report of Evaluation of the Functional Adult Literacy Programme in Uganda 1999.* (Kampala: Ministry of Gender Labour and Social Development in collaboration with World Bank Mission in Uganda).

Owusu, F. (2001). Urban impoverishment and multiple modes of livelihood in Ghana. *Canadian Geographer, 45*(3), 387.

Parthasarathy, D. and Chopde, V. K. (2000). *Building Social Capital: Collective action, adoption of agricultural innovations, and poverty reduction in the Indian semi-arid tropics.* (International Crops Research Institute for the Semi-Arid Tropics: Mali). http://www.eldis.org

Porter, G. (2003). NGOs and poverty reduction in a globalizing world: perspectives from Ghana. *Progress in Development Studies, 3*(2), 131–145.

Putnam, R. D. (2000). *Bowling Alone: The collapse and revival of American community.* (New York: Simon Schuster).

Raditloaneng, N. (2004). *Post Literacy and Poverty Eradication: Implications for adult education. Adult education and poverty reduction: A global priority.* (Gaborone: Department of Adult Education, University of Botswana).

Rodrik, D. (1999). *New Global Economy and Developing Countries: Making openness work.* (Baltimore: Johns Hopkins University Press).

SADC Council Of Non-Governmental Organizations (SADC-CNGO). (2002). Reducing Poverty in the SADC Region Through Collective Action: The role of NGOs. Paper presented to the SADC Council of Ministers, October.

Saegert, S. and Thomson, J. P. (2001). *Social Capital and Poor Communities.* (New York: Russell Sage Foundation).

Seeley, J. (2001). *Recognising Diversity: Disability and rural livelihoods approaches in India. Natural Resource Perspectives no. 72.* (London: Overseas Development Unit).

Slater, R. J. (2001). Urban agriculture, gender and empowerment: an alternative view. *Development Studies, 18*(5), 635–650.

United Nations Development Programme (UNDP). (2002). *Human Development Report 2002: Deepening democracy in a fragmented world.* (New York: Oxford University Press).

United Nations Development Programme (UNDP). (2003). *Millennium Development Goals: National reports a look through a gender lens.* (New York: UNDP).

United Nations Educational, Cultural And Scientific Organization (UNESCO). (2002). *Education for All: Is the world on track?* (Paris: UNESCO).

USAID. (2003). Girl's and Women's Education Policy Research Activity. (Office of Women in Development, United States Agency for International Development: Washington DC).

von Gleich, A. (2000). Poverty reduction strategies: The experience of Bolivia. In R. Halvorson-Quevedo and H. Schneider (eds.), *Waging the Global War on Poverty: Strategies and case studies.* (Paris: Development Centre OECD), pp. 115–139.

Wilenski, H. L. (2002). *Rich Democracies, Political Economy, Public Policy, and Performance.* (Berkeley: University of California Press).

World Bank. (2003). *Global Economic Prospects and the Developing Countries 2003.* (Washington, DC: World Bank).

World Bank. (2004). *World Bank Development Indicators 2004.* (Washington, DC: World Bank).

CHAPTER 16

Aligning Health Promotion and Adult Education for Healthier Communities

Barbara J. Daley

A dult education and health promotion are two fields that historically have developed along separate tracks. Health promotion has developed within the health care arena, more specifically from the areas of health education and public health, whereas adult education has developed more from education, learning, and psychology. Each has developed a philosophical and theoretical base separate from the other, and yet those philosophies and theories are often complementary. This chapter analyzes the concept of health promotion and discusses how the fields of health promotion and adult education can work together to foster the development of healthy communities.

The field of health promotion has grown and developed over the last two decades and is certainly not without controversy. The controversies in health promotion often relate back to the overall definition of health adopted by specific health promotion programs. The most commonly cited (and at the same time criticized) definition of health comes from the World Health Organization (WHO): a state of complete physical, mental, and social well-being, and not merely the absence of disease or infirmity (WHO, 1946). In this definition, health is viewed as a positive concept when it is defined as a state of well-being; at the same time health is differentiated from the implied negative states of disease and disability. It is helpful, in this definition, for health to be viewed as a multifaceted concept that includes physical, mental, and social aspects. Nevertheless, this definition has been criticized because health is viewed as the absence of disease rather than as a continuum where it can include aspects of long-term changes, successful aging, or differing levels of functioning following a disabling injury. Additionally, the definition has been criticized for its lack of attention to context and its almost exclusive focus on the individual.

Compare the WHO definition of health to the one developed at the fifth international conference on adult education in Hamburg, Germany. At this conference participants stated, "Health is essentially a social construct: it is created in the interaction between people and their environments in the process of everyday life: where people live, love, learn, work, and play" (UNESCO, 1997). In the UNESCO definition, we see that health is viewed as a concept intricately and inevitably intertwined with both the individual and the culture. Health here is viewed as a socially constructed concept whose meanings and interpretations depend on the individual, and his or her biological, mental, social, spiritual, or cultural state. Additionally, health is connected in this definition to the day-to-day living practices of individuals and to the environments in which they find themselves. This definition makes the environment and culture central to understanding the concept of health. These critiques and controversies around the definition of health are important because they often frame philosophies, views, and approaches of subsequent health promotion programs.

HEALTH PROMOTION

Health promotion has grown out of the field of health education, but it tends to be broader and take a more comprehensive view. Health education is often the domain of health care providers who view the education process as simply telling individuals what they need to do to maintain health, regain it, or prevent health problems. The expert knowledge of the health care provider is presented to clients or patients as information to be adopted in their daily lives. The process of health education typically is neglected in favor of the content that is presented to individuals. Traditional approaches to health education tend to focus on assisting individuals in simply acquiring information.

Health promotion, by contrast, tends to be a broader and more encompassing field. UNESCO (1997) has defined it this way: "Health promotion is the process of enabling people to increase control over their health through advocacy and intersectoral action. Health promotion is a dynamic and evolving concept which involves people in the context of their everyday lives, e.g. home, school, workplace, etc., and promotes the achievement of the highest level of physical, mental and social well-being for all" (p. 6).

What we see in this definition is emphasis on process, autonomy, control, advocacy, and action. The intent here is that health promotion deals with more than simply sharing health facts; it is the process whereby individuals and communities control their own health and advocate for solving health-related problems at the individual and community levels.

Downie, Tannahill, and Tannahill (1996) clarify the concept of health promotion even more by defining it this way: "Health promotion comprises efforts to enhance positive health and reduce the risk of ill-health, through the overlapping spheres of health education, prevention, and health protection" (p. 2). From this definition, they have created the model of health promotion diagrammed in Figure 16.1.

In this model, health education focuses on assisting individuals to assess or change knowledge, attitudes, and behaviors (Downie et al., 1996). The health education process here may include helping individuals gain information and

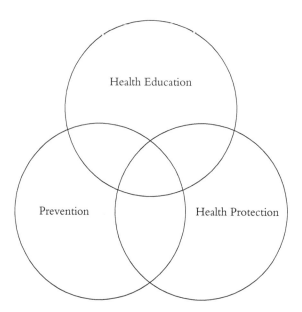

Figure 16.1. A Model of Health Promotion.

Source: Downie, R. S. et al. (1996) *Health promotion: Models and values* (2nd ed.). New York: Oxford University Press, p. 59, Fig. 19.1. Used by permission of Oxford University Press.

clarify values. The process is seen as participatory and recognizes the importance of the sociopolitical factors in health and health education. Additionally, the health education process envisioned by Downie et al. (1996) includes education that is disease-oriented, risk-factor-oriented, and health-oriented.

Prevention, in the Downie et al. model (1996), is viewed as "prevention of the onset or first manifestation of a disease process, or some other first occurrence, through risk reduction" (p. 51). Prevention also includes early detection, prevention of complications, and prevention of recurrence. What is unique about this view of prevention is that it includes illness and disease, as in more traditional models, but it also includes occurrences of other health issues, unwanted states, and unwanted phenomena. So the focus of prevention is much broader and incorporates other life states into the prevention idea.

Health protection, according to Downie et al. (1996), "comprises legal or fiscal controls, other regulations and policies and voluntary codes of practice, aimed at the enhancement of positive health and the prevention of ill-health" (p. 52). Included here, for example, is legislation on drinking and driving, cigarette taxes, environmental protections, and public policies that may impinge on health. These public policies may include such things as poverty, housing, transportation, employment, and safety concerns.

One of the strengths of the health promotion model in Figure 16.1 is the overlapping of the three areas of prevention, health protection, and health education. This overlap strengthens the idea of health promotion and more clearly demonstrates the complexities inherent in the process. For example, a specific health education program may be designed to teach individuals about developing healthy lifestyles, including activities to promote keeping blood pressure low. From a prevention standpoint, health care providers may participate in health screening programs designed to assist in identifying individuals at risk for high blood pressure or those who have high blood pressure and are unaware of it. From a protection standpoint, legislators and policy makers may be lobbied to provide funding for screening and education programs, as well as prescription blood pressure medications. As is seen in this example, the overlap of health education, protection, and prevention leads to a broader, more inclusive program that can include individuals as well as communities.

Health promotion also encompasses a greater focus on healthy communities. The healthy communities movement was initiated in 1986 by the WHO. A foundation of that movement is the Ottawa Charter for Health Promotion (1986), which defines the prerequisites for health as peace, shelter, education, food, income, a stable ecosystem, sustainable resources, social justice, and equity. Wolf (2001) indicates that health promotion within the healthy communities movement can take many forms, including a "focus on reducing specific diseases or promoting specific preventive practices around a wide range of community identified health issues such as asthma, teen pregnancy, or substance abuse. Another set of healthy community initiatives address social problems such as community violence, domestic violence, and child abuse. A vibrant wing of healthy communities initiatives are focused on environmental issues promoting sustainable communities and fighting for environmental justice.... And yet another form of healthy communities focuses on civic engagement" (p. 6).

In reviewing Wolf's examples of healthy communities initiatives, one can see the overlapping aspects of health education, health protection, and prevention identified earlier.

The healthy communities movement has advanced the idea of health promotion by linking health education, prevention, and health protection with strategies and methodologies that community members can access to move forward toward the goal of fostering health promotion. In the United States, for example, the Department of Health and Human Services has created a national health promotion and disease prevention agenda called Healthy People 2010. It includes a focus on prevention of certain diseases but also incorporates broader objectives for developing health at the community level. In addition, specific steps have been created that incorporate the Healthy People 2010 objectives with strategies to create healthy communities. According to Flowers (1993), these steps are "1. Discover just how healthy the community is, 2. Conceive a vision of a healthier community, 3. Work out a way for the whole community to plan together, 4. Create a plan of action, 5. Decide how you will know whether the plan has worked, 6. Grow Partnerships and nurture leadership to carry out the plan, 7. Design specific projects to further the plan, and 8. Commit to improving the life of all members of the community" (para. 1).

The steps outlined by Flowers (1993) have been used in many communities. For example, Healthy Boston, one of the most established community organizations in the United States, completed a community assessment and used the information to create a vision and a plan that included building a coalition of twenty-one neighborhood groups to address issues of substance abuse, violence, economic development, job training, and family support. Because of this effort health fairs, job fairs, candidate forums, voter registration drives, and public forums on community health issues have been held (Flowers, 1996). In another example, citizens from Tillery, North Carolina, organized to address community issues identified in the community assessment. They have recruited physicians to their area; organized transportation; lobbied the state for changes in environmental practices; and volunteered to teach each other literacy, basic health care, healthy eating, and exercise (Flowers, 1996).

In summary, use of the Downie et al. (1996) health promotion model and the steps to developing a health community (Flowers, 1993) are a guide for adult educators on how they can work collaboratively with health education professionals in fostering the development of health communities.

ALIGNING HEALTH PROMOTION AND ADULT EDUCATION

In reviewing the definitions of health, health promotion, and healthy communities given here and the examples cited, one sees that the fields of health promotion and adult education could benefit from closer collaboration and greater alignment. Alignment is used here to mean a process of fine-tuning the fields of adult education and health promotion so they are in coordinated, parallel, and synergistic positions with each other. Aligning the fields of adult education and health promotion means the two fields work together and collaboratively toward the same goal. It means each field brings unique strengths to the process of creating healthy communities and at the same time brings unique contributions. Aligning the two fields does not mean that one takes over or usurps the other; rather, alignment means the fields of health promotion and adult education are moving in the same direction, using unique approaches to obtain the ultimate goal of creating a healthy community.

But the question remains: What specifically can adult and health educators do to move toward aligning their fields and establishing healthy communities? It seems that the fields of adult education and health promotion could work toward alignment in three major areas: program planning, teaching and learning, and research. To promote health and healthy communities, these three areas need to be operationalized in specific programs; adult educators are uniquely qualified to assist and support these endeavors.

Program Planning

In the current work on developing healthy communities, some concepts from program planning models have been employed. Conducting needs assessment, developing objectives, designing program delivery, and measuring outcomes are all some of the methods that have been employed to develop healthy community programs. What adult educators add to this process is the ability to do even more in-depth program planning in cooperation with various stakeholder groups. The purpose of this in-depth program planning is to bring about coordinated and collaborative change. As Caffarella (2002) identified, change is the driving force linking all types of educational and training programs for adults. The same is true for health promotion programs. These programs have as their purpose to bring about either individual change in health behavior or community-oriented change at a broader level. To accomplish this, skills in program design are vitally important.

To foster the change process, Caffarella (2002) developed an interactive program planning model that includes twelve components: "discerning the context for planning, building a solid base of support, identifying program ideas, sorting and prioritizing program ideas, developing program objectives, designing instructional plans, devising transfer-of-learning plans, formulating evaluation plans, making recommendations and communicating results, selecting formats, schedules, and staff, preparing budgets and marketing plans, and coordinating facilities and on-site events" (p. 34). They are all strategies that could be incorporated into developing health promotion and healthy community programs.

Specifically, devising transfer-of-learning plans seems to be a program planning component that is missing from health promotion programs. Adult educators understand that to achieve change on an individual or community level, transfer of learning must be integrated into the fabric of every educational program. One of the key issues in transfer of learning is that program planners often do not have control or influence over the factors that may inhibit learners from using new information learned once they return to their work site or community. However, combining a program planning model with a healthy community model creates an avenue to assess a spectrum of community needs and to work on the change process from multiple directions. For example, in a healthy community framework educators may plan a program to help new mothers learn about good nutrition for children. At the same time, nutritional changes may be initiated in school lunch programs, along with changes in methods for purchasing nutritious food for families. The idea here is that transfer of learning is considered in the educational program and variables that may affect the transfer are addressed in the healthy community model. This kind of collaboration has the potential to enhance the strength of what both adult educators and health educators bring to the program planning process.

To effectively plan programs advancing healthy communities also relies on involving a spectrum of people from groups within the community. The needs, concerns, and ideas of a variety of individuals will ultimately be incorporated into the programs developed. Thus, skills that entail involving stakeholders in the planning process, facilitating groups, group decision making, conflict resolution, and grassroots organizing are necessary. Adult and health educators can assist each other in this area. Most adult educators bring a solid grounding in group process skills that can be applied in the area of health promotion and healthy communities. Health educators bring a tremendous knowledge of group and community health needs. Coordinating the group knowledge and skills of adult and health educators has the potential again to strengthen and deepen the program planning function and hopefully lead to better health outcomes for the community.

Teaching and Learning

Adult educators also have a role to play in developing teaching and learning strategies for health promotion. Since health educators are most often health care practitioners first and educators second, they may not have had the opportunity to develop advanced skills in the area of teaching and learning. Adult educators could work with health educators to foster development of a more learner-centered approach to health education.

Developing health education programs with a learner-centered approach would rely on strategies to promote a more in-depth conceptual understanding of the content and methods linking learners' previous experience with new health education information. Concept maps (Novak, 1998; Novak & Gowin, 1984), discussion (Brookfield & Preskill, 1999), and dialogue (Mezirow, 1990; Mezirow & Associates, 2000) are all strategies that can support this approach. Additionally, added focus on developing reflective understanding can benefit health education programs, because it encourages the learner to link past and previous experiences with new information. Such strategies as critical incidents (Brookfield, 1995), journals (Boud, 2001; Mezirow, 1990), and teaching autobiographies (Dominicé, 1990) could be helpful in this process.

Many of the issues and controversies in the field of health promotion and the healthy communities movement are grounded in the values, beliefs, and assumptions held by individuals and groups. Again, adult educators may be helpful in promoting discussion and dialogue around these issues. Mezirow's theory of transformative learning (1990, 2000) offers one possible approach. Transformative learning focuses on assisting learners or groups to identify critical incidents in their lives, and then to reflect on the content, process, and premises of the assumptions underlying these events. Ultimately, the goal of this critical reflection process is to foster learning at a deeper level by developing an understanding of assumptions that may frame the actions of individuals or groups. This process of identifying assumptions may then permit a new perspective on actions to be taken. Mezirow's theory has been soundly criticized (Taylor, 1997) for its lack of attention to context and social action; yet Mezirow himself indicates there is nothing in his theory that prohibits application in these areas.

Transformative learning offers one of many possible approaches that adult educators could bring to the health promotion arena. Examining assumptions related to individual responsibility for health, the context of health promotion, the cost of health care, the balance of individual freedoms, and the common good may assist practitioners in developing balanced approaches to these issues.

In fact, portions of this transformative learning approach are currently being used in some health literacy programs around the world (Tappe & Galer-Unti, 2001). The American Cancer Society (1999) defines health literacy as "the capacity to obtain, interpret and understand basic health information and services and the competence to use such information and services in ways that enhance health" (n.p.). To reach this goal of health literacy, individuals and communities often need to engage in a process of critical reflection and learning. For example, a program in Scotland developed by Tett (2001) brought together people from a range of socioeconomically diverse areas. These individuals participated in a course titled Health Issues in the Community. During the course, individuals identified their own health care information needs and worked within groups to develop competence to meet these needs. This work often required the participants to reflect on their own beliefs about health, control of health care decisions, and sources of knowledge for health information. At the end of the course, participants then investigated a health care issue in their community. The topics included the impact of poverty on the health of women and families and the impact on housing as a health issue. The ultimate goal of these projects was community action. As Tett (2001) indicates, "Working with a community to increase self-determination and take control over its collective resources is an important task for educators. Building organizations, taking action to redistribute resources, ensuring that community voices are heard all have direct health benefits. This is because lack of control over one's own destiny promotes a susceptibility to ill health for people who live in difficult situations where they do not have adequate resources or support in their day-to-day lives" (p. 7).

Developing a health education program as described by Tett (2001) relies on a skilled facilitator who can bring together concepts of transformative learning, group dynamics, and social action—all areas in which adult educators have skills to bring to health promotion activities.

Finally, evaluation is also needed on incorporating adult education teaching methods in the area of health promotion. For example, adult educators could work with health educators to design programs around behavioral, cognitive, social, humanist, or constructivist learning orientations (Merriam & Caffarella, 1999). Evaluating the learning outcomes of health education programs designed and implemented from multiple orientations could assist educators in developing a better understanding of teaching methods that facilitate learning across various health issues, cultural groups, and contexts.

Research

Researching the connections among adult learning, adult education, health promotion, and healthy communities is an activity that requires the collaboration of both adult and health educators. There has been a significant amount of research in the area of health promotion, mostly in assessing program outcomes (Haber, 2002; Pelletier, 2001; Shohet, 2002) and outcomes of policy changes at a national level (Healthy People 2010, 2000; Pulliam & MacKenzie, 2003). There have also been some studies on the connections between health and learning. For example, Feinstein, Hammond, Woods, Preston, and Bynner (2003) investigated the effects of adult learning on measures of health and social capital. They used data from the National Child Development Study in Britain, which collected data from ten thousand individuals born in 1958. The focus of the study was to analyze changes in the participants' lives at thirty-three and forty-two. The outcomes considered in the study were changes in social and political attitudes, civic participation, health behaviors (smoking, alcohol consumption, and exercise), self-reported life satisfaction, and the onset and recovery from depression.

Study findings indicated that participation in adult learning plays an important role in contributing to the small shift in attitude and behavior taking place in the middle years of adulthood. For example, giving up smoking and increasing exercise were positive effects of participation in adult learning. An interesting finding was that taking leisure and vocational courses decreased alcohol consumption, whereas taking work-related courses increased alcohol consumption. Finally, study findings indicated that overall life satisfaction and well-being were increased with adult learning. However, when the sample was divided by gender, men had a statistically significant association between participation in adult learning and life satisfaction, but women did not.

The study conducted by Feinstein et al. (2003) needs to be replicated in numerous countries, because it addresses important issues connecting adult education, adult learning, and health. This type of research has the potential to inform health promotion practitioners, adult educators, and policy makers. The findings have implications for health education, health protection, and prevention as well. Additional research is also needed to understand more fully some of the interesting findings that emerged from this study.

Finally, as has just been suggested, research is needed in the areas of health protection and prevention. Adult educators have long been involved in leadership development, community development, participatory learning, and policy analysis. All types of studies related to these areas within health protection and prevention are needed, and adult educators are uniquely qualified in this area. This type of research has the potential to broaden the application of the health promotion model in Figure 19.1, and to create a positive link between adult education, health promotion, and healthy communities.

SUMMARY

As evidenced in this chapter, health promotion and adult education seem to be complementary concepts that could be aligned to focus on the development of healthy communities. The field of health promotion encompasses health education, health protection, and prevention, all areas in which adult educators have skills, abilities, and knowledge to bring to bear on both individual and community health issues. Adult educators have a role and a responsibility to work with health promotion practitioners in the areas of program planning, teaching and learning, and research. Alignment in these three areas could help foster the UNESCO (1997) position that "health is a basic human right. Investments in education are investments in health. Lifelong learning can contribute substantially to the promotion of health and the prevention of disease. Adult education offers significant opportunities to provide relevant, equitable and sustainable access to health knowledge" (p. 13).

REFERENCES

American Cancer Society. (1999). *National health education standards*. Washington, DC. Retrieved October 24, 2004, from http://www.cancer.org/cshe/csheintr.html.

Boud, D. (2001). Using journal writing to enhance reflective practice. In L. M. English & M. A. Gillen (Eds.), *Promoting journal writing in adult education* (pp. 9–17). New Directions for Adult and Continuing Education, No. 90. San Francisco: Jossey-Bass.

Brookfield, S. (1995). *Becoming a critically reflective teacher*. San Francisco: Jossey-Bass.

Brookfield, S., & Preskill, S. (1999). *Discussion as a way of teaching: Tools and techniques for democratic classrooms*. San Francisco: Jossey-Bass.

Caffarella, R. (2002). *Planning programs for adult learners: A practical guide for educators, trainers and staff developers* (2nd ed.). San Francisco: Jossey-Bass.

Dominicé, P. F. (1990). Composing education biographies: Group reflection through life histories. In J. Mezirow (Ed.), *Fostering critical reflection in adulthood* (pp. 194–212). San Francisco: Jossey-Bass.

Downie, R. S., Tannahill, C., & Tannahill, A. (1996). *Health promotion: Models and values* (2nd ed.). New York: Oxford University Press.

Feinstein, L., Hammond, C., Woods, L. Preston, J., & Bynner J. (2003). *The contribution of adult learning to health and social capital*. London: Centre for Research on the Wider Benefits of Learning, Institute of Education. (ED 478 951)

Flowers, J. (1993). Healthier communities: A compendium of best practices. *Healthcare Forum Journal, 36*(3). Retrieved January 22, 2005, from http://www.well.com/user /bbear/hc_compendium.html.

Flowers, J. (1996). Examples of healthier communities projects. Retrieved January 12, 2005, from http://www.well.com/user/bbear/hc_examples.html.

Haber, D. (2002). Health promotion and aging: Educational and clinical initiatives by the federal government. *Educational Gerontology, 28*, 253–262.

Healthy people 2010: Understanding and improving health (2nd ed.). (2000). Washington, DC: U.S. Government Printing Office. Retrieved October 24, 2004, from http://www.health.gov/healthypeople/.

Merriam, S., & Caffarella, R. (1999). *Learning in adulthood*. San Francisco: Jossey-Bass.

Mezirow, J. (1990). *Fostering critical reflection in adulthood*. San Francisco: Jossey-Bass.

Mezirow, J., & Associates. (2000). *Learning as transformation: Critical perspectives on a theory in progress*. San Francisco: Jossey-Bass.

Novak, J. (1998). *Learning, creating and using knowledge: Concept maps as facilitative tools in schools and corporations*. Mahwah, NJ: Erlbaum.

Novak, J., & Gowin, B. (1984). *Learning how to learn*. Cambridge: Cambridge University Press.

Ottawa Charter for Health Promotion. (1986). *Health Promotion, 1*(4), iii–v.

Pelletier, K. (2001). A review and analysis of the clinical and cost effectiveness studies of comprehensive health promotion and disease management programs at the worksite: 1998–2000 update. *American Journal of Health Promotion, 16*(2), 107–116.

Pulliam, L., & MacKenzie, R. (2003). *Health promotion and wellness in Canada: A review*. Calgary, Alberta, Canada: University of Calgary.

Shohet, L. (2002). *Health and literacy: Perspectives in 2002*. Nathan, Queensland Centre: Adult Literacy and Numeracy Australian Research Consortium. (ED 473 575)

Tappe, M. K., & Galer-Unti, R. A. (2001). Health educators' role in promoting health literacy and advocacy for the 21st century. *Journal of School Health*, 71(10), 477–482.

Taylor, E. (1997). Building on the theoretical debate: A critical review of the empirical studies of Mezirow's transformative learning theory. *Adult Education Quarterly*, 48(1), 34–59.

Tett, L. (2001, September). *Health concerns in communities and the wider benefits of learning: Perspectives from practice in Scotland*. Paper presented at the European Conference on Educational Research, Lisbon, Portugal. (ED 459 358)

UNESCO (United Nations Educational, Scientific, and Cultural Organization). (1997). *Health promotion and health education for adults. Adult learning in the context of environment, health and population*. Hamburg, Germany: Institute for Education. (ED 435 011)

WHO (World Health Organization). (1946). *Constitution*. New York: Author.

Wolf, T. (2001, August). *Healthy communities: Building communities from the ground up*. Paper presented at the annual meeting of the American Psychological Association, Washington, DC. (ED 479 140).

CHAPTER 17

Critiquing Human Resource Development's Dominant Masculine Rationality and Evaluating Its Impact

Laura L. Bierema

CHALLENGING DOMINANT MASCULINE RATIONALITY IN HUMAN RESOURCE DEVELOPMENT

Human resource development (HRD) is an emerging field of practice and research. Broadly concerned with the humans in organizations, HRD has historically been focused on issues related to the development of workers and the organization with regard to training, career development, and organization development (OD; McLagan, 1989). The field has decidedly humanistic roots traceable to the human relations movement and prominent in the creation of the field of OD (Burke, 1992; Greiner & Cummings, 2004; Porras & Bradford, 2004; Waclawski & Church, 2002; Wheatley, Tannenbaum, Yardley Griffin, & Quade, 2003; Wirtenberg, Abrams, & Ott, 2004). It is a field founded on employee advocacy, yet it is situated in a system saturated with sexism, racism, and managerialism.

I contend that HRD is at risk of becoming, or perhaps already is, co-opted into hegemonic practices of management that are rendering it unable to fulfill its pivotal role: humanistically facilitating development and change. Change agents strive to meet the cliché of "thinking outside the box," challenging the status quo, and innovating in ways that help us see problems and opportunities in new lights. Yet HRD is increasingly thinking "inside the box" of capitalism and masculine rationality making it ever more difficult for the profession to behave ethically, sustainably, or creatively.

The purpose of this article is to critique HRD's dominant philosophy, practices, and research; illustrate how they negatively affect women HRD practitioners and recipients; and recommend alternative conceptualizations of the field. This article is grounded in a critical feminist theoretical framework, draws on critical theory and critical management studies, and is inspired by my ongoing disenchantment with HRD's overreliance on "performative" ideas and practices.

The human resource (HR) field in general is an excellent candidate for a post-structural feminist analysis as it has been historically applauded as a welcome movement away from Taylorist scientific management and toward a more human and humane workplace (Storberg-Walker & Bierema, 2008). Yet I maintain that the field is at risk of perpetuating the very philosophy it rose to challenge. Although many of HR's innovations have been heralded as moving the workplace away from the external controls that have accompanied the rise of scientific management, today's HR innovations have also been critiqued for simply moving the locus of control more toward the internal and self-regulation, guided by what feminists call the panoptic gaze of the "other" as legitimate masculine authority. For instance, although workers today are valued for their whole person and treated humanely in the workplace, management has created means of worker surveillance such as monitoring communications, self-surveillance, 360-degree feedback, and self-directed work teams that might be viewed as a kinder gentler means of managerial control (Alvesson & Willmott, 1992). These measures are subtle means of maintaining White male power, a vestige of management.

This article presents one perspective, not a claim to one "truth." Through interrogating dominant views and proposing alternative ways of conceptualizing the field, I aim to attempt what Calas and Smircich (1999) describe as "help[ing] us to understand the exclusions on which writers need to rely to represent 'positive knowledge'" (p. 658). The goal of my work is to unsettle the settled ideas and practices that shape HRD.

▮ UNSETTLING HRD

I contend that HRD is strongly influenced by masculine rationality, meaning it identifies with masculine attributes such as being strong, mechanical, assertive, objective, and controlled. Masculinist rationality is an assumption that masculine traits of objectivity, aggressiveness, and performance are the standard and that adhering to them is a neutral behavior that should not be questioned. It is convenient for those in power, typically White males, to establish expectations that leave little room for others to question the prevailing standards that elite White males have themselves created. For instance, the definition "HRD is a process of developing and unleashing human expertise through organization development (OD) and personnel training and development (T&D) for the purpose of improving performance" (Swanson & Holton, 2001, p. 90) is focused on performance, a prevailing definition in HRD created by White males.

Society is steeped in masculine rationality and generally lives unquestioningly with its assumptions that promote inequitable social systems and practices such as management, capitalism, sexism, and racism. Naturally, masculine rationality trickles down to smaller social systems, including fields such as HRD. When masculine rationality is challenged, its challengers are often accused of being irrational by its beneficiaries who seek to maintain the privileges afforded by the status quo. My own critiques of HRD's performance orientation have been described as "contain[ing] gross errors and misunderstandings" (Swanson & Holton, 2001, p. 131). In part, I believe that performance-based HRD has become such a dominant voice in HRD because of its advocacy by powerful male figures in the field and its advancement by practitioners and researchers, both female and male. Our masculine, rational, and performative outlook privileges management— generally a male-dominated and controlled enterprise—and is also used in a competitive sense to build HRD's credibility among the management elite. It distresses me that the field is so uncritical of these linkages. Masculine rationality also silences other voices, particularly more feminist ones. Ruddick (1996) drawing on Code explains as follows:

> The ideals of rationality and objectivity that have guided and inspired theorists of knowledge throughout the history of western philosophy have been constructed through excluding the attributes and experiences commonly associated with femaleness and underclass status: emotion, connection, practicality, sensitivity, and idiosyncrasy (Code, 1993, p. 21). (p. 248)

The field's adoption of masculine rational frameworks and methods is apparent in its overreliance on economic models and performance-enhancing interventions. Its quest to prove its worthiness with management is also an effort to prove HRD's rationality. This pursuit has caused the field to dismiss other models and interventions that challenge the "rational HRD way."

One way this masculine rationality is evident is through HRD's omission of marginalized groups in its research. This problem was illuminated in Bierema and

Cseh's (2003) feminist analysis of more than 600 Academy of Human Resource Development conference articles from 1996 to 2000. They found that HRD research overwhelmingly excluded issues of equity and access in the workplace. Very few studies promoted diversity or emphasized issues of social justice. Women's voices and experience were ignored, as were asymmetrical power arrangements. Gender was rarely used as a category of analysis—even when data were collected by gender. Furthermore, organizational "undiscussables" such as sexism, racism, patriarchy, or violence received little attention in the literature, and HRD research has only weakly advocated change. They concluded that HRD research may be reproducing inequitable power relationships in organizations rather than restructuring them.

Not long after the publication of the Bierema and Cseh (2003) study, an editorial in *Human Resource Development Quarterly* appeared that was critical of the application of a feminist research framework because of an alleged "inherent bias." The editorial brazenly suggested "unisex research" as a way of avoiding such bias:

> The solution as I see it to the inherent bias of Feminist Research is to move on to Unisex Research. Unisex Research is proposed to be an overarching value on top of mature research methods to ensure that those methods are not distinguished or distinguishable on the basis of sex. Once in place, Unisex Qualitative Research projects, Unisex Case Study Research projects, Unisex Theory Building Research projects, etc., can take place with the threat of bias under better control. Thus, the generation of significant new knowledge without a sexual bias will advance our scholarly understanding of phenomena being investigated. (Swanson, 2004, p. 118)

This editorial provides a prime example of masculinist rationality and an exhibit of a powerful elite White male telling us what should, and *should not*, count for knowledge. He paints feminism as irrational, reactionary, and plain wrong. Yet he appears to overlook that he is also working from a theoretical framework. Yet because his is the "default" dominant masculine rational one, it is nearly invisible and above critique. "Unisex research," in my view, claims the stance of rationality by claiming that it is "an overarching value," "mature," "controlled," and superior to feminist methods. It disturbs me that the field easily accepts or ignores editorials like Swanson's, but it is indicative of HRD's general apathy toward power dynamics and their influence on organization life or interest in critique. If the field is to develop in a multifaceted manner, it is important to open up debate and welcome multiple conflicting understandings of it. Exploring critical HRD provides one avenue toward alternative conceptualizations and understandings of HRD.

▨ A CRITICAL HRD

HRD is a field that values reflective practice (Grieves, 2003; Yorks, 2005), questioning assumptions (Argyris, Putnam, & Smith, 1985; Senge, 1990), and embracing change (Burke, 1992; Schein, 1987, 1988). Yet when challenged to apply these tools to itself, HRD appears to adopt a resistant unreflective theory-in-use that significantly contradicts its espoused theory. Some scholars have recommended that HRD undertake a more rigorous critique of its principles and practices that incorporates critical theory (Elliott & Turnbull, 2003; Fenwick, 2004, 2005; Sambrook, 2003), but such calls have been largely ignored and in some cases, discouraged. Critical HRD receives more robust treatment in Great Britain where it has thread status at the International Critical Management Studies Conference and at the Academy of Management's Critical Management Studies special interest group. Critical HRD is slowly gaining traction at the Academy of Human Resource Development Conference, with 2009 representing the first time it has been officially recognized as a stream of research.

Elliot and Turnbull (2003) are concerned "that the methodological traditions that guide the majority of HRD research do not allow researchers to engage in studies that challenge the predominately performative and learning-outcome focus of the HRD field" (p. 971). They make a plea to open HRD theory to broader perspectives. I have proposed a starting point for considering critical HRD and offer this working definition:

> Critical HRD challenges performative HRD philosophy and practice arguing for a critical and socially conscious HRD that problematizes its precepts by challenging the commodification of employees; involving multiple stakeholders; contesting the nature of power relations; pursuing wide-ranging goals; providing alternative, nonoppressive, and holistic models for cultivating development in work context; and transforming the workplace.

The definition speaks to what I see as the major critiques of HRD:

- a performative philosophy
- the commodification of employees
- the allegiance to shareholders
- the ignoring of power relations
- the lack of alternative models and theories for HRD practice

Each of these elements will be discussed in the next sections.

HRD Is Performative

I contend that HRD is dominated by a performative philosophy that must be critiqued for how performativity has (mis)shaped the field. Performativity—a natural by-product of masculinist rationality—is a shift away from human values and toward efficiency and performance (Lyotard, 1984). Performativity has become the overarching goal in industrialized workplaces that have been downsized, smartsized, and globalized with "performance-enhanced" workers (note, this is not the same as Butler's, 1990, definition of performativity pertaining to gender performance). HRD has conformed to conventional management philosophy by devising methods of "unleashing human expertise" in ways that benefit the enterprise, defining "success" with linear rational measures and careful consideration of its return on investment, referring to workers as "resources" or "productivity brokers," providing unequal access to learning and development for marginalized workers, viewing employee development as primarily an "investment in human capital," giving lip service to issues of diversity, and demanding enhanced performance from fewer workers. This drive for performance has clouded HRD's focus on human development and sharpened its focus on productivity, performance, and profit. Blindly incorporating performativity into one's HRD repertoire may also be a deeper response to HRD's marginalized status in most organizations. Embracing performativity becomes a channel for enhancing HRD's secondary status and justifying its existence. Thus, HRD professionals master identities as "performance consultants" without a great deal of critical awareness about the orientation or the discourse itself.

Performativity has invigorated the rise of managerialism where those running an organization are afforded undeserved leeway to make decisions that are assumed to be rational, schooled, and ethical. Our society has fueled the rise of such management power by granting corporations more legal rights than citizens and valuing money and the life it brings on human systems (deGeus, 1997). Performativity also parallels other manifestations of patriarchy in that it is based on masculine rationality that strives to enhance power and control in the organization. "Performativity . . . carries the added message of masculinity: the commonsense expectations of men's behavior. That is, the competition, aggression, the functionality of performance measurement, all framed within notions of emotional control, rationality and endurance" (Whitehead, 1998, p. 212).

Holton (1999) contends, "Because many HRD practitioners have developmental values and roots, they view the notion of performance outcomes and accountability for developmental processes with disdain and avoid it" (p. 37).

I disagree and believe there is nothing inherently wrong with performance, but it needs to be balanced with other organizational and community variables and considered in the totality of the health of the organization using multifaceted critical criteria. The problem as I see, it is that performativity has eclipsed how HRD is defined, discussed, and delivered. To rectify the problem will require HRD to become more antiperformative in its stance.

HRD Commodifies Workers

Performance-based HRD often commodifies workers. Labor becomes commodity or commodified when it is done in exchange for something else. Commodification transforms work relationships into products that are bought and sold and preserves the masculine rational goals of profitability and performance. This transaction attitude toward labor grew out of industrialization and cultivated a very narrow concept of production (productivity, performance, and profit). Preindustrialization labor was important for subsistence and life, such as farming. Now, labor's value is as a commodity to be bought and sold with little or no consideration of its life-enhancing qualities. Hart (1992) highlights this contrast noting subsistence production values sustaining and improving life. Commodity production, conversely, values producing goods and services for profit. Hart alleges that commodity production erodes quality of life in the name of profit. HRD focused only on profit maximization creates the same effect, commodifying employees. This commodification is dehumanizing as employees learn to market themselves, increase their value to the organization, and improve performance. The organization responds in kind by forming a transaction-oriented relationship with workers where their labor can be easily bought or sold, and cast aside when it is no longer needed.

According to Basgen and Blunden (n.d.), the process of commodification has accelerated during recent decades. They describe the rise of women's paid labor as one example:

> "Women's work"—cleaning, cooking, caring, rearing, teaching, washing, sewing, and so on—is now carried out by women selling their labor power in factories ... and then purchasing the products on the market as commodities. This process is everywhere today; everything has a price tag, everything has become a commodity. (Basgen & Blunden, n.d.)

They cite the privatization of government services as another example of commodification. This is particularly evident in an age of school vouchers, corporate universities, privatized public transportation, health maintenance organizations, and other services that require the user to purchase them rather than the public to provide them through tax revenues. Human interaction is also being replaced by machines evident in daily activities such as banking, self-checking aisles at the grocery store, automated airline check-in, and the universally dreaded voice mail system. Employee identities have become commodities as well where corporate education programs may function to duplicate the organization within the person (Covaleski, Dirsmith, Heian, & Samuel, 1998), with educational programs aimed at instilling the organization's values, goals, and discourse, thus enhancing their marketability to the organization. The explosion of the knowledge economy and rise of learning organizations also suggests that knowledge is the latest thing to be commodified. Commodification is a prominent feature of the knowledge economy where there is,

> An emphasis on productive capacity with regard to knowledge and control as an asset in order to yield value to its owners. The intellectual nature of the commodity makes the control of labour in knowledge economies a key determinant of "profitability." Consequently, the efficient capture, control and exploitation of the surplus value of workers' labour is of central importance. (Fletcher, Boden, Kent, & Tinson, 2007, pp. 433–434)

People, or commodities that yield profit, are usually under surveillance to ensure they are being productive.

Commodification is a double-edged sword that has been described as inevitable in that it is simultaneously dehumanizing and freeing, requiring consumers to sacrifice a certain degree of human dignity but at the same time, giving them power in the market place. Commodification integrates people into capitalism in a situation where the market succeeds because of consumer dependence that becomes self-perpetuating. Technology and wealth creation have accelerated this process. Although corporations would not exist without profits, the performance improvement orientation loses sight of balancing human and organizational needs. This imbalance has caused HRD to align with organizational interests with the expectation that humans will follow suit, or else. There is also anticipation that the human needs should parallel those of the organization:

> When individual's needs are consistent with the organization's, there is no tension. When the individual's needs are not congruent with the organization's performance requirements, and the organization is providing the required learning experience, a tension exists and inevitably results in some degree of organizational control. For this

reason, learning professionals in HRD must balance practices that lead to the most effective adult learning with those that will lead to performance outcomes (Knowles, Holton, & Swanson, 1998, p. 122).

This demand for enhanced employee performance that is aligned with organization goals signifies the commodification of employee needs, learning, and autonomy.

HRD Is Beholden to Shareholders

Another critique of HRD is its failure to consider all of its stakeholders. Notably, HRD functions in a gray area where its practitioners are expected to satisfy management while simultaneously serving employees. The expectations of these two stakeholder groups may be contradictory, leaving the HRD practitioner in a no-win situation where personal ethical principles must be abandoned to achieve managerial expectations (Marsick, 1997). Korten (1996) observed in a speech to the Academy of Human Resource Development Conference that there is a "serious disconnect between your own values and the realities of life in many of the corporations in which you work" (p. 1). HRD tends to favor a stockholder orientation that is performative, placing value on economics and performance, only considering social responsibility when it is profitable or required by law. The stockholder orientation privileges managerial and organizational interests:

> A corporation is the private property of its stockholders and exists to create wealth and provide goods and services to the market. While obligated to comply with legal constraints, its primary goal is profitability; only secondarily is it to be concerned with goals, policies and strategies aimed at serving the needs of external publics. (Acar, Aupperle, & Lowy, 2001, p. 29)

A stockholder orientation generally favors procedures and processes that save or make money, at the expense of making the worker's life more difficult or unpleasant. Alternatively, the stakeholder orientation advocates for organizational social responsibility to widely affected parties. Freeman (1984) describes stakeholders as "any group or individual who can affect or is affected by the achievement of the organization's objectives" (p. 46), and suggests that corporations exist with society's permission and consequently must become a steward to external stakeholder groups. Clarkson (1995) defines primary stakeholders as those on whom a corporation depends for survival such as shareholders, investors, employees, customers, and suppliers. Secondary stakeholders as those who are influenced or affected by the organization but not engaged in transactions essential to the organization's survival.

A stakeholder perspective acknowledges that addressing multiple, sometimes conflicting needs is a process of negotiation in HRD where power relations play out among different groups with varying degrees of power. A critical HRD recognizes and values multiple stakeholders and seeks outcomes that matter for *all* parties. The contradictory nature of HRD work is not well understood or addressed in the literature or practice. Fenwick and Bierema (2008) explored how social responsibility commitments were understood and implemented by HR professionals in Canada and the United States. They found that the participants did not see the corporate social responsibility (CSR) initiative within their purview. Given our current era of corporate misbehavior, it is alarming that HR is not connecting CSR with recruitment, training, or development or seeing it as part of its mission.

Critical HRD is socially conscious HRD (Bierema & D'Abundo, 2004), which requires that organization practices be implemented democratically and involves a diverse range of stakeholders, including customers, employees, suppliers, and citizens in policy development and oversight. Critical HRD also recognizes that certain interests are privileged when decisions are made, questions who benefits from HRD, and ensures that stakeholders have voice or a "place at the planning table" (Cervero & Wilson, 2005). HRD can play a role in involving these parties in policy development and making the decision makers more aware of these groups as strategies are being formulated and implemented. Ultimately, management interests should be balanced and negotiated with others who are affected by the work of the organization.

HRD Ignores Power Relations

A more critical approach acknowledges that management is a political social practice that has been influenced by historical and cultural power relations. HRD's failure to recognize how some organization members are privileged while others are marginalized or disenfranchised by its work is problematic. Swanson's (2004) call for "unisex research" is an example of this nonrecognition. A critical HRD acknowledges that HRD is dominated by a masculine epistemology that has historically served to preserve power relations in a manner that marginalizes women and people of color. This masculine epistemology is manifested in HRD's performative value system that effectively devalues, ignores, and silences nondominant groups, preserving patriarchal power in both theory and practice.

Critical HRD rejects the technical rationalist perspective that managers and the managed should be naturally divided social positions. Vince (2003) argues that "HRD is clearly a political activity" (p. 1) and calls for a critical HRD that addresses emotions and politics, reflective practices, and a revised understanding of leadership practice. Sambrook (2003) predicts that as the critical study of HRD matures, we will hear more about HRD's role in promoting CSR and its more humanistic and emancipatory role in both helping individuals and transforming sociopolitical structures.

Power dynamics receive little attention in HRD education. To gain an understanding of how HRD and OD are power issues theoretically, I analyzed popular textbooks (Cummings & Worley, 2005; French & Bell, 1999; Gilley & Maycunich, 1998; Hargreaves & Jarvis, 2000; Phillips, 1999; Swanson & Holton, 2001; Walton, 1999; Yorks, 2005). Searches were made of the books' table of contents and subject indexes to see how the issue of power was being addressed. Only four of the eight reference power, and none substantively. Yorks (2005) refers to power once, and Walton (1999) refers to power four times. Cummings and Worley (2005) reference power on 5 pages of their 694 page volume. French and Bell (1999) only address power acknowledging "organization development has been criticized for not taking into account power in organizations" (p. 282) and conceding that OD is still in the early stages of understanding power. None of these books offer a thorough discussion of power or acknowledge that power structures are grounded in patriarchy and highly resistant to any initiatives that might threaten them, such as a robust attempt at addressing diversity.

> A key rationale for encouraging human resource developers to be critical lies in the realisation of how powerful managers now are in the world, yet how poorly traditional HRD education has prepared them for considering questions of power and responsibility. (Trehan, 2004, p. 30)

Traditional management and HRD education have reproduced prevailing relations of power and reinforced management superiority in organization life. "It is no longer acceptable that HRD educators allow managers to maintain the illusion that their choices and actions are without political consequences" (Trehan, 2004, p. 31). Overlooking dynamics that significantly affect the goals HRD hopes to achieve impinges our ability to be effective or implement lasting change.

So far, this article has argued that HRD is dominated by masculine rationality that compromises its goal of addressing humanistic equitable organization change. The field does a poor job of addressing diversity, acknowledging power dynamics, or considering alternative conceptual frameworks. A more critical HRD is proposed that critiques HRD's performative stance, commodification of workers, loyalty toward stockholders, and disregard of power relations—the real consequences of HRD's dominant masculine rationality. The next section illustrates how this orientation affects women, both those working in HRD and those served by it in organizations.

WOMEN IN HRD

Close your eyes for a moment and imagine an entry-level HRD practitioner. What does this person look like? Now, imagine a senior-level executive of HRD. In each instance, what did you see? Did you imagine a woman or a man? Did you picture a White person or a person of color? and What type of setting did you envision for your imaginary HRD people? It is likely you visualized women at the entry level and a White male at the executive level, both working in corporations. Why do we do that? Our gendered and race-based programming runs deep, just like our narrow views of what HRD is and where HRD is practiced.

Where are the women in HRD? Women populate the field and academic programs. Yet the top-level executive positions are held by men. The most widely recognized scholars are primarily White males who advocate performative theoretical frameworks valuing capitalistic, masculine, and rational models. Research has shown little movement into areas that call for attention related to sustainability and diversity. Few people in HRD seem to be alarmed by the field's constriction. Although the field appears dominated by masculine rationality, women have been involved in HRD throughout history.

Women's Place in HRD History

Historically, HR activities have been "women's work." In 1964, Miller and Coghill chronicled women's role in the evolution of personnel administration in the U.S. Personnel work grew because of the introduction of activities designed to improve the condition of workers along with the introduction of measures to enhance the internal efficiency of an organization. The growth of personnel work paralleled the rise of women in personnel management who were hired to promote employee betterment and welfare. Women also evolved the technical side of personnel work. Miller and Coghill suggest that women were channeled into personnel roles because they were similar to their roles in social reform movements in the decades leading to World War I. Women in personnel work held various titles such as "house mother," "matrons," "social secretary," and "employment manager."

Miller and Coghill (1964) offer observations on dynamics influencing women's movement into personnel administration. This work did not start out to be performative or masculine, but shifted that direction in parallel with industrialization:

- The social structure of post Civil War business elites lacked good role models for addressing the human side of problems associated with rapid industrialization. The available models were decidedly feminine: mother, nurse, teacher, and social worker.
- The most pressing humanitarian and public relations problems involved women and very young workers, reinforcing the role of women in creating industrial welfare work.
- The impulse toward "employee betterment" had religious roots, reinforcing the tendency to select women to direct that work, as religion was viewed as more within a "women's sphere" at the time.
- The rise of scientific management affected personnel work and a new association with a "hard" masculine field. This did not immediately preclude a good outlook for women, as witnessed by early scientific personnel managers such as Mary Gilson and Millicent Pond and consultants such as Katherine Blackford and Lillian Gilbreth.
- The input of military psychologists after World War I did much to diminish the earlier view of the personnel field as at least equally hospitable to women as to men.
- Employee welfare activities under the "American Plan" assumed more overtones of "exploit" (masculine image) than of "nurturance" (feminine image) that characterized the earlier less sophistical experience.
- Growth of the association between collective bargaining and personnel activities clearly diminished the opportunity for women to rise to the top in an occupation now dominated or threatened with domination by an overt, if qualified, "conflict" motif.

So historically, the HR function has feminine roots. Its focus shifted with industrialization when men took over these roles. Miller and Coghill (1964) close their article with the following observations:

> Today, although the personnel field may be regarded as less self-consciously "masculine" than such functions as production, engineering, finance and sales, women

operate at a competitive disadvantage. Still, their opportunities remain better here than in any of the other major specialized functions of management. "Getting along with people" is still an essential element of the job. In earlier times, training as a woman was seen as an asset in dealing with the problems of "humanizing" work organizations. Where so much lip service is paid to concern with the "whole man" it might be well to remember that the whole man is at least partly feminine. Given the stresses confronting members of large organizations now and in the immediate future as they face the implications of computerization, automation, reduced expense accounts, and related trauma, the personnel field may suffer from its decreasing reliance on women practitioners. (p. 44)

The Feminization of HRD

Miller and Coghill's (1964) words were written more than 40 years ago, yet they could have been written today. During the past 20 years or so, the HRD sector has become feminized and this is reflected in both pay scales and gender composition (Hanscome & Cervero, 2003). Although the field is feminized, it is dominated by masculine rationality, showing the power of patriarchal systems in society. HR is one of the few professions to have more female managers than male, yet men make more money and hold the top jobs. The Labour Force Survey 2001, based on a 1% sample of employees in the United Kingdom, found that women accounted for 57% of personnel, training, and industrial relations managers. The only higher proportions of women managers were health and social services managers (73%) and office managers (66%). The lowest percentage of women managers were among production and maintenance workers (6% to 7%). The survey also found a negligible number of female directors or CEOs (www.statistics.gov.uk). The survey results are summarized in Table 17.1.

In 2003, Hanscome and Cervero observed that although the HRD role has become more integrated and strategic, this growing importance of the function is not reflected in the current pay and prestige levels allotted to these functions managers, many of whom are women.

The HRD sector is similar to all other paid work domains in that "female dominated occupations pay less than male-dominated fields with similar educational requirements" (Jacobs & Blair-Loy, 1996, p. 209). In HRD circles, this pay differential is sometimes referred to as the feminization of HRD (Roos & Manley, 1996, p. 511).

Ackah and Heaton (2003) examined the career progression of human resource professionals among credentialed HR professionals. They explored the impact of the acquisition of a HR professional qualification on career progression for male and

Table 17.1.   Percentage of Women Managers by Industry

Variable	Percentage
Health and social services	73
Office managers	66
Personnel, training and industrial relations	57
Advertising and PR	45
Hospitality and leisure	45
Restaurant and catering	43
Financial institutions	37
Retail and wholesale	35
Shopkeepers	34
Quality and customer care	33
Financial managers and chartered secretaries	30
Distribution, storage and retail	27
Marketing and sales	21
ICT managers	17
Production works and maintenance	7
Production managers	6

SOURCE: *Office for National Statistics, Labour Force Survey, Spring 2001, Personnel Today, Reed Business Information United Kingdom, Ltd., a division of Reed Elsevier, Inc.*

female managers. They found that the careers of men and women do differ, with men receiving more internal promotions, whereas women were pursuing career progression in other organizations. Women were also found to be less successful in terms of earnings and more likely to perceive barriers to their careers such as lack of role models and more difficulties with self-confidence than men. The authors suggest their findings deserve consideration when designing curriculum to account for raising the confidence and aspirations of female managers.

A 2004 postal survey conducted among the Chartered Institute of Personnel and Development (CIPD) graduates examined the professional identities of human resource practitioners (Thompson, 2004). Her work was inspired by the dearth of women who hold top HR jobs, in spite of a near balance of midlevel managers when comparing women and men. She reported that although in 2002, 69% of all CIPD members were female, only 8.5% held senior executive or director positions, compared with 25% of the male membership. Her results suggested that women favor HR roles "more befitting personnel management than HRM" (p. 63) through their desire to help employees on maximizing profitability. Men, on the other hand, showed more proclivity toward profit maximization that she suggests may provide them a springboard toward upward levels of management. Furthermore, 72% of CIPD members are women as compared with only 28% of the 124,500 membership who are men (Tasker, 2005).

Tasker (2005) reports British figures from the Chartered Management Institute that reveal a significant pay gap between men and women in middle management HR posts. On average, women earn salaries of £41,000, whereas men earn £49,000. A recent U.S. HRD study yielded similar findings showing that women HRD practitioners' salaries lag behind those of men employed in the same job types by an average of $7,813 per year. In the entire range of HRD jobs presented in the article, men's salaries averaged $66,035 compared with women's $55,598 (Dobbs, 1999). "Gender Pay Differential in HR Salaries Is £8k" (2004) reported an £8k difference in pay between men and women in the United Kingdom because of the lack of women at the senior level. The report indicated, however, that women's pay is increasing at a faster rate than men's. Although there are fewer men in HR, their relative numbers increase with job seniority. Only 40% of HR directors are women that perpetuate the glass ceiling at the executive levels.

The "feminization of HRD" is noted further, according to statistics illustrating a 10-year trend that began in the 1980s in which men's entry into HRD-related categories decreased by 3.1%, whereas women's entry into HRD increased by 49.2% (Hanscome & Cervero, 2003; Roos & Manley, 1996). The more limited salary range in HRD job categories is one possible reason for the decline in men's entry into the field (Hanscome & Cervero, 2003; Roos & Manley, 1996) along with the lower prestige equated with HRD jobs (Hanscome & Cervero, 2003). HRD has historically served a more feminine function from the welfare-oriented programs that were a reaction to industrialization to more recent government-sponsored programs such as affirmative action and movements toward workplace equality. Men may be deterred from entering HRD because of concerns on restricted career mobility associated with the HRD sector given its reputation as a dead-end job not leading to advancement (Roos & Manley, 1996).

Women HRD Practitioners and Power

"Much of the current management and training literature is sparse about how issues of gender and power inform the day-to-day experiences of HRD managers" (Hanscome & Cervero, 2003, p. 511). Hanscome and Cervero (2003) observe that what exists tends to focus on diversity practices and strategies for scaling the career ladder. They contend, "Serious discussion about the real-life connections between gender and power at the organizational level is also absent in many HRD training texts" (p. 512). They surveyed several popular HRD textbooks (Cummings & Worley, 2005; Johns, 1996; Raymond, Hollenbeck, Gerhart, & Wright, 1996) and concluded the following:

> Women's workplace challenges were subsumed under the umbrella of organizational diversity or pay issues, thus seriously diluting the everyday problems that women experience. Although gender and power appear as separate listings in the indexes, they are not connected, as in cross-referencing or sub-indexing. As well, although power is linked to hierarchal structures, gender inequalities are only briefly mentioned in terms of the glass ceiling. (p. 512)

Hanscome and Cervero (2003) examined how gender and power influenced the interpersonal relationships among HRD managers through strategies HRD managers employed to negotiate day-to-day interactions. Five female and 5 male HRD managers were interviewed using critical incident techniques to explore specific workplace interactions. Two major conclusions of the study indicated that the experiences of female and male respondents regarding the exercise of power were profoundly different and that the strategies used by respondents generally reflected the gendered contexts of power.

The habitual disregard for gendered power relations in textbooks and research consequently results in organization inequalities and unfair management practices. One must look to literature outside HRD (such as, in adult education or critical management studies) for discussions of how gender and power shape organization life. Devos (1996) argues that a lack of critical perspectives in the literature on work-based training has resulted in sparse attention being given to issues of gender and power within organizations, noting that it results in a lack of an adequate framework for analyzing and understanding power dynamics. Lacking such analytical tools threatens to perpetuate oppressive organizational practices and structures. The irony of the feminization of HRD is that the field is dominated by masculine rationality—principles and practices that are often implemented by women—steeping the field in hegemony. Not only are women HRD workers marginalized in terms of pay, promotion, and prestige but also the very patriarchal policies they implement serve to prevent women from reaching their full career potential.

HRD for Women

Anna Quindlen (1997) once noted that women workers "spend their days doing a job most of their co-workers think they can't handle, and then they will go home and do another job most of their co-workers don't want." Her glum portrait sums up the situation of many women in the paid workforce where they must work twice as hard for half as much and simultaneously meet demands of family life.

This article has established that the HRD field is pervaded by masculine rationality that values performance over all other outcomes, and also that HRD has been feminized, evident in lower salaries and levels for women as compared with men. Women have not fared so well in this area as a profession, but what about women whom are served by HRD? Women play a key role in the global workplace, yet their work and influence are relatively invisible, even in HRD. The text *HRD Trends Worldwide* (Phillips, 1999) makes no mention of gender or women, and of the 16 trends identified, issues of diversity are strangely absent. The International Labour Organization (ILO, 1990) reports that women are excluded from high-profile training programs 38.8% of the time, yet more than 39% of employers feel this is a nonissue. In a 2007 report on Global Employment Trends for Women, the ILO concluded "More women than ever before are in work, but a persistent gap in status, job security, wages and education between women and men is contributing to the 'feminization of working poverty.'" Women are disadvantaged by HRD in terms of developmental opportunities, life–work balance, and diversity training, among other issues.

Women's Development

Women's developmental disadvantage is compounded by a hidden workplace curriculum that teaches them how to assimilate to a patriarchal culture and suppress their female identity (Bierema, 2002). Women and men receive different developmental experiences in their careers (Federal Glass Ceiling Commission, 1998; Knoke & Isho, 1998; Ohlott, Ruderman, & McCauley, 1994). In fact, Still (1985) found that men tend to be sent to training that is promotion-oriented whereas women receive training for functional skills for their current job. Male-dominated managerial hierarchies decrease women's opportunities for career encouragement and training (Tharenou, Latimer, & Conroy, 1994), and women do not have equal access to management development programs (Limerick & Heywood, 1993; Still, 1985). Just as in management, women tend to become sidelined and marginalized in management education and experiences that would groom them for ascending the career ladder. Women are also at a developmental disadvantage in the workplace because of the hidden curriculum that teaches them how to assimilate patriarchal culture, and expectations that they will suppress their female identity to succeed by masculine standards (Bierema, 2003; Hayes & Flannery, 2000). Social expectations for the "ideal worker" are gendered, and businesses define them through masculine criteria such as aggressiveness, independence, devotion, nonemotionality, and rationality (Rothausen-Vange, 2004).

Several authors have noted that although extensive research exists considering variables that hinder women's advancement, scarce literature exists about factors that facilitate such development (Hite & McDonald, 2004; Knorr, 2005; Osipow & Fitzgerald, 1996). Hite and McDonald (2004) also point out that the majority of research on women's careers focuses on college-educated managers, not nonmanagerial women. They conducted focus groups with 26 nonmanagerial women and found their participants adapted their career goals to meet other life circumstances; and that family responsibilities, job security, and organizational support systems influence their career success and satisfaction.

Hite and McDonald (2004) surveyed Black and White women managers and found differences in their perceptions of opportunities available based on race and gender. Black and White women share similar views when comparing opportunities between White women and men for getting hired, promoted, receiving salary increases, and other workplace challenges. When making comparisons with either men or women of color, White women were far more optimistic about the opportunities for people of color than were Black women. Hite and McDonald's study explores how issues of race are ignored among Whites and HRD practitioners.

Carter (2002) used phenomenological methods of heuristic inquiry to collaborate with nine midcareer women as coresearchers to explore learning in professional developmental relationships. She collected interview and journal data for 6 months. She found that women's developmental relationships are created and sustained largely through talk. Furthermore, they experience not only instrumental performance-based learning but also what Mezirow (1991) calls "transformative" learning—learning that significantly revises beliefs, attitudes, and values and results in a changed worldview or perspective. Carter has argued that her findings should call into question how managerial communication has been construed. She contents that it has been neglected as a developmental process.

Women's development is mitigated by a number of factors. Women's career development is different than men's and models are inadequate to describe it (Benko & Weisberg, 2007; Bierema, 1998; Farmer & Associates, 1997; Hewlett, 2007). The type of development women experience tends to keep them at midlevels rather than groom them for upward mobility, and development is not equal across racial groups. Yet Whites lack awareness about the systemic racism pervading HRD.

Life-Work Balance

Women's development and advancement are typically defined in male terms based on performative measures such as promotions, pay, and prestige. What is rarely asked, however, is how women define "success." Patriarchal organizations seem to have already defined it for them. O'Reilly (as cited in Tischler, 2004) concludes that success is not related to gender discrimination but, rather, how hard women choose to compete, noting the hardest competitors tend to be men. Yet who defines the terms of the competition? Why are these terms not being questioned? Top jobs require crushing demands of long work hours and travel. This workaholic value goes relatively unquestioned in the United States where we now clock more hours on the job than any other country on earth—500 hours a year more than the Germans and 250 hours more than the British (Tischler, 2004).

Women's family responsibilities have a major impact on the nature of their labor force participation (Davies & Thomas, 2000; Hochschild, 1997; Wilson, 1999). There is an assumption that family-friendly policies positively affect women's labor force participation. These policies are measured by level of public child care, parental leave arrangements, and other financial-related child support (van der Lippe & van Dijk, 2002). Rothausen-Vange (2004) argues that "ideal worker" images are masculine creating expectations that all employees are constantly available to employers making it difficult to simultaneously be available to the family. Making family a priority is still taboo for executive women. Rogier and Padgett (2004) validated this perception in their study of perceptions toward women working a flexible schedule. Participants reviewed a packet of materials simulating the personnel file of a female employee in an accounting firm who was seeking promotion from manager to senior manager. Participants perceived the female employee on the flexible schedule as less dedicated to her career and motivated to advance, although there were no differences in perceived capability. Brenda Barnes, formerly CEO of PepsiCo and the first woman executive who quit to spend more time with her children, "will be forever branded as The Woman Who Walked Away" notes Tischler (2004, p. 52), even though she continued serving on corporate boards and teaching at the university level while she was out of the workforce. Today, she is CEO of Sara Lee.

Trends in the labor market indicate that many women value autonomy, family–work balance, and maintaining a wider-ranging network than do men. In surveys of 4,700 workers in Britain and Spain, only 20% of women considered themselves "work centered" making careers a primary priority (55% of men in the study defined themselves as work centered; Hakim as cited in Tischler, 2004):

> Hordes of women refusing to play the career-advancement game aren't doing so because they can't hack it, but because they've lost faith in the institutions they've worked for and are tired of cultures driven by hairy-chested notions of how companies must function. (Tischler, 2004, p. 60)

Instead, women are leaving organizations to form their own businesses. The number of women-owned businesses increased by almost 90% during the 1990s (Korn/Ferry International, 2001). Organizations need to encourage the creation of alternative definitions of success and support and reward women's pursuit of success on their own terms.

Diversity Training

The American Society for Training and Development's 2002 state of the industry report ranked diversity as the second most prevalent concern of HRD professionals (VanBuren & Erskine, 2002), yet diversity training may falsely raise expectations, reinforce stereotypes, and create resentment among employees. Zhu and Kleiner (2000) identify several reasons for the failure of diversity training, including unrealistic goals, nonsupportive top management, national backlash (based on the erroneous assumption that it is White male bashing and the counter reaction of "reverse discrimination"), increased lawsuits, and few meaningful action steps. They offer corrective steps of stopping the denial of harassment and discrimination, removing the "diversity" label, establishing zero tolerance of discrimination and harassment policies, and demonstrating commitment at all levels of the organization.

The dominant diversity discourse heralds pluralism and multiculturalism, and it is generally believed that celebrating diversity is universally good. Yet Malik (2001) argues that the problem with embracing diversity and multiculturalism is it celebrates *difference* noting, "America is not multicultural; it is simply unequal" (p. 33). Campaigning for equality involves challenging accepted practices and policies, going against the grain, and seeking social transformation (Malik, 2001). Celebrating diversity on the other hand, "allows us to accept society as it is—all it says is 'we live in a diverse world, enjoy it.' It allows us to accept the divisions and inequalities that characterize the world today" (Malik, 2001, p. 34). Malik concludes that only in an equal society does difference have any meaning, because only in equal societies can difference be freely chosen. Given these problems with diversity training, organizations must ensure that such programs are carefully executed in an ethical, constructive, and sincere manner. Diversity programs also need to be sensitive to social context. This is increasingly important as the workplace globalizes.

This section has illuminated how HRD's dominant masculine rationality has affected women in HRD. HRD has been feminized, yet it continues to advance patriarchal practices and policies that marginalize women in organizations through unequal developmental opportunities, life-balance challenges, and ineffective diversity training. The next section identifies ways to challenge HRD's dominant masculinity.

CHALLENGING HRD'S DOMINANT MASCULINITY

This article began by offering a critique of HRD's narrow masculine rational orientation that is endangering the field's relevance and impact. Next, women working in the HRD profession and women who experience HRD were profiled to underscore how HRD's masculinist rational epistemology consequently marginalizes some workers. To conclude, I would like to raise questions and challenges to the field.

Many questions come to mind as we mire ourselves in new ways of thinking about HRD. How do we reconcile a field that has been feminized, yet remains dominated by performativity? I argue that the predominance of men at the top of the field perpetuates its passion with performativity and keeps women "in their place." How do we expand the discourse to include new conceptions of the field? How can HRD better serve women, people of color, and other marginalized groups? How can HRD be more sustainable? Who owns HRD? Who should evaluate HRD? How can HRD be more equitable? and How should HRD professionals be trained if we are seeking sustainable organizations? These are the questions HRD must grapple with if we intend to be relevant, representative, and responsible.

Identifying Sustainable HRD Models

The arduous work of challenging our HRD theories and practices can begin by conceptualizing and testing alternative frameworks and models for HRD. The dominant performance paradigm permeating HRD is objectionable because it has intellectually pigeonholed the field and represents masculine rational domination of it. We all understand the importance of organizations being profitable, yet HRD has helped perpetuate the development of a rigid and narrow view of profitability that is being exported globally (Johnson, 1998; Senge, 1990). This is alarming as consumption outpaces growth, corporate injustice is commonplace, jobs are outsourced to the lowest bidder, our natural resources are being depleted, the environment is polluted, and people starve when there is enough food in the world for everyone. Marjorie Kelly, cofounder of *Business Ethics* magazine, observed,

> We have words for racism and sexism, but wealth discrimination isn't fully recognized. It is a bias in favor of the wealthy and against labor, the environment, and the community. Concern for the public good must become the animating force of our economic order. (http://www.americanswhotellthetruth.org/pgs/portraits/Marjorie_Kelly.html)

Kelly's call for preserving the public good holds an important message for our work. Yet HRD practitioners do not see a clear role in promoting sustainability in their organizations (Fenwick & Bierema, 2008). A more optimistic view of HR's role in social responsibility is promoted by Lockwood (2004) who suggests that HRD leaders who are strategically implementing CSR programs have demonstrated return on investment, taken a role in promoting organization ethics, and built management and human capital into key business transactions. She reports that 63% of HR departments are spending on learning and training initiatives related to CSR, 40% are changing company policy in response to environmental issues, 36% are changing company policy in response to grassroots pressure to change certain business practices, and 32% are increasing involvement in social programs. She suggests that OD leaders can influence three primary standards of CSR—ethics, employment practices, and community involvement.

Critical approaches seek transformation that makes the world a more equitable place. A critical HRD could help transform management from a rational, bureaucratic, hierarchical, and masculine practice to one that is nonlinear, flat, and more parallel to natural models (Helgesen, 1990; Wheatley, 1992). It is not just the critical management studies paradigm calling for change. Transformation is being called for by even mainstream media and organizations. *Fortune* magazine recently ran the article advocating "tearing up the Jack Welch playbook" (Morris, 2006) arguing that a new set of rules is called for based on a historical context that demands agile, niche businesses, a customer and outward focus, a penchant for passionate workers, and managers who are courageous and soulful.

Hoque (2007) advocates a social business model for companies seeking to make a difference. "Social businesses have a humanitarian mission but are set up to earn a profit in a model superior to traditional philanthropy because it is self-sustaining" (p. 45). Goldman Schuyler (2004) advocates an organization health model that is holistic and concerned with creating organizations that promote well-being of workers, management, the organization, community, and other stakeholders. She argues that as organizational practitioners, we are most effective when the change process includes the following: (a) skills in organizational change and business, (b) a model for organizational health, and (c) practical theoretical approaches for maintaining individual health (encompassing physical, spiritual, and mental well-being). To help organizations through change in a way that promotes well-being, we need to help leaders attend to vision, teamwork, and individual development (Goldman Schuyler, 2004). It is also important to make sure the organization is providing resources for workers who are grappling with the changes themselves.

Advocating Responsibility

CSR goes hand-in-hand with sustainability. The atrocities of corporate crime have hurt countless people who put trust in their leaders. HRD professionals have escaped unscathed by ethical scandals such as Enron or the recent collapse of the financial markets, thanks to the world's preoccupation with profitability and performance. Yet the HR people who hired, trained, promoted, and monitored these corporate criminals are culpable. HRD needs to incorporate responsibility and sustainability into its repertoire.

The current environment is seeing pressure for organizations to be socially responsible, sustainable, and ethical. HRD is increasingly being called on to support these goals through well-managed programs, policies, and practices (Lockwood, 2004). Lockwood (2004) suggests that we can communicate the value of CSR through communications, employee relations, health, safety, and community relations.

The principle of social justice may take many forms. It requires us to consider "who benefits?" from HRD. Cervero and Wilson (2005) eloquently describe how competing interests and asymmetrical power relations can be negotiated. Dedication to social justice also assumes a wider commitment to redistributing power in society. This means that we also need to consider how HRD interventions will affect groups in the organization that have been historically marginalized because of class, race, gender, sexual orientation, religion, ethnicity, or other positionalities, and how the organization's actions will affect the wider community.

Creating New Measures of Organization "Health"

"Success" tends to be narrowly defined in terms of profitability in most organizations. An alternative HRD would help organizations be more accountable to stakeholders by ensuring a living wage was provided to all workers, and that "success" was redefined to mean more than profitability. HRD could lead in the development of instruments to evaluate organizations based on their overall health, ethics, environment, economics, stakeholders, fairness, diversity, social responsibility, sustainability, and living wage, not simply money earned. HRD also has the potential to help create employee-managed and owned organizations that are accessible to all employees regardless of gender, race, class, religion, physical ability, or sexuality. *Business Ethics* magazine (now CRO, *Corporate Responsibility Officer*) has developed rubrics to measure organizations' ethical behavior. Such rubrics are helpful as we create new means of measuring organizations' impact on the world.

Reconsidering "Who Owns HRD?"

Simply, following the basic tenets of critical HRD will result in new ways of thinking and practicing in the field. One unchecked assumption in HRD is that it is owned and controlled by the organization. Yet what future could we imagine for HRD that is sourced from elsewhere? Broadening our view to workforce development or countries that have national HRD policies provide important starting points for rethinking HRD ownership. What if HRD were community owned? It seems that ownership of knowledge and learning should be retained by citizens, both individuals and the community, rather than corporations.

With such a scenario, organizations would go to one public source for their HRD needs. In many ways, this would eliminate duplication of effort now occurring within organizations and provide opportunities for more out-of-the box thinking. Training and development would not be the first function to get cut and programs could be developed and delivered with less politicization. Women and people of color would have a more level-playing field when it came to receiving training for advancement rather than simply maintaining their current positions.

Although a community-owned HRD may be a fantasy, it offers an opportunity to imagine it in a new light and to consider possibilities we may never have imagined. It may not even be so far fetched in an environment where unchecked corporate greed has resulted in a worldwide collapse of financial markets. Creating a new source of HRD would require significant policy change and investment. The moment is ripe for alternative proposals where it is becoming increasingly evident that the modern organization is failing in a number of areas, including ethics, sustainability, and providing living wages to workers.

Meaningful evaluation of HRD practice should be conducted by stakeholders other than management, such as employees and communities. The venue for HRD practice has been exclusively corporate, at least in the mainstream discourse. HRD needs to broaden its horizons and focus on nonprofit organizations, professional associations, government, and small business as viable places for human development. Finally, HRD needs to critically assess whether it is working to institute masculine, rational, and performative management practices, or interrogate them in the name of meaningful lasting change. Bringing the stakeholders to the table is a key step in creating a more critical HRD.

Transforming HRD Curriculum

The influence of masculine rationality is evident in academic programs. The World Resources Institute and Aspen Institute (2005) released its biennial report *Beyond Grey Pinstripes* concluding that more business schools are improving at educating students about the social, environmental, and economic perspectives of business success in a competitive global economy, but it is still a significant minority. The report also found that more business schools offer courses in ethics, CSR, or environmental sustainability. The United States is not leading this charge however as three of the top-five ranked schools, and 12 of the top 30, are located outside the United States. The good news is that some business schools are advancing in this area. The bad news is that teaching and research on these topics is often marginalized or considered fringe from mainstream innovations.

Sustainability education is scarce in academic programs, including HRD. Not only is sustainability absent from the curriculum but also few academic programs offer courses in diversity or multiculturalism. Although it is likely that diversity is addressed in some current HRD courses, Kuchinke (2002) found that only 44% of programs covered diversity as a content area. Kuchinke further notes that although workforce diversity is one of several topics addressed in the HRD literature, it has not yet made the transition to being part of the core curriculum of graduate HRD programs, yielding a "gap between graduate education and emerging professional roles" (p. 140). Perhaps one reason academic HRD programs omit diversity content is because there are few HRD sources that adequately address it. Few HRD programs have taken the step to integrate critical perspectives, yet they will be increasingly important for academic programs that are training practitioners for global, diverse, and complex contexts.

Creating More Equitable HRD

Clearly, HRD is failing to sufficiently serve the learning and development needs of women, people of color, and other marginalized groups. Many HRD programs function to advance men in the organization and keep women and other marginalized groups from moving into coveted positions of power. HRD is dominated by performative discourse (Bierema, 2000; Rigg, Stewart, & Trehan, 2007), which may be one reason that it overlooks development that does not fit within the masculine productivity-oriented paradigm. As HRD practitioners, it is important to be mindful of this sexist performative bias and significantly more critical of how development programs are designed and distributed, and how they marginalize women by either ignoring them or channeling them into programs that are unhelpful in advancement. HRD needs a more holistic approach that considers multiple global stakeholders. We also need to consciously involve stakeholders in the decision-making process about development. All employees should have access to and control on their developmental experiences and these opportunities should be available across a range of levels in the organization. Programs should not only challenge the performative bias of the organization but also help its members achieve success on their own terms. Finally, organizations and HRD professionals have a social and ethical responsibility to honor all learners in their learning and development.

CONCLUSION

This article has challenged HRD's lack of engagement in critique of or debate on its theoretical frameworks. HRD is steeped in a masculine rational tradition that is preventing consideration of alternative conceptualizations of the field and perpetuating inequities. HRD's masculine rational blinders are putting the field at risk of becoming co-opted into hegemonic practices that are preventing it from fulfilling its goal of humanistically facilitating development and change. Ironically, HRD has become feminized, yet perpetuates masculine rational philosophies and practices. HRD's lack of self-critique or openness to alternative models may result in it becoming irrelevant, shallow, and unable to address the core political currents that dictate organization behavior, life, change, learning, and performance.

This article has attempted to unsettle our understandings of HRD and see the consequences of narrow conceptions of the field through women's experience as HRD professionals and HRD recipients. HRD's skewed focus toward masculine, managerial, and monetary interests results in abandonment of its humanitarian roots and prevents the field from serving as the organization conscience, change agent, or employee advocate. This state of affairs is a call for new ways of defining and doing HRD that are more critical, inclusive, and responsible.

REFERENCES

Acar, W., Aupperle, K. E., & Lowy, R. M. (2001). An empirical exploration of measures of social responsibility across the spectrum of organizational types. *International Journal of Organizational Analysis, 9*, 26–57.

Ackah, C., & Heaton, N. (2003). Human resource management careers: Different paths for men and women? *Career Development International, 8*(3), 134–142.

Alvesson, M., & Willmott, H. (Eds.). (1992). *Critical management studies.* London: Sage.

Argyris, C., Putnam, R., & Smith, D. M. (1985). *Action science: Concepts, methods, and skills for research intervention.* San Francisco: Jossey-Bass.

Basgen, B., & Blunden, A. (n.d.). *Encyclopedia of Marxism.* Retrieved July 13, 2004, from http:// www.marxists.org/glossary/index.htm

Benko, C., & Weisberg, A. (2007). *Mass career customization: Aligning the workplace with today's non-traditional workforce.* Boston: Harvard Business School Press.

Bierema, L. L. (Ed.). (1998). *Women's career development across the lifespan: Insights and strategies for women, organizations and adult educators.* New Directions for Adult and Continuing Education, No. 80. San Francisco: Jossey-Bass.

Bierema, L. L. (2000). Moving beyond performance paradigms in workplace development. In A. Wilson & E. Hayes (Eds.), *2000 handbook of adult and continuing education* (pp. 278–293). San Francisco: Jossey-Bass.

Bierema, L. L. (2002). The process of women's gender consciousness development. In *AHRD 2002: Proceedings of the Academy of Human Resource Development Conference* (pp. 177–184). Honolulu, Hawaii.

Bierema, L. L. (2003). The role of gender consciousness in challenging patriarchy. *International Journal of Lifelong Education, 22*, 3–12.

Bierema, L. L., & Cseh, M. (2003). Evaluating AHRD research using a feminist research framework. *Human Resource Development Quarterly, 14*, 5–26.

Bierema, L. L., & D'Abundo, M. L. (2004). HRD with a conscience: Practicing socially responsible HRD. *International Journal of Lifelong Education, 23*, 443–458.

Burke, W. W. (1992). *Organization development: A process of learning and changing* (2nd ed.). Reading, MA: Addison-Wesley.

Butler, J. (1990). *Gender trouble: Feminism and the subversion of identity*. New York: Routledge.

Calas, M. B., & Smircich, L. (1999). Past postmodernism? Reflections and tentative directions. *Academy of Management, 24,* 649–671.

Carter, T. (2002). The importance of talk to midcareer women's development: A collaborative inquiry. *Journal of Business Communication, 39,* 55–91.

Cervero, R., & Wilson, A. (2005). *Working the planning table: Negotiating democratically for adult, continuing and workplace education*. San Francisco: Jossey-Bass.

Clarkson, M.B.E. (1995). A stakeholder framework for analyzing and evaluating corporate social performance. *Academy of Management Review, 24,* 92–117.

Covaleski, M. A., Dirsmith, M. W., Heian, J. B., & Samuel, S. (1998). The calculated and the avowed: Techniques of discipline and struggles over identity in big six public accounting firms. *Administrative Science Quarterly, 43,* 293–327.

Cummings, T. G., & Worley, C. G. (2005). *Organization development and change* (8th ed.). Mason, OH: Thompson-Southwestern.

Davies, A., & Thomas, R. (2000). Gender and human resource management: A critical review. *International Journal of Human Resource Management, 11,* 1125–1136.

deGeus, A. (1997). *The living company: Habits for survival in a turbulent business environment*. Boston: Harvard Business School Press.

Devos, A. (1996). Gender, work and workplace learning. *Studies in Continuing Education, 18,* 110–121.

Dobbs, K. (1999). To have and have a lot: Trainers' salaries, 1999. *Training, 36*(11), 26–38.

Elliott, C., & Turnbull, S. (2003). Reconciling autonomy and community: The paradoxical role of HRD. *Human Resource Development International, 6,* 457–474.

Farmer, H. S., & Associates. (1997). *Diversity & women's career development: From adolescence to adulthood*. Thousand Oaks, CA: Sage.

Federal Glass Ceiling Commission. (1998). Washington, DC: U.S. Department of Labor.

Fenwick, T. J. (2004). Towards a critical HRD in theory and practice. *Adult Education Quarterly, 54,* 193–210.

Fenwick, T. J. (2005). Conceptions of critical HRD: Dilemmas for theory and practice. *Human Resource Development International, 8,* 225–238.

Fenwick, T. J., & Bierema, L. L. (2008). Corporate social responsibility: Issues for HRD engagement. *International Journal of Training and Development, 12,* 24–35.

Fletcher, C., Boden, R., Kent, J., & Tinson, J. (2007). Performing women: The gendered dimensions of the U.K. new research economy. *Gender, Work and Organization, 14,* 433–453.

Freeman, R. E. (1984). *Strategic management: A stakeholder approach*. Boston: Pitman.

French, W. L., & Bell, C. H. (1999). *Organization development: Behavioral science interventions for organization improvement* (6th ed.). Upper Saddle River, NJ: Prentice Hall.

Gender pay differential in HR salaries is £8k: Research blames absence of women at senior levels. (2004, September 30). *People Management*, p. 10.

Gilley, J. W., & Maycunich, A. (1998). *Strategically integrated HR: Partnering to maximize organizational performance*. Reading, MA: Addison-Wesley.

Goldman Schuyler, K. (2004). Practitioner—Heal thyself! Challenges in enabling organizational health. *Organization Management Journal—Emerging Scholarship, 1*(1), 28–37.

Greiner, L. E., & Cummings, T. G. (2004). Wanted: OD more alive than dead. *Journal of Applied Behavioral Science, 40*, 374–391.

Grieves, J. (2003). *Strategic human resource development*. London: Sage.

Hanscome, L., & Cervero, R. M. (2003). The impact of gendered power relations in HRD. *Human Resource Development International, 6*, 509–525.

Hargreaves, P., & Jarvis, P. (2000). *Human resource development handbook*. London: Kogan Page.

Hart, M. (1992). *Working and educating for life*. New York: Routledge.

Hayes, E., & Flannery, D. D. (2000). *Women as learners: The significance of gender in adult learning*. San Francisco: Jossey-Bass.

Helgesen, S. (1990). *The female advantage: Women's ways of leadership*. New York: Doubleday.

Hewlett, S. A. (2007). *Off-ramps and on-ramps: Keeping talented women on the road to success*. Boston: Harvard Business School Press.

Hite, L., & McDonald, K. (2004). Career aspirations of non-managerial women: Adjustment and adaptation. *Journal of Career Development, 29*, 221–235.

Hochschild, A. (1997). *The new time bind: When work becomes home and home becomes work*. New York: Metropolitan Books.

Holton, E. (1999). Performance domains and their boundaries. *Advances in Developing Human Resources, 1*, 26–46.

Hoque, F. (2007). Corporate social responsibility: Using a humanitarian business model. *Corporate Responsibility Officer, 2*(6), 45–46.

International Labour Organization. (1990). *Global employment trends for women*. Geneva: Author.

Jacobs, J. A., & Blair-Loy, M. (1996) Gender, race, local labor markets and occupational devaluation. *Sociological Focus, 29*(3), 209–230.

Johns, N. (Ed.). (1996). *Productivity management in hospitality and tourism: Developing a model for the service sector*. London: Cassell.

Johnson, H. T. (1998). Reflections of a recovering management accountant. In *Proceedings of the 1998 systems thinking in action conference* (pp. 68–79), San Francisco.

Knoke, D., & Isho, Y. (1998). The gender gap in company job training. *Work and Occupations, 25*, 141–167.

Knowles, M. S., Holton, E. F., & Swanson, R. A. (1998). *The adult learner: The definitive classic in adult education and human resource development*. Houston, TX: Gulf.

Knorr, H. (2005, February). *Factors that contribute to women's career development in organizations: A review of the literature*. Paper presented at the Academy of Human Resource Development International Conference (AHRD). Estes Park, CO.

Korn/Ferry International. (2001). *What women want in business: A survey of executives and entrepreneurs*. Los Angeles, CA: Author.

Korten, D. C. (1996, March). *When corporations rule the world*. Paper presented at the meeting of the Academy of Human Resource Development Conference, Minneapolis, MN.

Kuchinke, K. P. (2002). Institutional and curricular characteristics of leading graduate HRD programs in the United States. *Human Resource Development Quarterly, 13*, 127–143.

Limerick, B., & Heywood, E. (1993). Training for women in management: The Australian context. *Women in Management Review, 8*(3), 23–30.

Lockwood, N. R. (2004, December). Corporate social responsibility: HR's leadership role. *HR Magazine*. Retrieved August 2, 2008, from http://findarticles.com/p/articles/mi_m3495/ is_12_49/ai_n8583189

Lyotard, J. F. (1984). *The postmodern condition: A report on knowledge*. Minneapolis: University of Minnesota Press.

Malik, K. (2001, Spring). The perils of pluralism: A re-examination of the terms of engagement between races and cultures, and a plea for equality. *Diversity Factor*, 31–34.

Marsick, V. J. (1997). Reflections on developing a code of integrity in HRD. *Human Resource Development Quarterly, 8*, 91–94.

McLagan, P. (1989). Models for HRD practice. *Training & Development Journal, 43*(9), 49–59.

Mezirow, J. (1991). *Transformative dimensions of adult learning*. San Francisco: Jossey-Bass.

Miller, F. B., & Coghill, M. A. (1964). Sex and personnel managers. *Industrial & Labor Relations Review, 18*(1), 32–44.

Morris, B. (2006, July 11). New rule: Agile is best; being big can bite you. Old rule: Big dogs own the street. *Fortune*. Retrieved July 15, 2006, from http://money.cnn.com/2006/07/10/magazines/fortune/rule1.fortune/index.htm

Ohlott, P. J., Ruderman, M. N., & McCauley, C. D. (1994). Gender differences in managers' developmental job experiences. *Academy of Management Journal, 37*, 46–67.

Osipow, S. H., & Fitzgerald, L. F. (1996). *Theories of career development* (4th ed.). Boston: Allyn & Bacon.

Phillips, J. (1999). *HRD trends worldwide: Shared solutions to compete in a global economy*. Houston: Gulf.

Porras, J. I., & Bradford, D. L. (2004). A historical view of the future of OD: An interview with Jerry Porras. *Journal of Applied Behavioral Science, 40*, 392–402.

Quindlen, A. (1997). *Words of women quotations for success*. Retrieved from http://www.people.ubr.com/authors/by-first-name/a/anna-quindlen/anna-quindlen-quotes/it-makes-me-angry-to.aspx

Raymond, A. N., Hollenbeck, J. R., Gerhart, B., & Wright, P. M. (1996). *Human resources management: Gaining a competitive advantage*. New York: Irwin/McGraw-Hill.

Rigg, C., Stewart, J., & Trehan, K. (Eds.). (2007). *Critical human resource development: Beyond orthodoxy*. Essex, UK: Prentice Hall.

Rogier, S., & Padgett, M. (2004). The impact of utilizing a flexible work schedule on the perceived career advancement potential of women. *Human Resource Development Quarterly, 15*, 89–106.

Roos, A. P., & Manley, J. E. (1996). Staffing personnel: Feminization and change in human resource management. *Sociological Focus, 29*(3), 245–261.

Rothausen-Vange, T. J. (2004). Gender: Work-family ideologies and roles. *Organization Management Journal, 1*(1), 55–60.

Ruddick, S. (1996). Reason's femininity: A case for connected knowing. In N. Goldberger, J. Tarule, B. Clinchy, & M. Belenky (Eds.), *Knowledge, difference and power: Essays inspired by women's ways of knowing*. New York: Basic Books.

Sambrook, S. (2003, July 7–9). *A "critical" time for HRD?* Proceedings of the third International Critical Management Studies Conference. Lancaster, England.

Schein, E. H. (1987). *Process consultation, Vol. 2: Lessons for managers and consultants*. Reading, MA: Addison-Wesley.

Schein, E. H. (1988). *Process consultation Volume 1: Its role in organization development* (2nd ed.). Reading, MA: Addison-Wesley.

Senge, P. M. (1990). *The fifth discipline: The art and practice of the learning organization*. New York: Doubleday/Currency.

Still, L. V. (1985). *The status of women managers in Australian business: An exploratory study* (Women in Management Series, 2). Nepean College of Advanced Education, School of Business.

Storberg-Walker, J., & Bierema, L. L. (2008). An historical analysis of HRD knowledge: A critical review of The foreman: Master and victim of doubletalk. *Journal of European Industrial Training, 32*(6), 433–451.

Swanson, R. A. (2004). Unisex research. *Human Resource Development Quarterly, 15*, 117–119.

Swanson, R. A., & Holton, E. F. III, (2001). *Foundations of human resource development*. San Francisco: Berrett-Koehler.

Tasker, J. (2005, November 8). Why are there so many women in HR? *Personnel Today*, 18–21.

Tharenou, P., Latimer, S., & Conroy, D. (1994). How do you make it to the top? An examination of influences on women's and men's managerial advancement. *Academy of Management Journal, 37*, 899–931.

Thompson, A. (2004, September 30). Professional identities: The impact of gender on the HR role. *People Management, 10*(19), p. 63.

Tischler, L. (2004, February). Where are the women? *Fast Company*, Issue 79, pp. 52–55, 58, 60.

Trehan, K. (2004). Who is not sleeping with whom? What's not being talked about in HRD? *Journal of European Industrial Training, 28*(1), 23–38.

VanBuren, M., & Erskine, W. (2002). *The 2002 state of the industry report.* Alexandria, VA: American Society for Training and Development.

Van der Lippe, T., & Van Dijk, L. (2002). Comparative research on women's employment. *Annual Review of Sociology, 28,* 221–241.

Vince, R. (2003, July 7–9). *Towards a critical practice of HRD.* Proceedings of the third International Critical Management Studies Conference. Lancaster, England.

Waclawski, J., & Church, A. H. (Eds.). (2002). *Organization development: A data-driven approach to organization* change. San Francisco: Jossey-Bass.

Walton, J. (1999). *Strategic human resource development.* Essex, UK: Pearson Education.

Wheatley, M. (1992). *Leadership and the new science: Learning about organization from an orderly universe.* San Francisco: Berrett-Koehler.

Wheatley, M., Tannenbaum, R., Yardley Griffin, P., & Quade, K. (2003). *Organization development at work: Conversations on the values, applications and future of OD.* San Francisco: Pfeiffer.

Whitehead, A. (1998). Disrupted selves: Resistance and identity work in the managerial arena. *Gender and Education, 10,* 199–215.

Wilson, F. (1999). Genderquake? Did you feel the earth move? *Organization, 6,* 529–541.

Wirtenberg, J., Abrams, A., & Ott, C. (2004). Assessing the field of organization development. *Journal of Applied Behavioral Science, 40,* 465–479.

World Resources Institute and Aspen Institute. (2005). *Beyond grey pinstripes.* Retrieved July 07, 2006, from http://business.wri.org/newsrelease_text.cfm?NewsReleaseID=346

Yorks, L. (2005). *Strategic human resource development.* Mason, OH: Thomson Southwestern.

Zhu, J., & Kleiner, B. (2000). The failure of diversity training: Is there a better way to prevent workplace discrimination? *Nonprofit World, 18*(3), 12–14.

CHAPTER 18

Organizational Learning Communities and the Dark Side of the Learning Organization

Phillip H. Owenby

earning communities in organizations are nothing new. Indeed, one may argue that viable organizations are fundamentally made up of learning communities (de Geus, 1997; St. Clair, 1998). Learning communities in organizations have many forms and names—for example, learning networks (Poell, Van der Krogt, and Wildemeerch, 1999), project-based learning teams (Poell, Van der Krogt, and Warmerdam, 1998), self-directed work teams (Orsburn, Moran, Musselwhite, and Zenger, 1990), quality teams or circles (Walton, 1986), and action learning teams (Yorks, O'Neil, and Marsick, 1999). Other learning communities, such as formal or informal special interest groups of members of similar occupational or disciplinary backgrounds, are also common in organizations (Poell, Van der Krogt, and Wildemeerch, 1999). Perhaps the most discussed of all types of organizational learning communities in recent years is the learning organization (Senge, 1990a, 1990b; Watkins and Marsick, 1993). Many companies have become enamored of the learning organization concept—of turning the entire workforce into a grand learning community. Seizing on ideas that promise competitive advantage, this has fostered a headlong rush into varied initiatives such as corporate universities, knowledge management, knowledge transfer, and related practices (Jacques, 1996). For example, according to Jeanne Meister (1998), the number of corporate universities increased from about four hundred to over one thousand in the decade ending in 1998. I will argue in this chapter that learning communities in organizations—especially the so-called learning organization—are successful to the extent that they are horizontal in nature. I will further argue that deliberate attempts to establish learning organizations must consider the manifold aspects of power relations, including organizational structure, if they are to succeed in ways that maintain the commonly held values of adult educators.

LEARNING NETWORKS AS LEARNING COMMUNITIES

There are many possible ways to describe learning communities. However, the case could be made that any conceivable workplace learning community could be put in the framework of Poell, Van der Krogt, and Wildemeerch's (1999) four types of learning networks.

Four Types of Learning Networks

In the *vertical learning network,* managers and human resource development (HRD) staff direct and linearly plan the learning activities of employees around, for example, the development and implementation of a new policy, process, goal, or procedure. The result is a "task-specific" learning program that is "centrally organized" (p. 45). Quality circles and corporate universities easily fit this definition.

The *horizontal learning network,* in contrast, is an egalitarian, problem-focused community of learners attempting to "solve complex problems by reflecting on experiences, developing joint action theories, and bringing these into practice in an investigative manner" (Poell, Van der Krogt, and Wildemeerch, 1999, p. 45). Action learning teams and project-based learning teams easily fit the definition of this kind of network (Poell, Van der Krogt, and Warmerdam, 1998). Such teams are defined by the way through which they "organize [their] learning path" by diagnosing "existing conditions, developments, and problems. . . . data feedback and . . . . formulation of learning themes; and . . . [organizing] one or more learning projects" (p. 29). This is the ideal behind the learning organization concept.

The *external learning network,* the third kind, is "inspired by action theories developed outside the organization" (Poell, Van der Krogt, and Wildemeerch, 1999, p. 45). It is common among professionals whose practice inside the organization is often directed by professional associations outside the organization. For example, groups of physicians, nurses, psychologists, accountants, engineers, scientists, and others are organized around special occupational or disciplinary interests.

Last, in the *liberal learning network,* employees direct their own learning activities, mostly in an unstructured fashion. "They may team up with other learners for group reflection on their experiences, but basically all individual members create their own policies and practices" (Poell, Van der Krogt, and Wildemeerch, 1999, p. 46). Such networks would include learning communities organized around special interests, including electronic discussion groups. As a case in point, my own organization has recently attempted to facilitate learning communities by providing space for electronic newsgroups—similar to USENET Internet discussion groups—on its intranet servers.

Horizontal Learning Organizations

Poell, Van der Krogt, and Warmerdam (1998) help make the case that project-based learning teams can serve as nuclei for the formation of learning organizations. As members of such learning teams develop their learning networks, the interactions among these networks "gradually become institutionalized" (p. 33) into new organizational structures that influence both learning programs and the overall learning climate. These new organizational structures, I believe, are largely horizontal. Thus, the learning organization can be understood as an interactive and interparticipatory complex of smaller learning communities or networks. In other words, it can be seen as a grand horizontal learning community.

■ THE DARK SIDE OF THE LEARNING ORGANIZATION

Previously identified issues that affect adult learning in general also affect the functioning of learning communities or networks, especially in the case of vertical learning networks with their top-down direction of learning goals and structures (Poell, Van der Krogt, and Wildemeerch, 1999). These issues also affect the functioning of the learning organization, particularly when channeled through institutions such as corporate universities or more traditional HRD functions.

Power Interests and the Learning Agenda

Tisdell (1993), for example, describes how subtle issues of status and power resulting from classism, racism, and sexism affect relations in learning environments by influencing participation, relationships among learners and facilitators, and ultimately what is learned both explicitly and implicitly. Similarly, Mills, Cervero,

Langone, and Wilson (1995) reported how the planning of learning programs is influenced not only by available resources but also by organizational structure, culture, and power relationships. They point out that structure, culture, and power relationships operate through traditionalist interests to select which needs should be served in learning programs. Korten (1995) has pointed out how present-day corporations routinely sacrifice the interests of their employees to further corporate goals of profitability and competitive advantage in the new global economy. It could be argued that, to the extent that employee needs and interests are ignored, the corporation's attempt to deploy the collective learning power of its employees in order to obtain competitive advantage is merely a new form of worker exploitation.

Corporate Universities as Instruments of Corporate Control

In the case of corporate universities—which are in many ways admirable structures for unifying and focusing an organization's learning agendas to support its strategic business goals (Meister, 1998)—those same agendas are usually dominated by the views of executives, strategic planners, external consultants, and HRD experts. For example, a recent book entitled *Learning from the CEO: How Chief Executives Shape Corporate Education* (Meister, 2000) lists seven roles for chief executive officers in corporate learning organizations: visionary, sponsor, governor, subject matter expert, faculty, learner, and chief marketing agent. Interestingly, the role of governor is defined as taking "an active role in governing the corporate learning function, [reviewing] goals and objectives, and [providing] direction on how to measure the effectiveness of learning, and .... outcomes" (p. 5). Also interesting is how the role of faculty is defined as "thought leader .... for the entire organization" (p. 5). The book seems congratulatory of executives who champion learning, yet lacks critical awareness of their power to suppress competing agendas. And although it could be argued that most corporate universities and HRD staffs attempt to analyze learners' needs before planning and implementing learning programs, it could also be argued that the very methodologies chosen to gather and analyze learning needs are influenced by the interests of management. For example, Meister (2000) is quite clear that a primary focus of executive involvement in corporate learning is to increase "stockholder value" (p. 3). Executive-driven learning agendas can easily interfere with employee-driven learning agendas; according to recent Gallop findings employees' loyalty and retention are linked to the availability of learning and development opportunities not necessarily related to their present jobs (Buckingham and Coffman, 1999).

The Language of Power in Organizational Learning

Rees, Cervero, Moshi, and Wilson (1997) describe how organizational power interests shape the language that frames learning programs so that those interests are served rather than other, less powerful interests. Although their study focused on the way program planners exerted power through language, the implications are clear that the language employed in framing the agendas of organizational learning programs helps ensure that learning serves the dominant power interests. Indeed, the language chosen to express learning agendas works automatically and unconsciously to exclude competing agendas. In corporate learning organizations, management exercises a monopoly of language to serve the learning goals established externally to the employee-learner. This monopoly is exercised through statements of corporate mission, vision, values, strategic business objectives, and the formal learning objectives of education and training programs.

Organizational Learning as a Technology of Power

As a corporate educator and internal consultant, I have personally experienced the resistance and alienation of learners compelled to attend so-called continuous learning programs, which they had no voice in formulating and whose goals they felt were unrelated either to their daily work or their personal development goals. Far from feeling empowered in their learning (*empowerment* means allowing employees greater voice and participation in decision making about work-related issues), they felt coerced and disempowered. I would thus argue that the rhetoric of the learning organization, as in public educational institutions, constitutes a "technology of power" that is "given concrete expression in forms of knowledge that constitute the formal curriculum" (Giroux, 1990, p. 197).

CONTRADICTIONS IN THE QUEST FOR ORGANIZATIONAL LEARNING

Toffler (1980, 1990) has stated that over recent decades organizations have begun either consciously or unconsciously to respond to the shift from the *second wave* (smokestack-industrial) to the *third wave* (postindustrial or knowledge-based) world. Jacques (1996) has argued that the rhetoric of the learning organization is in some ways an inadequate attempt to address postindustrial management challenges by repackaging systems theory in faddist language. Whatever the merits of his position, I believe that organizational learning—as a specific strategy of response to such challenges—must be accompanied by changes in the structure of power relations in organizations if it is to be faithful to its claims.

According to Toffler (1990), the traditional hierarchical model of workplace governance does not fit the requirements for success for the new kind of knowledge worker. In addition, de Geus (1997), who is widely credited with establishing the concept of the learning organization, in describing the so-called *living company* flatly declares that "centralization of power.... reduces the learning capacity of an organization" (p. 190). What, then, is the result when traditionally hierarchical organizations attempt to implement a learning organization culture? Based on both personal experience in consulting in organizations and the published literature, I believe that the following dynamics come into play.

Critical Awareness Versus Surplus Control

First of all, organizational learning requires not only knowledge but also critical reflection and collaborative learning skills (Cranton, 1996). These skills may often be developed among an organization's members through formal training programs or through project assignments in problem solving, quality improvement, process improvement, or action learning teams. They may even be produced as a result of deliberate changes in the leadership style of individual managers—for example, in so-called fusion leadership, which emphasizes nonhierarchical, egalitarian approaches to organizational management (Daft and Lengel, 1998). Through such programs, employees develop knowledge-and perspective-sharing networks outside the organization's normal, hierarchical silos. However, once they have been acquired, these skills and networks can be directed at all facets of the organization, including how power and privilege benefit some members rather than others at the expense of total organizational efficacy. Such insights frequently come after instances when management tacitly punishes employees for attempting to apply in unforeseen ways the principles and techniques they learned in sanctioned learning programs. For example, an employee process improvement team will uncover cause-and-effect relationships affecting their performance that originate in management practices. Often, these same management practices originate in organizational mechanisms that manifest themselves in overly centralized controls (de Geus, 1997), leading to *surplus order,* which Toffler (1990) defines as the amount of power used to establish order "over and above that needed .... to function .... [and which is] imposed merely to perpetuate the regime" (p. 470) . Thus, surplus order can be viewed as surplus control or surplus power. Toffler believes that power exercised in this way is immoral. More important, employees themselves view surplus order as immoral and tend to become cynical and less productive the more they become aware of it.

Toffler's views are reinforced by philosopher John Rawls's (1971) theory of justice. It justifies exercising power and privilege only to the extent that they benefit the total membership of the society or organization. It is in often those very areas of surplus power in which opportunities for improvement are identified by critical reflection and learning. This is because surplus power consumes or redirects energy and resources away from other functions; therefore, it is an indirect tax on organizational productivity. For example, micromanagement is a classic exercise of surplus power through which management seeks to control all the actions of subordinates, preapprove all but the most trivial decisions, and control all information flow through hierarchical channels. Micromanagement can occur when managers jealously protect mechanisms of surplus control. It is almost always evident that there is micromanagement if work flow slows or stops when the manager is absent from the office. Interestingly, micromanagement has been identified as one of the top reasons why employees leave supervisors to seek jobs elsewhere (Buckingham and Coffman, 1999).

Organizational Learning Versus Organizational Lacunae

Because those who exercise surplus control are threatened by critical awareness, they are motivated (both overtly and covertly) to defend areas of organizational practice that are threatened by agents of organizational learning, such as workers, adult educators, trainers, or organizational development consultants. These agents may be unaware but sincere organizational citizens who reveal contradictions innocently or aware corporate "revolutionaries" who reveal contradictions deliberately and knowingly. Management may protect the status quo by suppressing or redirecting learning or inquiry, or suppressing or redirecting agents of organizational learning. Suppression can result in organizational *lacunae* or blind spots (Goleman, 1985). Lacunae are areas unavailable to observation and analysis as a result of shared complacency, disguise, or misdirection. Like the air we breathe, they are largely unnoticed. Further, the fact that they are unnoticed is also unnoticed. We do not know what we do not know. These lacunae operate to obstruct the implementation of the learning organization by sapping energy and resources through surplus control or by hiding opportunities for transformation. Employees may sabotage their own consciousness to avoid punishment. Organizational cynicism can increase through awareness of how power interests serve themselves and suppress learning. These lacunae also affect the organization overtly in the form of "busy work" teams or impressive-sounding but impotent or irrelevant initiatives (in terms of fundamental or heartfelt issues). For example, employees may be assigned to process improvement teams whose charters carefully restrict the issues available for inquiry; on the off-chance that team members find legitimate ways to go beyond the charter's intended limits, budgetary or other plausible reasons can usually be found for suppressing their recommendations.

Self-Deceptive Learning Organizations

Yet relatively trivial issues can yield returns when subjected to reflection and learning. Thus, organizations may deceive themselves into believing they are successful learning organizations. Power interests may even consent to overt changes in the formal organization, especially if they can help them gain advantage over competing interests. Corporate universities in particular can deceive themselves into believing that they are agents of fundamental change when in fact they are often allowed to function only to the degree that they may be co-opted by the deep structure of power relations in the organization.

OVERCOMING THE DARK SIDE

But it need not be this way. Employees, management, and other stakeholders all benefit from the success of learning organizations. Employees want the organization to succeed so that their jobs are protected, they gain satisfaction from their work, and they achieve personal developmental goals. Management wants security, continued influence over the direction of the organization, and the approval of stockholders and stakeholders. Stockholders and other stakeholders want to benefit from the success of management and employees in making the organization productive, profitable, and socially responsible. How can these interests be reconciled and served by the learning organization? The transition to the learning organization involves some growing pains.

Create a Vision

As a classic second-wave smokestack industry (Toffler, 1980), a large Southeastern company has been driven by many of the *powershift* issues identified by Toffler in 1990 to adapt to a third wave (knowledge industry) world. Since 1994, this company has undertaken initiatives designed to improve its social, environmental, and financial performance—changes that benefit its stakeholders and customers. Through its corporate university, it has also made available more continuous learning opportunities for its employees in information technology, critical problem solving skills, business awareness, environmental responsibility, leadership, teamwork, and individual development. Yet these initiatives, although laudable, did not address the issues of misused power and surplus control.

Champion New Values

In 1997, the company launched a fundamental transformation initiative to align individual and organizational behavior to its stated corporate values. This was a multifaceted initiative. First, every employee from the board of directors to the boilermakers attended a two-day workshop on interpersonal relations, communication, and other related topics; these were discussed in the context of basic values. Next an intensive awareness campaign was launched to highlight the values along with the message that it was not just OK but mandatory to hold everyone accountable for demonstrating the values in everyday work life. After that, a second phase of workshops was launched to target organizational leaders. These were accompanied by the message that leaders would be held accountable in their performance reviews for how they practice a set of "winning behaviors." Interestingly, these winning behaviors are directed toward the proper uses of power in leader-follower relationships. In tandem with this second phase of workshops, an "organizational health index" was developed using metrics derived from employee perception surveys in specific organizations. These are a kind of report card that compare organizations against statistically derived indices; scores below the control limits are colored red whereas those above are green. Managers who fail to improve the poor scores of their organizations fall under scrutiny and could risk losing their performance bonuses. A third phase of workshops is now being planned for other employees as well.

Do Not Miss the Point

This example demonstrates that a comprehensive effort to change the culture of power, when combined with a business plan that acknowledges the organization's responsibilities to all stakeholders as well as a continuous learning system for all employees, can create many—but not all—of the fundamental requisites for a healthy learning organization. To be sure, this company has attempted to graft these initiatives onto a top-down, hierarchical, second-wave organization that is little changed in management structure from the early decades of the twentieth century.

As a result, some interesting dynamics have been illuminated; the traditional manner in which power is structured and distributed interferes with the espoused values of the organization. Such structural contradictions are apparent when managers are punished for actions that conflict with the corporate values but also for failing to follow management practices of the traditionally vertical organizational hierarchy. This is the implicit contradiction that comes from placing horizontal values in a stubbornly vertical organizational framework.

CONCLUSION

Organizations that are thoroughly committed to transformational learning must provide the widest possible training in critical reflection and action inquiry to ensure the widest possible transformational consciousness among their members. They must commit to uncovering hidden power relationships and eliminating surplus control. They must struggle to correlate the formal organization with centers of power that promote rather than obstruct organizational learning. Finally, they must realize that the formal organization needs to parallel the fundamentally horizontal structure of the learning organization. In addition to their formal roles, corporate educators, trainers, and consultants are challenged to promote the political consciousness required for a healthy learning organization.

REFERENCES

Buckingham, M., and Coffman, C. *First Break All the Rules: What the World's Greatest Managers Do Differently.* New York: Simon & Schuster, 1999.

Cranton, P. "Types of Group Learning." In S. Imel (ed.), *Learning Groups: Exploring Fundamental Principles, New Uses, and Emerging Opportunities.* New Directions for Adult and Continuing Education, no. 71. San Francisco: Jossey-Bass, 1996.

Daft, R. L., and Lengel, R. H. *Fusion Leadership: Unlocking the Subtle Forces That Change People and Organizations.* San Francisco: Berrett-Koehler, 1998.

de Geus, A. *The Living Company: Habits for Survival in a Turbulent Business Environment.* Boston: Harvard Business School Press, 1997.

Giroux, H. A. "Critical Theory and the Politics of Culture and Voice: Rethinking the Discourse of Educational Research." In R. R. Sherman and R. B. Webb (eds.), *Qualitative Research in Education: Focus and Methods.* London: Falmer Press, 1990. (Originally published 1988.)

Goleman, D. *Vital Lies, Simple Truths: The Psychology of Self-Deception.* New York: Simon & Schuster, 1985.

Jacques, R. *Manufacturing the Employee: Management Knowledge from the 19th to 21st Centuries.* London: Sage, 1996.

Korten, D. C. *When Corporations Rule the World.* West Hartford, Conn.: Kumarian Press–San Francisco: Berrett-Koehler, 1995.

Meister, J. C. *Corporate Universities: Lessons in Building a World-Class Workforce.* New York: McGraw-Hill, 1998.

Meister, J. C. *Learning from the CEO: How Chief Executives Shape Corporate Education.* New York: Corporate University Exchange–Forbes Custom Publishing, 2000.

Mills, D. P., Cervero, R. M., Langone, C. A., and Wilson, A. "The Impact of Interests, Power Relationships, and Organizational Structure on Program Planning Practice: A Case Study." *Adult Education Quarterly*, 1995, *46*(1), 1–16.

Orsburn, J. D., Moran, L., Musselwhite, E., and Zenger, J. H. *Self-Directed Work Teams: The New American Challenge.* Homewood, Ill.: Irwin, 1990.

Poell, R. F., Van der Krogt, F. J., and Warmerdam, J.H.M. "Project-Based Learning in Professional Organizations." *Adult Education Quarterly*, 1998, *49*(1), 28–42.

Poell, R. F., Van der Krogt, F. J., and Wildemeerch, D. "Strategies in Organizing Work-Related Learning Projects." *Human Resource Development Quarterly*, 1999, *10*(1), 43–62.

Rawls, J. *A Theory of Justice.* Boston: Harvard University Press, 1971.

Rees, E. F., Cervero, R. M., Moshi, L., and Wilson, A. L. "Language, Power, and Construction of Adult Education Programs." *Adult Education Quarterly*, 1997, *46*(2), 63–77.

Senge, P. M. *The Fifth Discipline: The Art and Practice of the Learning Organization.* New York: Doubleday, 1990a.

Senge, P. M. "The Leader's New Work: Building Learning Organizations." *Sloan Management Review*, 1990b, *32*(1), 7–23.

St. Clair, R. "On the Commonplace: Reclaiming Community in Adult Education." *Adult Education Quarterly*, 1998, *49*(1), 5–14.

Tisdell, E. J. "Interlocking Systems of Power, Privilege, and Oppression in Adult Higher Education Classes." *Adult Education Quarterly*, 1993, *43*(4), 203–226.

Toffler, A. *The Third Wave.* New York: Bantam, 1980.

Toffler, A. *Powershift: Knowledge, Wealth, and Violence at the Edge of the 21st Century.* New York: Bantam, 1990.

Walton, M. *The Deming Management Method.* New York: Perigee-Putnam, 1986.

Watkins, K. E., and Marsick, V. J. *Sculpting the Learning Organization: Lessons in the Art and Science of Systemic Change.* San Francisco: Jossey-Bass, 1993.

Yorks, L., O'Neil, J., and Marsick, V. J. (eds.). *Action Learning: Successful Strategies for Individual, Team, and Organizational Development.* Advances in Developing Human Resources, no. 2. San Francisco: Berrett-Koehler, 1999.

CHAPTER 19

Negotiating Democratically for Educational and Political Outcomes

Ronald M. Cervero and Arthur L. Wilson

▧ WHY PLANNING TABLES MATTER

In this section we develop the planning table metaphor introduced in Chapter One as the central dynamic of program planning, and we explain why it can both account for people's lived experience and provide a guide to practical action. If program planning cannot be accurately depicted as a sequence of activities that begins with needs-assessment, moves through educational design, and ends with evaluation, then what do planners actually do? In place of the logic used in classical planning models, the starting point of our theory is that "people plan educational programs" (Cervero & Wilson, 1994a, 1996). Unlike the classical planning models, the theory offers an account of people's lived experiences when planning in social and organizational contexts. This starting point highlights the fundamentally social nature of program planning and focuses attention on where decisions are truly made about educational programs—namely, at "the planning table" (Cervero & Wilson, 1998).

Drawing Attention to What Matters

The planning table metaphor draws attention to the fundamental idea that people make judgments with others in social and organizational contexts that determine

291

the specific features of an educational program, such as its purpose, content, audience, and format (Cervero & Wilson, 1996). The planning table can be a physical one at which people make decisions about an educational program. More often, however, it is a metaphorical table, accounting for the judgments that people make with others in conversations on telephones, through e-mail and faxes, and sometimes privately in offices, hallways, and restrooms or at social gatherings. People make these judgments about the features of educational programs at multiple, historically developing, and intersecting planning tables. For example, in making decisions about the management education program, Pete and Joan worked at multiple planning tables. At one table, with the president, they made decisions about the overall need, purpose, and place for the program. At another table, they worked out the specific features of the educational design with George, the outside facilitator. At other planning tables, Pete had one-on-one meetings with three vice presidents as he sought approval for the key features of the program. The work at these planning tables was historically developing in the sense that each discussion crystallized additional judgments about the objectives, the activities, and the leadership for the program. For example, each of the three meetings that Pete and Joan had with the president built on decisions and discussions from the previous meetings. The work at these planning tables was intersecting in that Pete's efforts to gain approval from the vice presidents for certain program features provided important information and leverage as he worked the planning table with the president.

Drawing Attention to the Making of Judgments

A second reason for the planning table as an organizing theme is that it draws attention to when judgments are made that determine the features of an educational program. The history of the planning table for a program might have begun well before the "formal planning" was initiated. For example, the management education program at the Phoenix Company had been an annual event for several years. Thus, when Pete and Joan entered the president's office for their first planning meeting, their efforts were part of a long-standing set of traditions in the company about how the planning would occur as well as about the purposes and format for this program. These prior judgments about the uses of the annual retreat formed a strong frame around the possibilities for the one being planned. This attention to when judgments are made that determine the features of a program also shows that planning does not stop when a brochure is printed or an instructional design is written down. It is important to recognize that the instructional site itself forms a critical planning table for any educational program. For example, instructors often make judgments about the content during the program, ad hoc decisions are made about changing the design due to suggestions from the learners, mistakes are made by the facilitator in carrying out the design, and unexpected opportunities become available to the group in organizing the curriculum. Although these are generally thought of as "implementation" decisions, this distinction between planning and implementation misses the opportunity to see that learners are always at a planning table for any program. Although important judgments prior to the educational activity generally delimit what is possible for the educational agenda, people either support or change these decisions at the planning table with learners. The PI program provides a good example. The agenda for the afternoon of the second day called for a "concept mapping" activity, which had been successful in the previous two PI projects. However, when Cassie and Dougie sensed a rising anxiety among the participants, they decided at lunch to change this activity to a less structured one, allowing the teachers to continue the morning discussion.

Drawing Attention to the Character of Planning

A third reason for the planning table as an organizing theme is that it draws attention to the fundamentally social and political character of educational planning. Although some planning models urge educators to pay attention to context (Boone, Safrit, & Jones, 2002; Caffarella, 2002; Sork, 2000), they do not locate where and how political relationships play out in the planning process nor do they show specifically how to plan strategically within these relationships. By noting where judgments are made about a program, planning is moved out of the minds of individuals and into socially and politically constructed places (Wilson & Cervero, 2003). Most important, the planning table shows specifically and concretely where power operates to affect educational programs. Thus, the planning tables (both literal and metaphorical) are the central link between the individual person and the political and social structures within which people make judgments about a program's purposes, content, and audiences. In the SVP story, we see precisely how political relationships shaped the judgments about specific features of the Fundamentals of Valuation program. The organizational structure at the Society—specifically, the Professional Development Committee—provided the political frame for making decisions about the program. Indeed, the creation of the Professional Development Committee was a concrete political strategy used by the Society to change how decisions were made about education. Thus, membership in this committee mattered because it defined who sat at the planning table.

Arthur worked this politically constructed planning table to make the fundamental decisions about the program's purpose, audience, and general outlines of its format. The point is that people work planning tables structured by existing social and political relationships to make the judgments about an educational program's features.

Connecting the Domains of Planning

Finally, the planning table metaphor connects the technical, political, and ethical domains of planning (Cervero & Wilson, 1994a, 1994b; Sork, 2000). To have any hope of connecting ethical beliefs, political analyses, and technical skills, we must look to the planning tables where the real work gets done. Virtually all of the theory about planning educational programs separates the technical processes from the political and ethical realities that educators face. Indeed, these two dimensions of education often exist in parallel universes. In one dimension, education plays an important role in the ongoing distribution of knowledge and power in social and organizational contexts (Cervero & Wilson, 2001). The other dimension highlights the technical processes of planning, such as the development of surveys and focus groups to collect data from learners about their needs (Sork & Buskey, 1986; Wilson & Cervero, 1997). Separating these two dimensions of education into issues of ethics and power and issues of technique and practice has failed to give educators the tools and analyses necessary to plan responsibly. This separation produces a missed opportunity to offer practical strategies that educators can use to plan democratically in the face of the power relations that shape what is possible, or even imaginable, in social and organizational contexts. For example, when Pete and Joan discussed with George the idea of surveying people attending the program, they were addressing both technical and political issues. Although it was important to design a technically credible survey, it was equally important to determine how they would use this information to decide about the features of the program. Although people's technical knowledge and skills are critically important in planning (for example, about budgeting and instructional design), these processes are always embedded in political and ethical domains (Cervero & Wilson, 1996). As Forester (1989) so clearly points out: "Once reported or uttered, even the most technical judgment becomes an integral part of the political world; it becomes inescapably political, seeking legitimacy by appealing to the consent of those concerned with the merits of the case" (p. 72). That legitimacy is enacted at the planning tables where decisions are made that determine the features of educational programs.

▦ DIMENSIONS OF THE PLANNING TABLE

This section addresses four key dynamics that operate at the planning tables where educational programs are produced: (1) power relations enable and constrain people's access to and capacity to act at the planning table, (2) people represent interests at the table, (3) ethical commitments define who should be represented at the table, and (4) negotiation is the central practical action at the table. These four dynamics are linked to form a definition of program planning as a social activity in which people negotiate with and among interests at planning tables structured by socially organized relations of power. This activity produces programs that have educational and political outcomes for multiple stakeholders.

Power Relations Shape the Planning Table

By defining planning as a social activity, what matters most is which people are at the table deciding the features of an educational program. Planning tables do not simply arise out of people's minds but rather are firmly rooted in ongoing sociopolitical relationships and represent places where power is both produced and used (Wilson & Cervero, 2003). These power relations are fundamentally important because they influence whose interests are represented at the planning table. Power is defined in many different ways, but for our theory it has three important characteristics (Giddens, 1979; Isaac, 1987; Winter, 1996). First, power is a social and relational characteristic, not simply something that people "possess" and use on one another. Second, it is necessary to distinguish between power relations as a structural characteristic and people's exercise of their power, which is an individual activity. Third, although power relations are relatively stable, they are continuously negotiated at planning tables.

Power is the capacity to act, which is distributed to people by virtue of their position and participation in enduring social and organizational relationships (Apple, 1992; Giddens, 1979; Isaac, 1987; Winter, 1996). Recognizing that people have "power" means that they have a certain "capacity" to act, rooted in a specific socially structured relationship; such capacity to act is not simply a consequence of individual attributes. Here is an example of the relational nature of power: when Cassie was planning with Dougie, they had a roughly symmetrical power relationship in contrast to her greater power when she was making decisions with program participants and her lesser power with Ron. Even though she is the same person in each situation, her capacity to act is different because of the socially organized relations in which she is a participant. Another example is the fact that

Pete had much less capacity to act at the planning table with the president than at a planning table with the hourly employees at the Phoenix Company. Again, he is obviously the same person at each planning table, but his capacity to act is different based on his organizational role as vice president and his social position as a white male in relation to the others at the table.

Defining power as relational means that it frames all human interactions (Foucault, 1977; Giddens, 1979). Power is not specific to a particular form of relationship, such as the case where one person gets another person to do something she would not otherwise have done. Although this coercive relationship is the most common view of power, it is entirely too restrictive (Isaac, 1987; Wilson & Cervero, 2002; Winter, 1996). Even though many power relationships are highly asymmetrical forms of domination, there are also relationships in which the capacity to act is distributed relatively equally to all people at the table. For example, the six Valuation Discipline committees at the SVP had the same organizationally defined capacity to develop workshops, even though the exercise of that power varied by individuals and individual committees. We agree with Forester (1999), who concludes that "Where some focus on power as structuring and limiting, I take power to be enabling as well, a politically shifting relationship rather than a fixed position or possession" (p. 6; see also Isaac, 1987; Wilson & Cervero, 2002; Winter, 1996). These power relations matter because they shape who has the capacity to be represented at the planning tables where decisions are made about educational programs.

Although power both enables and constrains action, exercising power in concrete situations is always a form of negotiation among the various people involved (Cervero & Wilson, 1994a). Even in asymmetrical power relationships, there is always some form of negotiation in determining who is at the planning table and what happens there. As Giddens (1979, p. 149) argues, "However wide the asymmetrical distribution of resources involved, all power relations manifest autonomy and dependence in both directions." At Phoenix, although Pete clearly was in a subordinate relationship to the president, the organizational structure limited how the president could exercise his power, and it distributed to Pete the capacity for a "variety of modes of leverage, maneuvering, and strategic bargaining" (Isaac, 1987, p. 91). The outcome of people's exercise of power about and at the planning table cannot be predetermined, but is contingent on how people choose to use that power. Although Pete could have exercised his power to bring managers and workers to the planning table, he did not. However, he did exercise his power by hiring a consultant and by getting approval for his plans from the other vice presidents before going to the president. This example acknowledges the existence of preexisting power relationships, while showing that people always face the problem of how to achieve their interests by exercising their power.

The third important characteristic of our theory is that power itself is always being negotiated at the planning table (Cervero & Wilson, 1996, 1998). Although the preexisting structural capacity to act is relatively stable, it is affected by who gets to make decisions at the planning tables for an educational program. As Forester (1989) argues, "Every organizational interaction or practical communication (including the nonverbal) not only produces a result, it also reproduces, strengthening or weakening, the specific social working relationships of those who interact" (p. 71). Forester's observation highlights the point that educational planning always has two outcomes: (1) negotiations at the planning table focus on making decisions about the program's educational features, and (2) these negotiations either maintain or alter the social and political relationships of those who are included and excluded from the planning (Cervero & Wilson, 1998). Planners always negotiate with their own power and negotiate between and among the political relationships of other people to make judgments about the features and outcomes of an educational program. At the same time, planners also negotiate about the political relationships themselves, seeking to reinforce or alter them. People's political relationships are therefore not static, because they are continually acted upon through the negotiation practices themselves. For example, by not having the department managers directly negotiate for their interests in planning the retreat, Pete strengthened the existing power structure in regard to who (namely, executives) could articulate the needs for educational programs. In the SVP story the PDC effectively shifted decision making away from the Education Committee, which had traditionally designed educational programs for the Society, by acquiring authority to design and direct the new educational program. The effect that efforts at planning tables have on social and political relationships themselves, which are crucial for enabling planners to act, is an often overlooked outcome of the planning process.

People's Interests Play Out at the Planning Table

If power relations shape the planning tables and people's capacity to act there, then people seek to achieve their interests as they exercise power at these tables (Cervero & Wilson, 1994a, 1994b). People come to the table with a complex set of interests, which are "predispositions, embracing goals, values, desires, and other orientations and inclinations that lead a person to act in one direction or another" (Morgan, 1997, p. 161). Interests are the motivations and purposes that lead people to act in certain ways when confronted with situations in which they must make a judgment about what to do or say. Those involved in planning educational programs exercise their power in accordance with their own specific interests and the interests of others they represent at the table.

We need to make two important points about how interests play out at the planning table. First, the features of educational programs result from the interests that people negotiate at the planning table. For example, the features of the management education program were determined by the interests that Mr. Jones, Pete, Joan, and George represented at the planning table. Thus, educational programs are causally related to specific interests of the people who plan them (Cervero & Wilson, 1994a). We can now amplify the theory's starting point, saying that "people with interests plan programs." Second, although programs are causally related to people's interests, there is no sense in which the judgments about specific programmatic features are predetermined. Rather, these outcomes depend on which people are at the planning table, which and whose interests they represent, and how they choose to exercise power at the table. Because of these contingencies, for example, the Fundamentals of Valuation program could have had different purposes, objectives, methods, audiences, and locations than the ones actually selected. That it ended up being a three-day meeting to address the topic of Fundamentals, was held at a college campus, and included an examination all resulted from the power relations that shaped the planning tables, the interests that people brought to these tables, and the specific negotiations that occurred there.

Of the complex sets of interests that people represent at the planning table, some are related to educational outcomes, whereas others are related to social and political outcomes (Cervero & Wilson, 1998). The SVP leaders used professional development programs not only to educate the members, but also to create a clearer professional identity and add a revenue stream for the Society. The people at the Phoenix Company planning table had interests related to the educational outcomes of the program. They hoped that the program would give individuals the knowledge and skill to improve communication in the company as a whole. Thus, the expected educational outcomes include not only participants' knowledge but also their use of this knowledge to benefit the wider group, organization, or community. These same people also brought interests related to social and political outcomes to the planning table. By trying to bring learners to the planning table, George hoped not only to be seen as a good consultant so that he might be hired again in the future but also to promote his view that company workers needed to be involved in company decision making through participatory management. As a newly employed director of customer service, Joan hoped to use the program not only to gain more visibility in the company and to more clearly define her role, but also to change organizational patterns of interaction through experiential training activities. Pete's interests in the management education program included improving the status of his human resources office as well as improving communication in the company.

People's interests that are unrelated to educational outcomes are often labeled as "hidden agendas," which many believe should not affect the decisions that are made about educational programs. However, it is politically naïve and practically ineffective to ignore the many outcomes that people seek to achieve in planning educational programs. Indeed, this is one of the fundamental blind spots of almost all planning theories, which assume that programs are only about educational outcomes. Interests related to social and political outcomes cannot be wished away; they are as much a part of the planning process as interests related to educational outcomes. Indeed, the former are often more important, as people seek to achieve many diverse political outcomes at the planning table. As Pete worked the planning table to reposition himself and his department, he had to negotiate with George, who wanted to use the program to foster participatory management in the company. Arthur sought to represent learners and promote experiential learning and reflective practice, whereas SVP's leaders sought to use the program to increase membership and influence state and federal legislatures. Cassie and Dougie worked to change whose knowledge mattered in staff development.

Almost always, people at the planning table are representing the interests of others. For example, Arthur saw himself representing the interests of the learners when he negotiated the addition of interactive instructional techniques at the instructor training clinic. Very often the interests that people bring to the table are contradictory. For example, by intentionally excluding the executive vice president from the planning process, Pete's stated interest of improving communication in the company was outweighed by his personal interest of improving his standing with the president. Thus, the fundamental practical questions about interests at the planning table are, Whose interests are at stake in this program, and what are those interests? By asking these questions, people are able to anticipate, and therefore act, in ways that are both politically astute and practically effective in planning educational programs.

Who Should Be at the Planning Table?

Ethical Commitments in Action

Who sits at the planning table matters because there is a causal relationship among whose interests people represent there, the practical judgments that these people make, and the specific features of educational programs (Cervero & Wilson, 1994a). That educational programs are causally related to people's interests is no superfluous claim, for if program features were not determined by these interests, then what would determine them? Although evidence can, and in many cases should, inform these practical judgments, they are actually made by people seeking to achieve specific outcomes. Even more important, if program features were not produced by people's interests, then why would the programs matter? Educational programs matter because they create possible futures in the lives of people, organizations, and communities. These judgments can only be made based on the ethical commitments that people bring to the planning table about what these possible futures should be and how they can be achieved through education. Ethical commitments are not some metaphysical, disembodied set of principles but rather beliefs about how to act in the world (Flax, 1992; Forester, 1999; West, 1989). These ethical commitments are critical because as any experienced planner knows, "Hundreds of practical judgments must be made, but the labels of 'neutrality' or 'impartiality' hardly inform how those judgments ought to be made in diverse practical situations" (Forester, 1999, p. 190). To fully account for what matters in planning, then, a theory needs to address the ethical commitments that inspire people's actions at the table.

These commitments are played out in decisions about and at the uneven planning tables where people negotiate interests in planning programs. People enact their ethical commitments in practical settings by answering two basic questions: Who should benefit in what ways from educational programs, and whose interests should be represented at the planning tables where judgments are made about educational programs (Cervero & Wilson, 1994a, 2001)? In answering the first question, people's ethical commitments offer a priority order for the political analysis of whose interests are at stake. For example, whereas Mr. Jones might have believed that everyone at the Phoenix Company had a stake in the outcome of the retreat, his primary ethical commitment was to ensure that decisions made at the executive level were effectively communicated downward through the organization. Mr. Jones's beliefs about how to act were at odds with those of George, whose ethical commitment was to develop more participatory forms of management. The second question addresses people's social and political commitments about whose interests matter enough to be represented at the planning table. No evidence could have been used to decide if Pete should have brought representatives of the 1,200 employees to the planning table to identify the retreat's educational objectives. These two sets of ethical commitments, about who should benefit and who should be at the table, are intertwined. For example, Pete's beliefs about a communication problem helped determine the objectives because he was also able to determine who should sit (and not sit) at the table to develop objectives.

Ethical commitments are also deeply intertwined with the political relationships in the social and organizational settings where planning occurs. People's ethical commitments are typically enacted in a world of conflicting interests and unequal power relations, producing the uneven tables at which most planning occurs. This point is vitally important because if "ethical thinking is blind to the world of politics and pragmatism, then ethics, it seems, asks us to be saints and martyrs, not planners" (Forester, 1990, p. 253). Without ethical commitments about who should benefit and who should be at the planning table, those with the most power can exercise it to determine the features of a program and its educational and political outcomes. People's commitments are also important when adjudicating among the stakeholders' interests related to educational and political outcomes. These outcomes often present competing choices to people at the planning table. Pete had to decide whose definition of the communication problem would drive the retreat program. Would he base the definition of need on the president's view or would he engage managers who were the learners? Would he take the president's view because it was the right definition of the problem or because it would further his political interest to strengthen the human resources office? Pete's ethical commitment about whose interests matter and his political analysis of the situation framed his actions in planning the retreat.

People Negotiate at the Planning Tables

People undertake many forms of practical action when planning educational programs. One form is discussed by theories that focus on procedural tasks, such as writing a budget, visiting a possible site of instruction, and preparing an end-of-program evaluation survey. Planners often bring technical knowledge and rules of thumb to bear in addressing such tasks (Sork, 1996). For example, Cassie and Dougie knew that with twenty-four participants in this year's program, they needed to create two groups for many activities in order to facilitate participation. Although the SVP leaders did not expect to lose money, for the first offering of the

Fundamentals program the registration fee was set lower than the competition's programs to encourage participants to switch their allegiance to the SVP programs. Although such activity is typically thought of only in terms of technique, it also represents how planners bring their power and interests to bear in determining which tasks will be addressed and how.

The form of practical action that really matters is undertaken at the planning tables where people confer, discuss, and argue in making judgments about what to do to produce the important features of the educational program. Negotiation is the overall concept describing these interactions, not because there is always conflict involved but rather because all human interactions are, in part, political. Thus, negotiation is the social activity in which people interact at the planning table in order to reach agreement about what to do in relation to the educational program (Cervero & Wilson, 1994a). What makes such negotiations political is that they are neither neutral nor objective nor even simply technical, but rather represent how planners exercise power to represent their own and others' interests in shaping educational and political outcomes. Situations at the planning table may differ dramatically, from those where there is widespread agreement among people's interests to those where high levels of difference and conflict exist. Following Newman (1994), Baptiste (2000) classifies these "social transactions into one of three groupings … depending on the severity of conflict they exhibit" (p. 41) and argues that each situation calls for a different overall approach to negotiation. As people negotiate at the planning table, then, they need to be able to anticipate and read situations so that they can use an approach that matches the situation.

There are some situations at the planning table in which "two or more parties whose common interests outweigh any conflicting ones come together with a view to sharing information and solving problems to their mutual advantage" (Newman, 1994, p. 154). The negotiations undertaken in these situations are consultations because people treat each other as allies and friends, trust is high, and everyone works together in a mutually supportive way. The planning that Cassie, Dougie, and Ron undertook for the staff development program is a typical example of a consultation. In these situations the amount of power that people bring to the table is relatively unimportant because everyone has a similar set of interests driving their judgments. Everyone is "on the same page," so there is little or no worry that some may leverage their power to harm others at the table. Rather, decision making about the features of the educational program is a form of problem solving. For example, although the political relationships among

Pete, Joan, and Mr. Jones were highly asymmetrical, their common interests far outweighed their conflicting ones. Thus, their negotiations about the management retreat were consultative: friendly, noncoercive, and virtually free of conflict. Out of these consultations, they made judgments about the need, purpose, audience, facilitators, and location of the retreat.

Moving along the continuum, there are situations at the planning table "where two or more parties with both common and conflicting interests come together to talk with a view to reaching agreement" (Newman, 1994, p. 153). The negotiations undertaken in these situations are bargaining because it is likely that the final set of agreements about the program will not address everyone's interests. People in situations that call for a bargaining strategy need each other, however, and will seek to find, if not to maximize, areas of common interests. Unlike in consultations, the amount of power that people have at the table now matters. Whose interests finally prevail when bargaining at the planning table is strongly influenced by people's political relationships. In fact, "one party may lose out badly in the negotiation and another may gain considerably" (Newman, 1994, p. 153) based on how people choose to exercise their power. An example of this outcome occurred when Pete and George were bargaining over the purpose of the retreat. Their interests conflicted in that George understood the retreat objective as trying to develop more participatory forms of management. Pete (as a representative of top management) did not share this agenda, and he used his power in this situation to focus the retreat on helping managers run better meetings. In situations that call for bargaining, there are many different strategies, ranging from withholding information and using power to keep items off the agenda to efforts by people at the table to educate others about their interests.

At the other end of the continuum lie those situations marked by a great deal of conflict among people at the planning table. These are situations "in which parties whose conflicting interests outweigh any common ones engage with one another, each with a view to winning—that is, furthering its own interests or gaining ascendancy for its own viewpoint" (Newman, 1994, p. 154). The negotiations undertaken in these situations are disputes, which "arise when talks have broken down; when distrust is open and rampant; when the battle lines are drawn, and when opposing sides seek actively, freely, and knowingly to frustrate each other's causes" (Baptiste, 2000, p. 43). In these situations, the amount of power that people bring to the table is vital to both the strategy that needs to be used and the likelihood that a person will achieve her objective. The person who has power in a highly asymmetrical relationship can simply exercise that power in a variety of ways to achieve her interests. In a dispute at the SVP, a governor in a budget meeting demanded to know how this new education program was going to be funded, because there was not a budget line item for Arthur's position or for the program's start-up costs. Because he was the Society president and the PDC chair, the president had the power to respond that the Society was going to offer this program even without any visible means of financial support. However, if a person has little power in an asymmetrical relationship, she will need to counteract that power at the planning table. For example, Pete explicitly kept Brad away from the retreat planning tables. He was able to counteract Brad's power by working directly with the president, who signed off on all decisions for the retreat. Pete's alliance with the president at the planning table was an effective strategy in this dispute.

NEGOTIATING DEMOCRATICALLY AT THE PLANNING TABLE

This section builds on the planning table metaphor to address the issue of "how to do planning well in a messy, politicized world" (Forester, 1999, p. 10). It moves from accounting for people's lived experience to providing a guide for practical action based on an ethical commitment to substantively democratic planning.

Negotiating at the Educational and Political Intersection

All planning models offer a guide for planning that addresses key questions of educational needs, objectives, instructional design, and evaluation. As explained in Chapter One, however, these models provide little guidance for the common practical situations in which people pursue outcomes at the planning table related to their social and political interests. Indeed, these other interests are generally considered to be "noise" that impedes good planning. Yet, any guide to practical action must address the complete picture at the planning table, including the multiple outcomes that people seek to achieve as well as the social and political relationships that make planning possible. Thus, any guide to responsible planning "requires attention to both the substantive issues at hand and the relationships that link the parties who care about those issues" (Forester, 1999, p. 65).

People responsible for planning educational programs are at the nexus of two evolving sets of negotiations (Cervero & Wilson, 1994b, 1998). Thus they need "to develop the double vision that students of negotiation consider second nature:

the ability to pay attention not only as narrower 'technicians' to the 'substance at hand' (what we are negotiating about), but also to the 'relationships between parties' (how we are negotiating this)" (Forester, 1999, p. 89). The "substance at hand" in educational planning involves the actual features of the educational program necessary to produce educational outcomes. Planners must always stay aware of many important substantive issues, such as the educational need, the audience, the market for the program, and the program evaluation. At the same time, they must pay attention to the "relationships between parties," focusing on social and political relationships among people both at the planning table and not at the table and the multiple outcomes that people seek to achieve there. Recognizing opportunities and resolving the dilemmas and contradictions arising from the intersection of these two sets of negotiations is the fundamental political and ethical problem of educational planning (Cervero & Wilson, 1998). While planners must necessarily address political relationships at this intersection, an ethical commitment to substantively democratic planning prevents the stress on politics from degenerating into a "disempowering relativism" (Hart, 1992, p. 157) in which "might makes right."

Committing Ethically to Substantively Democratic Planning

As these two sets of negotiations intersect at the table, planners enact an ethical commitment about who should be at the table and who should benefit from the educational program. Our vision of good planning is based on an ethical commitment to nurturing substantively democratic planning across both levels of negotiations (Cervero & Wilson, 1994a, 1994b). At the level of substantive negotiations, this commitment should produce programs that enlarge rather than restrict people's life chances. At the level of negotiations about people's social and political relationships, planners should focus on the democratic construction of the planning table. Youngman's (1996) advice that there is always a space to work out an ethical commitment to substantive democratic planning cuts across both levels: "Adult educators work in a wide variety of situations, ranging from institutions of the state to organizations of civil society. Their scope for a critical practice varies accordingly. However, it is our contention that spaces can be found in all situations if adult educators are clear about their social goals and how these can be embodied in their day-to-day activities" (p. 4). These spaces exist in negotiating about either a program's substantive features or the social and political relationships at the planning table.

An ethical commitment to substantively democratic planning means that all people who are affected by an educational program should "be involved in the deliberation of what is important" (Apple, 1992, p. 11). As Frankel (1977) says of Dewey's democratic vision, "Democracy is a procedure for melding and balancing human interests. The process need not be conducted, and at its best is not conducted, without regard for truth and facts.... Its controlling purpose is collective action, not the accreditation of propositions as true" (p. 20). Thus, a democratizing process means simply that real choices about what collective action to take for the educational program will be put before people at the planning table. By arguing for an ethical commitment to substantively democratic planning, we explicitly align our theory with an intellectual-practical tradition in American education that "rests on a recognition of the importance of a fully political and educative notion of democracy that recaptures the collective struggle by citizens to build institutions in participatory ways" (Carlson & Apple, 1998, p. 9). This tradition builds on both Dewey's vision for democratic forms of education and more recent attempts to reinterpret this vision in a way that recognizes the threats to democratic education posed by the asymmetrical power relationships embedded in existing social, racial, cultural, political, and economic systems (Apple, 1990; Collins, 1991; West, 1989).

The ethical commitment to substantively democratic planning is not an abstract one, because as Apple (1990) points out, "Democracy is not a slogan to be called upon when the 'real business' of our society is over, but a constitutive principle that must be integrated into all of our daily lives" (p. xvi). Substantively democratic planning is to be distinguished from the techniques of formal democracy, such as voting. In educational planning terms, formal democracy might mean arranging people's chairs in a circle around a friendly planning table and asking them what they want to learn. However, imagine what would happen if the hourly worker, manager, and venture capitalist were placed around the planning table and treated as equals under the guise of equal opportunity. In situations of conflicting interests, this would ensure that those who have the most power would see their interests manifested in the educational program. Substantive democracy insists on the recognition that systems of power and privilege do not stop at the doors of the social and organizational contexts in which programs are offered (Cervero & Wilson, 2001). People's efforts at the planning table should be guided by the principle of "pragmatics with vision" (Forester, 1993, p. 39), which stresses the need to hold firm in democratic values, matching planning strategies to social and political relationships to nurture that commitment.

The principle of "pragmatics with vision" requires planners to recognize that in nurturing democratic planning, different situations call for different forms of negotiation (Cervero & Wilson, 1994a; Forester, 1989). The same action could nurture democratic planning in one situation and thwart it in another. For example, although both sets of negotiations are often mutually supportive in consultative situations, planners will encounter bargaining situations in which there are trade-offs across these two levels of negotiations. Worse yet, they can encounter dispute situations in which there are even more restrictive strategies that can be used to enact democratic planning at either level. Many of the planning activities for the staff development program were undertaken in consultative situations, in which the planners and learners often refashioned the instructional design of the retreats to meet changing needs. However, the wigger incident clearly presented a bargaining situation in which getting people to talk with one another was a major struggle. In contrast to these situations, if Pete and Joan had brought managers and other employees to meet with Mr. Jones about the program, a substantively democratic planning process would have resulted only if the Phoenix Company presented a consultative situation in which the interests were consensual and political relationships symmetrical. Because the situation was not consultative, the program would probably have been the same in all respects because of the enormous amount of power the president had in the situation. Thus, Pete and Joan would have had to recognize that they faced a bargaining situation at the planning table before they could use a negotiation strategy that would enfranchise the interests of all stakeholders in constructing the program. In the SVP story, initially Arthur was the only one to raise the question of learner needs, and he did so in a consultative fashion, assuming that his being hired as an educator meant that the Society would draw upon that expertise. Because the members of the PDC felt they understood what aspiring valuators needed to learn, they designed curricula and courses representing what they thought would best enhance the professional status of their association and its members. Arthur misread these political relationships and had relatively little power in the organization; therefore, he was unable to promote learner involvement.

These examples illustrate that people need not only an ethical commitment, but also a commitment that is linked with a political analysis, because "good intentions when blind to the context of action can lead directly to bad results" (Forester, 1990, p. 253). However, saying that planners need to negotiate at both levels and take account of the context does not solve the problems of planning. Rather, to say that program planning is political should begin the discussion, not end it. As Forester argues (1999), "No realistic discussion of planning is possible without taking power into account in several forms. If we are to analyze power as a political, and thus alterable, reality rather than as an unchangeable metaphysical ether, let us stop rediscovering and instead assess practically, comparatively, and prescriptively what different actors can do about it" (p. 9). To that end, we propose that planners should work the planning table to produce both educational and political outcomes by using negotiation strategies that honor "democratic deliberations rather than restrict them" (Forester, 1999, p. 9).

CONCLUSION

We have used Part One to show how planners' perspectives shape their practical action. Throughout much of the last century one perspective in particular, the "classical viewpoint" (Cervero & Wilson, 1994a; Schubert, 1986), has dominated the way we have theoretically understood and practically imagined the work of planning. That viewpoint, representing theoreticians' attempts to address what they have considered as "practical" questions, has indeed helped focus planners' attention on important aspects of their work. Nevertheless, one of the great limitations of this viewpoint has been its failure to understand the nature of practical action in real settings.

We offer a different perspective that puts people at the center of planning action. Working the planning table is at the heart of our theoretical claims about what matters when people plan educational programs in social and organizational contexts. These contexts are structured by power relations and provide the ground on which planners negotiate interests to produce both educational and political outcomes. In the face of power, we continually argue for the ethical commitment to nurture a substantively democratic process when planning programs. This understanding of people acting in context not only accounts for planners' experiences but also provides the best opportunity to produce educational programs that enlarge people's life chances in the real world.

REFERENCES

Apple, M. W. (1990). *Ideology and curriculum* (2nd ed.). New York: Routledge.

Apple, M. W. (1992). The text and cultural politics. *Educational Researcher*, *21*(7), 4–11, 19.

Baptiste, I. (2000). Beyond reason and personal integrity: Toward a pedagogy of coercive restraint. *Canadian Journal for the Study of Adult Education, 41*(1), 27–50.

Boone, E. J., Safrit, R. D., & Jones, J. (2002). *Developing programs in adult education: A conceptual programming model* (2nd ed.). Prospect Heights, IL: Waveland.

Caffarella, R. S. (2002). *Planning programs for adult learners: A practical guide for educators, trainers, and staff developers* (2nd ed.). San Francisco: Jossey-Bass.

Carlson, D., & Apple, M. W. (1998). *Power, knowledge, pedagogy: The meaning of democratic education in unsettling times.* Boulder, CO: Westview Press.

Cervero, R. M., & Wilson, A. L. (1994a). *Planning responsibly for adult education: A guide to negotiating power and interests.* San Francisco: Jossey-Bass.

Cervero, R. M., & Wilson, A. L. (1994b). The politics of responsibility: A theory of program planning practice for adult education. *Adult Education Quarterly, 45,* 249–268.

Cervero, R. M., & Wilson, A. L. (Eds.). (1996). *What really matters in adult education program planning: Lessons in negotiating power and interests.* New Directions for Adult and Continuing Education, No. 69. San Francisco: Jossey-Bass.

Cervero, R. M., & Wilson, A. L. (1998). Working the planning table: The political practice of adult education. *Studies in Continuing Education, 20*(1), 5–21.

Cervero, R. M., & Wilson, A. L. (2001). At the heart of practice: The struggle for knowledge and power. In R. M. Cervero, A. L. Wilson, & Associates, *Power in practice: Adult education and the struggle for knowledge and power in society* (pp. 1–20). San Francisco: Jossey-Bass.

Collins, M. (1991). *Adult education as vocation: A critical role for the adult educator.* London: Routledge.

Flax, J. (1992). The end of innocence. In J. Butler & J. W. Scott (Eds.), *Feminists theorize the political* (pp. 445–463). New York: Routledge.

Forester, J. (1989). *Planning in the face of power.* Berkeley: University of California Press.

Forester, J. (1990). Evaluation, ethics, and traps. In N. Krumholz & J. Forester (Eds.), *Making equity planning work: Leadership in the public sector* (pp. 241–260). Philadelphia: Temple University Press.

Forester, J. (1993). *Critical theory, public policy, and planning practice.* Albany: State University of New York Press.

Forester, J. (1999). *The deliberative practitioner: Encouraging participatory planning processes.* Cambridge, MA: MIT Press.

Foucault, M. (1977). *Discipline and punish: The birth of the prison* (A. Sheridan, Trans.). New York: Vintage.

Frankel, C. (1977). John Dewey's social philosophy. In S. M. Cahn (Ed.), *New studies in the philosophy of John Dewey* (pp. 3–44). Hanover, NH: University Press of New England.

Giddens, A. (1979). *Central problems in social theory: Action, structure, and contradiction in social analysis.* Berkeley: University of California Press.

Hart, M. (1992). *Adult education and the future of work.* New York: Routledge.

Isaac, J. C. (1987). *Power and Marxist theory: A realist view*. Ithaca, NY: Cornell University Press.

Morgan, G. (1997). *Images of organization* (2nd ed.). Thousand Oaks, CA: Sage.

Newman, M. (1994). *Defining the enemy: Adult education in social action*. Sydney: Stewart Victor.

Schubert, W. (1986). *Curriculum: Perspective, paradigm, and possibility*. New York: Macmillan.

Sork, T. J. (1996). Negotiating power and interests in planning: A critical perspective. In R. M. Cervero & A. L. Wilson (Eds.), *What really matters in adult education program planning: Lessons in negotiating power and interests* (pp. 81–99). New Directions for Adult and Continuing Education, No. 69. San Francisco: Jossey-Bass.

Sork, T. J. (2000). Planning educational programs. In A. L. Wilson & E. Hayes (Eds.), *Handbook of adult and continuing education: New edition* (pp. 171–190). San Francisco: Jossey-Bass.

Sork, T. J., & Buskey, J. H. (1986). A descriptive and evaluative analysis of program planning literature, 1950–1983. *Adult Education Quarterly, 36*, 86–96.

West, C. (1989). *The American evasion of philosophy: A genealogy of pragmatism*. Madison: University of Wisconsin Press.

Wilson, A. L., & Cervero, R. M. (1997). The song remains the same: The selective tradition of technical rationality in adult education program planning theory. *International Journal of Lifelong Education, 16*(2), 84–108.

Wilson, A. L., & Cervero, R. M. (2002). The question of power and practice. In K. Kunzel (Ed.), *International yearbook of adult education* (pp. 209–226). Cologne: Bohlau-Verlag.

Wilson, A. L., & Cervero, R. M. (2003). A geography of power, identity, and difference in adult education curriculum practice. In R. G. Edwards & R. Usher (Eds.), *Space, curriculum, and learning* (pp. 123–138). Greenwich, CT: Information Age Publishing.

Winter, S. L. (1996). The "power" thing. *Virginia Law Review, 82*(5), 721–835.

Youngman, F. (1996). A transformative political economy of adult education: An introduction. In P. Wangoola & F. Youngman (Eds.), *Towards a transformative political economy of adult education: Theoretical and practical challenges* (pp. 3–32). DeKalb: Northern Illinois University, LEPS Press.

PART FOUR

THE CHANGING LANDSCAPE OF ADULT LEARNING

Adult learning is the glue that holds an otherwise incredibly diverse field of practice together. Whether engaged in continuing professional education, learning to read, returning to higher education, enhancing work-related skills, or just strolling through a museum, adults are learning. The more we understand how adults learn, the more effective we can be in our practice as adult educators. As with the other parts of this book, the six chapters are not intended to comprehensively cover what we know about learning; rather, we have chosen selections on adult learning that allow readers to sample some of the newer thinking about adult learning. Three selections are generally about learning—the nature of reflection, social learning, and transformative learning—and three selections are more specifically about a particular aspect of adult learning—the role of emotions, mass media and learning, and non-Western perspectives on learning and knowing.

Much of our learning is embedded in the experiences we have in our everyday lives. Reflection on our experiences is often what leads us to know that we have learned something, something which leads to our thinking about or doing things differently. Chapter 20, from Michael Newman's well-known book *Defining the Enemy,* is a discussion of the meaning of reflection. He traces the various conceptions of reflection from reflection as pondering, to reflection as self-disclosure, to its roles in praxis, in experiential learning, and so on.

Reflection, and in particular critical reflection, is key to understanding transformative learning. In Chapter 21, Cranton nicely summarizes the issues around Mezirow's theory of transformative learning (TL) and reviews some of the more recent conceptualizations of TL. Drawing from both Freire and Habermas, Mezirow's theory of transformative learning has been just that—a theory in progress that has captured the interest of practitioners, scholars, and researchers. Through biannual conferences on transformative learning; a journal devoted to this type of learning; and hundreds of articles, books, and proceedings, TL is surely one of the most studied areas of adult learning today.

As Cranton notes, many have observed that transformative learning, at least Mezirow's version of TL, has often been seen and critiqued for its focus on the individual and cognitive rationality. In Chapter 22, Niewolny and Wilson present "an alternative to the discourse of individualism." They explore ways in which adults learn in and with the social world. Social learning can mean anything from Bandura's notion of modeling behavior, to group learning, to how informal and nonformal learning is characterized, to experiential and context-based learning, and so on. Their exploration helps broaden our notion of adult learning as more than an individual, rational endeavor. As they point out, learning as a social activity is really a political endeavor as issues of power, privilege, and one's positionality all come into play. This position reflects the perspective of Freire and others in popular education and critical pedagogy that all education is political.

That learning is more than a cognitive activity is also quite apparent in Chapter 23, in which Dirkx discusses the affective, emotional, and embodied dimensions of learning. Many aspects of our practice, such as group activities, evaluation, even certain content matter such as math, often elicit powerful emotional responses. Further, emotional intelligence, transformative learning, and spirituality and learning have strong emotional components. He maintains that it is through acknowledging and processing these emotional and physical reactions that we are able to connect with the self. This dimension to learning is often spontaneous and serendipitous, but it is frequently what makes learning so profound and meaningful.

Yet another perspective on adult learning, one that we rarely account for when studying adult learning, are the ways in which media and technology are influencing "the thought and actions of people . . . at a level unprecedented in human history." In Chapter 24, Guy makes a persuasive case that global networks of mass media shape our ideas about the world. The problem with this global system of informal adult education is that only a few powerful elites are in control of this system, and learners are steered away from critical and socially conscious forms of learning and social action.

In Chapter 25, Merriam and Kim discuss non-Western perspectives on learning and knowing. While in Chapter 24 Guy makes the point that globalization, technology, and media have colluded to shape our thinking about the world and in so doing threaten both democracy and diversity, the same forces have led to our world being connected economically, culturally, technologically, and educationally as never before. One benefit of globalization has been a growing awareness of other systems and perspectives on learning and knowing. In contrast to Western ideas about how knowledge is constructed, what counts as legitimate knowledge, and how people learn, non-Western and indigenous knowledge systems emphasize learning that is communal; that is, it is the responsibility of all in the service of developing the community. Here learning is lifelong and informal, and it is holistic, involving the mind, the body, and the spirit.

Adult learning is hard to capture in a selection of readings. What we have tried to do here is to present the reader with glimpses of a variety of issues and perspectives that we hope will stimulate thought and discussion about the rich and diverse ways of looking at this very fundamental component of all of adult education practice. Since adult learning covers the spectrum from basic education to the synthesis and evaluation of ideas, this is a vital engagement for us all.

FOR REFLECTION AND DISCUSSION

1. Some feel that reflection is integral to learning. What are the different types of reflection and how important is reflection to learning? Can we learn without systematic or conscious reflection?

2. What is your understanding of transformative learning? How common a phenomenon is it? Describe an experience you or someone you know has had with transformative learning. How closely does the experience match Mezirow's model?

3. Adult learning is more than information processing through the brain. Describe a learning experience that involves the body, emotions, and/or spiritual dimensions.

4. Globalization, the interconnectedness of economies, peoples, cultures, and information, is not new. What is new is the breadth and speed at which these connections occur. Discuss how globalization can be viewed both negatively and positively in relation to our understanding and our practice of adult learning.

5. Consider how a collage is a grouping together of a collection of artifacts or objects to convey the complexity of a phenomenon. If adult learning is the phenomenon, in addition to the six different ways of thinking about adult learning presented here, what *other* perspectives, models, or theories of adult learning would you add to convey a comprehensive look at adult learning?

CHAPTER 20

Reflection Disempowered

Michael Newman

R eflecting on experience would seem to make sense. In the last twenty
years reflection has been accorded an increasingly important place in adult
learning, and many adult educators now see their major role as that of helping
learners reflect on and learn from events, behaviours and emotions experienced.
These events, behaviours and emotions may be from the learners' own lives, or
they may be created or triggered through visits, encounters, exercises, games,
simulations, or role-plays organised especially for the learning event. Educators
may employ a range of methods and techniques to aid this reflection, including
structured discussions, small group work, pair work, listening exercises, and report
and journal writing. One of the skills this modern adult educator must have is
that of helping people debrief their experiences—that is, of helping people talk
out, think about, come to understand, and draw insight and conclusions from an
experience.

However the meaning adult educators give to reflection has undergone a
number of changes. It started as a concept very much within the liberal tradition
of education, was injected with a charge of high emotion from the field of
psychotherapy, was politicised, was gradually wrested back by the humanists,
and is currently being taken over by latter-day behaviourists. In the process an
intellectual activity concerned with imagination, intuition and insight has been
diminished.

In the liberal adult education tradition the learner read, or listened to the
teacher, and then found time to think over what she or he had read or heard. In
this sense reflection really meant much the same as pondering. It was understood

315

that through careful thought we would arrive at rational conclusions, deeper understandings of universal truths, or finer appreciations of the aesthetic aspects of our culture. Reflection was seen as both a natural activity and as evidence of the existence of the enlightened mind. It was also seen as a discrete activity, preceding and separate from any action one might take as a result of conclusions reached or decisions taken in the course of that reflection.

In the 1960s adult education adopted a whole range of experiential techniques from the field of psychotherapy that encourage self-disclosure. These techniques rendered reflection a much more emotionally charged and much less orderly activity. As we have seen in an earlier chapter, Carl Rogers attests to the joy it gave him to "free curiosity" in his learner-patients, to "unleash a sense of enquiry" and to "permit individuals to go charging off in new directions dictated by their own interests" (Rogers, 1983, pp. 120–121).

In developing his concept of praxis, Paulo Freire politicised reflection. Radical adult educators, drawing on Marxist and socialist discourse to inform their practice, had employed the word *praxis* but it was Freire in the 1960s and 70s who made it current in the adult education profession as a whole. In Freire's concept, reflection and action are both contained in praxis and cannot be isolated one from the other. The two activities fuse into one dynamic process in which the learners act on themselves and on their world, bringing about a change in their own consciousness and in the way they engage with other people, organisations, institutions and objects around them. Freire was working with people whose consciousness he perceived as "naïve" or constructed by others and who lived in conditions of oppression. Praxis was a process of action-reflection by which they began liberating themselves from their false consciousness and from their oppression.

In the 1970s and 80s Donald Schön, working with practitioners in corporate and professional fields, began separating reflection out from action again. He was interested in practitioners who could think on their feet, and adjust their practice accordingly, and he called this process reflection-in-action. Action and reflection coincide, but are clearly separate concepts in that reflection becomes a mode of monitoring and adjusting action. Schön (1983, 1987) envisages the practitioner reflecting "in and on" her or his practice to identify tacit norms that underlie judgements, implicit theories that inform behaviour, feelings that have impelled particular actions, modes of thought that have been used, and roles that have been constructed.

Freire's concept of praxis and Schön's reflection-in-action are very different. The actors in praxis are groups of people defined by their common oppression, their culture, their class and their history. The actors in Schön's reflection-in-action are individual practitioners, normally operating in professional contexts. In praxis, reflection, acting, the generation of new knowledge and the development of new understandings are indivisibly part of a process that changes both the people involved and the society of which they are a part. Reflection-in-action is a process in which practitioners use reflection to adjust and adapt their performances so as to make both themselves and the systems or organisations in which they operate function more effectively. Freire envisages praxis as a process with the potential of bringing about social, even revolutionary, change. Schön's reflection-in-action is also seen as capable of bringing about change in both the practitioner and the organisation, but it is not presented as a process that might challenge the society of which the practitioner and the organisation are parts.

David Boud, Rosemary Keogh and David Walker (1985) separate reflection even further from action. The model they develop very clearly implies a chronological sequence. Experience comes first, then the reflective process, then the outcomes. There may be interplay and some to-ing and fro-ing between the first two stages leading to more experiences and more reflection, but all three stages are depicted as encircled, separate and happening one after the other.

Boud and Walker revisit and develop this model in a later paper (1992). They accept that in the earlier model they concentrated on reflection after the event and did not give enough consideration to the roles reflection could play in the lead up to a learning experience, and during the experience itself. In a revision of the model they envisage both learners and facilitators using reflective processes to prepare for the learning in a number of ways. They also refer to Schön's concept of reflection-in-action and propose a role for reflection during the experience. Here, however, they do not appear to accept Schön's idea of a continuous reflection both in and on practice. They come to the conclusion that the learner at the moment of reflection is by definition detached from the experience:

> There is a fundamental tension between becoming fully immersed in an event and standing back to witness our own actions. The former is required if we are to be a full player in the event. The latter is implicit in the concept of reflection (1992, p. 271).

This leads them to maintain the sequential relationship between reflection and experience even during the learning event. The learner is offered prearranged and discrete periods of time in which to withdraw from the experience and reflect. Reflection during experience is actually reflection during breaks in the experience.

> In practice, there are many opportunities for reflection within planned learning activities. Natural breaks in the flow of events, time-out activities and exercises of a reflective nature can all be scheduled as part of the overall structure (1992, p. 271).

When considering reflection after the event, Boud and Walker retain the description of the reflective process they and Keogh included in their 1985 model. The process comprises three clusters of reflective activity: returning to the experience; attending to feelings; and re-evaluating the experience. Under "re-evaluating the experience," Boud, Keogh and Walker (1985) propose:

- relating what has become known to what is already known
- integrating new knowledge with old
- mentally testing our understandings in new contexts and
- making the knowledge gained our own.

Gone is the gentle magic of reflection as pondering, or the political promise of reflection as conscientization, or simply the idea that letting the mind play over what happened might produce some kind of insight. In their place is a list of mental actions to perform.

In Freire, reflection is part of a political process, part of learning for liberation. In Schön, reflection has a political colour too, in that it is presented as a mode of monitoring practice that will help the practitioner work more effectively within the corporate, professional and political structures of a capitalist culture. In Boud, Keogh and Walker reflection is an aid to experiential learning, with the political context of the learning and the social condition of the learners unspecified. They envisage the outcomes of their kind of reflective learning as being "new perspectives on experience," "change in behaviour," "readiness for application" and "commitment to action." The language is vague and I am tempted to ask: Perspectives that are new in what way? What kind of change in behaviour? Readiness for application to what? Commitment to what kind of action? Socialist action? Selfish action? Charitable action? Racist action? Once again, I suspect, we have encountered the humanists' faith that the outcomes from this kind of experiential learning will be expressive of some human and moral essence that resides in us all, and so, although unspecified, will necessarily be good ones.

Peter Jarvis argues that reflection is "to a great extent socially constrained" (1987a, p.112) and in his description of reflection he links it with reasoning.

> Reflection...means a process of deep thought, both a looking backwards to the situation being pondered upon and a projecting forward to the future, being both a process of recall and reasoning (p. 87).

He emphasises this link in a diagrammatic "model of the learning processes" by placing "reasoning and reflecting" in the same box (p. 25).

Jarvis' model has a number of factors and processes that he argues can be related in different ways and that can occur in different sequences, and his intention is clearly to present a model that can help us understand the fluid and variable nature of learning. However, a result of arguing that reflection is socially constrained is to imply that it is in itself an activity that can be learned. This is reinforced by linking it closely to reasoning, which in some respects can be regarded as a skill. And then by listing reflection along with a number of other activities such as memorisation, evaluation, practice and experimentation Jarvis is moving perilously close to describing reflection as a competency.

In his explication of his model and his discussion of reflection it is clear that this is not Jarvis' intention. He devotes much more time to a discussion of reflection than to any of the other factors or processes in his model; and in that discussion he canvasses a wide range of definitions and interpretations of reflection. However I express my disquiet because his model may be open to exploitation by the mechanists in our trade.

Indeed, others have gone further than Jarvis. In *Developing a Competent Workforce* (1992) Andrew Gonczi identifies a number of "higher order competencies":

> analytical and planning skills, logical and critical thinking, the ability to turn abstract ideas into concrete strategies, the ability to work in a team, communication capacities, a desire to produce high quality products (p. 4).

Later in the same book Paul Hager cites a definition of critical thinking as "reasonable reflective thinking that is focussed on deciding what to believe or do" (Hager, 1992, p. 152). In the course of reading the book, then, it is possible to draw the inference that reflective thinking is simply part of a definition of critical thinking which is itself simply another competency listed along with the ability to work in a team and a desire to produce high quality products. Reflection, a potentially emancipatory activity of the intellect that can encompass reverie, flights of fancy, insight, and intuition as well as reasoning, becomes another tool of commerce and industry.

Mechthild Hart has given a name to this process of turning activities of the intellect into utilitarian competencies. She notes that, in the training of people for business careers in recent years in the United States, "liberal learning skills" such as questioning, analysing problems and exercising judgment have been separated out and taught without reference to their traditional liberal arts content or context. It is a phenomenon she describes as "the gutting of liberal education" (1992, pp. 65–68).

REFERENCES

Boud, D., Keogh, R., and Walker, D. (eds.). (1985) *Reflection: Turning Experience into Learning*, Kogan Page Ltd., London

Boud, D. and Walker, D. (1992). "In the midst of experience: developing a model to aid learners and facilitators," in Harris, R. and Willis, P. *Striking a Balance: Adult and Community Education in Australia Towards 2000*, Centre for Human Resource Studies, University of South Australia and the South Australian Branch of the Australian Association of Adult and Community Education

Gonczi, A. (ed.) (1992). *Developing a Competent Workforce*, National Centre for Vocational Education Research, Adelaide

Hager, P. (1992). "Teaching Critical Thinking" in Gonczi, A. (ed.), *Developing a Competent Workforce*, National Centre for Vocational Education Research, Adelaide

Hart, M. (1992). *Working and Educating for Life: Feminist and International Perspectives on Adult Education*, Routledge, London

Jarvis, P. (1987a). *Adult Learning in the Social Context*, Croom Helm, Beckenham, Kent

Rogers, C. (1983). *Freedom to Learn for the 80s*, Charles E. Merrill Publishing, New York

Schön, D. (1983). *The Reflective Practitioner*, Temple Smith, London

Schön, D. (1987). *Educating the Reflective Practitioner*, Jossey-Bass, San Francisco

CHAPTER 21

A Theory in Progress

Patricia Cranton

A s is indicated in the subtitle of the book Mezirow edited in 2000, transformative learning theory is a theory in progress. Nowhere is this more evident than in the proceedings of the International Transformative Learning Conferences (for example, see Wiessner, Meyer, Pfhal, and Neuman, 2003). First initiated in 1998 by Victoria Marsick and Jack Mezirow, the purpose of the conference was and continues to be one of expanding and elaborating on transformative learning theory. The book based on the first conference (Mezirow and Associates, 2000) made several of these perspectives accessible to scholars and practitioners in the field.

The earliest critics of transformative learning theory focused on Mezirow's failure to address social change and his selective interpretation of Habermas's work (Collard and Law, 1989), his neglect of power issues (Hart, 1990), his disregard for the cultural context of learning (Clark and Wilson, 1991), and his overemphasis on rational thought (Dirkx, 1997). These issues remain at the center of debates today.

Baumgartner (2001) uses Dirkx's (1998) four-lens approach to understanding the directions in which transformative learning theory has moved. One lens has Freire's (1970) perspective as its foundation; that is, transformative learning can be seen as having liberation from oppression as its goal and social justice as its orientation. The second lens is Mezirow's (2000) concentration on rational thought and reflection as central to a process of responding to a disorienting dilemma, questioning and revising assumptions, engaging in discourse, and acting on a new perspective. The third lens is a developmental approach to transformative learning (Daloz, 1999). Here the process is intuitive, holistic, and contextually based; it is a transitional journey that takes place within a social environment. And finally, the fourth lens through which transformative learning can be viewed is one in which learning is linked to spirituality (Dirkx, 2001a, 2001b; Tisdell and Tolliver, 2001). Dirkx describes transformative learning as soul work; other writers link it to specific practices such as Buddhist meditation (Robinson, 2004) and yoga (Cohen, 2003). The popularity of a half-day postconference workshop on spirituality and transformative learning led by Wiessner, Dirkx, and Tisdell at the 2003 International Transformative Learning Conference speaks to the power of this perspective.

In this chapter, I group the directions in which transformative learning theory has developed in a slightly different way, though I do find Dirkx's four lenses very helpful. I first describe the introduction of connected and relational learning into the theory, and I provide some thoughts on transformative learning in relation to social change. These perspectives stretch the basic rationalistic views of Mezirow's theory and open the door for alternative ways of understanding transformative learning, yet they rely primarily on reflection to mediate the learning processes and, in this sense, are an extension of the emphasis on critical reflection. I then discuss the application of transformative learning theory to groups and organizations and review how transformative learning can be seen as an approach to worldviews on globalization and environmentalism. I describe the extrarational approach, which represents a fundamental challenge to critical reflection as a way of knowing by suggesting that transformative learning is mediated by unconscious processes beyond the level of rational and conscious awareness. Finally, I summarize some of the research on transformative learning by drawing on E. Taylor's (2000a, 2000b) important reviews and the offerings from both the International Transformative Learning Conferences and the *Journal of Transformative Education*.

CONNECTED KNOWING

It is not just in regard to transformative learning theory that there has been considerable debate about whether learning is connected and relational or independent and autonomous (see MacKeracher, 2004, for example). Traditional learning theory focuses on how an individual person learns, and although the context of the learning may be considered, it is generally about that person, not that person learning in and from relationships with others. This sounds odd, given the emphasis on groups and interactive methods in adult education, but learning has long been seen as an individual process even though discussion and group work may be used to get there. Perhaps the roots of this lie in behaviorism, with its emphasis on the individual organism, or perhaps they lie in the models of assessment that drive educational systems. Intelligence and aptitude are always measured individually, and scoring systems are based on comparison and competition among individuals. Evaluation of learning is an individual thing in education from the first grade through to doctoral studies. I have listened to many college instructors agonize over how to grade students when they are engaged in group projects.

Western society values individualism. Every aspect of our life is influenced by this value, including how we think about learning (see for example, Brookfield, 2005). It should not be too big a surprise that we respect autonomous, independent learning. Since Gardner (Gardner, Kornhaber, and Wake, 1996) introduced multiple intelligences, one of which is interpersonal intelligence, and Goleman (1998) brought the concept of emotional intelligence to our attention, there has been some change in our collective perspective. In training programs and workplace education, more emphasis is placed on how people learn to work together. But still, this is primarily about how an individual person learns to work with others, not learn in relation to others.

Feminist writers (Tisdell, 2000a, 2000b) and theorists interested in gender differences in learning (Hayes and Flannery, 2000) emphasize relational or connected learning. Women tend to learn differently, they propose; women learn through relationships with others, through nurturing and caring, and by connecting with each other (Belenky and Stanton, 2000). Belenky and Stanton critique traditional transformative learning theory on this and related bases. They suggest that although Mezirow presumes relations of equality among participants in discourse, most human relationships are asymmetrical. This has serious consequences, especially for women. Dualistic thinking (male-female, thinking-feeling, public-private) serves to create hierarchies in which one pole of the dichotomy is prized and the other devalued. We must, the authors argue, replace dualistic categories with integrative thinking.

Drawing on Belenky's well-known earlier research with her colleagues (Belenky, Clinchy, Goldberger, and Tarule, 1986), Belenky and Stanton (2000) describe six developmental stages of knowing for women: silenced, received knowers, subjective knowers, separate knowers, connected knowers, and constructivist knowers. It is the distinction between separate knowing and connected knowing that is of greatest interest to the authors in examining implications for transformative learning theory. The traditional theory, they suggest, places separate knowing in a central role. Unlike separate knowers, who follow lines of reasoning and look for flaws in logic to create more defensible knowledge, connected knowers suspend judgment and struggle to understand others' points of view from their perspective. They look for strengths not weaknesses in another person's point of view. Belenky and Stanton write, "The more Connected Knowers disagree with another person the harder they will try to understand how that person could imagine such a thing, using empathy, imagination and storytelling as tools for entering into another's frame of mind" (p. 87). They see this as a radically different stance in which the goal is to see holistically, not analytically.

Some recent research validates this understanding of transformative learning. For example, Carter (2000) found that transformation occurred primarily through developmental relationships among the upper-level management women she studied. In describing several types of relationships reported on by her participants, Carter labels one of these as a love relationship—a deep, intimate sharing of experiences and feelings over a sustained period of time. Others of Carter's participants maintained relationships in their memory with loved ones who had died. Gilly (2004) reports on an experience of transformative education among members of a doctoral peer group in which she finds collaboration and relationship to be the central aspects of transformation. In a careful, detailed self-study, J. Clark (2005) dedicates one chapter to the important role of friendship in transformative learning. Clark goes so far as to say that transformative learning could not take place without friendship.

I see some danger in proposing that women engage in transformative learning in one way. To suggest that women learn one way and men another way could be seen as stereotyping, and, given that the way women's learning is depicted is a way that is less valued in our society, this could also serve to further marginalize women. English (2004) speaks well to this issue in reporting on her study of women's learning in volunteer organizations. J. Cohen (2004) describes the stories of transformation in an adult education program that is explicitly designed to incorporate autonomy and connection.

It seems quite reasonable to suggest that different people engage in transformative learning in different ways and that some are more likely to learn through relationships, but I grow cautious when this is drawn along gender lines.

SOCIAL CHANGE

Transformative learning theory has long been criticized for not paying enough attention to social change. Although Mezirow (1991, 2000) draws on the works of Freire and Habermas, both of whom have social change as a central goal, Mezirow clearly believes that individual transformation precedes social transformation. Collard and Law (1989), Cunningham (1992), and Hart (1990) were among those who objected to this view early on in the development of the theory.

Social reform has long been a goal of adult education. Two examples come immediately to mind. In Canada, the Antigonish movement was founded by Father Jimmy Tompkins and Father Moses Coady in the late 1920s as a way of helping ordinary people foster economic development through cooperatives and credit unions. Using mass meetings, study groups, kitchen meetings, and community courses, the leaders of the movement sought to "help the people build greater and better democratic institutions" (Coady, 1939, p. 3). The six principles of the Antigonish movement were: (1) individual needs are primary and need to be developed in social contexts, (2) the root of social reform lies in education, (3) individuals are most concerned with economic needs and education must start there, (4) group settings are most suitable to education, (5) social reform both causes and is dependent on change in social and economic institutions, and (6) a full, self-actualized life for everyone in the community is the aim of the movement.

The second example, of course, is the Highland Folk School (now called the Highlander Research and Education Center) founded in the United States by Myles Horton and his colleagues in 1932. As was the case in the Antigonish movement, the goal was to provide education for ordinary people as a way of effecting social change. The development of literacy skills was seen to be one way of fostering both social and personal transformation. Horton's goal was to bring people together to challenge oppressive organizations and governments. Based on interviews with eight current educators from the Highlander Research and Education Center, Ebert, Burford, and Brian (2003) describe nine facets of practice relevant to transformative education: (1) providing a safe place to encourage discourse and reflection, (2) assuming participants bring a wealth of knowledge and experience, (3) helping people discover they are not alone, (4) facilitating critical thinking, (5) helping people develop voice and the confidence to act, (6) solving problems through synergy, (7) encouraging lifelong and diverse learning for change, (8) promoting the idea that everyone is an important member of a community, and (9) implementing continuous improvement.

Writers and theorists who emphasize social action see critical reflection without social action as "a self-indulgent form of speculation that makes no real difference to anything" (Brookfield, 2000, p. 143). Mezirow (2000) distinguishes between educational tasks—helping people become aware of oppressive structures and learn how to change them—and political tasks, which force economic change. This distinction is helpful. It is not the case that Mezirow is saying that social action is not the responsibility of adult educators or the product of transformative learning. He is saying that educators go about making a difference in the world by helping learners learn how to make a difference in the world. Still, this does not fully address the link between transformative learning and social action.

In a review of the work of bell hooks and Angela Davis, Brookfield (2003) concludes that both women see transformative learning as ideology critique. The purpose of transformative education is to "help people uncover and challenge dominant ideology and then learn how to organize social relations according to noncapitalist logic" (p. 224). In social action, disequilibrium is present in all relationships. Transformation includes not only structural change in the individual's way of seeing himself or herself and the world, but also structural change in the social world that provides the context for the individual's life. Newman (1994) places the emphasis solidly on the social structures when he proposes that we should study not the oppressed, but oppression. In his writing on critical theory, Brookfield (2005) takes a similar stance. Ideology critique describes the ways in which people come to recognize uncritically assimilated assumptions and beliefs. The role of adult educators is to help people see how these ideologies (assumptions and beliefs) have been imposed on them without their knowledge and how they justify and maintain economic and political inequity (p. 13).

Merriam and Caffarella (1999) credit both Mezirow and Freire as being the leading theorists in transformative learning, with Freire focusing more on social change than Mezirow. Torres (2003) follows Freire's (1970) view of transformative learning as an instrument for social justice. He raises an interesting paradox. Democracy implies participation based on the assumption of equality among people. Yet people need to be educated in democratic participation. Knowing how to engage in discourse, collaborate with others, and exercise democratic rights and obligations is both a precondition of and a product of democratic participation. Torres argues that "transformative social justice should be based on unveiling the conditions of alienation and exploitation in society, thereby creating the basis for the understanding and comprehension of the roots of social behaviour" (2003, p. 429). He does not, however, deny the importance of what he calls self-transformation, a process by which we rethink our past and gain an understanding of the formation of our self. Understanding our present condition allows us to see the limitations and possibilities of being a "self-in-the-world" (p. 429).

GROUPS AND ORGANIZATIONS

Group and organizational transformation has been a recent line of inquiry. Yorks and Marsick (2000) have focused their research on action learning and collaborative inquiry, two group learning strategies employing reflection and action aimed at producing transformational organizational learning. Similarly, Kasl and Elias (2000) report on transformative learning within the context of group learning and organizational change. It is sometimes difficult to distinguish between transformative learning with social change as a goal and group learning. Scott (2003) helps clarify this when she says that "transformation includes structural changes in the psyches of persons and in the structures of society" (p. 281). Following Kegan's (2000) constructivist-developmental approach, Scott sees a collective movement occurring toward higher mental functions.

Although learning in groups has a long history in adult education, the idea that a group as an entity can learn is relatively new. Kasl, Marsick, and Dechant (1997) claim that a group, as a system, can create knowledge for itself. The popular work on learning organizations follows this model. The idea began with the work of Argyris and Schön (1974) and was popularized by Senge (1990), among others. But it was the work of Watkins and Marsick (1993) that connected the learning organization to transformative learning. Yorks and Marsick's (2000) work on organizational transformation is based on action learning and collaborative inquiry. Action learning involves learning in small groups or teams by working on a real project or problem in the organization. Collaborative inquiry sounds similar—it is defined as a "process consisting of repeated episodes of reflection and action through which a group of peers strives to answer a question of importance to them" (p. 266). There is an emphasis on co-inquiry, democratic process, and holistic understanding of the experience. According to Yorks and Marsick, organizations transform along several dimensions: the nature of the environment, the vision or mission of the organization, their products or services, the organizational structure, management of the organization, and how members of the organization see their roles.

Fenwick (1998) is quite critical of this perspective. She suggests that those who write about learning organizations are likely to be closely aligned with the organization's goals, but visions and goals of the ordinary person working within the organization may be very different. She also argues that it is not reasonable to describe an organization as a unitary, intelligent entity. It is not unitary, nor is it bounded and stable—it contains multiple subgroups, different cultures, and a continually changing workforce.

Can groups learn and transform? Kasl and Elias's (2000) writing is based on the premise that they can. They use two concepts to support this assumption: that individuals, groups, and organizations all share common characteristics, and the idea of a group mind. Kasl and Elias include both critical reflection and discernment as central processes in their conceptualization of transformative learning. Discernment begins with receptivity and appreciation and moves to seeing patterns of relational wholeness. "Frames of reference are transcended rather than analyzed" (p. 231). Transformative learning becomes an expansion of consciousness that is collective as well as individual. Using a case study, Kasl and Elias illustrate that processes usually ascribed to individuals can provide a model for understanding and interpreting group learning.

ECOLOGICAL VIEW

O'Sullivan and his colleagues from the Transformative Learning Centre at the Ontario Institute for Studies in Education provide an unusual and intriguing approach to transformative learning. Their broad vision spans the individual, relational, group, institutional, societal, and global perspectives: "Transformative learning involves experiencing a deep, structural shift in basic premises of thought, feelings, and actions. It is a shift of consciousness that dramatically and permanently alters our way of being in the world. Such a shift involves our understanding of ourselves and our self-locations; our relationships with other humans and with the natural world; our understanding of relations of power in interlocking structures of class, race and gender; our body awareness; our visions of alternative approaches to living; and our sense of possibilities for social justice and peace and personal joy" (Transformative Learning Centre, 2004).

O'Sullivan (2003) is careful to say that he does not see transformative learning as an individual process, but rather a personal process that is carried out in "integrally webbed totalities" (p. 337). Central to his understanding is that we are part of the whole. What we should strive for is a planetary community that holds together without collapsing and obliterating human diversity.

In Sweden, the Holma College of Integral Studies takes a similar approach to understanding transformative learning (Gunnlaugson, 2003). The college provides a one-year intensive adult education program in personal and global well-being studies, drawing participants who are looking for personal and collective transformation. An emphasis on "learning to love life in all forms first, then extending this love out from the personal to more universal horizons" (p. 326) allows students to develop what is described as an "integrally informed" education. Gunnlaugson follows O'Sullivan's (2003) thinking in proposing that there is a pressing need to contemplate "our collective evolutionary destiny from the vantage point of the history of planet Earth" (p. 324).

EXTRARATIONAL APPROACH

It is perhaps the extrarational approach to transformative learning that holds the most promise for expanding the theory, given how different it is from Mezirow's original work. Even though they may not label it as extrarational, many of the new writers in the field are drawn to something beyond the cognitive way of processing (Herman, 2003; Lennard, Thompson, and Booth, 2003). If we can integrate this way of understanding transformation with Mezirow's work rather than treating it as an opposing position, I think we will have made good steps in the direction of developing a unifying, holistic theory (Cranton and Roy, 2003).

Boyd and Myers (1988; Boyd, 1985, 1989) were early proponents of using Jungian psychology to explain transformative learning. They describe a process of discernment in which symbols, images, and archetypes play a role in personal illumination. Boyd (1989) reports on a method of working in small groups in which individuals struggle to deal with unconscious content. The group itself affects the way individual members create images, identify personal dilemmas, and relate developmental phases to personal stages. Boyd defines personal transformation as "a fundamental change in one's personality involving conjointly the resolution of a personal dilemma and the expansion of consciousness resulting in greater personality integration" (p. 459). In 1991, Boyd suggests that transformation is an inner journey of individuation, the process of learning through reflection on the psychic structures that make up one's uniqueness. That Boyd's early writing is frequently cited twenty years later shows how it resonates with many people's experience of transformation.

More recently, Dirkx (2001a, 2001b) has taken up the torch of extending transformative learning theory beyond the ego-based, rational, and objective traditional approach. Dirkx (1997) provides the compelling view that transformative learning involves very personal and imaginative ways of knowing—the way of mythos rather than logos. Dirkx draws on Hillman's (2000) and Moore's (1996) writings on soul and Jung's ([1921] 1971) concept of individuation.

Transformative learning involves imaginative and emotional ways of knowing, says Dirkx (1997). Mythos reflects a facet of knowing that we can see in symbols, images, stories, and myths. Framing learning as a problem of critical self-reflection leads us to neglect the emotional, spiritual, and imaginative aspects of transformation, and yields a limited, fragmented perspective rather than a holistic, whole-person understanding. Boyd (1991) talks of "transformative education" in order to maintain holism, and similarly, the founders of the *Journal of Transformative Education* chose that title deliberately so as to be inclusive, integrative, and holistic (Markos and McWhinney, 2004).

It is one thing to say this and another to understand what it means in relation to both theory and practice. Dirkx (1997) describes soul through examples of experiences rather than through a definition—being awestruck by a sunset, or gripped by pain and helplessness in the face of another's suffering. We experience soul through art, music, and film. It is that magic moment, defining moment, that transcends rationality and gives depth, power, mystery, and deep meaning to the connection between the self and the world. In nurturing soul, we attend to not only the intellectual aspects of the learning environment, but to the emotional, spiritual, social, and physical aspects as well. We pay attention to the small, everyday occurrences (Dirkx, 2000), listen to individual and collective psyches, understand and appreciate images, and honor the multifaceted dimensions of learning.

Jung ([1921] 1971, p. 448) defines individuation as the process by which individuals differentiate themselves from the general, collective society. It involves becoming aware of and considering the psychic structures of anima, animus, ego, shadow, and the collective unconscious. People come to see how they are both the same as and different from others. Transformation through individuation occurs whether we are conscious of it or not. However, when we participate in it consciously and imaginatively, we develop a deepened sense of self and an expansion of consciousness. Transformation is the emergence of the Self.

The process of individuation, becoming conscious of what is unique about oneself, involves differentiating ourselves from people we have admired and modeled ourselves on—parents, teachers, and mentors (Sharp, 2001). Individuality and group identity are incompatible. According to transformative learning theory, individuals come to question assumptions and perspectives that were uncritically absorbed from family, community, and culture. This sounds very much like differentiating ourselves from others upon whom we have modeled ourselves, except that according to Mezirow, it is a conscious, cognitive, rational, problem-solving process, and according to the Jungian perspective, it is an intuitive, emotional, and often not even a voluntary journey. Jung writes, "The developing personality obeys no caprice, no command, no insight, only brute necessity: it needs the motivating force of inner or outer faculties" (cited in Sharp, 2001, p. 66).

As different as the paths are, it seems they are going to the same place. If we want, as we say we do, a holistic theory of transformative learning, then both paths can be valid. Those among us who strive to develop theories to explain others' learning are also human beings looking at ourselves and the world through the lens of our meaning perspectives. It should not be too surprising that this results in different ways of seeing the journey. Jung ([1921] 1971), in his work on psychological type preferences, tells the story of different people taking the same trip. One person may wax eloquently about the beauty of the landscape; another may focus on the restaurants in the area and describe the many good meals he had; someone else may have noticed neither the landscape nor the restaurants, but have spent time getting to know the people and understanding their culture. So it is, I think, with the development of transformative learning theory.

RESEARCH ON TRANSFORMATIVE LEARNING

With the International Conference on Transformative Learning in its sixth year and the *Journal of Transformative Education* in its third volume, the amount of accessible research on transformative learning has begun to grow exponentially. Prior to the existence of these vehicles for dissemination, much of the research in the area would have been not easily available but for the efforts of E. Taylor (2000a, 2000b), who conscientiously read, summarized, critiqued, and integrated the many graduate theses in the field. In this brief overview of the research, I draw heavily, and with gratitude, on Taylor's work.

Taylor outlines eight themes from the research published up until 2000: (1) transformative learning is uniquely adult; (2) transformative learning appears to be a linear, but not necessarily step-wise process; (3) the nature of a frame of reference and how it transforms is unclear; (4) a disorienting dilemma usually initiates transformative learning; (5) critical reflection is significant to transformative learning; (6) discourse is equally dependent on relational ways of knowing; (7) context plays an important role in shaping transformative learning, but the influence of culture has not been well investigated; and (8) some characteristics of a learning environment that fosters transformative learning have been identified, but more work needs to be done in this area. Essentially, the research supports Mezirow's (2000) theoretical description, with the possible exception of the importance of relational ways of knowing. However, even here, Mezirow (2003) has now elaborated on the conditions of discourse to include interpersonal skills, social relationships, and emotional intelligence. We must keep in mind that Taylor chose to review only those studies that referred directly to Mezirow's conceptualization of transformative learning, though some studies also included other theoretical models as well.

Based on his review, Taylor suggests future directions for research: (1) in-depth analyses of specific components of transformative learning that tend to be overlooked in the broader studies—for example, feelings such as anger, happiness, and shame, the management of emotions, and changes in behavior following transformation; (2) studies of how transformative learning is fostered in classrooms; and (3) new and varied research designs and data collection techniques, including longitudinal research, observer participation, collaborative inquiry, action research, and quantitative studies.

It is difficult to find research reports that do not, at least in part, have Mezirow's work as a foundation. I include a few examples here, with no intention of providing a comprehensive review. Some of the research on spirituality and transformative learning refers to the work of Dirkx (1997), English and Gillen (2000), and Palmer (1998), for example, rather than to the more cognitive, rational, traditional transformative learning theory. Tisdell (2000b) studied a multicultural group of women adult educators and reports on five themes in their experience: (1) a spiral process of moving beyond the spiritual values of their culture of origin; (2) spirituality as a life force providing interconnectedness and wholeness; (3) the presence of a higher power that facilitates healing and gives courage to take new action; (4) the importance of an integrated and balanced approach to living and a commitment to action for social change; and (5) the development of authentic identity.

I found the latter theme related to authenticity and the integration of personal identity and spirituality to be of special interest in light of my own research. In a study of twenty-two educators over a three-year period, a colleague and I found evidence that the development of an authentic identity as a teacher can be a transformative process (Cranton and Carusetta, 2004).

Tisdell and Tolliver (2001) later take the results of Tisdell's (2000b) study and explore the implications for transformative learning in adult higher education. They suggest that there has been little discussion of the role of spirituality in teaching for social transformation and propose the importance of (1) the authenticity of teachers and students, (2) an environment that allows for the exploration of the cognitive, the affective or relational, and the symbolic or spiritual dimensions, and (3) the limitations of the adult learning environment and that transformation is an ongoing process that takes time (p. 368).

As I mention earlier in this chapter, Gilly's (2004) research on the nature of a "living learning group" (p. 236) shows the importance of relational, collaborative, and egalitarian group work in transformative learning. The group moved from being a collection of individuals to being a community of practice where the "processes of transforming experience into knowledge were habituated" (p. 236). In relating her study to the literature, Gilly found that the more cognitive rational approach (Cranton, 1994; Mezirow, 2000) did not address important aspects of her experience.

SUMMARY

Transformative learning theory has benefited greatly over the years from the contributions of scholars from a variety of perspectives. Many researchers and writers emphasize relational, connected knowing over individual, autonomous learning. From this perspective, transformative learning has a different emphasis and perhaps a different outcome. Subjective discussion (rather than rational discourse) encourages participants to share their experiences in a nonjudgmental way, and connected knowing involves working hard to understand others rather than looking for flaws in others' reasoning.

Social change lies at the heart of the history of adult education. In the 1920s and 1930s, adult education practice and theory was about helping people challenge oppressive organizations and governments. Those who criticize Mezirow's work on the basis of his ignoring social action as a goal of transformative learning may be overlooking his desire to help people learn how to change oppressive structures rather than to change them himself—his distinction between educational and political tasks—as well as overlooking his own commitment to that work. Nevertheless, it is the case that adult education theory in general and transformative learning theory in particular has moved away from social issues and toward an emphasis on individual learning in recent decades. Brookfield's (2005) four traditions of criticality are helpful in understanding how both personal and social transformation are a part of what we do in adult education.

The idea that groups and organizations as entities can learn and transform provides yet another perspective on the theory (Kasl and Elias, 2000). I accept that groups and organizations change and develop, but I question the concept of a "group mind," and therefore I question the idea that groups transform in the way individuals transform. Group transformation is an intriguing idea, but I think it needs to be better situated in transformative learning theory or perhaps named differently.

O'Sullivan's broad vision of transformative learning theory, with its goal of striving for a planetary community, may have the potential of opening up our understanding of transformation so as to integrate all perspectives. I suggest that we need to explore how this vision is related to the existing alternative ways of describing transformation.

The extrarational approach put forth by Dirkx and others provides us with an intriguing and complementary way of understanding the central process of transformation. It brings in imagination, intuition, soul work, and emotion as ways in which people come to see themselves and their world in a new light. As different as the extrarational approach is from Mezirow's cognitive rational description of transformative learning, the two need not be viewed as contradictory. I do not intend to gloss over the differences between these viewpoints—the processes involved and the expected outcomes of each are fundamentally different. For example, if one views transformation as individuation, the outcome is self-knowledge and a more individuated personality. But each of these ways of understanding transformation can be descriptive of the experiences of different individuals or even of the same individual on different occasions.

Transformative learning theory is not only a theory in progress in terms of how people are thinking about and elaborating on it. It is also a theory in progress in relation to the expanding body of research that is supporting and asking questions of the theoretical developments. Much of the research supports Mezirow's understanding of transformation, but that may be in part because the reviews we rely on to make sense out of the field emphasize studies that are based on this approach. Research that includes spirituality, relational knowing, and authenticity are beginning to help us grasp how the various perspectives complement and elaborate on each other. Perhaps most important, the individuals who are involved in the continued development of transformative learning theory (see, for example, Wiessner, 2004) are engaged in intentional efforts to expand our thinking.

REFERENCES

Argyris, C., and Schön, D. A. *Theory in Practice: Increasing Professional Effectiveness.* San Francisco: Jossey-Bass, 1974.

Baumgartner, L. M. "An Update on Transformational Learning." In S. Merriam (ed.), *The New Update on Adult Learning Theory.* New Directions for Adult and Continuing Education, no. 89. San Francisco: Jossey-Bass, 2001.

Belenky, M. F., Clinchy, B. M., Goldberger, N. R., and Tarule, J. M. *Women's Ways of Knowing: The Development of Self, Voice, and Mind.* New York: Basic Books, 1986.

Belenky, M., and Stanton, A. "Inequality, Development, and Connected Knowing." In J. Mezirow, and Associates (eds.), *Learning as Transformation: Critical Perspectives on a Theory in Progress.* San Francisco: Jossey-Bass, 2000.

Boyd, R. D. "Trust in Groups: The Great Mother and Transformative Education." In L. S. Walker (ed.), *Proceedings of the Annual Midwest Research-to-Practice Conference in Adult and Continuing Education.* Ann Arbor: University of Michigan, 1985.

Boyd, R. D. "Facilitating Personal Transformation in Small Groups." *Small Group Behavior,* 1989, *20*(4), 459–474.

Boyd, R. D. *Personal Transformation in Small Groups: A Jungian Perspective.* London: Routledge, 1991.

Boyd, R. D., and Myers, J. B. "Transformative Education." *International Journal of Lifelong Education,* 1988, 7, 261–284.

Brookfield, S. "Transformative Learning as Ideology Critique." In J. Mezirow, and Associates (eds.), *Learning as Transformation: Critical Perspectives on a Theory in Progress.* San Francisco: Jossey-Bass, 2000.

Brookfield, S. "The Praxis of Transformative Education: African American Feminist Conceptualizations." *Journal of Transformative Education,* 2003, *1*(3), 212–226.

Brookfield, S. *The Power of Critical Theory: Liberating Adult Learning and Teaching.* San Francisco: Jossey-Bass, 2005.

Carter, T. *The Voice of Relationship: Transformative Learning Through Developmental Relationships in the Lives of Mid-Career Women.* Unpublished doctoral dissertation, George Washington University, 2000.

Clark, J. E. *Scholarly Writing: A Personal Odyssey.* Unpublished doctoral dissertation, Ontario Institute for Studies in Education, 2005.

Clark, M. C., and Wilson, A. L. "Context and Rationality in Mezirow's Theory of Transformational Learning." *Adult Education Quarterly,* 1991, *41*(2), 75–91.

Coady, M. M. *Masters of Their Own Destiny.* New York: Harper and Brothers, 1939.

Cohen, J. B. "Hatha-Yoga and Transformative Learning— The Possibility of a Union?" Paper presented at the Fifth International Conference on Transformative Learning, Teachers College, Columbia University, 2003.

Cohen, J. B. "Late for School: Stories of Transformation in an Adult Education Program." *Journal of Transformative Education,* 2004, *2*(2), 242–252.

Collard, S., and Law, M. "The Limits of Perspective Transformation: A Critique of Mezirow's Theory." *Adult Education Quarterly*, 1989, *39*, 99–107.

Cranton, P. *Understanding and Promoting Transformative Learning*. San Francisco: Jossey-Bass, 1994.

Cranton, P., and Carusetta, E. "Developing Authenticity as a Transformative Process." *Journal of Transformative Education*, 2004, *2*(4), 276–293.

Cranton, P., and Roy, M. "When the Bottom Falls out of the Bucket: Toward a Holistic Perspective on Transformative Learning." *Journal of Transformative Education*, 2003, *1*(2), 86–98.

Cunningham, P. "From Freire to Feminism: The North American Experience with Critical Pedagogy." *Adult Education Quarterly,* 1992, *42*(3), 180–191.

Daloz, L. *Mentor: Guiding the Journey of Adult Learners*. San Francisco: Jossey-Bass, 1999.

Dirkx, J. "Nurturing Soul in Adult Education." In P. Cranton (ed.), *Transformative Learning in Action: Insights from Practice*. New Directions for Adult and Continuing Education, no. 74. San Francisco: Jossey-Bass, 1997.

Dirkx, J. "Transformative Learning Theory in the Practice of Adult Education: An Overview." *PAACE Journal of Lifelong Learning,* 1998, 7, 1–14.

Dirkx, J. "After the Burning Bush: Transformative Learning as Imaginative Engagement with Everyday Experience." In C. A. Wiessner, S. Meyer, and D. Fuller (eds.), *Challenges of Practice: Transformative Learning in Action*. Proceedings of the Third International Conference on Transformative Learning, Teachers College, Columbia University, 2000.

Dirkx, J. "Images, Transformative Learning and the Work of Soul." *Adult Learning*, 2001a, *12*(3), 15–16.

Dirkx, J. "The Power of Feelings: Emotion, Imagination, and the Construction of Meaning in Adult Learning." In S. Merriam (ed.), *The New Update on Adult Learning Theory*. New Directions for Adult and Continuing Education, no. 89. San Francisco: Jossey-Bass, 2001b.

Ebert, O., Burford, M. L., and Brian, D. "Highlander: Education for Change." *Journal of Transformative Education*, 2003, *1*(4), 321–340.

English, L. "Feminine/Feminist: A Poststructural Reading of Relational Learning in Women's Social Action Organizations." In D. Clover (ed.), *Proceedings of the Joint International Conference of the Adult Education Research Conference and the Canadian Association for Studies in Adult Education* (pp. 136–141). University of Victoria, British Columbia, May, 2004.

English, L., and Gillen, M. (eds.). *Addressing the Spiritual Dimensions of Adult Learning: What Educators Can Do*. New Directions for Adult and Continuing Education, no. 85. San Francisco: Jossey-Bass, 2000.

Fenwick, T. "Questioning the Concept of the Learning Organization." In S. M. Scott, B. Spencer, and A. M. Thomas (eds.), *Learning for Life: Canadian Readings in Adult Education*. Toronto: Thompson, 1998.

Freire, P. *Pedagogy of the Oppressed*. New York: Herder and Herder, 1970.

Gardner, H., Kornhaber, M. L., and Wake, W. K. *Intelligence: Multiple Perspectives.* New York: Harcourt Brace, 1996.

Gilly, M. S. "Experiencing Transformative Education in the 'Corridors' of a Nontraditional Doctoral Program." *Journal of Transformative Education*, 2004, *2*(3), 231–242.

Goleman, D. *Working with Emotional Intelligence.* New York: Bantam Books, 1998.

Gunnlaugson, O. "Toward an Integral Education for the Ecozoic Era: A Case Study in Transforming the Glocal Learning Community of Holma College of Integral Studies." *Journal of Transformative Education,* 2003, *2*(4), 313–335.

Hart, M. "Critical Theory and Beyond: Further Perspectives on Emancipatory Education." *Adult Education Quarterly,* 1990, *40*, 125–138.

Hayes, E., and Flannery, D. *Women as Learners: The Significance of Gender in Adult Learning.* San Francisco: Jossey-Bass, 2000.

Herman, L. "Engaging the Disturbing Images of Evil." In C. A. Wiessner, S. R. Meyer, N. Pfhal, and P. Neaman (eds.), *Transformative Learning in Action: Building Bridges Across Contexts and Disciplines.* Proceedings of the Fifth International Conference on Transformative Learning, Teachers College, Columbia University, 2003.

Hillman, J. "Peaks and Vales." In B. Sells (ed.), *Working with Images.* Woodstock, CT: Spring Publications, 2000.

Jung, C. *Psychological Types.* Princeton: Princeton University Press, 1971. (Originally published in 1921.)

Kasl, E., and Elias, D. "Creating New Habits of Mind in Small Groups." In J. Mezirow, and Associates (eds.), *Learning as Transformation: Critical Perspectives on a Theory in Progress.* San Francisco: Jossey-Bass, 2000.

Kasl, E., Marsick, V. J., and Dechant, K. "Teams as Learners: A Research-Based Model of Team Learning." *Journal of Applied Behavioral Science,* 1997, *33*, 227–246.

Kegan, R. "What 'Form' Transforms? A Constructive-Developmental Approach to Transformative Learning." In J. Mezirow, and Associates (eds.), *Learning as Transformation: Critical Perspectives on a Theory in Progress.* San Francisco: Jossey-Bass, 2000.

Lennard, D., Thompson, T., and Booth, G. "The Artist's Inquiry: Fostering Transformative Learning Through the Arts." In C. A. Wiessner, S. R. Meyer, N. Pfhal, and P. Neaman (eds.), *Transformative Learning in Action: Building Bridges Across Contexts and Disciplines.* Proceedings of the Fifth International Conference on Transformative Learning, Teachers College, Columbia University, 2003.

MacKeracher, D. *Making Sense of Adult Learning* (2nd ed.). Toronto: University of Toronto Press, 2004.

Markos, L., and McWhinney, W. "Editors' Perspectives: Building On and Toward a Shared Vision." *Journal of Transformative Education,* 2004, *2*(2), 75–79.

Merriam, S., and Caffarella, R. *Learning in Adulthood: A Comprehensive Guide.* San Francisco: Jossey-Bass, 1999.

Mezirow, J. *Transformative Dimensions of Adult Learning.* San Francisco: Jossey-Bass, 1991.

Mezirow, J. "Learning to Think Like an Adult." In J. Mezirow, and Associates (eds.), *Learning as Transformation: Critical Perspectives on a Theory in Progress*. San Francisco: Jossey-Bass, 2000.

Mezirow, J. "Transformative Learning as Discourse." *Journal of Transformative Education*, 2003, *1*(1), 58–63.

Mezirow, J., and Associates (eds.). *Learning as Transformation: Critical Perspectives on a Theory in Progress*. San Francisco: Jossey-Bass, 2000.

Moore, T. *The Re-enchantment of Everyday Life*. New York: HarperCollins, 1996.

Newman, M. *Defining the Enemy: Adult Education in Social Action*. Sydney, Australia: Victor Stewart, 1994.

O'Sullivan, E. "The Ecological Terrain of Transformative Learning: A Vision Statement." In C. A. Wiessner, S. R. Meyer, N. Pfhal, and P. Neaman (eds.), *Transformative Learning in Action: Building Bridges Across Contexts and Disciplines*. Proceedings of the Fifth International Conference on Transformative Learning, Teachers College, Columbia University, 2003.

Palmer, P. *The Courage to Teach: Exploring the Inner Landscape of a Teacher's Life*. San Francisco: Jossey-Bass, 1998.

Robinson, P. "Meditation: Its Role in Transformative Learning and the Fostering of an Integrative Vision for Higher Education." *Journal of Transformative Education*, 2004, *2*(2), 107–122.

Scott, S. "The Social Construction of Transformation." *Journal of Transformative Education*, 2003, *1*(3), 264–284.

Senge, P. M. *The Fifth Discipline: The Art and Practice of the Learning Organization*. New York: Doubleday, 1990.

Sharp, D. *Digesting Jung: Food for the Journey*. Toronto: Inner City Books, 2001.

Taylor, E. "Analyzing Research on Transformative Learning Theory." In J. Mezirow, and Associates (eds.), *Learning as Transformation: Critical Perspectives on a Theory in Progress*. San Francisco: Jossey-Bass, 2000a.

Taylor, E. "Fostering Transformative Learning in the Adult Education Classroom: A Review of the Empirical Studies." In C. A. Wiessner, S. Meyer, and D. Fuller (eds.), *Challenges of Practice: Transformative Learning in Action*. Proceedings of the Third International Conference on Transformative Learning, Teachers College, Columbia University, 2000b.

Tisdell, E. J. "Feminist Pedagogies." In E. Hayes and D. Flannery (eds.), *Women as Learners: The Significance of Gender in Adult Learning*. San Francisco: Jossey-Bass, 2000a.

Tisdell, E. J. "Spirituality and Emancipatory Adult Education in Women Adult Educators for Social Change." *Adult Education Quarterly*, 2000b, *50*(4), 308–335.

Tisdell, E. J., and Tolliver, D. E. "The Role of Spirituality in Culturally Relevant and Transformative Adult Education." *Adult Learning*, 2001, *12*(3), 13–14.

Torres, C. A. "Paulo Freire, Education and Transformative Social Justice Learning." In C. A. Wiessner, S. R. Meyer, N. Pfhal, and P. Neaman (eds.), *Transformative Learning in Action: Building Bridges Across Contexts and Disciplines.* Proceedings of the Fifth International Conference on Transformative Learning, Teachers College, Columbia University, 2003.

Transformative Learning Centre. The Transformative Learning Centre, Retrieved from http://www.oise.utoronto.ca/~tlcentre/index.htm, November, 2004.

Watkins, K., and Marsick, V. J. *Sculpting the Learning Organization: Lessons in the Art and Science of Systemic Change.* San Francisco: Jossey-Bass, 1993.

Wiessner, C. A. "Where Have We Been? Where Are We Going? A Critical Reflection on a Collaborative Inquiry." *SCUTREA 2005 Conference Proceedings*, University of Sheffield, UK, 2004.

Wiessner, C. A., Meyer, S. R., Pfhal, N., and Neuman, P. (eds.). *Transformative Learning in Action: Building Bridges Across Contexts and Disciplines.* Proceedings of the Fifth International Conference on Transformative Learning, Teachers College, Columbia University, 2003.

Yorks, L., and Marsick, V. J. "Organizational Learning and Transformation." In J. Mezirow, and Associates (eds.), *Learning as Transformation: Critical Perspectives on a Theory in Progress.* San Francisco: Jossey-Bass, 2000.

CHAPTER 22

"Social Learning" for/in Adult Education?

A Discursive Review of What It Means for Learning to Be "Social"

Kim L. Niewolny and Arthur L. Wilson

INTRODUCTION AND PURPOSE

"Social learning" has been recognized as an important perspective for understanding and problematizing the relationships between learning as a social process and social contexts in the areas of adult, extension, and community education for several years. Literature ranging from Jarvis (1987) and Brookfield (2005) to Fenwick (2000), Foley (1999), and Usher, Bryant, and Johnston (1997) has emphasized a wide range of societal conditions, structures, and practices as defining characteristics of socials forms of adult learning. Historically, several groups of learning theories have been identified as "social learning" theories in adult education scholarship including experiential learning (e.g., Fenwick, 2000), cultural-historical activity theory (e.g., Sawchuk, 2003a), situated cognition (e.g., Lave, 1988), social learning theory (e.g., Bandura, 1977), and transformative learning (e.g., Mezirow, 1991). Other influential dimensions of "social learning" include emancipatory learning (e.g., Hart, 1990), distributed learning (e.g., Lea & Nicoll, 2002), informal learning (e.g., Field & Spence, 2000), lifelong learning (e.g., Edwards, 2006), and participatory learning (e.g., Leeuwis, & Pyburn, 2002). According to Jarvis (2006) and Merriam, Caffarella, and Baumgartner (2007), this extensive literature has become fairly visible as a foundation for exploring the societal dimensions of adult education in a variety of formal, non-formal, and informal learning settings.

Despite what appears to be a welcomed move toward increasing our understanding of those social aspects and circumstances in which people learn, conceptual clarification of "social learning" remains scarce in adult education scholarship. We argue that this lack of elucidation not only limits our understanding of the ways in which adults learn in/with the social world but enables the (re)production of asocial, individualistic conceptions of adult learning, as explained by "psychologism" and its parent discourse, individualism (Usher, Bryant, & Johnston, 1997, p. xiii). Individualism is a modernist framework best explained by the "Enlightenment ideal of the autonomous subject-person" (Finger & Asún, 2001, p. 117). A major premise for adult educators critical of the prevailing discourse of individualism is that learning does not occur "just inside the head." "Social learning" has become a catch phrase used by adult educators to demonstrate how learning is something more than a psychological activity characterized by individuals accumulating knowledge and skills to be transferred across time and space (Niewolny & Wilson, 2009). But what does it mean when adult educators say learning is social? Put another way, what is "social learning" for/in adult education? We argue that "social learning" should be viewed less as a particular learning tradition and more like a discourse of learning that is framed by relations of power that constitute its formation. Our paper is, therefore, focused on the discursive construction of "social learning" to better understand this emerging discourse and its significance for organizing and developing adult education as an alternative to the discourse of individualism.

METHODOLOGY

We refrain from reviewing the "social learning" literature as a distinct tradition of theory and practice in adult education; instead; we (re)locate the literature within a discursive framework by drawing upon the project of critical discourse analysis (CDA). While it is difficult to treat CDA as a unified framework, it is often explained as a form of discourse critique influenced by the techniques of applied linguistics and theoretical insights of (post)structuralist theory (Niewolny & Wilson, 2008). According to Gee (1999) and Fairclough (2003), CDA enables us to critically reveal larger formations of discourse and power in our everyday educational settings. Our approach to CDA is grounded in the scholarship of Fairclough (1992) and Foucault (1972). A key assumption of CDA in this view is that discourse and social practices are linked together and to wider social structures by taking into account the heterogeneous and historicized nature of discourse (Foucault, 1972), and the textual, discursive practice, and social practice dimensions of discourse analysis (Fairclough, 1992). For Luke (1995), this form of discourse critique is described as a bridging together of the "macro approaches to discourse with more microanalytical text analyses" (p. 10).

Following Foucault (1972) and Fairclough (1992), we examined the discourse of "social learning" for its underlying structure of meaning which, in turn, constitutes regimes of truth about what it means for learning to be "social" in adult education literature. This approach not only emphasizes the kinds of investigations that have focused on social aspects of adult learning but exemplifies what Foucault (1972) would describe as an underlying uniformity of meaning despite the apparent diversity of what has been said about "social learning" for/in adult education. Our analysis involved paying careful attention to the ways in which meanings of "socialness" are constructed and legitimated in some ways while not in others. We identified several themes of "socialness" from the literature to frame the analysis: nature of context, experience, mediation, social action, social purpose, and social positioning (Edwards, 2006; Fenwick, 2000; Foley, 1999; Jarvis, 1987; Lave, 1988; Lea & Nicoll, 2002; Salomon & Perkins, 1998; Sawchuk, 2003a; Usher, Bryant, & Johnston, 1997).

Building on earlier insights (Niewolny & Wilson, 2006, 2009; Wilson, 1993), we examined empirical and conceptual writings in the areas of "cultural historical-activity theory," "distributed learning," "emancipatory learning," "experiential learning," "lifelong learning," "situated cognition/learning," "sociocultural learning," "social leaning," "informal/non-formal learning," "participatory learning," and "transformative learning." In the tradition of CDA, we acknowledge that this corpus of literature is a discursive construction embedded in our own assumptions and perspectives. We further recognize that while the corpus comprises the bulk of the adult "social learning" literature, it does not capture all that has been written about "social learning" theory and practice.

▪ MAPPING THE DISCOURSE OF "SOCIAL LEARNING"

"Social learning" is nothing new to educators. According to Salomon and Perkins (1998) and Wenger (1998), research in the field of education has shed a good deal of light on the ways in which learning—as a social phenomenon—is constituted by social behavior, experience, activity, mediation, positionality, and context. Adult educators have actively contributed to the "social learning" conversation. An initial reading of the "social learning" literature in adult education illustrates how "this" kind of learning is, on the one hand, many things to many people, depending on perspective. On the other hand, however, if viewed as a discourse of adult learning, we begin to see how "this" construction of power and knowledge is actually a discursive strategy employed by adult educators to challenge the established promotion of psychological theories of adult learning that understand learning as something that occurs "inside" the mind of the individual. Yet we argue that this discourse is too susceptible to misappropriation and consequently circumscribed by the larger discursive construction of individualism currently circulating in adult education scholarship. That is to say, our findings begin to reveal that while adult educators are increasingly investigating adult learning as a social or sociocultural phenomenon by drawing upon several frameworks and concepts rooted in "socialness," this discourse is actually a weak manifestation of resistance to the discourse of individualism, as exemplified in behaviorist, cognitive, and constructivist psychology. For the purpose of this paper, we limit the remaining discussion to two discursive positions that begin to illustrate the insecure nature in which the discourse currently operates. Before we share those crucial points, we briefly sketch the discursive configuration of the literature that frames the discussion by following Fairclough's (1992) notion of "conditions of discourse practice."

Focusing on the discursive ways in which literature emerges in adult education circles, our analysis demonstrates how the discourse appears to be broadly constituted though an array of conceptual camps and venues. First, we found that adult educators have liberally appropriated "social learning" to designate everything from the kind of learning that occurs through modeling behavior (Bandura, 1977), to group learning (Imel, 1999), to participatory learning in and for community organizing and sustainable development (Falk, 2001; Leeuwis & Pyburn, 2002), to learning as a situated and/or sociocultural experience (Alfred, 2003; Sawchuk, 2003a; Wilson, 1993), to a kind of learning that characterizes the in/non-formality of adult learning (Field & Spence, 2002), to learning that has transformative power for purposes of social action and emancipation from oppressive conditions (Foley, 1999; Mezirow, 1991; Hart, 1990; O'Sullivan, Morrrell, & O'Connor, 2002), to learning that falls within the purview of mobility and distribution as explained by globalizing processes and postmodernism (Edwards & Usher, 2008; Usher, Bryant, & Johnston, 1997). Second, we located explicit and implicit meanings of "social learning" in numerous journals, texts, and edited contributions in the general areas of adult learning, adult and community education, lifelong learning, and community development; therefore, we argue that the discourse is widely circulated in adult education literature. Third, we learned that these meanings are variably characterized with such terminology as context-based learning, emancipatory learning, experiential learning, distributed learning, informal/non-formal learning, participatory learning, sociocultural learning, situated learning, social learning, and transformative learning. Finally, our point is amplified by the way in which the discourse is anchored in a diverse range of theoretical traditions including behaviorism, constructivism, feminism, Marxism, and postmodernism (Fenwick, 2000; Jarvis, 1987, 2006; Sawchuk, 2003b).

Drawing specifically upon the notion of "interdiscursivity" (Fairclough, 1992; Foucault, 1972), two discursive positions stand out from our analysis that indicate how the literature is poorly situated to challenge the (re)production of asocial, individualistic conceptions of adult learning. First and foremost, we revealed that not all social theories of adult learning operate outside of the prevailing psychological perspective. For example, it is no secret that Bandura's (1977) popular social learning theory illustrates the behaviorist response to understanding people learning from each other in social settings through observation: "Bandura's theory has a particular relevance to adult learning in that it accounts for both the learner and the environment in which he or she operates. Behavior is a function of the interaction of the person with the environment" (Merriam & Caffarella, 1999, p. 260). While adult educational research grounded in this theoretical perspective purports to incorporate the "learner and environment" as a valuable contribution to theory and practice, it is the way in which the social context is defined as a "container-like" variable that is of concern in this discussion. This functionalist amalgamation of the individual and the social clearly suggests that such a "social" perspective of adult learning is nothing more than an "add-on" to existing cognitive and behaviorist frameworks. On the one hand, it might be argued that this strategy is taken-up by educators to better build conceptual linkages with historically neglected dimensions, such as social factors as "external learning factors" (Lent & Brown, 1996, p. 312). On the other hand, however, as we have argued elsewhere (Niewolny & Wilson, 2006, 2009; Wilson, 2005), this "add-on" approach is more accurately described as a misuse of "socialness" that discursively limits us from fully exploring how learning occurs as a socially dynamic and culturally mediated activity embedded in and constituted by relations of power. In this view, we located several other efforts that employ this "add-on" strategy, most particularly in the area of situated learning (e.g., Daley, 2002; King, 2003).

The second discursive position characterizes the way in which "socialness" is dis/articulated as a political construction of adult learning. Without a doubt, some adult educators have not only taken up social learning approaches but have attempted to theorize an array of social, cultural, and historical perspectives as critical perspectives of adult learning (e.g., Barton & Tusting, 2005; Brookfield, 2005; Finger & Asún, 2001; Foley, 1999; Hart, 1990; O'Sullivan, Morrrell, & O'Connor, 2002; Sawchuk, 2003a; Sawchuk, Duarte, & Elhammoumi, 2006). Our reading of the literature suggests that politicized frameworks, such as emancipatory learning (Hart, 1990), have garnered much attention as viable social learning frameworks through references made to three themes: learning for social responsibility, learning for emancipation, and learning as ideological resistance. Focusing particularly on the way in which "social learning" is positioned as an ideological-discursive practice, we learned that several authors explicitly and implicitly draw upon "social learning" as an ideological-discursive strategy to challenge the role of expertism in technology and science as a leading development agenda (Falk, 2001; Leeuwis, & Pyburn, 2002; Wals, 2007). In this view, according to Wals (2007), social learning enables educators and community organizers to engage in the process of resisting and transforming hegemonic and oppositional ideologies and discourses, particularly as they relate to the struggle for sustainability.

While it is encouraging to discover that the role of power informs "social learning" discourse, we revealed that critically oriented frameworks overall are largely positioned at the periphery and therefore not visible as central ideas for understanding adult learning. Drawing upon Foley (1999), we argue that this inferior position makes it difficult for adult educators to recognize that learning is much more than a "technical and value-neutral process" characterized by individualistic conceptions of adult education (p. 2). Usher, Bryant, and Johnston (1997) further argue that such positioning limits our capacity to understand the interrelated relationships among social practices, selves, and the contemporary sociocultural context, as a guiding adult learning principle. This failure to fully articulate "social learning" as a political discourse is most evident in the ways in which critical readings of situated cognition and cultural-historical activity theory have been consistently overlooked by adult educators, thus ignoring the role of social action and cultural reproduction as the theoretical basis for conceptualizing the explicitly politicized nature of people learning in *and* with context(s) (Niewolny & Wilson, 2006, 2009; Wilson, 1993, 2005).

■ IMPLICATIONS FOR THEORY/PRACTICE

Our paper is an argument for viewing "social" learning not as a particular learning tradition but more like a discourse of learning that is framed by relations of power/knowledge in adult education literature that constitutes its formation. With this discursive lens firmly in place, we argue that while it is promising that adult educators are increasingly committed to the ongoing discussion of social theories of learning, albeit with different perspectives and purposes, the conceptual fuzziness that surrounds the discourse remains troubling if we are to more robustly understand how adults learn embedded in and distributed across socially and culturally structured relations of power (Niewolny & Wilson, 2009). It is our hope that this paper contributes to the understanding of "social learning" and its significance for organizing and developing adult education as an alternative to the prevailing discourse of individualism, as explained by behaviorist, cognitive, and constructivist psychology. This review of the literature, therefore, attempts to challenge the status quo while proposing new possibilities as we move toward theorizing the multifarious and political nature of "socialness" in the theory and practice of adult education.

REFERENCES

Alfred, M. (2003). Sociocultural contexts and learning: Anglophone Caribbean immigrant women in U.S. postsecondary education. *Adult Education Quarterly*, *53*(4), 242–260.

Bandura, A. (1977). *Social learning theory*. Englewood Cliffs, NJ: Prentice Hall.

Barton, D., & Tusting, K. (Eds.). (2005). *Beyond communities of practice: Language, power, and social context*. Cambridge, UK: Cambridge University Press.

Brookfield, S. (2005). *The power of critical theory: Liberating adult learning and teaching*. San Francisco: Jossey-Bass.

Edwards, R. (2006). Beyond the moorland? Contextualising lifelong learning. *Studies in the Education of Adults*, *38*(1), 25–36.

Edwards, R., & Usher, R. (2008). *Globalisation and pedagogy: Space, place and identity*. London: Routledge.

Daley, B. (2002). Context: Implications for learning in professional practice. In M. Alfred (Ed.). *Learning in sociocultural contexts: Implication for adult, community and workplace education* (pp. 79–88). San Francisco: Jossey-Bass.

Fairclough, N. (1992). *Discourse and social change*. Cambridge, UK: Polity Press.

Fairclough, N. (2003). *Analyzing discourse: Textual analysis for social research*. London: Routledge.

Falk, I. (Eds). *Learning to manage change: Developing regional communities for a local-global millennium*. National Centre for Vocational Education Research: Adelaide.

Fenwick, T. (2000). Expanding conceptions of experiential learning: A review of the five contemporary perspectives on cognition. *Adult Education Quarterly, 50*(4), 243–272.

Field, J. & Spence, L. (2000). Informal learning and social capital. In F. Coffield (Ed.), *The necessity of informal learning* (pp. 32–42). Bristol: The Policy Press.

Finger, M., & Asún, J. (2001). *Adult education at the crossroads: Learning our way out*. London: Zed Books.

Foley, G. (1999). *Learning in social action: A contribution to understanding informal education*. London: Zed Books.

Foucault, M. (1972). *The archaeology of knowledge*. New York: Pantheon.

Gee, J. (1999). *An introduction to discourse analysis: Theory and method*. London: Routledge.

Hart, M. U. (1990). Liberation through consciousness raising. In J. Mezirow & Associates (Eds.), *Fostering critical reflection in adulthood: A guide to transformative and emancipatory learning* (pp. 47–73). San Francisco: Jossey-Bass.

Imel, S. (1999). Using groups in adult learning: Theory and practice. *Journal of Continuing Education in the Health Professions, 19*(1), 54–61.

Jarvis, P. (1987). *Adult learning in the social context*. London: Croom Helm.

Jarvis, P. (2006). *Towards a comprehensive theory of human learning*. London: Routledge.

King, K. (2003). Learning the new technologies: Strategies for success. In K. King & P. Lawler (Eds.), *New perspectives on designing and implementing professional development for teachers of adults* (pp. 49–58). San Francisco: Jossey-Bass.

Lave, J. (1988). *Cognition in practice: Mind, mathematics, and culture in everyday life*. Cambridge, UK: Cambridge University Press.

Lea, M., & Nicoll, K. (Eds.). (2002). *Distributed learning: Social and cultural approaches to practice*. London: Routledge.

Leeuwis, C., & Pyburn, R. (Eds.) (2002). *Wheelbarrows full of frogs: Social learning in rural resource management*. Assen, Netherlands: Koninklijke Van Gorcum.

Lent, R., & Brown, S. (1996). A social cognitive framework for career choice counseling. *Career Development Quarterly, 44*, 310–321.

Luke, A. (1995). Text and discourse in education: An introduction to critical discourse analysis. In M. Apple (Ed.), *Review of research in education, 21*, 3–48. Washington, DC: AERA.

Merriam, S., & Caffarella, R. (1999). *Learning in adulthood* (2nd ed.). San Francisco: Jossey-Bass.

Merriam, S., Caffarella, R., & Baumgartner, L. (2007). *Learning in adulthood: A comprehensive guide* (3rd ed.). San Francisco: Jossey-Bass.

Mezirow, J. (1991). *Transformative dimensions of adult learning*. San Francisco: Jossey-Bass.

Niewolny, K., & Wilson, A. (2006). (Re)situating cognition: Expanding sociocultural perspectives in adult education. In *Proceedings of the 47th Annual Adult Education Research Conference* (pp. 276–281). St. Paul, MN: University of Minnesota.

Niewolny, K., & Wilson, A. (2009). What happened to the promise? A critical (re)orientation of two sociocultural learning traditions. *Adult Education Quarterly*, *60*(1), 26–45.

O'Sullivan, E., Morrrell, A., & O'Connor, M. (Eds.). (2002). *Expanding the boundaries of transformative learning: Essays on theory and praxis.* New York: Palgrave.

Salomon, G., & Perkins, D. (1998). Individual and social aspects of learning. *Review of Research in Education*, *23*, 1–24.

Sawchuk, P. (2003a). *Adult learning and technology in working-class life.* Cambridge, UK: Cambridge University Press.

Sawchuk, P. (2003b). Informal learning as speech-exchange system: Implications of knowledge production, power, and social transformation. *Discourse and Society*, *14*(3), 291–307.

Sawchuk, P., Duarte, N., & Elhammoumi, M. (Eds.). (2006). *Critical perspective on activity: Explorations across education, work, and everyday life.* Cambridge, UK: Cambridge University Press.

Usher, R., Bryant, I., & Johnston, R. (1997). *Adult education and the postmodern challenge.* London: Routledge.

Wals, A. (2007). *Social learning towards a sustainable world: Principles, perspective, and praxis.* Wageningen: Wageningen Academic Publishers.

Wenger, E. (1998). *Communities of practice: Learning, meaning, and identity.* Cambridge, UK: Cambridge University Press.

Wilson, A. (1993). The promise of situated cognition. In S. Merriam (Ed.), *An update on adult learning* (pp. 71–80). San Francisco: Jossey-Bass.

Wilson, A. (2005). Activity theory. In L. English (Ed.), *Encyclopedia of adult education* (pp. 25–30). Houndshill, Hampshire, UK: Palgrave Macmillan.

CHAPTER 23

The Meaning and Role of Emotions in Adult Learning

John M. Dirkx

In an online graduate class in education, a middle-aged white woman wrote in her journal that she was so angry with her team members that she could have put her foot right through the computer.

On returning from a kitchen remodeling class at a home improvement store, a thirty-year-old African American man remarked that it was a great class because he felt safe enough in the context to ask what might seem to others as really stupid questions, and participating made him feel confident he could take on the home project he was planning.

A fifty-five-year-old White man, recently laid off from his manufacturing job and now in a community college developmental education math class, angrily complained to the teacher about having to learn fractions and bitterly asked her where in his world he would ever have to add and subtract fractions.

At break during a professional development conference for adult basic education, a forty-year-old Native American woman, who has been teaching in her program for fifteen years, remarked to her colleague that she really enjoyed the opportunity to hear what others were doing to address some of the problems she confronted in her teaching. She said she felt affirmed by listening to the stories of others but also excited to be able to try out some of their suggestions.

In an English Language Learning (ELL) class, the teacher, a forty-five-year-old woman of eastern European descent, was confronted with the angry outbursts of one of her adult students. Later she reported that she felt herself growing very angry at this student during this episode and almost lashed out at her during class.

These brief descriptions of incidents within settings of adult learning illustrate the powerful role that emotions can play in the lives of both teachers and learners (Schutz, Hong, Cross, and Osbon, 2006). They clearly animate processes of teaching and learning and at times become so powerful that they seem to blot out virtually everything else happening at the time.

But what do these emotionally laden experiences mean? Are they aberrant blips on the landscape of adult learning, distractions from the real work of teaching and learning? Do they represent unavoidable by-products of the struggles that are part of teaching and learning and, as such, need to be accepted but their disruptive potentials minimized? Or are they somehow constitutive of the very learning processes themselves, integral to the meaning making in which the learners and the teachers are engaged? What do the emotional experiences of adults within these settings tell us about them as teachers and learners, the processes of learning, and the contexts in which these experiences occur? What role does affect have in learning?

Educators have long been interested in the role of feeling, affect, and emotion in learning (Jones, 1968; Rogers, 1969; Salzberger-Wittenberg, Henry, and Osborne, 1983), and historically adult education has recognized their importance in adult learning (Brookfield, 1986; Lindeman, 1926). Within the past fifteen to twenty years, the emotional aspects of teaching and learning in adulthood have become a major theme in the scholarly literature and professional development programs. For example, while preparing the final draft of this chapter, I received an e-mail from the National Association for Adults with Special Learning Needs announcing an upcoming webinar titled, "Emotions: Supporting the Critical Prerequisite to Learning." While emphasizing the positive contribution that emotion and affect make on learner motivation and self-esteem, emotions are nonetheless widely recognized as a kind of baggage that impedes effective teaching and learning. As one adult learner, talking about the tensions and issues in her dislocated worker retraining group, recently told me, "Yeah, I know we are all struggling. They just need to get it off their chest, so they concentrate on getting something out of this."

Stemming from a broader discourse on emotions and the emotional self (Lewis and Haviland-Jones, 2000; Lupton, 1998), recent work in adult and continuing education reflects a re-visioning of the role of emotions in adult learning. Increasingly rejecting the notion of emotion as a barrier to reason and knowledge, this work suggests a more integral, central, and holistic role of emotion in reason, rationality, learning, and meaning making (Jarvis, 2006; Merriam, Caffarella, and Baumgartner, 2007). This volume contributes to the emerging conversation and explores various ways in which the emotional self is manifest within diverse settings of adult learning. In doing so, we hope to honor and give voice to the importance of this often neglected dimension of adult learning.

In this chapter, I provide a brief theoretical foundation for our exploration of affect-laden experiences in adult learning. While I rely on multiple sources and disciplines to develop this overview, the study of emotions is a vast and historically situated enterprise. In these few pages, I can only acknowledge some important themes that resonate in our conversations today about and practices with adult learning. Following a brief description of the various ways affect and emotion can be expressed in the adult learning enterprise, I briefly discuss three interrelated issues: the nature and meaning of emotion, the changing understanding of the role of emotion in human experience, and the integration of emotion in adult learning.

WAYS IN WHICH EMOTION IS MANIFEST IN ADULT LEARNING

Adult learners experience affect and emotion in a range from positive and energizing to negative and distracting. Emotions are also experienced in other ways as well, such as anger over something in the educational environment that may energize the learning experience or elation that blinds one to more difficult aspects of the experience. Learners may also experience emotions arising from within or evoked by the learning environment itself, or they may be struggling with personal issues around family, relationships, or work. Learning-related emotional issues among individuals often reflect a history of emotional experiences or trauma, of which learners may be variably aware, such as being humiliated by certain teachers in certain subjects or experiencing physical, sexual, or emotional abuse by persons in authority.

In one form or another, emotional issues never seem very far from the surface in adult learning contexts. The social and relational nature of these contexts often fosters, elicits, or implicitly encourages learners to give voice or expression to this underlying affect or emotion. Helping learners understand and make sense of these emotion-laden experiences within the context of the curriculum represents one of the most important and most challenging tasks for adult educators.

Perhaps the most common expression of strong emotions in adult learning occurs around areas of conflict, in which there may be profound disagreement of values or interest. Differences among students regarding values or interests, such as how to best proceed with a group project, often lead to feelings of anger or frustration, as in the opening example. Such emotional expressions are often bounded by the curricular contexts in which the disagreement surfaces, but they may create an affect that endures for the remainder of that particular setting or even beyond.

So-called personality conflicts among learners can result in emotional tones that color the learning experiences. For example, some learners might find the behaviors of another learner annoying in some way, and the behaviors gradually wear on them over time. Their feelings may then surprisingly erupt in powerful ways within the learning group, such as a verbal attack on the individual or indirectly on the teacher, who may be perceived as doing little or nothing about this annoying person.

Learning tasks and anticipation of being evaluated often precipitate emotional reactions among learners. They may feel anxious about doing well on a test, fear failure, or perceive themselves as unable to meet expectations. At times, the structure of the learning experience itself can foster various emotional reactions among students, some of whom may complain that not enough direction and structure are being provided, while others might feel equally strong about there being too much. Some students will express joy and elation about finally seeing the light about some problem or learning task, while others may feel overwhelmed by the multiplicity of demands within their lives. At times, students may give voice within the learning setting to the strong feelings and emotions being evoked by these various issues. Teachers may be the unwitting targets of such feelings, and they may react angrily at what they perceive as an attack on them by the students, as in the earlier example of the ELL teacher.

Occasionally curricular content stimulates powerful emotions among adult learners. For example, the subject of math often evokes considerable anxiety among many adult learners. Stories or examples included in the curriculum might bring to life for some learners painful or joyful experiences within their distant past. A teacher may precipitate affect-laden memories of earlier instructors or mentors or of one's parents. In other situations, the learning setting may simply represent a holding environment for the learners' difficult experiences within their families and relationships, or at work. These emotions often run the gamut from sadness and joy to anger and excitement.

Over twenty years ago, Brookfield (1986) characterized the adult discussion group as a psychodynamic battleground. While stretching the military metaphor a bit, Brookfield's comment underscores the profoundly emotional, affect-laden context in which adult learning occurs. The chapters in this volume suggest that the emotional contexts for adult learning and the experience of the emotional self stretch across a wide variety of settings for adult learning.

Emotion, affect, and feeling are all used to describe various aspects of these contexts. In some instances, it may be important to stress subtle differences to which these terms refer. In educational discourse, however, these terms are used fairly interchangeably, and no attempt is made in this volume to differentiate among these terms. Some emotions are experiences in a fairly focused and time-limited way within particular contexts, such as an angry reaction to being cut off in traffic or feeling insulted by what someone says in group discussion. Other emotions seem more diffuse and less restricted to particular contexts. Feeling blue or generally excited often reveals emotions about something, but we tend to have more difficulty describing just what it is we are feeling blue about or why on some days we feel so happy and upbeat. This latter form of emotional experience may be referred to as moods. They too are important in teaching and learning and often find expression in particular ways, such as interactions with others, our interest and motivation in learning, or the care we give to our work. Therefore, in this volume, we are interested in emotions, feelings, affect, and mood as they influence, shape, and constitute the nature and quality of adult learning experiences.

THE NATURE AND MEANING OF EMOTION

The authors of the following chapters share a constructive and holistic view of emotions in adult learning, However, educators have not always looked favorably on the manifestation of emotions and feelings within the learning process. Reflecting the widespread influence of the enlightenment and the growth of scientific ways of knowing, emotions have for many years been regarded as largely undesirable within teaching and learning settings, that is, as obstacles to reason and the development of knowledge. Many educators still regard their manifestation within the learning process as a distinctly negative development, and they seek ways to avoid or mitigate their expression.

Others perceive the expression of emotions as perhaps necessary but only as a means of ventilating and allowing the learners to refocus on the learning task. Teachers who admit to this orientation suggest that it is important to let learners get things off their chest so that they may be able to devote their energies to learning what is contained within the curriculum (Dirkx and Spurgin, 1992). At the hint of affect-laden conflict, disagreement, or powerful expressions of emotionality, learners and educators alike, in many different educational contexts, tend to feel their stomach tighten, their pulse quicken, and their breathing grow more shallow and constrained. Even expressions of so-called positive emotions, such as joy or elation, are often regarded as pleasant interruptions of an otherwise sober environment.

Increasingly, however, educators are acknowledging the powerful role emotions and affect play in the adult learning process. In their widely popular text, Merriam, Caffarella, and Baumgartner (2007) demonstrate the growing recognition of emotion in various theories and models of adult learning. Jarvis (2006) devotes an entire chapter to the interrelationship of emotions and learning, suggesting that "emotions can have a considerable effect on the way we think, on motivation and on beliefs, attitudes and values" (p. 102).

Depending on whose writings you read and what discipline the scholar represents, the meaning of emotion and what is considered an emotion vary widely. Some theorists argue for a view of emotions that largely represents an innate or inherent perspective. These scholars argue that emotional states are, for the most part, physiological responses to particular stimuli, as evidenced in the flight-or-fight response to situations that evoke fear (Lupton, 1998). They are, in effect, manifestations of the lower parts of our brains (Jarvis, 2006; Lupton, 1996). In a simplistic sense, an unanticipated encounter with a mountain lion along a quiet bubbling stream evokes an involuntary emotional arousal of fear that precipitates a strong desire to flee.

Cognitive theorists adhere to a somewhat less essentialist view, allowing that emotional behavior remains an essentially physiological response to external stimuli but often mediated by processes of judgment and assessment or appraisal. In a sense, emotional expressions represent complex processes of neurophysiological arousal and cognitive processing that lead to certain conclusions about the meaning of certain stimuli within one's environment. It is the cognitive appraisal that allows us to conclude that despite being scared to death by an encounter with a mountain lion, the last thing we would want to do in that situation is run.

Others, however, claim that emotions are fundamentally social constructions and entirely dependent on the particular contexts in which they are manifest. From this point of view, emotions are "always experienced, understood and named via social and cultural processes" (Lupton, 1998, p. 15). Fear as an emotional response to the encounter of a mountain lion is therefore the result of a learned or acquired meaning schema. Learning to be very careful around hot stoves after having an unpleasant experience with one at an earlier point in one's life exemplifies this learned, constructed process.

Scholars representing this perspective are particularly interested in the implications that emotional experiences and expression hold for one's sense of self and one's relationships with others and the broader world. Lupton (1998) argues that within this group, positions reflect what she refers to as the "weak or less relativistic thesis" and the "strong thesis" (p. 15). While the former admits to a small range of emotions they consider naturally occurring and biologically given, the latter insists that emotion is, fundamentally and irreducibly, a "sociocultural product, wholly learnt and constructed through acculturation" (p. 15).

That is, the weak thesis might posit that we will naturally experience fear as a result of something like an encounter with a mountain lion, the consequence of the activities of the lower parts of our brain. But making sense of that fear within that particular situation is learned or acquired through one's social and cultural contexts. Proponents of the strong thesis would argue that one's emotional response to the encounter of a mountain lion in the depths of the forest is entirely the result of a set of meanings and relationships acquired over time within particular social and cultural contexts. As a child, we might have been read numerous fairy tales of similar creatures stalking unlikely innocents and making a quick lunch of them. These earlier experiences continued to be reinforced by similar myths and stories in popular culture of late adolescence and young adulthood. As an adult, the literal mountain lion might have morphed into more symbolic images, such as greedy corporations, heartless employers, and terrorists from other lands.

Emerging recently as a third major approach to understanding emotion is the idea of the emotional self as embodied, of recognizing, as Lupton (1998) suggests, the role that our flesh and blood play in emotion. But this perspective emphasizes more than just emotion as a bodily sensation. Rather, "embodiment is integral to, and inextricable from, subjectivity" (p. 32). From this viewpoint, emotion represents both the experience of particular body states and our interpretation or construction of these states as mediated by sociocultural processes.

For example, I might be in a curriculum meeting with colleagues in which we are reviewing proposed revisions in our graduate program. The meeting seems to be going well, but I gradually become aware of tightness in the back of my neck and shoulders. I might initially shrug it off as the product of my posture or the chair in which I am sitting, and I shift my weight and position. As the meeting proceeds, however, I notice that the tightness has become more, rather than less, pronounced. At the same time, I become aware of feeling vaguely uncertain about what is going on in the meeting, and the good feeling about the meeting I had earlier now evaporates. Before I know it, we seem to have two factions arguing heatedly about what seem to me quite obscure and innocuous points of the proposed curriculum plan. I recognize and interpret this tightness and discomfort in my body as a manifestation of anxiety. My experience of this emotion is the result of both attending to a physical sensation and framing this sensation within a broader discourse that leads to my naming it and experiencing it as anxiety.

Within the educational literature, the notion of embodied emotion is part of a broader conversation on embodied learning or knowing (Horn and Wilburn, 2005). According to Merriam, Caffarella, and Baumgartner (2007), "Embodied learning has a strong emotional or feeling dimension" (p. 194). It represents a theory of knowledge production that "depends on being in a world that is inseparable from our bodies, our language, and our social history" (Varela, Thompson, and Rosch, 1991, p. 149). Embodied learning represents a more holistic way of understanding learning and knowing (Barlas, 2001; Merriam, Caffarella, and Baumgartner, 2007) and is reflected in the work of scholars in adult and continuing education as well (Brooks and Clark, 2001; Chapman, 1998; Clark, 2001; Schlatner, 1994). Central to these views of embodied learning and knowing is the idea of the experience of emotion as embodied.

Variations of one or more of these three perspectives are evident in the growing discourse on emotion and adult learning (Jarvis, 2006; Merriam, Caffarella, and Baumgartner, 2007). In general, this discourse reflects an understanding of emotion as a neurophysiological response to an external or internal stimulus, occurring within and rendered meaningful through a particular sociocultural context and discourse, and integral to one's sense of self.

THE ROLE OF EMOTION IN HUMAN EXPERIENCE

Reflecting the influence of Cartesian dualism of mind and body and the growth of modernity, emotion has for many years been regarded as separate from both our cognitive and bodily processes, and an anathema to reason and knowing. Over the past twenty years, however, more holistic conceptions of the emotional self have become increasingly common. This holistic understanding of the emotional self implicates our emotions in an active process of knowing, suggesting a positive and "intelligent" role for them in our lives and, in particular, in adult learning.

Goleman's writing (1995) on the idea of emotional intelligence contributed significantly to a popular revision of the role of emotion in our private and social worlds. He suggests that human learning is constituted by both rational and emotional ways of knowing, but both are deeply integrated and bound up with one another. Emotional intelligence reflects self-awareness of one's own feelings and emotions, as well as those of others.

Emotional intelligence conveys the idea of emotions as something to be managed and used in our encounters with the outer world. Other scholars, however, attribute to emotion a more intrinsic intelligence, a way of knowing that augments or works in coordination with more traditional means of reason and cognition. In particular, feminist theory has been a major force in re-visioning our understanding of the role of emotions in our lives, rejecting the view of emotions as an obstacle to reason and knowledge, and helping to shape a deeper understanding of the role of emotions in the development of moral knowledge (Gorton, 2007). This re-visioning process has occurred largely within the broader focus of embodied knowing and learning (Merriam, Caffarella, and Baumgartner, 2007) and reflects conceptions of embodied emotion (Lupton, 1998).

Martha Nusbaum (2001) argues that emotions are characterized by a certain kind of intelligence and help us discern and make our way through our worlds. She rejects the widely popular image, carried over from the enlightenment, and its mind-body dualism, that emotions represent alien forces that invade and disrupt conscious, rational thought. Solomon (2007), who has explored and written about the emotions for many years, consistently links emotions to meaning in our lives. Similar to Nusbaum, Solomon rejects the idea of emotions as something happening to us or that they are, in a literal sense, irrational. Rather, he argues, emotions are intimately bound up with judgments we make, and they represent strategies for living these judgments within the world. "We live our lives through emotions," Solomon (2007) writes, "and it is our emotions that give our lives meaning" (p. 1).

Post-Jungians also emphasize the important role that emotions play in rendering meaning to our lives. While Solomon and Nusbaum represent a group of scholars that accord emotions an integral role in our rational understandings of the world, post-Jungian scholars such as Hillman (1975) and Watkins (2000) stress the importance of emotions to imaginative engagement with the world. Essentially, they argue, we can know ourselves and the world meaningfully only through the images that we create. These images are intimately bound up with our emotional experiences of the world. For these scholars, emotions represent expressions and ways of coming to know one's unconscious self, the fundamental source of meaning and creativity in our lives.

EMOTION AND ALTERNATIVE WAYS OF KNOWING IN ADULT LEARNING

Constructive and holistic approaches to emotion in adult learning represent what we may essentially consider as ways of knowing that challenge historical dominance of reason and scientific ways of knowing. These alternate ways of knowing are evident in theories of experiential learning, whole person learning, embodied learning, transformative learning, and spiritual experience. Emotional dimensions of our experiences represent central themes in theories of experiential learning. In particular, several authors (Boud, Keogh, and Walker, 1985; Boud and Miller, 1996; Beard and Wilson, 2002) provide suggestions for helping adult learners work through some of the emotions and feelings arising within their learning contexts.

Relying on the work of Heron (1992), Yorks and Kasl (2002) propose a phenomenological perspective to experiential learning. In this view, experience is regarded as "a process, an encounter with the world" (p. 182). Their theory of whole person learning posits a more holistic understanding of learning through experience and the foundational role of affect in this process (Yorks and Kasl, 2006).

Embodied learning suggests a way of experiential knowing that "depends on being in a world that is inseparable from our bodies, our language and our social history" (Varela, Thompson, and Rosch, 1991, p. 149). This approach stresses the importance of somatic awareness and recognizes the body as a source of knowledge about one's self and one's relationship to the world. Embodied learning is characterized by a strong emotional or feeling dimension (Merriam, Caffarella, and Baumgartner, 2007). Emotions convey a deep and intimate connection with our world, and this connection is often manifest neurophysiologically through the body.

Transformative learning theories incorporate aspects of experiential, whole person, and embodied learning. Although we lack consensus on a clear definition of transformative learning, most would agree that it represents a fundamental change or shift in our understanding of ourselves or our relationship with the world in which we live (Boyd and Myers, 1988; Cranton, 2006; Mezirow and Associates, 2000; O'Sullivan, 1999). Prompted by what is widely perceived as the rational and cognitive emphasis in Mezirow's (1991) theory of transformative learning (Cranton, 2006; Merriam, Caffarella, and Baumgartner, 2007), numerous scholars have been exploring the emotional or affective processes involved in transformative learning. In particular, Boyd and his colleagues (Boyd, 1991; Boyd and Myers, 1988; Dirkx, 2001, 2006) argue for the centrality of emotional processes in the expansion of consciousness and integration of personality, key dynamics of their view of transformative learning. Yorks and Kasl (2006) provide guidelines on how expressive ways of knowing can foster the growing awareness of emotion and emergence of transformative learning.

Finally, growing attention to spirituality in adult and higher education (English, Fenwick, and Parsons, 2003; Kazanjian and Laurence, 2002; Tisdell, 2003) also demonstrates a re-visioning of the role of emotions in human experience and learning, and stresses alternative ways of knowing (Palmer, 1993). Here, again, no consensus exists on a definition of spirituality. In general, however, a deep and abiding search for meaning is often associated with a process of developing or making explicit a connection with something greater than one's self, to community, a transcendent energy, or a divinity (English, Fenwick, and Parsons, 2003). Palmer (1993) argues that a sensitivity to feelings is essential to fostering the kind of spiritual journey that he believes education can or should represent. In contrast to our common practice of evading, suppressing, or otherwise not attending to feelings in teaching and learning, Palmer encourages us to create space within our educational environments where giving voice to emotion-laden issues becomes an integral part of a community of truth.

CONCLUSION

In the following chapters, the authors explore ways in which emotion is manifest in a variety of contexts of adult learning. These discussions offer a vision for integrating emotion within alternative ways of knowing in adult and higher education. They include programs for academically underprepared adults, adult learners returning to higher education, multicultural education, online education programs, workplace learning, nonformal learning, and the role of the arts in adult learning. From the perspectives of these various practice contexts, contributors explore a deeper understanding of the role that emotions play in contributing to and expressing one's sense of self as practitioner and as learner. The authors provide a consideration of key theoretical perspectives on how emotion constitutes our subjectivity or sense of self as adult learners and practitioners, and the various ways in which the emotional self is manifest within several different contexts of adult learning. Contributors discuss methods and strategies within various contexts that may be used to help practitioners and learners make sense of potentially powerful emotions evoked within the learning experience and how these experiences can help learners develop a deeper understanding of themselves.

REFERENCES

Barlas, C. "Learning-Within-Relationship as Context and Process in Adult Education." In R. O. Smith and others (eds.), *Forty-Second Annual Adult Education Research Conference and Proceedings*. East Lansing: Michigan State University, 2001.

Beard, C., and Wilson, J. P. *The Power of Experiential Learning: A Handbook for Educators and Trainers*. London: Kogan Page, 2002.

Boud, D., Keogh, R., and Walker, D. *Reflection: Turning Experiences into Learning*. London: Kogan Page, 1985.

Boud, D., and Miller, N. *Working with Experience: Animating Learning*. London: Routledge, 1996.

Boyd, R. D. *Personal Transformation in Small Groups: A Jungian Perspective*. New York: Routledge, 1991.

Boyd, R. D., and Myers, J. G. "Transformative Education." *International Journal of Lifelong Education,* 1988, 7 (4), 261–284.

Brookfield, S. *Understanding and Facilitating Adult Learning*. San Francisco: Jossey-Bass, 1986.

Brooks, A., and Clark, C. "Narrative Dimensions of Transformative Learning." In R. O. Smith and others (eds.), *Forty-Second Annual Adult Education Research Conference and Proceedings*. East Lansing: Michigan State University, 2001.

Chapman, V. L. "Adult Education and the Body: Changing Performances of Teaching and Learning." In J. C. Kimmel (ed.), *Thirty-Ninth Annual Adult Education Conference Proceedings*. San Antonio: University of the Incarnate Word and Texas A&M, 1998.

Clark, M. C. "Off the Beaten Path: Some Creative Approaches to Adult Learning." In S. B. Merriam (ed.), *The New Update on Adult Learning Theory*. New Directions for Adult and Continuing Education, no. 89. San Francisco: Jossey-Bass, 2001.

Cranton, P. *Understanding and Promoting Transformative Learning: A Guide for Educators of Adults*. San Francisco: Jossey-Bass, 2006.

Dirkx, J. M. "The Power of Feelings: Emotion, Imagination, and the Construction of Meaning in Adult Learning." In S. B. Merriam (ed.), *The New Update on Adult Learning Theory*. New Directions for Adult and Continuing Education, no. 89. San Francisco: Jossey-Bass, 2001.

Dirkx, J. M. "Engaging Emotions in Adult Learning: A Jungian Perspective on Emotion and Transformative Learning." In E. Taylor (ed.), *Fostering Transformative Learning in the Classroom: Challenges and Innovations*. New Directions in Adult and Continuing Education, no. 109. San Francisco: Jossey-Bass, 2006.

Dirkx, J. M., and Spurgin, M. "Implicit Theories of Adult Basic Education Teachers: How They Think About Their Students." *Adult Basic Education: An Interdisciplinary Journal for Adult Literacy Educators,* 1992, 2, 20–41.

English, L. M., Fenwick, T. J., and Parsons, J. *Spirituality of Adult Education and Training*. Malabar, Fla.: Krieger, 2003.

Goleman, D. *Emotional Intelligence: Why It Can Matter More Than IQ.* New York: Bantam Books, 1995.

Gorton, K. "Theorizing Emotion and Affect." *Feminist Theory,* 2007, *8* (3), 333–348.

Heron, J. *Feeling and Personhood: Psychology in Another Key.* Thousand Oaks, Calif.: Sage, 1992.

Hillman, J. *Re-Visioning Psychology.* New York: HarperCollins, 1975.

Horn, J., and Wilburn, D. "The Embodiment of Learning." *Educational Philosophy and Theory,* 2005, *37* (5), 745–760.

Jarvis, P. *Toward a Comprehensive Theory of Human Learning.* London: Routledge, 2006.

Jones, R. M. *Fantasy and Feeling in Education.* New York: HarperCollins, 1968.

Kazanjian, V. H., and Laurence, P. L. (eds.). *Education as Transformation: Religious Pluralism, Spirituality, and a New Vision for Higher Education in America.* New York: Peter Lang, 2002.

Lewis, M., and Haviland-Jones, J. M. (eds). *Handbook of Emotions.* (2nd ed.) New York: Guilford Press, 2000.

Lindeman, E. C. *The Meaning of Adult Education.* New York: New Republic, 1926.

Lupton, D. *The Emotional Self: A Sociocultural Exploration.* Thousand Oaks, Calif.: Sage, 1998.

Merriam, S. B., Caffarella, R. S., and Baumgartner, L. M., *Learning in Adulthood: A Comprehensive Guide.* San Francisco: Jossey-Bass, 2007.

Mezirow, J. *Transformative Dimensions of Adult Learning.* San Francisco: Jossey-Bass, 1991.

Mezirow, J., and Associates. *Learning as Transformation: Critical Perspectives on a Theory in Progress.* San Francisco: Jossey-Bass, 2000.

Nusbaum, M. *Upheavals of Thought: The Intelligence of Emotions.* Cambridge: Cambridge University Press, 2001.

O'Sullivan, E. *Transformative Learning: Educational Vision for the 21st Century.* London: Zed, 1999.

Palmer, P. *To Know as We Are Known: Education as a Spiritual Journey.* New York: HarperSanFrancisco, 1993.

Rogers, C. R. *Freedom to Learn.* Columbus, Ohio: Charles E. Merrill, 1969.

Salzberger-Wittenberg, I., Henry, G., and Osborne, E. *The Emotional Experience of Teaching and Learning.* London: Routledge and Kegan Paul, 1983.

Schlatner, C. "The Body in Transformative Learning." In M. Hymans, J. Armstrong, and E. Anderson (eds.), *Thirty-Fifth Annual Adult Education Research Conference Proceedings.* Knoxville, Tenn.: University of Knoxville, 1994.

Schutz, P. A., Hong, J. Y., Cross, D. I., and Osbon, J. N. "Reflections on Investigating Emotion in Educational Activity Settings." *Educational Psychology Review,* 2006, *18,* 343–360.

Solomon, R. C. *True to Our Feelings: What Emotions Are Really Telling Us.* New York: Oxford University Press, 2007.

Tisdell, E. J. *Exploring Spirituality and Culture in Adult and Higher Education.* San Francisco: Jossey-Bass, 2003.

Varela, F., Thompson, E., & Rosch, E. *The Embodied Mind: Cognitive Science and Human Experience.* Cambridge, Mass.: MIT Press, 1991.

Watkins, M. *Invisible Guests: The Development of Imaginal Dialogues.* Woodstock, Conn.: Spring, 2000.

Yorks, L., and Kasl, E. "Toward a Theory and Practice for Whole-Person Learning: Reconceptualizing Experience and the Role of Affect." *Adult Education Quarterly,* 2002, *52,* 176–192.

Yorks, L., and Kasl, E. "I Know More Than I Can Say: A Taxonomy for Using Expressive Ways of Knowing to Foster Transformative Learning." *Journal of Transformative Education,* 2006, *4*(1), 43–64.

CHAPTER 24

Adult Education and the Mass Media in the Age of Globalization

Talmadge C. Guy

S ome forty years ago, Marshall McLuhan (McLuhan & Fiore, 1967) offered the insight that the medium is the message. Studying the impact of advertisers on consumers, McLuhan argued that it was the medium of TV, radio, or news that shapes the messages that consumers receive. A corollary to that insight is the notion that whoever controls the medium is in control of the message. As advertisers sought to secure the market for their products, to control the medium meant the message would influence the behavior of people.

In this chapter, I argue that the power of the media to influence the thought and actions of people is at a level unprecedented in human history. Additionally, I argue that the concentrated power of the media has the consequence of steering consumers (learners) away from critical, socially conscious forms of learning and social action. Media and technology have combined so as to produce a powerful global communications network that shapes our relationships and our ideas about the world in which we live.

Because they are so pervasive, these global communications networks of the mass media in effect become systems of informal adult education. Supported by telecommunications technology, the media transcend space and time to reach a global audience almost instantaneously. The advantage for owners of media is that they possess the capability to manipulate, enforce, and reinforce the messages they prefer for a large-scale audience on a global level. The ability to use communication technologies to disseminate prescribed ways of seeing the world is a powerful tool. The noted scholar of technologies and communication Neil Postman (1992) makes this point in saying that "our understanding of what is real is different which is another way of saying that embedded in every tool is an ideological bias, a predisposition to construct the world as one thing rather than another, value one thing over another, to amplify one sense or skill or attitude more loudly than another" (p. 13).

MEDIA CONCENTRATION AND GLOBALIZATION

Ownership of mass media organizations is increasingly concentrated in the hands of fewer and more powerful corporations and owners (Albarran, 1998; Herman & McChesney, 1997). In the United States, for example, it is possible to speak of the "Big Five": Viacom, News Corporation, Time Warner, General Electric, and Walt Disney, major players in the mass media industry that control such media outlets as television, radio, publishing, magazines, cinema, newspapers, bookstores, and video stores. These five corporations alone account for hundreds of billions of dollars in annual revenue, and the trend is upward as the rapid pace of acquisition and merger continues (Albarran, 1998; Herman & McChesney, 1997). Data on the growth of mass media illustrate both the size and reach of the major media corporations, which cover virtually every conceivable form of information development, production, and distribution (Herman & McChesney, 1997).

A significant factor in the continuing concentration of the media is regulatory support through the policies of the Federal Communications Commission (FCC) and congressional action as represented by the Telecommunications Act of 1996 (McChesney, 2004). Federal policy as evidenced by regulatory and legislative actions serves to reduce restrictions on ownership of media within major markets. In a move that would have further accelerated media mergers, the FCC last year approved rule changes allowing monopoly ownership of TV and newspaper outlets in the same city. Fortunately, a recent federal appeals court ruling has forestalled this change by asking the FCC to reconsider its rule change. At the time of this writing, the Bush administration had decided to back off its efforts to relax regulation on media control in urban markets (Labaton, 2005). Given the trends toward increasing concentration, one wonders how long this stay of regulatory relaxation will hold.

Media studies draw primarily on two theoretical traditions, in political economy and in cultural studies (Louw, 2001). The political economy approach stresses the need to analyze communication contextually, or as bound to the locations where they are made. Research informed by this theoretical lens focuses on the social location of people and the social relations between them, and the resulting struggles over dominant meanings within society. According to Louw (2001), researchers who employ a political economy approach to media studies are interested in "mapping out human relationships and the way some individuals gain more power than others through their positioning relative to others, and to their position relative to media production and circulation systems. Within such a framework, meaning-making is implicated in contextually-rooted processes of struggle and power acquisition. Gaining access to the means of communicative production/circulation . . . is both derivative of power and a means for accumulating power" (p. 4).

Therefore power relationships between individuals and historically constituted groups are fundamental to understanding the struggle to control the production and dissemination of meanings.

The cultural studies approach to media studies focuses on deconstructing texts and coding systems as a way of revealing hidden ideological orientations in messages being conveyed from producer to consumer. Louw (2001) says: "The cultural studies insight that humans swim in a sea of meanings that is the outcome of a process of semiosis provides a useful point of departure. We are born into pools of pre-constituted meanings and internalize these as we are socialized and learn to communicate. Various communication pools have merged as clusters or structures of meaning that have congealed over time. These communicative pools are coding styles or circulation patterns that have taken on identifiable forms which we call societies or cultures" (p. 3).

Various historically constituted groups have clusters of meaning that are distinct and frequently in conflict. As individuals are socialized into particular cultural groups, their subjectivity is constituted within a sociocultural and historical context on the basis of the distinct meaning sets they internalize.

GLOBAL MEDIA AND THE CONTROL OF CONSCIOUSNESS

The control of media production is a central concern here because control of media translates into control of meanings produced and disseminated by the media. The power exercised by those in control of the media is fundamentally symbolic (Louw, 2001). To exercise broad control over the thoughts and desires of the public is to exercise power in a way that is difficult to resist because the locus of power appears diffused. The reason for this has to do with what it means for media to become global.

According to Louw, the global nature of media represents a new stage of capitalism: global network capitalism. The information age that we so readily recognize in advanced technological societies requires a new kind of cultural capital to gain access to information required to do important work. This cultural capital is distinguished from that of the earlier managerial era of capitalism, where professional managers work in and through highly bureaucratized forms of organization in both the economic and the political sectors. Global network capitalism involves development and extension of far-reaching information networks and the growing privatization of decision making. In managerial capitalism, decision making is taken, in public and private domains, by a clearly identifiable body: corporate boards or commissions, or bureaus of government. This form of organization evolves under the new terms of globalization. Louw (2001) states, "The Fordist hierarchical company therefore breaks down and is replaced with a confederated network or global web" (p. 62). As the media move to become more global, the locus of media control can be more difficult to identify.

Frankfurt School critical theorists were among the first to offer a systematic analysis of the consumer society that depended on new modes of social integration and control (Kellner, 1989). Adorno and Horkheimer (1991) theorized the emergence of what they called "culture industries," referring to the products and processes of mass culture. Culture industries manipulate consumers' needs through production and arrangement of powerful cultural symbols. It was argued that a main function of culture industries was to shape the needs, attitudes, and behavior of individuals so that they could assume roles as consumers in a society where consumption was becoming vitally important for economic growth.

By the 1950s, mass consumption had become a reality, and with it came increased scholarly interest on the part of social theorists looking at problems of hegemony and domination in advanced capitalist societies. The challenge for the managers of capital was to develop institutional capacity to consistently influence the consciousness of the public (Kellner, 1989). Adorno and Horkheimer (1991) argued that the mass media were a central part of the machinery of the culture industry of modern capitalism, designed to intentionally influence the consciousness of the public to buy the goods and services produced. Consumers' needs are satisfied through orchestration of market forces to satisfy the demands for profit.

They suggested that culture industries give rise to two things: cultural homo-geneity and predictability in cultural taste. Cultural homogeneity resulted from mass-produced consumer products, where the public was increasingly restricted to a set number of choices of any product. Reduced competition resulting from consolidation of capital within specific markets therefore led to a narrowing of choices, producing in turn increasing cultural homogeneity. A second consequence of the growth in culture industries was predictability in cultural taste. Predictability was essential for producers to ensure that products would turn a profit. These two consequences meant that consumers' attention was increasingly turned to a narrower range of choices, determined by producers. Ideally, producers could control markets through manipulating consumer preferences.

In *One-Dimensional Man,* Herbert Marcuse states: "The irresistible output of the entertainment and information industry carries with them prescribed attitudes and habits, certain intellectual and emotional reactions which bind the consumer more or less pleasantly to the producers and, through the latter, to the whole. The products indoctrinate and manipulate; they promote a false consciousness which is immune against its falsehood—it becomes a way of life" (1991, pp. 26–27).

As products that satisfy predefined needs are supplied, consumers' wants and desires are turned to those commodities that give great pleasure and enjoyment. Who hasn't seen the fast sports car, or the luxurious villa of the rich and famous, or the designer clothes that we long for? The consequence of what economists call "pent up" consumer demand is that consumers buy at an unprecedented rate, even borrowing money to acquire the commodities that advertisers say they "need." In the United States consumer debt is at a historical high, reaching more than $2 trillion in credit and car loan debt. This figure translates into more than $18,000 per American household (Federal Reserve, 2004).

Another consequence of manipulating consumer consciousness is that citizens are distracted from asking fundamental questions about the use of economic and political power in society. As Adorno and Horkheimer (1991) argue, culture industries are able to forestall or even prevent formation of more critical sensibilities. Culture industries, in effect, override the development of aesthetic, moral, and political imagination. For them, authentic culture has taken over the utopian function of religion, which is to keep alive the human desire for a better world beyond the confines of the present. Authentic culture holds the key to unlock the prison house of mass culture. However as they point out, mass culture produces norms of behavior that are difficult to challenge: "Today anyone who is incapable of talking in the prescribed fashion, that is of effortlessly reproducing the formulas, conventions and judgments of mass culture as if they were his own, is threatened and his very existence, suspected of being an idiot or an intellectual" (p. 79).

In the search for cultural homogeneity, predictability, and profit, managers of capital deprive culture of its critical function. Commercialization devalues ethnic culture by turning it into just another commodity, like athletic shoes or deodorant or a soft drink. Instead, mass production entails colonization of independent thought and critical consciousness.

Marcuse (1991) identified mass production and market manipulation of need as the key to social integration in advanced capitalist society. By controlling the thoughts of the individual, the market could gain control of the individual. This was fundamental to producing a person who would want the items made available through the production process, even if those items were somehow deprecating, injurious, or offensive. Thus we are confronted with a dilemma: given the choice to critique, to condemn, to combat the dehumanizing forces of the market-driven, global media, we must forgo the pleasures that accompany the capitalist values of consumerism and materialism that influence behavior.

An Illustration: *The Matrix*—"Ignorance Is Bliss"

This dilemma is brought into sharp relief in the cult trilogy *The Matrix* (1999), when Cypher Reagan decides to betray the liberated humans to the Agents of the Matrix. The Matrix is an elaborate neural interactive simulation, a computer-generated dream world, the product of an elaborate computer program. Its purpose is control—that is, to enslave human beings to a world of machines who have taken over most of the surface of the planet Earth. Through the biological functioning of their nervous systems, human beings who are plugged into the Matrix provide energy for the machines who rule the Earth. In the world of the Matrix, humans are grown instead of born. However, there is a society of human beings who have been liberated from the Matrix. Their aim is to destroy it and to free all human kind from the system of control. Morpheus is a leader among the liberated. He is captain of a ship that ventures into the Matrix to liberate individuals. A member of Morpheus's crew, Cypher Reagan, turns against the free. Why? Reality is too harsh, too bare, too unexciting. The struggle for freedom is too demanding, too hard. He decides to give up freedom in favor of the sensory pleasures afforded by the Matrix. Exclaiming "Ignorance is bliss!" Cypher agrees to betray Morpheus and free humankind by striking a bargain with the gatekeepers of the Matrix, supercomputer programs called "agents."

In *The Matrix* we are presented with a quite contemporary and relevant moral dilemma: Is it better to surrender to the Matrix, a world of delusion and illusion in which the sensory pleasures abound but where humans have no control over their lives? Or is it preferable to be liberated in mind and body, only to realize that life must be a continuous struggle against the system of control that will seek to colonize humankind?

As might be argued, then, media can play a role in raising issues for critical thought. However, it is the case that *The Matrix* was never quite the stunning success it might have been and received mixed reviews in the media. As this case might suggest, the potential for the critical function of the media rests largely on the control of the market response.

Discovering Unexpected Cultural Homogeneity: *Behind Enemy Lines*

As a second example, in the movie *Behind Enemy Lines* (2001) fighter pilot Chris Burnett is shot down behind enemy lines in Bosnia. In a bold rescue, his commander sends help—but not before pilot Burnett has to take evasive action to escape hostile forces. While attempting to hide, Burnett encounters a group of underground fighters who give him a ride to escape the Bosnian forces in search of him. Not understanding each other because of language differences, one of the young underground rebels finally exclaims "Snoop Dogg," "NWA." Immediately recognizing a cultural common ground of hip hop music and rap stars, the young pilot understands he is in safe hands.

The relevance of this small scene for the present discussion has to do with the fact that in a desolate, war-torn, remote village in Bosnia the reach of American media is evident as the young teenage rebel quickly identifies with his American counterpart through a shared interest in rap music. This episode is a small instance of a larger, pervasive global process: the spread of a globalized mass media industry(-ies) and the homogenization of culture.

Appropriation and Domestication of Hip Hop: A Global Phenomenon

To further illustrate, as I write these words on a Friday morning in mid-April, I turn to read one of the headlines in the online version of the *New York Times:*

"For Colombia's Angry Youth, Hip Hop Helps Keep It Real" (Ferrero, 2004). The article says:

> What they see as hip-hop culture, with its baggy jeans and big jewelry, is high urban fashion. Rap has taken over at parties where salsa or boleros once ruled. Even major radio stations are offering hip-hop-oriented shows.
>
> "I like the rhythm, the beat, the boom, boom, boom," said Waira Zamora, 19, a university student. "I can listen to rap all night long."
>
> The biggest sellers remain Americans, artists like 50 Cent and the group NWA. Some American rappers, like Eminem, have had phenomenal success here, selling even more albums than better-known stars of more traditional popular music, like cumbia.

Where does rap come from? What are the social and political issues that give rise to its popularity? Rap music began in New York City in the 1970s. Its appeal stems from the rhythmic cadences and the lyrical richness from black males whose distinctive and patterned ways of behaving reflect an oppositional stance toward white mainstream America (Fordham, 1999). Although rap music has received lots of negative criticism, it has become a major international industry, generating billions of dollars in sales with a global marketing reach (Cashmore, 1997). It has transcended the boundaries of the ghetto to become an international force in popular and capitalist culture (Gilroy, 1998). In its early formation, rap music constituted a strong countercritique against mainstream American culture. This critical dimension has been eroded as rap became engulfed by the lure of money fed through the pipeline of major culture industries. As rap continues its global expansion, this expansion can be understood only in relationship to the technological innovation and capitalist organization on which the culture industries depend. As in the United States, the political critique initially represented by rappers in Colombia is becoming domesticated and colonized such that rap music becomes another avenue for importation of American mass culture.

What these examples demonstrate is that American popular culture (in this case the American hip hop scene) is beginning to have a global impact. This is not incidental or accidental but a manifestation of the development of global media networks accompanying the broader process of economic globalization. One area of concern for globalization critics has been the homogenization of culture and its attendant celebration of capitalist cultural values (consumerism, materialism, instant gratification, sexuality, and money).

■ STANDARDIZATION: THE ESSENCE OF MASS CULTURE

Frankfurt School critical theorists have argued that mass culture and popular culture are essentially the same. Popular culture is the product of mass culture processes. It loses its critical function by not taking any explicit political position. Adorno outlines how this occurs using the example of popular music. There are essentially three aspects of the process: standardization, passive listening, and psychological adjustment to the status quo.

Standardization occurs once a musical pattern has proved successful in the marketplace; it is exploited to commercial exhaustion. Once the details of the song become popular, they can be interchanged with details from another song. In this sense popular music is a mechanical reproduction of a formulaic approach to cultural expression. However, it's not in the best interest of the music industry to have every hit seem like every other hit. So, to conceal this process of standardization, the music industry engages in what Adorno and Horkheimer call "pseudo individualization," where each hit has something of its own distinctiveness.

Passive listening is induced partly as a result of the process of standardization. Popular hits have a certain repetitiveness and predictability. You can mentally skip out on one phrase or part of a song and happily rejoin it at a later point and achieve the same relative degree of aesthetic satisfaction. Adorno and Horkheimer (1991) argue that this passive quality in listening confirms the world as it is. Popular music operates on a kind of confused dialectic: to consume it demands inattention and distraction, while its consumption produces in the consumer inattention and distraction.

Psychological adjustment to the status quo occurs as a kind of social integration. Music fans feel a sense of connectedness to the music, and through the music to each other. Adorno and Horkheimer claim that this adjustment manifests itself in two major sociopsychological types of mass behavior: the rhythmically obedient and the emotional. The former dances, distracted by the rhythm, to his or her own exploitation. The latter dances in spite of the knowledge that those who are exploited remain oblivious to the real conditions of existence.

Although popular culture is now widely understood as more complex and multifaceted than Adorno and Horkheimer's depiction of it (for example, see Storey, 2003), the power of the mass media to co-opt and commodify popular culture appears to be very much in accord with Adorno and Horkheimer's characterization of it. In effect, popular culture's critical dimension is domesticated and colonized.

Let's apply Adorno and Horkheimer's analysis to the evolution of hip hop as a cultural trend. Hip hop began in the 1970s as a radical, oppositional, politically conscious musical movement to give voice to the disaffection felt by many African Americans living in poverty in America's central cities. However, circumstances have changed since hip hop's early days. Boyd (1997) argues that "affirmative action rappers" were influenced by the civil rights and black power movements of the 1960s and 1970s and were overtly political in their music. The current generation of rappers—Reaganomic rappers—were influenced by the harsh social and economic consequences of the conservative social policies of the 1980s. Reaganomic rappers respond to the growing victimization and marginalization of African Americans living in ghettos across America. As a consequence, the current generation of rappers strive for personal enrichment and fame rather than political commentary. As its popularity and marketability increase, rap music has lost its criticality in favor of being marketable and profitable. As Kelly (1999) observes: "The six major record firms have a quasi-colonial relationship with the black Rhythm Nation of America that produces hip hop and other forms of black music. Despite the names of a few big money-makers—Suge Knight, Sean Combs, and Russell Simmons . . . rap, like most black music, is under the corporate control of whites and purchased mostly by whites" (paragraph 1).

The issue of control is evident in the selection, development, representation, and production of rap stars and their music. In the process of bringing rap music to market, the culture industry turns critical potential into prepackaged forms that hold the promise of generating revenue.

As Adorno and Horkheimer (1991) observe, "The assembly-line character of the culture industry, the synthetic, planned method of turning out its products" (p. 81) assures owners of media a return on investment and in so doing removes any insightful critique of the existing power structure.

MASS MEDIA, MASS CULTURE, AND ADULT EDUCATION

The global mass media clearly have power to select, produce, and disseminate those meanings that serve the interest of the elite. But what is the import of this for adult educators? I identify four conceptual and policy areas of concern to adult educators: (1) the mass media as informal education, (2) the media as pedagogical tool, (3) the media as a threat to diversity, and (4) the media as a threat to democracy.

The Mass Media as Informal Education

A major development of the presence and influence of the media is that they are becoming a significant if not primary source of information and learning for adults. Cortes (1981) observed that learning outside schooling is becoming a kind of fifth estate, a "massive, ongoing, informal curriculum of families, peer groups, neighborhoods, churches, organizations, institutions and mass media, and other socializing forces that educates all of us throughout our lives" (p. 13). Conceptualizing the mass media as an educational sector points to the need to critique and understand how it operates. This is consistent with how adult educators have sought to understand schooling and its impact on adult learning.

Cortes (1994) conceptualized the mass media curriculum as promoting particular images. Through repetition, these images—essentially ideologically driven views of the world—set the norm for what matters in society. He asks key questions: How do corporate elites describe the opportunity structure? How does the system really work? Who wields power and authority? Herman and Chomsky (1988) extend these questions in asking whose interests are represented by the major media outlets' portrayal of news. The diet of predigested, predefined, and smartly packaged messages produced by the mass media in all areas of media control, news, entertainment, and advertising serves to educate the masses so as to reproduce and crystallize existing power relations in society. The educational impact of the media is not neutral.

The Media as Pedagogical Tool

A second area of concern for adult educators relates to the policy prescriptions of educational bodies to use the media as a source of information for educational purposes. Article 10 of the Hamburg Declaration on Adult Learning says:

> 10. The new concept of youth and adult education presents a challenge to existing practices because it calls for effective networking within the formal and non-formal systems, and for innovation and more creativity and flexibility. Such challenges should be met by new approaches to adult education within the concept of learning throughout life. Promoting learning, using mass media and local publicity, and offering impartial guidance are responsibilities for governments, social partners and providers. The ultimate goal should be the creation of a learning society committed to social justice and general well-being. [UNESCO Institute for Education, 1997]

In this statement (emphasis added), the media are seen in an atheoretical and instrumental light as impartial conveyors of information rather than shapers of meaning on behalf of those who control the media.

I would argue that a more critical stance be taken, given the earlier analysis. What is required is an in-depth analysis of the media. As was suggested, an important starting point is analysis of the patterns of ownership and control of the media through a political economy frame (Louw, 2001). The mass media indeed may serve as a source of information for learners, but educators must be critical in their use of the media and not simply view them as a passive tool for accessing information. Critical media literacy is a necessary step toward addressing the underlying issues of control, homogenization, and conformity produced by the media. Therefore the Hamburg Declaration statement to use the media in an impartial way is problematic because it masks the underlying issue of power and control that works against free, open, and critical consideration of issues relevant to learners.

The Media as a Threat to Diversity

The portrayal of historically marginalized groups through the media continues to be problematic. Stereotypical portrayals of African Americans, Native Americans, other ethnic or linguistic minorities, and women is cause for concern as the mass media extend their reach globally. As studies have shown, popular perceptions about racial, gender, and class differences are shaped in significant ways by the media (Guerrero, 1993; Mantsios, 1998; Wolf, 1991).

Representation of the poor, women, African Americans, Native Americans, Hispanics, Arabs, and other persons of non–European descent serves to reinforce stereotypes. The mass perception of members of these groups is that they are lazy, violent, or passive. We live in a society where we are separated by income, race, language, sexual orientation, and nationality. We cannot come to learn about other people without some kind of information, either through personal contact or through information we glean from various sources. As Holtzman (2004) points out, the media are the most common source of information we have about diversity, and they are laden with stereotypes and biases with respect to ethnic, racial, and cultural groups. Developing the critical skills to navigate through the flood of images and messages we receive every day is an imperative if, as a society, we are to adequately address the problems of racism, sexism, classism, and ethnocentrism that continue to plague us. There is a key role for adult education in this process.

The Media as a Threat to Democracy

In his analysis of the mass media, McChesney (2004) reviews the well-known Jeffersonian assertion about well-functioning democracies: they rely on an informed citizenry, "and having such a citizenry is the media's province" (p. 17). In modern complex societies, however, there is a constant struggle between those in power and those not. In an ideal circumstance, the media would ensure that information flows reflect the interests of all groups so that the public interest of democracy is served. As McChesney observes, "the crucial tension lies between the role of the media as profit-maximizing commercial organizations and the need for the media to provide the basis for informed self government" (p. 17).

Adult educators committed to the open and free flow of ideas—especially progressive and egalitarian forms of resistance to conformity, homogeneity, and submission to authority—will in the end be left with the task of organizing educational activities that attempt to overcome this tendency. The representation of multiple perspectives on any given issue of social consequence must be of concern when the media become the major source of information for citizens. To the extent that ownership, organization, and operation of mass media do not support the open and free flow of information and perspectives, democracy suffers. The threat comes in two forms: first, the owners and controllers of media are likely to be resistant to any effort that aims at significant diversity in perspective, or economic egalitarian and culturally pluralistic forms of social life.

Second, as learners come increasingly under the influence of media control of consciousness, they will view attempts to supply multiple perspectives on a range of public issues as impractical, unrealistic, or utopian. The possible result, as was the case with Cypher Reagan, will be to simply opt for the path of most pleasure and least resistance to conformity.

■ CLOSING COMMENTS

Adult educators should take a more critical stance toward the mass media and their power to shape the social arrangements and consciousness of individuals who would otherwise be asserting their rights and demands for equity, were it not for the power and influence of the global media through the culture industries. This, I believe, requires adult educators to become more media-conscious, to engage in a critical examination of media that includes ideology critique (Brookfield & Preskill, 1999).

The growing concentration of media ownership and control of the production of meaning has led some media scholars to assert that the media essentially function so as to serve up consumers to producers (Louw, 2001). This concentration represents a real threat because of long-standing assumptions in the field resting on the idea that learning is continuous throughout life. Further, although adult educators play a central role in planning, delivering, and evaluating educational programs, this role is being eroded by the effect of the mass media, especially on the younger generation. As historian Joseph Kett (1994) pointed out, adult education is becoming more central to modern life, whereas adult educators are becoming more marginal. In turning thought away from a critical examination of social issues to the processes and techniques of acquisition and consumption, the global mass media exercise considerable control of thought; we adult educators will be tacitly complicit in the process unless and until, as a field, we incorporate media analysis into our research and our practice. In short, scholars, activists, and practitioners should increasingly focus on the mass media and their potential for promoting or inhibiting learning aimed at progressive social change.

REFERENCES

Albarran, A. B. (1998). *Global media economics: Commercialization, concentration, and integration of world media markets.* Ames: Iowa State University Press.

Adorno, T. W., & Horkheimer, M. (1991). The culture industry: Enlightenment and mass deception. In T. W. Adorno & J. M. Bernstein (Eds.), *Selected essays on mass culture.* London: Routledge.

Boyd, T. (1997). *Am I black enough for you? Popular culture from the 'hood and beyond.* Bloomington: Indiana University Press.

Brookfield, S. D., & Preskill, S. (1999). *Discussion as a way of teaching: Tools and techniques for democratic classrooms.* San Francisco: Jossey-Bass.

Cashmore, E. (1997). *The black culture industry.* New York: Routledge.

Cortes, C. E. (1981). The societal curriculum: Implications for multiethnic education. In J. A. Banks (Ed.), *Education in the 80s: Multiethnic education.* Washington, DC: National Education Association.

Cortes, C. E. (1994). Knowledge construction and popular culture: The media as multicultural educator. In J. A. Banks & C. A. McGee Banks (Eds.), *Handbook of research on multicultural education.* New York: Macmillan.

Federal Reserve. Statistical release, G.19, consumer credit. [http://www.federalreserve.gov /releases/g19/20041207/]. Dec. 7, 2004.

Ferrero, J. For Colombia's angry youth, hip hop helps keep it real. *New York Times*. [http://www.nytimes.com/2004/04/16/international/americas/16bogo.html?hp]. Apr. 16, 2004.

Fordham, S. (1999). Ebonics as guerilla warfare. *Anthropology and Education Quarterly*, *30*(3), 272–293.

Gilroy, P. (1998). It's a family affair. In G. Dint (Ed.), *Black popular culture*. New York: NewPress.

Guerrero, E. (1993). *Framing Blackness: The African American image in film*. Philadelphia: Temple University Press.

Herman, E. S., & Chomsky, N. (1988). *Manufacturing consent: The political economy of the mass media*. New York: Pantheon.

Herman, E. S., & McChesney, R. W. (1997). *The global media*. London: Cassell Books.

Holtzman, L. (2004). Mining the invisible: Teaching and learning media and diversity. *American Behavioral Scientist*, *48*(1), 108–118.

Kellner, D. (1989). *Critical theory, Marxism, and modernity*. Baltimore: Johns Hopkins University Press.

Kelly, N. (1999). Political economy of black music. *Black Renaissance/Renaissance Noire*, *2*(2), 9–21. [http://www.hartford-hwp.com/archives/45a/358.html].

Kett, J. (1994). *The pursuit of knowledge under difficulties: From self-improvement to adult education in America, 1759–1990*. Stanford, CA: Stanford University Press.

Labaton, S. The media business: U.S. backs off relaxing rules for big media. *New York Times*. http://query.nytimes.com/gst/abstract.html?res=F10C11FF3F5F0C7B8ED DA80894DD404482&incamp=archive:search. Jan. 28, 2005.

Louw, P. E. (2001). *The media and cultural production*. Thousand Oaks, CA: Sage.

Mantsios, G. (1998). Media magic: Making class invisible. In M. Andersen & P. H. Hill-Collins (Eds.), *Race, gender, and class: An anthology*. (4th ed.). Belmont, CA: Wadsworth.

Marcuse, H. (1991). *One-dimensional man: Studies in the ideology of advanced industrial society*. Boston: Beacon Press.

McChesney, R. (2004). *The problem of the media: U.S. communication politics in the 21st century*. New York: Monthly Review Press.

McLuhan, M., & Fiore, Q. (1967). *The medium is the message*. New York: Random House.

Postman, N. (1992). *Technopoly: The surrender of culture to technology*. New York: Knopf.

Storey, J. (2003). *Inventing popular culture: From folklore to globalization*. Cambridge, MA: Blackwell.

UNESCO Institute for Education. Hamburg declaration on adult learning: The agenda for the future. [http://www.unesco.org/education/uie/confintea/pdf/ con5eng.pdf]. 1997.

Wolf, N. (1991). *The beauty myth*. New York: Morrow.

CHAPTER 25

Non-Western Perspectives on Learning and Knowing

Sharan B. Merriam and Young Sek Kim

> *The elder's opinion is truth. All power, all truth comes up from the roots of the*
> *family tree, the dead ancestors, to the trunk, the elders, and passes up to parents and*
> *children, the branches, leaves and flowers.*
>
> —HAMMINGA, 2005, P. 61

As the image conveys, what counts as knowledge and truth in an African context is deeply embedded in the community and is a product of age and experience. This view is in contrast to "the western strategy of convincing with *arguments*. From the African point of view, arguments are a sign of weakness, of lack of power and vitality. A good, forceful truth does not need arguments. . . . Truth is not argued for but *felt* . . . as a force coming from the speaking human" (Hamminga, 2005, p. 61; emphasis in original).

This is but one example of how another epistemological system or worldview differs from what we in Western society are accustomed to in our understanding of adult learning. The purpose of this chapter is to introduce readers to systems of learning and knowing different from our Western perspective. Many of these systems predate Western science by thousands of years, and even today they are held by the majority of the world's peoples. We first discuss the growing awareness of non-Western perspectives. This discussion is followed by three themes characterizing adult learning in non-Western systems. We close with a discussion of how familiarity with these perspectives can extend our understanding and practice as adult educators and learners.

▒ GLOBALIZATION AND THE NON-WESTERN WORLD

While we were writing this chapter, the U.S. economy teetered on the brink of a recession. Stock markets in Asia, Europe, and Latin America fell and rose in sync with U.S. swings and adjustments. There can be no doubt that what happens in one part of the world today affects the rest of the world. We are in an era of globalization, of being interconnected economically, culturally, technologically, and educationally with the rest of the world. Through the global economy, technology, travel, and immigration and migration, we come into contact with people from all over the world.

This awareness of our interconnectedness has also been sharpened by our concern with how humans are affecting the health of the planet itself. As O'Sullivan (1999) points out, our science and technology has afforded us "extraordinary control.... We command nuclear energy. We travel into space. We know the genetic coding process. We are also in the process of destroying the carrying capacity of the earth for our species as well as the larger biotic world" (p. 180). Indeed, "it would be difficult to find an educational system in the world that was not in the midst of a navigational solution in the turbulent waters of change that globalization has brought about" (Hilgendorf, 2003, p. 72).

Many writers advocate more of a global if not a cosmic consciousness, and we can learn what this is from non-Western systems of thought. Historically, however, "we have labeled cultures as retrograde for having a larger cosmology embedded in mythic structures" and in so doing have "established western scientific thinking as superior to the thinking of other existing cultures" (O'Sullivan, 1999, p. 181). So-called Western knowledge is a relatively recent phenomenon, first spread through colonization and then through globalization. Anchored in classical Greek thought, the dominance of Western knowledge has resulted in nonattention to, if not outright dismissal of, other systems, cosmologies, and understandings about learning and knowing. Only recently have we witnessed a growing interest in learning as an embodied, spiritual, or narrative phenomenon (see the chapters in this volume), or as something structured by a wholly different worldview (Johansen and McLean, 2006; Merriam, 2007).

The terms *Western* and *non-Western* are of course problematic, beginning with the fact that setting up dichotomies in the first place is a very Western activity. Further, many indigenous peoples live in Western countries. Imperfect as it is, our use of non-Western might be thought of as a shorthand reference to systems of thought different from what we in the West have come to assume about the knowledge base of adult learning theory.

Encompassed within our use of the term *non-Western* are what are known as "indigenous" knowledge systems. Dei, Hall, and Rosenberg (2000) identify these characteristics as common to many indigenous cultures: "Seeing the individual as part of nature; respecting and reviving the wisdom of elders; giving consideration to the living, the dead, and future generations; sharing responsibility, wealth, and resources within the community; and embracing spiritual values, traditions, and practices reflecting connections to a higher order, to the culture, and to the earth" (p. 6). Our discussion of non-Western perspectives of learning and knowing thus includes indigenous knowledge systems and major philosophical and religious systems of thought. Of course, how we categorize these systems is less important than recognizing that non-Western worldviews do have something to tell us about learning and knowing.

LEARNING AND KNOWING FROM NON-WESTERN WORLDVIEWS

A number of writers have compared Western and non-Western or indigenous knowledge systems. Burkhart (2004) points out that knowledge in a Western paradigm is defined by propositional statements, that is, "that something is so" (p. 19). Propositional knowledge is usually written, considered true, separate from the self, and permanent. Indigenous knowledge is that which we know in experience; it is "the kind of knowledge we carry with us." It is "embodied knowledge" (p. 20).

The notion that knowledge itself is fundamentally different in Western and non-Western systems leads to a difference in how knowledge is constructed, how people "learn" and the best way to instruct, that is, enable people to learn what they need to know. From reading widely, and indeed from experiencing different systems ourselves, we have selected three themes for attention: learning is communal, learning is lifelong and informal, and learning is holistic.

Learning Is Communal

In 2006, author Melissa Fay Greene published the true story of Haregewoin Teferra, an Ethiopian woman who dealt with the death of her husband and daughter by providing a refuge for children of AIDS-stricken families. Greene titled the book after an African proverb, *There Is No Me Without You.* Indeed, not only is learning a communal activity in many non-Western countries, so too is construction of one's identity. This same idea is echoed in Native American thought: "We are, therefore I am." Burkhart (2004) explains:

> In Western thought we might say that my experiences and thoughts count more than your experiences because I have them and you cannot. But if we are *WE,* then this constraint seems rather trivial. The hand may not have the same experiences as the foot, but this hardly matters if we understand them not as feet and hands but as this body. If it is through the body, or the people, that understanding arises, then no one part need shape this understanding [p. 26].

From this communal perspective, learning is the responsibility of all members of the community because it is through this learning that the community itself can develop.

This notion of community and interdependence plays out in a Buddhist worldview as a form of systems theory wherein in a work setting it is important "to look at the interrelationships between ourselves, our clients, and other members of the organization. Buddhism recognizes that nothing exists in isolation; everything and everyone is the product of the interactions between other things and people" (Johansen and Gopalakrishna, 2006, p. 343).

The Hindu worldview extends this notion of community even further. In writing about the Hindu perspective on learning in the workplace, Ashok and Thimmappa (2006) point out that "individuals, organizations, society, the universe, and the cosmos are all interrelated and integrated. The development of human resources is thus viewed in terms of facilitating the individual to realize oneself and to understand the intricate relationship between the individual and his or her role in the organization, the role of the organization in the society, society in the universe, and the universe within the cosmos" (p. 329).

The individual then, does not learn for his or her own development, but for what can be contributed to the whole. In some cultures, our Western notion of personal independence and empowerment is considered immature, self-centered, and detrimental to the group (Nah, 1999). So intertwined is the individual with the community that isolation or expulsion from some communities is considered to be "worse than dying" (Hamminga, 2005, p. 59).

Related to this communal and interdependent understanding of learning is the view that one's learning must benefit the community. Human resource development (HRD) in many non-Western countries serves to develop individual employees and the corporation but is as well considered instrumental in "nation building." Today in China, national policy is promoting a learning society to address social issues that have emerged from China's exploding market economy. The goal of this lifelong learning society is the very Confucian ideal of creating a harmonious society.

In addition to learning itself being embedded in the community and for the enhancement of the community rather than the individual, in some non-Western systems one has an obligation to share what has been learned. In Islam, for example, "if there is no medical doctor to serve a community, then it is obligatory upon the community to send one or more of its members for medical training, and failure to do so will result in each member sharing the community sin" (Kamis and Muhammad, 2007, p. 28). There is an obligation to share what is learned; in many non-Western communities it is the responsibility of members to both teach and learn. In commenting on several non-Western traditions presented in his book, Reagan (2005) observed that the notion of some adults being teachers with "specialized knowledge and expertise not held by others" (p. 249) was an "alien" concept.

Learning Is Lifelong and Informal

Whispered into the ear of a newborn Muslim infant is the Muslim call to prayer; they are also the last words whispered to a dying family member. So is characterized the Muslim's lifelong journey of learning. "Muslims believe that God's knowledge is infinitely vast...like a drop of water in the sea; one can never complete acquiring it" (Kamis and Muhammad, 2007, pp. 34–35). This belief translates into Muslims' emphasis on learning both sacred and secular knowledge throughout their lives.

It is important to note that even though some Western scholars do promote a seamless vision of lifelong learning, one that spans the whole of a person's life, it is more commonly thought of as something for adults to engage in. Boshier (2005) has observed that in general, in the West "lifelong learning is nested in an ideology of vocationalism. Learning is for acquiring skills enabling the learner to work harder, faster and smarter and to help their employer compete in the global economy.... It is nested in a notion of the autonomous free-floating individual learner as consumer and mostly abdicates responsibility for the public good" (p. 375).

This more formal, market-driven version of lifelong learning is quite different from what non-Western traditions refer to when speaking of learning as lifelong. For example, from a Buddhist worldview one is consciously mindful, attending to everything in daily life throughout life, and the learning that accrues from this mindfulness is its own reward. The motivation to learn "does not rest on getting anything in particular or on being competitive with others . . . . Motivation comes out of a noble, altruistic goal for the learning, rather than a less inclusive and more selfish one of an economic or competitive nature" (Johnson, 2002, p. 110). Indeed, this mindfulness is a journey that extends through "innumerous" lives (Shih, 2007, p. 109). Likewise, Hindus see themselves on a continuous journey of learning that leads to being liberated from the cycle of rebirth and death (Thaker, 2007). Yet another perspective, Confucianism, views learning as a never-ending process toward becoming fully human (Kee, 2007).

Lifelong learning and its connection to the communal, interdependent nature of learning is particularly visible in non-Western indigenous cultures. Avoseh (2001) speaks to the interaction between being an active citizen in the community and lifelong education in traditional African society. Education "was a lifelong process that could not be separated from the rest of life's activities. Its purpose was to empower the individual to be an active member of the community" (p. 482). Indeed, lifelong learning is so embedded in the community "that anyone who fails to learn, among the Yorubas for instance, is regarded as *oku eniyan* (the living dead)" (p. 483).

What is also clear about non-Western understandings of lifelong learning is that very little of it is lodged in formal institutional settings. Lifelong learning in non-Western settings is community-based and informal. Though certainly the majority of lifelong learning is informal even in the West, the difference is that most Westerners neither recognize nor value learning that is embedded in everyday life. Most Westerners think of learning as that which occurs in a formal teacher-directed classroom with a prescribed curriculum.

By contrast, lifelong learning in non-Western societies is structured by a community problem or issue. Resources in the form of people and materials are brought together to assess the problem and try out solutions. Such learning is "evaluated" by how effective the strategy is in addressing the problem. Fasokun, Katahoire, and Oduaran (2005) write about the informal nature of lifelong learning in Africa: informal learning "involves learning through experience under enabling conditions that facilitate the development of knowledge, skills, attitudes, aptitudes, values and interests. This is done to enhance performance, bring about change or solve practical problems" (p. 36).

The prevalence of informal learning is not to say that formal (often Western) education is not valued at all. Globalization especially has stimulated more demand for formal educational training throughout the world. However, although the West tends to conflate learning with education and formal schooling ("a tendency reflected in our concern with formal certification and degrees rather than with competence per se"), such a perspective is "far less common in non-Western traditions" (Reagan, 2005, p. 248).

Learning Is Holistic

"I think, therefore I am." Descartes's famous maxim captures the West's emphasis on learning as a cognitive process, one that takes place in the brain. Since the seventeenth century, the mind has been privileged as the site of learning and knowing. Even more recent understandings of knowing posit construction of knowledge as a process of mentally reflecting on experience. Only recently have we in adult education given serious attention to somatic knowing, that is, learning through the body, and the place of one's spirit in learning (see chapters in this volume).

If there's anything that non-Western systems of learning and knowing have in common, it's the notion that learning involves not only the mind but the body, the spirit, and the emotions. There is no separation of the mind from the rest of our being. In a discussion of the place of spirituality in Maori curriculum, for example, Fraser (2004) recounts how their holistic perspective is pictured by the Maori as their traditional meeting house. "The four walls of the house are a metaphor for the dimensions of each person. In this model, well-being (or *hauora*) comprises four components: the physical, the mental and emotional (taken as one), the social and the spiritual . . . . All four dimensions are necessary for strength and symmetry and . . . there are reciprocal influences between each one" (p. 89). Like the Maori, Native Americans see all life as interconnected, as in a circle where "everything . . . is connected to everything," and "learning must proceed in a cumulative and connected manner" (Allen, 2007, p. 51).

In non-Western traditions, learning and education are in the service of developing more than just the mind. Equally important is developing a moral person, a good person, a spiritual person, who by being part of the community uplifts the whole. In the Navajo tradition, "knowledge, learning, and life itself are *sacred, inseparable, and interwoven parts of a whole.* The quality of each determines the quality of the other" (Benally, 1997, p. 84; italics in original). In contrast, the West "separates secular and sacred knowledge and thus fragments knowledge. Consequently, some learning is forgotten soon after academic program requirements are met because it was never grounded or connected to life processes" (p. 84). Because indigenous peoples do not separate the sacred from the secular, it is not at all "personally or communally troubling" that human experiences, "especially 'religious' experiences, are not reducible to objects or logic" (Wildcat, 2001, p. 53).

Unlike the West, which privileges abstract and theoretical knowledge, non-Western traditions privilege experience in the everyday world. Learning that occurs in the experience is holistic; it has not just cognitive but physical, emotional, and sometimes spiritual dimensions, all of which are kept in balance. The Hindu tradition of Yoga, for example, employs the mind, body, and spirit in concert to work toward enlightenment. Buddhists seek a "middle way," or balance between body and mind in pursuing enlightenment. Native Americans use the medicine wheel to capture the idea of balancing the four components of a whole person (spiritual, emotional, physical, and mental): "When each aspect is developed equally, an individual is considered well-balanced and in harmony" (Hart, 1996, p. 66). The treatment of disease (dis-ease) assumes that the person is out of balance. Such notions of balance and harmony "extend to others, the family, the community, the natural and spirit worlds, to all that is living" (p. 67).

Given that learning is embedded in the context of everyday experience, active participation in everyday activities and the rites and rituals of a community are seen as conduits to learning. Learning occurs through observation of others and through practicing what is being learned. Adults are role models for younger people. In Buddhist, Hindu, Islamic, and Confucian traditions, the learner is expected to emulate teachers, sages, or more accomplished practitioners of the tradition.

Many other sources are readily recognized as mechanisms for learning in non-Western traditions. Stories, myths, and folklore define one group from another and one's place in the larger society. Rituals, symbols, music, art, theater, and even dreams and visions are also considered sources of knowledge. Ntseane (2007) notes that it is common practice in Botswana for traditional healers to rely on dreams in which spirits of the ancestors "instruct the healer on how to heal the patient and with what herbs" (p. 127).

The holistic nature of learning in non-Western traditions is of course interrelated with learning being a lifelong journey, a journey in community with others. At some level, most adult educators recognize that learning can be more than formal schooling, and knowledge can be more than abstract cognition. We turn now to how becoming acquainted with non-Western perspectives can enhance our practice.

NON-WESTERN PERSPECTIVES AND OUR PRACTICE OF ADULT LEARNING

Our exposure to non-Western perspectives of learning and knowing can influence our practice as adult educators in three ways: approaching learning holistically, valuing learning embedded in everyday life, and being responsive to learners from other cultures.

First, non-Western perspectives of learning and knowing model a holistic approach to learning, one that recognizes the interrelationship among an adult learner's body, cognition, emotion, and spirituality. Sina, a Muslim philosopher and physician in the eleventh century, for example, believed that body and emotions are closely connected; therefore a student's body can benefit when educators help students have positive emotions (Gunther, 2006). In the American Indian perspective, emotion is the foundation where we can develop a relationship between what we are learning and why we are learning it; love for people and one's land has been a primary reason for learning (Cajete, 2005). When Fraser (2004) reviewed adult learning from the perspective of the Maori, who value spirituality, she suggested that adult educators need to encourage adult learners to reflect on the meaning and purpose of life. Because the adult learner's body, cognition, emotion, and spirituality are closely interrelated, in Western society adult learners are likely to have more meaningful learning experiences if these interconnections are attended to.

Second, familiarity with non-Western perspectives of learning and knowing suggests that adult educators in Western society might place more value on learning embedded in everyday life. Because non-Westerners believe that knowledge is embedded in experiences in everyday life, they do not value what is learned in formal school settings more than what is learned in daily life. Indigenous knowledge is about what people learn in experience and deals with real problems and issues in community. Rather than emphasizing prefixed curriculum-driven learning, formal certification, and degrees, we in the West might make more visible the nonformal and informal learning that even here characterizes the majority of adult learning.

In American Indian society, for example, there is no general knowledge; each individual constructs his or her own knowledge "through patient observation and contemplation and not by question-formulation and hypothesis-testing" (Burkhart, 2004, p. 23). In addition, in Latin America, influenced by liberation theology, the grassroots community organization offers nonformal and informal learning opportunities for the poor where knowledge is transmitted in one-to-one small groups or through performance (Conceiçã and Oliveria, 2007). Western societies, which assume knowledge exists in the form of abstraction, often neglect how each individual's construction of specific knowledge in real life is valuable and how adults can teach and learn from each other to solve real-life problems outside the classroom. In practice, adult learners can be more encouraged to build their own knowledge, which can be put to use not by hypothesis testing or question formulation in the classroom but by observing and contemplating their unique experiences in real life.

Third, being familiar with non-Western perspectives of learning and knowing helps adult educators better understand how adult learners from non-Western societies act and think. With advances of technology and transportation, adult educators in Western societies are coming into contact with students who have other than Western worldviews. Many Asian learners, for example, adhere to a Confucian worldview that positions learning within the hierarchical structures of human relationships; such structures are designed to achieve a harmonious social order (Kee, 2007). Teachers thus have authority and power over students in this hierarchy. Confucianism assumes that students need to receive knowledge from teachers, without critique, and then memorize it. In Confucianism, criticizing a teacher's opinion or having opinions different from those of classical works was seen as breaking the harmonious social order; therefore, students from Confucian cultures need more guidance to think critically or engage in creative expression, both of which are valued in Western society (Yang, Zheng, and Li, 2006).

In collectivist cultures in Africa, an individual needs to take responsibility for others; individual interests are always less important than communal interests (Ntseane, 2006). For example, HIV/AIDS prevention strategies that emphasize a community problem (an ethical concern with the suffering of others) are more effective than strategies focusing on an individual health problem (the fear of death; Ntseane, 2006). Therefore, adult education practices that aim for self-actualization or personal growth would not resonate well with students from African or other collectivist cultures.

CONCLUSION

Our exposure to non-Western perspectives on learning and knowing broadens our understanding of adult learning and enhances our practice as educators in a global society. We hope that this chapter is just a starting point, encouraging you to look around and notice more diverse ways of learning and knowing. A more inclusive practice can enrich our lives and the lives of learners with whom we work.

REFERENCES

Allen, P. G. "American Indian Indigenous Pedagogy." In S. B. Merriam (ed.), *Non-Western Perspectives on Learning and Knowing* (pp. 41–56). Malabar, Fla.: Krieger, 2007.

Ashok, H. S., and Thimmappa, M. S. "A Hindu Worldview of Adult Learning in the Workplace." *Advances in Developing Human Resources*, 2006, *8*(3), 329–336.

Avoseh, M.B.M. "Learning to Be Active Citizens: Lessons of Traditional Africa for Lifelong Learning." *International Journal of Lifelong Education*, 2001, *20*(6), 479–486.

Benally, H. J. "The Pollen Path: The Navajo Way of Knowing." In R. P. Foehr and S. A. Schiller (eds.), *The Spiritual Side of Writing* (pp. 84–94). Portsmouth, N.H.: Boynton/Cook, 1997.

Boshier, R. "Lifelong Learning." In L. M. English (ed.), *International Encyclopedia of Adult Education* (pp. 373–378). New York: Palgrave Macmillan, 2005.

Burkhart, B. Y. "What Coyote and Thales Can Teach Us: An Outline of American Indian Epistemology." In A. Waters (ed.), *American Indian Thought* (pp. 15–26). Victoria, Aus.: Blackwell, 2004.

Cajete, G. "American Indian Epistemologies." In M.J.T. Fox, S. C. Lowe, and G. S. McClellan (eds.), *Serving Native American Students* (pp. 69–78). San Francisco: Jossey-Bass, 2005.

Conceiçã, S.C.O., and Oliveria, A.M.F. "Liberation Theology and Learning in Latin America." In S. B. Merriam (ed.), *Non-Western Perspectives on Learning and Knowing* (pp. 41–56). Malabar, Fla.: Krieger, 2007.

Dei, G. J., Hall, B. L., and Rosenberg, D. G. "Introduction." In G. J. Dei, B. L. Hall, and D. G. Rosenberg (eds.), *Indigenous Knowledges in Global Contexts* (pp. 3–17). Toronto: University of Toronto Press, 2000.

Fasokun, T., Katahoire, A., and Oduaran, A. *The Psychology of Adult Learning in Africa.* Hamburg, Germany: UNESCO Institute for Education and Pearson Education, South Africa, 2005.

Fraser, D. "Secular Schools, Spirituality and Maori Values." *Journal of Moral Education*, 2004, *33*(1), 87–95.

Greene, M. F. *There Is No Me Without You: One Woman's Odyssey to Rescue Africa's Children.* New York: Bloomsbury, 2006.

Gunther, S. "Be Masters in That You Teach and Continue to Learn: Medieval Muslim Thinkers on Educational Theory." *Comparative Education Review*, 2006, *50*(3), 367–388.

Hamminga, B. "Epistemology from the African Point of View." In B. Hamminga (ed.), *Knowledge Cultures: Comparative Western and African Epistemology* (pp. 57–84). Amsterdam and New York: Rodopi, 2005.

Hart, M. A. "Sharing Circles: Utilizing Traditional Practice Methods for Teaching, Helping, and Supporting." In S. O'Meara and D. A. West (eds.), *From Our Eyes: Learning from Indigenous Peoples* (pp. 59–72). Toronto, Ont.: Garamond Press, 1996.

Hilgendorf, E. "Islamic Education: History and Tendency." *Peabody Journal of Education,* 2003, *78*(2), 63–75.

Johansen, B-C. P., and Gopalakrishna, D. "A Buddhist View of Adult Learning in the Workplace." *Advances in Developing Human Resources,* 2006, *8*(3), 337–345.

Johansen, B.-C. P., and McLean, G. W. "Worldviews of Adult Learning in the Workplace: A Core Concept in Human Resource Development." *Advances in Developing Human Resources,* 2006, *8*(3), 321–328.

Johnson, I. "The Application of Buddhist Principles to Lifelong Learning." *International Journal of Lifelong Education,* 2002, *21*(2), 99–114.

Kamis, M., and Muhammad, M. "Islam's Lifelong Learning Mandate." In S. B. Merriam (ed.), *Non-Western Perspectives on Learning and Knowing* (pp. 21–40). Malabar, Fla.: Krieger, 2007.

Kee, Y. "Adult Learning from a Confucian Way of Thinking." In S. B. Merriam (ed.), *Non-Western Perspectives on Learning and Knowing* (pp. 153–172). Malabar, Fla.: Krieger, 2007.

Merriam, S. B. (ed.). *Non-Western Perspectives on Learning and Knowing.* Malabar, Fla.: Krieger, 2007.

Nah, Y. "Can a Self-Directed Learner Be Independent, Autonomous and Interdependent?: Implications for Practice." *Adult Learning,* 1999, *11*, 18–19, 25.

Ntseane, G. "Western and Indigenous African Knowledge Systems Affecting Gender and HIV/AIDS Prevention in Botswana." In S. B. Merriam, B. C. Courtenay, and R. M. Cervero (eds.), *Global Issues and Adult Education: Perspectives from Latin America, Southern Africa, and the United States* (pp. 219–230). San Francisco: Jossey-Bass, 2006.

Ntseane, G. "African Indigenous Knowledge: The Case of Botswana." In S. B. Merriam (ed.), *Non-Western Perspectives on Learning and Knowing* (pp. 113–136). Malabar, Fla.: Krieger, 2007.

O'Sullivan, E. *Transformative Learning.* Toronto: University of Toronto Press, 1999.

Reagan, T. *Non-Western Educational Traditions: Indigenous Approaches to Educational Thought and Practice* (3rd ed.). Hillsdale, N.J.: Erlbaum, 2005.

Shih, J. "Buddhist Learning: A Process to Be Enlightened." In S. B. Merriam (ed.), *Non-Western Perspectives on Learning and Knowing* (pp. 99–112). Malabar, Fla.: Krieger, 2007.

Thaker, S. N. "Hinduism and Learning." In S. B. Merriam (ed.), *Non-Western Perspectives on Learning and Knowing* (pp. 57–74). Malabar, Fla.: Krieger, 2007.

Wildcat, D. R. "The Schizophrenic Nature of Metaphysics." In V. Deloria, Jr., and D. Wildcat, *Power and Place: Indian Education in America* (pp. 47–55). Golden, Colo.: American Indian Graduate Center and Fulcrum Resources, 2001.

Yang, B., Zheng, W., and Li, M. "Confucian View of Learning and Implications for Developing Human Resources." *Advances in Developing Human Resources,* 2006, *8*(3), 346–354.

NEW DISCOURSES SHAPING CONTEMPORARY ADULT EDUCATION

Historically, adult education as a field of study has emerged as one where theories have been developed in specific, contextualized, and value-laden situations. There is no single overarching theory of adult education, and there are numerous sets of assumptions or principles masquerading as theory. New discourses in adult education, such as those reflected in the selections comprising Part Five, appear to make this point: A theory of adult education in some encompassing and universal sense is probably undesirable since diversity in the practical realm would seem best supported by diversity in theorizing. However, the absence of a universal theory does not negate the need for formal theories or the theorizing they can inspire. A turn to theory provides us with new languages and new ideas that help us to investigate lived, learned, and perhaps all too comfortable ways of knowing and acting that may be exclusionary and limiting. Brookfield (1992) speaks to the need for reflective practitioners to examine their informal theorizing through the lens of formal theories (universal analysis) and to engage in comparative analysis of the different informal theories they generate working in similar contexts (particular analysis). It is in this spirit that we invite readers to sample the diversity of new modes of discourse in our field whereby adult educators bring formal theories to bear on research, advocacy, activism, and practices in classrooms and other contexts. We hope this turn to theory and theorizing will help reflective practitioners to critique contemporary forms of adult learning and education.

In Chapter 26, Chapman's passionate and provocative argument reflects this spirit. Using the medium of a critical personal narrative, she speaks in particular to graduate students finding their way into formal theory and theorizing. Contrasting the dearth of theory and theorizing in academic adult education with a burgeoning theoretical landscape in academe in general, Chapman grapples with a twofold question: Does theory travel and what does this mean for adult education? In answering this question, she considers what theory and theorizing offer to adult education as praxis and to moving the field of study and practice forward.

Reflecting the notion that theory does indeed travel, Sandlin, in Chapter 27, brings cultural studies to bear on theorizing in adult education. Noting an interest in consumerism in adult education since the mid-1990s, she focuses specifically on the notion of *culture jamming,* which is a cultural-resistance strategy used by anticonsumption social movements that oppose consumerism. She discusses how these movements practice critical adult education through informal learning. For example, she points out that the Adbusters Media Foundation uses its magazine, *Adbusters,* as a forum for social dissent to consumerism. As she elucidates the concept of culture jamming, Sandlin situates it as a political form of popular pedagogy with critical intentions as she explores how community is created, how bodies and emotions are engaged, and how politics are enacted. She concludes with a discussion of what this pedagogy means for adult learners and critical adult education.

In Chapter 28, Kilgore explores what it means to engage in the teaching-learning interaction in adult education from a postmodern perspective that considers the positionalities of educators and learners, knowledge construction, and the influence of power in an instructional setting. For reflective practitioners concerned with roles and positionalities, she rearticulates the roles of the educator and the learner as she shapes postmodern pedagogy as a situated and collaborative way of knowing and learning. Using an autoethnographical account that describes her own experience of self, students, and classroom culture, she informs readers that there are key consequences to using postmodern pedagogy: the diffusion of power and the rejection of the traditional social positions of the educator and learner in the educator-learner relationship. She concludes with a reflection of what this means for adult educational practice and the role of educators in it.

As theory continues to travel in this section, it is explored as a resistance to conventions and norms that constitute barriers to an inclusive social world. In Chapter 29, Hill exemplifies this theme. Working in the complex intersection of theory, activism, and practice around sexual orientation and gender identity, Hill uses a queer critical postmodern lens and the tensions embodied and embedded in it to address a pivotal question: What are the concrete implications of issues of sexual difference and gender identity for adult education theory and practice? Viewing all education as political, Hill explores the notion of activism as an adult educational practice in which theorizing is linked to democratic participation. Reminding readers of the still harsh lived realities of so many sexual and gender minorities, Hill speaks to the possibility of adult education as a liberatory practice that emphasizes mediation, resistance, and proactive political engagement. He demonstrates his understanding of activism as an adult educational practice in a discussion of macropractices that involve coalition building and organizational and community interventions, and micropractices that involve resistances in everyday life. Hill concludes by considering the price of engaging in a politics of queer resistance as he calls on educators and activists to mobilize and problem solve.

In Chapter 30, Grace and Wells, using arts-informed education as a form of social learning as resistance, speak to the importance of such informal, community-based education in on-the-ground work to make life better for sexual-minority youth and young adults. Using a critical social-learning model informed by Freirean pedagogy of *just ire,* they speak to the work they do to help participants in their projects to become activists and leaders who start to change their own lives as part of a larger process of improving conditions for sexual-minority citizens. For readers interested in the practice of adult education as social education, Grace and Wells discuss how a by-learner-for-learner approach and coalition engendered education frame two arts-informed educational projects that they directed. They describe how a pedagogy of just ire can be used by learners to self-educate, educate others, problem solve, and work for social and cultural change. In a perspective reflecting Hill's understanding of activism as an adult educational practice, Grace and Wells conclude that advocacy and empowerment are the first steps in critical social pedagogy aimed at advancing sexual-minority inclusion.

We believe that the articles comprising this section demonstrate that theory and theorizing cannot be segregated from practice. We agree with Giroux's (1997) assertion that "the act of theorizing cannot be abstracted from the conditions we inherit or the problems that emerge in the face of specific historical conditions"

(p. 254). Thus it is important to learn about formal theories and to engage in theorizing as a personal and pedagogical act. We encourage readers to engage in this process as they work through readings in this section so they may think more deeply about their own educational experiences and practices and the degrees to which they have included all learners.

FOR REFLECTION AND DISCUSSION

1. While some readers may characterize theory as abstract and alienating, theory can be useful as a language of engagement that allows us to take part in understanding the contexts in which we live, learn, and work and how we might mediate them. Theory's language of critique helps us to problematize and raise questions. Its language of possibility helps us to think about potential solutions in a specified context. How do contexts inform and shape our educational projects? How do theory and theorizing help us to make sense of contexts and improve our educational practices? Select an area of practice in adult education and consider how theory can inform this practice.

2. How does theory help us to shape ourselves as inclusive educators and practitioners who are able to mediate adult learning and education as a political and ethical practice? How does theory help us to increase space and place for diverse identities and communities in an enhanced adult learning culture?

3. How do these readings help shape your understanding of the parameters of adult learning and education today? How do the components of the field of study and practice represented in this section of the book add perspective and value to the field?

4. How do we overcome a history of political neglect of particular groups in adult education? Can we move beyond field fragmentation and make a case for holistic adult learning and education that advances education for citizenship and empowerment?

REFERENCES

Brookfield, S. (1992). Developing criteria for formal theory building in adult education. *Adult Education Quarterly 42*(2), 79–93.

Giroux, H. A. (1997). *Pedagogy and the politics of hope: Theory, culture, and schooling.* Boulder, CO: Westview Press.

CHAPTER 26

Attending to the Theoretical Landscape in Adult Education

Valerie-Lee Chapman

M any of you know that I tend to use what I call "critical personal narrative" to frame and contextualize my work; I won't disappoint you. I am going to begin with a story. Back in about 1998, when I was a full-time student engaged in graduate work for my Ph.D. at the University of British Columbia, I felt I'd taken all the courses on adult education I really wanted, and I decided to travel a bit—become a transdisciplinarian, border crosser, all those ghastly trendy words—and so I registered for courses over in human geography. I had to go there because nobody in my department was teaching anything like that, and neither was anyone else in the faculty of education, and I knew there were things and ideas and theories I needed to help me understand and explain the work and scholarship I wanted to do in my area of university adult education. I turned up for my first three classes, all of which were taught by eminent scholars in their discipline, full of excitement.

And that was when I found out how the rest of the academy views education—poorly—and that actually my subfield, adult education, wasn't even something they had heard of, nor did they want to hear about it. I had to sort of interview with each of the professors; in preliminary meetings; they were all concerned that I wouldn't have the theoretical or intellectual foundations to take their course and succeed in it. Not that they cared that much—remember, no andragogical perspectives out there on campus—but they didn't want the class held up by some stumbling student. As one of them told me kindly, "We've had students from education before, and they're sadly ... lacking. We expect ours to have read Benjamin, Said, Foucault, Derrida, at the very least, and be able to discuss their work." Now, I did notice that there wasn't a woman in that list, but I figured I knew just enough about the others to bluff my way through. For the first 4 weeks, I didn't say a word. Then, I did because I realized I was just as bright as the other students and a lot more generous too in terms of classroom etiquette. It was difficult to explain my perspective in those classes, not simply because the content was so different or because it was an applied rather than a pure field but rather because I always had to borrow the theoretical framing from another discipline—sociology, geography, history, or anthropology—and that was when I realized how little theory education produces and how little of that emanates from adult education: practically none at all! My geography professors finally acknowledged that an educator could do theory—on their terms—but it was never a really comfortable experience; the students resented me because when it was my turn to introduce the week's reading and pose the discussion questions, I made them do some group work so there was at least more than one voice heard in the room. They didn't like that. Collaborative learning doesn't let you show off to the professor. See ... we can tell them some things!

One of the questions posed in that course was "Does theory travel?" That's what I want to focus on in these brief remarks. Edward Said (1984) believed not: He said that "theory has to be grasped in the place and time out of which it emerges" (pp. 241–242). He emphasized that those situations are always changing and that no theory can totally explain the place from which it travels, nor can it always explain in the place to which it is transported. Before considering the dilemma that this has created for adult education as a field of study, let me just say what I think theory is: nothing too hard, nor scary, nothing so difficult it becomes counterproductive to try to even pick it up and use it, and nothing, for sure, that any scholar, faculty or student should be diffident about trying out. Social theory (which is what we are concerned with here, education being a social kind of enterprise) is a collection of overlapping, contending, and colliding discourses, or ways of speaking, thinking, and acting, that tries to reflect explicitly on how social life is constituted and to make social practices intelligible. I'd also situate myself and my theory as critical—that is, I am concerned with the multiple discourses of critical theory, which seek to make social life and practices not just intelligible but also better. So let's go back to the question of how and where theory travels and what that has to do with adult education.

In their recent article in *Adult Education Quarterly*, Milton, Watkins, Studdard, and Burch (2003) discuss the factors affecting change in adult education graduate programs in the United States. (I'd like to point out that there is a rest of the world, and in some parts of it, there are actually graduate adult education programs too, but that's another story for another day.) It's a good read and I'll probably share it with my classes: good background on the growth last century of graduate programs and the difficulties in institutionalizing and then trying to establish a scholarly basis for the study and practice of adult education. There's a good deal on the challenges that adult education programs face, and many of us know those by heart, so I won't rehearse them here. The one thing they don't talk about is the challenge adult education has to face in terms of being taken seriously theoretically, either by its faculty and students or by the rest of the academy. In fact, that article is a really fine example of good adult education scholarship. It explains its field, rigorously and well, and then fails to apply it theoretically ... or maybe I am just greedy for explanations beyond the self-evident.

This is what we produce, and it's good, too. But it's the rest of the academy that is deciding whether we need to be considered a part of it or whether, like those geographers at the University of British Columbia, it's probably best if we don't even try to survive because ... what theory do we have or use anyway? For the academy judges by the theory and scholarship emerging from a particular field and discipline—can't be helped, that's the nature of academic discourse and its self-construction. We stand or fall by the weight others attribute to our scholarship. If you don't believe me, do a bit of reading around promotion and tenure guidelines.

Now, from the beginnings of adult education, with all those black and black and blue books [respectively, Jensen, Liveright, & Hallenbeck, 1964, referred to widely as "the black book" because of the color of its cover, and the much-criticized Peters, Jarvis, & Associates, 1991, referred to by some as "the black and blue book" because of its bruised reputation], and with all its andragogical perspectives, learning orientations, social constructions, and so on and so on, one thing is clear: If theory didn't travel, there wouldn't have been an adult education field of study. The founders of the discipline drew from psychology, sociology, history, a bit of philosophy (but not much ... too hard), and still do, and when absolutely pushed, a pinch of critical theory, really foreign in that it comes all the way from Frankfurt, is thrown in to make it culturally relevant or critical.

What has adult education sent back in terms of theory? Not much. Our heroines and heroes tend to come from somewhere else, too—like Paolo Freire and bell hooks, for example. OK. We've maybe adapted and reshaped psychological and social concepts to turn out some material on transformational learning or the ways people really plan programs. We now and then get carried away and even mention power, but sometimes ... we just play it safe and weigh in to current educational debates, such as what is cultural relevance or critically reflective practice ... but we've always been so half-hearted about theory that we're just really tokenist.

As a student and as a faculty member, when I say this sort of thing, I'm always being reminded that our audience—our consumer—is a "practitioner" ... there's the unspoken ... that practitioners don't need theory, just more practice. Well, practice makes practice, not perfection and definitely not intelligibility. Remember my definition of *social theory*—it should make the social world and its practices intelligible, that is, understandable and better. We do no favors to ourselves, or our students, to steer them away from theory. I saw a hunger for theory in junior scholars in adult education, in the bright and the not-so-bright, in the classes I took, and I see it now, in the ones I teach. Many of us want to use some theory to understand how things work, and we want explanations. We also want to be good at what we do, whether that's teaching, planning, leading, learning, and scholarship, and so we should attend to matters of improving practice and using theory.

I was thrilled when the new handbook (Wilson & Hayes) came out in 2000, to see that for once, adult education seemed to be a venturing field, not just waiting for theory to come to it, but going out to get it, and bring it back and use it, to make our work intelligible and better. I hear, though, that some said this was all too hard, students couldn't understand it. And I think their instructors couldn't understand it. Or wouldn't. Too foreign, too much distance? We should just churn out more of the same—more studies about motivation, participation, learning styles, orientations, and so on. Maybe more about who isn't served by adult education but not too much on that ... not too critical, just enough to show we can hit the diversity index.

Well, I think we need more of the kind of material in that handbook. If we want to exist, we need to not just take theory but produce it. Wouldn't it be better to encourage our students and our colleagues to be good at theory and practice, to try new things, to think differently, and, against the ways we've always thought, to see where it takes us. Now, I do want to emphasize (remember all the men in that geographers list?) that traveling is a very different activity, depending on your color, gender, sexuality, and ability. As bell hooks (1992) reminds us so eloquently, travel is an imperial metaphor: It's not easy for White, middle-class folks to understand and find room in that metaphor for the way people of color travel, with the memories of the "*Middle Passage,* the *Trail of Tears,* the landing of Chinese immigrants at Ellis Island, the forced relocation of Japanese Americans, or the plight of the homeless" (pp. 343–344). People of color, women, gay people, disabled people: we travel differently and our theories travel differently. We need to continually take that into account. We don't need more androcentric, Eurocentric, heterocentric, or chronocentric theories.

But we should still not stay home, surrounded by our old, well-worn theories. We need to get out more, invite more novel theories home for dinner, bring them into our classes and, yes, challenge ourselves and our students out of the comfort of the known and easily understood. If we want there to be an adult education field that is seen and understood and accepted in the academy, one that works to make things intelligible and better, we need some theory to do it. Otherwise, what will we turn out? As we get merged with educational administrators, human resource developers, technologists, and the legions of the K–12 empires, we can choose to turn out robots or Dilberts ... or students who travel into new work and new classrooms and are welcomed there because they can think, they can theorize, they can critique, because they can make themselves understood and they can make it different.

This isn't as perfect a speech as I had planned, I could have practiced it more, but you know, my hope comes from the fact that I was asked to make it. One of my students said of me, "Dr. Chapman is tough, she makes us think, but that's good. And we like the way she says 'a–dult.'" What else can I say? Oh, thank you to my friends ... travel well.

REFERENCES

hooks, b. (1992). Representing whiteness in the black imagination. In L. Grossberg, C. Nelson, & P. Treichler (Eds.), *Cultural studies* (pp. 338–346). New York: Routledge.

Jensen, G., Liveright, A. A., & Hallenbeck, W. (1964). *Adult education: Outlines of an emerging field of university study.* New York: Adult Education Association of the U.S.A.

Milton, J., Watkins, K. E., Studdard, S. S., & Burch, M. (2003). The ever widening gyre: Factors affecting change in adult education graduate programs in the United States. *Adult Education Quarterly, 54,* 23–41.

Peters, J. M., Jarvis, P., & Associates. (1991). *Adult education: Evolution and achievements in a developing field of study.* San Francisco: Jossey-Bass.

Said, E. (1984). *The world, the text and the critic.* London: Faber and Faber.

Wilson, A. L., & Hayes, E, R. (Eds.). (2000). *Handbook of adult and continuing education.* San Francisco: Jossey-Bass.

Editors' Note with Tom Sork, University of British Columbia: The opening general session of the 2003 Detroit meeting of the Commission of Professors of Adult Education (CPAE) consisted of a panel discussion, organized by Juanita Johnson-Bailey of the University of Georgia, with the title "Dilemmas Within Adult Education Graduate Programs: The Changing Theoretical, Philosophical, Social, and Economic Landscapes." Valerie-Lee Chapman, then assistant professor of adult education at North Carolina State University, had agreed to present remarks on the changing theoretical landscape. Less than 2 weeks before the meeting, Valerie was diagnosed with lung cancer. Although her treatment prevented her from attending the conference, she asked that her remarks be read to the group by Tom Sork, who had worked with Valerie during her graduate studies at the University of British Columbia. The editors of *Adult Education Quarterly* were encouraged by CPAE participants to publish the talk. They asked Valerie to submit her remarks for the forum section of the journal. She had intended to do so, but her treatment and the rapid progress of cancer prevented her from completing the task. Valerie died on September 4, 2004. What appears here is a lightly edited version of her wry, insightful, and irreverent observations about her own experiences as a graduate student and her hopes for how we might take up the task of theorizing in adult education.

CHAPTER 27

Popular Culture, Cultural Resistance, and Anticonsumption Activism

An Exploration of Culture Jamming as Critical Adult Education

Jennifer A. Sandlin

S ince the mid-1990s, adult educators have become increasingly interested in consumption and consumerism and how they relate to adult learning and adult education. For instance, Robin Usher, Ian Bryant, and Rennie Johnston (1997) have urged adult educators to start taking consumption seriously; they point out that we are all "affected by consumer culture and consumerist discourse and images" (p. 15). Kaela Jubas (2006) has investigated what it means to be a "critical consumer-citizen" (p. 200) through an exploration of how the process of shopping socializes adults to be consumers while at the same time offering possibilities to resist consumerism and to learn about democratic citizenship. And I (Sandlin, 2004, 2005a) have explored how consumer education can been seen as a political site where learners can craft particular points of view on and relationships with consumer culture. Although educators of adults are starting to explore issues of consumption, much work remains to be done.

Adult educators also have become increasingly interested in popular culture as a site of informal learning. Paul Armstrong (2000, 2005), Stephen Brookfield (1986), Elizabeth Tisdell and Patricia Thompson (2006), Robin Wright (2006),

Peter Jarvis (2005), and myself (Sandlin, 2005b) view the mass media in general, and specific forms of mass media such as soap operas, television, and popular magazines, as forms of public education. These realms of informal adult education are often neglected by adult educators although they are widespread and gaining in popularity. Armstrong (2000) argues that adult educators must learn to "recognize and value a wide range of informal learning" (p. 16), including the learning centered on the products of popular culture.

In this chapter I examine adult education and learning as it intersects with both consumerism and popular culture. I focus on a growing social movement of individuals who are concerned about consumerism and who are confronting consumption through cultural resistance in and through popular culture. I concentrate specifically on how these anticonsumption social movements are practicing critical adult education in largely informal realms of learning, through a cultural-resistance strategy called *culture jamming*. I use as examples two such groups, *Adbusters* magazine and Reverend Billy and the Church of Stop Shopping, exploring them as critical sites of adult education and learning. I also discuss culture jamming as a form of popular pedagogy, as described by Henry Giroux (2004) and Elizabeth Ellsworth (2005).

POPULAR CULTURE, CULTURAL RESISTANCE, AND PUBLIC PEDAGOGY

John Storey (2006) argues that there are many definitions of *popular culture*, including culture that is well liked by many people, "inferior culture" (p. 5) (or what is left over after we cull out "high culture"), commercial culture produced for mass consumption, folk culture emanating from "authentic" working-class people, and a political site of struggle between dominant and subordinate social groups. This last definition most accurately captures the way I view popular culture. I draw heavily from the view of popular culture that is grounded in a Gramscian cultural-studies framework. In this view, popular culture does not consist simply of cultural commodities such as film, television shows, and magazines (Storey, 1999, 2006). Rather, these commodities are the raw materials, provided by the culture industries, that people use to create popular culture. Storey (2006) states, "We need to see ourselves—all people, not just vanguard intellectuals—as active participants in culture: selecting, rejecting, making meanings, attributing value, resisting and, yes, being duped and manipulated" (p. 171). This perspective on popular culture thus conceptualizes it as an active, rather than a passive, process.

Also contained within a Gramscian view is the idea that what is important about popular culture is not its aesthetics but its politics—that is, its intersection with power (Bennett, 1998). Thus, popular culture is a site of conflict, where individuals resist, negotiate, and accommodate power relations. Stephen Duncombe (2002) explains this idea:

> Both the culture we enjoy and the culture in which we live provide us with ideas of how things are and how they should be, frameworks through which to interpret reality and possibility. They help us account for the past, make sense of the present and dream of the future. Culture can be, and is, used as a means of social control. More effective than any army is a shared conception that the way things are is the way things should be. The powers-that-be don't remain in power by convincing us that they are the answer, but rather that there is no other solution. But culture can be, and is, used as a means of resistance, a place to formulate other solutions. In order to strive for change, you have first to imagine it, and culture is the repository of imagination (p. 35).

In other words, popular culture is always at once a site of hegemonic power and of political resistance.

Much has been written about how popular culture works to inculcate dominant values in individuals (Giroux, 1999). Therefore, instead of focusing on how popular culture reproduces inequalities, I describe here how it works as a means of resistance. *Resistance* consists of acts of opposition to dominant culture that contain within them a critique of domination and a struggle for self and social emancipation (Giroux, 2001). Resistance celebrates the power of human agency and stresses the fact that individuals are not simply passive victims of social structures. Resistance theories explore how people struggle with societal structures and create their own meanings through these negotiations (Solorzano and Delgado Bernal, 2001). In short, they focus on the power of human agency to question, reject, modify, or incorporate dominant ideologies and cultures; to critique oppression; and to work toward social justice (Giroux, 2001).

Cultural resistance is defined by Duncombe (2002) as "culture that is used, consciously or unconsciously, effectively or not, to resist and/or change the dominant political, economic and/or social structure" (p. 5). Raymond Williams (1973) states that through cultural resistance people can create and maintain ideas that oppose those of the dominant society. Examples of cultural resistance—or using popular culture to resist—include the activities of subcultures such as the mods, rude boys, teddy boys, and skinheads of 1960s Britain, as described by

Dick Hebdige (1979); more recent subcultures including punk "straightedgers" and "ravers," or youth who are part of rave scenes; various forms of alternative and counter-hegemonic music from hip hop to Riot Grrrl bands; and 'zines and other DIY (do-it-yourself) magazines. Duncombe (2002) explains that individuals and groups practicing cultural resistance actively engage in creating popular culture, crossing the line "from consumer to creator" (p. 4). He also argues that cultural resistance provides a free space for creating new ideas to resist the dominant culture, helps build community, and can provide entrée into political resistance and can itself become political resistance. In exploring cultural resistance, Duncombe (2002) also urges us to pay attention to its educational process—that is, to focus on how politics is conveyed through popular culture—through examining the roles played by cultural content, form, and interpretation and the activity of cultural creation.

These views of popular culture and resistance are echoed by educational scholars who focus on popular culture as a site of learning. *Public pedagogy* refers to the education provided by popular culture; popular culture teaches audiences and participants through the ways it represents people and issues and the kinds of discourses it creates and disseminates. Culture is where "identities are continually being transformed and power enacted" (Giroux, 2000, p. 354). Ellsworth's (2005) current perspectives on public pedagogy are especially helpful in exploring how culture jamming works in adult education. Ellsworth urges educators to pay attention to informal sites of learning such as public art installations and museums—what she calls "anomalous places of learning"—and to focus on their "pedagogical hinges"—the aspects that make them powerful sites of learning and teaching (p. 5). I borrow from Ellsworth a way of thinking of education within popular culture as an ongoing, active, creative process. To Ellsworth, public pedagogy works best when it creates transitional spaces—that is, when it helps us connect our inner realities to people, objects, and places outside ourselves.

CULTURE JAMMING AS CRITICAL PUBLIC PEDAGOGY

I am currently in the process of collecting and analyzing data for a study of culture jamming as a site of adult learning. In this chapter I share some initial insights that begin to reveal how culture jamming works. I focus specifically on two culture-jamming groups, Adbusters Media Foundation and Reverend Billy and the Church of Stop Shopping. *Adbusters* is a magazine produced by the

Adbusters Media Foundation, based in Vancouver. The magazine has two main themes—the ways in which marketing and mass media colonize space and the ways in which global capitalism and rampant consumption are destroying natural environments (Rumbo, 2002). A reader-supported, not-for-profit magazine with an international circulation of eighty-five thousand, *Adbusters* contains reader-supplied letters and articles, commentaries by activists from around the world, and photographs and stories highlighting readers' social dissent. *Adbusters* also hosts a Web site (www.adbusters.org) where activists can read about anticonsumption campaigns; download activist resources and flyers for distribution; and post and read information about their own and others' activism.

Bill Talen, whose stage character is Reverend Billy, is a political-theater artist who adopts the persona of a Southern evangelical preacher. Reverend Billy, leader of the Church of Stop Shopping, stages "retail interventions" and political performances in public spaces and retail stores along with the Stop Shopping Gospel Choir. He also writes "intervention manuals" such as the "Starbucks Invasion Kit" and other scripts that activists can use in their own public-theater jams. He stages "comic theatrical service[s]" (Lane, 2002, p. 60), structured as comic church services, with "readings from the saints (or the devils), public confessions, collective exorcisms, the honoring of new saints, donations to the cause, a lively choir, and a rousing sermon" (Lane, 2002, p. 61). During these services he performs a call-and-response style of preaching as the audience responds with "Hallelujah!" and "Amen!"

Culture jamming has been called an "insurgent political movement" (Harold, 2004, p. 190) that works against "the advertising-saturated, corporate-ruled consumer culture" (Bordwell, 2002, p. 237). The phrase *culture jamming* was coined in 1984 by the San Francisco–based electronica band Negitivland in reference to the illegal interruption of ham-radio signals (Carducci, 2006), but many culture jammers see themselves as descendents of the Situationists, a 1950s European anarchist group led by Guy Debord (Harold, 2004). Members of this group were concerned with fighting the "spectacle" of everyday life—"modern society's 'spectacular' level of commodity consumption and hype" (Lasn, 1999, p. 100). The spectacle stifles spontaneity, free will, and active living and replaces them with prepackaged experiences (Lasn, 1999). Culture jammers, like the Situationists before them, reject the passive consumption of consumer culture and seek to be active creators who live authentically.

Culture jamming takes many forms; it includes such cultural activities as producing and disseminating "subvertisements," hosting and participating in virtual protests using the internet, enacting "placejamming" projects (in which public spaces are reclaimed), and participating in DIY (do it yourself) political theater and "shopping interventions." Culture jamming "seeks to undermine the marketing rhetoric of multinational corporations, specifically through [such] practices as media hoaxing, corporate sabotage, billboard 'liberation,' and trademark infringement" (Harold, 2004, p. 190). I see these various modes of culture jamming as constituting "anomalous pedagogies." I believe the educational power of culture jamming lies in its ability to open "transitional spaces" through creativity and cultural production, create community, engage with the learner and the "teacher" corporeally, and provide entrée into and enact politics. I further locate culture jamming's pedagogical hinge in the ways it creates possibilities for change in audience members.

Opening Transitional Spaces Through Cultural Production

As a form of cultural resistance, culture jamming is a free space where artists and activists can "experiment with new ways of seeing and being" and where they can "develop tools and resources for resistance" (Duncombe, 2002, p. 5). *Adbusters*, for instance, encourages submissions from readers; most of the content of the magazine is created and contributed by readers. Reverend Billy invites audience participation during his "revivals"; through his Web site (www.revbilly.com) audience members can discuss issues such as consumerism and strategies for creating awareness among ordinary consumers. Reverend Billy's Web site hosts scripts of performance pieces that audience members can take, change, and enact in their local contexts. Reverend Billy also encourages his audiences to create and enact their own performance art. Culture jammers are redefining what it means to "read" a magazine and to enter into a "shopping experience."

Culture jammers thus alter the ways in which public space and popular-culture commodities and experiences are created and used. Culture jammers create *transitional spaces,* which are spaces of play, creativity, and cultural production; transitional spaces help us bridge the boundaries between the self and the other. When we are in those spaces, "we are entertaining strangeness and playing in difference. We are crossing that important internal boundary that is the line between the person we have been but no longer are and the person we will become" (Ellsworth, 2005, p. 62). Culture jammers turn typically passive activities into active ones. In doing so they are creating culture rather than simply absorbing it. They redefine themselves and their relationships with consumption; they redefine possibilities for the future. As one reader/contributor to *Adbusters* wrote, "Another world is possible" ("Another World," 2003, p. 50).

Creating Community

As culture is created by culture jammers, it is also shared among them. Duncombe (2002) states that popular culture thus "becomes a focal point around which to build a community" (p. 6). Ellsworth (2005) argues that an important part of the education for democracy that takes place in public spaces is that it puts us in relation to each other "in ways we have never been before" (p. 95). I believe that both the act of creating culture together and the sharing of that culture help culture jammers and their audiences create community. Participating in culture jamming—for instance, in "liberating" billboards by changing the content of their messages—creates a powerful community for those doing the jamming. Culture jammers also offer audience members ways of relating to each other that they have never experienced before.

Engaging the Body and the Emotions

According to Ellsworth (2005), effective pedagogy must engage the entire learner. Part of the power of culture jamming as adult education lies in its ability to engage both the body and the emotions in a process of "becoming." First, the act of culture jamming often literally involves the body. For instance, one of Reverend Billy's "retail interventions," posted on his Web site, is a culture-jamming activity targeted at Starbucks. During this intervention, entitled "It's a Party! Bump and Grind the Buckheads," jammers filling a Starbucks store proceed to dance, strip, and hand out pamphlets. Reverend Billy explains the physical sensations that culture jamming ignites when he tries to reach his audience with his anticonsumption message. Audience members have to "embody the fun [of not consuming]. It all comes down to the decision, what sort of dance am I involved in here? Where are my arms, where are my hands? How far is my voice reaching, what am I saying? It's all physical. It's the physical-spiritual" (Reverend Billy, quoted in Ashlock, 2005). Second, culture jammers engage both their own and their audiences' emotions as they conduct their jams. For instance, one audience member explained his emotional reaction to one of Reverend Billy's public appearances, stating how suddenly feeling alive stirred up a sense of hope that is leading him to reconceptualize his identity.

Enacting Politics

Cultural resistance can provide an entrée into political resistance and can itself become political resistance (Duncombe, 2002). In fact, part of culture jamming's effectiveness as pedagogy is its ability to help participants engage in politics. When political resistance is presented or enacted through culture—and especially through a fun, exciting experience of culture—it can seem more friendly and perhaps less threatening than other forms of political protest. Duncombe (2002) argues that "because cultural resistance often speaks in a more familiar and less demanding voice than political dissent it makes this move ... easier. In this way cultural resistance works as a sort of stepping stone into political activity" (p. 6).

Culture jamming itself can also be considered political resistance, as it plays with and challenges dominant ways of doing, seeing, and experiencing culture. Duncombe (2002) argues that politics is essentially a cultural discourse— "a shared set of symbols and meanings that we all abide by" (p. 6). The politics of culture is conveyed through its content, form, interpretation, and the activity of production (Duncombe, 2002). Thus when culture jammers alter that discourse, shake it up, and envision new, more democratic discourses—change the content, the form, the ways it is interpreted, and the activities of its production—they are, in fact, enacting political resistance.

Culture Jamming's Pedagogical Hinge

All the pedagogical capacities thus far discussed involve leading learners to a moment of *détournement* (a turning around), in which they are no longer who they used to be but are caught off guard with the possibility of becoming someone different. I thus believe that the pedagogical hinge of culture jamming—an important learning moment—occurs when audience members experience détournement. *Adbusters* founder Kalle Lasn (1999) argues that culture jamming helps provide a new way of looking at the world; Lasn describes détournement as "a perspective-jarring turnabout in your everyday life" (p. xvii). He believes that détournement helps provide people with new choices about how to live and how to be: "You are—everyone is—a creator of situations, a performance artist, and the performance, of course, is your life, lived in your own way.... Many times a day, each of us comes to a little fork in the path. We can then do one of two things: act the way we normally, reflexively act, or do something a little risky and wild, but genuine. We can choose to live our life as 'a moral, poetic, erotic, and almost spiritual refusal' [Plant, 1992, p. 8] to cooperate with the demands of consumer culture" (p. 101).

Activists, through their culture jamming, are seeking to ignite détournement, to incite authenticity. As one culture jammer writing in *Adbusters* stated, "Is your life a project? Do you give a shit about anything? Can you still get angry? Be spontaneous?" ("Is Your Life a Project?" 2005). Détournement thus works as a form of transitional space in that it "opens up the space and time between an experience and our habitual response to it. It gives us time and space to come up with some other way of being in relation at that moment. It introduces a stutter, a hesitation. It jams the binary logics that keep self/other, inner/outer, individual/social locked in face-to-face opposition. It is a space where the skin-to-skin face-off between self and other has been pried apart so that a reordering of self and other can be set in motion and so that we might go on relating to each other at all" (Ellsworth, 2005, p. 64).

CONCLUSION

Nadine Dolby (2003), writing primarily for the K–12 educational realm, argues that educators who are concerned with democracy must extend their conception of teaching and learning "well beyond the schoolhouse" (p. 276). As educators of adults, we have long recognized the importance of the learning and education that goes on outside formal institutions. However, we are still largely ignoring the public pedagogy of popular culture, including the many ways in which adult learners are using cultural resistance to create democratic and empowering forms of popular culture and public spaces. We need to recognize the important learning that is happening outside formal adult education spaces in the realms of popular culture. The culture jammers I have described in this chapter are providing adult education, specifically with regard to the politics of consumption. These examples can be useful to adult educators, especially those interested in social justice.

First, they show how adults as learners are shaped by and actively re-create popular culture. Culture jammers "talk back" to and through popular culture—they name and make problematical the kinds of social relations and ideologies constructed through popular-culture commodities and experiences. They illustrate how we can view such commodities and experiences not as a fixed text that learners consume but as ongoing events or experiences (Giroux and Simon, 1989). These culture jammers also show how adult learners remake and appropriate the meanings of popular-culture commodities and experiences. As adult educators, we need to recognize this important aspect of identity formation and learning; we must include learners' engagement with popular culture when we draw on and build on their experiences, a hallmark of adult education practice. Paraphrasing Giroux and Simon (1989), we need to ask whether learners are able to see a connection between what we do in class and the lives they live outside of class, and we must devise ways to bring aspects of learners' lived culture into our classrooms.

Second, because critical adult education should be about the construction and production of knowledge, not just the consumption of it, the culture-jamming groups highlighted in this chapter can act as examples of classroom "prefigurative communities" (Epstein, 2002, p. 333). Social activist groups often try to structure their organizations and activities to be models for, or to prefigure, the kind of ideal society they are striving to create. Culture jammers participate in the creation of culture and knowledge, enact politics, open transitional spaces, create community, and engage their whole selves—intellect, body, and emotions. Culture jamming as pedagogy is an active "doing" rather than a passive "theorizing" (Hartley, 2002, p. 54). Culture jammers see culture as an active, two-way process; they refuse to be passive recipients of corporate-produced culture and instead produce their own (Hartley, 2002). In critical adult education classrooms, learners should be creating their own knowledges and cultures—becoming cultural producers, building new, more democratic cultural realities and spheres (Giroux, 2004). This depiction of culture jamming as education thus embodies what critical adult education could look like.

REFERENCES

"Another World." *Adbusters #49,* 2003, *11* (5), 50.

Armstrong, P. "All Things Bold and Beautiful: Researching Adult Learning Through Soaps." In T. J. Sork, V. Chapman, and R. St. Clair (eds.), *Proceedings of the 41st Annual Adult Education Research Conference.* Vancouver: University of British Columbia, 2000.

Armstrong, P. "*The Simpsons* and Democracy: Political Apathy, Popular Culture, and Lifelong Learning as Satire." In R. Hill and R. Kiely (eds.), *Proceedings of the 46th Annual Adult Education Research Conference.* Athens: University of Georgia, 2005.

Ashlock, J. "Shopocalypse Now!: Q+A with Reverend Billy." *RES Magazine,* 2005, *8.* Retrieved Jan. 5, 2007, from http://www.res.com/magazine/articles/shopocalypsenowqa withreverendbilly_2005–05–19.html.

Bennett, T. *Culture: A Reformer's Science.* Thousand Oaks, Calif.: Sage, 1998.

Bordwell, M. "Jamming Culture: Adbusters' Hip Media Campaign Against Consumerism." In T. Princen, M. Maniates, and K. Conca (eds.), *Confronting Consumption.* Cambridge, Mass.: MIT Press, 2002.

Brookfield, S. D. "Media Power and the Development of Media Literacy: An Adult Educational Interpretation." *Harvard Educational Review,* 1986, *56*(2), 151–170.

Carducci, V. "Culture Jamming: A Sociological Perspective." *Journal of Consumer Culture,* 2006, *6*(1), 116–138.

Dolby, N. "Popular Culture and Democratic Practice." *Harvard Educational Review,* 2003, *73*(3), 258–284.

Duncombe, S. *Cultural Resistance Reader.* New York: Verso, 2002.

Ellsworth, E. *Places of Learning: Media, Architecture, and Pedagogy.* New York: Routledge, 2005.

Epstein, B. "The Politics of Prefigurative Community." In S. Duncombe (ed.), *Cultural Resistance Reader.* New York: Verso, 2002.

Giroux, H., and Simon, R. I. (Eds.) *Popular Culture, Schooling, and Everyday Life.* New York: Bergin & Garvey, 1989.

Giroux, H. A. *The Mouse That Roared: Disney and the End of Innocence.* Lanham, Md.: Rowman & Littlefield, 1999.

Giroux, H. A. "Public Pedagogy as Cultural Politics: Stuart Hall and the 'Crisis' of Culture." *Cultural Studies,* 2000, *14*(2), 341–360.

Giroux, H. A. *Theory and Resistance in Education: Towards a Pedagogy for the Opposition.* New York: Bergin & Garvey, 2001.

Giroux, H. A. "Cultural Studies, Public Pedagogy, and the Responsibility of Intellectuals." *Communication and Critical/Cultural Studies,* 2004, *1*(1), 59–79.

Harold, C. "Pranking Rhetoric: 'Culture Jamming' as Media Activism." *Critical Studies in Media Communication,* 2004, *21*(3), 189–211.

Hartley, J. *Communication, Cultural and Media Studies: The Key Concepts.* New York: Routledge, 2002.

Hebdige, D. *Subculture: The Meaning of Style.* London: Methuen, 1979.

"Is Your Life a Project?" *Adbusters #49,* 2005, *11*(5), 88–89.

Jarvis, C. "Real Stakeholder Education? Lifelong Learning in the Buffyverse." *Studies in the Education of Adults,* 2005, *37*(1), 31–46.

Jubas, K. "The Trouble with Shopping: Discourses, Practices and Pedagogies of the Consumer-Citizen." In M. Hagen and E. Goff (eds.), *Proceedings of the 47th Annual Adult Education Research Conference.* Minneapolis: University of Minnesota, 2006.

Lane, J. "Reverend Billy: Preaching, Protest, and Postindustrial Flânerie." *Drama Review,* 2002, *46*(1), 60–84.

Lasn, K. *Culture Jam: How to Reverse America's Suicidal Consumer Binge—and Why We Must.* New York: HarperCollins, 1999.

Plant, S. *The Most Radical Gesture.* New York: Routledge, 1992.

Rumbo, J. D. "Consumer Resistance in a World of Advertising Clutter: The Case of *Adbusters.*" *Psychology Marketing,* 2002, *19*(2), 127–148.

Sandlin, J. A. "Consumerism, Consumption, and a Critical Consumer Education for Adults." In R. St. Clair and J. A. Sandlin (eds.), *Promoting Critical Practice in Adult Education.* New Directions for Adult and Continuing Education, no. 102. San Francisco: Jossey-Bass, 2004.

Sandlin, J. A. "Culture, Consumption, and Adult Education: Refashioning Consumer Education for Adults as a Political Site Using a Cultural Studies Framework." *Adult Education Quarterly,* 2005a, *55*(3), 165–181.

Sandlin, J. A. "'Spend Smart, Live Rich'? A Critical Analysis of the Consumer Education Lifestyle Magazine *Budget Living* and Its Readers' Forums." In R. Hill and R. Kiely (eds.), *Proceedings of the 46th Annual Adult Education Research Conference.* Athens: University of Georgia, 2005b.

Solorzano, D. G., and Delgado Bernal, D. "Examining Transformational Resistance Through a Critical Race and Latcrit Theory Framework." *Urban Education,* 2001, *36*(3), 308–342.

Storey, J. *Cultural Consumption and Everyday Life: Cultural Studies in Practice.* New York: Oxford University Press, 1999.

Storey, J. *Cultural Theory and Popular Culture.* (4th ed.) Athens: University of Georgia Press, 2006.

Tisdell, E. J., and Thompson, P. M. "*Crash*-ing into Pop Culture in Dealing with Diversity: Adult Education and Critical Media Literacy About Movies and Television." In M. Hagen and E. Goff (eds.), *Proceedings of the 47th Annual Adult Education Research Conference.* Minneapolis: University of Minnesota, 2006.

Usher, R., Bryant, I., and Johnston, R. *Adult Education and the Postmodern Challenge.* New York: Routledge, 1997.

Williams, R. "Base and Superstructure in Marxist Cultural Theory." *New Left Review,* 1973, *82*, 3–16.

Wright, R. R. "A Different Definition of 'Boob-Tube': What Dr. Catherine Gale, of *The Avengers*, Taught Women." In M. Hagen and E. Goff (eds.), *Proceedings of the 47th Annual Adult Education Research Conference.* Minneapolis: University of Minnesota, 2006.

CHAPTER 28

Toward a Postmodern Pedagogy

Deborah Kilgore

One evening in a university classroom, I sat among a group of students, listening intently to a student's description of a problem that she wanted the rest of us to solve, in order to demonstrate some of her thoughts about group learning processes. Her description of the scenario was spare, and she gave no guidance toward learning what we needed to learn to solve the problem. While I waited for the exercise to begin, I thought about what I had just voluntarily relinquished. To a degree I had given up the social position of teacher and the control such a position implies. I also thought about what I had taken up. To a degree I had taken up the social position of student and the dependence this position implies.

As the exercise unfolded, something developed collectively, distinct from the individual social positions of the various group members. Early interactions were chaotic, with various people calling out suggestions, sometimes interrupting one another. Fairly quickly, though, we developed a rhythm in which different individuals or pairs took the lead temporarily to guide the rest of us through a particular aspect of the learning process. Piece by piece we solved the problem, incorporating the contributions of each of our group members, sometimes in a temporal order, sometimes with simultaneous activities going on in various parts of the room.

I should add that we were all wearing blindfolds. This unique challenge to sighted people helped pull us out of our usual ways of taking up social positions in the adult education classroom, with the teacher either leading the way or delegating leadership roles in an orderly fashion to students. I use the terms *teacher* and *student* to refer to social positions rather than the people who take up these positions. Social positions, like teacher and student, are defined by the relations of power in which they are situated. To take up these positions is an act of individual agency and an acknowledgment of the legitimacy of the power relations among them (Bourdieu, 1990). When I became a faculty member in a university, I agreed to play by certain rules in order to remain in that position. Students enrolled in the university, in the classes I teach, have also agreed to certain conditions of the social position of student. To reject the rules outright would be to reject the position.

Yet rejecting such positions is a postmodern thing to do. In the example of that evening class, that rejection required an extreme measure—the use of blindfolds—for the students and me to at least partially reject our respective positions briefly and thus get closer to a postmodern way of being in the adult education classroom. Here I refer to the adult education classroom as a group of individuals who take up the roles of teacher(s) and students engaged together in a formal educational effort situated within an institution. An adult education classroom might be a graduate course in a university, a nine-week job training program funded by the state, or a leadership development workshop sponsored by a corporate employer. When I give examples here, I specifically refer to the adult education classrooms in which I take on the role of teacher: graduate courses in a U.S. research-oriented university.

In this chapter I will discuss how adult educators might move toward a postmodern pedagogy involving some degree of rejection of social positions like teacher and student, resulting in the emergence of a local, collective way of knowing and learning. I will describe the consequences of a postmodern understanding of knowledge: the death of the teacher, the subversion of the student, and the diffusion of power. In my tentative conclusions, I will speculate about what such conditions mean in practice and where postmodern adult educators might go from here.

POSTMODERN KNOWING

As a way of knowing the world, postmodernism is distinct in particular from modern thought. Postmodernists remind us that all modern ways of knowing, whether humanist, capitalist, feminist, Marxist, Christian, or critical theoretical, rest on some set of transcendental truths about being and knowing. Postmodernists take issue with the validity of these or any over-arching explanations (Hemphill, 2001; Usher and Edwards, 1994; Lyotard, 1993). They say that any knowledge presented as such could be hegemony, taking certain conditions of human life in society to be normal and fair even though they serve the interests of some people at the expense of others (Cahoone, 1996; Kilgore, 2001; Tierney, 1997).

Instead of universal truths, postmodernists focus on multiple, local forms of truth (Rosenau, 1992). These "stories of the Other" (Giroux, 1993, p. 478) can help us to understand the arbitrary nature of our assumptions about the way people are or ought to be, by offering alternative understandings. With a complete reconfiguration in the way we think we know the world comes a change in the adult education classroom, the social positions of teacher and student, and the power relationship between them.

The first major reconfiguration of knowing in postmodernism is that there is no longer anything grand or universal to know and that the teacher's authority to know only exists within an authority-granting institution and by the will of the members who play by its rules. For example, when I write a syllabus and when students read it and follow it, we all are engaged in a process that grants me authority. Postmodernism calls out this process as one of any number of processes, none of which is objectively better than another at identifying who knows better. Toward a postmodern pedagogy, we would subvert normative rules by using blindfolds and other surprising interventions that unfasten us from the reinforcing practices associated with our positions of relative authority and relative subordination.

The second major reconfiguration of knowing in postmodernism is the recognition that knowledge is multifaceted (Bagnall, 1999); there is more than one way to know something and more than one thing to know about it. Every text, whether it is a learning event, a book or article, a lecture or discussion, contains within it the potential for multiple meanings (Rosenau, 1992). We must reconcile ourselves to the idea that the teacher does not know everything; in fact, the teacher knows practically nothing in comparison with the many things that might be known. Toward a postmodern pedagogy, we would acknowledge that many interpretations of a text are possible; and we would support multiple readings and interpretations. We would "encourage the differing forms of language and thought adult learners may bring to the classroom" without expecting them to conform to "dominant cultural patterns" (Hemphill, 2001, p. 19).

The third major reconfiguration of knowing in postmodernism is a reallocation of where we think meaning authoritatively lies. Meaning no longer inhabits the texts students want to know about but rather lies within learners, who in their roles as students and teachers are readers and interpreters of those texts. By the same token, the learner is no longer a stable, centered individual (man) exploring (his) unlimited potential for enlightenment and self-actualization, as humanists assumed in the modern practice of adult education. Rather, the postmodern learner is "decentered" and "emergent" (Rosenau, 1992, p. 57). The postmodern learner is always becoming, always in process, always situated in a context that also is always becoming. The learner who inhabits the position of student lives up to master scripts about what being a student means (Bloom, 1998) but also participates in the creation of the meaning of the situated adult education classroom as it unfolds. Toward a postmodern pedagogy, we would not be concerned with such accomplishments as perspective transformation, which assumes a unified (and perhaps broken) self (Kilgore and Bloom, 2002). Instead, we would recognize the learner who takes up the position of student in the adult education classroom as someone who also occupies other social positions. This learner interprets and reinterprets what is going on in the adult education classroom not only as a student but also with regard to the rest of her or his many social roles (Clark and Dirkx, 2000). *Book learning*—the acquisition of whatever text the teacher is offering for students to consume—is but one way learners know the world around them.

The fourth major reconfiguration of knowing in postmodernism involves the relationship between knowledge and power. For postmodernists no one individual or group holds power over another; power is ever present in the relations among them. The adult education classroom is situated within an institution with normative rules of behavior; but teachers and students actively establish, maintain, reinforce, and break these rules (Usher, Bryant, and Johnston, 1997). Knowledge itself is the exercise of power (Pietrykowski, 1996). To know is to produce meaning, and the production of meaning is the production of power.

To understand power as something that we exercise rather than possess means giving up the notion that power flows from a centralized entity like the state, the university, or the teacher, turning to the production of social positions in the adult education classroom. The teacher and student are the product of a dynamic network of cultural and institutional practices that "increase the power of individuals at the same time as it renders them docile" (Sawicki, 1991, p. 22). There lies both our complicity with and resistance to oppression. Toward a postmodern pedagogy, we would acknowledge that what unfolds before us in the adult education classroom does so largely at our behest. We would be concerned with naming what makes us submissive and identifying what grants us power. We would move from there to the collective creation of what I think of as powerful knowledge, knowledge that is personally empowering and socially transforming.

In moving toward a postmodern pedagogy, we are most interested in shaking up the social positions of teacher and student and the power relationship between them. Such aspirations will require us to consider the death of the teacher, the subversion of the student, and the diffusion of power.

THE DEATH OF THE TEACHER

The transmission of truth is a nostalgic dream. We now recognize that the organized adult education classroom is heavily laden with many meanings drawn from its multilayered situation within a discipline, an established pedagogy, an institution, and the intersection of the many cultures and social positions that those present represent. Both teacher and student are challenged to make meaning of adult education, yet neither is in a great position to do so. The teacher is occupied with an attempt to mean something. The student is occupied with an attempt to decode the teacher's grading system.

Yet like other dualisms that poststructuralists (Seidman, 1994) have challenged, the teacher-student relation is suspect. First, such dualisms imply that the first term is somehow superior to the second. However, little distinguishes the teacher from the student, particularly in an adult education classroom. Teachers do not necessarily have more experience, knowledge, or wisdom than the students who enter their classrooms. Further, such dualisms imply that the second term represents everything that the first term is not. Yet many students who come to learn about adult education are themselves adult educators. Finally, such dualisms collapse all teachers and all students into two categories, extinguishing difference. Yet we know that teachers and students have many positions from which they make sense of the world, based at least in part on race, ethnicity, gender, class, age, physical ability, and sexual orientation (Sheared and Sissel, 2001).

Much writing on adult education pedagogy focuses on the teacher, the teacher's role in the adult education classroom, the teacher's style, and pedagogical approaches that the teacher can take to achieve the teacher's goals for students. To honor students we refer to them as *learners,* as if they weren't really subject to the teacher's pedagogical machinations at all.

What might our pedagogical texts look like if we began with the student and removed the teacher from the picture? One of our most influential pedagogical foundations—self-directed learning—already provides such a vision, with facilitators filling the space left by now-absent teachers. In this scenario we aspire to place students fully at the "depoliticized and decontextualized" (Grace, 2001, p. 264) center of their learning experience. However, as Johnson-Bailey (2002, p. 45) demonstrates in her research review, "learning environments are not neutral sites; they are instead driven in large part by the positionalities of the instructors and learners, with a conspicuous component of the makeup being race." A color-blind perspective removes the adult education classroom from its real-world context, where students' and teachers' locations in social relations of power matter (Johnson-Bailey and Cervero, 2000; Tisdell, 1998). Furthermore, the hegemony of late capitalism, and the maldistribution of power that accompanies it, has completely colonized such a pedagogical approach. Students become consumers experiencing "the same kind of freedom they enjoy in shopping malls," and adult educators "become increasingly de-skilled as they surrender their agency as teacher for the less pro-active role of broker of commodified educational services" (Collins, 1998, p. 83).

The point of deconstructing a dichotomy like teacher-student "is not to reverse the value of the signs" (Seidman, 1994, p. 204), that is, to make student superior to teacher. The point is to envision what it would be like to "make space for alternative democratic visions and discourses" (Grace, 2001, p. 267). Such an alternate vision will not occur simply by killing the teacher off. We must address the student.

THE SUBVERSION OF THE STUDENT

Naming the student is important because it reminds us that formal adult education almost never is a utopian democratic enterprise and that it is one that learners almost always enter into more or less involuntarily. Almost everything we do, from welfare-to-work job training to career-enhancing degree programs, is mandatory in light of what adults must do to acquire and maintain a certain standard of living under late capitalism.

However, the learner is only in small part a student (and teacher). The humanist vision of the learner privileges the socially subordinate position of student over other social positions. By "propelling the human subject to the center" (Rosenau, 1992, p. 47), that vision casts the learner as a unified individual self, one that must wholly and wholeheartedly take up the only position available to it in the adult education classroom, that of student.

Retheorizing subjectivity as multiple and contradictory creates many possibilities, not the least of which is the dissolution of the teacher-student divide. It helps us to explain why learners comply with the demands of their social positions as students and teachers even when such demands are oppressive (Clark and Dirkx, 2000). Adhering to the fantasy of the unitary self is isolating and causes us to aspire (and often fail) to be the good student, that is, the handsome, healthy, youthful yet not too young, white male student with middle-class values and a rational mind. Toward a postmodern pedagogy, we would acknowledge the multiple perspectives we derive from our experiences of race, ethnicity, gender, social class, age, physical ability, and sexual orientation; as well as positions we take up in our lives as workers, caregivers, and community activists. In this way we subvert the student and the stranglehold we have allowed him to have on the way we judge the value of our knowledge. With the death of the teacher and the subversion of the student, it becomes obvious that no one is left to own all the power.

THE DIFFUSION OF POWER

The modern concept of power is of something that one individual or group holds and exerts over another. The postmodern concept of power is quite different. Rather than possessing it, one exercises power (Sawicki, 1991): "Any individual, taken almost at random, can operate the machine" (Foucault, 1977, p. 202). Foucault's concept of power-knowledge is an acknowledgement of the "tremendous power in development, naming, and operation of knowledge" (Hemphill, 2001, p. 25). Every time we express knowledge, whether the knowledge the discipline presents to us or the knowledge we construct in opposition, we exercise power. Thus, the center of domination lies in our own practices.

As learners, teachers and students are situated within a community of practice that has a particular structure of power relations that "define possibilities for learning" (Lave and Wenger, 2002, p. 115). On the one hand, teachers and students come to understand what practicing successfully in the adult education classroom means, and this includes the tools and processes that are presented to them on their arrival and throughout their engagement. For example, teachers learn grading systems and pedagogical techniques while students learn study skills and time management methods. They develop all these competencies with an eye to established understandings of what should be learned and how. At the same time, teachers and students bring their own desires into the classroom, and "have a stake in its development as they begin to establish their own identity in its future" (p. 124). Depending on how the teachers and students—all learners—play it, the adult education classroom will be socially reproductive and productive of new knowledge. To produce what I call powerful knowledge, knowledge that is personally empowering and socially transforming, the class must meet two conditions. First, the adult education classroom must be explicitly situated. Second, the standard mode of operation in the adult education classroom should involve questioning, critique, and even rejection of established wisdom (Guile and Young, 2002).

TOWARD A POSTMODERN PEDAGOGY

In moving toward a postmodern pedagogy, we must bring into clarity the ideological context of the adult education classroom by questioning, critiquing, and sometimes even rejecting the social positions of teacher and student. To accomplish this we might first surprise ourselves out of such social positions. Second, we would open the adult education classroom to the many perspectives of the learners who engage in it, because without "diverse conversations about the nature of a particular phenomena" (Guile and Young, 2002, p. 362), we cannot hope to understand it. Third, we would stop fantasizing about an autonomous, unified learning self and instead acknowledge our multiple selves that are constantly in flux, that hold contingent and conflicting understandings of the adult education classroom. Fourth, we would seek to collectively construct out of this tentative, contingent, always-becoming tangle of interpretations, powerful knowledge that is personally empowering and socially transforming.

A postmodern pedagogy would include the recognition that adult education is a situated, collective learning process with difference at its core. A postmodern pedagogy would have us name our differences by acknowledging the institutional, cultural, and socioeconomic trajectories of each of our lives that have brought us into this adult education space. This includes our taking up and taking on the social positions of teacher or student within the situated adult education space and acknowledging the constraints of ideological logic that define these positions and this space. Acknowledging that this is so is not enough, and neither is pretending that it is not or imagining that we can shake it. Rather, analysis of such positions provides an opportunity to express power, to make the adult education classroom "a strategic site for intervention and change" (Tierney, 2001, p. 362). We must learn how to hear what we each have to say, across borders and outside an overarching hegemonic frame. Making difference central and then constructing a shared learning experience that aims to transcend hegemony while suspended within it is not an easy task.

After reading about the history of adult education as a field, students in my classes often become drawn into the task of delineating adulthood from childhood. But the interesting question about adult learners, of course, is not how they are different from children. Such a question stems from the modern practice of adult education, one that replaced one truth with another, along with a whole host of professionals to facilitate the transition. Rather, the interesting question about adult learners is the wonder of our experiences, the social positions we must or choose to take, and the influence on our learning of the intersection and interweaving of such life trajectories.

At the same time, we can do nothing with a wholly skeptical form of postmodernism that remains true only to death, as some have rightly criticized. We must not become paralyzed, particularly in late capitalism, where "global carpetbaggers" are "bent upon reaping short-term profits at the expense of ecological health and human dignity" (McLaren and Farahmandpur, 2000, p. 25). Yes, we must accept the annihilation of everything we thought was truth, but also we must be committed to developing new and moral meanings. We must step off the modern ledge, not to meet our demise but to fly.

REFERENCES

Bagnall, R. G. *Discovering Radical Contingency: Building a Postmodern Agenda in Adult Education.* New York: Peter Lang, 1999.

Bloom, L. R. *Under the Sign of Hope: Feminist Methodology and Narrative Interpretation.* Albany: State University of New York Press, 1998.

Bourdieu, P. *The Logic of Practice.* Translated by R. Nice. Stanford, Calif.: Stanford University Press, 1990.

Cahoone, L. (ed.). *Modernism to Postmodernism: An Anthology.* Cambridge, Mass.: Blackwell, 1996.

Clark, M. C., and Dirkx, J. M. "Moving Beyond a Unitary Self: A Reflective Dialogue." In A. L. Wilson and E. R. Hayes (eds.), *Handbook of Adult and Continuing Education.* San Francisco: Jossey-Bass, 2000.

Collins, M. *Critical Crosscurrents in Education.* Malabar, Fla.: Krieger, 1998.

Foucault, M. *Discipline and Punish: The Birth of the Prison.* New York: Vintage Books, 1977.

Giroux, H. "Postmodernism as Border Pedagogy: Redefining the Boundaries of Race and Ethnicity." In J. Natoli and L. Hutcheon (eds.), *A Postmodern Reader*. Albany: State University of New York Press, 1993.

Grace, A. P. "Using Queer Cultural Studies to Transgress Adult Educational Space." In V. Sheared and P. A. Sissel (eds.), *Making Space: Merging Theory and Practice in Adult Education*. Westport, Conn.: Bergin & Garvey, 2001.

Guile, D., and Young, M. "Beyond the Institution of Apprenticeship: Towards a Social Theory of Learning as the Production of Knowledge." In R. Harris, F. Reeve, A. Hanson, and J. Clarke (eds.), *Supporting Lifelong Learning. Vol. 1: Perspectives on Learning*. New York: Routledge, 2002.

Hemphill, D. F. "Incorporating Postmodernist Perspectives into Adult Education." In V. Sheared and P. A. Sissel (eds.), *Making Space: Merging Theory and Practice in Adult Education*. New York: Bergin & Garvey, 2001.

Johnson-Bailey, J. "Race Matters: The Unspoken Variable in the Teaching-Learning Transaction." In J. M. Ross-Gordon (ed.), *Contemporary Viewpoints on Teaching Adults Effectively*. San Francisco: Jossey-Bass, 2002.

Johnson-Bailey, J., and Cervero, R. M. "The Invisible Politics of Race in Education." In A. L. Wilson and E. R. Hayes (eds.), *Handbook of Adult and Continuing Education*. San Francisco: Jossey-Bass, 2000.

Kilgore, D. "Critical and Postmodern Perspectives on Adult Learning." In S. Merriam (ed.), *The New Update on Adult Learning Theory*. San Francisco: Jossey-Bass, 2001.

Kilgore, D., and Bloom, L. R. "'When I'm Down, It Takes Me a While': Rethinking Transformational Education Through Narratives of Women in Crisis." *Adult Basic Education*, 2002, *12*(3), 123–133.

Lave, J., and Wenger, E. "Legitimate Peripheral Participation in Communities of Practice." In R. Harris, F. Reeve, A. Hanson, and J. Clarke (eds.), *Supporting Lifelong Learning. Vol. 1: Perspectives on Learning*. New York: Routledge, 2002.

Lyotard, J.-F. "The Postmodern Condition: A Report on Knowledge." In J. Natoli and L. Hutcheon (eds.), *A Postmodern Reader*. Albany: State University of New York Press, 1993.

McLaren, P., and Farahmandpur, R. "Reconsidering Marx in Post-Marxist Times: A Requiem for Postmodernism?" *Educational Researcher*, 2000, *29*(3), 25–33.

Pietrykowski, B. "Knowledge and Power in Adult Education: Beyond Freire and Habermas." *Adult Education Quarterly*, 1996, *46*(2), 82–97.

Rosenau, P. M. *Postmodernism and the Social Sciences: Insights, Inroads, and Intrusions*. Princeton, N.J.: Princeton University Press, 1992.

Sawicki, J. *Disciplining Foucault: Feminism, Power, and the Body*. New York: Routledge, 1991.

Seidman, S. *Contested Knowledge: Social Theory in the Postmodern Era*. Cambridge, Mass.: Blackwell, 1994.

Sheared, V., and Sissel, P. A. (eds.). *Making Space: Merging Theory and Practice in Adult Education*. New York: Bergin & Garvey, 2001.

Tierney, W. G. *Academic Outlaws: Queer Theory and Cultural Studies in the Academy.* Thousand Oaks, Calif.: Sage, 1997.

Tierney, W. G. "The Autonomy of Knowledge and the Decline of the Subject: Postmodernism and the Reformulation of the University." *Higher Education*, 2001, *41*(4), 353–372.

Tisdell, E. J. "Poststructural Feminist Pedagogies: The Possibilities and Limitations of Feminist Emancipatory Adult Learning Theory and Practice." *Adult Education Quarterly*, 1998, *48*(3), 139–156.

Usher, R., Bryant, I., and Johnston, R. *Adult Education and the Postmodern Challenge.* New York: Routledge, 1997.

Usher, R., and Edwards, R. *Postmodernism and Education.* New York: Routledge, 1994.

CHAPTER 29

Activism as Practice

Some Queer Considerations

Robert J. Hill

As an adult educator, activist against oppression, member of a sexual minority, and a cultural worker, I am sometimes faced with this question: What are the concrete implications of lesbian and gay issues for adult education theory and practice? For me as an "out" scholar, an equally important question is how to work within adult education—which at times characterizes its theoretical frames as apolitical—with my belief that all education advocates something, that is, maintains or defends a cause. Educators' advocacy occurs in many different ways, from silently reinforcing the status quo to promoting activism. *Activism*—direct action contesting or upholding one side of a controversial issue—takes many positions along a continuum from engaging in education for social change to open protest and civil disobedience. Here I think through the issues of activism as practice, bringing about social change through educational practice.

My aim in this essay is to explore the implications that lesbian, gay, bisexual, transgender, and queer (LGBTQ) perspectives hold for my work, especially as they relate to the practice of adult education. I struggle with these terms because sexual minority categories are not easy to defend. In this chapter I employ the acronym LGBTQ to refer to persons with either fluid or distinct self-identities around sexual orientation and gender. The term *queer* itself has multiple uses and can refer to the entire collective of individuals of diverse sexualities. However, most often I use *queer* to describe a particular form of political dissidence that blurs the dominant binary gender distinction of male and female. Queer theory, a lens that mediates my activism as praxis, is a complex set of notions, a field of research and inquiry, and a process of action. It is rooted in a self-reflexive social, cultural, political, and historical context that acknowledges the legacy of feminism, lesbian and gay studies, and activism, as well as current trends in poststructuralism and critical postmodernism.

Destabilizing and challenging assumptions is inherent in the very concept of queer theory; it troubles the mainstream understandings of gender and human sexuality. It is a self-conscious, deliberate pulling apart of ideas of normality, with the ultimate goal of challenging identity. Recognizing that the boundaries around sex, sexual orientation, and gender are arbitrary, queer work seeks actively to destabilize these (see Bernstein and Reimann, 2001; Boone and others, 2000; Hill, 2001).

I am interested in the movement from theory to democratic participation. Embracing queer ideas has taken me more deeply into popular education and LGBTQ community development, not as theoretical approaches but as ways to do four things: subvert dominant notions; trouble assumptions; bring rigorous skepticism to so-called regimes of truth; and contest the tendency to domesticate, colonize, and sanitize difference. Queer notions model a process that can be applied to arenas of theory, practice, and research beyond those specifically involving sexual orientation or gender identity. As a progressive activist-scholar, I engage in advocacy work with adults to gain or deepen knowledge, behaviors, and values aimed at constructing a more just society and world. Activism as adult education practice, influenced by queer perspectives, allows interventions at the levels of community and society. It is work that intends to bring about immediate change in social structures and systems.

LGBTQ LIVED REALITY

Despite gains made since the 1969 Stonewall event that brought sexual minorities into greater public view, many societies and their representative governments still position LGBTQ people as pathological, criminal, or sinful—depraved and degenerate individuals who are a menace to public order. Our perceived moral status affects our access to full citizenship and the exercise of democracy. For a very long time, throughout the world, homophobia has subjected us to legal violence made up of discriminatory practices (Ungar, 2000). We have seen the consequences of being considered indecent, offensive, or anathema to public sentiments and social organization: marginalization and silencing at best, violence and death at worst. Additionally, rampant homophobia is more than prejudice; it is a system that punishes some but rewards others who support and sustain it, a situation known as heterosexual privilege. The response to this by LGBTQ individuals and communities includes silence, negotiation, resistance, and active construction of new politics. Adult education plays a key role in these strategies, involving not so much a movement from theory to practice but rather doing cultural work at the *confluence,* the meeting place of one with the other.

TAKING UP CRITICAL PRACTICE: QUEER IS AS QUEER DOES

The classifications *lesbian* and *gay* have become essentialized in stable, intact, and unitary identity categories—a situation unacceptable to the rigorous skepticism of queer ways. A claim for inclusion in existing social structures has been built on these categories, visible in the struggle for such things as gay marriage, lesbian adoptions, and open enlistment in the military. The queer movement emerged in the 1990s in response to unchallenged and oversimplistic lesbian and gay identities and the effort for inclusion. As a challenge to these notions, it continues to be about deploying, twisting, inverting, and turning them inside-out. Learning about things gay—formerly situated in the question "What truths do lesbian and gay knowledge provide?"—leads us to change the question to "For what pedagogical and political uses can this knowledge be deployed?" As an aside, in the world where to be heterosexual is to be normal, things straight are equally constructed as one-dimensional, monolithic, and unimpeachable—and as such, may be queered as well.

The term *critical* is used in multiple ways in the context of lifelong learning, but I use it to mean advocacy for empowerment and development of voice. Being queer and doing queer are inherently critical stances. By *queer* I refer to living out the notion that we can never adequately identify or codify identity; rather, it is about contingent knowledge whose meanings we must constantly reevaluate and reinterpret.

Queer shares with postmodern perspectives the refusal to be positioned as solitary and intact. Queer is a category that no one can ever fully own or possess because it requires shifting identity to practice. It explores the processes that make things supposedly normal in order to overturn them; and it announces and enacts alternatives to the sex, gender, identity, desire vectors of heterosexuality. Cohen (2001) and Talburt and Steinberg (2000) remind us that queer knowledge is knowledge that refuses to be complete. Queer epistemology leads to the belief that we can know nothing with certitude or finiteness. Queer is about being politically, culturally, and socially dissident.

The academy has taken up queer as the next darling of intellectuals in a way that has domesticated and tamed it. Merging theory with practice involves raising questions around the effects of this, which have made a safe and nonchallenging form of queer practice acceptable, losing sight of the fact that queer had its origins in radical educational projects, street rage, and direct action, including arrests and in-your-face politics. Its roots lie deeply in activism as the practice of adult education.

THE EBB AND FLOW OF QUESTIONS AND ANSWERS

Queer perspectives on adult education call us to be wary of categorization and open to fragmentation. Postmodernism offers methods to become skeptical—to challenge, complicate, disrupt, and redraw ideas, assumptions, beliefs, values, and discourses (Hemphill, 2001; Kerka, 1997). It encourages development of unruly perspectives and exposure of partial truths. St. Pierre and Pillow (2000) remind us of the need to be critical of structures of meaning and practice and to abandon the desire for a seamless narrative or cohesive identities. Postmodernism takes up a critical stance toward the status quo and contests regulation of identity, which is positioned as a contemporary, subtle form of oppression (Briton, 1996).

When working at the intersection of theory and practice, it is essential to ask fundamental *what if* questions, such as those of E. St. Pierre (personal communication, October 7, 2002) and St. Pierre, Hill, and Lewis (2003): What if the desire to know others is a colonial hope of speaking for (and possessing) the other? What if the Freirian notion of the redemptive value of knowledge is overrated? Is your truth my truth? Is one person's redemption another's vexation? What if empathy for sexual minorities is nothing more than forced intimacy that in the end appropriates the other and erases difference, difference that is a hallmark of queer perspectives? What if advocacy work is more about the cultural capital, privilege, and elitism of the one working for justice than getting out of the way of the dreams, desires, pleasures, joys, and angers of the "rescued"? To do queer work is in part to break the sanctioned public silence on questions of sexual practice. What if conflict and confrontation are the only means within the current cultural framework to establish difference? What if academic intervention is more violence by appropriation than salve for those we are engaging? What if as adult educators the project of delivering our objects of research (those we work with, on, for) to a readership in the service of knowledge production destroys the knowledge of those we research and the ways they have constructed meaning? What if we adult educators are naive when we think our liberal projects can liberate anyone without a revolutionary dismantling of a system that is beyond Band-Aids?

These questions are the essence of all that is queer. Federating the critical with the postmodern allows an ebb and flow of these and other questions and responses. It provides the space for answering questions and questioning answers so as to arrive at deeper understandings of what might constitute social justice for sexual minorities.

GLOCALIZING: THE INTERSECTION OF MICRO- AND MACROPRACTICE

A bumper sticker proclaims "Think Globally/Act Locally." The confluence of theory and practice means desiring and acting and participating in the "new" new social movement—called the convergence movement—constructed on this principle, which is sustained by convergence activism. It builds coalitions around antiglobalization, environmental justice, queer activism, the social construction of whiteness, third-wave feminism, anticapitalism, animal rights, and peace. It contests empire building, the so-called war on terrorism, racism, sexism, ethnocentrism, xenophobia, bigotry, and discrimination based on age, ethnicity, physical ability, sexual orientation and gender identity, creed, native language, and other forms of oppression.

This relatively recent movement has been inspired by globalization, the shifting boundaries between public and private space, growing income disparity, reactions to a nascent U.S. empire, and the emergence of new identities and new technologies (Shepard and Hayduk, 2002). It differs from "new social movements" (such as the lesbian and gay movement, the feminist movement) in that these have identity politics as their center, whereas the convergence movement is built on collective antioppression activism; it is a movement across differences. It represents the explosiveness of social tensions building over world capitalism, U.S. imperialism, and neoliberal market policies. It focuses on reconceptualizing truth as local, personal, and community-specific while acknowledging that local activity can transform global politics and that global actions have local implications.

Convergence activism offers knowledge to adult educators on the merits of coalitions without central control, nonhierarchical models, leaderless structures, flexible tactics, antiauthoritarianism, education in "cells," and antinormative and playful behaviors.

The term *glocal* describes the intersection of local and global concerns. Glocalization means that every specific local action has multiple global components; activism as practice is inherently international. Among others, "Queer radicals have opted to devote their energies to [this new movement] activism" (Highleyman, 2002, p. 112). This contrasts with most lesbian and gay organizations, which have resisted political action beyond the issues of sexuality and identity. Radical urban queers—mostly youth—are in part responsible for this shift. Highleyman points out, "the sight [in Seattle at the World Trade Organization protest] of a small group of Lesbian Avengers topless in the cold rain was among the most memorable images" (p. 114). All social protests since Seattle have contained an important, albeit small, queer presence.

Armed with notions of things glocal, I wade into the confluence of theory and queer postmodern criticality at both macro-and microlevels of practice. My macropractices are professionally directed organizational and community interventions. They are large-scale practices that have (potentially) direct effects on social structures, such as policy change. For example, it is important to have a queer presence (visibility) at antiwar rallies and peace protests and at actions against the neoliberal machine that is destroying the earth's ecology.

In another venue, at the university where I work as an out faculty member, lesbian, gay, and bisexual students who want to talk about their negative experiences on campus due to their (actual or perceived) sexual orientation frequently approach me. In response I organized a group of students, staff, and faculty to research safety and acceptance for LGBTQ learners at our institution. We discovered that their stories were the norm: our academy is not as welcoming as it could be for sexual minorities (Hill and others, 2002). Our committee drew policy recommendations in the report (available on-line) from students' experiences and aimed at structural changes that acknowledged all students' rights to difference—a very queer proposition.

Micropractices are those that we carry out in the course of daily life and everyday activities. Micropractices are within the "realm of original self-experience . . . the way a person lives, creates, and relates in the world" (Carr, 1977, p. 52). Micropractices take place in what Collins (1991, p. 93) calls the life-world, "made up of the routine day-to-day activities that are accomplished, effectively or otherwise, in a taken-for-granted manner." At this level, day by day practices challenge heterosexual privilege. But it is important not to allow meaning to become fixed in queer political projects nor to suspend skepticism while journeying throughout the day, for we can easily reproduce injustices and support the status quo in ways that marginalize and oppress others. It is here that notions of "troubling the everyday" are fruitful, as Collins (p. 94) writes, because it is essential for adults to "acquire the capacity to put aside the natural attitude of their everyday life-world and adopt a skeptical approach towards taken-for-granted innovations 'necessary for progress,' supposedly 'acceptable' impositions as the price of progress, and seemingly authoritarian sources of information that describe for us the landscapes of contemporary social reality."

THE POLITICS OF QUEER PRACTICE

Speaking out is a significant endeavor—provocation has its price. Being visible and articulate may carry serious penalties. Queer activists must believe in their words and acts because the effects of articulating and acting can have important ramifications, such as loss of family, friends, job, or housing, and can lead to marginalization and violence. Queer practice, however, is more than agitation and contest. It is assisting in the creation of new narratives that challenge what can be said and that interrogate taboos around sexuality, notions of the body, and identity for all groups. Instigating for social change means insinuating self and others into the social structure so as to fulfill one of John Dewey's notions of progressive education: to gain command of oneself to make positive social use of one's powers and abilities (Dewey, 1994).

Critical queer practice is transdisciplinary, investigating processes of normalization and their intersection with race, ethnicity, class, sexuality, and identity as categories of both experience and analysis. For example, African American lesbians' experiences are more than, and different from, layering race onto the categories of woman and lesbian. The intersection of sexual orientation, gender identity, and gender expression with race results in experiences that differ from those related to the individual elements.

Life at the contact zone of theory and activism manifests itself in numerous expressions. Some of the ways I deploy my privileged position to further critical queer consciousness include the following.

Queering Research

My research agenda explores processes and practices that try to push life's complex gender constructions—what it means to be female, what it means to be male, or what it means to be simultaneously neither or both—into the so-called normal patterns of U.S. culture. To do so is to contest the easy dualities of gender, and to interrogate the too easy answers with respect to the traditional binaries of male-female, men-women, gay-straight. Instead, a research-to-practice scheme must lead to the investigation of power relations and contest the social, political, economic, historical, and cultural contexts that define and sustain so-called normal sexuality, sexual orientation, and gender expression or identity. This is another example of queer work as a way to translate marginalized experiences and recognize the value of the knowledge found there. As a result I find myself engaged in research that assists transsexuals (Hill, 2000, 2002), sex workers, and other sexual nonconformists.

Queering Teaching

Differences are reflected in the backgrounds that students bring to learning situations (Moll, Tapia, and Whitmore, 1993). Bransford, Brown, and Cocking (1999) have shown that students come to the classroom with preconceptions about how the world works. Cultural and religious differences affect students' comfort level, which in turn has an impact on learning. Paulo Freire (Freire and Macedo, 1987, p. 127) advocates that educators should try to "live part of their dreams within their educational space." Doing queer cultural work at the crossing point of theory and activism as practice necessitates bringing it into the classroom. The confluence of theory and activism becomes a part of classroom performance in order to offer students new ways of seeing and being in the world. Activism also promotes ongoing dialogue among faculty, administrators, and higher education policymakers. Facilitating adult learning includes exposing student's attachments to heteronormativity, homophobia, and heterosexual privilege. The confluence of theory and activism as praxis demands that we think critically and teach subversively.

Queering the Internet

Internet social activism and advocacy takes many forms. These range from hacktivism (breaking into Web sites or databases and altering information for the purposes of disrupting them) to using listservs as tools for cyberactivism.

In the latter category, I use department, college of education, and university organization listservs to distribute resources and information that turn traditional gender binaries upside down. Reactions vary from silence to criticism to support. One recipient reported that my postings frequently stimulate her Web filter to send the message that they contain dangerous content. Another wrote, "We haven't met, but I wanted to thank you for your voice, presence and contributions.... I love seeing your postings on the list serve."

VISIBILITY: SEIZING OPPORTUNITIES TO MOBILIZE

For many people it is difficult to know oneself without first seeing oneself. In fact, some have argued that without visibility there is no history (Eaklor, 1997). Queer visibility is a quintessential and necessary political act and a critical practice in itself. Visibility work to broaden the scope of the term *minority* to include LGBTQ learners has met with mixed success. Life at the intersection of theory and practice means focusing on ways to ensure minority authenticity for our communities.

Other practices that lead to visibility include developing and implementing strategies for cultural competency in order to educate students, faculty, administrators, and counselors on sexual minority issues. Cultural competence is a set of congruent behaviors, attitudes, and policies that come together among professionals, enabling them to work effectively in cross-cultural situations (King, Sims, and Osher, n.d.).

For me queer practice has meant creating equitable classroom and work environments; assisting others to learn inclusive language; confronting behaviors that marginalize LGBTQ people; recognizing antigay bias; identifying the unique needs of members of the academy; helping to develop a program called Safe Space for LGBTQ students; working toward a permanent resource office for LGBTQ faculty, staff, and students; and actively recruiting openly LGBTQ students.

CRITICAL PRACTICE AS WILDNESS AND MISCHIEF: A KIND OF CONCLUSION

There is a certain irony in attempting to conclude a writing that purports to show the importance of being open and the shifting nature of discourse as queer theory positions it. The meeting of queer theory and practice as activism makes possible a larger vision of identity and liberation beyond the limiting roles and demands that the social mainstream mandates. Queer activism seeks to build a holistic revolutionary movement dedicated to fighting traditional gender roles, racism, patriarchy, and capitalism.

Challenging oppression requires disruptive knowledge, not simply more knowledge (Kumashiro, 2002). The *Queer Nation Manifesto* ([1990] 1997), circulated at the 1990 New York Pride Festival, opens, "How can I tell you? How can I convince you, Brother, Sister, that your life is in danger? That every day you wake up alive, relatively happy, and a functioning human being, you are committing a rebellious act. You as an alive and functioning Queer are a Revolutionary. There is nothing on this planet that validates, protects or encourages your existence. It is a miracle you are reading these words. You should by all rights be dead."

The award-winning African American director Marlin Riggs reminds us in his film *Tongues Untied* that men loving men is a revolutionary act. This can be extended to women loving women and to transgender and bisexual relationships.

Learning can be participatory, self-directed, collaborative, transformative, or conflictual. Queer notions of activism entail wildness and mischief, conjuring up our more raucous nature, but the stimulus for conflict need not be destructive. Many times *conflict*—a struggle between interdependent parties who perceive incompatible goals, scarce resources, or obstruction by one party that prevents another from achieving its aspirations (Zueschner, 1997)—leads to learning. Conflict-learning is the learning that occurs in situations of contest. The dissonance that sometimes results from inserting LGBTQ content into the learning environment has the potential for growth and development in those who encounter it.

An appeal to our wild side invokes a call to "reject inhibitions imposed by assumed meanings and to cultivate in their place the fiercely passionate and undomesticated side of our scholarly nature that challenges preconceived ideas" (Thomas, 1993, p. 7). As adult educators we are often faced with the choice of rigor or relevance (Argyris and Schön, 1991); life at the junction of queer critical postmodern theory and queer activism as practice allows for the exercise of both.

REFERENCES

Argyris, C., and Schön, D. "Participatory Action Research and Action Science Compared." In W. F. Whyte (ed.), *Participatory Action Research*. Thousand Oaks, Calif.: Sage, 1991.

Bernstein, M., and Reimann, R. "Queer Families and the Politics of Visibility." In M. Bern-stein and R. Reimann (eds.), *Queer Families, Queer Politics: Challenging Culture and the State*. New York: Columbia University Press, 2001.

Boone, J., and others (eds.). *Queer Frontiers: Millennial Geographies, Genders, and Generations.* Madison: University of Wisconsin Press, 2000.

Bransford, J. D., Brown, A. L., and Cocking, R. R. (eds.). *How People Learn: Brain, Mind, Experience, and School.* National Research Council. Washington, D.C.: National Academy Press, 1999.

Briton, D. *The Modern Practice of Adult Education: A Postmodern Critique.* Albany, N.Y.: SUNY Press, 1996.

Carr, D. "Husserl's Problematic Concept of the Life-World." In F. Elliston and P. McCormick (eds.), *Husserl Expositions and Appraisals.* Notre Dame, Ind.: University of Notre Dame Press, 1977.

Cohen, C. J. "Punks, Bulldaggers, and Welfare Queens: The Radical Potential of Queer Politics?" In L. Richardson, V. Taylor, and N. Whittier (eds.), *Feminist Frontiers 5.* New York: McGraw-Hill, 2001.

Collins, M. *Adult Education as Vocation: A Critical Role for the Adult Educator.* New York: Routledge, 1991.

Dewey, J. "My Pedagogic Creed." In A. Sadovnik, P. Cookson, and S. Semel (eds.), *Exploring Education: An Introduction to the Foundations of Education.* Needham Heights, Mass.: Allyn & Bacon, 1994.

Eaklor, V. L. "Without Visibility There Is No History." [http://las.alfred.edu/~hustud/eaklorwithoutvisessay.html]. 1997.

Freire, P., and Macedo, D. *Literacy: Reading the Word and the World.* New York: Bergin & Garvey, 1987.

Hemphill, D. F. "Incorporating Postmodernist Perspectives into Adult Education." In V. Sheared and P. A. Sissel (eds.), *Making Space: Merging Theory and Practice in Adult Education.* New York: Bergin & Garvey, 2001.

Highleyman, L. "Radical Queers or Queer Radicals? Queer Activism and the Global Justice Movement." In B. Shepard and R. Hayduk (eds.), *From ACT UP to the WTO: Urban Protest and Community Building in the Era of Globalization.* New York: Verso, 2002.

Hill, R. J. "Menacing Feminism; Educating Sisters." In T. J. Sork, V. Chapman, and R. St. Clair (compilers), *Proceedings of the 41st Annual Adult Education Research Conference.* Vancouver: University of British Columbia, 2000.

Hill, R. J. "Contesting Discrimination Based on Sexual Orientation at the ICAE Sixth World Assembly: 'Difference' Is a Fundamental Human Right." *Convergence,* 2001, *34*(2–3), 100–116.

Hill, R. J. "Dangerous Crossings: Transsexual Communities, Heteronormative Social Practices, and the Queer Struggle for Citizenship." Paper presented at the Education and Social Action Conference, University of Technology, Sydney, Australia, December 2002.

Hill, R. J., and others. *In the Shadows of the Arch: Safety and Acceptance of Lesbian, Gay, Bisexual, Transgendered, and Queer Students at the University of Georgia.* Athens, Ga.: Department of Adult Education, 2002. [http://www.uga.edu/globes/CCRG_report.pdf].

Kerka, S. "Postmodernism and Adult Education." *ERIC Trends and Issues Alert.* [http://ericacve.org/docgen.asp?tbl=tia&ID=105]. 1997. ED404549.

King, M. A., Sims, A., and Osher, D. "How Is Cultural Competency Integrated in Education?" [http://cecp.air.org/cultural/Q_integrated.htm#def]. n.d.

Kumashiro, K. *Troubling Education: Queer Activism and Antioppressive Pedagogy.* New York: RoutledgeFalmer, 2002.

Moll, L. C., Tapia, J., and Whitmore, K. F. "Living Knowledge: The Social Distribution of Cultural Sources for Thinking." In G. Salomon (ed.), *Distributed Cognitions.* Cambridge: Cambridge University Press, 1993.

Queer Nation Manifesto. New Haven, Conn.: Beloved Disciple Press, 1997. [http://members.aol.com/beldspress/qnation.htm]. (Originally published 1990.)

Shepard, B., and Hayduk, R. (eds.). *From ACT UP to the WTO: Urban Protest and Community Building in the Era of Globalization.* New York: Verso, 2002.

St. Pierre, E. A., Hill, R. J., and Lewis, J. "Advocacy Research: Tensions Between Critical and Postmodern Theories and Methods in Speaking for Others." Panel-workshop presented at the 16th annual conference on Interdisciplinary Qualitative Studies, Athens, Georgia, January 2003.

St. Pierre, E. A., and Pillow, W. (eds.). *Working the Ruins: Feminist Poststructuralist Theory and Methods in Education.* New York: Routledge, 2000.

Talburt, S., and Steinberg, S. R. (eds.). *Thinking Queer: Sexuality, Culture, and Education.* New York: Peter Lang, 2000.

Thomas, J. *Doing Critical Ethnography.* Qualitative Research Methods, vol. 26. Thousand Oaks, Calif.: Sage, 1993.

Ungar, M. "State Violence and Lesbian, Gay, Bisexual, and Transgender (lgbt) Rights." *New Political Science,* 2000, *22*(1), 61–75.

Zueschner, R. *Communicating Today.* Needham Heights, Mass.: Allyn & Bacon, 1997.

CHAPTER 30

Using Freirean Pedagogy of Just Ire to Inform Critical Social Learning in Arts-Informed Community Education for Sexual Minorities

André P. Grace and Kristopher Wells

W e explore Out Is In in this article, which is an informal, arts-informed, community education project that we developed and implemented to focus on sexual-minority youth and young adults, and their personal, educational, social, cultural, and civic needs. We use the term *sexual minorities* as an encompassing name for lesbian, gay, bisexual, intersexual, trans-identified, two-spirited, and queer (LGBITTQ) persons. We discuss how we created a critical social-learning model informed by Freirean pedagogy of just ire that can assist sexual-minority youth and young adults to become active participants who work to make a more accepting and accommodating world (Freire, 2004). We begin our exploration by discussing the place and need for critical social learning about sexual-minority differences in Canadian and U.S. academic adult education. Such learning, especially if applied in a more formal context, can inform academic adult education as social education. Next, we consider how the action dialectic of denouncing and announcing, which is the scaffolding for Freirean pedagogy of just ire, drives our critical social-learning model that frames our project's by-learner-for-learner approach and its mode of coalition-engendered education. We deliberate how Freire's action dialectic inspired our project participants to live out a pedagogy of just ire as they engaged in artistic expression as a means to inform, educate, problem solve, and fight for social and cultural change. We investigate how this action dialectic informed two artistic endeavors conducted as integral parts of the Out Is In project: the *Ideal School* art installation and *SASSY*, which stands for the *Summer Arts Studio Supporting Youth* program. We conclude with a political perspective that suggests advocacy and empowerment are first steps in a critical pedagogical engagement aimed at engendering sexual-minority inclusion in the Freirean context of fighting for social transformation.

▇ CRITICAL SOCIAL LEARNING ABOUT SEXUAL-MINORITY DIFFERENCES

Critical social learning that has focused on sexual-minority learners and their educational and civic needs has been incrementally making its way into adult education as a field of study and practice (Grace, 2001b; Grace & Hill, 2004). However, much of this work takes place in informal contexts (Hill, 2004). To move the formal field toward greater inclusivity, there is a need for academic adult education to investigate these contexts and build knowledge of diverse sexual orientations and gender identities; a need to investigate LGBITTQ social and cultural formations, problems, and projects that focus on identities, differences, survival, and collective action; and a need to explore LGBITTQ needs, desires, and concerns within a more inclusive understanding of education for citizenship (Grace, 2001a, 2005; Grace, Hill, Johnson, & Lewis, 2004).

There is precedent for such work in adult education, which, as social education, has historically been concerned with education for citizenship and social learning (Grace & Hill, 2004). Indeed, adult education in its critical social iterations has long called on educators to engage in innovative and experiential forms of social learning for cultural and community transformation (Allman, 2001; Cunningham, 1988; Foley, 1999; Holst, 2001; Jacobs, 2003). For this learning to contribute to social and cultural change as part of a radical praxis, "it must be infused, in all contexts, with an alternative educational approach, an approach that can be applied in informal or what may appear to be noneducational contexts" as well as formal ones (Allman, 2001, p. 85). Thus conceived, critical social learning has to intersect education with social action and cultural work as it focuses on ethics, awareness, agency, options, decisions, dreams, actions, and possible realities (Freire, 1998a, 1998b, 2004).

We consider a specific mobilization of these dynamics in this article as we explore the Out Is In project and its informal, arts-informed, critical social learning model that focuses on sexual-minority youth and young adults, and their educational, cultural, and civic needs. This community-based education project has aimed to help participants build the capacity and resiliency they need to be active participants who engage in cultural work for social transformation. Based in Edmonton, Alberta, this project is partially funded by Public Safety and Emergency Preparedness Canada's Community Mobilization Program. The project also receives funding and in-kind support from individual, university, business, and community sources. Project participants have been using the arts and artistic expression to raise both individual and community consciousness about LGBITTQ issues, and what they see as impediments to their individual development, inclusion, and social learning. Whatever artistic medium they use, project participants make it clear that heterosexism (the privileging of heterosexuality and its attendant oppression) and homophobia (aversion and hostility toward persons with same-sex attractions) are pervasive in the socially conservative province of Alberta, as elsewhere. As they expose these personal, social, and cultural millstones, they publicize efforts to overcome them by engaging in arts-informed cultural action for social transformation. Project participants build skills and capacities that are sustained within a by-learner-for-learner approach as well as through outreach efforts to meet the needs of other sexual-minority youth and young adults in various community settings. To enable this outreach, we, as part of a volunteer collective of Out Is In mentor-facilitators, provide participants with leadership training to assist them in running peer-led workshops and other learning activities. As the leaders of this collective, we also provide other mentor-facilitators with opportunities for training so we will all "*know* [what to do] to make viable even our first encounters with … [sexual-minority youth and young adults] whose humanity has been negated and betrayed, whose existence has been crushed" (Freire, 2004, pp. 57–58). Here we learn to engage the dialectic dynamic between fragility and resiliency in LGBITTQ lives. As Freire (2004) reminds us, "A life, where it is almost absent or negated, can only be woven through much stubbornness against need, threat, despair, injury, and pain" (p. 57).

With this perspective on a life diminished in mind, we would like to respond to a valid question that some readers might have at this point: Why should sexual-minority youth and young adults be subjects of discussion in an adult-education journal? As our research experience and interactions with youth (legally defined as 17 years old and younger in Canada) and young adults (legally defined as 18 years old or older) have shown us, many have been denied any luxury or frivolity associated with youth (Grace & Wells, 2001, 2005). Some of our research participants were kicked out of families and homes for disclosing their sexual orientation or gender identity in what proved to be a homophobic and violent environment. Although some became homeless and succumbed to the perils of living on the streets, others did find a way forward by living independently in rooming houses or apartments, albeit with government assistance. In our estimation, lived experience rushes the individual development of many sexual-minority youth and young adults so that chronological age belies the hard lives already endured. From this perspective, they deserve our attention in any casting of adult education as social education.

As researchers, we are obligated to protect sexual-minority youth from harm. In this regard, chronological age was a key criterion in choosing participants for the case-study research discussed later in this article. We only worked with research participants legally defined as young adults so parental or guardian permission to participate in our research was not required. Like other Canadian institutions, our university requires parental or guardian consent to conduct research with youth. In the case of sexual-minority youth, attempting to obtain this consent would be tantamount to a dependent's disclosure of a nonheteronormative sexual orientation or gender identity. In effect, in following ethical protocol, researchers could place these youth in danger. If parents or guardians are unaware of and subsequently fail to accept a dependent's sex, sexual, or gender differences, then they might become physically, mentally, and/or emotionally abusive. Because we have no way of knowing how parents or guardians might react, we only conduct research with young adults.

In situating Out Is In as an experiential form of contextualized social learning steeped in the inventiveness and informality of an arts-informed, community education project, we drew on Freire's (1998a, 1998b, 2004) political and pedagogical perspectives, especially as they are expressed in some of his final writings that his wife Nita brought together in the *Pedagogy of Indignation* (Freire, 2004). These writings capture Freire's understanding of pedagogy of just ire or legitimate anger, which he shaped within a politics that he soaked in hope and his belief that "changing the world is as hard as it is possible" (Freire, 2004, p. 14). Why did we turn to Freire's work? Although Freire did not pinpoint sexual orientation and gender identity as power relationships in his class-based work, his critical, sometimes radical research and writing are still important to researchers whose theorizing, activism, and cultural work focus on the disenfranchisement of sexual minorities, social learning, and education for full citizenship. Freire's (1998a) praxis emphasized ethics, democracy, inclusion, and civic courage. Recent critical queer scholarship recognizes the value of this praxis to sexual-minority studies and cultural work in communities. For example, Egan and Flavell (2006) relate that Freire's theorizing and cultural work have been important to those attempting to integrate critical understandings of culture, community, power, and agency in grassroots queer adult education. Hill (2004) values Freire's work in developing activism as a critical queer practice that employs experience and analysis to transgress sexual-minority oppression within a politics and practice of inclusion and accommodation.

In general, Freire's praxis can have significance for those working with the disenfranchised in any power category. Freire (1998a) demanded that we respect the knowledge and life experiences of the disenfranchised, and he challenged us to work collaboratively with them to explore their concrete realities, their experiences of violence, and the political and ideological implications of being excluded. Freire insisted on methodological rigor in doing this research, which included recognizing "the critical capacity, curiosity, and autonomy of the learner" in creating new knowledge (p. 33). In this regard, Freire wanted the disenfranchised as situated learners and historical subjects to know the value of research in intervening to change the world. Freire declared,

> I research because I notice things, take cognizance of them. And in so doing, I intervene. And intervening, I educate and educate myself. I do research so as to know what I do not yet know and to communicate and proclaim what I discover. (p. 35)

Valuing the Arts and Artistic Expression in Adult Education

When the formal field of study and practice in adult education inadvertently (in a hegemonic sense) or overtly polices the discourses and practices of marginalized groups, these groups often turn to informal education to find their way out (Foley, 1999; Hill 1995, 1996). In our own case, to counter memories of bad experiences with formal education (D'Augelli, 1998; Friend, 1998), we chose informal, arts-informed, community education as a means to help sexual-minority youth and young adults find a way to become more resilient so that they could insert themselves into the world with the intention of making it more LGBITTQ inclusive, accepting, and accommodating. This ambition is in keeping with a new millennial trend to emphasize the developmental assets and resiliency of sexual-minority learners in research (Savin-Williams, 2005). This accent on positive attributes replaces an earlier research emphasis that primarily focused on sexual-minority individuals as victims of heterosexism, homophobia, and transphobia. Fatalism permeated this earlier research. It found expression in despairing comments such as "It's your own fault for coming out and being too visible" and "If you want to fit in, assimilate and don't be so obvious." Such comments fuel hopelessness and helplessness, and they limit possibilities for transgressing systemic, institutional, and cultural heteronormativity.

As we explored how we would frame Out Is In, we perceived the arts as an energizing multimedium to enable critical social learning to transgress. Eisner (2004), a longtime advocate of valuing the arts in education, discusses how a turn to the arts expands choices:

> The arts teach students to act and to judge in the absence of rule, to rely on feel, to pay attention to nuance, to act and appraise the consequences of one's choices and to revise and then to make other choices. (p. 5)

From this perspective, Eisner (2004) advocates the development of aesthetic intelligence in which the arts advance values associated with expressive and relational learning. These values "include the promotion of self initiated learning, the pursuit of alternative possibilities, and the anticipation of intrinsic satisfactions secured through the use of the mind" (p. 7). For Out Is In project participants, artistic expression became a way to explore personally experienced outcomes and effects associated with being closeted about alternative sex, sexual, and gender differences. It helped them to explore feelings of being afraid and miserable, and how these feelings are linked to heterosexism, homophobia, transphobia, and the overt and subtle ways these forces bound sexual-minority lives. It facilitated thinking about the rule of heteronormativity, and how this hegemonic rule seeks to limit their life choices or contributes to making bad choices. It also facilitated thinking about life if heteronormativity was transgressed, and how this life would open up new choices and possibilities.

This emphasis on using the arts in education is finding a growing niche in adult education. Two recent publications demonstrate this trend. In her edited volume on artistic ways of knowing for *New Directions for Adult and Continuing Education,* Lipson Lawrence (2005) asserts that artistic expression expands the boundaries for knowing, learning, and comprehending culture and positionalities "holistically, naturally, and creatively, thus deepening understanding of self, [others], and the world" (p. 3). From this perspective, she maintains that artistic ways of knowing draw on the affective, somatic, and spiritual domains in the creative production of knowledge. She believes that this has the potential to expand possibilities for adult learning as a dialectical engagement between history and the present. We concur. For Out Is In project participants, this dialectical engagement helped them to see themselves in personally transforming ways that helped to counter a past in which they were invisible in families, schools, and communities. It also helped them to become agents of a better present in which they are visible, vocal, and proud as they mediate life in these three sociocultural sites.

In a special issue of *Convergence* devoted to the theme *the arts, social justice, and adult education,* editors Clover and Stalker (2005) locate the arts as a powerful medium in adult education and cultural work for social justice. Maintaining a position similar to Lipson Lawrence, they declare, "Engagement with and through symbolic, aesthetic media ... stimulates dialogue, critique, knowledge/learning, imagination and action by developing spaces of resistance, choice, accommodation, debate and control" (p. 4). For our project participants, artistic expression nurtured resistance, which, in turn, nurtured resilience as they found new energy in the hope and possibility of a more just world. Their artistic expression became a way to build what Hill (1996) calls fugitive knowledge to counter the ignorance that so often leads to fear and symbolic and physical violence toward LGBITTQ persons.

Freirean Pedagogy of Just Ire as a Way to Imbue the Out Is In Project

Studying and adapting Freire's (1998a, 1998b, 2004) political strategy animating a pedagogy of just ire to the Out Is In project, we developed a model of critical social learning aimed at progressive social and cultural changes that recognize, respect, and accommodate sex, sexual, and gender differences. In his strategizing, Freire imagined "a world that is less dehumanizing, more just, less discriminatory, and more humane" (Macedo, 2004, p. ix). His expression of legitimate anger was the "eruption of just ire" (Macedo, 2004, p. xi). Freire (1998a) stressed the importance of the right to convey legitimate anger.

> The kind of education that does not recognize the right to express appropriate anger against injustice, against disloyalty, against the negation of love, against exploitation, and against violence fails to see the educational role implicit in the expression of these feelings.... However, it is important to stress the "appropriateness" of this anger; otherwise it simply degenerates into rage and even hatred. (p. 45)

Freire reemphasizes this latter point: "Integral to right thinking is a generous heart, one that, while not denying the right to anger, can distinguish it from cynicism or unbalanced fury" (Freire, 1998a, p. 40). Newman (2006) asks us to be similarly cautious when he discusses how to develop a morality that urges us to act in the face of oppression. He warns us that anger can intensify hate, so we must be careful when we connect anger to hate. He suggests that two outcomes are possible. When anger and hatred are controlled, we can use them to impel humane social action for cultural transformation. However, problems arise when anger and hate are uncontrolled, as they are in the hands of fanatics and bigots. Newman insists that we should fear uncontrolled anger and hate and their inhumane outcomes. This is because notions like anger, hate, and even love can be manipulated as acts, emotions, or conditions, and their impulses and meanings can vacillate "mediated by our own actions and relationships, by the mass media, by our culture and by the various so-called social norms set by our political leaders, our churches and our many and various role models and 'moral guardians'" (p. 275).

In living out Freirean pedagogy of just ire through artistic expression, the Out Is In project has functioned to embody "the unity between art and education" (Freire, 2004, p. 80). For Freire, such alternative critical pedagogy gauges struggle and the possibility of change. It involves participant co-learners in consciousness-raising as part of a humanizing education that enables them to gain the critical tools needed to expose the systemic nature (the root causes) of oppression.

> A humanizing education is the path through which ... [participant co-learners] can become conscious about their presence in the world—the way they act and think when they develop all of their capacities, taking into consideration their needs, but also the needs and aspirations of others. (Freire, as quoted by Macedo, 2004, p. xx)

Denouncing and Announcing as the Key Action Dialectic in a Pedagogy of Just Ire

Within a pedagogy of just ire, "changing the world implies a dialectic dynamic between denunciation of the dehumanizing situation and the announcing of its being overcome" (Freire, as quoted by Macedo, 2004, p. xi). When people actively engage this dialectic, they insert themselves into the world as knowing subjects capable of engaging in "truly ethical and genuinely human actions" (Araújo Freire, 2004, p. xxx). In the Out Is In project, participants denounced the dehumanization of LGBITTQ persons in artistic expressions of just ire that were informed by presentations and discussions in which they explored the history of LGBITTQ exclusion and violence in Canada. Freire (2004) maintains that such a turn to history in developing critical pedagogy is crucial: "The study of the past brings to our conscious body's memory the reason for being of many present procedures, and it can help us, through a better understanding of the past, to overcome its marks" (p. 55).

In Canada, LGBITTQ history marks the present and affects LGBITTQ lives through the persistence of heterosexism, sexism, homophobia, and transphobia, and their violent expressions in symbolic and physical forms. This sociocultural negativity exists despite the fact that Section 15 (1) of the *Canadian Charter of Rights and Freedoms* has been in force to protect individual rights since 1985. It also exists despite the fact that in 1995 in *Egan and Nesbit v. Canada,* the Supreme Court of Canada unanimously agreed that sexual orientation is a protected category analogous to other characteristics like race and gender listed in that section (MacDougall, 2000). In reality, changes in law and legislation accepting and accommodating sexual minorities have been slow to permeate Canada's dominant culture and society. In general, sexual orientations and gender identities that lie outside the confines of heteronormativity remain problematic and often unacceptable, especially to social conservatives (Grace & Wells, 2001, 2004).

In light of this oppressive Canadian reality, many younger and older sexual-minority persons continue to experience symbolic violence, which includes shaming, harassment, name-calling, and rightist politico-religious denunciation; and physical violence, which includes a spectrum of criminal acts like assault and battery, rape, and murder (Grace & Wells, 2005; Janoff, 2005). In his statistical study of homophobic violence in Canada since 1990, Janoff (2005) includes a necrology of victims (1990–2004) who were variously beaten, kicked, strangled, suffocated, stabbed, shot, burnt, bludgeoned, dismembered, run over, or thrown off buildings. He notes that more than 40% of the perpetrators of these hate crimes were homophobic teenagers. In terms of violence directed toward LGBITTQ youth and young adults, the 2004 Ping national survey, which analyzed data gathered from 1,358 Canadians between the ages of 13 and 29, indicated that 23.8% had witnessed acts of symbolic and/or physical violence directed toward a sexual-minority person their own age (Wells, 2005). Moreover, many of those victimized remain silent about their experiences of violence and avoid seeking help from police, medical professionals, educators, or other authority figures and support persons. Why? They fear being ignored, or disbelieved, or rejected, and thus further victimized (MacDougall, 2000; Janoff, 2005). In general, whether they are victims of violence or not, many sexual-minority youth and young adults feel stigmatized and ashamed due to a still pervasive historical and cultural negativity toward their sex, sexual, and gender differences. Consequently, some act out of a sense of frustration, often exhibiting a range of self-destructive behaviors that may include social withdrawal, drug-and-alcohol abuse, suicide ideation or attempts, and physical and/or verbal aggression (Friend, 1998; McCreary Society, 1999; Ryan & Futterman, 1998). Moreover, some lash out themselves and become perpetrators of violence, perpetuating a vicious cycle of destructive antisocial behaviors (D'Augelli, 1998).

Yet, even in this milieu, increasing numbers of LGBITTQ youth and young adults are announcing their presence, naming and declaring their sex, sexual, and gender differences (Grace & Wells, 2005; Ryan & Futterman, 1998; Savin-Williams, 2005). They are also expressing their legitimate anger in the face of unrelenting heterosexism, sexism, homophobia, and transphobia. As well, they are announcing their plans to fight the stereotyping and exclusion they experience. This contestation of the historical reality of silence, exclusion, and disaffection is often undertaken without individual and social supports. In Edmonton, for example, very few structured social-learning opportunities have existed for sexual-minority youth and young adults (Grace & Wells, 2001). Thus, Out Is In fills a real void. In our political and pedagogical work, we make providing sexual-minority youth and young adults with resources and a support system a primary focus. Project mentor-facilitators engage participants in critical social learning about historical awareness, safety, well-being, resiliency, ethics, restorative justice, critique, intervention, and community building. This textured learning helps participants reflect on ways to develop as active participants in the world, thus countering their traditional status as fugitive objects. Cunningham (1988) has long supported such critical social-learning models that use informal educational initiatives to enable historically disenfranchised groups to transgress formal education and culture. She believes these models make social change possible.

> [As we assist] individuals in creating, disseminating, legitimating, and celebrating their own knowledge (including cultural knowledge), social change can occur—for two reasons. First, the participant-produced knowledge competes with, confronts, and forces change onto the official knowledge; second, the participants, in recognizing that they have produced and celebrated their own view of the world, empower them-selves. (p. 137)

As we created our social learning model, we proceeded knowing that an emancipatory pedagogy needs to be embodied and embedded in a process of reflection, revision, and critique; and that social learning must be from the bottom up to engender consciousness-raising (Birden, 2004; Freire, 1998a, 1998b, 2004). To enable this, critical social learning should be infused with "coalition-engendered education [that] clearly makes a more radical conceptual move by theorizing a sort of adult education that diffuses the teaching function" (Birden, 2004, p. 269). Living out this philosophy, Out Is In has expanded the teaching-learning inter-action to include other co-learners who share in teaching, consciousness-raising, and knowledge-building processes. For example, members of other LGBITTQ and allied groups like Edmonton's *Youth Understanding Youth* have been involved. When other groups come together with Out Is In, participants teach and learn from one another, drawing on personal knowledge and experience to solve problems. They engage such issues as how to survive when family or friends abandon them. Community agencies have also been involved. For example, *Planned Parenthood* has run safer-sex workshops on the hazards and root causes of risky sexual practices, and the Edmonton Police Service's *Hate and Bias Crime Unit* has helped partici-pants understand what hate incidents and crimes are, and how they might address them in a safe and confidential manner. With this kind of coalition-engendered education, social learning is generative, enhancing possibilities for critique and change (Birden, 2004).

LIVING OUT FREIREAN PEDAGOGY OF JUST IRE THROUGH ARTISTIC EXPRESSION

Freire's political and dialectical engagement with legitimate anger can inspire LGBITTQ cultural action for social transformation. Here, possibilities for action are deliberated and framed within a dialectical dynamic that denounces hetero-sexism, sexism, homophobia, and transphobia, and announces options to enhance LGBITTQ inclusion and accommodation. Following Freire's (2004) suggestion, Out Is In participants enter this process by refusing to be the objects of further injustice. Freire maintains that the "most fundamental lesson is the one of noncon-formity before injustice, the teaching that we are capable of deciding, of changing the world, of improving it" (p. 55). In learning this lesson, participants are encour-aged to build their capacity and resiliency so they can work in community with others to transform the world. We believe that engaging participants in artistic expression is integral to this developmental process, conveying what Freire calls "experience-built knowing" (p. 64). In this engagement, which is intended to develop self and community, participants focus on the person the self sees and the person that others see. They also focus on the world that is and the world that is desired. As participants express themselves, many experience catharsis. Some also experience healing as reality meets possibility, prompting them to think about new ways of being, becoming, and belonging in the world. From this perspective, critical social learning is happening in an alternative, richly textured space that contests "the willed erasure of [LGBITTQ] history" as it interrogates "how, substantively, historically, materially, ... [an anti-LGBITTQ world] came into being" (Sedgwick, 2003, pp. 14–15). This new and differently textured space has an "ineffaceable historicity" (p. 15) that challenges heteronormativity as it moves across an array of perceptual data, capturing moments in LGBITTQ history as possibility. As participants engage in artistic expression, they represent self, others, reality, and possibility in art forms that stimulate affect (a felt emotion) in both the artist and those engaging what the artist has created. This generates an intimacy between the perceptible and the emotive.

These dynamics are now explored in two artistic activities conducted as part of the Out Is In project: the Ideal School art installation and SASSY. As Out Is In's project leaders, we wanted to engage in research that would create a memory of the project and allow us to share aspects of the dynamics, intricacies, and outcomes of each activity with a wider audience. We conducted a case study of each activity, recruiting sexual-minority young adults (18 years old or older) from the group of 25 participants in our project. We asked these young adults to recount and reflect on their recent life histories as youth dealing with their sex, sexual, and gender differences.

We invited our research participants to provide informed consent after we discussed details of the research with them, including how the created research knowledge would be used. They were told that they had the freedom to withdraw from the research at any time. They were asked to participate in open-ended interviews, and we invited them to provide samples of their artwork, which then became prompts for discussion during the interview process. We chose a case-study design because it is conducive to deep analysis of the particular and the emergent in investigations of historically excluded groups (Gall, Borg, & Gall, 1996). To assist in constructing authentic meaning, we involved research participants in an iterative process in which they worked with us to correct, amend, edit, and interpret interview drafts. This process was aided by the fact that both the researchers and the research participants were intimately involved in the Out Is In project and had vested interests in its outcomes. Some of the knowledge created by two of our research participants, T. J. and Jen, is shared in this article.

The Ideal School Art Installation

The notion that representing self, others, reality, and possibility in art forms fuels affect infused the Ideal School art installation, which became Out Is In's first public art exhibition. It was held at the main branch of the Edmonton Public Library during Gay Pride Week in June 2004. The exhibition drew more than 300 visitors. Project participants worked with different media to create an art installation from several old school lockers. The locker art became a historical monument that denounced how their families, schools, and communities had often excluded them. In keeping with the action-dialectic infusing Freirean pedagogy of just ire, participants contested these artistic expressions by creating others that announced possibilities for rearticulating these spaces as sites of hope and possibility where sexual-minority differences could be affirmed, accommodated, and valued.

In creating the art installation, project participants transformed the old school lockers into a provocative visual display. Participants decorated the outside of the lockers to reflect how their teachers, classmates, parents, and communities viewed them, which often positioned them in stereotypical ways. They also decorated the inside of the lockers with images, collages, and dioramas to reflect their inner selves, which they often kept hidden from their families, friends, and teachers. The juxtaposition of the outer and often misrepresented self with the inner and often more secret self helped to create a profoundly textured and performative display that served to emphasize how heterosexism, sexism, homophobia, and transphobia constantly circulate to police and enforce heteronormative objectification. Moreover, juxtaposing these dualities was integral to a collective process of reclamation and resignification that the participants used to affirm their identities and integrity. Collectively, the lockers took on political and pedagogical meaning as they created a counternormative discourse that traced, supplemented, questioned, and critiqued the impact of heteronormativity on the lives of sexual minorities in schools as primary formal learning sites.

Various research participants provided us with reflections on the meaning of their artistic creations. For example, T. J., age 21, provided the following explanation of the symbols that he used to create his locker (see Figure 30.1). The eyeglasses on the outside of the locker represented the pair that he was ridiculed for wearing in junior high school. The purple felt background symbolized the purple sweat pants that he remembered being laughed at for wearing to school. T. J. had also cut out and pasted words and phrases from magazines that reflected his familial and schooling experiences. The phrases on the outside of his locker door included "obedient child," "sitting in judgment," "tolerable," "STOP, Mom Don't Look,"

Figure 30.1.   The Outside of T. J.'s Locker Door

and "worth much more." He scrawled the word "NERD" in dark black ink over these words and the purple felt background.

Opening T. J.'s locker door, dozens of pairs of eyes cut from magazines glared at the viewer (see Figure 30.2). They were staring outward, as if waiting and watching. The phrase "running scared" was written amid the eyes. Looking further, the viewer could see shards of broken glass and fragments of a smashed mirror glued to the inside walls of the locker (see Figure 30.3). A candle covered in dripping red wax stood in the middle of the locker; a purple crucifix hung in the background. There were few words inside the locker. The locker was stark with a shrine-like quality. It was composed of broken glass and disembodied photographs of T. J. with his face scratched out beyond recognition.

Reflecting on his artistic work as a means of representing his dehumanizing familial and educational experiences, and his coming to terms with his marginalized identity, T. J. stated,

> This locker project gave me a voice. I got to express the transition, to give a voice to me then, to that voiceless person who couldn't understand what was going on for himself. I got to reach out to him.

During the project I uncovered and developed artistic skills and vision that I never knew I even had. I was able to talk about my efforts to reconcile my sexual identity with my family's conservative Christian background. As I spoke about my challenges, it helped me to let go of a past of denying and disguising my gay orientation. It was a release. I felt that I could finally use my energy for infinitely more positive tasks.

With his reflection, T. J. engaged in the *"possibility of sense making available* within the discourses within a particular sense-making community" (Davies, 2004, pp. 4–5). Mentor-facilitators, project participants, and viewers constituted this sense-making community in the Ideal School art installation. In creating his locker art display, T. J. was immersed in a dual process of contesting objectification and growing into subjectivity. This complex process exemplifies how the very bodies, thoughts, and desires of sexual-minority persons are "gradually, progressively, really, and materially constituted through a multiplicity of organisms,

Figure 30.2.   The Inside of T. J.'s Locker Door

Figure 30.3.   The Inside of T. J.'s Locker

forces, energies, materials, desires, [and] thoughts" (Foucault, as cited in Davies, 2004, p. 5). As T. J. created his artwork, and as he discussed it with members of his sense-making community, it took on an intricate and performative role. He and those who viewed his locker display were involved in an affective, perceptual, and deeply textured mode of pedagogical address that could invoke legitimate anger and possibilities for change (Ellsworth, 1997; Sedgwick, 2003).

SASSY: The Summer Arts Studio Supporting Youth Program

During the remaining summer months of 2004, the Out Is In project participants brainstormed and developed another innovative arts-informed initiative called SASSY. Assisted by mentor-facilitators who shared their artistic skills, participants used arts-informed approaches to develop their capacities to address issues related to self, culture, reality, and possibility. Participants met twice a week. Their creative productions revealed the complexities of sorrow and joy marking their everyday lives. Two professors from our Faculty of Education—Dr. Mike Emme, an associate professor of art education, and Dr. Diane Conrad, an assistant professor of drama education—volunteered to mentor students. Dr. Conrad provided SASSY participants with access to a professional drama studio where they began each meeting with a physical warm-up activity to help them get their creative juices flowing. Inspired by the body movements and pulsating rhythms that they experienced, the SASSY participants would then make the transition to work on their photographic explorations of the self in personal and cultural contexts. Here, participants learned to use digital photography, computers, and photo-editing programs to develop artistic self-expressions that reflected their diverse identities and experiences. They would plan out and pose for images that they wanted to capture as photographs. Dr. Emme helped the SASSY participants create these self-portraits using a digital camera connected to a laptop computer. Each SASSY member helped others manipulate lights, set up props, and use computer imagery as they created visual narratives of the self.

In the SASSY program, artistic expression was coupled with honing communication skills. The artistic expression focused on building self-knowledge and self-confidence, and building knowledge of the self in relation to culture and how it works. To improve communication skills, participants engaged in writing exercises, public speaking, and developing critical listening skills. Here, they learned about the intricacies of speaking out and speaking about. This artistic and communicative work created expressive and affective learning for many participants. Of course, engaging in a self-focused artistic endeavor in an environment valuing peer collaboration can be a risky (ad)venture. SASSY participants had to proceed with care and compassion as individuals exposed their vulnerable selves. Jen, age 18, comments on her involvement.

> Art is very much a catalyst for me. I find it therapeutic when I put a lot of myself into creating a piece. It helps me learn to communicate how I'm feeling and to sort out my ideas and perceptions in my own head. SASSY was a very intense, look-deep-into-your-life-and-pull-out-who-you-are on-the-inside kind of work. It was very important to have a safe group setting because we all became somewhat vulnerable during the creative processes that we pursued. SASSY helped me to explore who I am as a queer person. I am better able to identify parts of myself. I know my wants and needs much more strongly because my involvement has given me the time, space, and means to look deeply into myself. I now have a much clearer idea of who I am.

After a summer of creativity, the final photographic self-portraits were ready for a showing at a local café, Café Mosaics, where the participants' photos were displayed for a month. SASSY members brainstormed for a name that would represent the diversity of the images of self and culture that comprised their collective display. In the end, they named their photo gallery *Queer View Mirror* (see Figure 30.4). They felt the term *queer* incorporated the group's array of sex, sexual, and gender differences, which they saw as emerging, changing, never fixed. Allied heterosexual participants also found space and place in this fluid mixture. For example, one young man who self-identified as heterosexual participated in SASSY with his bisexual girlfriend. For him, it was an opportunity to get to know people across a spectrum of sex, sexual, and gender differences. It was also an exercise in risk taking as he displayed his photographs at the café alongside those of other participants. The young man had to address the possibility of being perceived as perhaps someone other than heterosexual.

SASSY demonstrated that with the support of caring and compassionate mentor-facilitators and peer collaborators, LGBITTQ and allied youth and young

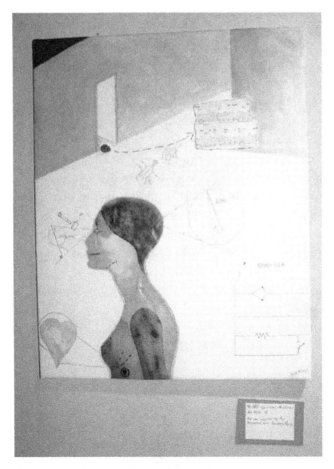

Figure 30.4. Visual Narratives as Self-Portraits: A Scene From the *Queer View Mirror* Exhibition

adults can build capacity and resiliency as they engage in informal education as communicative learning about self, others, and culture. However, although SASSY itself provided a safe space to learn and share, some participants did not feel safe enough to talk with families and friends about their involvement. Some simply told those close to them that they were taking a free art class at the university. This is a troubling reality. It reminds us that in large part, culture, families, and communities still lag behind the reality of LGBITTQ-inclusive laws and legislation and the fiction of LGBITTQ-positive movies and television when it comes to respecting and accommodating LGBITTQ persons.

CONCLUDING PERSPECTIVE: SAY "NO" TO BACKWARD FORCES

The Out Is In project advocated for LGBITTQ and allied youth and young adults as they explored self, culture, communities, and how power weaves through each. Although advocacy and empowering individuals were important elements, they were just starting points (Greene, 1995). For project participants, artistic expression became an intense medium for critical reflection and communicative learning. Greene (1995) speaks to the value of reflection, linking it to the possibility of transformation:

> It is not enough to emancipate individuals or to enable them to disclose their lived worlds for their enlightenment and our own. Lived worlds themselves must be open to reflection and transformation … [Individuals have] to open themselves to what they are making in common. Once they are open, once they are informed, once they are engaged in speech and action from their many vantage points, they may be able to identify a better state of things—and go on to transform. (p. 59)

Out Is In participants found the seeds for transformation in the artistic expression of their legitimate anger. This expression became an intervention, which, in the spirit of Freire (2004), is actively living out a pedagogy of just ire that "says *no* to backward forces" (p. 6).

REFERENCES

Allman, P. (2001). *Critical education against global capitalism: Karl Marx and revolutionary critical education*. Westport, CT: Bergin & Garvey.

Araújo Freire, A. M. (2004). Prologue. In P. Freire (Ed.), *Pedagogy of indignation* (pp. xxvii–xxxii). Boulder, CO: Paradigm.

Birden, S. (2004). Theorizing a coalition-engendered education: The case of the Boston women's health book collective's body education. *Adult Education Quarterly, 54*(4), 257–272.

Clover, D. E., & Stalker, J. (2005). Social justice, arts and adult education [Editorial for special issue]. *Convergence, 38*(4), 3–7.

Cunningham, P. M. (1988). The adult educator and social responsibility. In R. G. Brockett (Ed.), *Ethical issues in adult education* (pp. 133–145). New York: Teachers College Press.

D'Augelli, A. R. (1998). Developmental implications of victimization of lesbian, gay, and bisexual youths. In G. M. Herek (Ed.), *Stigma and sexual orientation: Understanding prejudice against lesbians, gay men, and bisexuals* (pp. 187–210). Thousand Oaks, CA: Sage.

Davies, B. (2004). Introduction: Poststructuralist lines of flight in Australia. *International Journal of Qualitative Studies in Education, 17*(1), 3–9.

Egan, J. P., & Flavell, A. J. (2006). Toward celebration through education: Queer Canadian adult education. In T. Fenwick, T. Nesbitt, & B. Spencer (Eds.), *Contexts of adult education: Canadian perspectives* (pp. 260–269). Toronto: Thompson Educational.

Eisner, E. W. (2004, October 14). What can education learn from the arts about the practice of education? *International Journal of Education & the Arts, 5*(4). Retrieved July 24, 2006, from http://ijea.asu.edu/v5n4/

Ellsworth, E. (1997). *Teaching positions: Difference, pedagogy and the power of address.* New York: Teachers College Press.

Foley, G. (1999). *Learning in social action: A contribution to understanding informal organization.* New York: Zed Books.

Freire, P. (1998a). *Pedagogy of freedom: Ethics, democracy, and civic courage.* Lanham, MD: Rowman & Littlefield.

Freire, P. (1998b). *Teachers as cultural workers: Letters to those who dare teach.* Boulder, CO: Westview.

Freire, P. (2004). *Pedagogy of indignation.* Boulder, CO: Paradigm.

Friend, R. A. (1998). Heterosexism, homophobia, and the culture of schooling. In S. Books (Ed.), *Invisible children in the society and its schools* (pp. 137–166). Mahwah, NJ: Lawrence Erlbaum.

Gall, M. D., Borg, W. R., & Gall, J. P. (1996). *Educational research: An introduction* (6th ed.). White Plains, NY: Longman.

Grace, A. P. (2001a). Being, becoming, and belonging as a queer citizen educator: The places of queer autobiography, queer culture as community, and fugitive knowledge. *Proceedings of the 20th Annual Conference of the Canadian Association for the Study of Adult Education*, 100–106.

Grace, A. P. (2001b). Using queer cultural studies to transgress adult educational space. In V. Sheared & P. A. Sissel (Eds.), *Making space: Merging theory and practice in adult education* (pp. 257–270). Westport, CT: Bergin & Garvey.

Grace, A. P. (2005). Reparative therapies: A contemporary clear and present danger across minority sex, sexual, and gender differences. *Canadian Woman Studies, 24*(2, 3), 145–151.

Grace, A. P., & Hill, R. J. (2004). Positioning queer in adult education: Intervening in politics and praxis in North America. *Studies in the Education of Adults, 36*(2), 167–189.

Grace, A. P., Hill, R. J., Johnson, C. W., & Lewis, J. B. (2004). In other words: Queer voices/dissident subjectivities impelling social change. *International Journal of Qualitative Studies in Education, 17*(3), 301–323.

Grace, A. P., & Wells, K. (2001). Getting an education in Edmonton, Alberta: The case of queer youth. *Torquere, Journal of the Canadian Lesbian and Gay Studies Association, 3,* 137–151.

Grace, A. P., & Wells, K. (2004). Engaging sex-and-gender differences: Educational and cultural change initiatives in Alberta. In J. McNinch, & M. Cronin (Eds.), *I could not speak my heart: Education and social justice for gay and lesbian youth* (pp. 289–307). Regina, CANADA: Canadian Plains Research Centre, University of Regina.

Grace, A. P., & Wells, K. (2005). The Marc Hall prom predicament: Queer individual rights v. institutional church rights in Canadian public education. *Canadian Journal of Education, 28*(3), 237–270.

Greene, M. (1995). *Releasing the imagination: Essays on education, the arts, and social change.* San Francisco: Jossey-Bass.

Hill, R. J. (1995). Gay discourse in adult education: A critical review. *Adult Education Quarterly, 45*(3), 142–158.

Hill, R. J. (1996). Learning to transgress: A social-historical conspectus of the American gay lifeworld as a site of struggle and resistance. *Studies in the Education of Adults, 28*(2), 253–279.

Hill, R. J. (2004). Activism as practice: Some queer considerations. In S. Imel & J. M. Ross-Gordon (Series Eds.) & R. St. Clair & J. A. Sandlin (Vol. Eds.), New directions for adult and continuing education: No. 102. *Promoting critical practice in adult education* (pp. 85–94). San Francisco: Jossey-Bass.

Holst, J. D. (2001). *Social movements, civil society, and radical adult education.* London: Bergin & Garvey.

Jacobs, D. (Ed.). (2003). *The Myles Horton reader: Education for social change.* Knoxville: The University of Tennessee Press.

Janoff, D. V. (2005). *Pink blood: Homophobic violence in Canada.* Toronto, Canada: University of Toronto Press.

Lipson Lawrence, R. (2005). Knowledge construction as contested terrain: Adult learning through artistic expression. In S. Imel & J. M. Ross-Gordon (Series Eds.) & R. Lipson Lawrence (Vol. Ed.), New directions for adult and continuing education: No. 107. *Artistic ways of knowing: Expanded opportunities for teaching and learning* (pp. 3–11). San Francisco: Jossey-Bass.

MacDougall, B. (2000). *Queer judgments: Homosexuality, expression, and the courts in Canada.* Toronto, Canada: University of Toronto Press.

Macedo, D. (2004). Foreword. In P. Freire (Ed.), *Pedagogy of indignation* (pp. ix–xxv). Boulder, CO: Paradigm.

McCreary Centre Society. (1999). *Being out: Lesbian, gay, bisexual, & transgender youth in BC: An adolescent health survey.* Burnaby, BC: Author.

Newman, M. (2006). *Teaching defiance: Stories and strategies for activist educators.* San Francisco: Jossey-Bass.

Ryan, C., & Futterman, D. (1998). *Lesbian and gay youth: Care & counseling.* New York: Columbia University Press.

Savin-Williams, R. C. (2005). *The new gay teenager.* Cambridge, MA: Harvard University Press.

Sedgwick, E. (2003). *Touching feeling: Affect, pedagogy, performativity.* Durham, NC: Duke University Press.

Wells, K. (2005). *Gay–straight student alliances in Alberta schools: A guide for teachers.* Edmonton, Canada: Alberta Teachers' Association.

Name Index

A

Abrahams, D., 141
Abrams, A., 247
Acar, W., 255
Ackah, C., 260
Acosta, A., 170
Adeya, C. N., 225–226
Adorno, T. W., 366, 367,
  371, 372
Ahmed, M., 221
Albarran, A. B., 364
Aldana Mendoza, C., 155,
  156, 162
Aldridge, F., 214
Alfred, M., 343
Allen, P. G., 384
Allman, P., 157, 215, 216, 437
Althusser, L., 207
Alvesson, M., 248
Apple, M., 61, 80, 166, 213,
  295, 306
Applebaum, B., 158
Apps, J. W., 47
Araújo Freire, A. M., 443
Arendt, H., 116
Argyris, C., 251, 327, 433
Aristotle, 174, 209
Armstrong, P., 401, 402
Aronowitz, S., 129, 130, 131

Aronson, E., 164
Ashlock, J., 407
Ashok, H. S., 381
Asún, J., 341, 345
Atwood, R. B., 78
Aupperle, K. E., 255
Austin, R., 149, 153
Avoseh, M. B. M., 383
Axford, R. W., 39, 46, 48, 50

B

Badat, S., 140, 143, 146
Bagnall, R. G., 415
Ball, S. J., 126
Bandura, A., 340, 343, 344
Banks, J., 70
Bannerji, H., 196
Baptiste, I., 82, 302, 303
Barber, S. L., 88, 89
Barlas, C., 356
Barton, D., 345
Basgen, B., 253
Bauman, Z., 115
Baumgartner, L. M., 321, 340,
  350, 354, 356, 357, 358
Beard, C., 358
Beck, U., 114, 188
Beder, H., 58
Beeghley, E. L., 212

Belenky, M., 323
Bell, C., 134
Bell, C. H., 257
Bell, D., 34, 35, 69
Benally, H. J., 384
Benko, C., 265
Bennett, T., 403
Bergevin, P., 37, 41, 47, 48
Bernstein, M., 425
Bierema, L. L., 247, 248,
  249–250, 256, 264, 265,
  269, 273
Bird, E., 191
Birden, S., 445, 446
Blair-Loy, M., 260
Blakely, R. J., 36, 40, 41
Bloom, L. R., 416
Blunden, A., 253
Boden, R., 254
Boone, E. J., 293
Boone, J., 425
Booth, G., 329
Bordwell, M., 405
Borg, W. R., 447
Boshier, R., 59, 382
Boud, D., 241, 317–318, 358
Boulmetis, J., 87
Bourdieu, P., 210, 213, 414
Bowles, S., 213

459

Subject Index

Millennium Development Goal (United Nations), 204, 219
Mindfulness, 382–383
Miner Teachers College, 74
Minority groups: democracy and, 194, 195, 196; human resource development and, 256; media representations of, 374; theory building and, 398–399
Moods, 353
Moorland-Spingarn Archives, 70, 79
Moral progress, 157–158
Motherwork, 191, 192, 193
Motivation, of learners: in Buddhist worldview, 383; emotions and, 350, 354; research of, 50
Multiculturalism, 151, 163, 267
Multiple intelligences, 323
Munnomu kabi, 227
Music: cultural resistance in, 404; globalization of, 369–370, 371; in non-Western worldviews, 385
Mythos, 330
Myths, 385

N

Narrative education, 20–32
National Actions to Implement Lifelong Learning in Europe (European Commission), 122–123
National Association for Adults with Special Learning Needs, 350
National budgets, 177
National Center for Education Statistics (NCES), xvii
National Child Development Study, 243
National Colored Women's Clubs, 68
National Conference on Adult Education and the Negro, 73
National Council of the YMCA, 74–75

National Slum Dwellers Federation, 146
National Society for Performance and Instruction, 90
National Union Catalog of Manuscript Collections, 70
Native Americans, 381, 384, 386
Natural resources: conflicts over, 171–172; conservation of, 175; effects of globalization on, 173
Natural science, 125
Navajo tradition, 384
Nazism, 116
NCES. *See* National Center for Education Statistics
Nchimishi, 225
Necrophily, 25
Need fulfillment, 173–175, 176, 178
Negitivland, 405
Negotiations, 296, 297, 301–308
Negro As Artist program, 81
Negro Folk Education Project, 81
Neoliberalism, 108, 109
Nepal, 190
New Directions for Adult and Continuing Education, xviii
New Historical Project, 176
New Labour government, 133, 134
New social movements, 428
New York Pride Festival, 433
New York Public Library, 70
New York Times, 369–370
News Corporation, 364
News programs, 373
Newspapers. *See* Mass media
Nigeria, 224
The Ninth Man (National Council of the YMCA), 74–75
Noetic societies, 41
Nongovernmental organizations (NGOs), 226–227

Non-Western worldviews, 380–387
Normative orientation, 139
North America, 211, 214
Nuclear submarines, 198
Nutrition programs, 240

O

Obedience, 223
Objectivity, 125
Observation, 386
Obsolete knowledge, 36
Oil crisis, 34
Omega Psi Phi, 68
One-Dimensional Man (Marcuse), 367
Online courses, 197
Ontario Institute for Studies in Education, 328
Oppression: in banking concept of education, 21–32; disruptive knowledge and, 433; in First World countries, 155; free market and, 176; ideology critique and, 157, 158; knowledge production and, 40, 41; postmodern pedagogy and, 416–417; purpose of adult education and, 48; reflection and, 317; social class and, 213; student experiences of, 162; transformative learning and, 326
Organization development, 257, 269
Organization health model, 270, 271
Organizational health, 288
Organizational learning, 286–287
Organizational structure, 296
Organizational transformation, 327–328
Ottawa Charter for Health Promotion, 237–238
Our Common Future (World Commission on Environment and Development), 175

CPSIA information can be obtained
at www.ICGtesting.com
Printed in the USA
BVHW012107250322
632490BV00010B/84